D0964377

The Social Writings of Jack London

The Social Writings of Jack London

Edited, with a biographical study,
by **PHILIP S. FONER**

Citadel Press   **Secaucus, N.J.**

Copyright 1947, © 1964 by The Citadel Press
All rights reserved
Published by Citadel Press
A division of Lyle Stuart Inc.
120 Enterprise Ave., Secaucus, N.J. 07094
In Canada: Musson Book Company
A division of General Publishing Co. Limited
Don Mills, Ontario
Manufactured in the United States of America
ISBN 0-8065-0886-8

Originally published as Jack
London: *American Rebel*

Preface

In the biographical sketch on Jack London which appears in the fourteenth edition of the *Encyclopaedia Brittanica* there is the following revealing paragraph:

> *His novels and other writings fall sharply into two classes—those which he wrote for money, as he frankly admitted in his letters, and those whose sincerity and militancy made him at one time the American Socialist best known outside the U.S.A.* The Iron Heel (*1907*), The War of the Classes (*1904*), Revolution and other Essays (*1910*) *are chief of these latter;* The Iron Heel *has had an enormous circulation in the Old World. With these should be classed* The People of the Abyss (*1903*), *a valuable sociological study of London's East End.*

All over Europe and Asia and in outlying parts of the world thousands of copies of these works still circulate annually and continue to stimulate progressive thinking and to inspire social and political reforms. Yet in his own country the social writings of Jack London have been permitted to lie buried. Search the vast majority of American book stores and libraries, and one will find only a stray copy here and there of any of the titles mentioned above.

It is the aim of the present volume to restore to the American reading public a body of writings which have accelerated the social progress of the past half-century. During the feverish years preceding World War I these writings, distributed widely in pamphlet form, were an integral part of the labor and socialist movements. Hatred of oppression and the vision of a society which would abolish profit, exploitation and inequality, run as a constant through these pages. Over and over again these themes recur in his novels, stories and essays. What emerges, however, is not preachment, but real men, women and children and the ebb and flow of their dramatic struggles against social evils. For Jack London brought to these writings the sensitivity of a poet, the polemical skill of a pamphleteer, the magic of a master-craftsman in words and the analytical power and sweep of an acute student and interpreter of social forces.

Upton Sinclair spoke the truth when he said that Jack London's social writings "constitute him one of the great revolutionary figures in our history." These writings occupy an important place in the long American tradition of protest and revolt, a tradition associated with the names of other American rebels—Jefferson and Paine, Emerson and Thoreau, Whittier and Whitman. It is true that the oft-cited contradictions in Jack London produced decided flaws in his social philosophy and ultimately weakened his attachment to the main source of strength in American life, the people themselves. But in spite of these shortcomings, Jack London was one of the outstanding interpreters and champions of the American socialist movement prior to the First World War. In the biographical study which accompanies this collection of London's social writings, I have sought to relate in detail his unique contributions to this movement. I concern myself chiefly with those aspects of his life and writings in which he played the role of a social rebel. Other aspects of his life and work have been dealt with in various studies, whereas this side of his career has been comparatively neglected.

I am grateful to Mrs. Charmian Kittredge London for permission to reprint the sections from *The Iron Heel, Martin Eden, The People of the Abyss* and *John Barleycorn,* the story "South of the Slot," the review of *The Jungle,* and various letters by Jack London as well as excerpts from his diaries. I also wish to express my gratitude to Mr. Irving Shepard for supervising the arrangements for the use of this material.

I am indebted to Mr. Upton Sinclair, of Monrovia, California, for permission to reprint the introduction by Jack London to *The Cry for Justice.*

I wish to express my thanks to Doubleday and Company for permission to quote from Irving Stone's *Jack London: Sailor on Horseback* and from Joan London's *Jack London and His Times.*

I am indebted to Mr. Eugene Schwab for furnishing me with a copy of an inscription by Jack London in the volume *Martin Eden* in his possession. It is a pleasure to express my appreciation to Mr. John Metcalfe, Principal Librarian of the Public Library of New South Wales, Sydney, Australia who kindly furnished me with a copy of the article, "Strike Methods" by Jack London, published in the Sydney *Star*.

PHILIP S. FONER

New York City

Contents

Jack London: American Rebel
    BY *Philip S. Foner*   3

FICTION

The Iron Heel   133
    The Philomaths, 133 . . . The Vortex, 149 . . . The
General Strike, 156 . . . The Beginning of the End, 164
. . . Last Days, 170 . . . The End, 175 . . . The Scar-
let Livery, 181 . . . In the Shadow of Sonoma, 186 . . .
The Roaring Abysmal Beast, 190 . . . The Chicago
Commune, 195 . . . The People of the Abyss, 205 . . .
Nightmare, 215 . . . The Terrorists, 220

The Apostate   222
The Dream of Debs   240
South of the Slot   258
The Strength of the Strong   273
In the Laundry
    A SELECTION FROM *Martin Eden*   287

AUTOBIOGRAPHICAL WRITINGS

In the Powerhouse
    A SELECTION FROM *John Barleycorn*   307

Tramp Days
    SELECTIONS FROM *My Life in the Underworld*   314
    A Reminiscence and a Confession, 314 . . . "Holding
    Her Down," 325 . . . "Pinched," 339 . . . The "Pen,"
    350
How I Became a Socialist   362
In the London Slums
    SELECTIONS FROM *The People of the Abyss*   366
    Preface, 366 . . . The Descent, 367 . . . Those on the
    Edge, 373 . . . The Carter and the Carpenter, 376 . . .
    Carrying the Banner, 384 . . . The Management, 387
What Life Means to Me   392

NEWSPAPER ARTICLES

Explanation of the Great Socialist Vote of 1904   403
Something Rotten in Idaho   407
Strike Methods: American and Australian   411

ESSAYS

What Communities Lose by the Competitive System   419
Wanted: A New Law of Development   431
The Class Struggle   446
The Scab   460
The Tramp   474
Revolution   488

REVIEWS AND COMMENTS

"The Octopus"   507
"Fomá Gordyéeff"   512
"The Jungle"   517
Introduction to "The Cry for Justice"   525

    Sources   529
    Supplementary Material   533
    Bibliography   557

Jack London
American Rebel

Jack London: American Rebel

BY Philip S. Foner

"No American writer," said Fred Lewis Pattee of Jack London, "has had a career more representative of his time." To this one should add that no American writer was a more articulate and splendid spokesman for his time. For it was Jack London more than any other writer of his day, who broke the ice that was congealing American letters and brought life and literature into a meaningful relation to each other.

The end of the nineteenth century found the nation in a state of great social and political unrest. It found expression in the rise of the labor movement, furious battles between labor and capital, and the political conflict between farmers, workers and small business men on the one hand and the powerful monopolies on the other. Yet throughout this turbulent period there was a curious dichotomy between literature and life. Anyone dependent upon American letters to guide him would have obtained the most confused and inaccurate conceptions of the life led by more than sixty millions of Americans and of the major problems confronting them. He would find that the American people were concerned solely with romantic love sometimes enacted in remote times by men and women in costume who addressed each other as "thee" and "thou," or in imagined principalities of Europe like Zenda or Graustark where gilt-uniformed officers wooed beautiful heroines on marbled terraces. If the romance was set in contemporary America it was all in the fragrance of new-mown hay or of magnolias surrounding white-columned verandas. The teeming life of the industrial city produced the formula of the poor boy who married the boss's daughter and was taken into the firm.

Of the grinding poverty of the workers, of wretched housing, low wages, long hours and unsanitary working conditions, of child labor, of the ruthless industrial and financial tycoons, the literature of the day said little. By an almost universal agreement among editors and publishers they were considered unmentionable and unfit for literary presentation. Theodore Dreiser, recalling his early days as a journalist in New York, has recorded in *A Book About Myself* his reactions to the failure of contemporary literature to deal faithfully with American life:

> *In a kind of ferment or fever due to my necessities and desperation, I set to examining the current magazines and fiction and articles to be found therein*—Century, Scribner's, Harper's. *I was never more confounded than by the discrepancy existing between my own observations and those displayed here, the beauty and peace and charm to be found in everything, the complete absence of any reference to the coarse and the cruel and the terrible. How did it happen that these remarkable persons, geniuses of course, one and all, saw life in this happy roseate? Was it so and was I all wrong?* . . . *They seemed to deal with phases of sweetness and beauty and success and goodness such as I rarely encountered.* . . .
>
> *When I think of the literary and social snobbery and bosh of that day, its utter futility and profound faith in its own goodness, as opposed to facts of its own visible life, I have to smile.*

Beginning with Rebecca Harding Davis' "Life in the Iron Mills" in *The Atlantic* of April, 1861, probably the earliest treatment of the lives of industrial workers that approached realism, American fiction since the Civil War had occasionally piped a rather feeble note of social criticism. Elizabeth Stuart Phelps' *The Silent Partner*, Edward Bellamy's *Looking Backward*, and William Dean Howells' *A Traveler from Altruria*, were among the books published before 1890 which attempted to get close to real life in America. But these were drowned in the avalanche of fiction which depicted only the pleasant side of life, and shied away from the harsh, the sordid, the real. Even Howells himself wrote that "the more smiling aspects of life are the more American."

Here and there a few Americans attempted to introduce Tolstoy, Zola, Turgeniev, Flaubert, Ibsen, Sudermann, Hauptmann and other

European realists to the American reading public and to recommend their methods to American writers. But they came against the stone wall of editorial opposition which insisted that American authors repeat the time-worn formulas of the pseudo-romance. Realism was condemned as indecent; literature must be "suited to maiden ears and eyes," and there must be an end to the "disposition which may well be called alarming, to trifle with the marriage relation." It was not art but contented itself "with photographing the transitory surfaces of life." It was pessimistic, depressing, and degrading, and no writer had "a right to make this beautiful, puzzling, sad world any more mournful than it is for everybody else." Most important of all, it was critical of contemporary society and filled with revolutionary ideas. "All this hacking at wealth," cried Maurice Thompson, a leading champion of the romantic school of literature, "and all this apostrophizing of poverty is not the spirit of Christ; it is in the spirit of communism, socialism and anarchy. . . ."

Upon this scene there stepped several young writers who at the turn of the century blazed new trails in American literature. Influenced by the European naturalistic and realistic tradition, and conscious of the growing class conflicts in their own country, they resolved to introduce into the thin, pale, bloodless, sentimental, insipid writing of the day, themes, characters and styles which were reflections of American life itself. At the same time, new and daring figures, like Frank A. Munsey, John Brisbane Walker and S. S. McClure, entered the magazine field. Aware of the startling technological advances which were reducing the cost of publishing, these men began to think in terms of huge circulation at low prices to a mass audience as yet untapped. To attract and hold this new audience these men vied with each other in publishing vital literature, replete with meaning for the times. *Munsey's, McClure's* and *Cosmopolitan* at ten cents a copy made the older magazines, purveying tranquil fiction and sedate essays to an exclusive public and selling for twenty-five and thirty-five cents, appear uninspired. Furthermore, the stronger organization of labor and the growth of the socialist movement brought into being a chain of radical periodicals, *The Appeal to Reason, The Comrade, Wilshire's Magazine,* the *International Socialist Review,* which offered a medium for material which was too strong even for the popular magazines and which formed a rallying point for a new school of American writers.

This new trend in American literature made its debut with the publication at the author's expense of Stephen Crane's *Maggie: A Girl of the Streets* in 1893. Six years later, Frank Norris, a devoted disciple of Emile Zola, laid the plans for his "Epic of Wheat" which in three novels would tell the story "of this huge Niagara of wheat," from its growth and harvesting in the West, through the speculation in the Chicago Wheat Pit, to its mission of feeding India's starving millions during a famine. Only two of the books, *The Octopus* and *The Pit*, were completed, for Norris died before he could start the third.

Crane and Norris were the pioneers of realism in modern American literature, but their writings did not reflect the most important issue confronting the American people in their day—the furious battle between labor and capital. Nor were they interested chiefly in protesting economic evils in society. In dedicating a copy of *Maggie* to a Baptist minister, Crane wrote: "It tries to show that environment is a tremendous thing in this world, and often shapes lives regardlessly. If I could prove that theory I would make room in heaven for all sorts of souls (notably an occasional street girl) who are not confidently expected to be there by many excellent people." But with the efforts of the working class to change their environment and to make room for a better society on earth, Crane was not concerned. Even Norris, for all his compassion and sense of justice, did not write to mobilize the people in the battle against economic injustice. Evils existed in society, to be sure, but they were subordinate to the all-prevailing, inevitable goodness of nature. Thus he wrote in the final paragraph of his greatest novel, *The Octopus*, the story of a futile uprising of San Joaquin Valley farmers against the Southern Pacific Railroad:

> *Falseness dies; injustice and oppression in the end of everything fade and vanish away. Greed, cruelty, selfishness and inhumanity are short-lived; the individual suffers, but the race goes on. Annixter dies, but in a far-distant corner of the world a thousand lives are saved. The larger view always and through all shams, all wickedness, discovers the Truth that will, in the end, prevail, and all things, surely, inevitably, resistlessly, work together for good.*

But another American writer was emerging who was interested not only in exposing cruelties and oppressions in the economic system, but in remaking it and building a new and better social order. This was Jack London. Like Crane and Norris he was a realist, but unlike them he was also a socialist, and from his belief in Marxism as a philosophy of history he drew the ability to describe, better than any of his predecessors or his contemporaries and most of those who followed him, the modern social struggle out of which would inevitably come the regeneration of mankind. London was not the equal of Crane or Norris in literary finish nor in balanced characterization; his style was often melodramatic and his writing was frequently marred by flaws of structure, but it achieved stature by its sheer intensity of conviction and its great love for the working people and their aspirations. London knew the life of which he wrote; knew how workers lived and talked and how to transfer the details of their lives to the printed page with amazing fidelity. And the workers read this writing, reread it and passed it along until the pages were shredded. In the January, 1929 issue of the *New Masses*, Martin Russak wrote:

> *A real proletarian writer must not only write about the working class, he must be read by the working class. A real proletarian writer must not only use his proletarian life as material; his writing must burn with the spirit of revolt. Jack London was a real proletarian writer—the first and so far the only proletarian writer of genius in America. Workers who read, read Jack London. He is the one author they have all read, he is one literary experience they all have in common. Factory workers, farm hands, seamen, miners, newsboys read him and read him again. He is the most popular writer of the American working class.*

Before Jack London, the fiction dealing with the working class was characterized by sympathy for labor and the underprivileged, but chiefly in the spirit of Christian principles of brotherhood, proclaiming as its message that if only labor and capital could be persuaded to follow the teachings of Christ, all social and economic problems could be solved. Most of these writers were convinced that injustices existed in our economic system, and against these injustices they protested, but they had no wish to change the system itself; or if they did, through idealistic, utopian schemes. For the most part, too, these writers were not workers themselves writing of their own experiences. They wrote about the working class as interested but objective observers, hoping as humanitarians to improve the living conditions of labor without shaking the economic structure. Frequently they discussed trade unions and strikes, but only to prove that force of any kind brought disaster upon the workers. Most of this writing ended with a sentimental plea to soften the hearts of the capitalists and infuse them with a belated spirit of brotherly love.

Life itself led Jack London to reject this approach in his writing. As a newsboy, sailor, mill-hand, stoker, tramp, and janitor, he came to know all there was to know about the life of the underdog. He knew what it meant to be one of the disinherited, to be chained to the deadening routine of the machine and to soul-destroying labor for an insufficient reward. Consequently he swept aside not only the literature that pretended that ours is a society of sweetness and light, but also that which contended that the inculcation of the spirit of Christian fellowship would put an end to class controversy. He did not oppose labor organization nor balk at the strike as a weapon of labor; rather, he took his heroes and heroines from the labor movement and wove his plots within their struggles. His own proletarian background had taught him that the individual worker was powerless in the face of the greed of the ruling class. He was not content to appeal for the end of poverty and ignorance and disease; he called for the destruction of the system which was responsible for these evils. He poured into his writings all the pain of his life, the fierce hatred of the bourgeoisie that it had produced in him, and the conviction it had brought to him that the world could be made a better place to live in if the exploited would rise up and take the management of society out of the hands of the exploiters. Even after he had established his fame and money-making power in the popular magazines, he did not forget his proletarian origins. He risked the rewards of his years of labor on the road up from poverty and obscurity to write socialist essays and revolutionary stories and novels. He became the most successful writer of his day, but he remained the most radical writer in American literature.

Jack London was born in San Francisco, California on January 12, 1876, the son of William Henry Chaney, an itinerant astrologer and Flora Wellman, a spiritualist. When he was eight months old, his mother married John London, a migrant worker and farmer, and took her young son to the London flat in the working-class section south of Market Street. From his foster-father Jack Chaney took the name by which he is known to history.

When Jack London came into the world it was in the midst of the crisis which began in September, 1873 when the banking house of

Jay Cook and Company closed its doors. By the time he was a year old hundreds of thousands of workers were jobless and the employed were forced to submit to reduction of wages ranging from forty to sixty per cent. All over the country homeless workers, the tramps of the 'seventies, wandered about picking up odd jobs when they were fortunate, but mainly living in shacks and gleaning the garbage heaps for food. In San Francisco, communities of homeless workers dotted the outskirts of the city living on food "that a humane man would hesitate about throwing to his dog."

The depression did not leave the London family untouched. During the first five years of Jack's childhood the family moved about constantly while John London tried his hand at various occupations. At times they were fairly well off, but they never knew security. And the constant moving about—the family changed its residence five times in as many years—provided additional hardships for the youngster. Each time the family moved, Jack had to make new friends, and very often during his childhood he was to know what it meant to have no playmates.

In 1880 the family, penniless after an unsuccessful grocery store venture, tried its hand at raising corn and other vegetables on a twenty-acre farm in Alameda. From there they moved to a desolate ranch in San Mateo where they were to remain for the next three years, in hardships that dwarfed anything they had hitherto experienced. London calls this the hungriest period in his life. So hungry was he that at one time he stole a tiny piece of meat from a girl's lunch-basket. It was with the greatest effort that he stopped himself from retrieving the unwanted scraps of meat that his schoolmates threw to the ground. Years later he wrote of this period in his life:

> I had been poor. Poor I had lived. I had gone hungry on occasion. I had never had toys nor playthings like other children. My first memories of life were pinched by poverty. The pinch of poverty had become chronic. . . . And only a child, with a child's imagination, can come to know the meaning of things it has long been denied.

When Jack was eight, the family moved to Livermore Valley. Here he discovered "the authentic passion of his life," the love of books. His teacher loaned him Washington Irving's *The Alhambra*. He scoured the homes of his neighbors and came upon Paul du Chaillu's

Explorations and Adventures in Equatorial Africa and Ouida's *Signa*, the romantic story of an Italian peasant lad who rose to fame as a composer. He read everything and anything he could lay his hands on, although most of his literary fare consisted of dime novels and old newspaper serials featuring the adventures of "poor but virtuous shopgirls." Next year when the family moved back to Oakland, he made the acquaintance of the Oakland Public Library and every moment he could spare found him buried in a book. He read all the time, at meals, after meals, on the way to and from school and during recess. If hunger had not interfered, he would have sat with his books all day long "and read, and read, and read, and read."

But John London was once again out of work, and it was up to Jack to furnish food for the poverty-stricken family. He awoke at 3 A.M. to deliver newspapers, after which he went on to school. After school hours he delivered the evening papers. Week-ends he worked on an ice wagon, in a bowling alley, and as a porter. All of his earnings he turned over to his family.

What time he could spare from his work, from school and from his reading, he spent at the water-front seeking an escape from the humdrum of his life. By scraping together nickels and dimes he managed to accumulate enough money to buy an old boat first and later a second-hand skiff. Every spare moment found him in the saloons supplementing his formal education by what he learned from the water front characters, or taking ever longer sails on the treacherous San Francisco Bay.

When he was graduated, at the age of thirteen, from the Oakland grammar school, he was named class historian, and chosen to deliver a speech at the graduation exercises. But his clothes were too ragged for the acceptance of honors, and Jack did not even show up formally to receive his diploma. The financial situation in the London household put high school out of the question, for Jack's earnings were now urgently needed to supplement the family income. For a year he continued selling papers morning and night, plus whatever odd jobs he could pick up. Then his foster-father was struck by a train and seriously hurt. The family moved again, this time to a broken down cottage on the Estuary surrounded by shacks built of driftwood.

He found work in a cannery in West Oakland. His pay—ten cents an hour—was so low that even a ten-hour shift did not net him enough for the family's pressing needs. So he worked overtime, standing at the same machine for eighteen and twenty hours at a stretch. Once he worked for thirty-six consecutive hours, after which, as was his custom, he walked home, unable to spare the money for carfare.

For several months he continued the back-breaking routine—up in the morning at half-past five, at the machine until after dark, home from work, numb with fatigue and in bed after midnight. And then both his mind and body rebelled. The vision of being tied to the machine for the rest of his life and gradually sapped of all vitality and ambition horrified him and he sought escape. His life on the water front had made him familiar with the ways of the oyster pirates who raided the beds owned by a few companies in Lower Bay and sold their loot for high prices on the Oakland docks. A man who owned his own boat, he knew, could make as much in one night as he brought home in several months' work at the cannery. And instead of the monotonous work at the machine he would be out on a boat in the company of hard-fisted, hard-drinking men. At one stroke, his financial problems would be solved and his love of adventure satisfied.

So Jack London, not yet fifteen, borrowed $300 from Mammy Jenny, his Negro wet-nurse, and bought the *Razzle-Dazzle,* a fast sloop owned by French Frank, one of the older pirates. The next night Jack made his first raid on the oyster-beds. French's sixteen-year-old girl-friend, Mame, queen of the oyster pirates, and eighteen other water front characters with names like Spider, Big George, Young Scratch Nelson, Whiskey Bob, and Nicky the Greek made up the crew. The following morning he was back in Oakland selling the loot. In one night he had made three months' cannery wages. Within a short time he paid Mammy Jenny back her loan.

For a year or more he sailed San Francisco Bay, robbing oyster-beds, living recklessly and, between raids, reading books borrowed from the public library. Any night he might receive a bullet through his head from the rifles of the Fish Patrol or a knife in his back from the hand of some drunken member of his crew. But to Jack all this was secondary to the new-found adventure and the ability to make money easily. Within six months he became known as the Prince of the Oyster Pirates. A little while later he added the title, Prince of the Drunkards. He got drunk on raw whiskey whenever he was not on raids, and although he made as much as $180 in a night's raid, he was constantly broke. He no longer contributed to his family; the saloons received the money which should have gone for food and rent. The water front gave the fifteen-year-old "Prince" no more than a year to live!

Along the Oakland water front [writes F. L. Pattee] *the old salts will even now be recounting ripping tales of the young "daredevil London," who could drink any man down at the bar, and knock any two of them down at once, who had the temerity to refuse his invitation to "line-up."*

Jack might have been able to forget his sordid childhood and wretched boyhood in drink. But raw whiskey almost ended his career at fifteen. One morning at 1 A.M. he accidentally fell into the water. He had been drinking for three weeks continuously. A fit of despondency seized him and he decided to drown himself. All night long he swam and floated in the bay, waiting for exhaustion to carry him under. But, sobered by the cold water, he changed his mind. This was no solution to his problems. He struck out across the current, and daylight found him, completely exhausted, fighting the tides off Mare Island. A few minutes more and all would have been over. Fortunately, a Greek fisherman hauled him in, unconscious.

A few days after the rescue, while running in a load of oysters, Jack was hailed by a State officer and offered an opportunity to become a deputy for the Fish Patrol to police the same waters he had so skilfully pillaged. The pay was fifty per cent of the fines collected. Jack accepted and soon experienced the same joy in sailing the waters of the Bay as a Patrol officer that he had known as a pirate.

He worked for the Fish Patrol for almost a year. But the more he had to do with it the more disgusted he became with the politicians who controlled it. It sickened him to discover that the officials were crooked and venal and not men who received their offices through ability and public service.

His disillusionment quickened his desire for a change. In January, 1893, Jack shipped out aboard the *Sophie Sutherland* headed for Korea, Japan and Siberia. On board ship he used his fists to win acceptance as an equal by the hard-bitten seamen who regarded boys as door mats to be stepped upon and slaves to cater to their whims. He had signed on as an able-bodied seaman, and though he knew enough to cover himself, he also understood the resentment of the older men who had gone through all the hard knocks of life to gain a similar rating. He won them over with his wit, his fists and his daring exploits. One night, when drunk, he swam all alone through the ink-black harbor of Yokohama, a feat which almost cost him his life but established him in the eyes of the older men.

Seven months at sea were enough. He returned to San Francisco, stopped to buy a round of drinks for former friends, bought a second-hand hat, coat and vest, a few shirts and two suits of underclothes, and went directly to Oakland. There he found the family on the verge of starvation. Jack paid the bills and turned the rest of his savings over to his mother. Then he set out to look for a job.

But while Jack London had been hunting seals off the Siberian coast, drinking and listening to the yarns of sealers and sailors, and, after a sufficient number of whiskeys, brawling with the natives, the severest economic crisis America had yet experienced swept the nation. By the time he returned to Oakland the panic of 1893 had paralyzed the industrial structure, knocked the bottom under wages, and reduced to idleness three million workers. He saw jobless men everywhere, wandering through the city in search of work, only to be joined by workers being discharged from the places where they applied. He saw thousands standing in line all night waiting for work at ten cents an hour.

The only work Jack could find was in a jute mill where for ten hours of back-breaking labor he earned one dollar. At his side were children, some eight years of age, earning a little over thirty cents for the same working day. He stayed on for several months, hoping each week to receive the dollar and a quarter a day the owners of the mill had promised him.

After a day spent in the mill Jack was in no condition to think of anything besides getting to bed. Yet it was under such conditions that he published his first story. Years later he told reporters how he got his start as a writer:

> In my fitful school days I had written the usual composition which had been praised in the usual way, and while working in the jute mills I still made an occasional try. The factory occupied thirteen hours of my day, and being young and husky, I wanted a little for myself, so there was not much left for composition. The San Francisco Call offered a prize for a descriptive article. My mother urged me to try for it, and I did, taking for my subject, "Typhoon off the Coast of China."
>
> Very tired and sleepy and knowing I had to be up at 5:30, I began the article at midnight and worked straight on until I had written 2,000 words, the limit of the article, but with my idea only half worked out. I continued, adding another 2,000

words before I had finished, and the third night I spent in
cutting out the excess, so as to bring the article within the
conditions of the contest. The first prize came to me, and my
success seriously turned my thoughts to writing, but my blood
was still too hot for a settled routine.

On November 12, 1893, the *San Francisco Call* announced that the
five judges had unanimously awarded the twenty-five dollars first
prize to "Story of a Typhoon off the Coast of Japan, by John London
aged 17—address—1321 Twenty-second Avenue, Oakland."

After another effort at a sea tale brought no response from the
Call, Jack resigned himself to his job at the jute mill. But not for long.
The promised raise did not materialize, and he realized he was rapidly
getting nowhere. He quit, deciding to learn a trade. Trade school
was out of the question, for he had to earn money to support the
family. The next best thing was to get into some industry, start at
the bottom and work himself up. He hit upon the field of electricity,
which was just making its influence felt in American industry.

When Jack applied for a job at the power plant of the Oakland
Street Railway, he was overjoyed to discover that the superintendent
sympathized with young men who were not afraid of hard work and
were willing to do anything to get a start. He gave Jack the job of
feeding coal to the enormous furnaces, assuring him that in time
he would become an oiler, an assistant to the mechanics, and eventually, depending, of course, on himself, he might go clear to the top.
Jack added the rest himself—promotion after promotion and finally
the hand of the boss's daughter in marriage. Later he wrote of himself: "I formulated a gospel of work which put Carlyle or Kipling
to shame. I was as faithful a wage slave as ever capitalist exploited.
My joyous individualism was dominated by orthodox bourgeois
ethics. . . ."

So it was with real zest that he started to shovel coal in day and
night shifts, thirteen hours a day, twenty-nine days a month, for
thirty dollars a month. Hour after hour, day and night, he would
fill his iron wheelbarrow with coal, push it to the scales where he
would weigh the load, then off to the fire room to dump the coal.

The cannery and jute mill seemed child's play compared to this;
the work was so hard that even his robust frame, his "physique of
twisted steel," began to break under it. He simply could not understand how human beings could be expected to work so hard. One of

the firemen broke the news to him. When the superintendent saw that Jack was willing to do any amount of work to break into the trade, he had fired two men, one on the day shift and the other on the night shift, and had given the ambitious young man both of their jobs. Thus he saved fifty dollars a month.

This discovery did not cause London to quit immediately. He decided to show the superintendent that he could take it. And the loss of such a fine worker would be regretted the more deeply when he finally left. But a few days later he changed his mind. The same fireman showed him a newspaper item. It was a story of a suicide. One of the coal passers whose job Jack had unwittingly taken had killed himself, because, jobless, he could not bear watching his wife and children starve. Jack quit.

The nightmare of toil was filling in the details in Jack London's education in the class struggle. His first reaction, however, was a horror of manual labor of any sustained sort. The only choice left him by society was to kill himself by overwork or to become a tramp. He became a tramp.

This was in the spring of 1894 at a time when the ranks of the unemployed were swollen by thousands every week, when strikes of exploited workers were shaking the nation to its foundation, and when farmers were joining the chorus of national discontent in protest against forty-nine cent wheat, seven-cent cotton and twenty-six cent corn. All over the country there arose the wail of hunger from men, women and children calling upon the government to step into the situation and provide for the needs of the unemployed. But in Congress there was no awareness that the problem of unemployment and relief was any concern of the national government. "Millions for armories and the military instruction of the young," complained B. O. Flower, editor of the liberal magazine, *The Arena*, "but not one cent to furnish employment to able-bodied industry in its struggle to escape the terrible alternative of stealing or starving—such seems to be the cry of government in the United States today. . . ." Flower suggested an extensive program of public works to relieve unemployment authorized under the general welfare clause of the Constitution, a proposal which had already been advanced in December, 1893 at the convention of the American Federation of Labor.

While these ideas were being discussed in liberal magazines and at labor conventions, masses of unemployed workers were making their way by foot, rail or water to Washington, there to register emphatic dissatisfaction with the conditions of the country and to demand redress of the grievances of a whole people. From hamlet and city the armies of the Commonweal were recruited, and the spring of 1894 saw them marching down from New England, straggling in from California, Arizona and Texas, and tramping through the late snow-storms in the Alleghanies. All told about 10,000 men were on the march throughout the country with Washington as their destination.

The originator of the descent upon Washington was Jacob Sechler Coxey, a wealthy manufacturer of Massillon, Ohio who formulated a plan under which the National Government was to issue $500,000,000 in legal tender notes to be expended for the employment of citizens on a huge nation-wide road-building program. A companion measure to the good roads bill advocated issuance of legal tender notes for city streets and public buildings on the security of non-interest-bearing bonds to be authorized by any State, county or town. The two bills were introduced into Congress on March 19, 1894, by Senator Peffer, Populist, of Kansas.

Six days later Coxey's army, a "petition in boots" for the passage of the bills, left Massillon for Washington. Within a few days the idea spread like wildfire to every section of the country, and local "armies" were organized which would march across the states, picking up recruits as they went and joining Coxey in Washington. In his ad-dress to the American Railway Union Convention in June, 1894 Eugene V. Debs portrayed this mass procession in vivid language:

> Out of work, out of money and without food, ragged, friend-less and homeless, these Commonwealers began their march to the capital city of the nation while Congress is in session. . . . Faster and still faster they rallied as the bugle call echoed through the land. They walk, they ride, they float ; the storms beat upon them, their tents their skins ; their couch the mother earth, their pillows stones. Some fall by the way and are buried by their comrades, unknelled and unsung, to sleep their last sleep in unknown and forgotten graves. But the survivors press forward to Washington, and as they march, recruits start up from almost every center of population in all of the land, from mountains and valley, from hill and dale, from abandoned mine and silent factory, shop and forge—they come and tramp to the muffled drum—funeral march of their throbbing hearts. The cry is, "On to Washington," where, on the marble steps of the

nation's capitol, in their rags, and barefooted, they would pe-
tition Congress to enact laws whereby they might perpetuate
their wretched existence by toil—laws that would rekindle
the last remaining sparks of hope, that their future would be
relieved of some of the horrors of hunger and nakedness. . . .

The largest of the unemployed armies was organized in San Francisco by Colonel William Baker who was soon replaced by General
Charles T. Kelly, a compositor in a San Francisco printing establishment. By April the army had recruited fifteen hundred men, "genuine
laboring men," said the San Francisco *Chronicle*, "who are now
struggling by every honest means to better their condition." On
April 7 the army sped towards Utah in freight cars. At Chautauqua
Park, Iowa, Kelly's army was joined by the eighteen-year-old Jack
London.

Jack had first made the acquaintance of Kelly's army while they
were stranded in Oakland. He mingled with the men as they marched
about the town mobilizing public support against the mayor who had
ordered them out of town and the railroad officials who had refused
to give them free transportation. He quickly decided to join the industrial army. The aims of the movement did not deeply concern
him. Here was simply a chance to see more of the world at no cost to
himself. With a ten-dollar gold piece in his pocket, contributed by his
sister Eliza, he set out for the freight yards only to find that several
hours earlier the army had been bundled into boxcars by the police,
the fire department and a contingent of deputies, and sent on its way
to Sacramento. Off he went with others who had been left behind to
catch up with the army at Sacramento, but again he missed it. Instead of turning back to Oakland, Jack decided to beat his way east
until he caught up with Kelly and his men, and then, he exulted *"On
to Washington."*

He already knew "all about this tramp business" when he started
out with his chum, Frank Davis, to pursue Kelly's army. Two years
before he had met a group of "road kids" and joined their gang to
get his first taste of the road. For several weeks he moved along with
them, beating his way across the Sierras into Nevada and back, earned
the moniker of Sailor Kid, learned to beg, to roll drunks, and the
other techniques involved in riding the freights and dodging the
bulls. He was in the company of boys who were the victims of poverty and broken homes, but his knowledge of social problems was not

greatly enhanced by this adventure. It was to be reserved for his next hoboing experience to arouse in him an understanding of the social and economic forces which turned men and boys into tramps. The first indication that Jack London gives anywhere of a social consciousness is the note in his diary written a few days after he and his companion had started out after the first detachment of Kelly's army:

> *The road has no more charms for Frank. The romance & adventure are gone, and nothing remains but the stern reality of the hardships to be endured. Though he has decided to turn West again I am sure the experience has done him good, broadened his thoughts, given him a better understanding of the low strata of society, & surely will have made him more charitable to the tramps he will meet hereafter when he is in better circumstances. He starts West and I start East tonight. . . . I Am going to brake coal on the engine from here to Carlin, 131 miles.*

Jack pushed eastward in box cars, in the ice box of a refrigerator car, on the roofs of coaches, suffering from heat and cold and other discomforts. In his penciled scrawl he noted in his diary that in the desert "the days are burning & the nights freezing cold"; that he "woke up at 3:30 A.M. half froze to death"; that his feet "were so cold that it took half an hour's brisk walk to restore circulation"; that it "was so cold on the train that night that the brakeman did not care to bother me," and that he rode the blind baggage through a blizzard with snow so thick that "one could not see over a rod ahead." He also recorded the problems involved in dodging brakemen on an Overland Limited:

> *We made a 45 mile run to Elko & a 23 mile run to Peko where they tried to ditch us. We went out ahead but the brakeman rode the blind out. We waited till the train had almost run by when two of us jumped the palace cars & decked them while the third went underneath on the rods. I climbed forward two cars to the other fellow & [asked him] to come on along the decks to the blind but he said that it was too risky. I went forward about five cars & as the brakeman was on the platform I could proceed no further and escape observation. I waited & when the train stopped I climbed down & ran ahead to the blind. The brakeman rode her out but I took the next one*

*behind him, & when he jumped off to catch me I ran ahead &
took the platform he had vacated. The fellow on the roof with
me got ditched, but I made her into Wells, the end of the
division where they put on a double header. The brakeman was
after us like a blood hound, so I climbed on the engine &
passed coal through to Terrace, the end of that division.*

When he finally caught up with Kelly and joined the rear rank of
the "first Regiment of the Reno Industrial Army," Jack found it
difficult to accept discipline and act as part of an organization. He
was still too much of an individualist to work with others for the
common good, and after all he was out for adventure, not for Congressional legislation for the unemployed. He stole out of camp each
night in violation of orders. After the army took to boats down the
Des Moines River, Jack and nine other individualists from his company went ahead of the rest. Flying American flags, they would approach a town or a group of farmers on the banks of the river, proclaim
themselves the "advance boat," dispatched by General Kelly to ar-
range for supplies, and demand provisions gathered for the army. They
took the cream of everything offered by sympathetic farmers and
townspeople, leaving the remains for the hundreds of men who arrived a half a day or a day later. For three hundred miles they lived
well, but, as Jack ruefully admitted years later, "the main army . . .
starved." Naturally, General Kelly who, unlike Jack London did not
look upon the expedition as a lark, was furious, and sent horsemen
down the banks of the river warning farmers and townspeople against
the ten pirates. Thereafter the individualists were greeted by constables and dogs whenever they ran up their American flags and went
into their act. Jack and his colleagues gave up and returned to the
army.

As the going got rougher, desertions became common. And when
the army learned that on May 1st General Coxey and two other
leaders had been arrested in Washington and brought into court for
having violated "the peace and Government of the United States"
because they unlawfully entered upon the grounds of the Capitol
and "did then and there step upon certain growing plants, shrubs,
and turf . . . ," the demoralization increased. On May 18 Jack wrote
in his diary: "We passed a miserable day on the water with a chilling
wind and driving rain. In the afternoon we camped in Missouri where
we passed a miserable night." Six days later, he remarked: "We went

supperless to bed. Am going to pull out in the morning. I can't stand starvation." The next morning he deserted at Hannibal, Missouri.

Jack roamed the country as a hobo, riding the rails to Chicago, then to New York, begging for food on the way and sleeping in fields or in barns when he was not in a boxcar. His first impressions of New York were anything but pleasant. He soon became aware of the misery that lay underneath its glamor. He arrived in midsummer during a week of scorching weather. With him in the park at night were men, women and children escaping their stifling tenement rooms. The hunger and want written on their faces stayed with him for a long time.

He spent his afternoons in the City Hall Park reading damaged books which he bought from push-cart men for a few cents each and drinking ice-cold, sterilized milk sold at a penny a glass. During one of his sessions in the park a policeman approached the "meek and studious milk-drinking hobo," and, without warning, struck him a severe blow over the head with his club, knocking him down. He managed to struggle to his feet and disappear before the policeman could nab him. He had no desire to spend thirty days on Blackwells Island for resisting an officer.

A few days later Jack was in jail in Niagara Falls as a vagrant. The next morning he was sent to the Erie County penitentiary for thirty days, summarily dispatched to prison, along with fifteen other men, by a judge who did not even bother to ask a routine, "guilty or not guilty." Jack London was beginning to learn the meaning of the term, class justice. The month in prison filled in other essential details in his education in the class struggle. When he emerged from prison he knew his status in society.

Through the influence of a convict friend, Jack was made a trusty. He thus had freedom to get a complete picture of life in the Pen. He saw men robbed and beaten to death; he saw prisoners throw fits and go mad; he saw bestial tortures inflicted upon inmates by sadistic guards, and he saw the filthy, unsanitary conditions under which the prisoners were compelled to live. He saw the penal system, not re-forming criminals, but actually making them worse criminals as it instilled in them the determination to revenge themselves on a society which had treated them worse than beasts. He himself ventured no protest against these conditions at this time; indeed, he acted as any other trusty, getting what he could for himself and making the con-victs pay for favors. But the suffering he witnessed bit deep, and in later years he was to write brilliant, scathing indictments of prison conditions.

As soon as he was released, Jack hopped the cars of the Canadian Pacific and worked his way back to the west coast. But this was a new Jack London. The road, as he called these several months of hoboing, marks the turning point in his life. New ideas had presented themselves which were to be vastly significant in his development. The tramps he had met had treated him as an equal in spite of his youth. They had told him their stories. He had listened intently to the labor men and thinkers who were on the march with him. He learned that these men had once been as young, as strong, as fearless as he. The capitalists had used these poor "work beasts" for their gain and kicked them into the gutter or sent them to jail when they no longer provided profits. Jack saw ahead to the time when a similar fate might be his; when, instead of light-hearted vagabondage, he would be riding the rails and begging for food and shelter from necessity. He knew now that he too was a member of what the sociologists called the submerged tenth at the bottom of the social pit, and that the only way in which he could avert the scrap heap when his time came was to develop his brain, since muscles were used up so quickly.

But Jack emerged from his "life in the underworld" with more than a formula for self-elevation. The class struggle became a reality in these tramping journeys. He understood that there was something basically wrong with a society which exhausted so many people for the profits of the wealthy after which they could look forward only to misery and degradation. What if he could save himself from such a fate by playing the game properly? There would still be millions of young people like himself condemned by the existing system to the fate of the road.

As they rode the baggage cars together the men talked about these problems. Some said that there was nothing to do, for the forces which controlled society were too powerful to be beaten. But Jack heard others talk of the great strength of the working class when it was organized and how it had been able throughout history to wrest concessions from the capitalists. They spoke of socialism, of the writings of Karl Marx and Frederick Engels. In every country in the world, they told him, there existed movements based upon Marxian socialist theory which were engaged in the struggle to overthrow the present economic system and usher in a new society where the products of man's labor would be used for the benefit of all. Here in his own country, too, they assured him, there had existed such movements for nearly half a century.

American socialism before the 1890's, when Jack London became interested in the movement, had already enjoyed an exciting history. As in Europe it had its beginnings in utopian experiments founded upon the theories of Robert Owen and Charles Fourier. Marxian or Scientific Socialism was brought to the United States by German immigrants who arrived in the late 'forties and throughout the 'fifties, many of them refugees from the reaction which followed the abortive revolution of 1848. In October, 1857 the Communist Club of New York was formed with a constitution which required all members to "recognize the complete equality of all men—no matter of what color or sex," and to "strive to abolish the bourgeois property system . . . and substitute for it a sensible system under which participation in the material and spiritual pleasures of the earth would be accessible to everyone and corresponding, as much as possible, to his needs." Meanwhile, Americans were becoming familiar with the name of Karl Marx through his contributions to the *New York Tribune,* the most widely circulated newspaper in the country.

Before and during the Civil War the Marxists played a significant role in the struggle to overthrow Negro slavery and, after the war, they made their influence felt in the local and national trade unions which emerged during the course of the conflict. Yet throughout these years the growth of the socialist movement was limited by the character of its membership. It consisted mainly of German workers and intellectuals many of whom simply transferred to America what they had learned in Germany without attempting to understand the differences between the two countries. V. L. Rosenberg, Secretary of the Socialist Labor Party, put it quite candidly in 1885: "Let us not conceal the truth: the Socialist Labor Party is only a German colony, an adjunct of the German-speaking Social Democracy." A year later Engels himself criticized the German-American socialists for failing properly to integrate their movement among the American masses:

> *The Germans have not understood how to use their theory as a lever which could set the American masses in motion; they do not understand the theory themselves for the most part and treat it in a doctrinaire and dogmatic way, as some-*

> *thing which has got to be learnt off by heart but which will then*
> *supply all needs without more ado. To them it is a* credo, *and*
> *not a guide to action. Added to which they learn no English on*
> *principle. Hence the American masses had to seek out their*
> *own way. . . .*

Despite these shortcomings, socialist thought grew enormously in the United States during the very years Jack London was learning the realities of the class struggle as a worker in the jute mill, cannery and power house, and as a hobo on the road. The pent-up bitterness of workers, farmers and small business men over the power of growing monopoly caused them to turn an attentive ear to proposals for far-reaching changes in the existing social system. The publication of Edward Bellamy's *Looking Backward* in January, 1888, at the height of the intense industrial conflict of the decade, lent impetus to this growing interest in a new social system. Hundreds of thousands read this utopian account of the operations of a cooperative commonwealth in the United States in the year 2000, and overnight Nationalist groups, seeking "to nationalize the functions of production and distribution," sprang up everywhere, linked together loosely through correspondence and exchange of lectures, and recruiting their membership mainly from the urban middle class.

Although the short-lived Nationalist movement had little in common with scientific socialism and Bellamy himself went to great pains to point out that he was no Marxist, it did contribute to the growth of the socialist movement in this country. Not a few Nationalists moved into the Socialist Labor Party (in too many cases taking with them much more of Bellamy's utopianism and emphasis on gradual evolutionary reforms than they did of Marxism), and *Looking Backward* continued for many years to constitute for many Americans their first introduction to socialism.

Among those who moved from the Nationalist movement to the Socialist Labor Party, the most important was Daniel De Leon. A brilliant writer and a man of broad culture, De Leon rapidly became the most prominent figure in the Socialist Labor Party. As editor of *The People*, the Party's organ, and as a national lecturer for the Party, De Leon did much to lift the Socialist Labor Party out of the narrow confines of the German-speaking element. In the 1890's the Socialist Labor Party still was mainly based upon foreign-born workmen, but it had set up numerous English-speaking groups. Lecturers

for the Party went all over the country to speak at "cross roads,
school houses, street corners, on Commons, before debating societies,
reform or radical clubs, or wherever an audience can be gathered to
listen to the gospel of socialism."

The dawn of Jack London's interest in socialism coincided with the
beginnings of the transformation of the socialist movement from small
groups of men and women scattered about the country, who centered
most of their activities around foreign-language newspapers, into a
gigantic organization of protest which brought home to hundreds of
thousands of the American people, through a chain of newspapers
and magazines in the English language, the message that the utiliza-
tion of the vast American wealth for the community rather than individual profit could produce a saner, more just and more durable
society. To this remarkable growth Jack London through his writings
and speeches was to make a valuable contribution.

On his return to Oakland from his tramping journey, Jack London
had decided coolly and irrevocably what his course would be. Immediately he set about acquiring the formal education which, for a
time, he believed indispensable to reaching his goal of selling the
products of his brain. In 1895, at the age of nineteen, he entered Oakland High School. He supported himself as best he could, mowing
lawns, running errands, beating carpets, and assisting the school
janitor.

Still he managed to find time to pursue further the interest in
socialism which the discussion on the road had aroused in him. One
of his associates had often mentioned *The Communist Manifesto,* so
he obtained a copy of the pamphlet from the library. He was astounded by what he read. He found all the questions that had been
piling up in his mind during his life as a newsboy, factory hand, pirate
and hobo clearly answered in the revolutionary pamphlet written by
Marx and Engels in 1847. His own experience in the class struggle,
he now saw, was no accident. He learned that throughout all history
there had existed a conflict between opposing forces and that he lived
in the era of the final conflict. From the pamphlet lying before him
he copied into his notebook the words:

> *The whole history of mankind has been a history of contests*
> *between exploiting and exploited; a history of these class*
> *struggles shows the evolution of economic civilization just as*

Darwin's studies show the evolution of man; with the coming of industrialism and concentrated capital a stage has been reached whereby the exploited cannot attain its emancipation from the ruling class without once and for all emancipating society at large from all future exploitation, oppression, class distinctions and class struggles.

He learned also, as he read further in the *Manifesto,* why previous attempts to change society into Socialism failed; how the laws of capitalist society itself force workers into organizations of their own choosing; why the bourgeoisie loses the power to remain the ruling class; and the real meaning of the so-called eternal truths like freedom and justice. He discovered, too, that there was more to the program of Scientific Socialism than a "square deal for the underdog," that it called for the abolition of private property and the collective ownership of the means of production and distribution. Now he not only began to understand the past of society, but also to see clearly the direction in which present society was moving.

One paragraph in the *Manifesto* appealed especially to Jack. He underlined with his heavy pencil the passionate words ending with the powerful battlecry:

> *The socialists disdain to conceal their aims and views. They openly declare their ends can be attained only by a forcible overthrow of all existing conditions. Let the ruling class tremble at the socialistic revolution. The proletarians have nothing to lose but their chains. They have a world to gain. Working men of all countries, unite!*

Jack never forgot these words. He used them in one form or another in street-corner speeches, in addresses before University audiences, in talks to businessmen's groups and Women's Clubs, and in his revolutionary essays, short stories and novels. He had only contempt for those socialists who wished to tone down this final paragraph of the *Manifesto,* contending that it had lost most of its original significance.

Jack London may have read little else of Marx and Engels, but it was from the *Manifesto,* with its inimitable clarity, that he obtained the fundamental concepts of his socialism. Some of the principles of Marxism that went counter to his own preconceived prejudices, he either ignored, shunted aside or distorted so that often he would mar the insight that he obtained from the *Manifesto* with absurdities. But three basic concepts which he drew from his initial reading of this pamphlet were never to leave him, even after he resigned from the Socialist Party—the belief in the class struggle; the conviction that private ownership of the means of production and the interest of the majority of the people were opposed; and confidence in the inevitable emergence of Socialism.

Now that he knew that he was a socialist, Jack began to search out the movement in his community. He joined the Henry Clay Debating Society to which came the cream of Oakland's intellectual progressives, and participated in discussions on economic issues with young lawyers, doctors, musicians and University students. He was invited to join the Socialist Labor Party branch in Oakland, became an active member, and proclaimed that his proudest possession was his Party card.

The Socialist Labor Party of Oakland had been organized in 1892 by a group of middle class intellectuals. They included a few former Abolitionists who in their quest for a new Cause had hit upon socialism, several ministers who saw in socialism a means of reviving the spirit of early Christianity, a number of exiled German socialists, and one or two former members of the British Socialist Labor Party. Much of the branch's activities was taken up with theoretical discussions, but some of the members were active propagandists, speaking on street corners and at open air meetings.

Jack participated eagerly in the discussions, but noticed the absence of workingmen. Young as he was, he had already experienced more of the class struggle than many of the members of his branch, and this, plus his reading of *The Communist Manifesto,* had convinced him that however important the middle class intellectuals were in the struggle for socialism, it would rest mainly on the shoulders of the working class to conduct the consistent class-conscious battle against capitalism. He decided to go where the workers were, attended meetings of trade unions and other workingmen's organizations, listened to the discussions and talked to them about socialism. These early contacts with the labor movement in California were to fill an important gap in his thinking. He himself had never belonged to a trade union, nor had he hitherto understood too much of the importance of organization for the working-class. Indeed, when his foster-father, John London, had worked as a scab during the great railroad strike of 1894, Jack had seen nothing to condemn in the act.

Now, however, he was to become a passionate convert to trade union-ism, and this was both to deepen his class-consciousness and to give to his writings on socialism a reality which was absent from the disser-tations of many intellectuals in the movement.

Not long after he joined the Party, Jack made his first speech in public. The Mayor of Oakland, yielding to reactionary pressure, an-nounced that there would be no more permits issued to the Socialist Labor Party for outdoor meetings. The Party decided to test the issue by conducting an outdoor meeting without a permit, leaving it up to the courts to decide the constitutionality of the Mayor's decree. Jack volunteered to speak, chancing an arrest and a possible jail sentence. But when he mounted the soap-box he got stage-fright, stammered a few incoherent sentences, and turning to his friend, Jim Whitaker, cried, "My God, Jim, I can't do it." Jim took his place. Later when a patrol wagon drew up, Jack again stepped on the soap-box, waiting to be arrested. Charged with speaking without a permit, he was let off with a stern lecture and a warning of imprisonment if it happened again.

The following day the Oakland papers played up the story, calling Jack "The Boy Socialist," a name that was picked up and applied to him for years.

All this time, Jack was at high school. He mingled little with his fellow-students, partly because they were comparatively children, and also because he was ashamed of his poor clothes and lack of money. Once he became the school janitor even the meager contacts he had established were broken.

But the existence of a student literary magazine, *The Aegis*, com-forted him. Of the ten articles and stories he published in *The Aegis*, several came from his experiences on the road and one was his first socialist article. In this essay, "Optimism, Pessimism and Patriotism," published in 1895, Jack accused the "powers that be" of keeping edu-cation from the masses, because of their fear that it would arouse in them a spirit of revolt. He pointed to the evils of capitalism, the long hours and low wages and the social and moral degradation that flowed from these evils, and urged "ye Americans, patriots and optimists to awake! Seize the reins of a corrupted government and educate the masses."

The Members of the Board of Education had barely recovered from the shock of seeing a revolutionary article in the high school paper when Jack again publicly proclaimed his socialist views before the school. Although he was not a member of the graduating class, he was chosen one of the debaters at the graduating exercises. What topic was assigned to him for his speech is not known, but immediately following his opening remarks he launched into a socialist oration. He announced his conviction that the time had arrived for the destruction of the existing social order, and that he personally was prepared to use any means to achieve this end. Georgia Bamford, one of Jack's classmates, recalls that some in the audience feared that he might at any moment descend from the platform and tear into the well-dressed listeners.

This time the Board of Education demanded disciplinary action. But Jack never returned to Oakland High School. He felt that he could learn little about writing from his English teachers who disliked his style of writing. Besides, he was twenty years old and impatient with his slow progress at school.

On money borrowed from his sister, Eliza, Jack entered a preparatory school as a short-cut to the University. He covered ground so rapidly that he was well on the way to completing two years' work in one semester. But the director, fearing that his progress would be cited by the Universities as proof of the loose methods of preparatory schools, returned Jack's fee in full. He finished the cramming by himself, studying nineteen hours a day in order to take the entrance examinations in August. For three months he dug into English, history, algebra, geometry, literature and physics, the last without the aid of a laboratory. At first he also tried to keep up with Party meetings and lectures, but after two months he gave that up to concentrate on his studies. The second week of August, 1896 saw the end of the ordeal. He spent several days at the Berkeley campus plowing through the examinations, and then, completely exhausted but confident that he had passed, took his first fling in a year and a half, getting gloriously drunk.

Jack entered the freshman class at the University of California in September and remained for little more than one semester. John London was too ill to provide for the family, and Jack had once again to shoulder the responsibilities for the home. It is doubtful, however, if he left the Berkeley campus reluctantly. He seems rapidly to have become disgusted with the superficial political and social thinking of the professors and students, and to have become convinced that there was little the faculty could teach him that he could not obtain for himself. At any rate, the bitterness he displayed later towards the cloistered life of the University campus stemmed directly from his own experience at Berkeley.

On February 4, 1897 Jack was granted honorable dismissal from the University. He knew that he had to find a job, but first he tried his hand at writing. He had contributed nothing to the publications at the University, but his name had apeared in print signed to letters he had sent to the *Times* and *Item,* Oakland newspapers, advocating socialism as against the single taxers and the Populists in the election campaign of 1896. Now he again took to the typewriter and for several weeks, working day and night, turned out poetry, essays and stories. As rapidly as he finished a manuscript he sent it off East to the magazines. But only rejection slips came back. Finally, when the London family was down to its last dollar, he gave it up and took a job in the laundry of the Belmont Academy. For thirty dollars a month plus board and lodging he sorted, washed, starched and ironed shirts, collars, cuffs and trousers. Once again he experienced the exhausting life of the wage slave; once again he was too tired after a week's work to open a book; and once again it seemed that he was trapped, doomed to have his strength sucked dry by the machine and then to be tossed aside.

Suddenly there appeared a solution to his problems. Gold was discovered in the Klondike. Adventure and the lure of easy money beckoned. On July 25, 1897, Jack and his brother-in-law, financed by Eliza to the tune of fifteen hundred dollars, most of which came from a mortgage she had taken out on her house, set sail on the *Umatilla* for the Alaskan gold fields.

Jack's Alaskan adventures would have laid the average man low forever. He wrote later of one of his feats of strength:

> *I remember at the end of the twenty-eight-mile portage across Chilkoot from Dyea Beach to Lake Linderman, I was packing up with the Indians and outpacking many an Indian. The last pack into Linderman was three miles. I back-tripped it four times a day, and on each forward trip carried one hundred and fifty pounds. This means that over the worst trails I daily traveled twenty-four miles, twelve of which were under a burden of one hundred and fifty pounds.*

He was happy in the Klondike. The men he met were congenial and stimulating, and he learned much from their discussions. To his delight he found a wide interest in the camps in political and economic issues, with socialism the favorite topic of conversation. Fred Thompson, a close companion of his Klondike days, recalled later that Jack was too busy discussing socialism with the prospectors even to split wood. These discussions around camp fires paved the way for the organization of the Socialist Party in Alaska which grew so rapidly in a few years that George Goebel, the socialist candidate, came within forty votes of being elected the first territorial representative in Congress.

Jack was deeply impressed by various aspects of life in the Klondike. He was to make frequent reference later to the fact that the Indians in Alaska shared both poverty and wealth together so that no one in the tribe benefited at the expense of others. Again he appreciated the community conscience that developed among the individualistic miners by the sheer necessities of frontier life. These men worked hard, lived hard, and fought hard, but among them there was nothing of the pettiness and sordidness of the commercial world he had left behind. Nor were they restrained by conventions. When they found gold they spent it in orgies of dissipation; yet the next night they would calmly discuss their experiences as if nothing had happened. This type of life was always to appeal to Jack London, and often, he would contrast it with civilization and its established customs. "The grim Yukon life had failed to make Daylight hard," he wrote later in his novel, *Burning Daylight*. "It required civilization to produce this result."

Yet as a socialist London understood that life in the Klondike as he knew it was doomed, and that soon enough it would give way to a new Klondike which would be more efficient than the old. He concluded an article on "The Economics of the Klondike," published in *Review of Reviews* in January, 1900, with the prediction:

> *The new Klondike, the Klondike of the future, will present remarkable contrasts with the Klondike of the past. Natural obstacles will be cleared away or surmounted, primitive methods abandoned, and the hardship of toil and travel reduced to the smallest possible minimum. Exploration and transportation will be systematized. There will be no waste energy, no harum-scarum carrying on of industry. The frontiersman will yield to the laborer, the prospector to the mining engineer, the dog-driver to the engine-driver, the trader and speculator to the steady-going modern man of business; for these are the*

men in whose hands the destiny of the Klondike will be intrusted.

Jack mined no gold during his year's stay in the Klondike, but he learned enough from listening to the stories of those who did the mining and from his own observations of the life about him to earn a fortune in later years. He took careful notes on everything he heard and saw and these were to provide the material for the numerous stories that were to flow from his pen after his return to the States.

An attack of scurvy hastened his homeward journey. In June, 1898, when he had recovered sufficiently to travel, Jack started on the 1900 mile voyage down the Yukon River and along the Bering Sea in a small open boat. Nineteen days later the party arrived at St. Michael where Jack got a job as a stoker on a steamer bound for British Columbia. From there he beat his way to Oakland. He arrived home penniless to find John London dead and the responsibility for the family, augmented during his absence by his foster father's grandson, completely on his shoulders.

His first impulse was to write, to turn the raw material he had gathered in Alaska into finished stories. But he shoved the desire aside and began again the search for a job. He tried everything, willing to begin as a manual laborer, willing to go back into the laundry, but all he could pick up was the usual round of odd jobs washing windows and beating carpets. When the post office announced civil service examinations, he took the tests and passed.

In the meantime, while awaiting his appointment as a mail carrier, he turned again to writing. Four years later, when his success and fame were already assured, he wrote of those early heart-breaking efforts at "Getting into Print":

> . . . . let me state that I had many liabilities and no assets, no income, several mouths to feed, and for landlady, a poor widow woman whose imperative necessities demanded that I should pay my rent with some degree of regularity. This was my economic situation when I buckled on the harness and went up against the magazines.
>
> Further, and to the point, I knew positively nothing about it. I lived in California, far from the great publishing centers. I did not know what an editor looked like. I did not know a soul, with the exception of my own, who had ever tried to write anything, much less tried to publish it. . . .

I had no one to give me tips, no one's experience to profit by. So I sat down and wrote in order to get an experience of my own. I wrote everything—short stories, articles, anecdotes, jokes, essays, sonnets, ballads, vilanelles, triolets, songs, light plays in iambic tetrameter, and heavy tragedies in blank verse. These various creations I stuck into envelopes, enclosed return postage, and dropped into the mail. Oh, I was prolific. Day by day my manuscripts mounted up, till the problem of finding stamps for them became as great as that of making life livable for my widow landlady.

All my manuscripts came back. They continued to come back. The process seemed like the working of [a] soulless machine. I dropped the manuscript into the mail box. After the lapse of a certain approximate length of time, the manuscript was brought back to me by the postman. Accompanying it was a stereotyped rejection slip. A part of the machine, some cunning arrangement of cogs and cranks at the other end . . . had transferred the manuscript to another envelope, taken the stamps from the inside and pasted them outside, and added the rejection slip.

He sent off at least seven Alaskan stories and a twenty-thousand word serial for *Youth's Companion* before he received a letter from the *Overland Monthly* to whom he had sent the story, "To the Man on the Trail." Its appearance convinced him that this was the thing he had been waiting for:

I could not open the letter right away [he wrote later]. *It seemed a sacred thing. It contained the written word of an editor. The magazine he represented I imagined ranked in the first class. I knew it had a four-thousand word story of mine. What will it be? I asked. The minimum rate, I answered modest as ever; forty dollars of course. Having thus guarded myself against any kind of disappointment, I opened the letter and read what I thought would be blazed in letters of fire on my memory for all time. Alas! the years are few, yet I have forgotten. But the gist of the letter was coldly to the effect that my story was available, that they would print it in the next number, and that they would pay me for it the sum of five dollars.*

Five dollars! A dollar and a quarter a thousand! That I did

> *not die right there and then convinces me that I am possessed*
> *of a singular ruggedness of soul which will permit me to survive*
> *and ultimately qualify me for the oldest inhabitant.*
>
> *Five dollars! When? The editor did not state. I didn't have*
> *even a stamp with which to convey my acception or rejection*
> *of his offer. Just then the landlady's little girl knocked at the*
> *back door. Both problems were clamoring more compellingly*
> *than ever for solution. It was plain there was no such thing*
> *as a minimum rate. Nothing remained but to get out and shovel*
> *coal. I had done it before and earned more money at it. I re-*
> *solved to do it again. . . .*

But that very afternoon the postman brought him another letter, this time from *The Black Cat,* with the offer of forty dollars for a four-thousand-word story, provided he would consent to having it cut in half. He promptly forgot his coal-shoveling resolution, retrieved his bicycle, watch, and mackintosh from the pawnbroker, paid the landlady, the grocer and butcher, and continued "to whang away at the typewriter." The desire for self-expression, the aim to rise to the heights of literary fame completely consumed him, so that in spite of the rejection slips which followed his first success, in spite of his extreme poverty, in spite of his continued trips to the pawnbroker, when the Post Office on January 16, 1899 offered him an appointment at sixty-five dollars a month, he rejected it.

Four things, Jack decided, were necessary to become a great writer: good health, work, a philosophy of life, and sincerity. His health was good; the prodigious energy with which he attacked his writing has seldom been paralleled, but he still had to develop the clarity of his thinking and to deepen his philosophy of life. "If you think clearly," he wrote in 1903 in an article entitled "On the Writer's Philosophy of Life," "you will write clearly; if your thoughts are worthy, so will your writing be worthy. . . . If your knowledge is sparse or unsystematized, how can your words he broad or logical? And without the strong central thread of a working philosophy, how can you make order out of chaos? how can your foresight and insight be clear? how can you have a quantitative and qualitative perception of the relative importance of every scrap of knowledge you possess? And without all this how can you possibly be yourself? how can you have something fresh for the jaded care of the world?"

So he set out to systematize his thinking, to deepen his knowledge, to broaden his working philosophy of life, to "find out about this earth, this universe; this force and matter, and the spirit that glimmers up through force and matter from the maggot to Godhead," to gather up all he could of "history, evolution, ethics, and the thousand and one branches of knowledge." He read Boas and Frazer in anthropology, Darwin, Huxley and Wallace in biology, Adam Smith, Malthus, Ricardo, Bastiat, John Stuart Mill in economics, Aristotle, Gibbon, Hobbes, Locke, Hume, Hegel, Kant, Berkeley, Liebnitz, Nietzsche, Herbert Spencer, Haeckel and Kidd in history and philosophy. He reread Marx and Engels and devoured everything he could find on unemployment, the causes and cures of poverty, criminology and trade unionism.

How much of what he gulped down from these books remained with him and influenced his writing is difficult to determine exactly. But we do know that with the concepts of Marxism in his thinking were now to be amalgamated doctrines derived from Nietzsche, Spencer and Kidd.

All works on the Nietzschean world-conqueror, the strong and ruthless supermen, the blond beasts who were destined to be the rulers and emperors over all other men interested Jack London. He read and discussed several of the books by the archpriest of the cult of superman, *Thus Spake Zarathustra, The Will to Power, Genealogy of Morals, The Case of Wagner, The Antichrist*, and later wrote a preface for Leo Berg's *The Superman*. George Bernard Shaw's "philosopher-athlete" in *Man and Superman* appealed to Jack immensely.

The fact that so much of the Nietzschean philosophy, emphasizing as it did an aristocracy of supermen who would dominate the ordinary run of human beings, and flaunting its detestation of socialism and trade unionism, went counter to his socialist convictions did not bother Jack London. He took those aspects of Nietzsche which appealed to him and which he could, in his own fashion, reconcile with Marxism. After all, why could not the supermen work to bring about a system under which the average man would be benefited? "Why should there be one empty belly in all the world," he wrote in the essay "Wanted: A New Law of Development," "when the work of ten men can feed a hundred? What if my brother be not so strong as I? He has not sinned. Wherefore should he suffer hunger—he and his sinless little ones? Away with the old law. There is food and shelter for all, therefore let all receive food and shelter."

While it is true that the Nietzschean world-conqueror pops up somewhere in nearly all of his books, it still must be emphasized that London never fully accepted Nietzsche's philosophy. In his essay, "The Class Struggle," he says, speaking of the working class: "They refuse to be the 'glad perishers' so glowingly described by Nietzsche." In "How I became a Socialist," he burlesques Nietzsche's blond beast fetish: "I found there," he writes, referring to the down-and-outers among the unemployed, "all sorts of men, many of whom had once been as good as myself and just as *blond-beastly*; sailor-men, soldier-men, labor-men, all wrenched and distorted and twisted out of shape by toil and hardship and accident, and cast adrift by their masters like so many old horses." Again, in a footnote in *The Iron Heel*, London describes Nietzsche as a "mad philosopher who caught wild glimpses of truth, but who, before he was done, reasoned himself around the great circle of human thought and off into madness." Too many among London's critics have ignored these comments and have concluded that Nietzsche completely dominated his reason and conscience. Actually, London often warned against the Nietzschean philosophy, insisting that "individualism will destroy itself and will destroy America if it does not meet with Socialist opposition." Moreover, he contended that some of his most important writing was directed against Nietzsche's doctrines. Indeed, the last literary note Jack London ever penciled was to this effect: "Martin Eden and Sea Wolf, attacks on Nietzschean philosophy, which even the socialists missed the point of."

Herbert Spencer and the evolutionists of whom he was the philosophical spokesman and leader also deeply impressed Jack London. Yet, unlike the industrial and financial leaders of the country who became enthusiastic disciples of Spencer, he rejected those features of Spencer's philosophy which were used effectively against all reform movements. Whereas Spencer contended "that there shall not be a *forcible* burdening of the superior for the support of the inferior," London stressed the duty of the superior to work towards the achievement of a society which would allow all to grow to their full stature. Whereas Spencer condemned legislative interference with *natural* law, London advocated legislation outlawing factory employment of children and sweatshop wages for women workers and championed many other reforms which would eliminate evils stemming from the operation of natural law. Whereas Spencer held the rights of property to be absolute, London in speech, newspaper article, essay and book after book called for the overthrow of the system of private property.

Nothing that he read in Spencer and his disciples, Haeckel and Kidd, weakened London's belief in the inevitability of the class struggle under the capitalist system or his confidence in the ultimate triumph of socialism. From them he did obtain, however, pseudo-scientific justification for the most serious flaw in his thinking—the doctrine of white supremacy, a doctrine that was to remain with him to the end of his life. One of the persistently recurrent themes in London's stories is the supremacy over all other peoples of the white man. To the Solomon Islands on Copra and "black-birding" expeditions, to the Klondike in the grueling race for gold stakes, to the farthest north among the Eskimo tribes in Russia—over sea and mountain, sand and snow—the white man pursues through Jack London's stories his conquering way. And white man meant Nordic, and still more specifically, Anglo-Saxon. London did try to reconcile his belief in the superman with his socialism; he did reject those features of Nietzsche's and Spencer's philosophy which went counter to his conviction that all men, the strong and the weak, should unite in the struggle for socialism, but he never altered the doctrine that the white man was superior and that the earth belonged to him. There were even times when he argued that socialism was "devised for the happiness of certain kind of races," and that the socialist commonwealth should operate for the sole benefit of the Anglo-Saxon.

The amazing thing, however, is that so little of this actually entered into Jack London's writings and speeches for the socialist movement, for here he lowered the race barrier and called all men Comrades, the black and brown as well as the white. Yet perhaps it is not amazing at all, for during the most important period of his life, his activity and enthusiasm for the Cause drove out of his thinking, even if temporarily, those backward aspects of his philosophy that had no place in the make-up of a socialist. And as he drifted away from such activity and enthusiasm, they returned, weakening the validity of all that he did and wrote.

But this was still in the future. Meanwhile, he was trying desperately to make the grade as a writer. His success could be gauged by his trips to the pawnbroker. When checks from editors were scarce, Jack pawned his mackintosh and suit of clothes; when they became still scarcer, in went his bicycle, and finally when he was desperate he would turn over his typewriter. Then some story of his would be accepted, and he would redeem everything and start all over again. The following week back would go the mackintosh and suit of clothes, and in the next fortnight his bicycle and typewriter would keep them company. The *Overland Monthly* promised him seven dollars and fifty cents for every story they published, but Jack literally had to invade the office of the magazine and threaten violence before he could collect even five dollars for "The White Silence" published in February, 1899. After considerable correspondence he obtained seven-fifty each for "The Son of Wolf" which appeared in April, 1899 and "The Men of Forty Mile" the following month. With the publication of other stories, a poem and even an article or two in May and June, he was able to take his bicycle out of the pawnshop.

Twice during that terrible spring of 1899 when the family lived on beans and potatoes, when there were times that not even five cents or a slice of bread remained in the house, when he even offered to sell stories for a dollar to silence the creditors, Jack had turned down the Post Office appointment. Now it seemed that his faith in himself was justified. He was being talked about in Oakland, and even doubters had to admit that the boy with the second-hand suit and the torn mackintosh could write.

Most of the one thousand words he wrote undeviatingly every day, six days a week, went into the Alaskan stories and poems, but he also turned out socialist essays, one of which, "The Question of the Maximum," was purchased by an Eastern magazine but not published because the editor became frightened by its radical theme. Jack also used this essay as the basis of a lecture before a branch meeting of the Socialist Labor Party in Oakland. He told his comrades that the industrialized nations of the world were engaged in a race to dispose of their surplus commodities among the backward nations. Yet, since machinery was being sold to these same backward countries, they were also developing industry, even though at a slower pace, and would eventually also have a surplus. Inevitably, he predicted, great wars would occur as a result of the struggle over markets and colonies. But eventually the people would rise up and take over the means of production and distribution and put an end to the economic rivalries which led to wars. "The procession of ages," he concluded, "has marked not only the rise of man, but the rise of the common man. From the chattel slave, or the serf chained to the soil, to the highest seats in modern society, he has risen, rung by rung, amid the crumbling of the divine right of kings and the crash of falling sceptres. That he has done this, only in the end to pass into the perpetual slavery of the industrial oligarch, is something at which his whole past cries in protest. The common man is worthy of a better future, or else he is not worthy of his past."

The Oakland Socialists were so impressed with London's ability to analyze complex problems like the economic foundations of imperialism and the inevitable emergence of socialism from the contradictions within capitalism in simple, clear and vigorous language that they invited him to lecture to the Local every Sunday night. Jack promptly accepted, and although he was at his typewriter day and night trying to earn a living as a writer, he somehow managed to find the time to deliver these weekly talks. Moreover, despite his poverty he neither asked for nor expected to receive any compensation for this work.

In December, 1899 at a Socialist Labor Party meeting in San Francisco Jack first met Anna Strunsky, whose friendship during the next three years was to provide him with the intellectual stimulation that his active mind needed. She has given us an unforgettable picture of Jack London as he appeared at this time at the age of twenty-four, a picture that conveys a little of his magnetism and explains why those who once knew him could never forget him:

> I see him in pictures, steering his bicycle with one hand and with the other clasping a great bunch of yellow roses which he has just gathered out of his own garden, a cap moved back on his thick brown hair, the large blue eyes with their long lashes looking out star-like upon the world—an indescribably virile and beautiful boy, the kindness and wisdom of his expression somehow belying his youth.
>
> I see his face down among the poppies and following with his eyes his kites soaring against the high blue of the California skies, past the tops of the giant sequoias and eucalyptus which he so dearly loved.
>
> I see him becalmed on "The Spray," the moon rising behind us, and hear him rehearse his generalizations made from his studies in the watches of the night before of Spencer and Darwin. His personality invested his every movement and every

*detail of his life with an alluring charm. One took his genius
for granted, even in those early years when he was struggling
with his unequalled energies to impress himself upon the
world.*

Anna was a member of a large Russian Jewish family who had come
to the United States to escape the tsarist pogroms. They kept open
house in San Francisco and interesting people dropped in. Jack became a frequent visitor at her home and was moved by the warmth
displayed at the long dinner table. He told Anna that someday he too
would like to have a large home with many guests seated about enjoying themselves. Even now his home was "the Mecca of every
returned Klondiker, sailor or soldier of fortune" he had ever met.
"Some day," he wrote to her, "I shall build an establishment, invite
them all, and turn them loose upon each other. . . ." After learning of
the coldness of his own home environment, Anna understood what mo-
tivated this desire.

With Anna Strunsky Jack was brutally frank. He was a socialist,
he told her, but he was also a hard realist living in a chaotic jungle,
and he was determined to push to the top. ". . . . should you know
me," he wrote to her on December 21, 1899, "understand this: I, too,
was a dreamer, on a farm, nay, a California ranch. But early, at only
nine, the hard hand of the world was laid upon me. It has never relaxed. It has left me sentimental, but destroyed sentimentalism. It
has made me practical, so that I am known as harsh, stern, uncompromising. It has taught me that reason is mightier than imagination;
that the scientific man is superior to the emotional man. . . ." His
reason had convinced him, he assured her, that he could beat the
capitalists at their own game, and with cold-blooded efficiency he
would extract the most he could for the products of his brain. But, he
insisted, this was not simply for his own personal aggrandizement, for
he was confident that by so doing he would render the Cause a great
service, that it would have "certain propaganda value" to show the
Capitalists that "Socialists were not derelicts and failures."

Anna struggled hard to eliminate these contradictions in London's
thinking, tried to get him to understand that he could not play the
game of the capitalists without being corrupted by it.

> *This dream of his* [she recalled later] *even when projected
> and before it became a reality, was repellent to me. The greatest
> natures, I thought, the surest Social Democrats, would be*

*incapable of harboring it. To pile up wealth, or personal success—surely anybody who was a beneficiary of the Old Order
must belong to it to some extent in spirit and in fact!*

*So it was that our ancient quarrel, and many, many others,
took their rise in the same source—a doubt, not as to himself—
I never doubted the beauty and warmth and the purity of his
own nature—but as to the ideas and the principles which he
invited to guide his life. They were not worthy of him, I
thought; they belittled him and eventually they might eat
away his strength and grandeur.*

She lived to see her fears justified. "He paid the ultimate price for
what he received," she wrote a year after London's death. "His success was the tragedy of his life."

And success began to come. The *Atlantic Monthly* gave him the
stamp of approval of the most aristocratic literary magazine in the
country by purchasing his story, "An Odyssey of the North," and paying one hundred and twenty dollars for it. Then on December 21, 1899
he signed a contract with Houghton Mifflin and Company, a conservative Boston publishing house, for a volume of short stories. The
reader's report on his short stories explains why his writing was overcoming the qualms and prejudices of publishers accustomed to the
"prissy" literature of the day:

> *He uses the current slang of the mining camps a little too
> freely, in fact he is far from elegant, but his style has fresh
> ness, vigor, and strength. He draws a vivid picture of the ter
> rors of cold, darkness, and starvation, the pleasures of human
> companionship in adverse circumstances, and the sterling qual
> ities which the rough battle with nature brings out. The
> reader is convinced that the author has lived the life itself.*

Then some months went by without any sales to the magazines.
The pawnshop saw him again and the pinch of poverty made him cry
out in despair: "It's money that I want, or rather, the things money
will buy: and I can never possibly have too much." Still he turned
out articles on socialism that he knew no magazine would touch and
continued studying for future essays on the same subject. At the same
time he made speaking tours for the Party to Alameda, San Jose, and
other towns. His work for the magazines was hack-work but the time
he devoted to the Party was spent on work that he loved, and he was

completely frank with himself. On February 3, 1900 he wrote to Anna Strunsky: "Saturday night, and I feel good. Saturday night, and a good week's work done—hack work, of course. Why shouldn't I. Like any other honest artisan by the sweat of my brow. . . ."

He felt good, too, for still another reason. For some time Jack had been longing for a home, children, and respectability. Frustrated in his desire to marry his first love, Mabel Applegarth, he proposed to Bessie Maddern whom he had known for some time and who, he objectively concluded, would make a good wife and an intelligent companion. Bessie like Jack loved someone else, but like him, too, she was lonely and anxious for her own home. She accepted his proposal and a week later, in January, 1900, they were married.

The turn of the century found Jack's luck definitely changed for the better. *McClure's Magazine* bought two of his short stories and agreed to take all he could turn out. In April his first volume of short stories, *The Son of the Wolf,* was published. The critics hailed him as "a natural born story teller," said the book was "full of fire and feeling," and that it possessed "much of the imaginative power and dramatic force of Kipling," with a "tenderness of sentiment and quick appreciation of the finer sentiments of heroism that are seldom seen in Kipling." The book sold fairly well and McClure promptly agreed to advance Jack $125 a month while he worked on a full-length novel.

Marriage, his wife's pregnancy and the widening circle of friends who dropped in on him at all times put a heavy drain on his allowance from McClure and the royalties from his first book. So, in addition to his daily stint on the novel, he was forced to turn out light verse, humorous sketches, stories and reviews. He also found time to win the first prize of two hundred dollars in a contest sponsored by *Cosmopolitan Magazine* for the best article on "Loss by Lack of Co-operation" with a socialist essay, "What Communities Lose by the Competitive System." Jack had toned down the article to fit the mood of the editors and it hardly breathes the revolutionary fervor to be found in his later essays. Still it is a logical and calm appraisal of the evils of the competitive system, showing how competition makes for duplication of work, and why, because of the waste growing out of this duplication, a planned society is necessary. The essay was reprinted as a penny pamphlet by the Socialist Party of England.

On January 15, 1901 his daughter, Joan, was born. It took Jack some time to recover from his disappointment at not having a son, but the need to finish the novel drove everything else out of his mind. A few weeks after Joan was born the manuscript was forwarded to McClure. Both author and publisher agreed that it was a disappointing work. McClure decided not to publish the book, but to retrieve some of his investment, peddled it around among other houses and finally sold it to J. B. Lippincott and Company of Philadelphia under whose imprint it appeared in October, 1902.

The Daughter of the Snows, London's first novel, did not enhance his reputation, yet it is important in revealing certain trends in his writing. Frona Welse, the heroine of the book, returns to her home in Alaska after several years at school. The reader first meets her as she is being rowed from the steamer to the Alaskan town she has not seen in years, and immediately he is brought into contact with a new type of American heroine. Any other of the 1902 type would have blushed and fainted at the oaths and blasphemies poured out by the boatmen, but Frona is at home with them. Actually, she can hold her own with them in the toughest of work.

Through the character of her father, Jacob Welse, the trader, the reader grasps London's love of the community spirit on the frontier. When a famine threatens the miners, Welse says: "A Bonanza property, or a block of Bonanza properties, does not entitle you to a pound more than the oldest penniless 'sour-dough,' or the newest baby born. Trust me. As long as I have a pound of grub you will not starve. Stiffen up. Shake hands." Here is the frontier emphasis on a man's need rather than his possessions which London regarded so superior to what he saw in more civilized society.

From this high level of social thinking London descends to his doctrine of white supremacy. During a discussion Frona Welse expresses her belief in the superiority of the white man over the natives, pointing out that the white man had always been able to best the Indian. London not only permits her to win the argument but later has Vance Corliss, who originally disagreed with Frona, echo her views. In essence, they are the views of London himself.

The publication of *The Daughter of the Snows* marks the end of the first and most minor period in London's career as a writer. Before its appearance two other volumes of his short stories, *The God of His Fathers* and *Children of the Frost,* had come off the press. Three volumes of short stories and one novel in three years was no mean achievement for a young writer. Jack London was definitely on his way, but his greatest work still lay before him.

During these years when Jack London was striving to become a successful writer the socialist movement in the United States was undergoing important changes. It had gained a remarkable new leader when Eugene V. Debs embraced socialism and it operated through a new organization when the Socialist Party of the United States was formed.

Until the Pullman strike of 1894 Debs had been convinced that through progressive trade unionism the working class would be able to abolish poverty, unemployment, injustice and all of its other grievances. But the ruthlessness of the railroad companies and the eager cooperation of the national government in breaking the strike opened his eyes. As Debs himself put it: ". . . in the gleam of every bayonet and the flash of every rifle *the class struggle was revealed.*" Later, while in jail for having defied an injunction during the strike, he read many books and pamphlets dealing with social and economic problems, including the first volume of Marx's *Capital.* He emerged from jail a confirmed socialist.

In the election of 1896 Debs campaigned for William Jennings Bryan, believing "that the triumph of Mr. Bryan and free silver would blunt the fangs of the money power." Following McKinley's election, he devoted all of his time and energy to the socialist movement. When the Brotherhood of the Co-operative Commonwealth—a utopian scheme for colonizing some western states—was formed in the fall of 1896, Debs became the chief organizer. In June, 1897 he united the remnants of the American Railway Union and the Brotherhood of the Co-operative Commonwealth to form the Social Democracy of America. In a circular letter to his associates in the labor movement, he wrote:

> *The issue is Socialism versus Capitalism. I am for socialism because I am for humanity. We have been cursed with the reign of gold long enough. Money constitutes no proper basis of civilization. The time has come to regenerate society—we are on the eve of a universal change.*

Two months after the founding of the new party, the Jewish socialists of the East joined its ranks. These socialists had long been chafing under the domination of Daniel De Leon and the philosophy of the Socialist Labor Party under his leadership. They were opposed to De Leon's dual union tactics, his indifference to immediate demands,

his subordination of the Party to the industrial organization of the
workers and his intransigence and inability to work with anyone
who did not unreservedly accept his doctrines. Furthermore, the
lawyers and middle class intellectuals among the Jewish socialists
shared none of De Leon's revolutionary zeal and writhed under his
attacks against petty bourgeois elements in the Party. In the 1896
convention of the Socialist Labor Party the Jewish socialists had been
expelled because of their opposition to some of De Leon's policies.
In August, 1897 they voted to affiliate with the Social Democracy of
America.

In the summer of 1898 a split occurred in the Social Democracy over
the colonization plan. The anti-colonizationists favoring political action were defeated at the party's convention, but they bolted and
decided to organize a new socialist party to be composed only of those
who believed in the "principles and program of International Socialism." The group adopted as its name, The Social Democratic Party
of America. Debs went along with the bolters and toured the country
for the new party.

For a while there was hope that the Social Democratic Party and
the Socialist Labor Party would amalgamate and form a united socialist movement. Indeed, in order to promote the fusion, the National
Executive Board of the Social Democratic Party, of which Debs was
a member, requested the editor of its official organ not to accept
articles which attacked either the tactics or the personnel of De Leon's
organization. But the unity movement quickly dissolved. A major
break was occurring in the Socialist Labor Party as members everywhere rose up in revolt against the dictatorial methods of De Leon
and his sectarian policies. Early in 1900 these discontented elements,
led by Morris Hilquit, Job Harriman and Max Hayes, met in Roches-
ter, New York, appointed a committee to work for unification with
the Social Democratic Party and invited that organization to appoint
a committee for the same purpose. The Social Democratic Party first
referred to its membership the question: "Is union between the Social
Democratic Party and the Socialist Labor Party faction desirable?"
The vote, announced in May, 1900, was 939 for union and 1213
against. Nevertheless, the forces working for unity persisted and
temporary fusion was achieved with two separate Social Democratic
Parties functioning. In the political campaign of 1900 Debs was
nominated for President of the United States by both groups and
polled nearly a hundred thousand votes.

A year later those who had worked for a united socialist movement saw their hopes realized. In August, 1901, a resolution was adopted at a convention in New York attended by delegates from both groups proclaiming the birth of the new Socialist Party under the leadership of Eugene V. Debs, Victor Berger, and Morris Hilquit.

All of these developments since 1896 barely touched the socialist movement in Oakland and San Francisco. As far as Jack London himself was concerned we have only one statement which indicates any reaction on his part to what was taking place in the movement nationally. When the Social Democracy of America was first formed by Eugene V. Debs in June, 1897, he wrote to Ted Applegarth: "Organized labor headed by Debs and beginning with the American Railway Union, has commenced a change of front. The old methods of strikes and boycotts to obtain shorter hours and better pay has been abandoned. They now strike for political power, their openly avowed goal being the cooperative commonwealth. That is, the socialist propaganda in the United States is assuming greater proportions." It is hardly an acute observation and, as was to happen frequently in the future, Jack was allowing his imagination to run away with his judgment, but it does reveal that his interest in the movement was growing. Thereafter he expressed no views on the issues involved in the conflict inside the Socialist Labor Party, but he must have been a follower of Debs, for whom he had the greatest respect and admiration, and when the great majority of the Oakland Socialists left the Socialist Labor Party and affiliated with the Socialist Party, Jack London went along with them.

In 1901 the newly-organized Oakland Socialist Party nominated Jack London, already its most popular and most publicized member, for mayor. In accepting the nomination, the twenty-five-year-old candidate said: "It is we, the Socialists, working as a leaven throughout society, who are responsible for the great and growing belief in municipal ownership. It is we, the Socialists, by our propaganda, who have forced the old parties to throw as sops to the popular unrest certain privileges." Jack put up a good campaign, but he only gained a meager 245 votes.

If the voters of Oakland had read a story by Jack London published about the time he was running for mayor the chances are that he would have received still fewer votes. Irving Stone characterizes "The Minions of Midas" which appeared in *Pearson's Magazine* in

May, 1901, as a "proletarian" story and hails it as initiating socialist fiction writing in America. Actually, although the story contains phrases like "wage slaves," "Capitalist Class," and "industrial and social wrong," it is anything but "proletarian" in content and orientation and is more revealing of some of London's limitations as a socialist than of his contribution to socialist fiction.

The story is composed of seven letters written to the Money Baron, Eben Hale, by anonymous members of a class-conscious organization calling itself The Minions of Midas. They ask for twenty million dollars and promise to strike down various innocent people if he spurns their demand. In the midst of these murders, Eben Hale, who has refused to be intimidated, commits suicide.

The members of this terroristic organization may have been class-conscious wage-slaves, but their goal is purely a selfish one. They believe that because of their superiority they should be co-rulers of the earth along with the capitalists. They are not interested in changing society; they merely want to share the spoils with the capitalists and, to achieve this goal, they institute a reign of terror to mulct the millionaires of a large portion of their wealth. Nowhere is there even the slightest indication that this money will be used to right social evils. The group simply wants the money because it needs capital to compete with the great trusts and business combinations of the capitalists.

The Minions of Midas refer to themselves as "a new force" in society, but they have nothing in common with the real force emerging at this time represented by the labor and socialist movements. Indeed, those who were slandering trade unionists and socialists, charging that they sought to achieve their aims by the murder of innocent people, could have made good use of Jack London's so-called "proletarian" story.

Probably London tossed the story off as a piece of hack-writing or perhaps he gained a certain satisfaction from the idea that The Minions of Midas were fulfilling his own personal ambition of beating the capitalists at their own game. At any rate, the story reveals how much he had yet to learn as a socialist. There were one or two members of the Socialist Party of Oakland who recognized these weaknesses in London's thinking even at this early stage in his career and tried to influence him to eradicate them. But their voices were drowned in the chorus of approval that arose from the hero-worshipping elements in the Party, most of whom knew little of Marxism themselves, and were impressed by the thought that London was reaching circles with the socialist message that they could never approach.

This much, at least, is true. Jack London was being invited to talk to groups never before reached by the socialists on the Pacific Coast. He may have made few converts on such occasions, but he did reveal his contempt for the bourgeoisie in no uncertain terms. He was invited to speak to the Women's Press Association of San Francisco on Rudyard Kipling, and a crowded auditorium faced the handsome young writer when he arose to speak. He calmly told the distinguished audience that he had sent his article on Kipling to a magazine and, since he could not speak without his manuscript, he would talk to them on "The Tramp."

This lecture had originally been delivered before the Alameda Socialist Party, was to be published in *Wilshire's Magazine,* an independent socialist monthly in February-March, 1904, and was to appear in book form a year later as the second essay in *The War of the Classes.*

To the Women's Press Association, London demonstrated, by marshalling an array of facts, that the tramp was in reality a product of economic necessity, fulfilling a need in capitalist society. The army of surplus labor, he told the ladies, is needed when production increases and the ordinary workers cannot handle the work; it is needed to work on emergency projects and to meet the demands of seasonal employment, and finally, but most important, it is needed to act as a check on all employed labor. "That which maintains the integrity of the present industrial society," he declared, "more potently than the courts, police, and military is the surplus labor army." For if it did not exist, there would be no limit to what the workers might demand, and before long labor would control both the means of production and the state. The surplus army, he continued, is recruited from the less efficient workers who can no longer provide a profit for their employers, and from those who are thrown out of work because of an economic crisis or technological improvements. They had the choice of becoming actual slaves, by working for whatever pittance their employers will toss them, or going on the road. Many of them choose to become tramps, rebels against the social order that compelled them to follow this course.

London concluded his talk with a brilliant piece of satire. He saw but one way out of the dilemma confronting society arising from the existence of the surplus army—kill off this army and then there will be no unemployment and no tramps. But the ethics of capitalism forbids this; yet it is perfectly ethical to leave them to starve to death. So let them live. But don't tell the tramp to go to work: "As the scapegoat to our economic and industrial sinning, or to the plan of things, if you will, we should give him credit. Let us be just. He is so made. Society made him. He did not make himself."

When the lecture was published several socialists pointed to significant omissions in the brilliant analysis of unemployment in capitalist society and indicated that, instead of emphasizing the struggles of the oppressed classes, London stressed their helplessness in the hands of society. But the staid ladies of the Women's Press Association were too horrified to worry about such details. When the lecture ended, the audience was in an uproar. The well-dressed listeners attacked London with such heat that the Chairlady hurriedly adjourned the meeting to prevent fist-fights.

On July 21, 1902 London received a wire from the American Press Association asking if he were ready to go immediately to South Africa to report on the aftermath of the Boer War which had come to a close six weeks before. Jack leaped at the chance, accepted by telegraph within an hour, and left immediately for New York. On arriving in the Empire City he headed for the offices of the Macmillan Company, met George F. Brett, its president, and told him about the Kempton-Wace letters, a series of philosophical letters on love on which he and Anna Strunsky had been working for some time, and which is interesting today solely because they provide an excellent insight into London's backward ideas on women. Brett promptly accepted it for publication, and assured Jack that when he returned from South Africa Macmillan would publish all that he wrote.

In high spirits, Jack sailed on the *Majestic* for England. His jubilant frame of mind was due to more than his arrangement with Macmillan and the prospect of adventure that lay before him. His trip east had convinced him that the Cause was making progress. "I meet the men of the world in Pullman coaches, New York clubs, and Atlantic liner smoking rooms," he wrote to Anna Strunsky his second day on the boat, "and, truth, to say, I am made more hopeful for the Cause by their total ignorance and non-understanding of the forces at work. They are blissfully ignorant of the coming upheaval, while they have grown bitterer and bitterer towards the workers. You see, the growing power of the workers is hurting them and making them bitter while

it does not open their eyes." In the same letter, Jack outlined his plan
of operation during his stay in London. For two days he would sink
out of sight in the slums of the East End, to view the coronation of
King Edward from the standpoint of the slum people.

The two days were to stretch into six weeks. When the ship docked,
Jack was handed a cablegram from the Press Association cancelling
the engagement. He was left with a return ticket, but with little
money. Still Jack decided that it was a fortunate turn of events, for
now he could really examine the slums of London about which he had
heard and read so much.

Passing as an American sailor stranded in England, Jack bought
some second-hand clothes, rented a room in the East End and then
set out to investigate life in the slums, taking with him the criteria—
"That which made for more life, for physical and spiritual health,
was good; that which made for less life, which hurt, dwarfed, and
distorted life, was bad." Out of that experience came the terrible picture of poverty and misery, *The People of the Abyss*. It was a book
which was turned out white-hot from the boiling reservoirs of Jack
London's indignation. Speaking of it in a letter to a friend, he says,
"It is rather hysterical, I think," but in later years he is said to have
loved it most of all his books, because "no other book of mine took
so much of my young heart and tears as that study of the economic
degradation of the poor."

Though the book is replete with factual data which lend authenticity to the study, London was not content merely to survey the
scene as a sociologist, calmly taking notes and then presenting an
academic analysis of conditions. He got to know the people; he talked
with them, and knocked about with the sailor, the hop-picker, the
derelict and the pauper. ". . . I was out all night with the homeless
ones," he wrote to Anna Strunsky on August 25, 1902, "walking the
streets in the bitter rain, and, drenched to the skin, wondering when
dawn would come. Sunday I spent with the homeless ones, in the
fierce struggle for something to eat. I returned to my rooms Sunday
evening, after thirty-six hours continuous work and short one night's
sleep. . . . I am worn out and exhausted and my nerves are blunted
with what I have seen and the suffering it has cost me." His friend
Upton Sinclair reported that "for years afterwards the memories of
this stunted and depraved population haunted him beyond all peace."

London visited rooms which were mean, sordid and completely
lacking in sanitation, and learned that the people who occupied these

dwellings earned so little in return for back-breaking and heart-breaking toil that they could barely keep body and soul together; that the mortality rate in "this human hell-hole" was appalling. Suicides were so common that they passed unnoticed. Many of the slum dwellers lived for drink alone, but London points out that it was the misery of their lives that drove them to drink, crime and suicide.

But there were those who were worse off than the slum dwellers, the completely destitute who were without even the security of a filthy room. They were condemned to "Carrying the Banner," that is, walking the streets by night, routed out of every corner by the policeman's club. Some slept in the parks or on the benches along the Thames Embankment. Others waited in line long, dreary hours at workhouses for a chance at a mean cot, often to hear the callous cry, "Full-up," as they were about to approach the door. Then they departed for another workhouse where, too often, they met with the same response. London tells of one occasion, when after being turned away from one workhouse, he set out with a carter and a carpenter for another. The men had once been skilled workers, earning a fair living, but they were now too old to produce a profit for any employer. As they walked along, London noticed:

> *From the slimy, spittle-drenched side-walk, they were picking up bits of orange peel, apple skin, and grape stems, and they were eating them. The pits of green gage plums they cracked between their teeth for the kernels inside. They picked up stray crumbs of bread the size of peas, apple cores so black and dirty one would not take them to be apple cores, and these things these two men took into their mouths, and chewed them, and swallowed them; and this, between six and seven o'clock in the evening of August 20, year of our Lord 1902, in the heart of the greatest, wealthiest, and most powerful empire the world has ever seen.*

London was extremely critical of the workhouses. For a cot and a bit of supper and breakfast consisting of food unfit for human consumption, they worked the wretched men nearly to death. The Salvation Army operated a superior type of workhouse, but before one could get any food, he had to wait in line for two hours and another hour inside. Then he was forced to pray and listen to pious speeches before a scanty breakfast was served. Small wonder so many of these destitute men and women would go without food for days on end. Many became ill as their resistance to the rampant slum diseases was lowered. Once ill, their chances for recovery were negligible.

Throughout his investigation London sought an answer to the question, why are these people in the slums? Not by choice and not through laziness, he discovered, but old age, disease, or accidents which had reduced their labor value. Escape from the slums was difficult, for the tiny wages of these people simply did not permit them to live elsewhere. Then when they were thrown on society's scrap heap, through illness, age, accident, they had no resources on which to draw. Slow starvation was the common end.

This picture of the slums was obtained, moreover, in what was considered "good times," when business was prosperous, when the factory hands and the clerks were "normally" employed. "The starvation and lack of shelter I encountered," London wrote, "constituted a chronic condition of misery which is never wiped out, even in the periods of greatest prosperity."

London was not content simply to paint a devastating picture of the life of the poor. As a socialist he drew conclusions which the ordinary social worker or academician was wont to ignore. He compared the inhabitants of the British Isles with the primitive Indians of Alaska. Among the Innuit folks who lived along the banks of the Yukon River, he pointed out, chronic starvation is unknown. When there was a lack of food, all suffered; when there was plenty, all ate their fill. But in the civilized world one had too much and another too little. One man lived in a fine mansion, another slept in some dark doorway. Everywhere there was starvation in the midst of plenty.

> *The unfit and the unneeded!* [he wrote bitterly]. *The miserable and despised and forgotten, dying in the social shambles. The progeny of prostitution—of the prostitution of men and women and children, of flesh and blood, and sparkle and spirit; in brief, the prostitution of labor. If this is the best that civilization can do for the human, then give us howling and naked savagery. Far better to be a people of the wilderness and desert, of the cave and the squatting place, than to be a people of the machine and the Abyss.*

Why is it, London asked, that as civilization increased its producing power misery increased in direct ratio? The cause was mismanagement; the answer a socialist commonwealth. The profit motive must go. Society must be compelled to better the lot of the average man, capable as it is of a production of abundance. Society must be reorganized on a basis of production for use and not for profit. Once capitalist mismanagement is wiped out, the evil of the slums, of slow starvation, of disease, of death from malnutrition, will be wiped off the face of the earth.

The People of the Abyss, published by Macmillan in November, 1903, received mixed reactions from the critics. *The Nation* commented that London "describes the East End of London as Dante might have described the Inferno had he been a yellow journalist." The *Atlantic Monthly* considered it "deficient in the firmness and dignity of mood and touch which might have made it literature," while the *Bookman* accused the author of "snobbishness because of his profound consciousness of the gulf fixed between the poor denizens of the Abyss and the favored class of which he is the proud representative. . . ."

Other critics recognized the book for what it was, a major sociological study of the underprivileged deserving to stand besides Jacob Riis' *How the Other Half Lives* and Arthur Morrison's *Tales of Mean Street.* "This life," said *The Independent,* "has been pictured many times before—complacently and soothingly by Professor Walter A. Wyckoff, luridly by Mr. Stead, scientifically by Mr. Charles Booth. But Mr. London alone has made it real and present to us." A few months after the American publication of the book, Isaac Pitman's Sons, a conservative London publishing house, brought out a British edition. The English critics were favorably impressed, and agreed that Jack London had come closer to the heart of the East End slums than any other writer.

The People of the Abyss brought Jack London to the attention of the entire socialist movement in the United States. Previous to its appearance he was only well-known on the Coast. Then *Wilshire's* printed *The People of the Abyss* serially, beginning with the March, 1903 issue and running it through January, 1904. Thus several months before Macmillan released the book, socialists all over the country were reading London's burning indictment against capitalism, and overnight his name became a household word among Party members.

Jack London returned to California four months after he had left for England to pick up the responsibilities of a family man. In the winter of 1902 he was again the father of a daughter, and his disappointment at not having been presented with a son by Bessie made both of them ill. Then an idea for a story possessed him, and he forgot mother and daughter, and once again was at work nineteen hours a day, his only recreation being the Wednesday night open house for his friends.

In June, 1902, *Cosmopolitan* had published "Batard," London's story of a struggle between a dog, uncanny in his diabolic shrewdness, and his evil master, each biding his time to kill the other, each fearing and respecting the other to the end. Now he sat down to write a short story that would be a companion piece to "Batard." But what started out to be a four thousand word story grew into a full-length novel, which London, who had a genius for selecting just the right title, named *The Call of the Wild*. It was completed in thirty days and accepted immediately by the *Saturday Evening Post* which paid him two thousand dollars for the month's work. Though Brett of Macmillan liked the story, he did not care for the title and feared that the novel was too realistic to be popular with "the sentimentalist public." He, therefore, proposed that London sell the book outright to Macmillan for two thousand dollars, with the assurance that it would be published in an attractive format and heavily advertised. This, in turn, would increase the sale of London's books already published. The need for money to support his family, two servants and Mammy Jenny brought from Jack a quick acceptance of the offer.

It is not difficult to understand Brett's doubts about the success of *The Call of the Wild*. (It remained the title for the simple reason that no better one was proposed.) A generation brought up on animal stories like *Black Beauty* and familiar with the quaint animal characters of the *Uncle Remus Stories* of Joel Chandler Harris, was likely to be shocked at the savagery of the story of Buck, a cross between a St. Bernard and a Scotch-shepherd, who led the life of an ordinary dog until he was kidnapped and taken to the Klondike, and who, when the call of the wild asserted itself after the death of his master, is drawn back to life with the wolf-pack. But the publisher had overlooked the fact that the increased interest in natural history stimulated by men like Muir and Burroughs, and the growing taste for realism in literature, had created an audience for just such a type of story. Then again, the novel is endowed with such magic and imagination, it moves so swiftly to its logical end, and recreates so brilliantly the atmosphere appropriate to the moods of the animals, that no reader could possibly be unmoved. Thousands were soon to thrill to the struggle between Buck and Spitz for leadership of the team,

to the picture of the Arctic code of survival, to the huskies' "pride of
the trace," and to the bitter rivalry which culminated in a battle to
the death. Finally, there were passages of beauty, the equal of which
it is difficult to find in the literature of the day such as:

> *With the aurora borealis flaming coldly overhead, or the
> stars leaping in the frost dance, and the land numb and
> frozen under its pall of snow, the song of the huskies might have
> been the defiance of life, only it was pitched in a minor key,
> with long-drawn wailings and half sobs, and was more the
> pleading of life, the articulate travail of existence. It was an
> old song, old as the breed itself—one of the first songs of the
> younger world in a day when songs were sad. It was invested
> with the woe of unnumbered generations, this plaint by which
> Buck was so strangely stirred. When he moaned and sobbed,
> it was with the pain of living that was of old the pain of his
> wild fathers, and the fear and mystery of the cold and dark
> that was to them fear and mystery.*

Fortunately, the usual interpolations about white supremacy which
mar so much of London's work are absent in this book. In fact, it is
interesting in the light of his phobia about mixed breeds that London's brave and dignified dog hero should be a mongrel!

The critical response to *The Call of the Wild* was so overwhelmingly
favorable that ten thousand copies were sold the first day of publication. It was the first of London's books to be a best seller, and it
remains today the best known of his writings, having sold over six
million copies since 1903.

A month before *The Call of the Wild* was published, *The Critic*
carried an article by London, "The Terrible and Tragic in Fiction."
It concluded with a remark that was to loom large in London's future
development. "The pity of it," he wrote, "is that the writer-folk are
writing for bread first and glory after; and that their standard of
living goes up as fast as their capacity for winning bread increases,—
so that they never get around to glory,—the ephemeral flourishes,
and the great stories remain unwritten." *The Call of the Wild* assured
London the status of a highly paid author, yet the more money he
made the more he was to need with the result that in the end he
turned out material that had value only because it made money, and
the great stories in him also remained unwritten.

But that was to come much later. Meanwhile, he still devoted no small part of his writing time to work for the radical movement, for which he received nothing but the satisfaction of knowing that he was aiding the Cause.

The Comrade, an official Party publication founded in 1901 * was featuring a series of articles by well-known Party members on how they became Socialists. There were contributions by Father McGrady, the Rev. T. H. Hagerty, William T. Brown, Joshua Wanhope and other prominent socialists of the period. Naturally, Jack London was asked for his story, and in "How I Became a Socialist" he told of his experiences on the road, of his gradual realization of the fact that society took men of brawn and muscle, used them up and discarded them, and of his fear that someday this too would be his fate. He told how his rebellion against this system made him investigate possible cures, and led him to socialism. Since that day, he told his Party comrades, he had read many books on the subject, "but no economic argument, no lucid demonstration of the logic and inevitableness of Socialism affects me as profoundly and convincingly as I was affected on the day when I first saw the walls of the Social Pit rise around me and felt myself slipping down, down, into the shambles at the bottom."

The essay brought a flood of demands for articles from the socialist press and large batches of mail from comrades all over the country. Jack responded to both. For the socialist press he wrote a series of articles without either expecting or receiving any financial return. He personally answered every letter from comrades, opening each with "Dear Comrade," and closing, "Yours for the Revolution, Jack London." Two of the socialist essays written during this period illustrate Jack London's ability to take a difficult subject and so simplify it that even a political illiterate could understand it. Furthermore, they reveal his capacity for applying Marxism to American conditions.

In "The Class Struggle," published in the New York *Independent* of November 5, 1903, London sets out to destroy one of the cherished myths of American capitalism: that there is no class struggle in

---

* After reading the first issue of the magazine, London wrote joyfully to the editor: "My congratulations on your noteworthy first number. What with the *International Socialist Review* and *The Comrade,* I really feel a respectable member of society, able to say to the most finicky: 'Behold the literature of my party!' But, seriously, I must confess to a pleasant surprise at the work you have done." (*The Comrade,* November, 1901, Vol. I, no. 2, p. 32.)

American society. The believers in the myth are like ostriches with
their heads in the sand; because they cannot see the class struggle,
they refuse to recognize that it exists. He points out that the disap-
pearance of the frontier forced the superior workers, who usually rose
out of their class, to remain in the working class. At first they seek to
improve their conditions through individual efforts, but life teaches
them that as individuals they are powerless to combat the system
which exploits them. So they begin to play a leading role in the organization of labor, and soon these "ambitious young men, denied
the opportunity to rise from the working class, preach revolt to the
working class." The existence of trade unions, London argues, is
irrefutable proof of the presence of the class struggle. Capital wants
more profit and labor wants higher wages, and no amount of pretty
speechifying about the need for harmony between these two classes
can blunt the basic struggle that exists between them. In this struggle,
London is convinced, the workers will win out as soon as they understand that their class has little or nothing to gain from the old-line
political parties, build their own and take over control of the government. London is aware that many of the existing trade unions do not
understand that trade unionism divorced from political activity is
often futile, and he does not hesitate to call this to the attention of
the American labor movement. Trade unionism coupled with a correct political ideology, he concludes, will achieve a new social order
in America.

"The Scab," published in the *Atlantic Monthly* in January, 1904, is
further evidence of London's concern with major problems confronting the working class. Here again he stresses the existence of a class
struggle between labor and capital, and shows how the scab is an
inevitable feature of this struggle. Unfortunately, as the essay develops, its power dwindles. London's definition of a scab takes in so
much territory that one cannot be sure just what he has in mind. A
scab, he argues, "is one who gives more value for the same price than
another." He differentiates, to be sure, between the scab who is
utilized by employers to break strikes and a laborer who does more
work for the same wage than another. But the difference is somewhat
glossed over in the discussion, and the reader is led to the conclusion
that almost everybody scabs in a society where men struggle with one
another for food and shelter—worker against worker, capitalist
against capitalist and nation against nation. In fact, London concludes
that in a competitive society "the non-scab is a vanishing quantity."

In addition to the loose terminology, London's essay also suffers from a failure to analyze sufficiently the reasons why men scab on their fellow-workers. While he points out that the employers use scabs to destroy the organized power of labor, he leaves the impression that their main aim is to get low-paid workers, thus overlooking the fact that professional strike-breakers were being paid more for a month's work than the men on strike received during the entire year. Nor does he point out that the refusal of the craft unions to organize Negro and women workers often lead them to scab against their will.

Despite these weaknesses, however, the essay remains an important theoretical discussion of a phenomenon extremely common "in a society organized on a tooth-and-nail basis." At a time when Charles Elliot, President of Harvard University, was calling the scab "the American hero," Jack London was demonstrating that the strike-breaker was simply another mercenary in the army of the capitalists to crush the organizations of labor.

Some time later London wrote a description of a scab which, though it never could have found a place in the pages of the *Atlantic Monthly*, provided the labor movement with an eloquent and forceful weapon in its struggles and is still widely used today:

> *After God had finished the rattlesnake, the toad and the vampire, he had some awful substance left with which He made a SCAB. A SCAB is a two-legged animal with a corkscrew soul, a water-logged brain, and a combination backbone made of jelly and glue. Where others have hearts he carries a tumor of rotten principles.*
>
> *When a SCAB comes down the street men turn their backs and angels weep in heaven, and the devil shuts the gates of hell to keep him out. No man has a right to SCAB as long as there is a pool of water deep enough to drown his body in, or a rope long enough to hang his carcass with. Judas Iscariot was a gentleman compared with a SCAB. For betraying his Master, he had character enough to hang himself. A SCAB HASN'T!*
>
> *Esau sold his birthright for a mess of pottage. Judas Iscariot sold his Savior for thirty pieces of silver. Benedict Arnold sold his country for a promise of a commission, in the British Army. The modern strikebreaker sells his birthright, his country, his wife, his children, and his fellow-men for an unfulfilled promise from his employer, trust or corporation.*

Esau was a traitor to himself, Judas Iscariot was a traitor to his God. Benedict Arnold was a traitor to his country.
A STRIKEBREAKER IS A TRAITOR TO HIS GOD, HIS COUNTRY, HIS FAMILY AND HIS CLASS!

In the summer of 1903, London fell in love with Charmian Kittredge and abruptly left his wife and two daughters. Then he settled down to the writing of *The Sea Wolf*. On January 7, 1904, five days before his twenty-eighth birthday, he sailed for Yokohama on the *S.S. Siberia* to cover the Russo-Japanese war for the Hearst syndicate, leaving the manuscript of *The Sea Wolf* with his friend George Sterling who was to see it through the press.

The voyage was ill-fated from the start. While still on board ship, Jack came down with the grippe and, on top of this, hurt his ankle. Once in Japan he was unable to get to the scene of the actual fighting because of the strict Japanese regulations covering correspondents. Then he was arrested for taking pictures. To elude the censors and get his stories, he hired a native junk to take him to Chemulpo in Chosen (Korea). For six days and nights he was on a tiny boat in freezing weather with only cold native food to subsist on. An English photographer who saw him arrive at Chemulpo reported: "He was a physical wreck. His ears were frozen, his fingers were frozen, his feet were frozen." But, despite his condition, Jack pushed on towards the front, and finally, after weeks of travel through mud and ice, he reached the battle lines at Yalu. He was immediately ordered back and thrown into a military prison. Later he managed to get some dispatches through the censor, but he was convinced that he was a failure as a war correspondent. "Only in another war, with a white man's army may I hope to redeem myself," he wrote as he returned home in disgust.

That a "yellow, inferior race" like the Japanese could defeat the Russians, a white people, drove London frantic and, in his dispatches to the Hearst press, his lamentations came through clearly. In one dispatch which appeared in the *New York American and Journal* of June 12, 1904, he told of his sensations at the sight of a group of Russian prisoners:

> . . . *the sight I saw was a blow in the face to me. On my mind it had all the stunning effect of the sharp impact of a man's fist. There was a man, a white man, with blue eyes, looking at me. He was dirty and unkempt. He had been through a*

fierce battle. But his eyes were bluer than mine, and his skin
was as white. And there were other white men in there with
him, many white men.

I caught myself gasping. A choking sensation was in my
throat. These men were my kind. I found myself suddenly and
sharply aware that I was an alien among the brown men who
peered in through the windows at me. And I felt myself
strangely alone with those other men behind the window, felt
that my place was there inside with them in their captivity
rather than outside in freedom among the aliens.

All this, of course, was grist to the mills of the Hearst press then
engaged in a campaign against the "Yellow Peril" and for the exclusion of Asiatics from the United States, but the socialists in this
country found London's accounts of his Japanese experiences revolt-
ing. Some of his comrades in Oakland rebuked him for his race
chauvinism which, according to the reminiscences of one of the members of the branch, brought from London the retort: "What the devil!
I am first of all a white man and only then a Socialist."

When Jack returned from Japan, Bessie began divorce proceedings. With the press featuring every detail of his personal affairs, he
settled down at Glen Ellen with his mother, waiting until Bessie's
divorce became final so that he could marry Charmian Kittredge.

While Jack London was returning home from his trip to Japan,
the Socialist Party met in Chicago and nominated Eugene V. Debs
and Ben Hanford for President and Vice President of the United
States. The Party platform defined socialism as meaning that "all
those things upon which the people in common depend shall by the
people in common be owned and administered; that all production
shall be for the direct use of the producers." For its immediate program the Party pledged itself to work for shorter working days and
higher wages; for the insurance of the workers against accident, sickness and lack of employment; for pensions for aged and exhausted
workers; for the public ownership of the means of transportation,
communication and exchange; for the graduated taxation of incomes,
inheritances, franchises and land values; for the complete education of
children and the complete abolition of child labor.

The press ignored both the socialist candidates and platform until
the Democratic party rejected William Jennings Bryan as being too
radical, and in his stead nominated Judge Alton B. Parker of New

York on a conservative gold-standard platform. The action immediately put life into the socialist campaign, for it was obvious that
many voters, convinced that there was no difference between the
major parties, would be looking for a new avenue to express their
discontent. Debs issued a statement reminding "Democrats, progressives, liberals, humanitarians; you now have no place to go except
the Socialist Party."

But not even the most enthusiastic socialist was prepared for the
outcome of the election. Debs and Hanford gained almost a half
million votes; in California alone the vote for the socialist candidates
rose from 7,572 in 1900 to over 35,000 in 1904. The old-line politicians
were simply astounded, and all over the country newspapers and
magazines began to probe into the reasons for this astounding rise in
the socialist vote. The *San Francisco Examiner* called on Jack London,
whom it described as "one of the World's greatest authorities on
Socialism," for an explanation.

In his article London did not content himself with analyzing simply
the background of the national campaign of 1904. He told the readers
of the Hearst paper that socialism was not confined to one country,
but was an international movement which "had fastened upon every
civilized country in the world." He quoted from a message sent to
the Socialists of Russia by their comrades in Japan assuring them
that the war between their two countries was being conducted for
imperialist purposes, and which added, "but for us Socialists there
are no boundaries, race, country or nationality. We are comrades,
brothers and sisters, and have no reason to fight." Socialism, London
continued, was destined to grow stronger in the United States, for it
was a fundamental movement. Unlike Populism, which was doomed
to die quickly because it only scratched the surface of society's evils,
Socialism was "a revolutionary movement that aims to pull down
society to its foundations and upon a new foundation to build a
new society where shall reign order, equity and justice." The history
of society, he reminded his readers, was a history of class struggle, and
just as the capitalists overthrew the feudal lords so would the working class triumph over their class enemies: "That the working class
shall conquer (mark the note of fatalism) is as certain as the rising
of the sun."

London, of course, was letting his imagination run riot when he told
the readers of the *Examiner* that the vote cast for Debs "was the tally
of the American citizens who have raised the red banner of revolt."

The majority of these voters were simply voicing their dissatisfaction over the control of both major parties by big business and were more concerned with some of the immediate demands of the Socialist Party than with its ultimate goal. Still London's explanation of the great socialist vote in 1904 brought home to a large body of the American people that they were dealing with a world-wide phenomenon, a truly fundamental movement, and not a flash-in-the-pan. Furthermore, it is highly significant that London wrote so glowingly of the Japanese socialists and of their pronouncement that "for us Socialists there are no boundaries, race, country or nationality." Here again, when writing about the Cause that was so close to his heart, Marx and Engels rather than Nietzsche, Spencer, Kidd and Haeckel dominated his thinking.

Jack London was now a famous writer. *The Call of the Wild* had established his popularity, and his dispatches from Japan, headlined as they were in the Hearst newspaper chain, had made his name familiar to millions of Americans who did not usually read books. It is hardly surprising, then, that when *The Sea Wolf* was announced for publication, the advance sales totaled 40,000 copies before the book was off the press. It hit the best-sellers' list the moment it appeared in November, 1904. Critical acclaim was instant. Some reviewers found it a disgusting book, but the majority agreed that it was a work of "rare and original genius." Perhaps the most penetrating comment came from Ambrose Bierce, a fellow Californian, who wrote to George Sterling on February 18, 1905:

> *Yes, you sent me "The Sea Wolf." My opinion of it? Certainly—or a part of it. It is a most disagreeable book, as a whole. London has a pretty bad style and no sense of proportion. The story is a perfect welter of disagreeable incidents. Two or three (of the kind) would have sufficed to show the character of the man Larsen; and his own self-revealings by word of mouth would have "done the rest." Many of these incidents, too, are impossible—such as that of a man mounting a ladder with a dozen other men—more or less—hanging to his leg, and the hero's work of rerigging a wreck and getting it off a beach where it had stuck for weeks, and so forth. The "love" element, with its absurd suppressions and impossible proprieties, is awful. I confess to an overwhelming contempt for both sexless lovers.*

*Now as to the merits. It is a rattling good story in one way;
something is "going on" all the time—not always what one
would wish, but something. One does not go to sleep over the
book. But the great thing—and it is among the greatest of
things—is that tremendous creation, Wolf Larsen. If that is
not a permanent addition to literature, it is at least a permanent
figure in the memory of the reader. You "can't lose" Wolf Larsen. He will be with you to the end. So it does not really matter
how London has hammered him into you. You may quarrel
with the methods, but the result is almost incomparable. The
hewing out and setting up of such a figure is enough for a man
to do in one life-time. I have hardly words to impart my good
judgment of that work.*

Just what did London have in mind in creating that remarkable
character, Wolf Larsen? All of the critics saw in him the glorification
of the Nietzschean superman, and, at first glance, it is not difficult
to understand why. Wolf Larsen, captain of the *Ghost,* is a perfect
Nietzschean speciman, a man with a splendid body and a splendid
mind. He can jump six feet across the deck and land a fist into a deck
hand's body so that the deck hand will be lifted off his feet. He can
strangle a bull-necked mate as easily as wringing a floor mop. He can
squeeze a potato, and it will squirt "out between his fingers in
streams." He can brush his chief mate away with a back-handed sweep
of the arm, gentle enough, apparently, "but which hurls Johansen
back like a cork, driving his head against the well with a crash." Yet
he is also a philosopher. He has read Darwin and Spencer; he quotes
Browning, reads Ecclesiastes, and his shelves of books include Tenny-
son, Poe, DeQuincey and other classics. He spends hours in interminable discussions with Maud Brewster and Humphrey Van Weyden,
and nothing these two highly educated people say can confound him.
He holds his own in both worlds—the physical and the intellectual.

Yet a careful reading of the book reveals that behind the exciting
outward story is a message which none of the critics grasped—that
under the present system the individualist must end in self-
destruction. Torn by inner contradictions, unable to solve his own
problems, Wolf Larsen became bitter, warped and vicious, a fiend
who sadistically persecutes others. In the end the superman collapses,
paralyzed and rendered impotent by one of his recurring headaches,
his giant body and will of steel eaten away. His brutality, his ruth-

lessness are a mask for his inner weakness and fear. His ultimate self-destruction is a logical result of the failure of individualism.

This then, London stoutly maintained, was the message of *The Sea Wolf*. In 1915, a year before his death, he wrote to Mary Austin: ". . . Long years ago, at the very beginning of my writing career, I attacked Nietzsche and his super-man idea. This was in *The Sea Wolf*. Lots of people read *The Sea Wolf*, no one discovered that it was an attack upon the super-man philosophy." One can, of course, argue that it was London's duty so to present his message that it could not possibly be misinterpreted, yet it is significant that in many of the comments on London's writings which appeared after his death, the writers declared that, upon second reading, they found no difficulty in discerning London's social message in *The Sea Wolf*.

The years 1905–1907 marked the period of Jack London's greatest activity for the socialist movement. During these years he lectured frequently to socialist organizations, toured the East for the Intercollegiate Socialist Society, raised money for the movement and for various labor causes, wrote numerous essays and stories in which he brought the socialist message before the American reading public, and completed his most important contribution to the literature of socialism, *The Iron Heel*. Just how much all of this added up to as positive gains for the movement was a subject of debate among socialists; one group contended that through London's writings and speeches many Americans received their first introduction to socialism and became inspired converts; another group maintained that his unorthodox and outlandish conduct and flamboyant utterances antagonized respectable people, gave them an erroneous conception of the socialist movement, and that consequently he was more of a detriment than a benefit to the Cause.

There is some truth in both contentions, but in the main London, during these years, gave the socialist movement a needed stimulus. Much of the literature of the American socialist movement was either a curious mixture of reform, revolution and Christian socialism or dull translations of often tedious writings by European theoreticians. (The writings of Lenin, however, appeared not at all in the socialist literature of the period.) London supplied the movement with literature which was alive and vigorous; which applied Marxist theory to the American scene and explained socialism in terms which workers could read without the need of a dictionary to explain the meaning of words far removed from their everyday life. Even conservative critics admitted that London's socialist essays were written in such a "forcible and striking style" as to hold the attention even "of thousands who hate and fear his 'views'." Thus *Bookman* pointed out in its comments on *The War of the Classes,* a collection of London's socialist essays published in April, 1905: ". . . Certainly no other American writer, and probably no English writer, has produced something that can compare with it in forcefulness and literary merit."

But the American socialist movement was in need of what London had to say as well as how he said it. As the election returns in 1904 indicated, the influence of the Socialist Party was growing. No longer isolated from the main body of the American people by De Leon's opposition to immediate demands, the socialists were able to attract many in the countryside and the industrial cities who were losing faith in the major political parties, and who found in the platform of the Socialist Party demands similar to those which had brought them into the Populist movement. In Eugene V. Debs, moreover, the Socialist Party had a leader whose magnetic personality, brilliant oratory and tireless energy captured the hearts of thousands of workers and farmers. Finally, for the first time in American history, the socialists were moving outside the ranks of the foreign-born and appealing to the native-born. As early as December 9, 1902 the *Milwaukee Daily News,* a Democratic newspaper, declared:

> *The assumption that the Socialist party appeals alone to the foreign born voters is hardly borne out by the election returns, although it is quite true that until recently the socialist propaganda in the United States has been carried on largely by German Socialists. Since the party has taken the aggressive and occupied the field left vacant by the Populist party, it has drawn within its membership all classes and conditions of men—one of its most conspicuous champions being a millionaire and a Harvard graduate.*

Unwittingly, however, this same observation touched upon a major weakness in the Socialist Party which was to grow in importance as the years went by and to overshadow many of its positive contributions. The Party grew rapidly, running up its membership from a few thousand in 1901 to 42,000 in 1909 and to 118,000 in 1912, at the same time increasing its vote in national elections from 87,000 in 1900 to close to a million in 1912. The socialist movement was running at flood tide, but a considerable portion of the new membership came from outside the working-class—lawyers, doctors, dentists, preachers, educators, small manufacturers and business men and an occasional millionaire. Being persuasive speakers and excellent parliamentarians they quickly rose to leadership in the Party and came to control its policies, pushing the working-class members into the background. As one socialist put it, they were "soft and shifty stuff for Socialism to build on." Most of them knew little of Marxism, looked with horror upon revolutionary agitation among the masses, believed that with the capture of sufficient political offices through the ballot box socialism could rapidly be achieved, and preached an emotional propaganda filled with Christian ethics but ignoring the class-struggle.

It was in combating these reformist influences in the Socialist Party that Jack London was to make his greatest contributions as a writer and speaker. The strength, vigor, militant fire and forthright and fearless character of his speeches and writings were in sharp contrast to the propaganda spread by the middle-class intellectuals in the Party. As the *International Socialist Review*, organ of the left-wing elements in the Party, pointed out in discussing *The War of the Classes*:

> . . . *The trouble with London is that he is not the ordinary kind of a literary socialist. It would be easy to name a half dozen prominent writers of the last decade who have occasionally admitted that they were socialists, but their socialism was generally of such a mild inoffensive sort that it didn't hurt them much with their capitalist friends. London, however, is the genuine, old-fashioned, proletarian, class-struggle socialist. His socialism is like everything else about him, virile, combative and genuine to the backbone.*

Almost from the beginning of his career as a socialist, Jack London had seen the danger of the domination of the movement by the middle class intellectuals and had sought to identify himself closely with the working class. This he continued to do during the period of his greatest activity in the movement. In an address at a socialist meeting in Los Angeles in 1905, he repudiated the chairman's characterization of him as "a ripe scholar, a profound philosopher, a literary genius and the foremost man of letters in America," and said: "Before people had given me any of these titles with which the chairman so lavishly credits me, I was working in a cannery, a pickle factory, was a sailor before the mast, and spent months at a time looking for work in the ranks of the unemployed; and it is the proletarian side of my life that I revere the most, and to which I will cling as long as I live."

The amazing success of *The Sea Wolf* brought London requests for speaking engagements from all sorts of groups. The University of California invited him to address the student body. He accepted eagerly. He hated the cloister-like, ivory-tower atmosphere in which the students prepared for life, and was determined to hit them "a stinging blow, right between the eyes, and shake their mental processes a bit, even if I incurred the risk of being called a long-haired anarchist." So on January 20, 1905 he spoke to 3,500 people, most of them students, with President Wheeler in the chair. Instead of a discourse on literature he addressed the students and professors on "The Revolutionary Spirit of the American Proletariat," opening his speech with the words that were soon to ring throughout the country:

> *Yesterday morning I received a letter from a man in Arizona. It began, "Dear Comrade," and ended "Yours for the Revolution." I answered that letter this morning. I began, "Dear Comrade," and I ended, "Yours for the Revolution."*
>
> *There are 500,000 men in the United States beginning and ending their letters as our letters were begun and ended. There are 1,000,000 men in France, 3,000,000 men in Germany, and 6,000,000 men in the world beginning and ending their letters as ours were begun and ended.*
>
> *Now what do these facts mean? They mean that the Revolution is here, now. We are in it. It goes on every day. No man can escape it. Oh, it is great! There has been nothing like it in the world. Its battle cry is: "Workingmen of the world, unite. You have nothing to lose but your chains. You have a world to gain." Our Revolution was a merely local thing compared with it. The English revolution was a merely local thing compared to it. And so was the French Revolution. This Revolution is as wide as the earth. Its men clasp hands around the globe. The Japanese Socialist hails the Russian Socialist, and the German Socialist hails the French Socialist with the same word that we California Socialists hail each other, the noble word, COMRADE.*

Why were these men socialists, London asked? What was it that drove them "unceasingly to work for the Revolution, to go to prison for it, to go into exile for it, to die for it?" He told the students and professors of his experiences in the London slums when he was writing *The People of the Abyss,* reminding them that in the British capital alone, close to two million people lived on the poverty line and below it and another million "with one week's wages between them and pauperism," while in all of Europe sixty million people suffered from hunger and want. He quoted from the English scholar, Frederick W. Harrison who, after studying the condition of the poor in Europe, had concluded: "If this is to be the permanent condition of modern society, civilization must be held to bring a curse on the great majority of mankind." Then he urged his audience to read Robert Hunter's *Poverty,* a detailed study of social conditions in the United States and he quoted statistics from the book which had just been published by Macmillan, which proved that even in fairly prosperous years there were no less than ten million persons in this country who were "underfed, underclothed and poorly housed," that over a million and a half little children "were forced to become wage earners when they should still be in school," that about five million women found it necessary to work, that no less than one million workers were injured or killed each year while at work, and about ten million persons "now living, will, if the present ratio be kept up, die of the preventable disease, tuberculosis."

It was such facts, said London, and "the glorious ideas of Socialism" that kept the revolutionists unceasingly at work and it was this, too, that had convinced him "that the capitalist system which has so grossly and criminally mismanaged our industrial life must be swept away, and the Socialist system put in its place." He told them frankly what the socialists were striving to achieve: "We propose to destroy present-day civilization, that is, capitalist civilization, with its brutal struggle of man with man for life—by the ballot, where it is free, be it forever remembered—and replace it by a better civilization, a civilization whose principle shall be 'Each for all and all for Each.' "

London concluded his address with a direct appeal to the University students:

> *As I look over the universities of my land today, I see the students asleep, asleep in the face of the awful facts I have given you, asleep in the greatest revolution that has ever come*

*to the world. Oh, it is sad! Not long ago, revolutions began,
grew, broke out, in Oxford. Today Russian universities seethe
with revolution. I say to you, then: University men and women,
you men and women in the full glory of life, here is a cause
that appeals to all the romance in you. Awake to its call. Line
up! Line up! All the world despises a coward. Read our books.
Fight us, if you do not agree with us. But by all that is brave
and strong, show your colors! Line up! Line up! I say.*

London let his imagination soar when he said that there were six
million revolutionists in 1905 who closed their letters, "Yours for the
Revolution." But the bulk of the lecture was a carefully-documented
and vigorous indictment of capitalism, and it received wide publicity
in such socialist journals as the *Socialist Voice* of Oakland and the
Appeal to Reason.

A few days after his speech at the University of California there
came news of Bloody Sunday in St. Petersburg initiating the brutal
suppression of the revolutionary movement in Russia. London immediately announced his support of the Russian revolutionists and
joined with other leading comrades in issuing a call to the American
socialists to raise funds for the Russian revolution. This action, however, received little notice outside of the socialist press. Then London
spoke before a businessmen's club in Stockton and, in the course of
his remarks, proclaimed that the Russian revolutionists who had
assassinated several tsarist officials were his brothers. Immediately
the newspaper headlines throughout the country screamed: "Jack
London calls Russian Assassins his Brothers," and a clamor arose
demanding that he retract his statement, some newspapers even
threatening prosecution for treason unless he did so. But London
stood firm. He knew that the Russian Revolution of 1905 was an
uprising of the working class against capitalist oppression and Tsarist
tyranny and that under such an autocratic government it was inevitable that blood would flow when the exploited masses rose up to
overthrow their oppressors. As a revolutionary socialist, an inter-
nationalist, he acknowledged his comradeship with the Russian revolutionists. The shrieks of the bourgeois press did not move him.

The furore over his remarks before the Stockton businessmen was
no sooner off the front pages when he spoke again, quoted William
Lloyd Garrison, the great Abolutionist leader, as saying "To Hell
with the Constitution" when that document was utilized to defend

slavery, and pointed out that General Sherman Bell had said the
same thing in 1904 while helping to break the strike of ore miners in
Cripple Creek, Colorado. The press deliberately misquoted London;
the headlines this time screaming, "Jack London says to Hell with
the Constitution." It was useless for him to try to explain that he was
not the one who had made the remark; the editorials continued to
describe him as a wild-eyed fanatic bent on undermining the most
sacred institution in the United States.

These attacks had their effect on public opinion in California, for
when London ran again for Mayor of Oakland on the Socialist ticket
in the spring of 1905, he received only 981 votes. This was four times
his previous total, but it was hardly an impressive showing.

In the summer of 1905 Jack London wrote gleefully to George Bamford from his Hill Ranch near Glen Ellen in Sonoma County which
he had just built with his royalties from *The Sea Wolf:* "Oh, take
my word, there is no place like the country." A few months later he
was crossing the country to conduct a lecture tour for the socialist
cause in behalf of the Intercollegiate Socialist Society.

Inspired by the growth in the socialist vote in the 1904 presidential
election and by the world-wide repercussions of the Russian Revolution of 1905, a movement got under way to inculcate among college
men and women an understanding of socialism. The idea was first advanced by Upton Sinclair, a young Baltimorean who had gone through
the College of the City of New York without learning that there was
such a thing as a Socialist Party in the United States. This state of
affairs, he believed, should be remedied, and college students be made
aware of "this mighty new current in modern life." After some discussion with his friend, George Stroebel, it was decided to contact
well-known writers and educators to sponsor the organization. Jack
London was among the first to be contacted. He expressed immediate
interest, agreed to serve as a sponsor, and signed the call announcing
the formation of The Intercollegiate Socialist Society:

> *In the opinion of the undersigned* [went the call] *the recent
> remarkable increase in the Socialist vote in America should
> serve as an indication to the educated men and women in the
> country that Socialism is a thing concerning which it is no
> longer wise to be indifferent.*
>
> *The undersigned, regarding its aims and fundamental prin-*

*ciples with sympathy, and believing that in them will ultimately
be found the remedy for the far-reaching economic evils, propose organizing an association to be known as the Intercollegiate Socialist Society, for the purpose of promoting an
intelligent interest among college men and women, graduate
and undergraduate, through the formation of study groups in
the colleges and universities, and the encouraging of all legitimate endeavors to awaken an interest in Socialism among the
educated men and women of the country.*

The undersigned were William English Walling, graduate of the
University of Chicago, Thomas Wentworth Higginson, famous Boston author and graduate of Harvard, J. Phelps Stokes, a New York
millionaire, Charlotte Perkins Gilman, the great-granddaughter of
Lyman Beecher, Clarence S. Darrow, already making a reputation for
himself in law, B. O. Flower, the publisher of *The Arena*, Oscar
Lovell Triggs, Leonard D. Abbott, Jack London and Upton Sinclair.

At a meeting held in New York City on September 12, 1905, the
Society was formally established and Jack London, although not
present, was unanimously elected president, and Upton Sinclair and
J. Phelps Stokes, vice presidents. Jack's comrades were aware that
even though he might not be able to devote too much time to the
organization, his name had such great publicity value that it would
enable the Society to secure entry into places which otherwise might
close its doors upon anything labeled socialist.

Along with Eugene Debs, Charles Edward Russell, Sinclair, Walling, Stokes, and Higginson, London was asked to undertake a lecture
tour for the new organization, appearing at colleges, forums or on any
other available platform. He accepted, planning to couple his free
lectures for the society with talks before women's clubs and businessmen's associations where he would receive the handsome fees he needed
for land improvements on his ranch, the upkeep of his family, contributions to the Party, strike funds and labor defense funds, and the
building of the *Snark* with which he intended to sail around the world.
He started east on a Pullman, accompanied by a Korean valet.

From beginning to end the lecture tour was conducted in a blaze
of publicity. He was already one of the most romantic figures of the
period, personifying youth and courage, adventure, the sea, the Klondike and the road, and everyone knew that despite his handsome earnings as a writer he was a champion of the underdog. People flocked

to hear him and the youth of the country in white shirts with soft collars, tried to look like Jack London and to speak like his characters.

The unfavorable publicity, however, started early in the tour. His divorce became final on November 18, 1905. The next day in Chicago he married Charmian Kittredge only to find that the state law forbade the marriage for a year. When Jack learned of this, he told reporters: "I will get married in every State in the Union just as fast as I can— from one to another, if it is necessary." It was generally agreed that his haste in marrying Charmian was unseemly and this statement brought down upon London a deluge of criticism. In a sermon in Des Moines, Iowa, Dr. James A. Beebe attacked the Women's Club of the city for having invited London to lecture before them and fawning over a person who had "so lightly treated the marriage relation." "To lionize one who is guilty of moral laxity," he declared, "is to condone the offence." Although a number of women's clubs cancelled engagements and some socialists criticized him because the press was putting the blame for his "immorality" on his socialist views, London remained unperturbed. How he conducted his personal life, he asserted, was nobody's business but his own.

Some women's clubs may have been too shocked to hear London lecture, but whenever he spoke at a college or university he addressed capacity audiences. At Harvard two thousand university men—"the pick and flower of perhaps the most luxurious bourgeois society in the world"—packed the great room of the Union. Many were probably more amused than impressed, but London let them have it straight from the shoulder. Again he defended the Russian Revolutionists: "I speak and think of these 'assassins' in Russia as my comrades. So do all the comrades in America, and all the seven million comrades in the world. This is shown by the fact that we do back up all the comrades in Russia. They are not disciples of Tolstoy, nor are we. We are revolutionists."

From Harvard London went to New York where he addressed an exclusive group of extremely wealthy men and women. He was to use the incident several months later in the brilliant chapter of *The Iron Heel,* "The Philomaths." According to an account by Joshua Wanhope who attended the lecture to the wealthy New Yorkers, London concluded his speech with a vehement attack upon the audience:

> *You have been entrusted with the world; you have muddled and mismanaged it. You are incompetent, despite all your*

boastings. A million years ago the caveman, without tools, with small brain, and with nothing but the strength of his body, managed to feed his wife and children, so that through him the race survived. You, on the other hand, armed with all the modern means of production, multiplying the productive capacity of the cavemen a million times—you are incompetents and muddlers, you are unable to secure to millions even the paltry amount of bread that would sustain their physical life. You have mismanaged the world, and it shall be taken from you.

The "silk-stockinged audience," Wanhope recalled "murmured their perturbation, anger and impatience, but the unrelenting London went on":

Who will take it from you? We will! And who are we? We are seven million socialist revolutionists and we are everywhere growing. And we want all you have! Look at us! We are strong! Consider our hands! They are strong hands, and even now they are reaching forth for all you have, and they will take it, take it by the power of their strong hands; take it from your feeble grasp. Long or short though the time may be, that time is coming. The army is on the march, and nothing can stop it, that you can stop it is ludicrous. It wants nothing less than all you have, and it will take it; you are incompetent and will have to surrender to the strong. We are the strong, and in that day we shall give you an exhibition of power such as your feeble brains never dreamed the world contained!

"There was a loud murmur of protest and dissent," Wanhope continued, "and one or two respectable-looking persons choked up, and it seemed as if they were about to have apoplexy. London walked down from the rostrum through a sea of blasted, purple faces distorted with rage, but no attempt was made to detain him. . . . It was not until he was well out of earshot that some of the stunned audience plucked up enough courage to remark that 'he ought to be in jail.' "

Jack was gleeful. He wrote to Bamford: "Oh, I have some stories to tell you when I get back about my clashes with the masters of society!"

On January 26, 1906 London interrupted his stay in New York and went down to New Haven for a lecture at Yale. Dr. Alexander Irvine, minister of the Pilgrim Church in New Haven and secretary of the local Socialist Party, had persuaded the Yale Union, a debating society, to sponsor the lecture on condition that London would stay away from radical topics. Woolsey Hall was rented for the occasion, leaflets were distributed in factories and shops, and posters were plastered over the campus announcing the lecture. The New Haven comrade who had painted the poster showed London in a red turtle-neck sweater with a mass of flames as the background and con-spicuously featured as the title of the lecture the single word, "REVO-LUTION."

Needless to add, the next morning Yale was shocked. For a time it appeared that London would not be permitted to speak, but William Lyon Phelps, one of the younger professors and already a prominent member of the faculty, squashed the movement to cancel the lecture with the simple query, "Is Yale a monastery?"

Three thousand students, three hundred members of the faculty, and citizens of the community, including a group of workers who came to help out if there should be any trouble, packed Woolsey Hall to hear London speak on "Revolution." This famous lecture was an expansion of the talk on "The Revolutionary Spirit of the American Proletariat," delivered a year before at the University of California. It opened with a dramatic report of the millions enrolled in the army of socialism, and made the point that this international organized movement was unequalled in history. It represented a growing flame of revolt, with its own history and traditions and a vast body of scientific literature. The revolutionists addressed each other as "com-rades"; their red banner symbolized, not incendiarism, but the brotherhood of man, and would eventually destroy all national bound-aries. Wherever the law of the land permitted, the revolutionists fought to destroy the existing capitalist society peaceably, at the ballot-box, but where this was not permitted, and force was used against them, they resorted to force themselves, meeting violence with violence.

This huge revolutionary upsurge, London emphasized, was basically a working-class movement. Middle class and professional men were interested in the struggle to overthrow capitalism, but it was never-theless "a distinctly working-class revolt." The middle class was a perishing class, and only the workers would have the strength to carry through the battle for socialism to victory. "The workers of the world, as a class, are fighting the capitalists of the world, as a class," he told the Yale audience.

Then London analyzed the reason for the existence of this vast
socialist army and the necessity for a new social order. The present
structure of society, he pointed out, was inadequate to meet the needs
of humanity—witness unemployment, low wages and hunger. Even
the cave dweller lived in greater security than the hungry and homeless for whom the present social order had so little use. Yet, the most
incredible part of it all was that there was absolutely no need for
misery and starvation, for the means of production were more than
adequate to provide food, shelter and clothing for everyone. Still,
because of the mismanagement of the capitalist class, thousands upon
thousands went unsheltered, hungry and naked. To buttress his
point, London, throughout this section of his lecture, cited newspaper
reports, sociological studies and U.S. Bureau of Labor reports.

The capitalists were stupid as well as inefficient, he continued. They
believed that they could hold back the rising tide of revolution by
using violence against the workers—"bayonets, machine-guns, policemen's clubs, professional strike-breakers, and armed Pinkertons."
Yet by such tactics they were automatically converting more and
more workers into revolutionists.

The ruling class had failed to run the system properly. It was now
the turn of the working class. "The capitalist class has been indicted,"
London concluded. "It has failed in the management and its management is to be taken away from it. Seven million men of the working-
class say that they are going to get the rest of the working-class to
join with them and take the management away. The revolution is
here, now. Stop it who can."

The lecture is one of London's finest essays, presented in clear,
vigorous language, colorful and dramatic from beginning to end,
even while massing statistics to prove its thesis. Furthermore, its
pointed references to the importance of the working-class in the battle
to overthrow capitalism and his observations on the secondary role
of middle-class and professional men, were not lost on many members
of the Socialist Party. All told, like all of London's socialist essays,
it is still fresh and meaningful today more than forty years after it
was written.

In the middle of his prepared lecture at Yale, London interpolated
a bitter comment on the role of the American colleges and universities:

*I went to the University. I found the University, in the main,
practically wholly so, clean and noble, but I did not find the*

university alive. I found that the American university had this ideal, as phrased by a professor in Chicago University [Paul Shorey], namely: "The passionless pursuit of passionless intelligence"—clean and noble, I grant you, but not alive enough. . . . And the reflection of this university ideal I find— the conservatism and unconcern of the American people toward those who are suffering, who are in want. And so I became interested in an attempt to arouse in the minds of the young men of our universities an interest in the study of socialism. . . . We do not desire merely to make converts. . . . If collegians cannot fight for us, we want them to fight against us— of course, sincerely fight against us. But what we do not want is that which obtains today and has obtained in the past of the university, a mere deadness and unconcern and ignorance so far as socialism is concerned. Fight for us or fight against us! Raise your voices one way or the other; be alive!

When he finished, London received a tremendous ovation from the students and was carried off the platform on the shoulders of a group of Yale men. Even some of the faculty members shared this enthusiasm. "A Professor of Yale," Dr. Irvine once remarked, "told me a few days after the lecture that it was the greatest intellectual stimulus Yale had had in many years, and he sincerely hoped that London would return and expound the same program in the same hall." The press, to say the least, did not echo these sentiments. The New Haven papers were furious that the students had been exposed to the "rantings" of a socialist and the New York papers took up the cry. The *New York Times* devoted a long editorial on February 1, 1906 to London's speech at Yale in which it paid Jack a left-handed compliment, commending him "for the perfect frankness with which he tells his audiences what socialism is, and what it aims to accomplish." Unlike most of his comrades, said the *Times* piously, Jack London "does not croak socialism in timid disguises. He does not profess to regard it as a mere return to the principle of the golden rule, or as a reform altogether beneficent that will harm nobody and make all the world happier. Mr. Jack London's Socialism is bloody war—the war of one class in society against other classes. He says so. It is a destructive socialism. He glories in it." Then the *Times* calmly proceeded to distort London's remarks at Yale in the process of which Jack was quoted as saying: "If people object to our programme because of the Consti-

tution, then to hell with the Constitution. Yes, to hell with the
Constitution."

> *That is what Socialism means* [the *Times* concluded.] *It is
> to the accomplishment of these things that Socialism tends.
> Consciously or unconsciously, pretty much all Socialists want
> to see Mr. Jack London's reforms achieved, and to see them
> achieved in Mr. Jack London's way. . . . Very few Socialists,
> however, have Mr. Jack London's courage. Again we say, he
> must be commended for his courage and for his honesty. So-
> ciety can judge Socialism better and reach sounder conclusions
> upon its merits when it has a correct understanding of the
> nature of Socialism and the intentions of Socialists.*

London did not bother to answer the *Times*, but Upton Sinclair, in
a letter to the editor, sought to correct the "wrong impression" created
by the "quotation" from the Yale speech. When London referred to
the "blood-red banner" of revolution, wrote Sinclair, he "took pains
to explain to the audience that he meant it 'as a symbol of brotherhood of Man, and not of war and destruction' "; when he mentioned
the words "to hell with the Constitution," he was referring to the remarks of "a militia General who at one time held sway in the State
of Colorado," and when he talked of wresting power from the rulers,
"by war if necessary," he explained to the audience that "the Socialist
Party is a party of Constitutional agitation in countries where universal suffrage and free speech prevail, and that in countries where
these Constitutional rights are denied it resorts to force."

Sinclair also took the *Times* to task for implying that most Social-
ists shrank from stating their aims as courageously and frankly as did
Jack London. "I heard Jack London's address," Sinclair wrote sharply.
"I have heard and read many other Socialist addresses, and so far as
I know there is no such difference to be noted between them."

As Jack could have told him in advance, Sinclair's letter satisfied nobody. The newspapers continued to attribute to London the remark,
"To hell with the Constitution," and editorials still persisted in distorting his speeches by quoting excerpts out of context. On February
8, three days after Sinclair's letter appeared in the *Times*, the public
library in Derby Neck, Connecticut, withdrew from circulation all of
Jack London's works, making the following announcement: "As Jack
London publicly announces that he is an anarchist, devoting the
Constitution to hell and the government to destruction, we have

ordered all of his works withdrawn from circulation, and we urge not only other libraries to do likewise, but all lovers of their country to cease buying his books or taking magazines publishing his stories." Several other libraries responded immediately and all over the country arose the cry, "Boycott all magazines which contain stories by Jack London."

All this was to bring a decided slump in the sales of London's books. But what disturbed Jack much more than this was that it started a wave of consternation among the middle-class leaders of the Socialist Party who became frightened lest London's utterances be taken for the official position of the movement. When Jack quoted with approval Gene Debs' remark, "There is no good capitalist and no bad workingman," and when he talked of the class-struggle, a shudder ran through many right wing socialists. Fearing that the more timid members of the Party and its sympathizers were being antagonized by London's speeches, they were quick to disassociate themselves from his views. When J. G. Phelps Stokes introduced Jack to an audience at the Grand Central Palace in New York, he made it quite clear that he and other socialists did not agree with London that "the catastrophe which these things (the accumulation of wealth and power in the hands of the few, and the like) threaten will necessarily come upon us." The remark did not cause Jack to pull his punches. He was tired from a speaking trip to Florida and back, and was suffering from an attack of tonsilitis. Yet, as Upton Sinclair relates: "Amid the waving of red handkerchiefs, and in a voice of calm defiance he read to the city of New York his stunning 'Revolution'. . . ."

London continued with his lecture tour for the Intercollegiate Socialist Society, but on February 3, 1906 he fell seriously ill in St. Paul. The rest of his tour was cancelled and he returned to Glen Ellen. On February 22, he wrote to Anna Strunsky: "Back again after four months of lecturing. I rattled the dry bones some. Spoke at Yale, Harvard, Columbia, University of Chicago, and a lot of speeches for the Socialist Party." His lectures were never resumed.

While Jack London was by no means the only Socialist to popularize the Cause among college students, he, more than anyone, was the college man's idol and his lectures brought many of them closer to the movement. He himself felt that the work of the Intercollegiate Socialist Society was of great importance and disagreed sharply with those in the Party who believed that the organization should be disbanded. In every college where he lectured, he told George Bamford, he "found a number of socialistically inclined and non-Socialist students earnest and sincere, who were eager to form an Intercollegiate Socialist Society group," and if the Society had not existed nothing could have been accomplished. He admitted that not everyone who joined the Society was a full-fledged Socialist, but he was convinced "that the majority of the members will be hammered into Socialism. . . . In the meantime discussion will take place, reading is done, and the word 'Socialism' becomes a less misunderstood term in such a college."

London's lecture tour was important in still another respect. While most newspapers ignored London's carefully documented indictment of capitalism, concerning themselves with only a few phrases from his speeches which they could quote for their own purposes, a few did make an effort to check up on his facts. Thus when London cited the miserable wages of garment workers in Chicago in the course of his "Revolution" speech, concluding that "such wages means no childhood for the children, beastliness of living, and starvation for all," the *Chicago American* put its reporters to work to investigate the matter, and devoted several pages to their findings. The story opened:

> *Slaves in Chicago—slaves of the sweat shops, toiling all day long and making 15 cents—one family of three which earned a total of $2.50 as a total last week—a strong man who earned 95 cents in the same time—a woman who thinks $1.25 a week is a good wage and who supports two children on 90 cents a week—these were conditions discovered today by reporters for the* Chicago American *investigating the sweat shops of Chicago.*
>
> *Already enough facts have come to light to prove abundantly the assertion of Jack London, novelist and Socialist lecturer in a New York address, that many girls and women in Chicago earn only 90 cents a week.*
>
> *The* Chicago American *has found these statements to be true. There are many women in Chicago who earn no more than 90 cents a week. . . .*

Then followed a series of interviews with Italian garment workers which brought out the full details of the "beastliness" of their living. To London such newspaper articles were more important than the banning of his books by libraries and the boycotting of magazines featuring his stories, for he took pride in the fact that his lectures and essays were carefully documented with evidence secured through an

exhaustive source study. The newspapers liked to give the impression
that London was simply infatuated with the sound of radical slogans.
The truth is that London was a careful student of contemporary
society and when he sat down to write a socialist essay or story, he
drew on his vast collection of clippings from newspapers, magazines,
books and government reports. This material was in turn utilized by
socialists and trade unionists in their own talks and writings. "There
are enough striking illustrations and strong quotations between the
covers of this little book," said the *International Socialist Review* of
The War of the Classes, "to supply an army of soap box orators with
ammunition." London was overjoyed at such use of his material. "I'd
rather see every bit of Socialistic work I have done pirated, and given
a larger circulation . . . ," he wrote to Fred Bamford on June 26,
1906, "than to receive full credit for it and narrower circulation."

Even after his withdrawal from active work for the Intercollegiate
Socialist Society, London was to aid in the growth of the organization
through his essay, "What Life Means to Me," written expressly for
the Society and published as its first pamphlet. In this essay, probably
his finest piece of autobiographical writing, London looks back
through the years evaluating his own experiences up to the time that
he first gained a true perspective on life—the time that he was able
to see what part the philosophy of socialism played in his life. He
writes of his beginnings in the working class, and of the inner fire that
made him want to climb out of his class where everything seemed so
ugly into the ranks of those who wore beautiful clothes and had plenty
to eat and whose life was surely pure and noble and clean. But society
kept him from moving upwards and he was forced to work at every
conceivable job to keep alive. He learned that life was a business of
selling that which could make profit for others and he decided to sell
brains rather than muscle which wore out too quickly and did not
command a sufficiently high price. He came in contact with socialists
and, for the first time, life seemed worthwhile. He was among "great
souls who exalted flesh and spirit over dollars and cents, and to whom
the thin wail of the starved slum child meant more than all the pomp
and circumstance of commercial expansion and world empire." Finally,
as a "brain merchant" he climbed out of the pit, and found that those
on the top of the ladder were clean and beautiful, but that about them
was an air of hypocrisy that nauseated him. And above all he found
that they were not alive; that they had nothing to offer him. So he
returned to his comrades, content to work with them for the Revolu-

tion. Looking forward to that day, he predicts: "Then we'll cleanse the cellar and build a new habitation for mankind, in which there will be no parlor floor, in which all the rooms will be bright and airy, and where the air that is breathed will be clean, noble, and alive." He concludes with a reaffirmation of his faith in the inevitable triumph of socialism:

> And last of all, my faith is in the working-class. As some Frenchman has said, "The stairway of time is ever echoing with the wooden shoe going up, the polished boot descending."

In June the keel of the *Snark* was laid while London was busy at work on *The Iron Heel* and while he was contacting editors for the publication rights of stories and articles arising from his projected voyage to the South Seas. But he also took time off to write a review of Upton Sinclair's great muckraking novel of conditions in the Chicago meat-packing industry, *The Jungle*.

When the *Appeal to Reason*, late in 1905, serialized Sinclair's novel, London immediately expressed his enthusiasm for the work. "It has stirred me," he wrote to the author, "and made me sit right up time and again. There has been nothing done like it. You have my heartiest congratulations." A little later when Sinclair, who had found it impossible to secure a publisher and had decided to publish the book himself, appealed to London for aid, Jack responded with a resounding call to the readers of the *Appeal to Reason* urging them to send in advance orders to make possible the publication of the book. This call, published in the November 18, 1905 issue of the *Appeal to Reason*, is so full of London's enthusiasm that it merits quotation in full:

> *Dear Comrades:*
>
> *Here it is at last! The book we have been waiting for these many years! The "Uncle Tom's Cabin" of wage slavery! Comrade Sinclair's book, "The Jungle!" and what "Uncle Tom's Cabin" did for black slaves, "The Jungle" has a large chance to do for the wage-slaves of today.*
>
> *It is essentially a book of today. The beautiful theoretics of Bellamy's "Looking Backward" are all very good. They served a purpose, and served it well. "Looking Backward" was a great book. But I dare say that "The Jungle," which has no beautiful theoretics, is even a greater book.*

It is alive and warm. It is brutal with life. It is written of sweat and blood, and groans and tears. It depicts, not what man ought to be, but what man is compelled to be in our world, in the Twentieth Century. It depicts, not what our country ought to be, or what it seems to be in the fancies of Fourth of July spell-binders, the home of liberty and equality of opportunity; but it depicts what our country really is, the home of oppression and injustice, a nightmare of misery, an inferno of suffering, a human hell, a jungle of wild beasts.

And there you have the very essence of Comrade Sinclair's book—the jungle! And that is what he has named it. This book must go. And you, comrades, must make it go. It is a labor of love on the part of the man who wrote it. It must be a labor of love on your part to distribute it.

And take notice and remember, comrades, this book is straight proletarian. And straight proletarian it must be throughout. It is written by an intellectual proletarian. It is written for the proletarian. It is to be published by a proletarian publishing house. It is to be read by the proletariat. And depend upon it, if it is not circulated by the proletariat it will not be circulated at all. In short, it must be a supreme proletarian effort.

Remember, this book must go out in the face of the enemy. No capitalist publishing house would dare to publish it. It will be laughed at—some; jeered at—some; abused some; but most of all, worst of all, the most dangerous treatment it will receive is that of silence. For that is the way of capitalism.

Comrades, do not forget the conspiracy of silence. Silence is the deadliest danger this book has to face. The book stands on its own merits. You have read it, and you know. All that it requires is a hearing. This hearing you must get for it. You must not permit this silence. You must shout out this book from the housetops; at all times, and at all places. You must talk about it, howl about it, do everything but keep quiet about it. Open your mouths and let out your lungs, raise such a clamor that those in the high places will wonder what all the row is about and perchance feel tottering under them the edifices of greed they have reared.

All you have to do is to give this book a start. You have read the book yourselves, and you will vouch for it. Once it gets

*its start it will run away from you. The printers will be worked
to death getting out larger and larger editions. It will go out
by the hundreds of thousands. It will be read by every workingman. It will open countless ears that have been deaf to
Socialism. It will plough the soil for the seed of our propaganda. It will wake thousands of converts to our cause. Comrades, it is up to you!*

> *Yours for the Revolution,*
> *Jack London.*

Within a short time after this appeal was published, five thousand
advance orders (with funds enclosed) were received. The book was
published by the Jungle Publishing Company. Soon afterwards,
Doubleday, Page and Company, in spite of threats of law suits, decided to put it out under its imprint. As soon as the book appeared,
London wrote a glowing review for the Hearst papers, an emasculated
version of which was finally published in the *New York Journal* of
August 8, 1906. Furious at the censorship imposed upon him, London
sent the review to *Wilshire's Magazine* which printed it a month later
with the following editorial note appended:

*The full text of this remarkable review of the "Jungle" has
never before been published. It was originally sent by the reviewer to the Hearst papers and after lying unused for several
months was finally printed in an abbreviated and mutilated
condition, or, as the virile London says, "with the guts taken
out of it." Mr. London forwarded the review to this office, leaving it to us as to whether it should be published or not. We
believe that our readers will be interested in this powerful
synopsis of Sinclair's famous book, even if it is a trifle belated,
and it is therefore reproduced here.*

The Jungle rapidly became a best-seller, caused a nationwide furore
and brought about a Congressional investigation of the packing houses
of Chicago, yet it was London's enthusiastic support that started it
on its way to success. "If that book went all over the world," Sinclair
himself admitted, "it was Jack London's push that started it."

There were many sequels to London's action in the case of *The
Jungle*, and all so characteristic of him that they always remained in
the minds of those who knew him intimately as among the really
beautiful things in his life. "As I watched him, through the eleven

years that passed after that," wrote Upton Sinclair a year after London's death, "I saw that that action was not a single impulse, but an expression of his deepest nature. He was open-handedness incarnate; save only to editors and publishers whom he hated—on principle, be it said, as part of the class struggle! Towards young writers he was as a mother to a brood of children; perhaps he over-fed some of them with his praise. I know it was not enough to write of his pleasure in a note in the case of Lawrence's *Sons and Lovers,* his eager haste required a telegram! He knew all about the uphill fight a young radical had to make, and to such he gave both praise and money for the helping of the glorious cause. That is the thing for which I loved him most; I have saved it to the last, so that it may be the thing the reader carries away with him—the memory of a man strong, yet tender-hearted as a child, honest and open as daylight, generous as Mother Nature herself."

All this while, the *Snark* was costing London every penny he earned by his writings. So he wrote anything he could think of that would sell and furnish the money to pour into his boat. He was up to his neck in work. "Say," he wrote to Gaylord Wilshire on August 27, 1906, in answer to a request for an article, "if you had asked me for my wife or for my ranch, it would have been easier for me to have given them to you than for me to give you that article. I am so absolutely rushed to death with my work (writing), and with the stupendous volume of details of finishing building the boat and preparing for departure, that I cannot even *think* of what to write in such an article, must less find the *time,* in which to write it. Think! Why, all I can think about these days is how to make sea-anchors and oil-drags; how to make ice; how to make electricity; how to make gasoline engines go; how to store 1,000 gallons of gasoline on a small boat where there isn't room for 500 gallons. How to navigate— my God, man, do you realize that in a few short weeks we set sail, and I haven't had a bit of time in which to learn navigation? Time! If you can see any way to manage it, I'd sooner you sent me 200 hours of time than $200."

Jack was over-optimistic when he spoke of a few weeks; it was not to be until April 23 of the following year that he set sail out of the Golden Gate. During these months he kept writing and writing, to meet the mounting costs of his boat. The books and stories poured out one after another—*Moon-Face and other stories,* an unimportant collection, September, 1906; *White Fang,* a novel about a dog, half-

wolf, who through mistreatment becomes savage and through love
and kindness, becomes docile and loyal, September, 1906; *Scorn of
Women,* a play, November, 1906; *Before Adam,* a thrilling novel of
primitive life using an interesting dream device, February, 1907,
and numerous other short stories and articles including the series on
his tramping experiences in *Cosmopolitan Magazine* in 1907 under
the title "My Life in the Underworld" and published by Macmillan
in November, 1907 as *The Road.*

Pressed as he was to raise the thirty thousand dollars that went
into the building of the *Snark,* London's interest in the struggles of
the working-class remained undiminished. Three of his finest contributions to the literature of the radical movement were written during this harassing period: "The Apostate," "Something Rotten in
Idaho," and *The Iron Heel.*

London had been asked by an influential magazine to investigate
and write on conditions of child-labor in Southern cotton mills, but
bent on finishing *The Iron Heel* and tossing off material that would
raise money quickly, he had rejected the tempting offer. Still he could
not forget his own boyhood experiences in the jute mill, cannery
and laundry and, putting other work aside, he wrote a tale of uncompromising realism dealing with child labor, "The Apostate,"
which appeared in *Woman's Home Companion* in September, 1906
and became one of the most popular of the socialist pamphlets.

The title character is a boy of about seventeen, a bobbin winder in
a jute mill, stunted, a work-slave since the age of seven. The story
opens in the bedroom of a ramshackle home with the mother shaking
the boy to wake him up before dawn of a cold day, the boy fighting
for sleep and his mother warning him, "You'll be docked." Only a
writer who had gone through such experiences himself could convey
such a realistic picture of the boy's utter weariness. Equally effective
is the picture of the poverty-stricken home—the chill of the room,
the malodorous sink, the wretched coffee, the careful doling out of
the scanty food. As the five-thirty whistle blows, the scene shifts to
the mill. Here one meets the other children, some crippled, all under-
nourished and rickety and each with the inevitable hacking cough
from the lint. Here too is the harsh overseer, the superintendent who
allows himself to be deceived by the boys' ages. Johnny (the apostate-
to-be) is the star-worker, self-trained by years of monotonous work.

Morning after morning Johnny is "torn bodily by his mother from
the grip of sleep." At last, when he is about sixteen, comes illness and

a long convalescence. He sleeps and sleeps, and thinks. When well, he announces simply but irrevocably, that he will work no more. Despite his mother's tears, he walks out of the city, towards the open country. "He did not walk like a man," London writes. "He did not look like a man. He was a travesty of the human. It was a twisted and stunted and nameless piece of life that shambled like a sickly ape, arms loose-hanging, stoop-shouldered, narrow-chested, grotesque and terrible."

"Something Rotten in Idaho" grew out of the famous Moyer-Haywood-Pettibone case. The climax of years of class struggle in Idaho between the Western Federation of Miners and the corporations came on December 30, 1905 when former Governor Steunenberg, who had been responsible for much anti-labor violence during his administration, was assassinated by the explosion of a bomb attached to the gate of his ranch. The man who set the bomb, Harry Orchard, had a long criminal record; he was arrested, held incommunicado in jail, and then turned over to the Pinkerton Agency, which specialized in providing strike breakers and company police. Through a deal Orchard made with the Pinkertons, Charles Moyer, William "Big Bill" Haywood and George Pettibone, officers of the Western Federation of Miners, were arrested in Denver, kidnapped by the police of Idaho without extradition papers, locked in the state penitentiary in Boise, and charged with conspiracy to murder ex-Governor Steunenberg. All this, it soon became clear, had been secretly arranged by the Governors of Colorado and Idaho in collusion with the mining corporations.

Immediately the socialist and labor movements sprang to the defense of the three men, realizing that the blow was actually directed against the militant industrial union they led. Eugene V. Debs wrote a stirring call to action in the *Appeal to Reason:*

AROUSE YE SLAVES!

> *Murder has been plotted and is about to be executed in the name and under the form of law. Charles Moyer and William D. Haywood, of the Western Federation of Miners, are charged with the assassination of ex-Governor Frank Steunenberg, of Idaho, as a mere subterfuge to pounce upon them in secret, rush them out of the state by special train, clap them in the penitentiary, convict them upon the purchased, perjured testimony of villains, and then strangle them to death with the hangman's noose. If they attempt to murder Moyer, Haywood*

*and their brothers, a million revolutionists will meet them with
guns.*

President Theodore Roosevelt called Debs, Moyer and Haywood
undesirable citizens, but the movement in behalf of the three men
grew. Habeas corpus proceedings were started before a Federal District Court judge, and when the writ was denied, an appeal was
taken to the Supreme Court. But the highest judicial tribunal evaded
the appeal by taking a long summer vacation. Meanwhile, Moyer,
Haywood, and Pettibone remained in jail, bail having been denied.
Messages from socialists all over the world poured in on them. From
Maxim Gorky came the telegram: "Greetings to you, my brother
Socialists. Courage! The day of justice and deliverance for the oppressed of all the world is at hand."

Jack London's contribution to this struggle had already been made
in the form of contributions to the defense fund. Now came his
brilliant article, "Something Rotten in Idaho," which appeared in
the *Chicago Daily Socialist* on November 4, 1906 while the Supreme
Court was at last considering the appeal. It presented a clear-cut indictment of the capitalist system, of capitalist justice and the profit
motive. It is a considered, thoughtful, exciting and challenging article,
and compels the reader, no matter what his political convictions might
be, to draw the conclusion that three workers were in danger of dying
for a crime they had never committed because they stood "between
the mine owners and a pot of money." It ranks as one of the finest
pieces of working-class propaganda London ever turned out and stands
as a testimonial to his devotion to the labor movement and his readiness to use his great talent in its behalf. It was a major contribution
in the struggle which eventually resulted in the freeing of the three
men.

On December 3, 1906, the Supreme Court denied the appeal by a
vote of eight to one. A few months later, in February, 1907, London
spoke at a mass meeting, held under the auspices of the Socialist
Party, to commemorate the first anniversary of the kidnapping and to
push on the movement to free the victims. ". . . If the work of
freeing Moyer and Haywood and Pettibone is to be carried to a successful conclusion," he cried, "we must lift up not only our fingers but
our fists!" He qualified the statement the next day in an interview
with a reporter from the *San Francisco Examiner,* but if anyone
thought that this signified that Jack London had lost his belief in

militant socialism, the appearance of *The Iron Heel,* the most revolutionary novel in American literature, was swiftly to change his mind.

February of 1908 saw the book published which brought lasting fame to London's name the world over, *The Iron Heel,* a rare and prophetic novel. It was written during the summer of 1906 but it was the product of several years of thought and study. With an amazing insight into the mechanism of the capitalist system, London was able to catch tendencies in motion in modern society which went unnoticed by most of his socialist colleagues.

In his first important socialist essay, "The Question of the Maximum," London warned that the ruling class, faced by an economic crisis and the growing influence of socialism, might quickly place "a strong curb . . . upon the masses till the crisis were past." "It has been done before," he argued. "There is no reason why it should not be done again. . . . In 1871 the soldiers of the economic rulers stamped out, root and branch, a whole generation of militant socialists."

In 1903 London read W. J. Ghent's *Our Benevolent Feudalism* which, though written by a socialist sympathizer, ridiculed the contention of many socialists that the socialist society was about to be realized. It predicted instead a new feudalism dominated by the capitalists in which "labor will be bound to the machine in fashion similar to that in which the earlier serf was bound to the soil." In a review of Ghent's book for the *International Socialist Review,* London had urged his comrades to read and study its thesis with the hope that it would jar some of them out of the delusion that the capitalists were powerless to halt the advance of socialism.

Yet in his enthusiasm over the growth of the socialist movement, London forgot Ghent's prediction. In his explanation of the great socialist vote in 1904, written for the *San Francisco Examiner,* he declared that when the Socialist Party won control of the political machinery of the country at the ballot box, it would proceed "to confiscate, with or without remuneration, all the possessions of the capitalist class which are used in the production and distribution of the necessaries and luxuries of life." How the capitalists would meet this London did not pretend to know, but he was confident that they could not halt the advance of socialism in the United States for the simple reason that this was a new type of revolt, "a democratic re-

volt" which had to be "fought out with ballots," a "peaceable and
orderly revolt at the ballot box, under democratic conditions, where
the majority rules." Since the capitalists were in the minority, it
would be only a matter of time before the majority of the votes were
cast for the Socialist Party after which a new society, "run in the
interest of the working class," would be instituted.

London's faith in the triumph of "the democratic revolt" remained
unabated throughout most of 1905. Few members of the capitalist
class in the United States, he declared in his lectures, were aware of
the rising tide of revolution in the political world and those capitalists
who saw the threat to their power still believed that they could hold
it back by "bribery in every legislature for the purchase of capitalist
legislation, bayonets, machine-guns, policemen's clubs, professional
strike-breakers, and armed Pinkertons . . ." But such efforts were
futile since they only succeeded in turning more and more workers
into revolutionists. "The revolution is here, now," London declared
confidently. "Stop it who can!"

Yet the more London read and studied contemporary events, the
more he began to doubt a peaceful transition into socialism. The
brutal suppression of the Russian Revolution of 1905 convinced him
that the socialists had to face a fierce and violent struggle by the
capitalists to maintain their power. True, the United States was not
Russia, for here the workers had the right to vote and could pile up
majorities for the Socialist Party in elections. But what if the capitalists should deprive the people of their democratic rights and crush
the revolutionary movement by force of arms?

To his dismay, London found during his tour for the Intercollegiate
Socialist Society that most of the socialist leaders had not the slightest doubt that, faced by a workers' majority at the polls, the overawed capitalists would permit the socialists to take the control of the
means of production out of their hands. They were convinced that
capitalism in the United States soon would be peacefully voted out
of existence. Was not the Socialist Party making headway at the
polls? Were not mayors, aldermen, councilmen, and a few members of
state legislatures being elected on the socialist ticket? Next came
Congress, and as soon as the national legislature was dominated by the
socialists, socialism would be on the way in. "When we get Congress,"
London heard these socialists say, "we can get socialism."

London quickly saw through these delusions. He determined to
show these reformist socialists who naïvely believed that the revolu-

tion could be brought simply by electing enough socialist congressmen, that the capitalists would not sit by and calmly watch their control of society eliminated by legislative enactments. The capitalist
class then would resort to violence to prevent the "democratic revolt" from moving forward, would strike back with unprecedented
terror and fulfill W. J. Ghent's prediction of a new feudalism. Instead
of Ghent's "Benevolent Feudalism," however, there would emerge
the most brutal dictatorship in the history of mankind.

Into *The Iron Heel* London poured his indictment of the socialist
leaders for their failure accurately to assay the strength of the capitalists and to prepare to prevent them from abolishing democracy
when threatened by the victory of "the democratic revolt." Into this
novel he also put his belief in the eventual triumph of socialism, for
nothing that had happened in the world had lessened London's confidence that in the end the working class would triumph.

The Iron Heel is the name that London gives to the oligarchy of
American capitalists who seized power when there was danger of a
socialist victory at the polls. He describes the crushing of labor by this
oligarchy during the years between 1912 and 1932 and the terrible
and bitter conflict between the socialist underground and the forces
of dictatorship. In 1932, when the book ends abruptly, the Oligarchy
has undermined the first revolt of the socialist revolutionaries; but
secretly they plan the second revolt.

The novel purports to be derived from a manuscript discovered in
"the fourth century of the era of Brotherhood which dates the final
triumph of socialist democracy" when the promise of socialism is
being realized. It is written by Avis, the "gently nurtured wife" of
the leader of the second revolt, Ernest Everhard. Throughout the work
are footnotes which are intended to interpret various obsolete references for readers who live under socialism. The comments, drawn
from his extensive file of newspaper clippings and government documents, are devastating notes on conditions in Jack London's times and
are set forth with so keen a satiric sense as to give them place among
the most brilliant indictments of capitalism ever written. Through
this medium London presented his ablest application of Marxist
theory to American conditions.

He introduces his hero, Ernest Everhard as "a superman, a blond
beast such as Nietzsche described, and in addition he was aflame with
democracy." According to Ernest Untermann, who spent several years
with London on his ranch after 1910. Everhard was a composite of

three people: Jack London, Eugene V. Debs, and Untermann himself. Whomever London patterned his hero after he is not very important, for his characterization of him is a political one. We come
to know him through his political acts, his courage, his loyalty, his
comradeship and his devotion to the struggle for socialism and freedom. He starts as a wooden image rather than a real character, but
as the story unfolds he grows in reality until at the end we begin
to get close to him in a personal and intimate way.

Everhard is introduced to the reader at a dinner at the home of
John Cunningham, a distinguished physicist and professor at the
University of California at Berkeley. There he first meets his future
wife, Avis Cunningham, his host's daughter. A discussion develops
among some ministers present about the working class and its relation to the church. Everhard is quiet, listening. Finally he bursts out
with a scathing attack on the assembled churchmen, telling them
that they do not know what they are talking about, that they are
merely metaphysicians, each snug in a private world, and knowing
nothing of the real world about them. He goes further and charges
that the church preaches in the interest of the upper class, the class
that supports it. "You belong in the enemy's camp," he tells them
bluntly. "You have nothing in common with the working class. . . .
Be true to your salt and your hire; guard with your preaching, the
interests of your employers, but do not come down to the working
class and serve as false leaders. . . ."

Later in a separate discussion with Bishop Morehouse, Everhard
asserts that the church no longer teaches Christ, and that the workingmen do not wish to have anything to do with an institution which
"condones the frightful brutality and savagery with which the capitalist class treats the working class." He challenges the Bishop to
protest against the exploitation of labor, against children toiling in
the Southern cotton mills, and against other evils in society, assuring
him that it would cost him his post. The Bishop accepts the challenge,
determined to prove that the church was not silent in the midst of
human suffering. Everhard also challenges Avis Cunningham to learn
the full story of a worker in the Sierra Mills, in which the Cunning-
hams have investments, who lost his arm and was turned out without
a penny. Avis, too, accepts the challenge.

Avis' awakening to the realities of life occurs first. She visits Jackson, the worker who had lost his arm, discovers that accidents in the
Mills were quite common and that the maiming of hundreds of work-

ers, including children, could be traced to the negligence of the company. She also discovers that the evidence presented at the trial to
prevent Jackson from collecting damages was all fixed, and she hears
Colonel Ingram, the company lawyer, coolly admit that the injured
worker should have received damages. Then when Avis writes "a
quiet, restrained, dispassionate account" of Jackson's case in which
she simply sets forth the facts, she discovers that no newspaper will
publish her communication, and learns from a reporter friend that
all the papers are "solid with the corporations," and that any editor
who printed her material would lose his job.

Thus Avis begins "to see through the appearance of the society" in
which she has lived. And the reader gets a simple but dramatic lesson on factory conditions and on the control of the courts and the
press by the corporations. Later, along with Bishop Morehouse, the
reader learns of the control of the church by the same forces. When
the Bishop, having been shown the conditions of the working class in
his community, attempts to apply his Christianity literally—to feed
the poor, welcome the sinful and humble, and champion the cause
of the downtrodden, he is put in a madhouse.

Ernest Everhard is invited to speak before "The Philomaths," an
organization of the wealthiest business men of the community with
"a sprinkling of scholars to give it intellectual tone." He starts, hesi-
tant, to disarm his listeners into believing him a shy, innocent and
ignorant dreamer. He tells them of his life as a worker, and his
struggle to secure an education, of his contacts with the upper class
and of his consequent disillusionment. From novels he had read he had
thought them all fine, noble and intelligent. Instead he found them to
be crooked, rotten, selfish and stupid. He had seen ministers of the
Gospel dismissed because they refused to heed the biddings of the
wealthy, and professors "broken on the wheel of university subservience to the ruling class." In disgust he joined the socialist movement, and a new world opened before his eyes.

His audience remains unmoved; neither his denunciation of the
greed and stupidity of the upper class nor his exposition of the spirit
of the working class has touched them. Then Ernest tells them about
the revolution; he indicts the entire capitalist class, charging it with
mismanagement for compelling people to live in poverty when the
productive forces of society can provide all with a decent standard
of living. He tells them, too, of the determination of the working
class to take over the management of society from the capitalist class,

and he ends, as did London so often in his own lectures, with the
words: "This is the revolution, my masters. Stop it if you can."

The audience is instantly in an uproar. One after another they seek
to demolish Everhard's arguments, but he answers them with pitiless
logic and they resort to personal invective. Then one of the capitalists who has remained cool throughout the heated exchange rises
and says:

> *This, then, is our answer. We have no words to waste on
> you. When you reach out your vaunted strong hands for our
> palaces and purpled ease, we will show you what strength is.
> In roar of shell and shrapnel and in whine of machine-guns
> will your answer be couched. We will grind you revolutionists
> down under our heel, and we shall walk upon your faces. The
> world is ours, we are its lords, and ours it shall remain. . . .*

Everhard replies that the working class will triumph through the
power of the ballot. "What if you do get a majority, a sweeping majority, on election day," comes the immediate response. "Suppose we
refuse to turn the government over to you after you have captured
it at the ballot-box." Then, retorts Everhard, the answer of the working class on that day will come "in roar of shrapnel and in whine of
machine-guns. . . ."

At another meeting, this time of small business men and farmers,
Everhard calls the middle class "The Machine-Breakers." They
know that their existence as a class is rapidly coming to an end, and
in their desperate desire for survival are bent on turning back the
wheels of progress by breaking up the trusts. He tells them that they
are tilting against windmills, that they cannot turn back the tides of
economic evolution which made inevitable the rise of the trusts and
sounded the doom of the small capitalists. To their cry, "What are
we to do then?" he advises them to join the socialists, take over the
ownership of the trusts and utilize their abilities for the benefit of
all the people rather than for a handful of capitalists. Then he gives
them a lesson in Marxism, presenting arguments to prove that capitalism will inevitably break down under its own contradictions and
will give way to socialism. He bases this on a mathematical formula-
tion of the Marxist theory of surplus value. Since capitalists do not
pay their workers enough to permit them to buy back all that they
produce, a large surplus of manufactured goods is piled up each year.
The surplus must be exported. Yet soon every nation under capi-

talism will be in the same predicament, each having its own surplus to export. What then, he asks; and answers that in order to keep prices up and profits secure, it will be necessary to throw the surplus in the sea: "Throw every year hundreds of millions of dollars' worth of shoes and wheat and clothing and all the commodities of commerce into the sea."

Finally, Everhard warns his middle class audience that if they do not soon unite with the workers to achieve socialism, the entire population "will be crushed under the iron heel of a despotism as relentless and terrible as any despotism that has blackened the pages of the history of man."

It does not take long for Everhard's warning to be realized. The Oligarchy starts to crack down, using the entire force of the state to repress rebels and to still all voices which threaten its wealth and power. Social ostracism is the first weapon; then loss of jobs, finally bare-faced and brutal persecution. Vigilante groups, waving American flags and singing patriotic songs, destroy the socialist presses and break up the meetings of labor and radical groups. Strikes are viciously smashed by the police, the militia and the army; workers are wounded and killed and thousands of strikers are herded into concentration camps. The mass of the population is gradually enslaved, but no protests are uttered by the moulders of public opinion, the press, the church and the educators. Anyone who dares to lift his voice in behalf of freedom is deprived of his livelihood or imprisoned.

And while all this transpires the progressive groups are scarcely aware of the powerful forces they are combating and, because of the step-by-step character of the repression, are unable to foresee the ultimate goal of the Oligarchy—the compete overthrow of all democratic processes and the institution of a dictatorship. The socialists and the trade unionists still pin their faith on the ballot box as the solution. But Everhard warns them that the Iron Heel will trample the people's right to vote and that they must be prepared for revolutionary action to prevent it. "In this," writes London, "he was in advance of his party. His fellow-socialists could not agree with him. They still insisted that victory could be gained through the elections. . . . Ernest could not get them seriously to fear the coming of the Oligarchy. They were stirred by him, but they were too sure of their own strength. There was no room in their theoretical social evolution for an oligarchy, therefore the Oligarchy could not be." They would send him to Congress and all would be well.

Then the Plutocracy of America clashes with the German Plutocracy in competition for the same markets. The press and other
agencies whip up the war spirit since the ruling class hopes to divert
the workers from their enemy at home to its enemy abroad. But the
workers of both countries are not so easily fooled. They call a general
strike, and the war is stopped before a shot is fired. But the Oligarchy
still has a hidden weapon. It buys out the key unions by granting
them concessions in the form of higher wages, shorter hours and
better working conditions. The solidarity of labor is thereby broken,
and the weaker unions crushed.

And still the socialists and the trade union leaders cling to their
faith in the ballot. Only Everhard shakes his head. "How many
rifles have you got? Do you know where you can get plenty of lead?"
he asks when the socialists tell him they will triumph at the polls.

Events draw swiftly to a head. Fifty socialist congressmen are
elected. But they are powerless, being in the minority. Slowly the
work of destruction proceeds. The labor movement, split and weakened, is crushed; its leaders are arrested, jailed and secretly executed.
Finally, labor wakes up and makes a stand. But it is hopeless, for it
has come too late. The Iron Heel wreaks on the workers the most
awful vengeance. The Mercenaries, a professional soldiery, mow down
the revolutionists. In Chicago where a Commune is formed the bloody
warfare reaches its height. The city is left a shambles. Labor fights
to the last ditch, but to no avail. The socialists, led by Everhard,
resort to individual terrorism in their effort to fight back.

> And through it all moved the Iron Heel, impassive and de-
> liberate, shaking up the whole fabric of the social structure in
> its search for the comrades, combing out the Mercenaries, the
> labor castes, and all its secret services, punishing without
> mercy and without malice, suffering in silence all retaliations
> that were made upon it, and filling the gaps in its fighting line
> as fast as they appeared.

The book ends on this first defeat of the working class. This was followed by a second revolt, as crushingly defeated as was the first, but
the events of the book deal only with the first revolt. Everhard was
executed by the Oligarchy sometime during the year 1932, while making plans for the second revolt. He dies convinced that in the end
the Iron Heel will be crushed: "We have lost a battle, we shall win

the war. Lost for this time, but not forever! We have learned many things. Tomorrow the cause will rise once more, stronger in wisdom, and in discipline."

The closing sections of the novel in which London pictures the conditions of the masses after they are reduced to slavery, and portrays the work of the underground, are among the finest pieces of imaginative writing in all literature. The description of imaginary civil war in Chicago is masterly. It is unfortunate, however, that this section of the novel is weakened by London's treatment of the People of the Abyss as a "Roaring Abysmal Beast" moving about with only the aim of destruction in mind and powerless to serve any purpose other than that of providing cannon-fodder for the Mercenaries.

London spent several months writing *The Iron Heel,* fully aware that no publisher might accept it, that no magazine would dare to serialize it, that it would intensify the attacks upon him in the bourgeois press and seriously impair the sale of his other works. Yet he had to get this one book out of his system as his contribution to the success of the social revolution and his warning to the socialist movement that reformism would lead to world-wide disaster for the working class. Fortunately, Macmillan agreed to publish it. Brett's only request was that London delete a footnote which might land both author and publisher in jail. Jack's reply was characteristic: "If they find me guilty of contempt I'd be only too glad to do six months in jail, during which time I could write a couple of books and do no end of reading."

The book met with instant derision by the majority of the critics. The *Indianapolis News* was one of the few papers to praise it. "Power is certainly the keynote of this book," it said. "Every word tingles with it; it is so strong that it is almost brutal. But it is a great book, one that deserves to be read and pondered. . . . The lift of the book sweeps the reader to his feet; it contains a mighty lesson and a most impressive warning." Elsewhere the book was denounced as reckless sensationalism, dishonest, a dull tract masquerading as a novel. *The Dial* declared that "such books as this . . . have a mischievous influence upon unbalanced minds, and we cannot but deplore their multiplication." *The Independent* concluded that "semi-barbarians, to whom this sort of stuff appeals, may possibly tear down our civilization; they will never lay a single brick of a nobler civilization." *The Outlook* summed up the viewpoint of the press with the observation:

". . . as a work of fiction it has little to commend it, and as a socialist tract it is distinctly unconvincing."

The socialists were divided in their reactions. The more militant leaders like Eugene Debs, Bill Haywood and Mary Marcy praised it unstintingly and urged that its lessons be taken to heart by the entire movement. But the middle class leaders of the Party were even more vehement in their denunciations than the bourgeois critics. Here the Socialist Party was making headway at the polls and along came Jack London and took the edge off these victories with the pessimism and black despair of *The Iron Heel*. What would happen to those who had joined the movement because they were led to believe that in this country socialism was a matter of a few years of peaceful transition from capitalism and who were convinced that though the capitalists would resist, the will of the voters at the ballot box would prevail? Writing in the *International Socialist Review*, John Spargo admitted that there was literary skill in "this ingenious and stirring romance," but disagreed violently with those socialists who hailed it as a "great addition to the literature of Socalist propaganda." "The picture he gives," Spargo went on, "is well calculated, it seems to me, to repel many whose addition to our forces is sorely needed; it gives a new impetus to the old and generally discarded cataclysmic theory; it tends to weaken the political Socialist movement by discrediting the ballot and to encourage the chimerical and reactionary notion of physical force, so alluring to a certain type of mind . . ."

London emphatically denied that his message in *The Iron Heel* signified an abandonment on his part of a belief in political action. "I believe there is much to be gained by entering political campaigns," he told a socialist reporter several years later. "The real advantage, in my opinion, is the great opportunity to educate the workers to an understanding of the wrong of the present system and the meaning of class consciousness." In the same interview he repeated the basic message of *The Iron Heel*:

> *History shows that no master class is ever willing to let go without a quarrel. The capitalists own the governments, the armies and the militia. Don't you think the capitalists will use these institutions to keep themselves in power? I do.*

It was the capitalist class not the workers, London insisted, who would use violence; in their attempt to prevent the democratic will of the people from being exercised they would institute a reign of ter-

ror to destroy the movements that threatened their power. The years
have proved Jack London's picture in *The Iron Heel* to be tragically
correct. We have but to substitute the word "fascism" for "oligarchy"
and *The Iron Heel* becomes a living picture of what actually happened
in the past two decades. It is true that London did not foresee the
brutal forms which fascism would take in our time. Yet, despite many
differences between what happened in Germany, Italy and Spain and
what is pictured in this book, it is probably the most amazingly
prophetic work of the twentieth century. Since the advent of fascism,
radicals the world over have come to realize the validity of Jack London's prophecies. In 1924, after fascism had come to Italy, Anatole
France wrote in an introduction to a new edition of *The Iron Heel*:
"Alas, Jack London had that particular genius which perceived what
is hidden from the common herd, and possessed a special knowledge
enabling him to anticipate the future. He foresaw the assemblage of
events which is but now unrolling to our view."

Jack London was not in the country when *The Iron Heel* appeared.
On April 23, 1907 he hoisted Jimmy Hopper's football sweater for a
pennant and sailed for Hawaii and the South Seas on what was to
be a seven year voyage around the world. The *Socialist Voice* of Oakland bade him a mixed farewell:

> *Goodby, Jack, Goodby! The* Snark, *flying the red flag,
> weighed anchor April 22, and Jack London and his wife are
> now at sea. Roosevelt will be glad to know there is one less
> "undesirable citizen" in the country. To us Comrade London's
> departure is a source both of congratulation and regret. Lon-
> don goes into a field of wider usefulness to the cause of social-
> ism, and we are glad. Our only regret is that we shall miss his
> cheering personal contact.* Socialist Voice *has had many oc-
> casions to be grateful to Comrade London for substantial aid,
> as well as for encouragement. We hope the old world will wag
> right for you, Jack, and send you back to us the same big-
> hearted, clear-headed, hard-fisted fellow you now are. Good
> Luck!*

Amidst incredible chaos and danger, with his boat threatening any
moment to sink under him, and his crew sea-sick, London sat down
and began work on *Martin Eden.* The twenty-eight days before
Hawaii was reached was one long nightmare. But there was the con-

solation that now at last in Hawaii he could do his daily stint on the
novel, turn out articles about the voyage for the magazines and newspapers and write short stories without worrying about leaks, non-
functioning bathrooms, spoiled food and filthy quarters. Moreover, the
warm welcome extended to London and his crew by the "sweet people" of the "sweet land" made him forget the terrible voyage. One
week was spent gathering material for an article on the leper island,
Molokai, written at the request of the lepers with whom Jack and
Charmian mingled freely. This article, "The Lepers of Molokai," in
which he paid tribute to these outcasts who managed to create a
happy community on the island, is one of the most sensitive pieces of
writing to come out of the cruise.

But while Jack was adventuring in Hawaii, the Marquesas and
Tahiti, his estate at home was being run into the ground by his
sponging fair-weather friends and relatives. So much of his money
was being squandered that in the first week of 1908, while in Tahiti,
he learned that all he had in the world was sixty-six dollars. Yet a
month before he had received almost six thousand dollars in royalties.

Jack decided to return to San Francisco to straighten out his affairs.
He set sail from Tahiti on the *S.S. Mariposa,* landed in San Francisco,
immediately wired Brett at Macmillan for an advance against the
almost completed *Martin Eden,* paid off the most pressing of his
debts, put his affairs into a semblance of order, and within ten days
was back on the *Mariposa* for Tahiti to pick up the threads of his
projected seven-year voyage around the world. He left behind him
scores of enraged socialists who castigated him for deserting the
movement.

There are many contradictions in the life of Jack London, but it is
difficult to find one that equals his conduct in the South Seas. Everywhere he went, Fiji, the Marquesas, Samoa, and Hawaii, wherever he
could gather a group of white men together, he would lecture them
on Revolution and expound the class struggle and the battle for
socialism. Yet he took part in the "blackbirding" expeditions which
recruited natives as slave laborers for the copra * plantations. And in
none of the articles or stories which came out of the cruise of the *Snark*
is there any criticism of the effects of the white man's "civilization"
upon the natives.

On one score London was consistent: come what might, through
periods of skin ulcers and yaws, he continued his daily output of a

* Copra. The dried coconut palm kernel used in soap making.

thousand words. But against malaria even he was helpless, and for months he was as often on his back as on his feet. By September, 1908 he was in constant pain, the victim of a strange disease which no one could diagnose. Finally, too ill to seek further adventure, he arranged with a retired sea captain to watch over the *Snark,* and engaged passage for himself, Charmian, Martin Johnson and his servant, Makata, for Sydney, Australia.

London spent five weeks in a Sydney hospital, but to no avail; his affliction baffled Australian specialists. He remained in Sydney five more months, too sick to do much writing or reading. Yet it is amazing that in spite of a malady which caused his hands to swell to twice their natural size and his skin to peel off in layers, he turned out a penetrating article for the Sydney *Star* contrasting strike methods in the United States and Australia. No one reading the article could possibly guess that the author was a sick and discouraged young man. It has the old London vitality; the vigorous assertion of the class struggle; the indictment of capitalism for mismanagement, and the prediction that "the future belongs to labor." London answers the question, "Will industrial peace ever come?" with the observation:

> And the only answer is that it will never come so long as the present system of industrial production obtains. Human nature will not change. Capital will continue to want all it can get, and labor will continue to want all it can get. And on both sides they will fight for it. No, the lion and the lamb will never lie down together in vegetarian pastures.
>
> "Then must we forever endure the irrational anarchy of strikes and lockouts?" some one asks. Not so, is the answer. There are two ways by which industrial peace may be achieved. Either capital will own labor absolutely, and there will be no more strikes, or labor will own capital absolutely, and there will be no more strikes. . . ."

In contrast with his treatment of this theme in *The Iron Heel,* it is interesting to note that London was now convinced that it was "illogical to think of capital absolutely owning labor," for this "would mean chattel slavery, a trend backward to primeval night out of which civilisation has emerged." Evidently while he could predict fascism in his novel, London really could not conceive that mankind would permit these horrors to come to pass. He was spared the revelation that that which he termed "illogical" would become a reality.

London decided to get home to California and sent Martin Johnson
to the Solomon Islands to bring the *Snark* back to Sydney. There she
was sold at auction for $3,000 and put into service as a blackbirder
among the Solomon Islands. This was the end of a ship built by a man
who just a few weeks before had written in the Sydney *Star:* "It
would seem from reading the past, that the future belongs to labor."
On July 23, 1909, two and a quarter years after he had set sail with
such enthusiasm for a voyage around the world, Jack London landed
in San Francisco, discouraged, his health shot to pieces, deeply in
debt, and the magazines and newspapers convinced that his best writing was behind him.

During his twenty-five months' experience in the South Seas, London
wrote three books which can be regarded as direct products of the
voyage: the articles that made up *The Cruise of the Snark*, the stories
in *South Sea Tales* and the novel *Adventure*. With the exception of
"The Lepers of Molokai" in *The Cruise of the Snark* and four of the
stories in *South Sea Tales*, these books added little to London's literary stature. And so much of this writing is saturated with his chau-
vinistic conceit of the supremacy of the Anglo-Saxon race that these
books also added little to his stature as a socialist. In only four stories
—"The House of Mapuhi," "Mauki," "Samuel," and "The Seed of
McCoy"—is the native population portrayed sympathetically. In all
the rest, the native is servile and the white man the master.

Martin Eden, as we have seen, was started and completed during
the voyage, but it is based entirely on London's earlier life and is in
no sense a product of the expedition. Yet long after all of the articles
and most of the stories which came directly from the voyage would be
forgotten, *Martin Eden* would still be counted among the great American novels.

It is, of course, the most autobiographical of Jack London's novels,
dealing with the self-education of a sailor and recounting in the
process most of London's own struggles to become a writer. The title
character, a poorly-educated sailor, saves the life of Arthur Morse, a
well-to-do young man. He is introduced into Morse's home, a place of
wealth and culture, where he meets Mrs. Morse, a typical "good wife
and mother" of the upper middle class, Mr. Morse, a well-intentioned
but unimaginative business man, Arthur's brothers, pleasant young
college-boys with no vitality in them, and Ruth, the "pale, ethereal
creature with wide spiritual blue eyes and a wealth of golden hair"

whom he likens "to a pale gold flower upon a slender stem" and promptly worships. Awkward and embarrassed, ungrammatical and crude though he is, there is about him such virility and an air of romance arising from harsh adventures in far places of the world, that Ruth, to her horror, feels the strong attraction of his physical being. Martin's love for her and his admiration for her gracious way of life, stimulate him to educate himself and become a cultured individual able to move about with ease in her home. Ruth tutors and advises him at first, but is soon outstripped by a more intense intellect which, thwarted for twenty years, seizes upon culture with all its pent-up force. With an incredible hunger, Martin devours Spencer, Darwin, Huxley, Marx, Hegel and a huge and varied body of socio-logical, philosophical and literary works.

It is not long before Martin Eden begins to see through the bourgeois hypocrisy of the Morse family and to realize that Ruth, his idol, shares their narrowness and smugness. But his love for her becomes more understanding as he recognizes her intellectual and human in-adaquacies. Their engagement is a blow to the father and mother, but they decide to say nothing, biding their time in the belief that the uncouth Eden will dispose of himself.

Burning to become a writer, Martin Eden devotes over a year of gruelling labor and incredible self-denial to his chosen task—living in a hovel on the meagre meals he cooks himself, sleeping five hours a night and besieging the editors with manuscripts. But he receives neither encouragement nor understanding and sympathy from Ruth. On various occasions he reads her some of his stories whose quality she is totally unable to judge. She recognizes the power of the writing, but not the beauty in its realism; indeed, his attempts at beauty in realism provoke her indignant comments "degrading" and "nasty."

The break between the two comes with Martin's persistent refusal, in the face of constant rejections by the editors, to surrender his literary ambition and take a job. Just on the verge of his becoming a successful writer, Ruth breaks the engagement.

Brissenden, the consumptive poet and cynic, alone recognizes Martin Eden's gifts, and he seeks to persuade him to join the socialist movement, predicting disillusionment for Martin if he does succeed as a writer and has nothing to hold him to life. But Martin Eden refuses to heed his advice. "As for myself," he says ,"I am an individualist. I believe the race is to the swift, the battle to the strong. Such is the lesson I have learned from biology, or at least I think I have learned. As I said, I am an individualist, and individualism is the hereditary and eternal foe of socialism."

Brissenden dies before his prophecy is fulfilled. A controversial essay which has a phenomenal sale brings Martin's name to the attention of the editors, and he is overwhelmed with requests for material. Martin throws back at the editors the dozens of manuscripts which have been rejected and this time they are gobbled up. He becomes rich overnight even though he has written nothing new. The desire to beat the enemy at his own game becomes his major concern.

But soon a great weariness overtakes him. He is invited to the wealthiest homes for dinner, but now that he no longer fasts by necessity, it leaves him unmoved. He is indifferent even to Ruth, and refuses to renew their relationship when she comes to see him. Basically his spiritual weariness arises from his resentment that no one except Brissenden (who is dead) has respected him before he was publicly recognized. He hates the thought that he is being recognized not for his ability but because his name is in demand.

> *Invitations to dinner poured in on Martin; and the more they poured, the more he puzzled. He sat, the guest of honor, at an Arden Club banquet, with men of note whom he had heard about and read about all his life; and they told him how, when they had read "The Ring of Bells" in the* Transcontinental, *and "The Peri and the Pearl" in* The Hornet, *they had immediately picked him for a winner. My God! and I was hungry and in rags, he thought to himself. Why didn't you give me a dinner then? Then was the time. It was work performed. If you are feeding me now for work performed, why did you not feed me then when I needed it? Not one word in "The Ring of Bells," nor in "The Peri and the Pearl" has been changed. No; you're not feeding me now for work performed. You are feeding me because everybody else is feeding me and because it is an honor to feed me. You are feeding me now because you are herd animals; because you are part of the mob; because the one blind, automatic thought in the mob-mind just now is to feed me. And where does Martin Eden and the work Martin Eden performed come in in all this? he asked himself plaintively, then arose to respond cleverly and wittily to a clever and witty toast.*

As Brissenden had predicted, Martin Eden's success was more

disillusioning to him than all his previous defeats. He refuses to write
another word, winds up his business affairs, and sails for the South
Seas. Enroute, however, weariness overcomes him and he slips through
a porthole and vanishes into the midnight depths:

> *Down, down, he swam until his arms and legs grew tired and
> hardly moved. He knew that he was deep. The pressure on his
> ear-drums was a pain, and there was a buzzing in his head.
> His endurance was faltering, but he compelled his arms and
> legs to drive him deeper until his will snapped and the air
> drove from his lungs in a great explosive rush. The bubbles
> rubbed and bounded like tiny balloons against his cheeks and
> eyes as they took their upward flight. Then came pain and
> strangulation. This hurt was not death, was the thought that
> oscillated through his reeling consciousness. Death did not
> hurt. It was life, the pangs of life, this awful, suffocating feel-
> ing; it was the last blow life could deal him.*
>
> *His wilful hands and feet began to beat and churn about,
> spasmodically and feebly. But he had fooled them and the
> will to live that made them beat and churn. He was too deep
> down. They could never bring him to the surface. He seemed
> floating languidly in a sea of dreamy vision. Colors and radi-
> ances surrounded him and bathed him and pervaded him.
> What was that? It seemed a lighthouse; but it was inside his
> brain—a flashing, bright white light. It flashed swifter and
> swifter. There was a long rumble of sound, and it seemed to
> him that he was falling down a vast and interminable stair-
> way. And somewhere at the bottom he fell into darkness. That
> much he knew. He had fallen into darkness. And at the instant
> he knew, he ceased to know.*

The reaction of the critics bewildered and angered Jack London.
It was not so much that hardly any reviewer had a good word to say
for the book or that they sneered at the plot and declared that he
was "quite at sea" when he tried "to write about that ordinary society
which is variously described as decent, as respectable, as cultured, or
as good, and, in his language, as bourgeois." This he had come to
expect. What aroused his anger was that most of the critics, including
Socialist reviewers, attacked the novel as an apology for individualism
and as proof that London had abandoned his belief in socialism. Again
and again London was to assert that *Martin Eden* was the most mis-

understood of all his books. In the flyleaf of one copy of the book he wrote on April 4, 1910: "This is a book that missed fire with a majority of the critics. Written as an indictment of individualism, it was accepted as an indictment of socialism; written to show that man cannot live for himself alone, it was accepted as a demonstration that individualism made for death. Had Martin Eden been a socialist he would not have died." A few years later in *John Barleycorn* he pointed out that when pessimism overwhelmed him and he was about to seek Martin Eden's way out, one thing had saved him—the People!

> *I meditated suicide coolly, as a Greek philosopher might. My regret was that there were too many dependent directly upon me for food and shelter for me to quit living. But that was sheer morality. What really saved me was the one remaining illusion—THE PEOPLE.*
>
> *The things that I had fought for and burned my midnight oil for, had failed me. Success—I despised it. Recognition—it was dead ashes. Society, men and women above the ruck and muck of the water-front and the forecastle. I was appalled by their unlovely mental mediocrity. Love of woman—it was like the rest. Money—I could sleep in only one bed at a time, and of what worth was an income of a hundred porter-houses a day when I could eat only one? Art, culture—in the face of the iron facts of biology such things were ridiculous, the exponents of such things only the more ridiculous.*
>
> *From the foregoing it can be seen how very sick I was. I was born a fighter. The things I had fought for had proved not worth the fight. Remained the PEOPLE. My fight was finished, yet something was left still to fight for—the PEOPLE.*
>
> *But the PEOPLE saved me. By the PEOPLE I was handcuffed to life. There was still one fight left in me, and there was the thing for which to fight. I threw all precaution to the winds, threw myself with fiercer zeal in the fight for socialism. . . .*

The critics, however, can hardly be blamed for missing London's message in *Martin Eden;* indeed, it is likely that the average reader today still comes away from the book without the slightest conception that it was meant to be an attack on individualism. Actually, if it was London's aim to make converts for socialism in *Martin Eden* he chose peculiar ways of doing it. It is true that in the description of the discussion at the rooms of Kreis, a professor fired from the university for his radical views, there is a brilliant contrast between the superficial conversation at the Morse's and the keen witty remarks of the "rebels of one variety or another." But of the entire group only Brissenden is a socialist. And London's picture of Brissenden, the one socialist with whom Martin Eden has any real contact, is scarcely one to arouse enthusiasm for the movement. Brissenden explains that he is a socialist "because socialism is inevitable; because the present rotten and irrational system cannot endure; because the day is past for your man on horseback." But he has only contempt for the people, refers to them as "slaves," and freely admits: "Of course I don't like the crowd, but what's a poor chap to do?" Nothing in Brissenden reminds one of Ernest Everhard in *The Iron Heel* who is drawn to socialism by his love for the people and a determination to share in their struggles.

The only other socialist described in some detail in *Martin Eden* is a speaker at an open meeting of the Oakland local of whom London writes: "The speaker, a clever Jew, won Martin's admiration at the same time that he aroused his antagonism. The man's stooped and narrow shoulders and weazened chest proclaimed him the true child of the crowded ghetto, and strong on Martin was the age-long struggle of the feeble, wretched slaves against the lordly handful of men who had ruled over them and would rule over them to the end of time. To Martin this withered wisp of a creature was a symbol. He was the figure that stood forth representative of the whole miserable mass of weaklings and inefficients who perished according to biological law on the ragged confines of life. They were the unfit. . . ." But London does not tell us that the speaker is a "symbol" of the exploitation of labor under capitalism, nor does he even reveal what there was about him that won Martin's admiration. It is hardly surprising then that so many readers have left the account of the meeting of the Oakland local with the feeling that socialists were indeed "queer" people. How the reader can then possibly conclude that the tragedy of Martin Eden's life lay in his refusal to associate himself with such people is something which Jack London never bothered to explain.

Thus while *Martin Eden* is today regarded by many critics to be Jack London's most mature work and while it does contain a brilliant picture of the struggles of a worker to become educated, to make a living by writing, to become a success, it is also in many ways one of the least successful of his works. For it has been seized upon time and again to prove exactly the opposite of what the author said he wished to demonstrate.

Three short stories written soon after *Martin Eden* was completed were proof that London had not lost his ability to bring his message home clearly to his readers, and consequently all three, "The Dream of Debs," "South of the Slot" and "The Strength of the Strong," received much more attention in the socialist movement than the autobiographical novel.

"The Dream of Debs," published in the *International Socialist Review* in January-February, 1909, is an extremely readable and exciting story of a nation-wide general strike as seen through the eyes of the rich in San Francisco. The events take place sometime in the 1940's after the American Federation of Labor has been destroyed by its class-collaborationist president and its place taken by the I.L.W., "the biggest and solidest organization of labor the United States has ever seen." Every detail of the strike has been worked out in advance; it is conducted in an orderly and peaceful manner and the workers win by starving the capitalists into submission.

The description of events during the strike reveals that London had done considerable reading on the tactics of a general strike. Transportation is dead; the rich join the poor on the bread lines; hordes of city dwellers leave San Francisco and the countryside is devastated and cleaned out, and finally, after the outburst of violence among the slum people and the upper classes, the Employers' Association is forced to come to terms with the I.L.W. and the strike is over. The rich narrator's closing sentence, is typical of the reaction of employers at all stages in the history of the labor movement: "The tyranny of organized labor is getting beyond human endurance. Something must be done."

In a review of Leroy Scott's *The Walking Delegate* in the *San Francisco Examiner* of May 28, 1905, London had sharply criticized leaders of the American Federation of Labor "whose corrupt dealings throw much of odium upon the trade union movement," and had stressed that such leaders shared no small part of the responsibility for the exploitation of labor. Now in "The Dream of Debs" he demonstrated how a militant labor movement, led by honest men, could gain important victories for the working class. True, he exaggerated the supineness of the government in the face of the general strike and his love of the romantic led him to show the workers carrying out their plans with all the secrecy of a small, underground group. But with these exceptions the story is realistically handled and emerges as a remarkable piece of working-class propaganda clothed as fiction. It was reprinted in pamphlet form and received a wide circulation in labor circles, especially among the members of the I.W.W. after whom London had modelled the militant trade union which led the general strike.

"South of the Slot," published in the *Saturday Evening Post* of May 22, 1909, is a tale of the class struggle in San Francisco. The "Slot" is an iron crack along Market Street, separating the town into two residential sections—one for the rich, and one for the poor. Literally it is the class line of society.

Freddie Drummond, sociology professor at the University of California, an academic, slightly anemic, self-satisfied young writer, takes to crossing the Slot to study social conditions. He assumes the disguise of a truck driver and the name "Big" Bill Totts, a husky, boisterous worker, good fellow and good union man.

As Freddie Drummond he becomes engaged to a registerite damsel named Catherine Van Vorst. As Bill Totts he takes part in strike struggles and becomes friendly with Mary Condon, militant head of the Glove Workers' Union No. 974.

The two personalities come into direct conflict one day when Freddie Drummond and Catherine Van Vorst are driving in her automobile to visit a Boys' Club and are caught between striking workers and the police. The scabs driving the meat wagons are halted by a traffic jam created by a sympathetic coal-driver and teamster. As Freddie and Catherine look on, the police appear to be winning. A policeman has reached the top of the barricade, and has seized a worker. Freddie can stand it no longer. It is "Big" Bill Totts who leaps out of the car, onto the barricade and goes in punching for the workers, knocking down the policeman. Against the police "his onslaught was like a whirlwind. A rush of three more policemen gained the top [of the coal wagon stopped during the fight] and locked with Bill Totts in a gigantic clinch, during which his scalp was opened up by a club, and coat, vest, and half his starched shirt was torn from him. But the three policemen were flung wide and far, and Bill Totts, raining down lumps of coal, held the fort"

After the battle Bill Totts swings out of sight with Mary Condon on his arm. Thus the dual roles have been united in the heat of the class struggle, and a new labor leader arises, Bill Totts by name.

It is a magnificent working-class story showing the inevitable conflict between a worker's personality and the passionless, conservative
professor. In addition, it has one of the most exciting descriptions of
a street fight between workers and police ever written.

"The Strength of the Strong," published in *Hampton's Magazine*
in May, 1910, is one of the best of Jack London's propaganda stories
and is among the finest parables in American literature, ranking
with Edward Bellamy's "Parable of the Water Tank." The story is
set in pre-historic times, in an age when men have just begun to
abandon homes in the trees. Long Beard, an elder of the tribe, teaches
the younger men the meaning of unity and cooperation by a tale of
the old days, of his own youth. Once the tribe consisted of individual
families each hostile and afraid of the other, and each fending for
itself. But they learned the value of cooperation when a united tribe,
the Meat-Eaters, attacked and almost destroyed them. They saw that
"each Meat-Eater had the strength of ten for the ten had fought as
one man." So the tribe held council, drew up a system of self-defense
and formulated a code of laws.

But disunity returned. Among the tribe were the few who were
more interested in their own comfort than in the general welfare.
At first there was plenty to eat for all, but the few greedy ones amassed
all the land and forced the others to work for them. The son of the
chief, Dog-Tooth, demanded to be chief when his father died; another, Big-Fat, who could speak with the spirits of the dead set himself
up as the representative of the gods, and still another, Little Belly,
invented a fish-trap which enabled him to corner the market. The surplus was so great that the workers were no longer paid in kind but in
money. "But," Long Beard recalls, "this was the strange thing: as the
days went by we who were left worked harder and harder, and yet did
we get less and less to eat." The more money the exploiting members
of the tribe accumulated, the less there was for the workers, and the
more the workers produced, the less food they had to eat. As the
surplus increased, wages went still lower and the workers could not
afford to buy back the very food they had produced. So while they
went hungry, food was destroyed to keep prices high.

Inevitably the workers became discontented with their lot, and this
discontent flared into rebellion. But some of the workers were given
favored positions as guards and ordered to kill the rebels. The church
condemned the rebels and preached that God had decreed that the
wiser must rule over the rest. And the Bug, who had gained a reputa-

tion as a singer, sang that the Fish-Eaters were God's chosen people
and that it was His will that they destroy the Meat-Eaters. Forgetting
their hunger and their grumbling, the workers clamored to be led
against the Meat-Eaters. They did not heed the words of one of the
workers, Split-Nose, who cried that their real enemies were the rulers
of the tribe, that they should take away the power and wealth of the
rich, and that they should join forces with the Meat-Eaters instead
of fighting them. When the Bug sang that Split-Nose was a menace to
the tribe, the starving workers joined in stoning him to death.

But in the end, disunited, weakened by starvation and disease, the
workers were unable to resist their enemies. The Meat-Eaters came
over the divide and destroyed the tribe. Long Beard, who managed to
escape, concludes:

> *Some day . . . all the fools will be dead, and then all live
> men will go forward. The secret of the strength of the strong
> will be theirs, and they will add their strength together, so that
> of all the men in the world not one will fight with another. . . .
> And all men will be brothers, and no man will lie idle in the
> sun and be fed by his fellows.*

London made effective use of the past to build his indictment of
capitalism, and his simplicity of plot and style as well as his story-
telling ability made "The Strength of the Strong" an ideal propaganda piece. Soon after its appearance in *Hampton's Magazine,* it
was reprinted as a pamphlet by Charles H. Kerr Company of Chicago, the socialist cooperative publishing house, and became one of
the classics of socialist literature.

When London returned from Australia he found the newspapers and
magazines hostile or disinterested. But it was not long before he was
back in favor with the reading public and being sought after by
editors. The California climate helped him to recuperate and when he
discovered that the mysterious disease that had afflicted him was
caused by nothing more than the ultra-violet rays of the tropical sun,
he recaptured his old vitality. He picked up his routine and again
turned out a thousand words a day six days a week.

What flowed from Jack London's pen after his return from the
South Seas, with a few exceptions, were no better than pot-boilers.
Nor is this surprising, considering the growing demand on his pocket-
book. The quality of what he wrote did not, in the main, concern him.

He was interested only in the money it would bring in for the upkeep
of his ranch and the support of his relatives and numerous retainers
who sucked him dry. "I have no unfinished stories," he said frankly
during an interview in 1911. "Invariably I complete every one I start.
If it's good, I sign it and send it out. If it isn't good, I sign it and send
it out." And he had grown to hate his work:

> *I loathe the stuff when I have done it* [he wrote to Upton
> Sinclair]. *I do it because I want money and it is an easy way to
> get it. But if I could have my choice about it I never would
> put pen to paper—except to write a Socialist essay to tell the
> bourgeois world how much I despise it.*

But he no longer had a choice. Money as such, he wrote in *John
Barleycorn,* meant nothing to him. Yet the continuous financial demands made upon him compelled him to earn money by his writing,
regardless of whether or not he had any inspiration. By the summer
of 1910 he was buying story plots from Sinclair Lewis, rejecting those
which were not suited to his temperament and others because he was
"too lazy to dig up the requisite data or atmosphere." To young
writers eager to learn the secret of success in the profession, he would
reply advising them to take their time and, if necessary, to spend a
day on a paragraph. But he himself could no longer follow his own
advice. Writing was a means of making money, and the more he
wrote the more the money poured in. The quality no longer mattered.

Of course, London had become so adept that even at his worst he
is eminently readable. And in some of the books he wrote in the last
years of his life like *Burning Daylight, John Barleycorn, The Valley of
the Moon* and *The Star Rover,* there are sections which show that he
could still tell a vivid story in a wholly convincing way. Moreover, the
descriptions of high finance in *Burning Daylight,* the picture of the
life of the workers and of the flaming labor troubles in Oakland in
The Valley of the Moon, and the terrible indictment of society for
its treatment of criminals in *The Star Rover,* are proof that London
had not entirely lost the ability to present an important social message. Unfortunately, the realistic observations in these books are
usually obscured by unrealistic plots and preposterous characters, the
stories often run to seed after promising beginnings, and the writing
too frequently reflects London's backward racial prejudices. The
truth is that never again was Jack London to attain the literary heights

of *The Sea Wolf* and *Martin Eden* or the class-consciousness of *The Iron Heel.*

The decline in London's writings coincides with the waning of his activity in the socialist movement. He contributed financially to the Party and when he drove down to Santa Rosa once a week for relaxation he would discuss socialism with anyone at the bar and "would say things in the presence of judges, chamber of commerce executives and businessmen about how corrupt the capitalist system was." But other than that he did little for the movement, devoting most of his energies to fantastic ventures that he seemed to need to take his mind off the pot-boilers. He grew eucalyptus trees; he raised horses; he tried to make arid land fertile; he made his ranch a combination agricultural laboratory and model community, a utopian colony where he employed men with a genuine love for the soil and built cottages for his workers and schools for their children. But failure after failure struck at him. The money poured out, as through a sieve, and no results were realized.

On August 18, 1913, the magnificent "Wolf House," on which London had spent over $70,000, was completed. The workmen cleaned up and left. During the night the house burned to the ground. From this blow he never recovered. The outer stone shell of the house, which was all that remained of the magnificent mansion, was a symbol of what was left of Jack London.

Many of London's comrades viewed the tragedy as a judgment from heaven against a socialist for building a castle. They resented his having poured so much money into the house, believing that his extravagance gave the Cause unfavorable publicity and that it was hardly fitting for a socialist to spend so much to satisfy personal whims when the Party was desperately in need of funds. London, who always believed that the possession of wealth did not make him a capitalist, replied that he had built the house with money earned by his own labor.

The justification convinced few people, yet it is true that all his wealth came from his own labor. He had no investments and he exploited no one. Furthermore, his generosity was widely known. When he was building "Wolf House" he gave explicit orders that no man applying for work was to be turned away. Every Wobbly who journeyed westward stopped in for a handout at Jack London's place in the Valley of the Moon, and his ranch was a veritable refuge for all the down-and-outers who passed through California. His financial contributions to the movement and to special labor causes continued.

Still the cry that he was an "apostate Socialist" continued and increased as he moved further and further away from the Party. The finishing touch came with his changing attitude towards the Mexican Revolution.

In February, 1911, Jack London had addressed a letter to the "dear, brave comrades of the Mexican Revolution" who had revolted against the dictatorship of General Porfirio Diaz. The stirring letter, first published in the socialist press, had the characteristic London flair:

> *We socialists, anarchists, hobos, chicken thieves, outlaws and undesirable citizens of the United States are with you heart and soul in your efforts to overthrow slavery and autocracy in Mexico. You will notice we are not respectable in these days of the reign of property. All the names you are being called, we have been called. And when graft and greed get up and begin to call names, honest men, brave men, patriotic men and martyrs can expect nothing else than to be called chicken thieves and outlaws.*
>
> *So be it. But I for one wish that there were more chicken thieves and outlaws of the sort that formed the gallant band that took Mexicali, of the sort that is heroically enduring the prison holes of Diaz, of the sort that is fighting and dying and sacrificing in Mexico today.*
>
> *I subscribe myself a chicken thief and revolutionist,*
>
> *Jack London.*

A few weeks later London again expressed his solidarity with the Mexican revolutionists in a newspaper interview during which he also revealed his opposition to American imperialism in Mexico. "I hope the people of the United States," he declared after American troops had been dispatched to Mexico, "will resent this latest action of the United States government in proposing to overawe the Mexican revolutionists, but I'm afraid they will not. The action of the government is logical. It regards dollars, not democracy, and therefore it will send its troops to protect its dollars. It may be necessary to send troops into Mexico to crush the rebellion. Diaz is afraid all hell may break loose. If the United States government wants to invade Mexico, it can find plenty of legal pretexts, but it would be a burning shame.

It might end the revolution, but it certainly cannot crush the revolutionary spirit in Mexico."

London's sympathy for the Mexican Revolution also found expression in one of the short stories written during this period of his career, "The Mexican," published in the *Saturday Evening Post* on August 12, 1913. It describes the work of the Junta operating in the United States in support of the coming Mexican Revolution and, in particular, of one of the members of the organization, the eighteen-year-old Felipe Rivera, who becomes a prize fighter to raise money for guns for the Revolution. In the course of his masterful description of the fight between Rivera and Danny Ward, the coming lightweight champion, London uses the flash-back technique to show what was behind the revolutionary movement in Mexico. As Rivera sits in his corner awaiting the arrival of Danny Ward and his retinue, his mind goes back to his childhood:

> *He saw the white-walled, water-power factories of Rio Blanco. He saw the six thousand workers, starved and wan, and the little children, seven and eight years of age, who toiled long shifts for ten cents a day. He saw the perambulating corpses, the ghastly death's heads of men who labored in the dye rooms. He remembered that he had heard his father call the dye rooms the "suicide holes," where a year was death. . . .*
>
> *Big, hearty Joaquin Fernandez! A large place he occupied in Rivera's visions. He had not understood at the time, but, looking back, he could understand. He could see him setting type in the little printery, or scribbling endless hasty, nervous lines on the much-cluttered desk. And he could see the strange evenings, when workmen, coming secretly in the dark like men who did ill deeds, met with father and talked long hours where he, the muchado, lay not always asleep in the corner. . . .*
>
> *But more visions burned before the eye of Rivera's memory. The strike, or rather, the lockout, because the workers of Rio Blanco had helped their striking brothers of Puebla. The hunger, the expeditions in the hills for berries, the roots and herbs that all ate and that twisted and pained the stomachs of all of them. And then the nightmare; the waste of ground before the company's store; the thousands of starving workers; General Rosalio Martinez and the soldiers of Porfirio Diaz; and the death-spitting rifles that seemed never to cease spitting,*

*while the workers' wrongs were washed and washed again in
their own blood. And that night! He saw the flatcars, piled
high with the bodies of the slain, consigned to Vera Cruz, food
for the sharks of the bay. Again he crawled over the grisly
heaps, seeking and finding, stripped and mangled, his father
and his mother. His mother he especially remembered—only
her face projecting, her body burdened by the weight of dozens
of bodies. Again the rifles of the soldiers of Porfirio Diaz
cracked, and again he dropped to the ground and slunk away
like some hunted coyote of the hills.*

These visions enable Rivera to stand up under Danny Ward's brutal
punishment and, in the end, to knock out the coming champion. Battered and bruised though he is, Rivera is happy. The five thousand
dollar purse is his. "The guns were his. The revolution could go on."

Two years later Jack London was to hail American action against
the Mexican Revolution. After a series of revolutions and counter-
revolutions, during which American oil and financial interests ma-
neuvered to move in and control the Mexican economy, an incident
occurred which produced American intervention. An affront to an
American naval officer in Tampico was followed by a demand by the
United States that the American flag be saluted. Huerta, then in
power, refused and, on April 21, 1914, American troops seized Vera
Cruz.

In 1911 Jack London would have seen through the "legal pretexts"
which the United States used to justify its flagrant imperialism, would
have joined with other socialists and the trade unions in opposing the
unwarranted action of the Wilson administration, and would have
hailed the fact that when President Wilson asked Congress for permission to raise the army to war strength for the purpose of sending
an expedition to Mexico, Meyer London, the socialist congressman
from New York, cast the only vote recorded in the negative. But Jack
London was too tired, too deeply involved with his ranch and his
retinue of laborers and servants, and had moved too far away from
the active life of the Party, to be concerned about the revolution any
longer. So, on April 16, 1914, when *Collier's Weekly* wired him an
offer of $1100 a week and expenses to report the "war" he jumped at
the chance. He left the next day for Galveston where he was scheduled
to receive his credentials from Washington and from which port he
was to sail by army transport to Vera Cruz.

At Galveston he was forced to wait for his credentials. General Funston, it appeared, was not anxious to bestow a war correspondent's credentials on a man who two years before was reported to have denounced the military life and to have advised everyone to stay out of the army.

In October, 1913 the *International Socialist Review* had carried an article entitled "The Good Soldier" by Jack London. It urged "young men" not to enlist in the armed forces, declared that "the good soldier" never tried "to distinguish right from wrong," and if "ordered to fire down a crowded street when the poor was clamoring for bread, he obeys and sees the gray hairs of age stained with red and the life tide gushing from the breasts of women, feeling neither remorse nor sympathy. . . ." The article concluded:

> *No man can fall lower than a soldier—it is a depth beneath which he cannot go. Keep the boys out of the army. It is hell. Down with the army and the navy. We don't need killing institutions. We need life-giving institutions.*

The article, which was reprinted under London's name and widely distributed by the I.W.W., caused a furore. London, however, kept quiet until he discovered that the article was the cause of the withholding of his credentials. Then he publicly denied authorship of this "canard," and, in a letter dated August 5, 1916, stated that he had been denying responsibility for the article for years and argued that his books, newspaper reports, writings on prize-fighting and his war correspondence proved how ridiculous it was to accuse him of having written "The Good Soldier." "My opinion," he concluded, "is that it behooves a country or nation like the United States to maintain a reasonable preparedness for defense against any country or nation that at any time may go out upon the way of war to carve earth space for itself out of weaker and unprepared nations."

Whether or not Jack London actually wrote "The Good Soldier" will never be known since other articles were published in his name which he did not write. Yet it is difficult to believe that the *International Socialist Review* would have published the article under his name unless they had reasonable assurance that it expressed London's sentiments; nor did he protest the publication when it appeared. Again, parts of the article are reminiscent of his descriptions of the guards at the coronation of King Edward in *The People of the Abyss:* "Myriads of men, splendid men, the pick of the people, whose sole

function in life is to blindly obey, and blindly to kill and destroy and
stamp out life."

By the time London got to Mexico there was no war to report.
After the Marines had landed and occupied Vera Cruz, the United
States accepted the intervention of the ABC Powers—Argentina,
Brazil and Chile. The Huerta government made its apologies, the
American flag was saluted, reparations were promised and the threat-
ened war was over before it had actually started. London was reduced
to writing human interest articles which are important only in re-
vealing how far he had travelled in his attitude towards the Mexican
Revolution since 1911 and as further examples of his race chauvinism.
Describing a meeting between a Mexican Lieutenant and an American
Lieutenant, London wrote: "The Mexican Lieutenant strove to add
inches to himself by standing on top of a steel rail. But in vain. The
American still towered above him. The American was—well, American." In another article, he concluded: "To paraphrase Kipling the
consistency of these half-breeds is to know no consistency."

Something of the socialist left in him kept asking whether it was
not ridiculous to solve international problems by warfare, and he
admitted that "War is a silly thing for a rational, civilized man to
contemplate." But he justified American intervention with the comment that rational men could not be expected to settle problems in a
rational way when others insisted on doing it "by violent means."
Then he asked: "But in the meantime—and there you are—what
would have been the present situation if the United States had long
since disarmed? Somehow, I, for one, cannot see the picture of
Huerta listening to and accepting the high ethical advice of the United
States."

London saw nothing in the Mexican Revolution other than the universal desire to rob, pillage and loot, and to "shake down" the American oil interests "who had found and developed the oil-fields." It was
America's duty, he argued, to save Mexico from "the insignificant
portion of half-breeds who are causing all the trouble." Why bother
to justify American armed intervention because "of a failure in formal courtesy about a flag?" London got down to brass tacks:

> *The exotic civilization introduced by America and Europe
> is being destroyed by a handful of rulers who do not know how
> to rule, who have never successfully ruled, and whose orgies at
> ruling have been and are similar to those indulged in by*

drunken miners sowing the floors of barrooms with the un-fortunate gold dust.

The big brother can police, organize, and manage Mexico. The so-called leaders of Mexico cannot. And the lives and happiness of a few million peons as well as the many millions yet to be born, are at stake.

The policeman stops a man from beating his wife. The humane officer stops a man from beating his horse. May not a powerful and self-alleged enlightened nation stop a handful of inefficient and incapable rulers from making a shambles and a desert of a fair land wherein are all the natural resources for a high and happy civilization?

Granting even that London sincerely believed that American intervention would be of immeasurable benefit to the Mexican people and that they would be happier and economically better off as an American territory, how could one who had indicted the capitalists for mismanagement and for causing misery and poverty for their own people believe that these same capitalists would institute an era of plenty for the Mexican people? Certainly Jack London knew that even as he wrote the economy of Mexico was largely in the hands of American capitalists who used their control to keep the Mexican masses poverty-stricken. Who, after all, had owned the factories of Rio Blanco which he had described in "The Mexican," and who had been responsible for the slaughter of the workers in these factories when they had gone on strike?

Unlike Jack London, the American Socialist Party had not changed its attitude towards the Mexican Revolution. On April 16, 1914, the very same day that *Collier's Weekly* had wired London asking him to cover the war in Mexico, the *New York Call*, the official organ of the Socialist Party of New York, declared: "In spite of commercial interests and all this honorable piffle (about the honor of the nation), this war need not occur. President Wilson, tied down to the ideals of his class, may not be able to stop it. But the American working class can stop it." The day after the Marines landed at Vera Cruz, the National Executive Committee of the Socialist Party wired President Wilson denouncing the intervention. "The workers of the United States have no quarrel with the workers of Mexico," the telegram asserted. And in *The Masses,* a leading Socialist magazine, John Reed, who had spent four months with Pancho Villa's army in Mexico, cried out that intervention would destroy the gains of the Mexican Revolution and called upon the people to oppose the war.

Jack London's Mexican articles aroused a storm of fury in the radical press all over the country. Even the liberal *Nation* expressed amazement. "That an eminent apostle of red revolution," it observed, "should audibly be licking his chops over millions of gold dollars wrested from its rightful owner, the Mexican peon, by the predatory ministers of international capital, is somewhat disconcerting." John Kenneth Turner, a leading socialist, bluntly charged in the *Appeal to Reason* that London had been bribed by the "flattering good fellowship" of the oil interests to turn out "a brief for the oil man, a brief for intervention, a brief for what Mexicans call 'Yankee Imperialism.'"

Upton Sinclair was a good deal kinder. A year after London's death, he recalled the series of articles from Mexico which had caused radicals "to turn from him in rage." But, Sinclair was convinced, these articles in *Collier's Weekly* did not signify that London had fallen away from socialism. Rather they meant that he had fallen "under the spell of the efficiency of oil engineers." "But I felt certain," Sinclair added, "that the exponent of capitalist efficiency who counted upon Jack London's backing was a child playing in a dynamite factory . . ." Unfortunately, the articles themselves hardly bear out this interpretation. At the same time, it is not necessary to subscribe to John Kenneth Turner's analysis of the motives behind London's articles. Jack London had not been won over by the good fellowship of the oil men. Nor had he been subsidized by them to write this material. His own way of life had produced the change. He had lost contact with the people; he had grown wealthy, had forgotten his lessons in socialism and his own lectures and essays on imperialism; and, as a tired and confused man, no longer bothered to look beneath the surface for basic causes. Perhaps his daughter, Joan London, analyzed it best when she wrote: "His was a more tragic sellout, for he had been subsidized, bought body and soul, by the kind of life he had thought he wanted, and it was destroying him."

Jack London returned from Mexico in the summer of 1914 a sick man, physically and mentally. He was weary and disillusioned and constantly searching for a haven where he could get away from it all and just rest. His land now came to mean everything to him, for he was turning away more and more from the activities that had once buoyed

up his spirits and had "handcuffed" him to life. "I am weary of everything," he told a reporter for the *Western Comrade*, a small socialist
paper. "I no longer think of the world or the movement (the social
revolution) or of writing as an art. I am a great dreamer, but I dream
of my ranch, of my wife. I dream of beautiful horses and fine soil in
Sonoma County. And I write for no other purpose than to add to the
beauty that now belongs to me. I write a book for no other reason
than to add three or four hundred acres to my magnificent estate. I
write a story with no other purpose than to buy a stallion. To me, my
cattle are far more interesting than my profession. My friends don't
believe me when I say this, but I am absolutely sincere." When the reporter asked him what he intended to do, London replied: "I feel
that I have done my part. Socialism has cost me hundreds of thousands
of dollars. When the time comes I'm going to stay right on my ranch
at Glen Ellen and let the revolution go to blazes. I've done my part."
Then as an afterthought, he added: "That's the way I feel now. I
suppose when the time comes I'll let my emotions get the best of my
intellect and I'll come down from the mountain top and join the fray."

But Jack London stayed on the "mountain top" until his death. In
February, 1915, hoping that the sun would cure his illness, he and
Charmian sailed for Hawaii. They spent severable enjoyable months
there and Jack's health improved. London took time off from his
writing to mingle with the "smart set." The business and social crowd
in Honolulu lionized him. In return, he spoke appreciatively of their
charities for the natives, a practice he had hitherto always condemned
in his socialist writings. Again he was roundly criticized by socialists
and liberals in the United States.

It was while in Hawaii that Jack London produced his final piece of
socialist writing, the introduction to Upton Sinclair's anthology, *The
Cry for Justice*. Sinclair had sent him the manuscript of his collection
of excerpts on social justice and asked London to write a foreword to
the volume. London replied promptly. The introduction, dated at
Honolulu, March 6, 1915, is one of the most moving and poetic
pieces to come from London's pen. Sinclair considered it "one of the
finest things he ever did," and believed that some paragraphs from the
introduction "might be carved upon his monument." London saw this
anthology of writings dealing with the struggle of the common people
for freedom throughout the ages as a Bible for the working-class which
would inspire understanding and sympathy and which, in turn, would
invariably lead to service in the cause of humanity. London wrote:

*He, who by understanding becomes converted to the gospel
of service, will serve truth to confute liars and make of them
truth-tellers; will serve kindness so that brutality will perish;
will serve beauty to the erasement of all that is not beautiful.
And he who is strong will serve the weak that they may become
strong. He will devote his strength, not to the debasement and
defilement of his weaker fellows, but to the making of opportunity for them to make themselves into men rather than into
slaves and beasts.*

*It is so simple a remedy, merely service. Not one ignoble
thought or act is demanded of any one of all men and women
in the world to make fair the world. The call is for nobility of
thinking, nobility of doing. The call is for service, and, such
is the wholesomeness of it, he who serves all, best serves himself.*

We can agree with Upton Sinclair that "such words and actions
based upon them make precious his memory and will preserve it as
long as anything in American literature is preserved." For these lines
of Jack London, written at a time when he was a sick and weary man,
bring us the essence of the man and the message of his life. Despite his
many shortcomings, he did serve justice and the working class faithfully in accordance with his lights. When one least expected it, there
would come from his pen such an eloquent utterance as to cause one to
forgive him his vacillations and his weaknesses. Such an utterance is
the introduction to Sinclair's *The Cry for Justice,* and of a piece with
it is the moving letter he wrote a few years before his death to the
Central Labor Council of Alameda County:

*I cannot express to you how deeply I regret my inability to
be with you this day. But, believe me, I am with you in the
brotherhood of the spirit, as all you boys, in a similar brotherhood of the spirit, are with our laundry girls in Troy, New
York.*

*Is this not a spectacle for gods and men?—the workmen of
Alameda County sending a share of their hard-earned wages
three thousand miles across the continent to help the need of a
lot of striking laundry girls in Troy!*

*And right here I wish to point out something that you all
know, but something that is so great it cannot be pointed out*

too often, and that grows every time that it is pointed out,—
AND THAT IS, THE STRENGTH OF ORGANIZED
LABOR LIES IN ITS BROTHERHOOD. There is no
brotherhood in unorganized labor, no standing together
shoulder to shoulder, and as a result unorganized labor is as
weak as water.

And not only does brotherhood give organized labor more
fighting strength but it gives it, as well, the strength of right-
eousness. The holiest reason that men can find for drawing to-
gether into any kind of organization is BROTHERHOOD.
And in the end nothing can triumph against such an organi-
zation. Let the church tell you that servants should obey their
masters. This is what the church told the striking laundry girls
of Troy. Stronger than this mandate is brotherhood, and the
girls of Troy found out when the boys of California shared
their wages with them. (Ah, these girls of Troy! Twenty weeks
on strike and not a single desertion from their ranks! And ah,
these boys of California, stretching out to them, across a con-
tinent the helping hand of brotherhood!)

And so I say, against such spirit of brotherhood, all machina-
tions of the men-of-graft-and-grab-and-the-dollar are futile.
Strength lies in comradeship and brotherhood, not in a throat-
cutting struggle where every man's hand is against man. This
comradeship and brotherhood is yours. I cannot wish you good
luck and hope that your strength will grow in the future, be-
cause brotherhood and the comrade-world are bound to grow.
The growth cannot be stopped. So I can only congratulate you
boys upon the fact that this is so.

Yours in the brotherhood of man,
Jack London.

Who, after all, but Jack London at those times when he forgot his
fetish about Anglo-Saxon supremacy could write so warm and human
a tribute to the plain working people of our country? One can certainly agree with Upton Sinclair when he wrote: "It was a fact that
you could never give Jack London up; he had a mind, a terrific mind,
which worked unceasingly, and impelled him irresistibly; he had a
love of truth that was a passion, a hatred of injustice that burned
volcanic fires."

Back in California, London threw himself into work, and between February and April, 1916, two books came off the press—*The Acorn-Planter*, his third play, and *The Little Lady of the Big House*, a novel carrying forward the back-to-the-land idea which London had advanced in *The Valley of the Moon* as the solution for the problems of modern industrial society. Neither of these books added to London's stature as a writer. They were written, it must be remembered, by a man who had soured on everything and everyone, and to whom the very act of writing was a nightmare. "You may think that I am not telling the truth," he told Emanuel Julius of the *Western Comrade*, "but I hate my profession. I detest the profession I have chosen. I hate it, I tell you, I hate it!" He continued in the same vein:

> *I assure you that I do not write because I love the game. I loathe it. I cannot find words to express my disgust. The only reason I write is because I am well paid for my labor—that's what I call it—labor. I get lots of money for my books and stories. I tell you I would be glad to dig ditches for twice as many hours as I devote to writing if only I could get as much money. To me, writing is an easy way to make a fine living. Unless I meant it, I wouldn't think of saying a thing like this, for I am speaking for publication. I am sincere when I say that my profession sickens me. Every story that I write is for the money that will come to me. I always write what the editors want, not what I'd like to write. I grind out what the capitalist editors want, and the editors buy what the business and editorial departments permit. The editors are not interested in the truth. . . .*

Once there had been a time when he could drop his hack-work and turn out an essay or story for *The Comrade, Wilshire's Magazine* or the *International Socialist Review*, and feel invigorated by the thought that thousands of workers would be reading his material and soapbox orators would be using it in their speeches. But now he was too sick, too tired to care. More and more he needed the stimulation of whiskey to make life bearable.

But John Barleycorn was beginning to take its toll. His uremia became worse. Once again he hoped that the Hawaiian sun would effect a cure. In January, 1916, he sailed for Honolulu. Sitting in his stateroom he dictated his resignation from the Socialist Party to Charmian. Perhaps he knew that he was signing his death-warrant, for he did not forward it immediately. Then, after debating with himself whether to mail it or not, he decided to cut himself off completely from the Cause which had been so dear to him for more than twenty years, and sent the letter of resignation to the Oakland local:

Honolulu, March 7, 1916.

Glen Ellen
Sonoma County, California
Dear Comrades:

I am resigning from the Socialist Party, because of its lack of fire and fight, and its loss of emphasis upon the class struggle.

I was originally a member of the old revolutionary up-on-its-hind-legs, a fighting, Socialist Labor Party. Since then, and the present time, I have been a fighting member of the Socialist Party. My fighting record in the Cause is not, even at this late date, already entirely forgotten. Trained in the class struggle, as taught and practised by the Socialist Labor Party, my own highest judgment concurring, I believed that the working class, by fighting, by never fusing, by never making terms with the enemy, could emancipate itself. Since the whole trend of Socialism in the United States during recent years has been one of peaceableness and compromise, I find that my mind refuses further sanction of my remaining a party member. Hence, my resignation.

Please include my comrade wife, Charmian K. London's resignation with mine.

My final word is that liberty, freedom and independence are royal things that cannot be presented to nor thrust upon race or class. If races and classes cannot rise up and by their own strength of brain and brawn, wrest from the world liberty, freedom and independence, they never in time can come to these royal possessions . . . and if such royal things are kindly presented to them by superior individuals, on silver platters, they will not know what to do with them, will fail to make use of them, and will be what they have always been in the past . . . inferior races and inferior classes.

Yours for the Revolution,
Jack London.

No one in the Socialist Party was surprised by London's resignation; he had been drifting away from the movement ever since his return from the South Seas. Nonetheless, not a few socialists were annoyed that the man who had gone down to Mexico on a United States warship and then had written articles advocating American annexation of the land below the Rio Grande should decry the lack of revolutionary spirit in the Socialist Party. But those who questioned the sincerity of London's criticism of the Party overlooked the fact that however inconsistent he was in other respects as a socialist, London had never wavered in his insistence that socialist propaganda must be forthright and fearless and in his critical attitude towards the politicians in the leadership of the movement who were taking the Party along the road of expediency, opportunism and reformism. A year before he resigned, he told a reporter for the *Western Comrade* that he was deeply perturbed by the policy of compromise openly advocated by many Party leaders:

> *I became a Socialist when I was seventeen years old. I am still a Socialist, but not of the refined, quietistic school of socialism. The Socialists, the ghetto Socialists of the East, no longer believe in the strong, firm socialism of the early days. Mention confiscation in the ghetto of New York and the leaders will throw up their hands in holy terror. I still believe the Socialists should strive to eliminate the capitalist class and wipe away the private ownership of mines, mills, factories, railroads and other social needs.*
>
> *I do not believe that Socialists should soften and yield, eventually becoming mere reformers whose greatest desire is economy in government and low taxes, and the like. They should take upon themselves the task of doing away with the robbing capitalist system, do away with the profit system and place the workers in possession of the industries.*

London was among the earliest socialists, though not the only one, to perceive that reformism was steadily gaining ground among the leadership of the Socialist Party. In an article entitled "The Danger Ahead" published in the *International Socialist Review* of January, 1911, Eugene V. Debs had warned that the Party was in danger of becoming "permeated and corrupted with the spirit of bourgeois reform to an extent that will practically destroy its virility and efficiency as a revolutionary organization." On February 20, 1915, the *American*

Socialist featured an article which emphasized that the Party was becoming a "reformist political party . . . entirely lacking in class consciousness and revolutionary ideals. . . . Our party offices are being filled by men who appear to be far more solicitous for votes, political offices, and the good opinion of our enemies, than for the furtherance of those principles which make for the Revolution." And in April, 1916, one month after London's resignation, the *International Socialist Review* charged that the movement was dominated by middle class leaders "who spend precious time proving the post office and Panama Canal Socialist enterprises. From this type come suggestions that the class struggle, that impregnable fortress of the revolutionary workers, be dropped as obsolete because, presumably it is unpopular in the drawing rooms of the ultra respectable middle class. . . . To be brief, they would sugarcoat the pill so effectively that the masters might some day step down gracefully and fall in line ! ! ! We are getting yards of this sort of thing in a supposedly Socialist press."

Instead of resigning, London could have thrown in his lot with the left-wing forces who shared his conviction that the Party had lost its militancy and joined them in seeking to check compromise tendencies and build a truly revolutionary movement. Yet the tragedy of London's position was that he no longer fitted anywhere in the movement. If his belief in revolutionary socialism made it impossible for him to work with the conservative socialists, his attitude towards the World War which had broken out in the summer of 1914 made it equally impossible for him, had he wished to do so, to cooperate with the left-wing socialists.

When the news of the European conflict reached the United States, socialists condemned it as an imperialist war and offered sympathy to their comrades across the ocean. On August 12, 1914, the National Executive Committee issued a manifesto extending the sympathy of the American Party "to the workers of Europe in their hour of trial, when they have been plunged into a bloody and senseless conflict by ambition-crazed monarchs, designing politicians and scheming capitalists. The workers have no quarrel with each other but rather with their ruling classes." Again, in December, 1914, the Committee proposed the Socialist Party Anti-War Manifesto which declared that while the immediate causes of the war were "thoughts of revenge . . . imperialism and commercial rivalries . . . secret intrigue . . . lack of democracy . . . vast systems of military and naval equip-

ment . . . jingo press . . . powerful armament interests," the fundamental cause was the capitalist system. This position was endorsed in
a referendum vote in September, 1915 by a large majority of the
membership.

This enraged Jack London. From the beginning of the war he had
announced his support of the Allies and had refused to accept the
position that it was a capitalist war. Germany was the "Mad Dog of
Europe"; the Allies had to be supported. If England was defeated, he
was prepared to go "into the last ditch" with her. The cause of the
war, as he saw it, was simple: "I believe that the present war is being
fought out to determine whether or not men in the future may continue in a civilized way to depend upon the word, the pledge, the
agreement, and the contract." He brushed aside the fact that millions
would die in the course of the conflict: "As regards a few million terrible deaths, there is not so much of the terrible about a quantity of
deaths as there is about the quantity of deaths that occur in peace
times in all countries in the world, and that has occurred in war
times in the past." "Civilization," he wrote, "at the present time is
going through a Pentecostal cleansing that can only result in good for
humankind."

Soon enough other socialists in America were to echo London's sentiments and his call for the entrance of the United States into the war
on the Allied side. Ironically enough, they were precisely the forces
in the Socialist Party whom London had condemned for advocating a
policy of compromise and for their abandonment of a militant, revolutionary program. The left-wing socialists continued to insist that
the carnage in Europe was the result of rival imperialisms in quest of
markets for exploitation. However much they agreed with London's
criticism of reformist tendencies in the Socialist Party, they could
have little to do with one who took such a jingoistic attitude towards
the war.

The Socialist Party replied to London's letter of resignation in a
sharply-worded article entitled "How You Can Get Socialism" which
appeared in the *New York Call* of March 27, 1916:

> *The Socialist Party never spends much time in lamenting
> over those who occasionally quit its ranks, nor will it do so
> now. Mr. London's letter, unfortunately, is couched in such
> vague and general terms that no one can be sure what he means.
> London is a fighter. Good. For some reasons not stated, he*

realized his fighting record in the cause is a closed chapter. He has of late found the party too peaceable for his taste. He quits it and goes elsewhere to find a battlefield.

Doubtless this sounds odd to us and to most party members. Yet doubtless London is sincere. The reasons may be local or personal, or both. We don't know Glen Ellen, and we do know Jack London. The name of the place does sound rather too idyllic to harmonize with the author of The Sea Wolf *and* The Call of the Wild.

We can only assure him that, however tediously peaceable membership in Glen Ellen may be, the workingmen in mine and shop and factory who make up the rank and file of the Socialist Party are fighting—not always an exhilarating, romantic, spectacular fight—not always the sort of fight that makes good copy for the magazines or good films for the movies—but the steady, unflinching, uncomplaining, unboasting, shoulder to shoulder and inch-by-inch fight that uses the fighters up one by one and sends them to the soon-forgotten graves, but that gains ground for those who fill up the ranks as they fall, that undermines the enemy's defenses and wears him down and keeps on wearing him down until the time comes for breaking his line and making the grand dash that shall end the war.

Live long, Friend London, and keep the pugnacious spirit, that, when the way to victory has been prepared by the unheralded millions, you may be with us once more on that dramatic day. We shall go on doing our best to hasten it for you.

It was an angry reply, and it stung London. As the months passed he grew more embittered over the attacks against him for having deserted the Cause. He was convinced that in a few years the Socialists "will have entirely forgotten that a fellow named Jack London ever did a stroke to help along." A few months after his resignation he wrote bitterly: ". . . because the socialists and I disagreed about opportunism, ghetto politics, class consciousness, political slates, and party machines, they too, have dismissed all memory, not merely of my years of fight in the cause, but of me as a social man, as a comrade of men, as a fellow they ever embraced for having at various times written or said things they described as doughty blows for the Cause. On the contrary, by their only printed utterances I have seen, they deny I ever struck a blow or did anything for the Cause, at the same time affirming that all the time they knew me for what I was—a Dreamer."

His discouragement was intense. Without the movement he drifted aimlessly. Like Martin Eden he now had no reason to continue living.

During all these months, as if by habit, he was writing stories that he would never see in print and most of which it would have been better to have destroyed. Six volumes of London's works were to appear after his death: * *The Human Drift*, unimportant sociological essays; *Jerry of the Islands* and *Michael, Brother of Jerry*, both inferior dog stories; *The Red One* and *On the Makaloa Mat*, collections of short stories not one of which is outstanding; and *Hearts of Three*, a movie story written for Hearst's *Cosmopolitan* for which he received $25,000 but which was never filmed.

Hawaii could no longer cure London. He returned to Glen Ellen, his body bloated with disease, pain-wracked and miserable. He was desperately lonely and made vain overtures for friendly relations with his former wife and his two daughters. His drinking, always excessive, reached new extremes. The inevitable end was drawing near.

On the morning of November 22, 1916, Jack London was found in a coma. The doctors ascribed his state to an overdose of morphine, deliberately taken. He never recovered, responding only once during the treatments and then relapsing into unconsciousness. At about seven in the morning he died. His ashes were buried on a hill on his ranch as he had directed his sister Eliza only two weeks before.

In the announcements to the press London's death was attributed to "a gastro-intestinal type of Uremia." But, as Upton Sinclair pointed out in a letter to R. W. Francis, September 21, 1932: "Several of Jack London's intimates knew that he had committed suicide." The manner of his death London had forecast years before: "Yet suicide, quick or slow, a sudden spill or a gradual oozing away through the years, is the price which John Barleycorn exacts. No friend of his ever escapes making the just, due payment." The prophecy he had made in *Martin Eden*, the final victory of the "white logic," was fulfilled.**

* The last book published before London's death was *Turtles of Tasman* which appeared in September, 1916. It was a collection of several stories and a play previously published in magazines.

** In February, 1914, the *Medical Review of Reviews* featured a "Sym-

The *New York Times'* obituary made no mention that he had ever been a socialist. A day later, in an editorial, the *Times* again omitted the word "socialism" but did remark that "he was at once happiest and least effective when the artist became the preacher." "By Jack London's death," the editorial concluded, "American letters suffer a heavy loss, as by his life they incurred a heavy debt."

The socialist journals carried more moving tributes. His inconsistencies were forgiven, his resignation from the Party was attributed to his state of health, and the main emphasis was placed upon the great contribution he had made through his writing and speeches, his never-failing generosity to the fund drives and his devotion to the working-class and its struggles. *The Masses* commented: "Jack London brought true science and the pulse of revolution for the first time into English fiction. . . ." *The Intercollegiate Socialist* observed: "In the untimely passing of our Comrade Jack London our Society has lost one of its pioneers, our first president, and for a long time our earnest friend and helper. . . . During his last years his efforts have mainly been directed to his literary work, but he was still young, and our Society might well have expected a renewal of his help in later years." In April, 1917 the *International Socialist Review* carried a tribute to Jack London which might well have been inscribed on the rock that stood over his ashes:

> *Our Jack is dead!*
> *He who arose from us*
> *And voiced our wrongs;*
> *Who sang our hopes,*
> *And bade us stand alone,*
> *Nor compromise, nor pause;*
> *Who bade us dare*
> *Reach out and take the world*
> *In our strong hands.*
> *Comrade! Friend!*
> *Who let the sunshine in*
> *Upon dark places.*
> *Great ones may not understand,*

---

posium on Euthanasia." Jack London's contribution went: "Man possesses but one freedom, namely the anticipating the day of his death. Should collective man (the state) rob individual man of this one freedom? I believe not. I believe in the individual's right to cease to live. . . ."

Nor grant you now
The measure of your mede;
But, in the days to come,
All men shall see.
Father of Martin Eden
And the Iron Heel—
Yes, men shall know
When we arise
And fight to victory!

Jack London was only 40 when he died, and he began publishing at the start of the century; yet in those 16 years he wrote nineteen complete novels, eighteen books of compiled short stories and articles (152 in all), three plays and eight books autobiographical and sociological. He wrote too much, and in the end too hurriedly. If he wanted a fine saddle horse or a yawl, a story purchased it. Caught up in a system which offered huge rewards for a writer with a name, yet hating this system for the misery it produced for so many people, he ended up in a mass of confusion and contradiction. With the waning of his socialist activity and his drift away from the working class and working class ideas in his last years, Jack London lost the inspiration and the ability to write valid literature. But in spite of all this, he remains one of America's most significant writers because he concerned himself with the vital problems of his age. Of working class origin, he was the first American writer to portray his class sympathetically and one of the few to use literature for building the foundations of a future society. He was not educated in a formal sense, but his comprehension was so great that he rose above educated men in ability and power to portray in his writings the fundamental issues of our times. The spirit of the common people of America, heroic, fiery and adventurous, will live forever in the pages of his rebel stories, novels and essays.

Fiction

The Iron Heel

EDITOR'S NOTE: *The sections of* The Iron Heel *reprinted below begin with the exciting lecture delivered by Ernest Everhard to an audience of millionaires. They end with the complete dominance of the Oligarchy over the people and the crushing of the First Revolt of the working class. All of the events after the lecture to "The Philomaths" are foreshadowing the triumph of the Oligarchy, but only Ernest Everhard, the militant socialist, grasps the significance of these events. He warns the socialists and the trade unionists that the capitalists will not capitulate before a popular triumph at the polls; he urges them to prepare to prevent the ruling class from depriving the people of their democratic rights and instituting an era of unprecedented despotism. But his repeated warnings fall on deaf ears. Then, in several masterly and unforgettable chapters, Jack London tells how Everhard's predictions are fulfilled. Step by step he traces the rise of despotism and the destruction of democracy and describes the terrible and bitter conflict between the socialist underground and the forces of dictatorship as symbolized by the Iron Heel. The novel concludes with an unfinished sentence which restates the theme of the story: "the magnitude of the task" of creating a socialist society.*

For a detailed discussion of The Iron Heel, see pages 87–97.

THE PHILOMATHS

Ernest was often at the house. Nor was it my father, merely, nor the controversial dinners, that drew him there. Even at that time I flattered myself that I played some part in causing his visits, and it was

not long before I learned the correctness of my surmise. For never
was there such a lover as Ernest Everhard. His gaze and his hand-
clasp grew firmer and steadier, if that were possible; and the question that had grown from the first in his eyes, grew only the more
imperative.

My impression of him, the first time I saw him, had been unfavorable. Then I had found myself attracted toward him. Next
came my repulsion, when he so savagely attacked my class and me.
After that, as I saw that he had not maligned my class, and that the
harsh and bitter things he said about it were justified, I had drawn
closer to him again. He became my oracle. For me he tore the sham
from the face of society and gave me glimpses of reality that were as
unpleasant as they were undeniably true.

As I have said, there was never such a lover as he. No girl could
live in a university town till she was twenty-four and not have love
experiences. I had been made love to by beardless sophomores and
gray professors, and by the athletes and the football giants. But not
one of them made love to me as Ernest did. His arms were around
me before I knew. His lips were on mine before I could protest or
resist. Before his earnestness conventional maiden dignity was ridiculous. He swept me off my feet by the splendid invincible rush of him.
He did not propose. He put his arms around me and kissed me and
took it for granted that we should be married. There was no discussion
about it. The only discussion—and that arose afterward—was when
we should be married.

It was unprecedented. It was unreal. Yet, in accordance with Ernest's test of truth, it worked. I trusted my life to it. And fortunate
was the trust. Yet during those first days of our love, fear of the
future came often to me when I thought of the violence and im-
petuosity of his love-making. Yet such fears were groundless. No
woman was ever blessed with a gentler, tenderer husband. This gentle-
ness and violence on his part was a curious blend similar to the one
in his carriage of awkwardness and ease. That slight awkwardness!
He never got over it, and it was delicious. His behavior in our
drawing-room reminded me of a careful bull in a china shop.[1]

[1] In those days it was still the custom to fill the living rooms with bric-a-brac.
They had not discovered simplicity of living. Such rooms were museums, en-
tailing endless labor to keep clean. The dust-demon was the lord of the household. There were a myriad devices for catching dust, and only a few devices
for getting rid of it.

It was at this time that vanished my last doubt of the completeness of my love for him (a subconscious doubt, at most). It was at the Philomath Club—a wonderful night of battle, wherein Ernest bearded the masters in their lair. Now the Philomath Club was the most select on the Pacific Coast. It was the creation of Miss Brentwood, an enormously wealthy old maid; and it was her husband, and family, and toy. Its members were the wealthiest in the community, and the strongest-minded of the wealthy, with, of course, a sprinkling of scholars to give it intellectual tone.

The Philomath had no club house. It was not that kind of a club. Once a month its members gathered at some one of their private houses to listen to a lecture. The lecturers were usually, though not always, hired. If a chemist in New York made a new discovery in say radium, all his expenses across the continent were paid, and as well he received a princely fee for his time. The same with a returning explorer from the polar regions, or the latest literary or artistic success. No visitors were allowed, while it was the Philomath's policy to permit none of its discussions to get into the papers. Thus great statesmen—and there had been such occasions—were able fully to speak their minds.

I spread before me a wrinkled letter, written to me by Ernest twenty years ago, and from it I copy the following:

"Your father is a member of the Philomath, so you are able to come. Therefore come next Tuesday night. I promise you that you will have the time of your life. In your recent encounters, you failed to shake the masters. If you come, I'll shake them for you. I'll make them snarl like wolves. You merely questioned their morality. When their morality is questioned, they grow only the more complacent and superior. But I shall menace their money-bags. That will shake them to the roots of their primitive natures. If you can come, you will see the cave-man, in evening dress, snarling and snapping over a bone. I promise you a great caterwauling and an illuminating insight into the nature of the beast.

"They've invited me in order to tear me to pieces. This is the idea of Miss Brentwood. She clumsily hinted as much when she invited me. She's given them that kind of fun before. They delight in getting trustful-souled gentle reformers before them. Miss Brentwood thinks I am as mild as a kitten and as good-natured and stolid as the family cow. I'll not deny that I helped to give her that impression. She was very tentative at first, until she divined my harmlessness. I am to receive a handsome fee—two hundred and fifty dollars—as befits the man who, though a radical, once ran for governor. Also, I am to wear evening dress. This is compulsory. I never was so apparelled in my life. I suppose I'll have to hire one somewhere. But I'd do more than that to get a chance at the Philomaths."

Of all places, the Club gathered that night at the Pertonwaithe house. Extra chairs had been brought into the great drawing-room, and in all there must have been two hundred Philomaths that sat down to hear Ernest. They were truly lords of society. I amused myself with running over in my mind the sum of the fortunes represented, and it ran well into the hundreds of millions. And the possessors were not of the idle rich. They were men of affairs who took most active parts in industrial and political life.

We were all seated when Miss Brentwood brought Ernest in. They moved at once to the head of the room, from where he was to speak. He was in evening dress, and, what of his broad shoulders and kingly head, he looked magnificent. And then there was that faint and unmistakable touch of awkwardness in his movements. I almost think I could have loved him for that alone. And as I looked at him I was aware of a great joy. I felt again the pulse of his palm on mine, the touch of his lips; and such pride was mine that I felt I must rise up and cry out to the assembled company: "He is mine! He has held me in his arms, and I, mere I, have filled that mind of his to the exclusion of all his multitudinous and kingly thoughts!"

At the head of the room, Miss Brentwood introduced him to Colonel Van Gilbert, and I knew that the latter was to preside. Colonel Van Gilbert was a great corporation lawyer. In addition, he was immensely wealthy. The smallest fee he would deign to notice was a hundred thousand dollars. He was a master of law. The law was a puppet with which he played. He moulded it like clay, twisted and distorted it like a Chinese puzzle into any design he chose. In appearance and rhetoric he was old-fashioned, but in imagination and knowledge and resource he was as young as the latest statute. His first prominence had come when he broke the Shardwell will.[2] His

[2] This breaking of wills was a peculiar feature of the period. With the accumulation of vast fortunes, the problem of disposing of these fortunes after death was a vexing one to the accumulators. Will-making and will-breaking became complementary trades, like armor-making and gun-making. The shrewdest will-making lawyers were called in to make wills that could not be broken. But these wills were always broken, and very often by the very lawyers that had drawn them up. Nevertheless the delusion persisted in the wealthy class

fee for this one act was five hundred thousand dollars. From then
on he had risen like a rocket. He was often called the greatest lawyer
in the country—corporation lawyer, of course; and no classification
of the three greatest lawyers in the United States could have ex-
cluded him.

He arose and began, in a few well-chosen phrases that carried an
undertone of faint irony, to introduce Ernest. Colonel Van Gilbert
was subtly facetious in his introduction of the social reformer and
member of the working class, and the audience smiled. It made me
angry, and I glanced at Ernest. The sight of him made me doubly
angry. He did not seem to resent the delicate slurs. Worse than that,
he did not seem to be aware of them. There he sat, gentle, and stolid,
and somnolent. He really looked stupid. And for a moment the
thought rose in my mind, What if he were overawed by this imposing
array of power and brains? Then I smiled. He couldn't fool me. But
he fooled the others, just as he had fooled Miss Brentwood. She
occupied a chair right up to the front, and several times she turned
her head toward one or another of her *confrères* and smiled her
appreciation of the remarks.

Colonel Van Gilbert done, Ernest arose and began to speak. He
began in a low voice, haltingly and modestly, and with an air of
evident embarrassment. He spoke of his birth in the working class, and
of the sordidness and wretchedness of his environment, where flesh
and spirit were alike starved and tormented. He described his ambitions and ideals, and his conception of the paradise wherein lived
the people of the upper classes. As he said:

"Up above me, I knew, were unselfishnesses of the spirit, clean and
noble thinking, keen intellectual living. I knew all this because I read
'Seaside Library' [8] novels, in which, with the exception of the villains and adventuresses, all men and women thought beautiful
thoughts, spoke a beautiful tongue, and performed glorious deeds. In
short, as I accepted the rising of the sun, I accepted that up above me
was all that was fine and noble and gracious, all that gave decency and
dignity to life, all that made life worth living and that remunerated
one for his travail and misery."

---

that an absolutely unbreakable will could be cast; and so, through the generations, clients and lawyers pursued the illusion. It was a pursuit like unto that
of the Universal Solvent of the mediæval alchemists.

[8] A curious and amazing literature that served to make the working class
utterly misapprehend the nature of the leisure class.

He went on and traced his life in the mills, the learning of the horseshoeing trade, and his meeting with the socialists. Among them, he said, he had found keen intellects and brilliant wits, ministers of the Gospel who had been broken because their Christianity was too wide for any congregation of mammon-worshippers, and professors who had been broken on the wheel of university subservience to the ruling class. The socialists were revolutionists, he said, struggling to overthrow the irrational society of the present and out of the material to build the rational society of the future. Much more he said that would take too long to write, but I shall never forget how he described the life among the revolutionists. All halting utterance vanished. His voice grew strong and confident, and it glowed as he glowed, and as the thoughts glowed that poured out from him. He said:

"Amongst the revolutionists I found, also, warm faith in the human, ardent idealism, sweetnesses of unselfishness, renunciation, and martyrdom—all the splendid, stinging things of the spirit. Here life was clean, noble, and alive. I was in touch with great souls who exalted flesh and spirit over dollars and cents, and to whom the thin wail of the starved slum child meant more than all the pomp and circumstance of commercial expansion and world empire. All about me were nobleness of purpose and heroism of effort, and my days and nights were sunshine and starshine, all fire and dew, with before my eyes, ever burning and blazing, the Holy Grail, Christ's own Grail, the warm human, long-suffering and maltreated but to be rescued and saved at the last."

As before I had seen him transfigured, so now he stood transfigured before me. His brows were bright with the divine that was in him, and brighter yet shone his eyes from the midst of the radiance that seemed to envelop him as a mantle. But the others did not see this radiance, and I assumed that it was due to the tears of joy and love that dimmed my vision. At any rate, Mr. Wickson, who sat behind me, was unaffected, for I heard him sneer aloud, "Utopian." [4]

[4] The people of that age were phrase slaves. The abjectness of their servitude is incomprehensible to us. There was a magic in words greater than the conjurer's art. So befuddled and chaotic were their minds that the utterance of a single word could negative the generalizations of a lifetime of serious research and thought. Such a word was the adjective *Utopian*. The mere utterance of it could damn any scheme, no matter how sanely conceived, of economic amelioration or regeneration. Vast populations grew frenzied over such phrases as "an honest dollar" and "a full dinner pail." The coinage of such phrases was considered strokes of genius

Ernest went on to his rise in society, till at last he came in touch
with members of the upper classes, and rubbed shoulders with the men
who sat in the high places. Then came his disillusionment, and this
disillusionment he described in terms that did not flatter his audience.
He was surprised at the commonness of the clay. Life proved not to
be fine and gracious. He was appalled by the selfishness he encountered, and what had surprised him even more than that was the absence of intellectual life. Fresh from his revolutionists, he was shocked
by the intellectual stupidity of the master class. And then, in spite
of their magnificent churches and well-paid preachers, he had found
the masters, men and women, grossly material. It was true that they
prattled sweet little ideals and dear little moralities, but in spite of
their prattle the dominant key of the life they lived was materialistic.
And they were without real morality—for instance, that which Christ
had preached but which was no longer preached.

"I met men," he said, "who invoked the name of the Prince of
Peace in their diatribes against war, and who put rifles in the hands
of Pinkertons [5] with which to shoot down strikers in their own factories. I met men incoherent with indignation at the brutality of prize-
fighting, and who, at the same time, were parties to the adulteration of
food that killed each year more babes than even red-handed Herod
had killed.

"This delicate, aristocratic-featured gentleman was a dummy director and a tool of corporations that secretly robbed widows and
orphans. This gentleman, who collected fine editions and was a patron
of literature, paid blackmail to a heavy-jowled, black-browed boss of
a municipal machine. This editor, who published patent medicine advertisements, called me a scoundrelly demagogue because I dared
him to print in his paper the truth about patent medicines.[6] This man,
talking soberly and earnestly about the beauties of idealism and the
goodness of God, had just betrayed his comrades in a business deal.
This man, a pillar of the church and heavy contributor to foreign
missions, worked his shop girls ten hours a day on a starvation wage
and thereby directly encouraged prostitution. This man, who endowed chairs in universities and erected magnificent chapels, perjured

[5] Originally, they were private detectives; but they quickly became hired
fighting men of the capitalists, and ultimately developed into the Mercenaries
of the Oligarchy.

[6] *Patent medicines* were patent lies, but, like the charms and indulgences of
the Middle Ages they deceived the people. The only difference lay in that the
patent medicines were more harmful and more costly.

himself in courts of law over dollars and cents. This railroad magnate broke his word as a citizen, as a gentleman, and as a Christian, when he granted a secret rebate, and he granted many secret rebates. This senator was the tool and the slave, the little puppet, of a brutal uneducated machine boss; [7] so was this governor and this supreme court judge; and all three rode on railroad passes; and, also, this sleek capitalist owned the machine, the machine boss, and the railroads that issued the passes.

"And so it was, instead of in Paradise, that I found myself in the arid desert of commercialism. I found nothing but stupidity, except for business. I found none clean, noble, and alive, though I found many who were alive—with rottenness. What I did find was monstrous selfishness and heartlessness, and a gross, gluttonous, practised, and practical materialism."

Much more Ernest told them of themselves and of his disillusionment. Intellectually they had bored him; morally and spiritually they had sickened him; so that he was glad to go back to his revolutionists, who were clean, noble, and alive, and all that the capitalists were not.

"And now," he said, "let me tell you about that revolution."

But first I must say that his terrible diatribe had not touched them. I looked about me at their faces and saw that they remained complacently superior to what he had charged. And I remembered what he had told me: that no indictment of their morality could shake them. However, I could see that the boldness of his language had affected Miss Brentwood. She was looking worried and apprehensive.

Ernest began by describing the army of revolution, and as he gave the figures of its strength (the votes cast in the various countries), the assemblage began to grow restless. Concern showed in their faces, and I noticed a tightening of lips. At last the gage of battle had been thrown down. He described the international organization of the socialists that united the million and a half in the United States with the twenty-three millions and a half in the rest of the world.

"Such an army of revolution," he said, "twenty-five millions strong,

[7] Even as late as 1912, A.D., the great mass of the people still persisted in the belief that they ruled the country by virtue of their ballots. In reality, the country was ruled by what were called *political machines*. At first the machine bosses charged the master capitalists extortionate tolls for legislation; but in a short time the master capitalists found it cheaper to own the political machines themselves and to hire the machine bosses.

is a thing to make rulers and ruling classes pause and consider. The cry of this army is: 'No quarter! We want all that you possess. We will be content with nothing less than all that you possess. We want in our hands the reins of power and the destiny of mankind. Here are our hands. They are strong hands. We are going to take your governments, your palaces, and all your purpled ease away from you, and in that day you shall work for your bread even as the peasant in the field or the starved and runty clerk in your metropolises. Here are our hands. They are strong hands!' "

And as he spoke he extended from his splendid shoulders his two great arms, and the horseshoer's hands were clutching the air like eagle's talons. He was the spirit of regnant labor as he stood there, his hands outreaching to rend and crush his audience. I was aware of a faintly perceptible shrinking on the part of the listeners before this figure of revolution, concrete, potential, and menacing. That is, the women shrank, and fear was in their faces. Not so with the men. They were of the active rich, and not the idle, and they were fighters. A low, throaty rumble arose, lingered on the air a moment, and ceased. It was the forerunner of the snarl, and I was to hear it many times that night—the token of the brute in man, the earnest of his primitive passions. And they were unconscious that they had made this sound. It was the growl of the pack, mouthed by the pack, and mouthed in all unconsciousness. And in that moment, as I saw the harshness form in their faces and saw the fight-light flashing in their eyes, I realized that not easily would they let their lordship of the world be wrested from them.

Ernest proceeded with his attack. He accounted for the existence of the million and a half of revolutionists in the United States by charging the capitalist class with having mismanaged society. He sketched the economic condition of the cave-man and of the savage peoples of to-day, pointing out that they possessed neither tools nor machines, and possessed only a natural efficiency of one in producing power. Then he traced the development of machinery and social organization so that to-day the producing power of civilized man was a thousand times greater than that of the savage.

"Five men," he said, "can produce bread for a thousand. One man can produce cotton cloth for two hundred and fifty people, woollens for three hundred, and boots and shoes for a thousand. One would conclude from this that under a capable management of society modern civilized man would be a great deal better off than the cave-man. But is he? Let us see. In the United States to-day there are fifteen million [8] people living in poverty; and by poverty is meant that condition in life in which, through lack of food and adequate shelter, the mere standard of working efficiency cannot be maintained. In the United States to-day, in spite of all your so-called labor legislation, there are three millions of child laborers.[9] In twelve years their numbers have been doubled. And in passing I will ask you managers of society why you did not make public the census figures of 1910? And I will answer for you, that you were afraid. The figures of misery would have precipitated the revolution that even now is gathering.

"But to return to my indictment. If modern man's producing power is a thousand times greater than that of the cave-man, why then, in the United States to-day, are there fifteen million people who are not properly sheltered and properly fed? Why then, in the United States to-day, are there three million child laborers? It is a true indictment. The capitalist class has mismanaged. In face of the facts that modern man lives more wretchedly than the cave-man, and that his producing power is a thousand times greater than that of the cave-man, no other conclusion is possible than that the capitalist class has mismanaged, that you have mismanaged, my masters, that you have criminally and selfishly mismanaged. And on this count you cannot answer me here to-night, face to face, any more than can your whole class answer the million and a half of revolutionists in the United States. You cannot answer. I challenge you to answer. And furthermore, I dare to say to you now that when I have finished you will not answer. On that point you will be tongue-tied, though you will talk wordily enough about other things.

"You have failed in your management. You have made a shambles of civilization. You have been blind and greedy. You have risen up (as you to-day rise up), shamelessly, in our legislative halls, and declared that profits were impossible without the toil of children and babes. Don't take my word for it. It is all in the records against you. You have lulled your conscience to sleep with prattle of sweet ideals and dear moralities. You are fat with power and possession, drunken with success; and you have no more hope against us than have the

[8] Robert Hunter, in 1906, in a book entitled "Poverty," pointed out that at that time there were ten millions in the United States living in poverty.

[9] In the United States Census of 1900 (the last census the figures of which were made public), the number of child laborers was placed at 1,752,187.

drones, clustered about the honey-vats, when the worker-bees spring upon them to end their rotund existence. You have failed in your management of society, and your management is to be taken away from you. A million and a half of the men of the working class say that they are going to get the rest of the working class to join with them and take the management away from you. This is the revolution, my masters. Stop it if you can."

For an appreciable lapse of time Ernest's voice continued to ring through the great room. Then arose the throaty rumble I had heard before, and a dozen men were on their feet clamoring for recognition from Colonel Van Gilbert. I noticed Miss Brentwood's shoulders moving convulsively, and for the moment I was angry, for I thought that she was laughing at Ernest. And then I discovered that it was not laughter, but hysteria. She was appalled by what she had done in bringing this firebrand before her blessed Philomath Club.

Colonel Van Gilbert did not notice the dozen men, with passion-wrought faces, who strove to get permission from him to speak. His own face was passion-wrought. He sprang to his feet, waving his arms, and for a moment could utter only incoherent sounds. Then speech poured from him. But it was not the speech of a one-hundred-thousand-dollar lawyer, nor was the rhetoric old-fashioned.

"Fallacy upon fallacy!" he cried. "Never in all my life have I heard so many fallacies uttered in one short hour. And besides, young man, I must tell you that you have said nothing new. I learned all that at college before you were born. Jean Jacques Rousseau enunciated your socialistic theory nearly two centuries ago. A return to the soil, forsooth! Reversion! Our biology teaches the absurdity of it. It has been truly said that a little learning is a dangerous thing, and you have exemplified it to-night with your madcap theories. Fallacy upon fallacy! I was never so nauseated in my life with overplus of fallacy. That for your immature generalizations and childish reasonings!"

He snapped his fingers contemptuously and proceeded to sit down. There were lip-exclamations of approval on the part of the women, and hoarser notes of confirmation came from the men. As for the dozen men who were clamoring for the floor, half of them began speaking at once. The confusion and babel was indescribable. Never had Mrs. Pertonwaithe's spacious walls beheld such a spectacle. These, then, were the cool captains of industry and lords of society, these snarling, growling savages in evening clothes. Truly Ernest had shaken them when he stretched out his hands for their money-bags, his hands that had appeared in their eyes as the hands of the fifteen hundred thousand revolutionists.

But Ernest never lost his head in a situation. Before Colonel Van Gilbert had succeeded in sitting down, Ernest was on his feet and had sprung forward.

"One at a time!" he roared at them.

The sound arose from his great lungs and dominated the human tempest. By sheer compulsion of personality he commanded silence.

"One at a time," he repeated softly. "Let me answer Colonel Van Gilbert. After that the rest of you can come at me—but one at a time, remember. No mass-plays here. This is not a football field.

"As for you," he went on, turning toward Colonel Van Gilbert, "you have replied to nothing I have said. You have merely made a few excited and dogmatic assertions about my mental caliber. That may serve you in your business, but you can't talk to me like that. I am not a workingman, cap in hand, asking you to increase my wages or to protect me from the machine at which I work. You cannot be dogmatic with truth when you deal with me. Save that for dealing with your wage-slaves. They will not dare reply to you because you hold their bread and butter, their lives, in your hands.

"As for this return to nature that you say you learned at college before I was born, permit me to point out that on the face of it you cannot have learned anything since. Socialism has no more to do with the state of nature than has differential calculus with a Bible class. I have called your class stupid when outside the realm of business. You, sir, have brilliantly exemplified my statement."

This terrible castigation of her hundred-thousand-dollar lawyer was too much for Miss Brentwood's nerves. Her hysteria became violent, and she was helped, weeping and laughing, out of the room. It was just as well, for there was worse to follow.

"Don't take my word for it," Ernest continued, when the interruption had been led away. "Your own authorities with one unanimous voice will prove you stupid. Your own hired purveyors of knowledge will tell you that you are wrong. Go to your meekest little assistant instructor of sociology and ask him what is the difference between Rousseau's theory of the return to nature and the theory of socialism; ask your greatest orthodox bourgeois political economists and sociologists; question through the pages of every text-book written on the subject and stored on the shelves of your subsidized libraries; and from one and all the answer will be that there is nothing congruous between the return to nature and socialism. On the other hand, the unanimous affirmative answer will be that the return to nature and socialism are diametrically opposed to each other. As I say, don't take my word for it. The record of your stupidity is there in the books, your own books that you never read. And so far as your stupidity is concerned, you are but the exemplar of your class.

"You know law and business, Colonel Van Gilbert. You know how to serve corporations and increase dividends by twisting the law. Very good. Stick to it. You are quite a figure. You are a very good lawyer, but you are a poor historian, you know nothing of sociology, and your biology is contemporaneous with Pliny."

Here Colonel Van Gilbert writhed in his chair. There was perfect quiet in the room. Everybody sat fascinated—paralyzed, I may say. Such fearful treatment of the great Colonel Van Gilbert was unheard of, undreamed of, impossible to believe—the great Colonel Van Gilbert before whom judges trembled when he arose in court. But Ernest never gave quarter to an enemy.

"This is, of course, no reflection on you," Ernest said. "Every man to his trade. Only you stick to your trade, and I'll stick to mine. You have specialized. When it comes to a knowledge of the law, of how best to evade the law or make new law for the benefit of thieving corporations, I am down in the dirt at your feet. But when it comes to sociology—my trade—you are down in the dirt at my feet. Remember that. Remember, also, that your law is the stuff of a day, and that you are not versatile in the stuff of more than a day. Therefore your dogmatic assertions and rash generalizations on things historical and sociological are not worth the breath you waste on them."

Ernest paused for a moment and regarded him thoughtfully, noting his face dark and twisted with anger, his panting chest, his writhing body, and his slim white hands nervously clenching and unclenching.

"But it seems you have breath to use, and I'll give you a chance to use it. I indicted your class. Show me that my indictment is wrong. I pointed out to you the wretchedness of modern man—three million child slaves in the United States, without whose labor profits would not be possible, and fifteen million under-fed, ill-clothed, and worse-housed people. I pointed out that modern man's producing power through social organization and the use of machinery was a thousand times greater than that of the cave-man. And I stated that from these two facts no other conclusion was possible than that the capitalist

class has mismanaged. This was my indictment, and I specifically
and at length challenged you to answer it. Nay, I did more. I proph-
esied that you would not answer. It remains for your breath to smash
my prophecy. You called my speech fallacy. Show the fallacy, Colonel
Van Gilbert. Answer the indictment that I and my fifteen hundred
thousand comrades have brought against your class and you."

Colonel Van Gilbert quite forgot that he was presiding, and that
in courtesy he should permit the other clamorers to speak. He was on
his feet, flinging his arms, his rhetoric, and his control to the winds,
alternately abusing Ernest for his youth and demagoguery, and savagely attacking the working class, elaborating its inefficiency and
worthlessness.

"For a lawyer, you are the hardest man to keep to a point I ever
saw," Ernest began his answer to the tirade. "My youth has nothing
to do with what I have enunciated. Nor has the worthlessness of the
working class. I charged the capitalist class with having mismanaged
society. You have not answered. You have made no attempt to answer. Why? Is it because you have no answer? You are the champion
of this whole audience. Every one here, except me, is hanging on your
lips for that answer. They are hanging on your lips for that answer
because they have no answer themselves. As for me, as I said before, I
know that you not only cannot answer, but that you will not attempt
an answer."

"This is intolerable!" Colonel Van Gilbert cried out. "This is insult!"

"That you should not answer is intolerable," Ernest replied gravely.
"No man can be intellectually insulted. Insult, in its very nature, is
emotional. Recover yourself. Give me an intellectual answer to my
intellectual charge that the capitalist class has mismanaged society."

Colonel Van Gilbert remained silent, a sullen, superior expression
on his face, such as will appear on the face of a man who will not
bandy words with a ruffian.

"Do not be downcast," Ernest said. "Take consolation in the fact
that no member of your class has ever yet answered that charge." He
turned to the other men who were anxious to speak. "And now it's
your chance. Fire away, and do not forget that I here challenge you
to give the answer that Colonel Van Gilbert has failed to give."

It would be impossible for me to write all that was said in the
discussion. I never realized before how many words could be spoken
in three short hours. At any rate, it was glorious. The more his op-

ponents grew excited, the more Ernest deliberately excited them. He had an encyclopædic command of the field of knowledge, and by a word or a phrase, by delicate rapier thrusts, he punctured them. He named the points of their illogic. This was a false syllogism, that conclusion had no connection with the premise, while that next premise was an impostor because it had cunningly hidden in it the conclusion that was being attempted to be proved. This was an error, that was an assumption, and the next was an assertion contrary to ascertained truth as printed in all the text-books.

And so it went. Sometimes he exchanged the rapier for the club and went smashing amongst their thoughts right and left. And always he demanded facts and refused to discuss theories. And his facts made for them a Waterloo. When they attacked the working class, he always retorted, "The pot calling the kettle black; that is no answer to the charge that your own face is dirty." And to one and all he said: "Why have you not answered the charge that your class has mismanaged? You have talked about other things and things concerning other things, but you have not answered. Is it because you have no answer?"

It was at the end of the discussion that Mr. Wickson spoke. He was the only one that was cool, and Ernest treated him with a respect he had not accorded the others.

"No answer is necessary," Mr. Wickson said with slow deliberation. "I have followed the whole discussion with amazement and disgust. I am disgusted with you, gentlemen, members of my class. You have behaved like foolish little schoolboys, what with intruding ethics and the thunder of the common politician into such a discussion. You have been out-generalled and outclassed. You have been very wordy, and all you have done is buzz. You have buzzed like gnats about a bear. Gentlemen, there stands the bear" (he pointed at Ernest), "and your buzzing has only tickled his ears.

"Believe me, the situation is serious. That bear reached out his paws to-night to crush us. He has said there are a million and a half of revolutionists in the United States. That is a fact. He has said that it is their intention to take away from us our governments, our palaces, and all our purpled ease. That, also, is a fact. A change, a great change, is coming in society; but, haply, it may not be the change the bear anticipates. The bear has said that he will crush us. What if we crush the bear?"

The throat-rumble arose in the great room, and man nodded to

man with indorsement and certitude. Their faces were set hard. They
were fighters, that was certain.

"But not by buzzing will we crush the bear," Mr. Wickson went on
coldly and dispassionately. "We will hunt the bear. We will not reply
to the bear in words. Our reply shall be couched in terms of lead. We
are in power. Nobody will deny it. By virtue of that power we shall
remain in power."

He turned suddenly upon Ernest. The moment was dramatic.

"This, then, is our answer. We have no words to waste on you.
When you reach out your vaunted strong hands for our palaces and
purpled ease, we will show you what strength is. In roar of shell and
shrapnel and in whine of machine-guns will our answer be couched.[10]
We will grind you revolutionists down under our heel, and we shall
walk upon your faces. The world is ours, we are its lords, and ours
it shall remain. As for the host of labor, it has been in the dirt since
history began, and I read history aright. And in the dirt it shall remain so long as I and mine and those that come after us have the
power. There is the word. It is the king of words—Power. Not God,
not Mammon, but Power. Pour it over your tongue till it tingles
with it. Power."

"I am answered," Ernest said quietly. "It is the only answer that
could be given. Power. It is what we of the working class preach.
We know, and well we know by bitter experience, that no appeal for
the right, for justice, for humanity, can ever touch you. Your hearts
are hard as your heels with which you tread upon the faces of the
poor. So we have preached power. By the power of our ballots on
election day will we take your government away from you—"

"What if you do get a majority, a sweeping majority, on election
day?" Mr. Wickson broke in to demand. "Suppose we refuse to
turn the government over to you after you have captured it at the
ballot-box?"

"That, also, have we considered," Ernest replied. "And we shall give
you an answer in terms of lead. Power, you have proclaimed the king
of words. Very good. Power it shall be. And in the day that we sweep
to victory at the ballot-box, and you refuse to turn over to us the
government we have constitutionally and peacefully captured, and you

[10] To show the tenor of thought, the following definition is quoted from
"The Cynic's Word Book" (1906 A.D.), written by one Ambrose Bierce, an
avowed and confirmed misanthrope of the period: "Grapeshot, *n. An argument
which the future is preparing in answer to the demands of American Socialism.*"

demand what we are going to do about it—in that day, I say, we shall answer you; and in roar of shell and shrapnel and in whine of machine-guns shall our answer be couched.

"You cannot escape us. It true that you have read history aright. It is true that labor has from the beginning of history been in the dirt. And it is equally true that so long as you and yours and those that come after you have power, that labor shall remain in the dirt. I agree with you. I agree with all that you have said. Power will be the arbiter, as it always has been the arbiter. It is a struggle of classes. Just as your class dragged down the old feudal nobility, so shall it be dragged down by my class, the working class. If you will read your biology and your sociology as clearly as you do your history, you will see that this end I have described is inevitable. It does not matter whether it is in one year, ten, or a thousand—your class shall be dragged down. And it shall be done by power. We of the labor hosts have conned that word over till our minds are all a-tingle with it. Power. It is a kingly word."

And so ended the night with the Philomaths.

THE VORTEX

Following like thunder claps upon the Business Men's dinner, occurred event after event of terrifying moment; and I, little I, who had lived so placidly all my days in the quiet university town, found myself and my personal affairs drawn into the vortex of the great world-affairs. Whether it was my love for Ernest, or the clear sight he had given me of the society in which I lived, that made me a revolutionist, I know not; but a revolutionist I became, and I was plunged into a whirl of happenings that would have been inconceivable three short months before.

The crisis in my own fortunes came simultaneously with great crises in society. First of all, father was discharged from the university. Oh, he was not technically discharged. His resignation was demanded, that was all. This, in itself, did not amount to much. Father, in fact, was delighted. He was especially delighted because his discharge had been precipitated by the publication of his book, "Economics and Education." It clinched his argument, he contended. What better evidence could be advanced to prove that education was dominated by the capitalist class?

But this proof never got anywhere. Nobody knew he had been

forced to resign from the university. He was so eminent a scientist that such an announcement, coupled with the reason for his enforced resignation, would have created somewhat of a furor all over the world. The newspapers showered him with praise and honor, and commended him for having given up the drudgery of the lecture room in order to devote his whole time to scientific research.

At first father laughed. Then he became angry—tonic angry. Then came the suppression of his book. This suppression was performed secretly, so secretly that at first we could not comprehend. The publication of the book had immediately caused a bit of excitement in the country. Father had been politely abused in the capitalist press, the tone of the abuse being to the effect that it was a pity so great a scientist should leave his field and invade the realm of sociology, about which he knew nothing and wherein he had promptly become lost. This lasted for a week, while father chuckled and said the book had touched a sore spot on capitalism. And then, abruptly, the newspapers and the critical magazines ceased saying anything about the book at all. Also, and with equal suddenness, the book disappeared from the market. Not a copy was obtainable from any bookseller. Father wrote to the publishers and was informed that the plates had been accidentally injured. An unsatisfactory correspondence followed. Driven finally to an unequivocal stand, the publishers stated that they could not see their way to putting the book into type again, but that they were quite willing to relinquish their rights in it.

"And you won't find another publishing house in the country to touch it," Ernest said. "And if I were you, I'd hunt cover right now. You've merely got a foretaste of the Iron Heel."

But father was nothing if not a scientist. He never believed in jumping to conclusions. A laboratory experiment was no experiment if it were not carried through in all its details. So he patiently went the round of the publishing houses. They gave a multitude of excuses, but not one house would consider the book.

When father became convinced that the book had actually been suppressed, he tried to get the fact into the newspapers; but his communications were ignored. At a political meeting of the socialists, where many reporters were present, father saw his chance. He arose and related the history of the suppression of the book. He laughed next day when he read the newspapers, and then he grew angry to a degree that eliminated all tonic qualities. The papers made no mention of the book, but they misreported him beautifully. They twisted

his words and phrases away from the context, and turned his sub-
dued and controlled remarks into a howling anarchistic speech. It
was done artfully. One instance, in particular, I remember. He had
used the phrase "social revolution." The reporter merely dropped
out "social." This was sent out all over the country in an Associated
Press despatch, and from all over the country arose a cry of alarm.
Father was branded as a nihilist and an anarchist, and in one cartoon
that was copied widely he was portrayed waving a red flag at the head
of a mob of long-haired, wild-eyed men who bore in their hands
torches, knives, and dynamite bombs.

He was assailed terribly in the press, in long and abusive editorials,
for his anarchy, and hints were made of mental breakdown on his
part. This behavior, on the part of the capitalist press, was nothing
new, Ernest told us. It was the custom, he said, to send reporters
to all the socialist meetings for the express purpose of misreporting
and distorting what was said, in order to frighten the middle class
away from any possible affiliation with the proletariat. And repeatedly
Ernest warned father to cease fighting and to take to cover.

The socialist press of the country took up the fight, however, and
throughout the reading portion of the working class it was known
that the book had been suppressed. But this knowledge stopped with
the working class. Next, the "Appeal to Reason," a big socialist publishing house, arranged with father to bring out the book. Father was
jubilant, but Ernest was alarmed.

"I tell you we are on the verge of the unknown," he insisted. "Big
things are happening secretly all around us. We can feel them. We do
not know what they are, but they are there. The whole fabric of
society is a-tremble with them. Don't ask me. I don't know myself.
But out of this flux of society something is about to crystallize. It is
crystallizing now. The suppression of the book is a precipitation.
How many books have been suppressed? We haven't the least idea.
We are in the dark. We have no way of learning. Watch out next for
the suppression of the socialist press and socialist publishing houses.
I'm afraid it's coming. We are going to be throttled."

Ernest had his hand on the pulse of events even more closely than
the rest of the socialists, and within two days the first blow was
struck. The *Appeal to Reason* was a weekly, and its regular circulation amongst the proletariat was seven hundred and fifty thousand.
Also, it very frequently got out special editions of from two to five
millions. These great editions were paid for and distributed by the

small army of voluntary workers who had marshalled around the
Appeal. The first blow was aimed at these special editions, and it was
a crushing one. By an arbitrary ruling of the Post Office, these editions
were decided to be not the regular circulation of the paper, and for
that reason were denied admission to the mails.

A week later the Post Office Department ruled that the paper was
seditious, and barred it entirely from the mails. This was a fearful
blow to the socialist propaganda. The *Appeal* was desperate. It devised a plan of reaching its subscribers through the express companies,
but they declined to handle it. This was the end of the *Appeal*. But
not quite. It prepared to go on with its book publishing. Twenty thousand copies of father's book were in the bindery, and the presses
were turning off more. And then, without warning, a mob arose one
night, and, under a waving American flag, singing patriotic songs, set
ìire to the great plant of the *Appeal* and totally destroyed it.

Now Girard, Kansas, was a quiet, peaceable town. There had never
been any labor troubles there. The *Appeal* paid union wages; and, in
fact, was the backbone of the town, giving employment to hundreds
of men and women. It was not the citizens of Girard that composed
the mob. This mob had risen up out of the earth apparently, and
to all intents and purposes, its work done, it had gone back into the
earth. Ernest saw in the affair the most sinister import.

"The Black Hundreds [11] are being organized in the United States,"
he said. "This is the beginning. There will be more of it. The Iron Heel
is getting bold."

And so perished father's book. We were to see much of the Black
Hundreds as the days went by. Week by week more of the socialist
papers were barred from the mails, and in a number of instances the
Black Hundreds destroyed the socialist presses. Of course, the newspapers of the land lived up to the reactionary policy of the ruling
class, and the destroyed socialist press was misrepresented and vili-
fied, while the Black Hundreds were represented as true patriots and
saviours of society. So convincing was all this misrepresentation that
even sincere ministers in the pulpit praised the Black Hundreds while
regretting the necessity of violence.

History was making fast. The fall elections were soon to occur, and

[11] The Black Hundreds were reactionary mobs organized by the perishing
Autocracy in the Russian Revolution. These reactionary groups attacked the
revolutionary groups, and also, at needed moments, rioted and destroyed
property so as to afford the Autocracy the pretext of calling out the Cossacks.

Ernest was nominated by the socialist party to run for Congress. His chance for election was most favorable. The street-car strike in San Francisco had been broken. And following upon it the teamsters' strike had been broken. These two defeats had been very disastrous to organized labor. The whole Water Front Federation, along with its allies in the structural trades, had backed up the teamsters, and all had smashed down ingloriously. It had been a bloody strike. The police had broken countless heads with their riot clubs; and the death list had been augmented by the turning loose of a machine-gun on the strikers from the barns of the Marsden Special Delivery Company.

In consequence, the men were sullen and vindictive. They wanted blood, and revenge. Beaten on their chosen field, they were ripe to seek revenge by means of political action. They still maintained their labor organization, and this gave them strength in the political struggle that was on. Ernest's chance for election grew stronger and stronger. Day by day unions and more unions voted their support to the socialists, until even Ernest laughed when the Undertakers' Assistants and the Chicken Pickers fell into line. Labor became mulish. While it packed the socialist meetings with mad enthusiasm, it was impervious to the wiles of the old-party politicians. The old-party orators were usually greeted with empty halls, though occasionally they encountered full halls where they were so roughly handled that more than once it was necessary to call out the police reserves.

History was making fast. The air was vibrant with things happening and impending. The country was on the verge of hard times,[12] caused by a series of prosperous years wherein the difficulty of disposing abroad of the unconsumed surplus had become increasingly difficult. Industries were working short time; many great factories were standing idle against the time when the surplus should be gone; and wages were being cut right and left.

Also, the great machinist strike had been broken. Two hundred thousand machinists, along with their five hundred thousand allies in the metal-working trades, had been defeated in as bloody a strike as had ever marred the United States. Pitched battles had been fought with the small armies of armed strike-breakers [13] put in the field by

---

[12] Under the capitalist régime these periods of hard times were as inevitable as they were absurd. Prosperity always brought calamity. This, of course, was due to the excess of unconsumed profits that was piled up.

[13] *Strike-breakers*—these were, in purpose and practice and everything

the employers' associations; the Black Hundreds, appearing in scores of wide-scattered places, had destroyed property; and, in consequence, a hundred thousand regular soldiers of the United States had been called out to put a frightful end to the whole affair. A number of the labor leaders had been executed; many others had been sentenced to prison, while thousands of the rank and file of the strikers had been herded into bull-pens [14] and abominably treated by the soldiers.

The years of prosperity were now to be paid for. All markets were glutted; all markets were falling; and amidst the general crumble of prices the price of labor crumbled fastest of all. The land was convulsed with industrial dissensions. Labor was striking here, there, and everywhere; and where it was not striking, it was being turned out by the capitalists. The papers were filled with tales of violence and blood. And through it all the Black Hundreds played their part. Riot, arson, and wanton destruction of property was their function, and well they performed it. The whole regular army was in the field, called there by the actions of the Black Hundreds.[15] All cities and

---

except name, the private soldiers of the capitalists. They were thoroughly organized and well armed, and they were held in readiness to be hurled in special trains to any part of the country where labor went out on strike or was locked out by the employers. Only those curious times could have given rise to the amazing spectacle of one, Farley, a notorious commander of strike-breakers, who, in 1906, swept across the United States in special trains from New York to San Francisco with an army of twenty-five hundred men, fully armed and equipped, to break a strike of the San Francisco street-car men. Such an act was in direct violation of the laws of the land. The fact that this act, and thousands of similar acts, went unpunished, goes to show how completely the judiciary was the creature of the Plutocracy.

[14] *Bull-pen*—in a miners' strike in Idaho, in the latter part of the nineteenth century, it happened that many of the strikers were confined in a bull-pen by the troops. The practice and the name continued in the twentieth century.

[15] The name only, and not the idea, was imported from Russia. The Black Hundreds were a development out of the secret agents of the capitalists, and their use arose in the labor struggles of the nineteenth century. There is no discussion of this. No less an authority of the times than Carroll D. Wright, United States Commissioner of Labor, is responsible for the statement. From his book, entitled "The Battles of Labor," is quoted the declaration that *"in some of the great historic strikes the employers themselves have instigated acts of violence;"* that manufacturers have deliberately provoked strikes in order to get rid of surplus stock; and that freight cars have been burned by employers' agents during railroad strikes in order to increase disorder. It was out of these secret agents of the employers that the Black Hundreds arose; and it was they, in turn, that later became that terrible weapon of the Oligarchy, the agents-provocateurs.

towns were like armed camps, and laborers were shot down like
dogs. Out of the vast army of the unemployed the strike-breakers
were recruited; and when the strike-breakers were worsted by the
labor unions, the troops always appeared and crushed the unions.
Then there was the militia. As yet, it was not necessary to have recourse to the secret militia law. Only the regularly organized militia
was out, and it was out everywhere. And in this time of terror, the
regular army was increased an additional hundred thousand by the
government.

Never had labor received such an all-around beating. The great
captains of industry, the oligarchs, had for the first time thrown their
full weight into the breach the struggling employers' associations
had made. These associations were practically middle-class affairs,
and now, compelled by hard times and crashing markets, and aided
by the great captains of industry, they gave organized labor an awful
and decisive defeat. It was an all-powerful alliance, but it was an
alliance of the lion and the lamb, as the middle class was soon to learn.

Labor was bloody and sullen, but crushed. Yet its defeat did not
put an end to the hard times. The banks, themselves constituting one
of the most important forces of the Oligarchy, continued to call in
credits. The Wall Street [16] group turned the stock market into a
maelstrom where the values of all the land crumbled away almost in
nothingness. And out of all the rack and ruin rose the form of the
nascent Oligarchy, imperturbable, indifferent, and sure. Its serenity
and certitude was terrifying. Not only did it use its own vast power,
but it used all the power of the United States Treasury to carry out
its plans.

The captains of industry had turned upon the middle class. The
employers' associations, that had helped the captains of industry to
tear and rend labor, were now torn and rent by their quondam allies.
Amidst the crashing of the middle men, the small business men and
manufacturers, the trusts stood firm. Nay, the trusts did more than
stand firm. They were active. They sowed wind, and wind, and ever
more wind; for they alone knew how to reap the whirlwind and
make a profit out of it. And such profits! Colossal profits! Strong
enough themselves to weather the storm that was largely their own
brewing, they turned loose and plundered the wrecks that floated

[16] *Wall Street*—so named from a street in ancient New York, where was
situated the stock exchange, and where the irrational organization of society
permitted underhanded manipulation of all the industries of the country.

about them. Values were pitifully and inconceivably shrunken, and the trusts added hugely to their holdings, even extending their enterprises into many new fields—and always at the expense of the middle class.

Thus the summer of 1912 witnessed the virtual death-thrust to the middle class. Even Ernest was astounded at the quickness with which it had been done. He shook his head ominously and looked forward without hope to the fall elections.

"It's no use," he said. "We are beaten. The Iron Heel is here. I had hoped for a peaceable victory at the ballot-box. I was wrong. Wickson was right. We shall be robbed of our few remaining liberties; the Iron Heel will walk upon our faces; nothing remains but a bloody revolution of the working class. Of course we will win, but I shudder to think of it."

And from then on Ernest pinned his faith in revolution. In this he was in advance of his party. His fellow-socialists could not agree with him. They still insisted that victory could be gained through the elections. It was not that they were stunned. They were too cool-headed and courageous for that. They were merely incredulous, that was all. Ernest could not get them seriously to fear the coming of the Oligarchy. They were stirred by him, but they were too sure of their own strength. There was no room in their theoretical social evolution for an oligarchy, therefore the Oligarchy could not be.

"We'll send you to Congress and it will be all right," they told him at one of our secret meetings.

"And when they take me out of Congress," Ernest replied coldly, "and put me against a wall, and blow my brains out—what then?"

"Then we'll rise in our might," a dozen voices answered at once.

"Then you'll welter in your gore," was his retort. "I've heard that song sung by the middle class, and where is it now in its might?"

THE GENERAL STRIKE

Of course Ernest was elected to Congress in the great socialist landslide that took place in the fall of 1912. One great factor that helped to swell the socialist vote was the destruction of Hearst.[17] This the

[17] *William Randolph Hearst*—a young California millionaire who became the most powerful newspaper owner in the country. His newspapers were published in all the large cities, and they appealed to the perishing middle class and to the proletariat. So large was his following that he managed to take possession

Plutocracy found an easy task. It cost Hearst eighteen million dollars a year to run his various papers, and this sum, and more, he got back from the middle class in payment for advertising. The source of his financial strength lay wholly in the middle class. The trusts did not advertise.[18] To destroy Hearst, all that was necessary was to take away from him his advertising.

The whole middle class had not yet been exterminated. The sturdy skeleton of it remained; but it was without power. The small manufacturers and small business men who still survived were at the complete mercy of the Plutocracy. They had no economic nor political souls of their own. When the fiat of the Plutocracy went forth, they withdrew their advertisements from the Hearst papers.

Hearst made a gallant fight. He brought his papers out at a loss of a million and a half each month. He continued to publish the advertisements for which he no longer received pay. Again the fiat of the Plutocracy went forth, and the small business men and manufacturers swamped him with a flood of notices that he must discontinue running their old advertisements. Hearst persisted. Injunctions were served on him. Still he persisted. He received six months' imprisonment for contempt of court in disobeying the injunctions, while he was bankrupted by countless damage suits. He had no chance. The Plutocracy had passed sentence on him. The courts were in the hands of the Plutocracy to carry the sentence out. And with Hearst crashed also to destruction the Democratic Party that he had so recently captured.

With the destruction of Hearst and the Democratic Party, there

---

of the empty shell of the old Democratic Party. He occupied an anomalous position, preaching an emasculated socialism combined with a nondescript sort of petty bourgeois capitalism. It was oil and water, and there was no hope for him, though for a short period he was a source of serious apprehension to the Plutocrats.

[In 1905 William Randolph Hearst ran for Mayor of New York City on a Municipal Ownership platform and a year later was candidate for Governor on the Democratic and Independence League tickets. It took a few years for many progressives to realize that Hearst was only taking advantage of the popular discontent to increase the circulation of his newspapers and to advance his own political career. Soon enough he revealed his true role as one of the outstanding American spokesmen for reaction.—EDITOR.]

[18] The cost of advertising was amazing in those helter-skelter times. Only the small capitalists competed, and therefore they did the advertising. There being no competition where there was a trust, there was no need for the trusts to advertise.

were only two paths for his following to take. One was into the Socialist Party; the other was into the Republican Party. Then it was that we socialists reaped the fruit of Hearst's pseudo-socialistic preaching; for the great majority of his followers came over to us.

The expropriation of the farmers that took place at this time would also have swelled our vote had it not been for the brief and futile rise of the Grange Party. Ernest and the socialist leaders fought fiercely to capture the farmers; but the destruction of the socialist press and publishing houses constituted too great a handicap, while the mouth-to-mouth propaganda had not yet been perfected. So it was that politicians like Mr. Calvin, who were themselves farmers long since expropriated, captured the farmers and threw their political strength away in a vain campaign.

"The poor farmers," Ernest once laughed savagely; "the trusts have them both coming and going."

And that was really the situation. The seven great trusts, working together, had pooled their enormous surpluses and made a farm trust. The railroads, controlling rates, and the bankers and stock exchange gamesters, controlling prices, had long since bled the farmers into indebtedness. The bankers, and all the trusts for that matter, had likewise long since loaned colossal amounts of money to the farmers. The farmers were in the net. All that remained to be done was the drawing in of the net. This the farm trust proceeded to do.

The hard times of 1912 had already caused a frightful slump in the farm markets. Prices were now deliberately pressed down to bankruptcy, while the railroads, with extortionate rates, broke the back of the farmer-camel. Thus the farmers were compelled to borrow more and more, while they were prevented from paying back old loans. Then ensued the great foreclosing of mortgages and enforced collection of notes. The farmers simply surrendered the land to the farm trust. There was nothing else for them to do. And having surrendered the land, the farmers next went to work for the farm trust, becoming managers, superintendents, foremen, and common laborers. They worked for wages. They became villeins, in short—serfs bound to the soil by a living wage. They could not leave their masters, for their masters composed the Plutocracy. They could not go to the cities, for there, also, the Plutocracy was in control. They had but one alternative,—to leave the soil and become vagrants, in brief, to starve. And even there they were frustrated, for stringent vagrancy laws were passed and rigidly enforced.

Of course, here and there, farmers, and even whole communities of farmers, escaped expropriation by virtue of exceptional conditions. But they were merely strays and did not count, and they were gathered in anyway during the following year.[19]

Thus it was that in the fall of 1912 the socialist leaders, with the exception of Ernest, decided that the end of capitalism had come. What of the hard times and the consequent vast army of the unemployed; what of the destruction of the farmers and the middle class; and what of the decisive defeat administered all along the line to the labor unions; the socialists were really justified in believing that the end of capitalism had come and in themselves throwing down the gauntlet to the Plutocracy.

Alas, how we underestimated the strength of the enemy! Everywhere the socialists proclaimed their coming victory at the ballot-box, while, in unmistakable terms, they stated the situation. The Plutocracy accepted the challenge. It was the Plutocracy, weighing and balancing, that defeated us by dividing our strength. It was the Plutocracy, through its secret agents, that raised the cry that socialism was sacrilegious and atheistic; it was the Plutocracy that whipped the churches, and especially the Catholic Church, into line, and robbed us of a portion of the labor vote. And it was the Plutocracy, through its secret agents of course, that encouraged the Grange Party and even spread it to the cities into the ranks of the dying middle class.

Nevertheless the socialist landslide occurred. But, instead of a sweeping victory with chief executive officers and majorities in all legislative bodies, we found ourselves in the minority. It is true, we elected fifty Congressmen; but when they took their seats in the

[19] The destruction of the Roman yeomanry proceeded far less rapidly than the destruction of the American farmers and small capitalists. There was momentum in the twentieth century, while there was practically none in ancient Rome.

Numbers of the farmers, impelled by an insane lust for the soil, and willing to show what beasts they could become, tried to escape expropriation by withdrawing from any and all market-dealing. They sold nothing. They bought nothing. Among themselves a primitive barter began to spring up. Their privation and hardships were terrible, but they persisted. It became quite a movement, in fact. The manner in which they were beaten was unique and logical and simple. The Plutocracy, by virtue of its possession of the government, raised their taxes. It was the weak joint in their armor. Neither buying nor selling, they had no money, and in the end their land was sold to pay the taxes.

spring of 1913, they found themselves without power of any sort.
Yet they were more fortunate than the Grangers, who captured a
dozen state governments, and who, in the spring, were not permitted
to take possession of the captured offices. The incumbents refused to
retire, and the courts were in the hands of the Oligarchy. But this is
too far in advance of events. I have yet to tell of the stirring times of
the winter of 1912.

The hard times at home had caused an immense decrease in consumption. Labor, out of work, had no wages with which to buy. The
result was that the Plutocracy found a greater surplus than ever on
its hands. This surplus it was compelled to dispose of abroad, and,
what of its colossal plans, it needed money. Because of its strenuous
efforts to dispose of the surplus in the world market, the Plutocracy
clashed with Germany. Economic clashes were usually succeeded by
wars, and this particular clash was no exception. The great German
war-lord prepared, and so did the United States prepare.

The war-cloud hovered dark and ominous. The stage was set for a
world-catastrophe, for in all the world were hard times, labor troubles,
perishing middle classes, armies of unemployed, clashes of economic
interests in the world-market, and mutterings and rumblings of the
socialist revolution.[20]

The Oligarchy wanted the war with Germany. And it wanted the
war for a dozen reasons. In the juggling of events such a war would

---

[20] For a long time these mutterings and rumblings had been heard. As far
back as 1906 A.D., Lord Avebury, an Englishman, uttered the following in the
House of Lords: *"The unrest in Europe, the spread of socialism, and the ominous rise of Anarchism, are warnings to the governments and the ruling classes
that the condition of the working classes in Europe is becoming intolerable,
and that if a revolution is to be avoided some steps must be taken to increase
wages, reduce the hours of labor, and lower the prices of the necessaries of life."*
The *Wall Street Journal*, a stock gamesters' publication, in commenting upon
Lord Avebury's speech said: *"These words were spoken by an aristocrat and a
member of the most conservative body in all Europe. That gives them all the
more significance. They contain more valuable political economy than is to be
found in most of the books. They sound a note of warning. Take heed, gentlemen of the war and navy departments!"*
At the same time, Sydney Brooks, writing in America, in *Harper's Weekly*,
said: *"You will not hear the socialists mentioned in Washington. Why should
you? The Politicians are always the last people in this country to see what is
going on under their noses. They will jeer at me when I prophesy, and prophesy
with the utmost confidence, that at the next presidential election the socialists
will poll over a million votes."*

cause, in the reshuffling of the international cards and the making of
new treaties and alliances, the Oligarchy had much to gain. And,
furthermore, the war would consume many national surpluses, reduce
the armies of unemployed that menaced all countries, and give the
Oligarchy a breathing space in which to perfect its plans and carry
them out. Such a war would virtually put the Oligarchy in possession
of the world-market. Also, such a war would create a large standing
army that need never be disbanded, while in the minds of the people
would be substituted the issue, "America *versus* Germany," in place
of "Socialism *versus* Oligarchy."

And truly the war would have done all these things had it not been
for the socialists. A secret meeting of the Western leaders was held
in our four tiny rooms in Pell Street. Here was first considered the
stand the socialists were to take. It was not the first time we had put
our foot down upon war,[21] but it was the first time we had done so in
the United States. After our secret meeting we got in touch with the
national organization, and soon our code cables were passing back
and forth across the Atlantic between us and the International Bureau.

The German socialists were ready to act with us. There were over
five million of them, many of them in the standing army, and, in addition, they were on friendly terms with the labor unions. In both
countries the socialists came out in bold declaration against the war
and threatened the general strike. And in the meantime they made
preparation for the general strike. Furthermore, the revolutionary
parties in all countries gave public utterance to the socialist principle
of international peace that must be preserved at all hazards, even to
the extent of revolt and revolution at home.

The general strike was the one great victory we American socialists
won. On the 4th of December the American minister was withdrawn
from the German capital. That night a German fleet made a dash on

[21] It was at the very beginning of the twentieth century A.D., that the international organization of the socialists finally formulated their long-maturing
policy on war. Epitomized, their doctrine was: *"Why should the workingmen
of one country fight with the workingmen of another country for the benefit of
their capitalist masters?"*
On May 21, 1905 A.D., when war threatened between Austria and Italy, the
socialists of Italy, Austria, and Hungary held a conference at Trieste, and
threatened a general strike of the workingmen of both countries in case war
was declared. This was repeated the following year, when the "Morocco Affair"
threatened to involve France, Germany, and England.

Honolulu, sinking three American cruisers and a revenue cutter, and bombarding the city. Next day both Germany and the United States declared war, and within an hour the socialists called the general strike in both countries.

For the first time the German war-lord faced the men of his empire who made his empire go. Without them he could not run his empire. The novelty of the situation lay in that their revolt was passive. They did not fight. They did nothing. And by doing nothing they tied their war-lord's hands. He would have asked for nothing better than an opportunity to loose his war-dogs on his rebellious proletariat. But this was denied him. He could not loose his war-dogs. Neither could he mobilize his army to go forth to war, nor could he punish his recalcitrant subjects. Not a wheel moved in his empire. Not a train ran, not a telegraphic message went over the wires, for the telegraphers and railroad men had ceased work along with the rest of the population.

And as it was in Germany, so it was in the United States. At last organized labor had learned its lesson. Beaten decisively on its own chosen field, it had abandoned that field and come over to the political field of the socialists; for the general strike was a political strike. Besides, organized labor had been so badly beaten that it did not care. It joined in the general strike out of sheer desperation. The workers threw down their tools and left their tasks by the millions. Especially notable were the machinists. Their heads were bloody, their organization had apparently been destroyed, yet out they came, along with their allies in the metal-working trades.

Even the common laborers and all unorganized labor ceased work. The strike had tied everything up so that nobody could work. Besides, the women proved to be the strongest promoters of the strike. They set their faces against the war. They did not want their men to go forth to die. Then, also, the idea of the general strike caught the mood of the people. It struck their sense of humor. The idea was infectious. The children struck in all the schools, and such teachers as came, went home again from deserted class rooms. The general strike took the form of a great national picnic. And the idea of the solidarity of labor, so evidenced, appealed to the imagination of all. And, finally, there was no danger to be incurred by the colossal frolic. When everybody was guilty, how was anybody to be punished?

The United States was paralyzed. No one knew what was happening. There were no newspapers, no letters, no despatches. Every community was as completely isolated as though ten thousand miles of primeval wilderness stretched between it and the rest of the world. For that matter, the world had ceased to exist. And for a week this state of affairs was maintained.

In San Francisco we did not know what was happening even across the bay in Oakland or Berkeley. The effect on one's sensibilities was weird, depressing. It seemed as though some great cosmic thing lay dead. The pulse of the land had ceased to beat. Of a truth the nation had died. There were no wagons rumbling on the streets, no factory whistles, no hum of electricity in the air, no passing of street cars, no cries of newsboys—nothing but persons who at rare intervals went by like furtive ghosts, themselves oppressed and made unreal by the silence.

And during that week of silence the Oligarchy was taught its lesson. And well it learned the lesson. The general strike was a warning. It should never occur again. The Oligarchy would see to that.

At the end of the week, as had been prearranged, the telegraphers of Germany and the United States returned to their posts. Through them the socialist leaders of both countries presented their ultimatum to the rulers. The war should be called off, or the general strike would continue. It did not take long to come to an understanding. The war was declared off, and the populations of both countries returned to their tasks.

It was this renewal of peace that brought about the alliance between Germany and the United States. In reality, this was an alliance between the Emperor and the Oligarchy, for the purpose of meeting their common foe, the revolutionary proletariat of both countries. And it was this alliance that the Oligarchy afterward so treacherously broke when the German socialists rose and drove the war-lord from his throne. It was the very thing the Oligarchy had played for—the destruction of its great rival in the world-market. With the German Emperor out of the way, Germany would have no surplus to sell abroad. By the very nature of the socialist state, the German population would consume all that it produced. Of course, it would trade abroad certain things it produced for things it did not produce; but this would be quite different from an unconsumable surplus.

"I'll wager the Oligarchy finds justification," Ernest said, when its treachery to the German Emperor became known. "As usual, the Oligarchy will believe it has done right."

And sure enough. The Oligarchy's public defence for the act was that it had done it for the sake of the American people whose interests it was looking out for. It had flung its hated rival out of the world market and enabled us to dispose of our surplus in that market.

"And the howling folly of it is that we are so helpless that such idiots really are managing our interests," was Ernest's comment. "They have enabled us to sell more abroad, which means that we'll be compelled to consume less at home."

THE BEGINNING OF THE END

As early as January, 1913, Ernest saw the true trend of affairs, but he could not get his brother leaders to see the vision of the Iron Heel that had arisen in his brain. They were too confident. Events were rushing too rapidly to culmination. A crisis had come in world affairs. The American Oligarchy was practically in possession of the world-market, and scores of countries were flung out of that market with unconsumable and unsalable surpluses on their hands. For such countries nothing remained but reorganization. They could not continue their method of producing surpluses. The capitalistic system, so far as they were concerned, had hopelessly broken down.

The reorganization of these countries took the form of revolution. It was a time of confusion and violence. Everywhere institutions and governments were crashing. Everywhere, with the exception of two or three countries, the erstwhile capitalist masters fought bitterly for their possessions. But the governments were taken away from them by the militant proletariat. At last was being realized Karl Marx's classic: "The knell of private capitalist property sounds. The expropriators are expropriated." And as fast as capitalistic governments crashed, coöperative commonwealths arose in their place.

"Why does the United States lag behind?"; "Get busy, you American revolutionists!"; "What's the matter with America?"—were the messages sent to us by our successful comrades in other lands. But we could not keep up. The Oligarchy stood in the way. Its bulk, like that of some huge monster, blocked our path.

"Wait till we take office in the spring," we answered. "Then you'll see."

Behind this lay our secret. We had won over the Grangers, and in the spring a dozen states would pass into their hands by virtue of the elections of the preceding fall. At once would be instituted a dozen coöperative commonwealth states. After that, the rest would be easy.

"But what if the Grangers fail to get possession?" Ernest demanded. And his comrades called him a calamity howler.

But this failure to get possession was not the chief danger that Ernest had in mind. What he foresaw was the defection of the great labor unions and the rise of the castes.

"Ghent has taught the oligarchs how to do it," Ernest said. "I'll wager they've made a text-book out of his 'Benevolent Feudalism.' " [22]

Never shall I forget the night when, after a hot discussion with half a dozen labor leaders, Ernest turned to me and said quietly: "That settles it. The Iron Heel has won. The end is in sight."

This little conference in our home was unofficial; but Ernest, like the rest of his comrades, was working for assurances from the labor leaders that they would call out their men in the next general strike. O'Connor, the president of the Association of Machinists, had been foremost of the six leaders present in refusing to give such assurance.

"You have seen that you were beaten soundly at your old tactics of strike and boycott," Ernest urged.

O'Connor and the others nodded their heads.

"And you saw what a general strike would do," Ernest went on. "We stopped the war with Germany. Never was there so fine a display of the solidarity and the power of labor. Labor can and will rule the world. If you continue to stand with us, we'll put an end to the reign of capitalism. It is your only hope. And what is more, you know it. There is no other way out. No matter what you do under your old tactics, you are doomed to defeat, if for no other reason because the masters control the courts." [23]

[22] "Our Benevolent Feudalism," a book published in 1902 A.D., by W. J. Ghent. It has always been insisted that Ghent put the idea of the Oligarchy into the minds of the great capitalists. This belief persists throughout the literature of the three centuries of the Iron Heel, and even in the literature of the first century of the Brotherhood of Man. To-day we know better, but our knowledge does not overcome the fact that Ghent remains the most abused innocent man in all history.

[23] As a sample of the decisions of the courts adverse to labor, the following instances are given. In the coal-mining regions the employment of children was notorious. In 1905 A.D., labor succeeded in getting a law passed in Pennsylvania providing that proof of the age of the child and of certain educational qualifications must accompany the oath of the parent. This was promptly declared unconstitutional by the Luzerne County Court, on the ground that it violated the Fourteenth Amendment in that it discriminated between individuals of the same class—namely, children above fourteen years of age and children below. The state court sustained the decision. The New York Court of

"You run ahead too fast," O'Connor answered. "You don't know all the ways out. There is another way out. We know what we're about. We're sick of strikes. They've got us beaten that way to a frazzle. But I don't think we'll ever need to call our men out again."

"What is your way out?" Ernest demanded bluntly.

O'Connor laughed and shook his head. "I can tell you this much: We've not been asleep. And we're not dreaming now."

"There's nothing to be afraid of, or ashamed of, I hope," Ernest challenged.

"I guess we know our business best," was the retort.

"It's a dark business, from the way you hide it," Ernest said with growing anger.

"We've paid for our experience in sweat and blood, and we've earned all that's coming to us," was the reply. "Charity begins at home."

"If you're afraid to tell me your way out, I'll tell it to you." Ernest's blood was up. "You're going in for grab-sharing. You've made terms with the enemy, that's what you've done. You've sold out the cause of labor, of all labor. You are leaving the battle-field like cowards."

"I'm not saying anything," O'Connor answered sullenly. "Only I guess we know what's best for us a little bit better than you do."

"And you don't care a cent for what is best for the rest of labor. You kick it into the ditch."

"I'm not saying anything," O'Connor replied, "except that I'm president of the Machinists' Association, and it's my business to consider the interests of the men I represent, that's all."

And then, when the labor leaders had left, Ernest, with the calmness of defeat, outlined to me the course of events to come.

"The socialists used to foretell with joy," he said, "the coming of the day when organized labor, defeated on the industrial field, would come over on to the political field. Well, the Iron Heel has defeated the labor unions on the industrial field and driven them over to the

Special Sessions, in 1905 A.D., declared unconstitutional the law prohibiting minors and women from working in factories after nine o'clock at night, the ground taken being that such a law was "class legislation." Again, the bakers of that time were terribly overworked. The New York Legislature passed a law restricting work in bakeries to ten hours a day. In 1906 A.D., the Supreme Court of the United States declared this law to be unconstitutional. In part the decision read: *"There is no reasonable ground for interfering with the liberty of persons or the right of free contract by determining the hours of labor in the occupation of a baker."*

political field; and instead of this being joyful for us, it will be a source of grief. The Iron Heel learned its lesson. We showed it our power in the general strike. It has taken steps to prevent another general strike."

"But how?" I asked.

"Simply by subsidizing the great unions. They won't join in the next general strike. Therefore it won't be a general strike."

"But the Iron Heel can't maintain so costly a programme forever," I objected.

"Oh, it hasn't subsidized all of the unions. That's not necessary. Here is what is going to happen. Wages are going to be advanced and hours shortened in the railroad unions, the iron and steel workers unions, and the engineer and machinist unions. In these unions more favorable conditions will continue to prevail. Membership in these unions will become like seats in Paradise."

"Still I don't see," I objected. "What is to become of the other unions? There are far more unions outside of this combination than in it."

"The other unions will be ground out of existence—all of them. For, don't you see, the railway men, machinists and engineers, iron and steel workers, do all of the vitally essential work in our machine civilization. Assured of their faithfulness, the Iron Heel can snap its fingers at all the rest of labor. Iron, steel, coal, machinery, and transportation constitute the backbone of the whole industrial fabric."

"But coal?" I queried. "There are nearly a million coal miners."

"They are practically unskilled labor. They will not count. Their wages will go down and their hours will increase. They will be slaves like all the rest of us, and they will become about the most bestial of all of us. They will be compelled to work, just as the farmers are compelled to work now for the masters who robbed them of their land. And the same with all the other unions outside the combination. Watch them wobble and go to pieces, and their members become slaves driven to toil by empty stomachs and the law of the land.

"Do you know what will happen to Farley [24] and his strike-breakers? I'll tell you. Strike-breaking as an occupation will cease. There

[24] James Farley—a notorious strike-breaker of the period. A man more courageous than ethical, and of undeniable ability. He rose high under the rule of the Iron Heel and finally was translated into the oligarch class. He was assassinated in 1932 by Sarah Jenkins, whose husband, thirty years before, had been killed by Farley's strike-breakers.

won't be any more strikes. In place of strikes will be slave revolts. Farley and his gang will be promoted to slave-driving. Oh, it won't be
called that; it will be called enforcing the law of the land that compels
the laborers to work. It simply prolongs the fight, this treachery of the
big unions. Heaven only knows now where and when the Revolution
will triumph."

"But with such a powerful combination as the Oligarchy and the
big unions, is there any reason to believe that the Revolution will
ever triumph?" I queried. "May not the combination endure forever?"

He shook his head. "One of our generalizations is that every system founded upon class and caste contains within itself the germs of
its own decay. When a system is founded upon class, how can caste
be prevented? The Iron Heel will not be able to prevent it, and in the
end caste will destroy the Iron Heel. The oligarchs have already
developed caste among themselves; but wait until the favored unions
develop caste. The Iron Heel will use all its power to prevent it, but
it will fail.

"In the favored unions are the flower of the American workingmen.
They are strong, efficient men. They have become members of those
unions through competition for place. Every fit workman in the
United States will be possessed by the ambition to become a member
of the favored unions. The Oligarchy will encourage such ambition
and the consequent competition. Thus will the strong men, who might
else be revolutionists, be won away and their strength used to bolster
the Oligarchy.

"On the other hand, the labor castes, the members of the favored
unions, will strive to make their organizations into close corporations.
And they will succeed. Membership in the labor castes will become
hereditary. Sons will succeed fathers, and there will be no inflow of
new strength from that eternal reservoir of strength, the common
people. This will mean deterioration of the labor castes, and in the
end they will become weaker and weaker. At the same time, as an
institution, they will become temporarily all-powerful. They will be
like the guards of the palace in old Rome, and there will be palace
revolutions whereby the labor castes will seize the reins of power.
And there will be counter-palace revolutions of the oligarchs, and
sometimes the one, and sometimes the other, will be in power. And
through it all the inevitable caste-weakening will go on, so that in the
end the common people will come into their own."

This foreshadowing of a slow social evolution was made when Ernest was first depressed by the defection of the great unions. I never agreed with him in it, and I disagree now, as I write these lines, more heartily than ever; for even now, though Ernest is gone, we are on the verge of the revolt that will sweep all oligarchies away. Yet I have here given Ernest's prophecy because it was his prophecy. In spite of his belief in it, he worked like a giant against it, and he, more than any man, has made possible the revolt that even now waits the signal to burst forth.[25]

"But if the Oligarchy persists," I asked him that evening, "what will become of the great surpluses that will fall to its share every year?"

"The surpluses will have to be expended somehow," he answered; "and trust the oligarchs to find a way. Magnificent roads will be built. There will be great achievements in science, and especially in art. When the oligarchs have completely mastered the people, they will have time to spare for other things. They will become worshippers of beauty. They will become art-lovers. And under their direction, and generously rewarded, will toil the artists. The result will be great art; for no longer, as up to yesterday, will the artists pander to the bourgeois taste of the middle class. It will be great art, I tell you, and wonder cities will arise that will make tawdry and cheap the cities of old time. And in these cities will the oligarchs dwell and worship beauty.[26]

"Thus will the surplus be constantly expended while labor does the work. The building of these great works and cities will give a starvation ration to millions of common laborers, for the enormous bulk of the surplus will compel an equally enormous expenditure, and the oligarchs will build for a thousand years—ay, for ten thousand years. They will build as the Egyptians and the Babylonians never dreamed of building; and when the oligarchs have passed away, their great roads and their wonder cities will remain for the brotherhood of labor to tread upon and dwell within.[27]

[25] Everhard's social foresight was remarkable. As clearly as in the light of past events, he saw the defection of the favored unions, the rise and the slow decay of the labor castes, and the struggle between the decaying oligarchs and labor castes for control of the great governmental machine.

[26] We cannot but marvel at Everhard's foresight. Before ever the thought of wonder cities like Ardis and Asgard entered the minds of the oligarchs, Everhard saw those cities and the inevitable necessity for their creation.

[27] And since that day of prophecy, have passed away the three centuries of

"These things the oligarchs will do because they cannot help doing them. These great works will be the form their expenditure of the surplus will take, and in the same way that the ruling classes of Egypt of long ago expended the surplus they robbed from the people by the building of temples and pyramids. Under the oligarchs will flourish, not a priest class, but an artist class. And in place of the merchant class of bourgeoisie will be the labor castes. And beneath will be the abyss, wherein will fester and starve and rot, and ever renew itself, the common people, the great bulk of the population. And in the end, who knows in what day, the common people will rise up out of the abyss; the labor castes and the Oligarchy will crumble away; and then, at last, after the travail of the centuries, will it be the day of the common man. I had thought to see that day; but now I know that I shall never see it."

He paused and looked at me, and added:

"Social evolution is exasperatingly slow, isn't it, sweetheart?"

My arms were about him, and his head was on my breast.

"Sing me to sleep," he murmured whimsically. "I have had a visioning, and I wish to forget."

LAST DAYS

It was near the end of January, 1913, that the changed attitude of the Oligarchy toward the favored unions was made public. The newspapers published information of an unprecedented rise in wages and shortening of hours for the railroad employees, the iron and steel workers, and the engineers and machinists. But the whole truth was not told. The oligarchs did not dare permit the telling of the whole truth. In reality, the wages had been raised much higher, and the privileges were correspondingly greater. All this was secret, but secrets will out. Members of the favored unions told their wives, and the wives gossiped, and soon all the labor world knew what had happened.

It was merely the logical development of what in the nineteenth century had been known as grab-sharing. In the industrial warfare of

---

the Iron Heel and the four centuries of the Brotherhood of Man, and to-day we tread the roads and dwell in the cities that the oligarchs built. It is true, we are even now building still more wonderful wonder cities, but the wonder cities of the oligarchs endure, and I write these lines in Ardis, one of the most wonderful of them all.

that time, profit-sharing had been tried. That is, the capitalists had
striven to placate the workers by interesting them financially in their
work. But profit-sharing, as a system, was ridiculous and impossible.
Profit-sharing could be successful only in isolated cases in the midst
of a system of industrial strife; for if all labor and all capital shared
profits, the same conditions would obtain as did obtain when there
was no profit-sharing.

So, out of the unpractical idea of profit-sharing, arose the practical
idea of grab-sharing. "Give us more pay and charge it to the public,"
was the slogan of the strong unions. And here and there this selfish
policy worked successfully. In charging it to the public, it was
charged to the great mass of unorganized labor and of weakly organized labor. These workers actually paid the increased wages of
their stronger brothers who were members of unions that were labor
monopolies. This idea, as I say, was merely carried to its logical conclusion, on a large scale, by the combination of the oligarchs and the
favored unions.[28]

As soon as the secret of the defection of the favored unions leaked
out, there were rumblings and mutterings in the labor world. Next,
the favored unions withdrew from the international organizations and
broke off all affiliations. Then came trouble and violence. The members of the favored unions were branded as traitors, and in saloons
and brothels, on the streets and at work, and, in fact, everywhere,
they were assaulted by the comrades they had so treacherously deserted.

Countless heads were broken, and there were many killed. No
member of the favored unions was safe. They gathered together in
bands in order to go to work or to return from work. They walked
always in the middle of the street. On the sidewalk they were liable

---

[28] All the railroad unions entered into this combination with the oligarchs,
and it is of interest to note that the first definite application of the policy of
profit-grabbing was made by a railroad union in the nineteenth century A.D.,
namely, the Brotherhood of Locomotive Engineers. P. M. Arthur was for
twenty years Grand Chief of the Brotherhood. After the strike on the Pennsylvania Railroad in 1877, he broached a scheme to have the Locomotive Engineers make terms with the railroads and to "go it alone" so far as the rest of
the labor unions were concerned. This scheme was eminently successful. It
was as successful as it was selfish, and out of it was coined the word "arthuriza-
tion," to denote grab-sharing on the part of labor unions. This word "arthuriza-
tion" has long puzzled the etymologists, but its derivation, I hope, is now made
clear.

to have their skulls crushed by bricks and cobblestones thrown from windows and house-tops. They were permitted to carry weapons, and the authorities aided them in every way. Their persecutors were sentenced to long terms in prison, where they were harshly treated; while no man, not a member of the favored unions, was permitted to carry weapons. Violation of this law was made a high misdemeanor and punished accordingly.

Outraged labor continued to wreak vengeance on the traitors. Caste lines formed automatically. The children of the traitors were persecuted by the children of the workers who had been betrayed, until it was impossible for the former to play on the streets or to attend the public schools. Also, the wives and families of the traitors were ostracized, while the corner groceryman who sold provisions to them was boycotted.

As a result, driven back upon themselves from every side, the traitors and their families became clannish. Finding it impossible to dwell in safety in the midst of the betrayed proletariat, they moved into new localities inhabited by themselves alone. In this they were favored by the oligarchs. Good dwellings, modern and sanitary, were built for them, surrounded by spacious yards, and separated here and there by parks and playgrounds. Their children attended schools especially built for them, and in these schools manual training and applied science were specialized upon. Thus, and unavoidably, at the very beginning, out of this segregation arose caste. The members of the favored unions became the aristocracy of labor. They were set apart from the rest of labor. They were better housed, better clothed, better fed, better treated. They were grab-sharing with a vengeance.

In the meantime, the rest of the working class was more harshly treated. Many little privileges were taken away from it, while its wages and its standard of living steadily sank down. Incidentally, its public schools deteriorated, and education slowly ceased to be compulsory. The increase in the younger generation of children who could not read nor write was perilous.

The capture of the world-market by the United States had disrupted the rest of the world. Institutions and governments were everywhere crashing or transforming. Germany, Italy, France, Australia, and New Zealand were busy forming coöperative commonwealths. The British Empire was falling apart. England's hands were full. In India revolt was in full swing. The cry in all Asia was, "Asia for the Asiatics!" And behind this cry was Japan, ever urging and

aiding the yellow and brown races against the white. And while Japan
dreamed of continental empire and strove to realize the dream, she
suppressed her own proletarian revolution. It was a simple war of the
castes, Coolie *versus* Samurai, and the coolie socialists were executed
by tens of thousands. Forty thousand were killed in the street-
fighting of Tokio and in the futile assault on the Mikado's palace.
Kobe was a shambles; the slaughter of the cotton operatives by
machine-guns became classic as the most terrific execution ever
achieved by modern war machines. Most savage of all was the Japanese Oligarchy that arose. Japan dominated the East, and took to
herself the whole Asiatic portion of the world-market, with the exception of India.

England managed to crush her own proletarian revolution and to
hold on to India, though she was brought to the verge of exhaustion.
Also, she was compelled to let her great colonies slip away from her.
So it was that the socialists succeeded in making Australia and New
Zealand into coöperative commonwealths. And it was for the same
reason that Canada was lost to the mother country. But Canada
crushed her own socialist revolution, being aided in this by the Iron
Heel. At the same time, the Iron Heel helped Mexico and Cuba to
put down revolt. The result was that the Iron Heel was firmly established in the New World. It had welded into one compact political
mass the whole of North America from the Panama Canal to the
Arctic Ocean.

And England, at the sacrifice of her great colonies, had succeeded
only in retaining India. But this was no more than temporary. The
struggle with Japan and the rest of Asia for India was merely delayed. England was destined shortly to lose India, while behind that
event loomed the struggle between a united Asia and the world.

And while all the world was torn with conflict, we of the United
States were not placid and peaceful. The defection of the great unions
had prevented our proletarian revolt, but violence was everywhere.
In addition to the labor troubles, and the discontent of the farmers
and of the remnant of the middle class, a religious revival had blazed
up. An offshoot of the Seventh Day Adventists sprang into sudden
prominence, proclaiming the end of the world.

"Confusion thrice confounded!" Ernest cried. "How can we hope
for solidarity with all these cross purposes and conflicts?"

And truly the religious revival assumed formidable proportions.
The people, what of their wretchedness, and of their disappointment

in all things earthly, were ripe and eager for a heaven where industrial
tyrants entered no more than camels passed through needle-eyes.
Wild-eyed itinerant preachers swarmed over the land; and despite the
prohibition of the civil authorities, and the persecution for disobedi-
ence, the flames of religious frenzy were fanned by countless camp-
meetings.

It was the last days, they claimed, the beginning of the end of the
world. The four winds had been loosed. God had stirred the nations
to strife. It was a time of visions and miracles, while seers and proph-
etesses were legion. The people ceased work by hundreds of thousands
and fled to the mountains, there to await the imminent coming of
God and the rising of the hundred and forty and four thousand to
heaven. But in the meantime God did not come, and they starved to
death in great numbers. In their desperation they ravaged the farms
for food, and the consequent tumult and anarchy in the country districts but increased the woes of the poor expropriated farmers.

Also, the farms and warehouses were the property of the Iron Heel.
Armies of troops were put into the field, and the fanatics were herded
back at the bayonet point to their tasks in the cities. There they broke
out in ever recurring mobs and riots. Their leaders were executed for
sedition or confined in madhouses. Those who were executed went to
their deaths with all the gladness of martyrs. It was a time of madness.
The unrest spread. In the swamps and deserts and waste places, from
Florida to Alaska, the small groups of Indians that survived were
dancing ghost dances and waiting the coming of a Messiah of their
own.

And through it all, with a serenity and certitude that was terrifying, continued to rise the form of that monster of the ages, the Oligarchy. With iron hand and iron heel it mastered the surging millions,
out of confusion brought order, out of the very chaos wrought its own
foundation and structure.

"Just wait till we get in," the Grangers said—Calvin said it to us
in our Pell Street quarters. "Look at the states we've captured. With
you socialists to back us, we'll make them sing another song when we
take office."

"The millions of the discontented and the impoverished are ours,"
the socialists said. "The Grangers have come over to us, the farmers,
the middle class, and the laborers. The capitalist system will fall to
pieces. In another month we send fifty men to Congress. Two years

hence every office will be ours, from the President down to the local dog-catcher."

To all of which Ernest would shake his head and say:

"How many rifles have you got? Do you know where you can get plenty of lead? When it comes to powder, chemical mixtures are better than mechanical mixtures, you take my word."

THE END

When it came time for Ernest and me to go to Washington, father did not accompany us. He had become enamoured of proletarian life. He looked upon our slum neighborhood as a great sociological laboratory, and he had embarked upon an apparently endless orgy of investigation. He chummed with the laborers, and was an intimate in scores of homes. Also, he worked at odd jobs, and the work was play as well as learned investigation, for he delighted in it and was always returning home with copious notes and bubbling over with new adventures. He was the perfect scientist. . . .

And so it was that father kept on at our Pell Street quarters, while Ernest and I went to Washington. Except for the final consummation, the old order had passed away, and the final consummation was nearer than I dreamed. Contrary to our expectation, no obstacles were raised to prevent the socialist Congressmen from taking their seats. Everything went smoothly, and I laughed at Ernest when he looked upon the very smoothness as something ominous.

We found our socialist comrades confident, optimistic of their strength and of the things they would accomplish. A few Grangers who had been elected to Congress increased our strength, and an elaborate programme of what was to be done was prepared by the united forces. In all of which Ernest joined loyally and energetically, though he could not forbear, now and again, from saying, apropos of nothing in particular, "When it comes to powder, chemical mixtures are better than mechanical mixtures, you take my word."

The trouble arose first with the Grangers in the various states they had captured at the last election. There were a dozen of these states, but the Grangers who had been elected were not permitted to take office. The incumbents refused to get out. It was very simple. They merely charged illegality in the elections and wrapped up the whole situation in the interminable red tape of the law. The Grangers were powerless. The courts were the last recourse, and the courts were in the hands of their enemies.

This was the moment of danger. If the cheated Grangers became violent, all was lost. How we socialists worked to hold them back! There were days and nights when Ernest never closed his eyes in sleep. The big leaders of the Grangers saw the peril and were with us to a man. But it was all of no avail. The Oligarchy wanted violence, and it set its agents-provocateurs to work. Without discussion, it was the agents-provocateurs who caused the Peasant Revolt.

In a dozen states the revolt flared up. The expropriated farmers took forcible possession of the state governments. Of course this was unconstitutional, and of course the United States put its soldiers into the field. Everywhere the agents-provocateurs urged the people on. These emissaries of the Iron Heel disguised themselves as artisans, farmers, and farm laborers. In Sacramento, the capital of California, the Grangers had succeeded in maintaining order. Thousands of secret agents were rushed to the devoted city. In mobs composed wholly of themselves, they fired and looted buildings and factories. They worked the people up until they joined them in the pillage. Liquor in large quantities was distributed among the slum classes further to inflame their minds. And then, when all was ready, appeared upon the scene the soldiers of the United States, who were, in reality, the soldiers of the Iron Heel. Eleven thousand men, women, and children were shot down on the streets of Sacramento or murdered in their houses. The national government took possession of the state government, and all was over for California.

And as with California, so elsewhere. Every Granger state was ravaged with violence and washed in blood. First, disorder was precipitated by the secret agents and the Black Hundreds, then the troops were called out. Rioting and mob-rule reigned throughout the rural districts. Day and night the smoke of burning farms, warehouses, villages, and cities filled the sky. Dynamite appeared. Railroad bridges and tunnels were blown up and trains were wrecked. The poor farmers were shot and hanged in great numbers. Reprisals were bitter, and many plutocrats and army officers were murdered. Blood and vengeance were in men's hearts. The regular troops fought the farmers as savagely as had they been Indians. And the regular troops had cause. Twenty-eight hundred of them had been annihilated in a tremendous series of dynamite explosions in Oregon, and in a similar manner, a number of train loads, at different times and places, had been destroyed. So it was that the regular troops fought for their lives as well as did the farmers.

As for the militia, the militia law of 1903 was put into effect, and the workers of one state were compelled, under pain of death, to shoot down their comrade-workers in other states. Of course, the militia law did not work smoothly at first. Many militia officers were murdered, and many militiamen were executed by drumhead court martial. Ernest's prophecy was strikingly fulfilled in the cases of Mr. Kowalt and Mr. Asmunsen. Both were eligible for the militia, and both were drafted to serve in the punitive expedition that was despatched from California against the farmers of Missouri. Mr. Kowalt and Mr. Asmunsen refused to serve. They were given short shrift. Drumhead court martial was their portion, and military execution their end. They were shot with their backs to the firing squad.

Many young men fled into the mountains to escape serving in the militia. There they became outlaws, and it was not until more peaceful times that they received their punishment. It was drastic. The government issued a proclamation for all law-abiding citizens to come in from the mountains for a period of three months. When the proclaimed date arrived, half a million soldiers were sent into the mountainous districts everywhere. There was no investigation, no trial. Wherever a man was encountered, he was shot down on the spot. The troops operated on the basis that no man not an outlaw remained in the mountains. Some bands, in strong positions, fought gallantly, but in the end every deserter from the militia met death.

A more immediate lesson, however, was impressed on the minds of the people by the punishment meted out to the Kansas militia. The great Kansas Mutiny occurred at the very beginning of military operations against the Grangers. Six thousand of the militia mutinied. They had been for several weeks very turbulent and sullen, and for that reason had been kept in camp. Their open mutiny, however, was without doubt precipitated by the agents-provocateurs.

On the night of the 22d of April they arose and murdered their officers, only a small remnant of the latter escaping. This was beyond the scheme of the Iron Heel, for the agents-provocateurs had done their work too well. But everything was grist to the Iron Heel. It had prepared for the outbreak, and the killing of so many officers gave it justification for what followed. As by magic, forty thousand soldiers of the regular army surrounded the malcontents. It was a trap. The wretched militiamen found that their machine-guns had been tam-

pered with, and that the cartridges from the captured magazines did
not fit their rifles. They hoisted the white flag of surrender, but it was
ignored. There were no survivors. The entire six thousand were annihilated. Common shell and shrapnel were thrown in upon them
from a distance, and, when, in their desperation, they charged the
encircling lines, they were mowed down by the machine-guns. I talked
with an eye-witness, and he said that the nearest any militiaman approached the machine-guns was a hundred and fifty yards. The earth
was carpeted with the slain, and a final charge of cavalry, with tram-
pling of horses' hoofs, revolvers, and sabres, crushed the wounded
into the ground.

Simultaneously with the destruction of the Grangers came the
revolt of the coal miners. It was the expiring effort of organized labor.
Three-quarters of a million of miners went out on strike. But they
were too widely scattered over the country to advantage from their
own strength. They were segregated in their own districts and beaten
into submission. This was the first great slave-drive. Pocock [29] won
his spurs as a slave-driver and earned the undying hatred of the proletariat. Countless attempts were made upon his life, but he seemed to
bear a charmed existence. It was he who was responsible for the introduction of the Russian passport system among the miners, and
the denial of their right of removal from one part of the country to
another.

In the meantime, the socialists held firm. While the Grangers ex-
pired in flame and blood, and organized labor was disrupted, the socialists held their peace and perfected their secret organization. In
vain the Grangers pleaded with us. We rightly contended that any
revolt on our part was virtually suicide for the whole Revolution. The
Iron Heel, at first dubious about dealing with the entire proletariat

[29] Albert Pocock, another of the notorious strike-breakers of earlier years,
who, to the day of his death, successfully held all the coalminers of the country
to their task. He was succeeded by his son, Lewis Pocock, and for five generations this remarkable line of slave-drivers handled the coal mines. The elder Pocock, known as Pocock I., has been described as follows: "A long, lean head,
semicircled by a fringe of brown and gray hair, with big cheek-bones and a
heavy chin, . . . a pale face, lustreless gray eyes, a metallic voice, and a languid
manner." He was born of humble parents, and began his career as a bartender.
He next became a private detective for a street railway corporation, and by
successive steps developed into a professional strike-breaker. Pocock V., the
last of the line, was blown up in a pumphouse by a bomb during a petty revolt
of the miners in the Indian Territory. This occurred in 2073 A.D.

at one time, had found the work easier than it had expected, and would have asked nothing better than an uprising on our part. But we avoided the issue, in spite of the fact that agents-provocateurs swarmed in our midst. In those early days, the agents of the Iron Heel were clumsy in their methods. They had much to learn and in the meantime our Fighting Groups weeded them out. It was bitter, bloody work, but we were fighting for life and for the Revolution, and we had to fight the enemy with its own weapons. Yet we were fair. No agent of the Iron Heel was executed without a trial. We may have made mistakes, but if so, very rarely. The bravest, and the most combative and self-sacrificing of our comrades went into the Fighting Groups. Once, after ten years had passed, Ernest made a calculation from figures furnished by the chiefs of the Fighting Groups, and his conclusion was that the average life of a man or woman after becoming a member was five years. The comrades of the Fighting Groups were heroes all, and the peculiar thing about it was that they were opposed to the taking of life. They violated their own natures, yet they loved liberty and knew of no sacrifice too great to make for the Cause.[30]

[30] These Fighting groups were modelled somewhat after the Fighting Organization of the Russian Revolution, and, despite the unceasing efforts of the Iron Heel, these groups persisted throughout the three centuries of its existence. Composed of men and women actuated by lofty purpose and unafraid to die, the Fighting Groups exercised tremendous influence and tempered the savage brutality of the rulers. Not alone was their work confined to unseen warfare with the secret agents of the Oligarchy. The oligarchs themselves were compelled to listen to the decrees of the Groups, and often, when they disobeyed, were punished by death—and likewise with the subordinates of the oligarchs, with the officers of the army and the leaders of the labor castes.

Stern justice was meted out by these organized avengers, but most remarkable was their passionless and judicial procedure. There were no snap judgments. When a man was captured he was given fair trial and opportunity for defence. Of necessity, many men were tried and condemned by proxy, as in the case of General Lampton. This occurred in 2138 A.D. Possibly the most bloodthirsty and malignant of all the mercenaries that ever served the Iron Heel, he was informed by the Fighting Groups that they had tried him, found him guilty, and condemned him to death—and this, after three warnings for him to cease from his ferocious treatment of the proletariat. After his condemnation he surrounded himself with a myriad protective devices. Years passed, and in vain the Fighting Groups strove to execute their decree. Comrade after comrade, men and women, failed in their attempts, and were cruelly executed by the Oligarchy. It was the case of General Lampton that revived crucifixion as a legal method of execution. But in the end the condemned man found his executioner in the form of a slender girl of seventeen, Madeline Pro-

The task we set ourselves was threefold. First, the weeding out from our circles of the secret agents of the Oligarchy. Second, the organizing of the Fighting Groups, and, outside of them, of the general secret organization of the Revolution. And third, the introduction of our own secret agents into every branch of the Oligarchy—into the labor castes and especially among the telegraphers and secretaries and clerks, into the army, the agents-provocateurs, and the slave-drivers. It was slow work, and perilous, and often were our efforts rewarded with costly failures.

The Iron Heel had triumphed in open warfare, but we held our own in the new warfare, strange and awful and subterranean, that we instituted. All was unseen, much was unguessed; the blind fought the blind; and yet through it all was order, purpose, control. We permeated the entire organization of the Iron Heel with our agents, while our own organization was permeated with the agents of the Iron Heel. It was warfare dark and devious, replete with intrigue and conspiracy, plot and counterplot. And behind all, ever menacing, was death, violent and terrible. Men and women disappeared, our nearest and dearest comrades. We saw them to-day. To-morrow they were gone; we never saw them again, and we knew that they had died.

There was no trust, no confidence anywhere. The man who plotted beside us, for all we knew, might be an agent of the Iron Heel. We mined the organization of the Iron Heel with our secret agents, and the Iron Heel countermined with its secret agents inside its own organization. And it was the same with our organization. And despite

---

vence, who, to accomplish her purpose, served two years in his palace as a seamstress to the household. She died in solitary confinement after horrible and prolonged torture; but to-day she stands in imperishable bronze in the Pantheon of Brotherhood in the wonder city of Serles.

We, who by personal experience know nothing of bloodshed, must not judge harshly the heroes of the Fighting Groups. They gave up their lives for humanity, no sacrifice was too great for them to accomplish, while inexorable necessity compelled them to bloody expression in an age of blood. The Fighting Groups constituted the one thorn in the side of the Iron Heel that the Iron Heel could never remove. Everhard was the father of this curious army, and its accomplishments and successful persistence for three hundred years bear witness to the wisdom with which he organized and the solid foundation he laid for the succeeding generations to build upon. In some respects, despite his great economic and sociological contributions, and his work as a general leader in the Revolution, his organization of the Fighting Groups must be regarded as his greatest achievement.

the absence of confidence and trust we were compelled to base our every effort on confidence and trust. Often were we betrayed. Men were weak. The Iron Heel could offer money, leisure, the joys and pleasures that waited in the repose of the wonder cities. We could offer nothing but the satisfaction of being faithful to a noble ideal. As for the rest, the wages of those who were loyal were unceasing peril, torture, and death.

Men were weak, I say, and because of their weakness we were compelled to make the only other reward that was within our power. It was the reward of death. Out of necessity we had to punish our traitors. For every man who betrayed us, from one to a dozen faithful avengers were loosed upon his heels. We might fail to carry out our decrees against our enemies, such as the Pococks, for instance; but the one thing we could not afford to fail in was the punishment of our own traitors. Comrades turned traitor by permission, in order to win to the wonder cities and there execute our sentences on the real traitors. In fact, so terrible did we make ourselves, that it became a greater peril to betray us than to remain loyal to us.

The Revolution took on largely the character of religion. We worshipped at the shrine of the Revolution, which was the shrine of liberty. It was the divine flashing through us. Men and women devoted their lives to the Cause, and new-born babes were sealed to it as of old they had been sealed to the service of God. We were lovers of Humanity.

THE SCARLET LIVERY

With the destruction of the Granger states, the Grangers in Congress disappeared. They were being tried for high treason, and their places were taken by the creatures of the Iron Heel. The socialists were in a pitiful minority, and they knew that their end was near. Congress and the Senate were empty pretences, farces. Public questions were gravely debated and passed upon according to the old forms, while in reality all that was done was to give the stamp of constitutional procedure to the mandates of the Oligarchy.

Ernest was in the thick of the fight when the end came. It was in the debate on the bill to assist the unemployed. The hard times of the preceding year had thrust great masses of the proletariat beneath the starvation line, and the continued and wide-reaching disorder had but sunk them deeper. Millions of people were starving, while the oli-

garchs and their supporters were surfeiting on the surplus.[31] We called
these wretched people the people of the abyss,[32] and it was to alleviate
their awful suffering that the socialists had introduced the unemployed
bill. But this was not to the fancy of the Iron Heel. In its own way
it was preparing to set these millions to work, but the way was not our
way, wherefore it had issued its orders that our bill should be voted
down. Ernest and his fellows knew that their effort was futile, but
they were tired of the suspense. They wanted something to happen.
They were accomplishing nothing, and the best they hoped for was
the putting of an end to the legislative farce in which they were un-
willing players. They knew not what end would come, but they never
anticipated a more disastrous end than the one that did come.

I sat in the gallery that day. We all knew that something terrible
was imminent. It was in the air, and its presence was made visible by
the armed soldiers drawn up in lines in the corridors, and by the officers grouped in the entrances to the House itself. The Oligarchy was
about to strike. Ernest was speaking. He was describing the suffer-
ings of the unemployed, as if with the wild idea of in some way touching their hearts and consciences; but the Republican and Democratic
members sneered and jeered at him, and there was uproar and confusion. Ernest abruptly changed front.

"I know nothing that I may say can influence you," he said. "You
have no souls to be influenced. You are spineless, flaccid things. You
pompously call yourselves Republicans and Democrats. There is no
Republican Party. There is no Democratic Party. There are no Republicans nor Democrats in this House. You are lick-spittlers and

[31] The same conditions obtained in the nineteenth century A.D., under British
rule in India. The natives died of starvation by the million, while their rulers
robbed them of the fruits of their toil and expended it on magnificent pageants
and mumbo-jumbo fooleries. Perforce, in this enlightened age, we have much to
blush for in the acts of our ancestors. Our only consolation is philosophic. We
must accept the capitalistic stage in social evolution as about on a par with the
earlier monkey stage. The human had to pass through those stages in its rise
from the mire and slime of low organic life. It was inevitable that much of the
mire and slime should cling and be not easily shaken off.

[32] *The people of the abyss*—this phrase was struck out by the genius of
H. G. Wells in the late nineteenth century A.D. Wells was a sociological seer,
sane and normal as well as warm human. Many fragments of his work have
come down to us, while two of his greatest achievements, "Anticipations" and
"Mankind in the Making," have come down intact. Before the oligarchs, and
before Everhard, Wells speculated upon the building of the wonder cities,
though in his writings they are referred to as "pleasure cities."

panderers, the creatures of the Plutocracy. You talk verbosely in antiquated terminology of your love of liberty, and all the while you wear the scarlet livery of the Iron Heel."

Here the shouting and the cries of "Order! order!" drowned his voice, and he stood disdainfully till the din had somewhat subsided. He waved his hand to include all of them, turned to his own comrades, and said:

"Listen to the bellowing of the well-fed beasts."

Pandemonium broke out again. The Speaker rapped for order and glanced expectantly at the officers in the doorways. There were cries of "Sedition!" and a great, rotund New York member began shouting "Anarchist!" at Ernest. And Ernest was not pleasant to look at. Every fighting fibre of him was quivering, and his face was the face of a fighting animal, withal he was cool and collected.

"Remember," he said, in a voice that made itself heard above the din, "that as you show mercy now to the proletariat, some day will that same proletariat show mercy to you."

The cries of "Sedition!" and "Anarchist!" redoubled.

"I know that you will not vote for this bill," Ernest went on. "You have received the command from your masters to vote against it. And yet you call me anarchist. You, who have destroyed the government of the people, and who shamelessly flaunt your scarlet shame in public places, call me anarchist. I do not believe in hell-fire and brimstone; but in moments like this I regret my unbelief. Nay, in moments like this I almost do believe. Surely there must be a hell, for in no less place could it be possible for you to receive punishment adequate to your crimes. So long as you exist, there is a vital need for hell-fire in the Cosmos."

There was movement in the doorways. Ernest, the Speaker, all the members turned to see.

"Why do you not call your soldiers in, Mr. Speaker, and bid them do their work?" Ernest demanded. "They should carry out your plan with expedition."

"There are other plans afoot," was the retort. "That is why the soldiers are present."

"Our plans, I suppose," Ernest sneered. "Assassination or something kindred."

But at the word "assassination" the uproar broke out again. Ernest could not make himself heard, but he remained on his feet waiting for a lull. And then it happened. From my place in the gallery I saw noth-

ing except the flash of the explosion. The roar of it filled my ears and
I saw Ernest reeling and falling in a swirl of smoke, and the soldiers
rushing up all the aisles. His comrades were on their feet, wild with
anger, capable of any violence. But Ernest steadied himself for a moment, and waved his arms for silence.

"It is a plot!" his voice rang out in warning to his comrades. "Do
nothing, or you will be destroyed."

Then he slowly sank down, and the soldiers reached him. The next
moment soldiers were clearing the galleries and I saw no more.

Though he was my husband, I was not permitted to get to him.
When I announced who I was, I was promptly placed under arrest.
And at the same time were arrested all socialist Congressmen in
Washington, including the unfortunate Simpson, who lay ill with
typhoid fever in his hotel.

The trial was prompt and brief. The men were foredoomed. The
wonder was that Ernest was not executed. This was a blunder on the
part of the Oligarchy, and a costly one. But the Oligarchy was too confident in those days. It was drunk with success, and little did it dream
that that small handful of heroes had within them the power to rock
it to its foundations. To-morrow, when the Great Revolt breaks out
and all the world resounds with the tramp, tramp of the millions,
the Oligarchy will realize, and too late, how mightily that band of
heroes has grown.[33]

[33] Avis Everhard took for granted that her narrative would be read in her
own day, and so omits to mention the outcome of the trial for high treason.
Many other similar disconcerting omissions will be noticed in the Manuscript.
Fifty-two socialist Congressmen were tried, and all were found guilty. Strange
to relate, not one received the death sentence. Everhard and eleven others,
among whom were Theodore Donnelson and Matthew Kent, received life imprisonment. The remaining forty received sentences varying from thirty to
forty-five years; while Arthur Simpson, referred to in the Manuscript as being
ill of typhoid fever at the time of the explosion, received only fifteen years. It
is the tradition that he died of starvation in solitary confinement, and this
harsh treatment is explained as having been caused by his uncompromising
stubbornness and his fiery and tactless hatred for all men that served the despotism. He died in Cabañas in Cuba, where three of his comrades were also
confined. The fifty-two socialist Congressmen were confined in military fortresses scattered all over the United States. Thus, Du Bois and Woods were held
in Porto Rico, while Everhard and Merryweather were placed in Alcatraz, an
Island in San Francisco Bay that had already seen long service as a military
prison.

As a revolutionist myself, as one on the inside who knew the hopes and fears and secret plans of the revolutionists, I am fitted to answer, as very few are, the charge that they were guilty of exploding the bomb in Congress. And I can say flatly, without qualification or doubt of any sort, that the socialists, in Congress and out, had no hand in the affair. Who threw the bomb we do not know, but the one thing we are absolutely sure of is that we did not throw it.

On the other hand, there is evidence to show that the Iron Heel was responsible for the act. Of course, we cannot prove this. Our conclusion is merely presumptive. But here are such facts as we do know. It had been reported to the Speaker of the House, by secret-service agents of the government, that the socialist Congressmen were about to resort to terroristic tactics, and that they had decided upon the day when their tactics would go into effect. This day was the very day of the explosion. Wherefore the Capitol had been packed with troops in anticipation. Since we knew nothing about the bomb, and since a bomb actually was exploded, and since the authorities had prepared in advance for the explosion, it is only fair to conclude that the Iron Heel did know. Furthermore, we charge that the Iron Heel was guilty of the outrage, and that the Iron Heel planned and perpetrated the outrage for the purpose of foisting the guilt on our shoulders and so bringing about our destruction.

From the Speaker the warning leaked out to all the creatures in the House that wore the scarlet livery. They knew, while Ernest was speaking, that some violent act was to be committed. And to do them justice, they honestly believed that the act was to be committed by the socialists. At the trial, and still with honest belief, several testified to having seen Ernest prepare to throw the bomb, and that it exploded prematurely. Of course they saw nothing of the sort. In the fevered imagination of fear they thought they saw, that was all.

As Ernest said at the trial: "Does it stand to reason, if I were going to throw a bomb, that I should elect to threw a feeble little squib like the one that was thrown? There wasn't enough powder in it. It made a lot of smoke, but hurt no one except me. It exploded right at my feet, and yet it did not kill me. Believe me, when I get to throwing bombs, I'll do damage. There'll be more than smoke in my petards."

In return it was argued by the prosecution that the weakness of the bomb was a blunder on the part of the socialists, just as its premature explosion, caused by Ernest's losing his nerve and dropping it, was a blunder. And to clinch the argument, there were the several Congressmen who testified to having seen Ernest fumble and drop the bomb.

As for ourselves, not one of us knew how the bomb was thrown. Ernest told me that the fraction of an instant before it exploded he both heard and saw it strike at his feet. He testified to this at the trial, bu no one believed him. Besides, the whole thing, in popular slang, was "cooked up." The Iron Heel had made up its mind to destroy us, and there was no withstanding it.

There is a saying that truth will out. I have come to doubt that saying. Nineteen years have elapsed, and despite our untiring efforts, we have failed to find the man who really did throw the bomb. Undoubtedly he was some emissary of the Iron Heel, but he has escaped detection. We have never got the slightest clew to his identity. And now, at this late date, nothing remains but for the affair to take its place among the mysteries of history.[34]

IN THE SHADOW OF SONOMA

Of myself, during this period, there is not much to say. For six months I was kept in prison, though charged with no crime. I was a *suspect*—a word of fear that all revolutionists were soon to come to

---

[34] Avis Everhard would have had to live for many generations ere she could have seen the clearing up of this particular mystery. A little less than a hundred years ago, and a little more than six hundred years after her death, the confession of Pervaise was discovered in the secret archives of the Vatican. It is perhaps well to tell a little something about this obscure document, which, in the main, is of interest to the historian only.

Pervaise was an American, of French descent, who, in 1913 A.D., was lying in the Tombs Prison, New York City, awaiting trial for murder. From his confession we learn that he was not a criminal. He was warm-blooded, passionate, emotional. In an insane fit of jealousy he killed his wife—a very common act in those times. Pervaise was mastered by the fear of death, all of which is recounted at length in his confession. To escape death he would have done anything, and the police agents prepared him by assuring him that he could not possibly escape conviction of murder in the first degree when his trial came off. In those days, murder in the first degree was a capital offence. The guilty man or woman was placed in a specially constructed death-chair, and, under the supervision of competent physicians, was destroyed by a current of electricity. This was called electrocution, and it was very popular during that period. Anæsthesia, as a mode of compulsory death, was not introduced until later.

This man, good at heart but with a ferocious animalism close at the surface of his being, lying in jail and expectant of nothing less than death, was preknow. But our own nascent secret service was beginning to work. By the end of my second month in prison, one of the jailers made himself known as a revolutionist in touch with the organization. Several weeks later, Joseph Parkhurst, the prison doctor who had just been

---

vailed upon by the agents of the Iron Heel to throw the bomb in the House of Representatives. In his confession he states explicitly that he was informed that the bomb was to be a feeble thing and that no lives would be lost. This is directly in line with the fact that the bomb was lightly charged, and that its explosion at Everhard's feet was not deadly.

Pervaise was smuggled into one of the galleries ostensibly closed for repairs. He was to select the moment for the throwing of the bomb, and he naïvely confesses that in his interest in Everhard's tirade and the general commotion raised thereby, he nearly forgot his mission.

Not only was he released from prison in reward for his deed, but he was granted an income for life. This he did not long enjoy. In 1914 A.D., in September, he was stricken with rheumatism of the heart and lived for three days. It was then that he sent for the Catholic priest, Father Peter Durban, and to him made confession. So important did it seem to the priest, that he had the confession taken down in writing and sworn to. What happened after this we can only surmise. The document was certainly important enough to find its way to Rome. Powerful influences must have been brought to bear, hence its suppression. For centuries no hint of its existence reached the world. It was not until in the last century that Lorbia, the brilliant Italian scholar, stumbled upon it quite by chance during his researches in the Vatican.

There is to-day no doubt whatever that the Iron Heel was responsible for the bomb that exploded in the House of Representatives in 1913 A.D. Even though the Pervaise confession had never come to light, no reasonable doubt could obtain; for the act in question, that sent fifty-two Congressmen to prison, was on a par with countless other acts committed by the oligarchs, and, before them, by the capitalists.

There is the classic instance of the ferocious and wanton judicial murder of the innocent and so-called Haymarket Anarchists in Chicago in the penultimate decade of the nineteenth century A.D. In a category by itself is the deliberate burning and destruction of capitalist property by the capitalists themselves— see footnote 15 on page 154. For such destruction of property innocent men were frequently punished—"railroaded" in the parlance of the times.

In the labor troubles of the first decade of the twentieth century A.D., between the capitalists and the Western Federation of Miners, similar but more bloody tactics were employed. The railroad station at Independence was blown up by the agents of the capitalists. Thirteen men were killed, and many more were wounded. And then the capitalists, controlling the legislative and judicial machinery of the state of Colorado, charged the miners with the crime and came very near to convicting them. Romaines, one of the tools in this affair, like Pervaise, was lying in jail in another state, Kansas, awaiting trial, when he was approached by the agents of the capitalists. But, unlike Pervaise, the confession of Romaines was made public in his own time.

appointed, proved himself to be a member of one of the Fighting Groups.

Thus, throughout the organization of the Oligarchy, our own organization, weblike and spidery, was insinuating itself. And so I was kept in touch with all that was happening in the world without. And furthermore, every one of our imprisoned leaders was in contact with brave comrades who masqueraded in the livery of the Iron Heel. Though Ernest lay in prison three thousand miles way, on the Pacific Coast, I was in unbroken communication with him, and our letters passed regularly back and forth.

The leaders, in prison and out, were able to discuss and direct the campaign. It would have been possible, within a few months, to have effected the escape of some of them; but since imprisonment proved no bar to our activities, it was decided to avoid anything premature. Fifty-two Congressmen were in prison, and fully three hundred more of our leaders. It was planed that they should be delivered simultaneously. If part of them escaped, the vigilance of the oligarchs might be aroused so as to prevent the escape of the remainder. On the other hand, it was held that a simultaneous jail-delivery all over the land would have immense psychological influence on the proletariat. It would show our strength and give confidence.

So it was arranged, when I was released at the end of six months, that I was to disappear and prepare a secure hiding-place for Ernest. To disappear was in itself no easy thing. No sooner did I get my free-

---

Then, during this same period, there was the case of Moyer and Haywood, two strong, fearless leaders of labor. One was president and the other was secretary of the Western Federation of Miners. The ex-governor of Idaho had been mysteriously murdered. The crime, at the time, was openly charged to the mine owners by the socialists and miners. Nevertheless, in violation of the national and state constitutions, and by means of conspiracy on the parts of the governors of Idaho and Colorado, Moyer and Haywood were kidnapped, thrown into jail, and charged with the murder. It was this instance that provoked from Eugene V. Debs, national leader of the American socialists at the time, the following words: *"The labor leaders that cannot be bribed nor bullied, must be ambushed and murdered. The only crime of Moyer and Haywood is that they have been unswervingly true to the working class. The capitalists have stolen our country, debauched our politics, defiled our judiciary, and ridden over us rough-shod, and now they propose to murder those who will not abjectly surrender to their brutal dominion. The governors of Colorado and Idaho are but executing the mandates of their masters, the Plutocracy. The issue is the Workers versus the Plutocracy. If they strike the first violent blow, we will strike the last."*

dom than my footsteps began to be dogged by the spies of the Iron
Heel. It was necessary that they should be thrown off the track, and
that I should win to California. It is laughable, the way this was accomplished.

Already the passport system, modelled on the Russian, was developing. I dared not cross the continent in my own character. It was
necessary that I should be completely lost if ever I was to see Ernest
again, for by trailing me after he escaped, he would be caught once
more. Again, I could not disguise myself as a proletarian and travel.
There remained the disguise of a member of the Oligarchy. While
the arch-oligarchs were no more than a handful, there were myriads
of lesser ones of the type, say, of Mr. Wickson—men, worth a few
millions, who were adherents of the arch-oligarchs. The wives and
daughters of these lesser oligarchs were legion, and it was decided
that I should assume the disguise of such a one. A few years later this
would have been impossible, because the passport system was to become so perfect that no man, woman, nor child in all the land was
unregistered and unaccounted for in his or her movements.

When the time was ripe, the spies were thrown off my track. An
hour later Avis Everhard was no more. At that time one Felice Van
Verdighan, accompanied by two maids and a lap-dog, with another
maid for the lap-dog,[35] entered a drawing-room on a Pullman,[36] and
a few minutes later was speeding west.

The three maids who accompanied me were revolutionists. Two
were members of the Fighting Groups, and the third, Grace Holbrook,
entered a group the following year, and six months later was executed
by the Iron Heel. She it was who waited upon the dog. Of the other
two, Bertha Stole disappeared twelve years later, while Anna Roylston still lives and plays an increasingly important part in the Revolution.[37]

[35] This ridiculous picture well illustrates the heartless conduct of the masters.
While people starved, lap-dogs were waited upon by maids. This was a serious
masquerade on the part of Avis Everhard. Life and death and the Cause were
in the issue; therefore the picture must be accepted as a true picture. It affords
a striking commentary of the times.

[36] *Pullman*—the designation of the more luxurious railway cars of the period
and so named from the inventor.

[37] Despite continual and almost inconceivable hazards, Anna Roylston lived
to the royal age of ninety-one. As the Pococks defied the executioners of the
Fighting Groups, so she defied the executioners of the Iron Heel. She bore a
charmed life and prospered amid dangers and alarms. She herself was an exe-

Without adventure we crossed the United States to California.
When the train stopped at Sixteenth Street Station, in Oakland, we
alighted, and there Felice Van Verdighan, with her two maids, her
lap-dog, and her lap-dog's maid, disappeared forever. The maids,
guided by trusty comrades, were led away. Other comrades took
charge of me. Within half an hour after leaving the train I was on
board a small fishing boat and out on the waters of San Francisco
Bay. The winds baffled, and we drifted aimlessly the greater part of
the night. But I saw the lights of Alcatraz where Ernest lay, and
found comfort in the thought of nearness to him. By dawn, what with
the rowing of the fishermen, we made the Marin Islands. Here we lay in
hiding all day, and on the following night, swept on by a flood tide and
a fresh wind, we crossed San Pablo Bay in two hours and ran up
Petaluma Creek. . . .

THE ROARING ABYSMAL BEAST

. . . . The wholesale jail delivery did not occur until well along
into 1915. Complicated as it was, it was carried through without a
hitch, and as a very creditable achievement it cheered us on in our
work. From Cuba to California, out of scores of jails, military prisons,
and fortresses, in a single night, we delivered fifty-one of our fifty-
two Congressmen, and in addition over three hundred other leaders.
There was not a single instance of miscarriage. Not only did they
escape, but every one of them won to the refuges as planned. The one
comrade Congressman we did not get was Arthur Simpson, and he
had already died in Cabañas after cruel tortures.

The eighteen months that followed was perhaps the happiest period
of my life with Ernest. During that time we were never apart. . . .
During the long period of our stay in the refuge, we were kept closely
in touch with what was happening in the world without, and we were
learning thoroughly of the strength of the Oligarchy with which we
were at war. Out of the flux of transition the new institutions were
forming more definitely and taking on the appearance and attributes
of permanence. The oligarchs had succeeded in devising a govern-

---

cutioner for the Fighting Groups, and, known as the Red Virgin, she became
one of the inspired figures of the Revolution. When she was an old woman of
sixty-nine she shot "Bloody" Halcliffe down in the midst of his armed escort
and got away unscathed. In the end she died peaceably of old age in a secret
refuge of the revolutionists in the Ozark mountains.

mental machine, as intricate as it was vast, that worked—and this despite all our efforts to clog and hamper.

This was a surprise to many of the revolutionists. They had not conceived it possible. Nevertheless the work of the country went on. The men toiled in the mines and fields—perforce they were no more than slaves. As for the vital industries, everything prospered. The members of the great labor castes were contented and worked on merrily. For the first time in their lives they knew industrial peace. No more were they worried by slack times, strike and lockout, and the union label. They lived in more comfortable homes and in delightful cities of their own—delightful compared with the slums and ghettos in which they had formerly dwelt. They had better food to eat, less hours of labor, more holidays, and a greater amount and variety of interests and pleasures. And for their less fortunate brothers and sisters, the unfavored laborers, the driven people of the abyss, they cared nothing. An age of selfishness was dawning upon mankind. And yet this is not altogether true. The labor castes were honeycombed by our agents—men whose eyes saw, beyond the belly-need, the radiant figure of liberty and brotherhood.

Another great institution that had taken form and was working smoothly was the Mercenaries. This body of soldiers had been evolved out of the old regular army and was now a million strong, to say nothing of the colonial forces. The Mercenaries constituted a race apart. They dwelt in cities of their own which were practically self-governed, and they were granted many privileges. By them a large portion of the perplexing surplus was consumed. They were losing all touch and sympathy with the rest of the people, and, in fact, were developing their own class morality and consciousness. And yet we had thousands of our agents among them.[38]

The oligarchs themselves were going through a remarkable and, it must be confessed, unexpected development. As a class, they disciplined themselves. Every member had his work to do in the world, and this work he was compelled to do. There were no more idle-rich young men. Their strength was used to give united strength to the Oligarchy. They served as leaders of troops and as lieutenants and captains of industry. They found careers in applied science, and

[38] The Mercenaries, in the last days of the Iron Heel, played an important rôle. They constituted the balance of power in the struggles between the labor castes and the oligarchs, and now to one side and now to the other, threw their strength according to the play of intrigue and conspiracy.

many of them became great engineers. They went into the multitudinous divisions of the government, took service in the colonial possessions, and by tens of thousands went into the various secret
services. They were, I may say, apprenticed to education, to art, to
the church, to science, to literature; and in those fields they served
the important function of moulding the thought-processes of the nation in the direction of the perpetuity of the Oligarchy.

They were taught, and later they in turn taught, that what they
were doing was right. They assimilated the aristocratic idea from the
moment they began, as children, to receive impressions of the world.
The aristocratic idea was woven into the making of them until it
became bone of them and flesh of them. They looked upon themselves as wild-animal trainers, rulers of beasts. From beneath their
feet rose always the subterranean rumbles of revolt. Violent death
ever stalked in their midst; bomb and knife and bullet were looked
upon as so many fangs of the roaring abysmal beast they must dominate if humanity were to persist. They were the saviours of humanity,
and they regarded themselves as heroic and sacrificing laborers for
the highest good.

They, as a class, believed that they alone maintained civilization.
It was their belief that if ever they weakened, the great beast would
ingulf them and everything of beauty and wonder and joy and good
in its cavernous and slime-dripping maw. Without them, anarchy
would reign and humanity would drop backward into the primitive
night out of which it had so painfully emerged. The horrid picture of
anarchy was held always before their child's eyes until they, in turn,
obsessed by the cultivated fear, held the picture of anarchy before
the eyes of the children that followed them. This was the beast to be
stamped upon, and the highest duty of the aristocrat was to stamp
upon it. In short, they alone, by their unremitting toil and sacrifice,
stood between weak humanity and the all-devouring beast; and they
believed it, firmly believed it.

I cannot lay too great stress upon this high ethical righteousness of
the whole oligarch class. This has been the strength of the Iron Heel,
and too many of the comrades have been slow or loath to realize it.
Many of them have ascribed the strength of the Iron Heel to its system of reward and punishment. This is a mistake. Heaven and hell
may be the prime factors of zeal in the religion of a fanatic; but for
the great majority of the religious, heaven and hell are incidental to

right and wrong. Love of the right, desire for the right, unhappiness with anything less than the right—in short, right conduct, is the prime factor of religion. And so with Oligarchy. Prisons, banishment and degradation, honors and palaces and wonder-cities, are all incidental. The great driving force of the oligarchs is the belief that they are doing right. Never mind the exceptions, and never mind the oppression and injustice in which the Iron Heel was conceived. All is granted. The point is that the strength of the Oligarchy to-day lies in its satisfied conception of its own righteousness.[39]

For that matter, the strength of the Revolution, during these frightful twenty years, has resided in nothing else than the sense of righteousness. In no other way can be explained our sacrifices and martyrdoms. For no other reason did Rudolph Mendenhall flame out his soul for the Cause and sing his wild swan-song that last night of life. For no other reason did Hurlbert die under torture, refusing to the last to betray his comrades. For no other reason has Anna Roylston refused blessed motherhood. For no other reason has John Carlson been the faithful and unrewarded custodian of the Glen Ellen Refuge. It does not matter, young or old, man or woman, high or low, genius or clod, go where one will among the comrades of the Revolution, the motor-force will be found to be a great and abiding desire for the right.

But I have run away from my narrative. Ernest and I well understood, before we left the refuge, how the strength of the Iron Heel was developing. The labor castes, the Mercenaries, and the great hordes of secret agents and police of various sorts were all pledged to the Oligarchy. In the main, and ignoring the loss of liberty, they were better off than they had been. On the other hand, the great helpless mass of the population, the people of the abyss, was sinking into a brutish apathy of content with misery. Whenever strong proletarians asserted their strength in the midst of the mass, they were drawn

[39] Out of the ethical incoherency and inconsistency of capitalism, the oligarchs emerged with a new ethics, coherent and definite, sharp and severe as steel, the most absurd and unscientific and at the same time the most potent ever possessed by any tyrant class. The oligarchs believed their ethics, in spite of the fact that biology and evolution gave them the lie; and, because of their faith, for three centuries they were able to hold back the mighty tide of human progress—a spectacle, profound, tremendous, puzzling to the metaphysical moralist, and one that to the materialist is the cause of many doubts and reconsiderations.

away from the mass by the oligarchs and given better conditions by being made members of the labor castes or of the Mercenaries. Thus discontent was lulled and the proletariat robbed of its natural leaders.

The condition of the people of the abyss was pitiable. Common school education, so far as they were concerned, had ceased. They lived like beasts in great squalid labor-ghettos, festering in misery and degradation. All their old liberties were gone. They were labor-slaves. Choice of work was denied them. Likewise was denied them the right to move from place to place, or the right to bear or possess arms. They were not land-serfs like the farmers. They were machine-serfs and labor-serfs. When unusual needs arose for them, such as the building of the great highways and air-lines, of canals, tunnels, sub-ways, and fortifications, levies were made on the labor-ghettos, and tens of thousands of serfs, willy-nilly, were transported to the scene of operations. Great armies of them are toiling now at the building of Ardis, housed in wretched barracks where family life cannot exist, and where decency is displaced by dull bestiality. In all truth, there in the labor-ghettos is the roaring abysmal beast the oligarchs fear so dreadfully—but it is the beast of their own making. In it they will not let the ape and tiger die.

And just now the word has gone forth that new levies are being imposed for the building of Asgard, the projected wonder-city that will far exceed Ardis when the latter is completed.[40] We of the Revolution will go on with that great work, but it will not be done by the miserable serfs. The walls and towers and shafts of that fair city will arise to the sound of singing, and into its beauty and wonder will be woven, not sighs and groans, but music and laughter.

Ernest was madly impatient to be out in the world and doing, for our ill-fated First Revolt, that miscarried in the Chicago Commune, was ripening fast. Yet he possessed his soul with patience, and during the time for his torment, when Hadly, who had been brought for the purpose from Illinois, made him over into another man,[41] he revolved

[40] Ardis was completed in 1942 A.D., while Asgard was not completed until 1984 A.D. It was fifty-two years in the building, during which time a permanent army of half a million serfs was employed. At times these numbers swelled to over a million—without any account being taken of the hundreds of thousands of the labor castes and the artists.

[41] Among the Revolutionists were many surgeons, and in vivisection they at-tained marvellous proficiency. In Avis Everhard's words, they could literally make a man over. To them the elimination of scars and disfigurements was a trivial detail. They changed the features with such microscopic care that no

great plans in his head for the organization of the learned proletariat, and for the maintenance of at least the rudiments of education amongst the people of the abyss—all this, of course, in the event of the First Revolt being a failure.

It was not until January, 1917, that we left the refuge. All had been arranged. We took our place at once as agents-provocateurs in the scheme of the Iron Heel. I was supposed to be Ernest's sister. By Oligarchs and comrades on the inside who were high in authority, place had been made for us, we were in possession of all necessary documents, and our pasts were accounted for. With help on the inside, this was not difficult, for in that shadow-world of secret service identity was nebulous. Like ghosts the agents came and went, obeying commands, fulfilling duties, following clews, making their reports often to officers they never saw or coöperating with other agents they had never seen before and would never see again.

THE CHICAGO COMMUNE

As agents-provocateurs, not alone were we able to travel a great deal, but our very work threw us in contact with the proletariat and with our comrades, the revolutionists. Thus we were in both camps at the same time, ostensibly serving the Iron Heel and secretly working with all our might for the Cause. There were many of us in the various secret services of the Oligarchy, and despite the shakings-up and reorganizations the secret services have undergone, they have never been able to weed all of us out.

Ernest had largely planned the First Revolt, and the date set had been somewhere early in the spring of 1918. In the fall of 1917 we were not ready; much remained to be done, and when the Revolt was precipitated, of course it was doomed to failure. The plot of necessity was frightfully intricate, and anything premature was sure

---

traces were left of their handiwork. The nose was a favorite organ to work upon. Skin-grafting and hair-transplanting were among their commonest devices. The changes in expression they accomplished were wizard-like. Eyes and eyebrows, lips, mouths, and ears, were radically altered. By cunning operations on tongue, throat, larynx, and nasal cavities a man's whole enunciation and manner of speech could be changed. Desperate times give need for desperate remedies, and the surgeons of the Revolution rose to the need. Among other things, they could increase an adult's stature by as much as four or five inches and decrease it by one or two inches. What they did is to-day a lost art. We have no need for it.

to destroy it. This the Iron Heel foresaw and laid its schemes accordingly.

We had planned to strike our first blow at the nervous system of the Oligarchy. The latter had remembered the general strike, and had guarded against the defection of the telegraphers by installing wireless stations, in the control of the Mercenaries. We, in turn, had countered this move. When the signal was given, from every refuge, all over the land, and from the cities, and towns, and barracks, devoted comrades were to go forth and blow up the wireless stations. Thus at the first shock would the Iron Heel be brought to earth and lie practically dismembered.

At the same moment, other comrades were to blow up the bridges and tunnels and disrupt the whole network of railroads. Still further, other groups of comrades, at the signal, were to seize the officers of the Mercenaries and the police, as well as all Oligarchs of unusual ability or who held executive positions. Thus would the leaders of the enemy be removed from the field of the local battles that would inevitably be fought all over the land.

Many things were to occur simultaneously when the signal went forth. The Canadian and Mexican patriots, who were far stronger than the Iron Heel dreamed, were to duplicate our tactics. Then there were comrades (these were the women, for the men would be busy elsewhere) who were to post the proclamations from our secret presses. Those of us in the higher employ of the Iron Heel were to proceed immediately to make confusion and anarchy in all our departments. Inside the Mercenaries were thousands of our comrades. Their work was to blow up the magazines and to destroy the delicate mechanism of all the war machinery. In the cities of the Mercenaries and of the labor castes similar programmes of disruption were to be carried out.

In short, a sudden, colossal, stunning blow was to be struck. Before the paralyzed Oligarchy could recover itself, its end would have come. It would have meant terrible times and great loss of life, but no revolutionist hesitates at such things. Why, we even depended much, in our plan, on the unorganized people of the abyss. They were to be loosed on the palaces and cities of the masters. Never mind the destruction of life and property. Let the abysmal brute roar and the police and Mercenaries slay. The abysmal brute would roar anyway, and the police and Mercenaries would slay anyway. It would merely mean that various dangers to us were harmlessly destroying one another. In the meantime we would be doing our own work, largely un-hampered, and gaining control of all the machinery of society.

Such was our plan, every detail of which had to be worked out in secret, and, as the day drew near, communicated to more and more comrades. This was the danger point, the stretching of the conspiracy. But that danger point was never reached. Through its spy-system the Iron Heel got wind of the Revolt and prepared to teach us another of its bloody lessons. Chicago was the devoted city selected for the in-struction, and well were we instructed.

Chicago [42] was the ripest of all—Chicago which of old time was the city of blood and which was to earn anew its name. There the revo-lutionary spirit was strong. Too many bitter strikes had been curbed there in the days of capitalism for the workers to forget and forgive. Even the labor castes of the city were alive with revolt. Too many heads had been broken in the early strikes. Despite their changed and favorable conditions, their hatred for the master class had not died. This spirit had infected the Mercenaries, of which three regi-ments in particular were ready to come over to us *en masse*.

Chicago had always been the storm-centre of the conflict between labor and capital, a city of street-battles and violent death, with a class-conscious capitalist organization and a class-conscious work-man organization, where, in the old days, the very school-teachers were formed into labor unions and affiliated with the hod-carriers and brick-layers in the American Federation of Labor. And Chicago be-came the storm-centre of the premature First Revolt.

The trouble was precipitated by the Iron Heel. It was cleverly done. The whole population, including the favored labor castes, was given a course of outrageous treatment. Promises and agreements were broken, and most drastic punishments visited upon even petty offenders. The people of the abyss were tormented out of their apathy. In fact, the Iron Heel was preparing to make the abysmal beast roar. And hand in hand with this, in all precautionary measures in Chi-

---

[42] Chicago was the industrial inferno of the nineteenth century A.D. A curi-ous anecdote has come down to us of John Burns, a great English labor leader and one time member of the British Cabinet. In Chicago, while on a visit to the United States, he was asked by a newspaper reporter for his opinion of that city. "Chicago," he answered, "is a pocket edition of hell." Some time later, as he was going aboard his steamer to sail to England, he was approached by an-other reporter, who wanted to know if he had changed his opinion of Chicago. "Yes, I have," was his reply. "My present opinion is that hell is a pocket edi-tion of Chicago."

cago, the Iron Heel was inconceivably careless. Discipline was relaxed among the Mercenaries that remained, while many regiments
had been withdrawn and sent to various parts of the country.

It did not take long to carry out this programme—only several
weeks. We of the Revolution caught vague rumors of the state of
affairs, but had nothing definite enough for an understanding. In fact,
we thought it was a spontaneous spirit of revolt that would require
careful curbing on our part, and never dreamed that it was deliberately manufactured—and it had been manufactured so secretly, from
the very innermost circle of the Iron Heel, that we had got no inkling.
The counter-plot was an able achievement, and ably carried out.

I was in New York when I received the order to proceed immediately to Chicago. The man who gave me the order was one of the
oligarchs, I could tell that by his speech, though I did not know his
name nor see his face. His instructions were too clear for me to make
a mistake. Plainly I read between the lines that our plot had been discovered, that we had been countermined. The explosion was ready for
the flash of powder, and countless agents of the Iron Heel, including me, either on the ground or being sent there, were to supply that
flash. I flatter myself that I maintained my composure under the
keen eye of the oligarch, but my heart was beating madly. I could
almost have shrieked and flown at his throat with my naked hands
before his final, cold-blooded instructions were given.

Once out of his presence, I calculated the time. I had just the moments to spare, if I were lucky, to get in touch with some local leader
before catching my train. Guarding against being trailed, I made a
rush of it for the Emergency Hospital. Luck was with me, and I
gained access at once to comrade Galvin, the surgeon-in-chief. I
started to gasp out my information, but he stopped me.

"I already know," he said quietly, though his Irish eyes were flashing. "I knew what you had come for. I got the word fifteen minutes
ago, and I have already passed it along. Everything shall be done here
to keep the comrades quiet. Chicago is to be sacrificed, but it shall be
Chicago alone."

"Have you tried to get word to Chicago?" I asked.

He shook his head. "No telegraphic communication. Chicago is
shut off. It's going to be hell there."

He paused a moment, and I saw his white hands clinch. Then he
burst out:

"By God! I wish I were going to be there!"

"There is yet a chance to stop it," I said, "if nothing happens to the train and I can get there in time. Or if some of the other secret-service comrades who have learned the truth can get there in time."

"You on the inside were caught napping this time," he said.

I nodded my head humbly.

"It was very secret," I answered. "Only the inner chiefs could have known up to to-day. We haven't yet penetrated that far, so we couldn't escape being kept in the dark. If only Ernest were here. Maybe he is in Chicago now, and all is well."

Dr. Galvin shook his head. "The last news I heard of him was that he had been sent to Boston or New Haven. This secret service for the enemy must hamper him a lot, but it's better than lying in a refuge."

I started to go, and Galvin wrung my hand.

"Keep a stout heart," were his parting words. "What if the First Revolt is lost? There will be a second, and we will be wiser then. Good-by and good luck. I don't know whether I'll ever see you again. It's going to be hell there, but I'd give ten years of my life for your chance to be in it."

The Twentieth Century [43] left New York at six in the evening, and was supposed to arrive at Chicago at seven next morning. But it lost time that night. We were running behind another train. Among the travellers in my Pullman was comrade Hartman, like myself in the secret service of the Iron Heel. He it was who told me of the train that immediately preceded us. It was an exact duplicate of our train, though it contained no passengers. The idea was that the empty train should receive the disaster were an attempt made to blow up the Twentieth Century. For that matter there were very few people on the train—only a baker's dozen in our car.

"There must be some big men on board," Hartman concluded. "I noticed a private car on the rear."

Night had fallen when we made our first change of engine, and I walked down the platform for a breath of fresh air and to see what I could see. Through the windows of the private car I caught a glimpse of three men whom I recognized. Hartman was right. One of the men was General Altendorff; and the other two were Mason and Vanderbold, the brains of the inner circle of the Oligarchy's secret service.

[43] This was reputed to be the fastest train in the world then. It was quite a famous train.

It was a quiet moonlight night, but I tossed restlessly and could not sleep. At five in the morning I dressed and abandoned my bed.

I asked the maid in the dressing-room how late the train was, and she told me two hours. She was a mulatto woman, and I noticed that her face was haggard, with great circles under the eyes, while the eyes themselves were wide with some haunting fear.

"What is the matter?" I asked.

"Nothing, miss; I didn't sleep well, I guess," was her reply.

I looked at her closely, and tried her with one of our signals. She responded, and I made sure of her.

"Something terrible is going to happen in Chicago," she said. "here's that fake [44] train in front of us. That and the troop-trains have made us late."

"Troop-trains?" I queried.

She nodded her head. "The line is thick with them. We've been passing them all night. And they're all heading for Chicago. And bringing them over the air-line—that means business.

"I've a lover in Chicago," she added apologetically. "He's one of us, and he's in the Mercenaries, and I'm afraid for him."

Poor girl. Her lover was in one of the three disloyal regiments.

Hartman and I had breakfast together in the dining car, and I forced myself to eat. The sky had clouded, and the train rushed on like a sullen thunderbolt through the gray pall of advancing day. The very Negroes that waited on us knew that something terrible was impending. Oppression sat heavily upon them; the lightness of their natures had ebbed out of them; they were slack and absent-minded in their service, and they whispered gloomily to one another in the far end of the car next to the kitchen. Hartman was hopeless over the situation.

"What can we do?" he demanded for the twentieth time, with a helpless shrug of the shoulders.

He pointed out of the window. "See, all is ready. You can depend upon it that they're holding them like this, thirty or forty miles outside the city, on every road."

He had reference to troop-trains on the side-track. The soldiers were cooking their breakfasts over fires built on the ground beside the track, and they looked up curiously at us as we thundered past without slackening our terrific speed.

All was quiet as we entered Chicago. It was evident nothing had

[44] False.

happened yet. In the suburbs the morning papers came on board the
train. There was nothing in them, and yet there was much in them for
those skilled in reading between the lines that it was intended the
ordinary reader should read into the text. The fine hand of the Iron
Heel was apparent in every column. Glimmerings of weakness in the
armor of the Oligarchy were given. Of course, there was nothing definite. It was intended that the reader should feel his way to these glimmerings. It was cleverly done. As fiction, those morning papers of
October 27th were masterpieces.

The local news was missing. This in itself was a master-stroke. It
shrouded Chicago in mystery, and it suggested to the average Chicago
reader that the Oligarchy did not dare give the local news. Hints that
were untrue, of course, were given of insubordination all over the
land, crudely disguised with complacent references to punitive measures to be taken. There were reports of numerous wireless stations
that had been blown up, with heavy rewards offered for the detection
of the perpetrators. Of course no wireless stations had been blown
up. Many similar outrages, that dovetailed with the plot of the revolutionists, were given. The impression to be made on the minds of the
Chicago comrades was that the general Revolt was beginning, albeit
with a confusing miscarriage in many details. It was impossible for
one uninformed to escape the vague yet certain feeling that all the
land was ripe for the revolt that had already begun to break out.

It was reported that the defection of the Mercenaries in California
had become so serious that half a dozen regiments had been disbanded
and broken, and that their members with their families had been
driven from their own city and on into the labor-ghettos. And the
California Mercenaries were in reality the most faithful of all to their
salt! But how was Chicago, shut off from the rest of the world, to
know? Then there was a ragged telegram describing an outbreak of
the populace in New York City, in which the labor castes were joining, concluding with the statement (intended to be accepted as a
bluff) that the troops had the situation in hand.

And as the oligarchs had done with the morning papers, so had they
done in a thousand other ways. These we learned afterward, as, for
example, the secret messages of the oligarchs, sent with the express
purpose of leaking to the ears of the revolutionists, that had come
over the wires, now and again, during the first part of the night.

"I guess the Iron Heel won't need our services," Hartman remarked, putting down the paper he had been reading, when the train

pulled into the central depot. "They wasted their time sending us here. Their plans have evidently prospered better than they expected. Hell will break loose any second now."

He turned and looked down the train as we alighted.

"I thought so," he muttered. "They dropped that private car when the papers came aboard."

Hartman was hopelessly depressed. I tried to cheer him up, but he ignored my effort and suddenly began talking very hurriedly, in a low voice, as we passed through the station. At first I could not understand.

"I have not been sure," he was saying, "and I have told no one. I have been working on it for weeks, and I cannot make sure. Watch out for Knowlton. I suspect him. He knows the secrets of a score of our refuges. He carries the lives of hundreds of us in his hands, and I think he is a traitor. It's more a feeling on my part than anything else. But I thought I marked a change in him a short while back. There is the danger that he has sold us out, or is going to sell us out. I am almost sure of it. I wouldn't whisper my suspicions to a soul, but, somehow, I don't think I'll leave Chicago alive. Keep your eye on Knowlton. Trap him. Find out. I don't know anything more. It is only an intuition, and so far I have failed to find the slightest clew." We were just stepping out upon the sidewalk. "Remember," Hartman concluded earnestly. "Keep your eyes upon Kowlton."

And Hartman was right. Before a month went by Knowlton paid for his treason with his life. He was formally executed by the comrades in Milwaukee.

All was quiet on the streets—too quiet. Chicago lay dead. There was no roar and rumble of traffic. There were not even cabs on the streets. The surface cars and the elevated were not running. Only occasionally, on the sidewalks, were there stray pedestrians, and these pedestrians did not loiter. They went their ways with great haste and definiteness, withal there was a curious indecision in their movements, as though they expected the buildings to topple over on them or the sidewalks to sink under their feet or fly up in the air. A few gamins, however, were around, in their eyes a suppressed eagerness in anticipation of wonderful and exciting things to happen.

From somewhere, far to the south, the dull sound of an explosion came to our ears. That was all. Then quiet again, though the gamins had startled and listened, like young deer, at the sound. The doorways to all the buildings were closed; the shutters to the shops were up.

But there were many police and watchmen in evidence, and now and again automobile patrols of the Mercenaries slipped swiftly past.

Hartman and I agreed that it was useless to report ourselves to the local chiefs of the secret service. Our failure so to report would be excused, we knew, in the light of subsequent events. So we headed for the great labor-ghetto on the South Side in the hope of getting in contact with some of the comrades. Too late! We knew it. But we could not stand still and do nothing in those ghastly, silent streets. Where was Ernest? I was wondering. What was happening in the cities of the labor castes and Mercenaries? In the fortresses?

As if in answer, a great screaming roar went up, dim with distance, punctuated with detonation after detonation.

"It's the fortresses," Hartman said. "God pity those three regiments!"

At a crossing we noticed, in the direction of the stockyards, a gigantic pillar of smoke. At the next crossing several similar smoke pillars were rising skyward in the direction of the West Side. Over the city of the Mercenaries we saw a great captive war-balloon that burst even as we looked at it, and fell in flaming wreckage toward the earth. There was no clew to that tragedy of the air. We could not determine whether the balloon had been manned by comrades or enemies. A vague sound came to our ears, like the bubbling of a gigantic caldron a long way off, and Hartman said it was machine-guns and automatic rifles.

And still we walked in immediate quietude. Nothing was happening where we were. The police and the automobile patrols went by, and once half a dozen fire-engines, returning evidently from some conflagration. A question was called to the firemen by an officer in an automobile, and we heard one shout in reply: "No water! They've blown up the mains!"

"We've smashed the water supply," Hartman cried excitedly to me. "If we can do all this in a premature, isolated, abortive attempt, what can't we do in a concerted, ripened effort all over the land?"

The automobile containing the officer who had asked the question darted on. Suddenly there was a deafening roar. The machine, with its human freight, lifted in an upburst of smoke, and sank down a mass of wreckage and death.

Hartman was jubilant. "Well done! well done!" he was repeating, over and over, in a whisper. "The proletariat gets its lesson to-day, but it gives one, too."

Police were running for the spot. Also, another patrol machine had halted. As for myself, I was in a daze. The suddenness of it was stunning. How had it happened? I knew not how, and yet I had been looking directly at it. So dazed was I for the moment that I was scarcely aware of the fact that we were being held up by the police. I abruptly saw that a policeman was in the act of shooting Hartman. But Hartman was cool and was giving the proper passwords. I saw the levelled revolver hesitate, then sink down, and heard the disgusted grunt of the policeman. He was very angry, and was cursing the whole secret service. It was always in the way, he was averring, while Hartman was talking back to him and with fitting secret-service pride explaining to him the clumsiness of the police.

The next moment I knew how it had happened. There was quite a group about the wreck, and two men were just lifting up the wounded officer to carry him to the other machine. A panic seized all of them, and they scattered in every direction, running in blind terror, the wounded officer, roughly dropped, being left behind. The cursing policeman alongside of me also ran, and Hartman and I ran, too, we knew not why, obsessed with the same blind terror to get away from that particular spot.

Nothing really happened then, but everything was explained. The flying men were sheepishly coming back, but all the while their eyes were raised apprehensively to the many-windowed, lofty buildings that towered like the sheer walls of a canyon on each side of the street. From one of those countless windows the bomb had been thrown, but which window? There had been no second bomb, only a fear of one.

Thereafter we looked with speculative comprehension at the windows. Any of them contained possible death. Each building was a possible ambuscade. This was warfare in that modern jungle, a great city. Every street was a canyon, every building a mountain. We had not changed much from primitive man, despite the war automobiles that were sliding by.

Turning a corner, we came upon a woman. She was lying on the pavement, in a pool of blood. Hartman bent over and examined her. As for myself, I turned deathly sick. I was to see many dead that day, but the total carnage was not to affect me as did this first forlorn body lying there at my feet abandoned on the pavement. "Shot in the breast," was Hartman's report. Clasped in the hollow of her arm, as a child might be clasped, was a bundle of printed matter. Even in death she seemed loath to part with that which had caused her death; for when Hartman had succeeded in withdrawing the bundle, we found that it consisted of large printed sheets, the proclamations of the revolutionists.

"A comrade," I said.

But Hartman only cursed the Iron Heel, and we passed on. Often we were halted by the police and patrols, but our passwords enabled us to proceed. No more bombs fell from the windows, the last pedestrians seemed to have vanished from the streets, and our immediate quietude grew more profound; though the gigantic caldron continued to bubble in the distance, dull roars of explosions came to us from all directions, and the smoke-pillars were towering more ominously in the heavens.

THE PEOPLE OF THE ABYSS

Suddenly a change came over the face of things. A tingle of excitement ran along the air. Automobiles fled past, two, three, a dozen, and from them warnings were shouted to us. One of the machines swerved wildly at high speed half a block down, and the next moment, already left well behind it, the pavement was torn into a great hole by a bursting bomb. We saw the police disappearing down the cross-streets on the run, and knew that something terrible was coming. We could hear the rising roar of it.

"Our brave comrades are coming," Hartman said.

We could see the front of their column filling the street from gutter to gutter, as the last war-automobile fled past. The machine stopped for a moment just abreast of us. A soldier leaped from it, carrying something carefully in his hands. This, with the same care, he deposited in the gutter. Then he leaped back to his seat and the machine dashed on, took the turn at the corner, and was gone from sight. Hartman ran to the gutter and stooped over the object.

"Keep back," he warned me.

I could see he was working rapidly with his hands. When he returned to me the sweat was heavy on his forehead.

"I disconnected it," he said, "and just in the nick of time. The soldier was clumsy. He intended it for our comrades, but he didn't give it enough time. It would have exploded prematurely. Now it won't explode at all."

Everything was happening rapidly now. Across the street and half a block down, high up in a building, I could see heads peering out. I had just pointed them out to Hartman, when a sheet of flame and smoke ran along that portion of the face of the building where the heads had appeared, and the air was shaken by the explosion. In places the stone facing of the building was torn away, exposing the iron construction beneath. The next moment similar sheets of flame and smoke smote the front of the building across the street opposite it. Between the explosions we could hear the rattle of the automatic pistols and rifles. For several minutes this mid-air battle continued, then died out. It was patent that our comrades were in one building, that Mercenaries were in the other, and that they were fighting across the street. But we could not tell which was which—which building contained our comrades and which the Mercenaries.

By this time the column on the street was almost on us. As the front of it passed under the warring buildings, both went into action again —one building dropping bombs into the street, being attacked from across the street, and in return replying to that attack. Thus we learned which building was held by our comrades, and they did good work, saving those in the street from the bombs of the enemy.

Hartman gripped my arm and dragged me into a wide entrance.

"They're not our comrades," he shouted in my ear.

The inner doors to the entrance were locked and bolted. We could not escape. The next moment the front of the column went by. It was not a column, but a mob, an awful river that filled the street, the people of the abyss, mad with drink and wrong, up at last and roaring for the blood of their masters. I had seen the people of the abyss before, gone through its ghettos, and thought I knew it; but I found that I was now looking on it for the first time. Dumb apathy had vanished. It was now dynamic—a fascinating spectacle of dread. It surged past my vision in concrete waves of wrath, snarling and growling, carnivorous, drunk with whiskey from pillaged warehouses, drunk with hatred, drunk with lust for blood—men, women, and children, in rags and tatters, dim ferocious intelligences with all the godlike blotted from their features and all the fiendlike stamped in, apes and tigers, anæmic consumptives and great hairy beasts of burden, wan faces from which vampire society had sucked the juice of life, bloated forms swollen with physical grossness and corruption, withered hags and death's-heads bearded like patriarchs, festering youth and festering age, faces of fiends, crooked, twisted, misshapen monsters blasted with the ravages of disease and all the horrors of chronic innutrition—the refuse and the scum of life, a raging, screaming, screeching, demoniacal horde.

And why not? The people of the abyss had nothing to lose but the misery and pain of living. And to gain?—nothing, save one final, awful glut of vengeance. And as I looked the thought came to me that in that rushing stream of human lava were men, comrades and heroes, whose mission had been to rouse the abysmal beast and to keep the enemy occupied in coping with it.

And now a strange thing happened to me. A transformation came over me. The fear of death, for myself and for others, left me. I was strangely exalted, another being in another life. Nothing mattered. The Cause for this one time was lost, but the Cause would be here to-morrow, the same Cause, ever fresh and ever burning. And thereafter, in the orgy of horror that raged through the succeeding hours, I was able to take a calm interest. Death meant nothing, life meant nothing. I was an interested spectator of events, and, sometimes swept on by the rush, was myself a curious participant. For my mind had leaped to a star-cool altitude and grasped a passionless transvaluation of values. Had it not done this, I know that I should have died.

Half a mile of the mob had swept by when we were discovered. A woman in fantastic rags, with cheeks cavernously hollow and with narrow black eyes like burning gimlets, caught a glimpse of Hartman and me. She let out a shrill shriek and bore in upon us. A section of the mob tore itself loose and surged in after her. I can see her now, as I write these lines, a leap in advance, her gray hair flying in thin tangled strings, the blood dripping down her forehead from some wound in the scalp, in her right hand a hatchet, her left hand, lean and wrinkled, a yellow talon, gripping the air convulsively. Hartman sprang in front of me. This was no time for explanations. We were well dressed, and that was enough. His fist shot out, striking the woman between her burning eyes. The impact of the blow drove her backward, but she struck the wall of her on-coming fellows and bounced forward again, dazed and helpless, the brandished hatchet falling feebly on Hartman's shoulder.

The next moment I knew not what was happening. I was overborne by the crowd. The confined space was filled with shrieks and yells and curses. Blows were falling on me. Hands were ripping and tearing at my flesh and garments. I felt that I was being torn to pieces. I was being borne down, suffocated. Some strong hand gripped my shoulder in the thick of the press and was dragging fiercely at me.

Between pain and pressure I fainted. Hartman never came out of that entrance. He had shielded me and received the first brunt of the attack. This had saved me, for the jam had quickly become too dense for anything more than the mad gripping and tearing of hands.

I came to in the midst of wild movement. All about me was the same movement. I had been caught up in a monstrous flood that was sweeping me I knew not whither. Fresh air was on my cheek and biting sweetly in my lungs. Faint and dizzy, I was vaguely aware of a strong arm around my body under the arms, and half-lifting me and dragging me along. Feebly my own limbs were helping me. In front of me I could see the moving back of a man's coat. It had been slit from top to bottom along the centre seam, and it pulsed rhythmically, the slit opening and closing regularly with every leap of the wearer. This phenomenon fascinated me for a time, while my senses were coming back to me. Next I became aware of stinging cheeks and nose, and could feel blood dripping on my face. My hat was gone. My hair was down and flying, and from the stinging of the scalp I managed to recollect a hand in the press of the entrance that had torn at my hair. My chest and arms were bruised and aching in a score of places.

My brain grew clearer, and I turned as I ran and looked at the man who was holding me up. He it was who had dragged me out and saved me. He noticed my movement.

"It's all right!" he shouted hoarsely. "I knew you on the instant."

I failed to recognize him, but before I could speak I trod upon something that was alive and that squirmed under my foot. I was swept on by those behind and could not look down and see, and yet I knew that it was a woman who had fallen and who was being trampled into the pavement by thousands of successive feet.

"It's all right," he repeated. "I'm Garthwaite."

He was bearded and gaunt and dirty, but I succeeded in remembering him as the stalwart youth that had spent several months in our Glen Ellen refuge three years before. He passed me the signals of the Iron Heel's secret service, in token that he, too, was in its employ.

"I'll get you out of this as soon as I can get a chance," he assured me. "But watch your footing. On your life don't stumble and go down."

All things happened abruptly on that day, and with an abruptness that was sickening the mob checked itself. I came in violent collision with a large woman in front of me (the man with the split coat had vanished), while those behind collided against me. A devilish pandemonium reigned,—shrieks, curses, and cries of death, while above all rose the churning rattle of machine-guns and the put-a-put, put-a-put of rifles. At first I could make out nothing. People were falling about me right and left. The woman in front doubled up and went down, her hands on her abdomen in a frenzied clutch. A man was quivering against my legs in a death-struggle.

It came to me that we were at the head of the column. Half a mile of it had disappeared—where or how I never learned. To this day I do not know what became of that half-mile of humanity—whether it was blotted out by some frightful bolt of war, whether it was scattered and destroyed piecemeal, or whether it was escaped. But there we were, at the head of the column instead of in its middle, and we were being swept out of life by a torrent of shrieking lead.

As soon as death had thinned the jam, Garthwaite, still grasping my arm, led a rush of survivors into the wide entrance of an office building. Here, at the rear, against the doors, we were pressed by a panting, gasping mass of creatures. For some time we remained in this position without a change in the situation.

"I did it beautifully," Garthwaite was lamenting to me. "Ran you right into a trap. We had a gambler's chance in the street, but in here there is no chance at all. It's all over but the shouting. Vive la Revolution!"

Then, what expected, began. The Mercenaries were killing without quarter. At first, the surge back upon us was crushing, but as the killing continued the pressure was eased. The dead and dying went down and made room. Garthwaite put his mouth to my ear and shouted, but in the frightful din I could not catch what he said. He did not wait. He seized me and threw me down. Next he dragged a dying woman over on top of me, and, with much squeezing and shoving, crawled in beside me and partly over me. A mound of dead and dying began to pile up over us, and over this mound, pawing and moaning, crept those that still survived. But these, too, soon ceased, and a semi-silence settled down, broken by groans and sobs and sounds of strangulation.

I should have been crushed had it not been for Garthwaite. As it was, it seemed inconceivable that I could bear the weight I did and live. And yet, outside of pain, the only feeling I possessed was one of curiosity. How was it going to end? What would death be like? Thus did I receive my red baptism in that Chicago shambles. Prior to that, death to me had been a theory; but ever afterward death has been a simple fact that does not matter, it is so easy.

But the Mercenaries were not content with what they had done. They invaded the entrance, killing the wounded and searching out the unhurt that, like ourselves, were playing dead. I remember one man they dragged out of a heap, who pleaded abjectly until a revolver shot cut him short. Then there was a woman who charged from a heap, snarling and shooting. She fired six shots before they got her, though what damage she did we could not know. We could follow these tragedies only by the sound. Every little while flurries like this occurred, each flurry culminating in the revolver shot that put an end to it. In the intervals we could hear the soldiers talking and swearing as they rummaged among the carcasses, urged on by their officers to hurry up.

At last they went to work on our heap, and we could feel the pressure diminish as they dragged away the dead and wounded. Garthwaite began uttering aloud the signals. At first he was not heard. Then he raised his voice.

"Listen to that," he heard a soldier say. And next the sharp voice of an officer. "Hold on there! Careful as you go!"

Oh, that first breath of air as we were dragged out! Garthwaite did the talking at first, but I was compelled to undergo a brief examination to prove service with the Iron Heel.

"Agents-provocateurs all right," was the officer's conclusion. He was a beardless young fellow, a cadet, evidently, of some great oligarch family.

"It's a hell of a job," Garthwaite grumbled. "I'm going to try and resign and get into the army. You fellows have a snap."

"You've earned it," was the young officer's answer. "I've got some pull, and I'll see if it can be managed. I can tell them how I found you."

He took Garthwaite's name and number, then turned to me.

"And you?"

"Oh, I'm going to be married," I answered lightly, "and then I'll be out of it all."

And so we talked, while the killing of the wounded went on. It is all a dream, now, as I look back on it; but at the time it was the most natural thing in the world. Garthwaite and the young officer fell into an animated conversation over the difference between so-called modern warfare and the present street-fighting and sky-scraper fighting that

was taking place all over the city. I followed them intently, fixing up
my hair at the same time and pinning together my torn skirts. And
all the time the killing of the wounded went on. Sometimes the revolver shots drowned the voices of Garthwaite and the officer, and
they were compelled to repeat what they had been saying.

I lived through three days of the Chicago Commune, and the vastness of it and of the slaughter may be imagined when I say that in
all that time I saw practically nothing outside the killing of the people
of the abyss and the mid-air fighting between sky-scrapers. I really
saw nothing of the heroic work done by the comrades. I could hear
the explosions of their mines and bombs, and see the smoke of their
conflagrations, and that was all. The mid-air part of one great deed
I saw, however, and that was the balloon attacks made by our comrades on the fortresses. That was on the second day. The three disloyal regiments had been destroyed in the fortresses to the last man.
The fortresses were crowded with Mercenaries, the wind blew in the
right direction, and up went our balloons from one of the office buildings in the city.

Now Biedenbach, after he left Glen Ellen, had invented a most
powerful explosive—"expedite" he called it. This was the weapon the
balloons used. They were only hot-air balloons, clumsily and hastily
made, but they did the work. I saw it all from the top of an office
building. The first balloon missed the fortresses completely and disappeared into the country; but we learned about it afterward. Burton
and O'Sullivan were in it. As they were descending they swept across
a railroad directly over a troop-train that was heading at full speed
for Chicago. They dropped their whole supply of expedite upon the
locomotive. The resulting wreck tied the line up for days. And the
best of it was that, released from the weight of expedite, the balloon
shot up into the air and did not come down for half a dozen miles,
both heroes escaping unharmed.

The second balloon was a failure. Its flight was lame. It floated too
low and was shot full of holes before it could reach the fortresses.
Herford and Guinness were in it, and they were blown to pieces along
with the field into which they fell. Biedenbach was in despair—we
heard all about it afterward—and he went up alone in the third balloon. He, too, made a low flight, but he was in luck, for they failed
seriously to puncture his balloon. I can see it now as I did then, from
the lofty top of the building—that inflated bag drifting along the air,
and that tiny speck of a man clinging on beneath. I could not see the

fortress, but those on the roof with me said he was directly over it. I did not see the expedite fall when he cut it loose. But I did see the balloon suddenly leap up into the sky. An appreciable time after that the great column of the explosion towered in the air, and after that, in turn, I heard the roar of it. Biedenbach the gentle had destroyed a fortress. Two other balloons followed at the same time. One was blown to pieces in the air, the expedite exploding, and the shock of it disrupted the second balloon, which fell prettily into the remaining fortress. It couldn't have been better planned, though the two comrades in it sacrificed their lives.

But to return to the people of the abyss. My experiences were confined to them. They raged and slaughtered and destroyed all over the city proper, and were in turn destroyed; but never once did they succeed in reaching the city of the oligarchs over on the west side. The oligarchs had protected themselves well. No matter what destruction was wreaked in the heart of the city, they, and their womenkind and children, were to escape hurt. I am told that their children played in the parks during those terrible days and that their favorite game was an imitation of their elders stamping upon the proletariat.

But the Mercenaries found it no easy task to cope with the people of the abyss and at the same time fight with the comrades. Chicago was true to her traditions, and though a generation of revolutionists was wiped out, it took along with it pretty close to a generation of its enemies. Of course, the Iron Heel kept the figures secret, but, at a very conservative estimate, at least one hundred and thirty thousand Mercenaries were slain. But the comrades had no chance. Instead of the whole country being hand in hand in revolt, they were all alone, and the total strength of the Oligarchy could have been directed against them if necessary. As it was, hour after hour, day after day, in endless train-loads, by hundreds of thousands, the Mercenaries were hurled into Chicago.

And there were so many of the people of the abyss! Tiring of the slaughter, a great herding movement was begun by the soldiers, the intent of which was to drive the street mobs, like cattle, into Lake Michigan. It was at the beginning of this movement that Garthwaite and I had encountered the young officer. This herding movement was practically a failure, thanks to the splendid work of the comrades. Instead of the great host the Mercenaries had hoped to gather together, they succeeded in driving no more than forty thousand of the wretches into the lake. Time and again, when a mob of them was well in hand and being driven along the streets to the water, the comrades would create a diversion, and the mob would escape through the consequent hole torn in the encircling net.

Garthwaite and I saw an example of this shortly after meeting with the young officer. The mob of which we had been a part, and which had been put in retreat, was prevented from escaping to the south and east by strong bodies of troops. The troops we had fallen in with had held it back on the west. The only outlet was north, and north it went toward the lake, driven on from east and west and south by machine-gun fire and automatics. Whether it divined that it was being driven toward the lake, or whether it was merely a blind squirm of the monster, I do not know; but at any rate the mob took a cross street to the west, turned down the next street, and came back upon its track, heading south toward the great ghetto.

Garthwaite and I at that time were trying to make our way westward to get out of the territory of street-fighting, and we were caught right in the thick of it again. As we came to the corner we saw the howling mob bearing down upon us. Garthwaite seized my arm and we were just starting to run, when he dragged me back from in front of the wheels of half a dozen war automobiles, equipped with machine-guns, that were rushing for the spot. Behind them came the soldiers with their automatic rifles. By the time they took position, the mob was upon them, and it looked as though they would be overwhelmed before they could get into action.

Here and there a soldier was discharging his rifle, but this scattered fire had no effect in checking the mob. On it came, bellowing with brute rage. It seemed the machine-guns could not get started. The automobiles on which they were mounted blocked the street, compelling the soldiers to find positions in, between, and on the sidewalks. More and more soldiers were arriving, and in the jam we were unable to get away. Garthwaite held me by the arm, and we pressed close against the front of a building.

The mob was no more than twenty-five feet away when the machine-guns opened up; but before that flaming sheet of death nothing could live. The mob came on, but it could not advance. It piled up in a heap, a mound, a huge and growing wave of dead and dying. Those behind urged on, and the column, from gutter to gutter, telescoped upon itself. Wounded creatures, men and women, were vomited over the top of that awful wave and fell squirming down the face of it till they threshed about under the automobiles and against the legs of the soldiers. The latter bayoneted the struggling wretches, though one I saw who gained his feet and flew at a soldier's throat with his teeth. Together they went down, soldier and slave, into the welter.

The firing ceased. The work was done. The mob had been stopped in its wild attempt to break through. Orders were being given to clear the wheels of the war-machines. They could not advance over that wave of dead, and the idea was to run them down the cross street. The soldiers were dragging the bodies away from the wheels when it happened. We learned afterward how it happened. A block distant a hundred of our comrades had been holding a building. Across roofs and through buildings they made their way, till they found themselves looking down upon the close-packed soldiers. Then it was counter-massacre.

Without warning, a shower of bombs fell from the top of the building. The automobiles were blown to fragments, along with many soldiers. We, with the survivors, swept back in mad retreat. Half a block down another building opened fire on us. As the soldiers had carpeted the street with dead slaves, so, in turn, did they themselves become carpet. Garthwaite and I bore charmed lives. As we had done before, so again we sought shelter in an entrance. But he was not to be caught napping this time. As the roar of the bombs died away, he began peering out.

"The mob's coming back!" he called to me. "We've got to get out of this!"

We fled, hand in hand, down the bloody pavement, slipping and sliding, and making for the corner. Down the cross street we could see a few soldiers still running. Nothing was happening to them. The way was clear. So we paused a moment and looked back. The mob came on slowly. It was busy arming itself with the rifles of the slain and killing the wounded. We saw the end of the young officer who had rescued us. He painfully lifted himself on his elbow and turned loose with his automatic pistol.

"There goes my chance of promotion," Garthwaite laughed, as a woman bore down on the wounded man, brandishing a butcher's cleaver. "Come on. It's the wrong direction, but we'll get out somehow."

And we fled eastward through the quiet streets, prepared at every cross street for anything to happen. To the south a monster conflagration was filling the sky, and we knew that the great ghetto was burn-

ing. At last I sank down on the sidewalk. I was exhausted and could
go no farther. I was bruised and sore and aching in every limb; yet
I could not escape smiling at Garthwaite, who was rolling a cigarette
and saying:

"I know I'm making a mess of rescuing you, but I can't get head
nor tail of the situation. It's all a mess. Every time we try to break
out, something happens and we're turned back. We're only a couple
of blocks now from where I got you out of that entrance. Friend and
foe are all mixed up. It's chaos. You can't tell who is in those darned
buildings. Try to find out, and you get a bomb on your head. Try to
go peaceably on your way, and you run into a mob and are killed by
machine-guns, or you run into the Mercenaries and are killed by your
own comrades from a roof. And on the top of it all the mob comes
along and kills you, too."

He shook his head dolefully, lighted his cigarette, and sat down
beside me.

"And I'm that hungry," he added, "I could eat cobblestones."

The next moment he was on his feet again and out in the street
prying up a cobblestone. He came back with it and assaulted the
window of a store behind us.

"It's ground floor and no good," he explained as he helped me
through the hole he had made; "but it's the best we can do. You get
a nap and I'll reconnoitre. I'll finish this rescue all right, but I want
time, time, lots of it—and something to eat."

It was a harness store we found ourselves in, and he fixed me up a
couch of horse blankets in the private office well to the rear. To add to
my wretchedness a splitting headache was coming on, and I was only
too glad to close my eyes and try to sleep.

"I'll be back," were his parting words. "I don't hope to get an auto,
but I'll surely bring some grub,[45] anyway."

And that was the last I saw of Garthwaite for three years. Instead
of coming back, he was carried away to a hospital with a bullet
through his lungs and another through the fleshy part of his neck.

NIGHTMARE

I had not closed my eyes the night before on the Twentieth Century,
and what of that and of my exhaustion I slept soundly. When I first
awoke, it was night. Garthwaite had not returned. I had lost my watch

[45] Food.

and had no idea of the time. As I lay with my eyes closed, I heard the same dull sound of distant explosions. The inferno was still raging. I crept through the store to the front. The reflection from the sky of vast conflagrations made the street almost as light as day. One could have read the finest print with ease. From several blocks away came the crackle of small hand-bombs and the churning of machine-guns, and from a long way off came a long series of heavy explosions. I crept back to my horse blankets and slept again.

When next I awoke, a sickly yellow light was filtering in on me. It was dawn of the second day. I crept to the front of the store. A smoke pall, shot through with lurid gleams, filled the sky. Down the opposite side of the street tottered a wretched slave. One hand he held tightly against his side, and behind him he left a bloody trail. His eyes roved everywhere, and they were filled with apprehension and dread. Once he looked straight across at me, and in his face was all the dumb pathos of the wounded and hunted animal. He saw me, but there was no kinship between us, and with him, at least, no sympathy of understanding; for he cowered perceptibly and dragged himself on. He could expect no aid in all God's world. He was a helot in the great hunt of helots that the masters were making. All he could hope for, all he sought, was some hole to crawl away in and hide like any animal. The sharp clang of a passing ambulance at the corner gave him a start. Ambulances were not for such as he. With a groan of pain he threw himself into a doorway. A minute later he was out again and desperately hobbling on.

I went back to my horse blankets and waited an hour for Garthwaite. My headache had not gone away. On the contrary, it was increasing. It was by an effort of will only that I was able to open my eyes and look at objects. And with the opening of my eyes and the looking came intolerable torment. Also, a great pulse was beating in my brain. Weak and reeling, I went out through the broken window and down the street, seeking to escape, instinctively and gropingly, from the awful shambles. And thereafter I lived nightmare. My memory of what happened in the succeeding hours is the memory one would have of nightmare. Many events are focussed sharply on my brain, but between these indelible pictures I retain are intervals of unconsciousness. What occurred in those intervals I know not, and never shall know.

I remember stumbling at the corner over the legs of a man. It was the poor hunted wretch that had dragged himself past my hiding-place. How distinctly do I remember his poor, pitiful, gnarled hands as he lay there on the pavement—hands that were more hoof and claw than hands, all twisted and distorted by the toil of all his days, with on the palms a horny growth of callous a half inch thick. And as I picked myself up and started on, I looked into the face of the thing and saw that it still lived; for the eyes, dimly intelligent, were looking at me and seeing me.

After that came a kindly blank. I knew nothing, saw nothing, merely tottered on in my quest for safety. My next nightmare vision was a quiet street of the dead. I came upon it abruptly, as a wanderer in the country would come upon a flowing stream. Only this stream I gazed upon did not flow. It was congealed in death. From pavement to pavement, and covering the sidewalks, it lay there, spread out quite evenly, with only here and there a lump or mound of bodies to break the surface. Poor driven people of the abyss, hunted helots— they lay there as the rabbits in California after a drive.[46] Up the street and down I looked. There was no movement, no sound. The quiet buildings looked down upon the scene from their many windows. And once, and once only, I saw an arm that moved in that dead stream. I swear I saw it move, with a strange writhing gesture of agony, and with it lifted a head, gory with nameless horror, that gibbered at me and then lay down again and moved no more.

I remember another street, with quiet buildings on either side, and the panic that smote me into consciousness as again I saw the people of the abyss, but this time in a stream that flowed and came on. And then I saw there was nothing to fear. The stream moved slowly, while from it arose groans and lamentations, cursings, babblings of senility, hysteria, and insanity; for these were the very young and the very old, the feeble and the sick, the helpless and the hopeless, all the wreckage of the ghetto. The burning of the great ghetto on the South Side had driven them forth into the inferno of the street-fighting, and whither they wended and whatever became of them I did not know and never learned.[47]

[46] In those days, so sparsely populated was the land that wild animals often became pests. In California the custom of rabbit-driving obtained. On a given day all the farmers in a locality would assemble and sweep across the country in converging lines, driving the rabbits by scores of thousands into a prepared enclosure, where they were clubbed to death by men and boys.

[47] It was long a question of debate, whether the burning of the South Side ghetto was accidental, or whether it was done by the Mercenaries; but it is

I have faint memories of breaking a window and hiding in some shop to escape a street mob that was pursued by soldiers. Also, a bomb burst near me, once, in some still street, where, look as I would, up and down, I could see no human being. But my next sharp recollection begins with the crack of a rifle and an abrupt becoming aware that I am being fired at by a soldier in an automobile. The shot missed, and the next moment I was screaming and motioning the signals. My memory of riding in the automobile is very hazy, though this ride, in turn, is broken by one vivid picture. The crack of the rifle of the soldier sitting beside me made me open my eyes, and I saw George Milford, whom I had known in the Pell Street days, sinking slowly down to the sidewalk. Even as he sank the soldier fired again, and Milford doubled in, then flung his body out, and fell sprawling. The soldier chuckled, and the automobile sped on.

The next I knew after that I was awakened out of a sound sleep by a man who walked up and down close beside me. His face was drawn and strained, and the sweat rolled down his nose from his forehead. One hand was clutched tightly against his chest by the other hand, and blood dripped down upon the floor as he walked. He wore the uniform of the Mercenaries. From without, as through thick walls, came the muffled roar of bursting bombs. I was in some building that was locked in combat with some other building.

A surgeon came in to dress the wounded soldier, and I learned that it was two in the afternoon. My headache was no better, and the surgeon paused from his work long enough to give me a powerful drug that would depress the heart and bring relief. I slept again, and the next I knew I was on top of the building. The immediate fighting had ceased, and I was watching the balloon attack on the fortresses. Some one had an arm around me and I was leaning close against him. It came to me quite as a matter of course that this was Ernest, and I found myself wondering how he had got his hair and eyebrows so badly singed.

It was by the merest chance that we had found each other in that terrible city. He had had no idea that I had left New York, and, coming through the room where I lay asleep, could not at first believe that it was I. Little more I saw of the Chicago Commune. After watching the balloon attack, Ernest took me down into the heart of

---

definitely settled now that the ghetto was fired by the Mercenaries under orders from their chiefs.

the building, where I slept the afternoon out and the night. The third day we spent in the building, and on the fourth, Ernest having got permission and an automobile from the authorities, we left Chicago.

My headache was gone, but, body and soul, I was very tired. I lay back against Ernest in the automobile, and with apathetic eyes watched the soldiers trying to get the machine out of the city. Fighting was still going on, but only in isolated localities. Here and there whole districts were still in possession of the comrades, but such districts were surrounded and guarded by heavy bodies of troops. In a hundred segregated traps were the comrades thus held while the work of subjugating them went on. Subjugation meant death, for no quarter was given, and they fought heroically to the last man.[48]

Whenever we approached such localities, the guards turned us back and sent us around. Once, the only way past two strong positions of the comrades was through a burnt section that lay between. From either side we could hear the rattle and roar of war, while the automobile picked its way through smoking ruins and tottering walls. Often the streets were blocked by mountains of débris that compelled us to go around. We were in a labyrinth of ruin, and our progress was slow.

The stockyards (ghetto, plant, and everything) were smouldering ruins. Far off to the right a wide smoke haze dimmed the sky,—the town of Pullman, the soldier chauffeur told us, or what had been the town of Pullman, for it was utterly destroyed. He had driven the machine out there, with despatches, on the afternoon of the third day. Some of the heaviest fighting had occurred there, he said, many of the streets being rendered impassable by the heaps of the dead.

Swinging around the shattered walls of a building, in the stockyards district, the automobile was stopped by a wave of dead. It was for all the world like a wave tossed up by the sea. It was patent to us what had happened. As the mob charged past the corner, it had been swept, at right angles and point-blank range, by the machine-guns drawn up on the cross street. But disaster had come to the soldiers. A chance bomb must have exploded among them, for the mob,

---

[48] Numbers of the buildings held out over a week, while one held out eleven days. Each building had to be stormed like a fort, and the Mercenaries fought their way upward floor by floor. It was deadly fighting. Quarter was neither given nor taken, and in the fighting the revolutionists had the advantage of being above. While the revolutionists were wiped out, the loss was not one-sided. The proud Chicago proletariat lived up to its ancient boast. For as many of itself as were killed, it killed that many of the enemy.

checked until its dead and dying formed the wave, had white-capped and flung forward its foam of living, fighting slaves. Soldiers and slaves lay together, torn and mangled, around and over the wreckage of the automobiles and guns.

Ernest sprang out. A familiar pair of shoulders in a cotton shirt and a familiar fringe of white hair had caught his eye. I did not watch him, and it was not until he was back beside me and we were speeding on that he said:

"It was Bishop Morehouse."

Soon we were in the green country, and I took one last glance back at the smoke-filled sky. Faint and far came the low thud of an explosion. Then I turned my face against Ernest's breast and wept softly for the Cause that was lost. Ernest's arm about me was eloquent with love.

"For this time lost, dear heart," he said, "but not forever. We have learned. To-morrow the Cause will rise again, strong with wisdom and discipline."

The automobile drew up at a railroad station. Here we would catch a train to New York. As we waited on the platform, three trains thundered past, bound west to Chicago. They were crowded with ragged, unskilled laborers, people of the abyss.

"Slave-levies for the rebuilding of Chicago," Ernest said. "You see, the Chicago slaves are all killed."

THE TERRORISTS

It was not until Ernest and I were back in New York, and after weeks had elapsed, that we were able to comprehend thoroughly the full sweep of the disaster that had befallen the Cause. The situation was bitter and bloody. In many places, scattered over the country, slave revolts and massacres had occurred. The roll of the martyrs increased mightily. Countless executions took place everywhere. The mountains and waste regions were filled with outlaws and refugees who were being hunted down mercilessly. Our own refuges were packed with comrades who had prices on their heads. Through information furnished by its spies, scores of our refuges were raided by the soldiers of the Iron Heel.

Many of the comrades were disheartened, and they retaliated with terroristic tactics. The set-back to their hopes made them despairing and desperate. Many terrorist organizations unaffiliated with us sprang into existence and caused us much trouble.[49] These misguided people sacrificed their own lives wantonly, very often made our own plans go astray, and retarded our organization.

And through it all moved the Iron Heel, impassive and deliberate, shaking up the whole fabric of the social structure in its search for the comrades, combing out the Mercenaries, the labor castes, and all its secret services, punishing without mercy and without malice, suffering in silence all retaliations that were made upon it, and filling the gaps in its fighting line as fast as they appeared. And hand in hand with this, Ernest and the other leaders were hard at work reorganizing the forces of the Revolution. The magnitude of the task may be understood when it is taken into [50]

[49] The annals of this short-lived era of despair make bloody reading. Revenge was the ruling motive, and the members of the terroristic organizations were careless of their own lives and hopeless about the future. The Danites, taking their name from the avenging angels of the Mormon mythology, sprang up in the mountains of the Great West and spread over the Pacific Coast from Panama to Alaska. The Valkyries were women. They were the most terrible of all. No woman was eligible for membership who had not lost near relatives at the hands of the Oligarchy. They were guilty of torturing their prisoners to death. Another famous organization of women was The Widows of War. A companion organization to the Valkyries was the Berserkers. These men placed no value whatever upon their own lives, and it was they who totally destroyed the great Mercenary city of Belona along with its population of over a hundred thousand souls. The Bedlamites and the Helldamites were twin slave organizations, while a new religious sect that did not flourish long was called The Wrath of God. Among others, to show the whimsicality of their deadly seriousness, may be mentioned the following: The Bleeding Hearts, Sons of the Morning, the Morning Stars, The Flamingoes, The Triple Triangles, The Three Bars, The Rubonics, The Vindicators, The Comanches, and The Erebusites.

[50] This is the end of the Everhard Manuscript. It breaks off abruptly in the middle of a sentence. She must have received warning of the coming of the Mercenaries, for she had time safely to hid the Manuscript before she fled or was captured. It is to be regretted that she did not live to complete her narrative, for then, undoubtedly, would have been cleared away the mystery that has shrouded for seven centuries the execution of Ernest Everhard.

The Apostate

Now I wake me up to work;
I pray the Lord I may not shirk.
If I should die before the night,
I pray the Lord my work's all right.

AMEN

"If you don't git up, Johnny, I won't give you a bite to eat!"

The threat had no effect on the boy. He clung stubbornly to sleep, fighting for its oblivion as the dreamer fights for his dream. The boy's hands loosely clenched themselves, and he made feeble, spasmodic blows at the air. These blows were intended for his mother, but she betrayed practised familiarity in avoiding them as she shook him roughly by the shoulder.

"Lemme 'lone!"

It was a cry that began, muffled, in the deeps of sleep, that swiftly rushed upward, like a wail, into passionate belligerence, and that died away and sank down into an inarticulate whine. It was a bestial cry, as of a soul in torment, filled with infinite protest and pain.

But she did not mind. She was a sad-eyed, tired-faced woman, and she had grown used to this task, which she repeated every day of her life. She got a grip on the bedclothes and tried to strip them down; but the boy, ceasing his punching, clung to them desperately. In a huddle, at the foot of the bed, he still remained covered. Then she tried dragging the bedding to the floor. The boy opposed her. She braced herself. Hers was the superior weight, and the boy and bedding gave, the former instinctively following the latter in order to shelter against the chill of the room that bit into his body.

As he toppled on the edge of the bed it seemed that he must fall head-first to the floor. But consciousness fluttered up in him. He righted himself and for a moment perilously balanced. Then he struck the floor on his feet. On the instant his mother seized him by the shoulders and shook him. Again his fists struck out, this time with more force and directness. At the same time his eyes opened. She released him. He was awake.

"All right," he mumbled.

She caught up the lamp and hurried out, leaving him in darkness.

"You'll be docked," she warned back at him.

He did not mind the darkness. When he had got into his clothes, he went out into the kitchen. His tread was very heavy for so thin and light a boy. His legs dragged with their own weight, which seemed unreasonable because they were such skinny legs. He drew a broken-bottomed chair to the table.

"Johnny!" his mother called sharply.

He arose as sharply from the chair, and, without a word went to the sink. It was a greasy, filthy sink. A smell came up from the outlet. He took no notice of it. That a sink should smell was to him part of the natural order, just as it was a part of the natural order that the soap should be grimy with dishwater and hard to lather. Nor did he try very hard to make it lather. Several splashes of the cold water from the running faucet completed the function. He did not wash his teeth. For that matter he had never seen a tooth-brush, nor did he know that there existed human beings in the world who were guilty of so great a foolishness as tooth washing.

"You might wash yourself wunst a day without bein' told," his mother complained.

She was holding a broken lid on the pot as she poured two cups of coffee. He made no remark, for this was a standing quarrel between them, and the one thing upon which his mother was hard as adamant. "Wunst" a day it was compulsory that he should wash his face. He dried himself on a greasy towel, damp and dirty and ragged, that left his face covered with shreds of lint.

"I wish we didn't live so far away," she said, as he sat down. "I try to do the best I can. You know that. But a dollar on the rent is such a savin', an we've more room here. You know that."

He scarcely followed her. He had heard it all before, many times. The range of her thought was limited, and she was ever harking back to the hardship worked upon them by living so far from the mills.

"A dollar means more grub," he remarked sententiously. "I'd sooner do the walkin' and git the grub."

He ate hurriedly, half chewing the bread and washing the unmasticated chunks down with coffee. The hot and muddy liquid went by the name of coffee. Johnny thought it was coffee—and excellent coffee. That was one of the few of life's illusions that remained to him. He had never drunk real coffee in his life.

In addition to the bread, there was a small piece of cold pork. His mother refilled his cup with coffee. As he was finishing the bread, he began to watch if more was forthcoming. She intercepted his questioning glance.

"Now, don't be hoggish, Johnny," was her comment. "You've had your share. Your brothers an' sisters are smaller'n you."

He did not answer the rebuke. He was not much of a talker. Also, he ceased his hungry glancing for more. He was uncomplaining, with a patience that was as terrible as the school in which it had been learned. He finished his coffee, wiped his mouth on the back of his hand, and started to rise.

"Wait a second," she said hastily. "I guess the loaf can stand another slice—a thin un."

There was legerdemain in her actions. With all the seeming of cutting a slice from the loaf for him, she put loaf and slice back in the bread box and conveyed to him one of her own two slices. She believed she had deceived him, but he had noted her sleight-of-hand. Nevertheless, he took the bread shamelessly. He had a philosophy that his mother, what of her chronic sickliness, was not much of an eater anyway.

She saw that he was chewing the bread dry, and reached over and emptied her coffee cup into his.

"Don't set good somehow on my stomach this morning," she explained.

A distant whistle, prolonged and shrieking, brought both of them to their feet. She glanced at the tin alarm-clock on the shelf. The hands stood at half-past five. The rest of the factory world was just arousing from sleep. She drew a shawl about her shoulders, and on her head put a dingy hat, shapeless and ancient.

"We've got to run," she said, turning the wick of the lamp and blowing down the chimney.

They groped their way out and down the stairs. It was clear and cold, and Johnny shivered at the first contact with the outside air.

The stars had not yet begun to pale in the sky, and the city lay in blackness. Both Johnny and his mother shuffled their feet as they walked. There was no ambition in the leg muscles to swing the feet clear of the ground.

After fifteen silent minutes, his mother turned off to the right.

"Don't be late," was her final warning from out of the dark that was swallowing her up.

He made no response, steadily keeping on his way. In the factory quarter, doors were opening everywhere, and he was soon one of a multitude that pressed onward through the dark. As he entered the factory gate the whistle blew again. He glanced at the east. Across a ragged sky-line of housetops a pale light was beginning to creep. This much he saw of the day as he turned his back upon it and joined his work-gang.

He took his place in one of many long rows of machines. Before him, above a bin filled with small bobbins, were large bobbins revolving rapidly. Upon these he wound the jute-twine of the small bobbins. The work was simple. All that was required was celerity. The small bobbins were emptied so rapidly, and there were so many large bobbins that did the emptying, that there were no idle moments.

He worked mechanically. When a small bobbin ran out, he used his left hand for a brake, stopping the large bobbin and at the same time, with thumb and forefinger, catching the flying end of twine. Also, at the same time, with his right hand, he caught up the loose twine-end of a small bobbin. These various acts with both hands were performed simultaneously and swiftly. Then there would come a flash of his hands as he looped the weaver's knot and released the bobbin. There was nothing difficult about the weaver's knots. He once boasted he could tie them in his sleep. And for that matter, he sometimes did, toiling centuries long in a single night at tying an endless succession of weaver's knots.

Some of the boys shirked, wasting time and machinery by not replacing the small bobbins when they ran out. And there was an overseer to prevent this. He caught Johnny's neighbor at the trick, and boxed his ears.

"Look at Johnny there—why ain't you like him?" the overseer wrathfully demanded.

Johnny's bobbins were running full blast, but he did not thrill at the indirect praise. There had been a time . . . but that was long ago, very long ago. His apathetic face was expressionless as he lis-

tened to himself being held up as a shining example. He was the perfect worker. He knew that. He had been told so, often. It was a com-
monplace, and besides it didn't seem to mean anything to him any
more. From the perfect worker he had evolved into the perfect machine. When his work went wrong, it was with him as with the
machine, due to faulty material. It would have been as possible for a
perfect nail-die to cut imperfect nails as for him to make a mistake.

And small wonder. There had never been a time when he had not
been in intimate relationship with machines. Machinery had almost
been bred into him, and at any rate he had been brought up on it.
Twelve years before, there had been a small flutter of excitement in
the loom room of this very mill. Johnny's mother had fainted. They
stretched her out on the floor in the midst of the shrieking machines.
A couple of elderly women were called from their looms. The foreman
assisted. And in a few minutes there was one more soul in the loom
room than had entered by the doors. It was Johnny, born with the
pounding, crashing roar of the looms in his ears, drawing with his first
breath the warm, moist air that was thick with flying lint. He had
coughed that first day in order to rid his lungs of the lint; and for the
same reason he had coughed ever since.

The boy alongside of Johnny whimpered and sniffed. The boy's
face was convulsed with hatred for the overseer who kept a threatening eye on him from a distance; but every bobbin was running full.
The boy yelled terrible oaths into the whirling bobbins before him;
but the sound did not carry half a dozen feet, the roaring of the room
holding it in and containing it like a wall.

Of all this Johnny took no notice. He had a way of accepting things.
Besides, things grow monotonous by repetition, and this particular
happening he had witnessed many times. It seemed to him as useless
to oppose the overseer as to defy the will of a machine. Machines were
made to go in certain ways and to perform certain tasks. It was the
same with the overseer.

But at eleven o'clock there was excitement in the room. In an apparently occult way the excitement instantly permeated everywhere.
The one-legged boy who worked on the other side of Johnny bobbed
swiftly across the floor to a bin truck that stood empty. Into this he
dived out of sight, crutch and all. The superintendent of the mill was
coming along, accompanied by a young man. He was well dressed and
wore a starched shirt—a gentleman, in Johnny's classification of men,
and also, "the Inspector."

He looked sharp at the boys as he passed along. When he did so, he was compelled to shout at the top of his lungs, at which moments his face was ludicrously contorted with the strain of making himself heard. His quick eye noted the empty machine alongside of Johnny's, but he said nothing. Johnny also caught his eye, and he stopped abruptly. He caught Johnny by the arm to draw him back a step from the machine; but with an exclamation of surprise he released the arm.

"Pretty skinny," the superintendent laughed anxiously.

"Pipe stems," was the answer. "Look at those legs. The boy's got the rickets—incipient, but he's got them. If epilepsy doesn't get him in the end, it will be because tuberculosis gets him first."

Johnny listened, but did not understand. Furthermore he was not interested in future ills. There was an immediate and more serious ill that threatened him in the form of the inspector.

"Now, my boy, I want you to tell me the truth," the inspector said, or shouted, bending close to the boy's ear to make him hear. "How old are you?"

"Fourteen," Johnny lied, and he lied with the full force of his lungs. So loudly did he lie that it started him off in a dry, hacking cough that lifted the lint which had been settling in his lungs all morning.

"Looks sixteen at least," said the superintendent.

"Or sixty," snapped the inspector.

"He's always looked that way."

"How long?" asked the inspector quickly.

"For years. Never gets a bit older."

"Or younger, I dare say. I suppose he's worked here all those years?"

"Off and on—but that was before the new law was passed," the superintendent hastened to add.

"Machine idle?" the inspector asked, pointing at the unoccupied machine beside Johnny's, in which the part filled bobbins were flying like mad.

"Looks that way." The superintendent motioned the overseer to him and shouted in his ear and pointed at the machine. "Machine's idle," he reported back to the inspector.

They passed on, and Johnny returned to his work, relieved in that the ill had been averted. But the one-legged boy was not so fortunate. The sharp-eyed inspector hauled him out at arm's length from the bin truck. His lips were quivering, and his face had all the expression of one upon whom was fallen profound and irremediable disaster. The

overseer looked astounded, as though for the first time he had laid
eyes on the boy, while the superintendent's face expressed shock and
displeasure.

"I know him," the inspector said. "He's twelve years old. I've had
him discharged from three factories inside the year. This makes the
fourth."

He turned to the one-legged boy. "You promised me, word and
honor, that you'd go to school."

The one-legged boy burst into tears. "Please, Mr. Inspector, two
babies died on us, and we're awful poor."

"What makes you cough that way?" the inspector demanded, as
though charging him with crime.

And as in denial of guilt, the one-legged boy replied: "It ain't
nothin'. I jes' caught a cold last week, Mr. Inspector, that's all."

In the end the one-legged boy went out of the room with the inspector, the latter accompanied by the anxious and protesting superintendent. After that monotony settled down again. The long morning
and the longer afternoon wore away and the whistle blew for quitting
time. Darkness had already fallen when Johnny passed out through
the factory gate. In the interval the sun had made a golden ladder of
the sky, flooded the world with its gracious warmth, and dropped
down and disappeared in the west behind a ragged sky-line of housetops.

Supper was the family meal of the day—the one meal at which
Johnny encountered his younger brothers and sisters. It partook of
the nature of an encounter, to him, for he was very old, while they
were distressingly young. He had no patience with their excessive and
amazing juvenility. He did not understand it. His own childhood was
too far behind him. He was like an old and irritable man, annoyed
by the turbulence of their young spirits that was to him arrant silli-
ness. He glowered silently over his food, finding compensation in the
thought that they would soon have to go to work. That would take
the edge off of them and make them sedate and dignified—like him.
Thus it was, after the fashion of the human, that Johnny made of
himself a yardstick with which to measure the universe.

During the meal, his mother explained in various ways and with
infinite repetition that she was trying to do the best she could; so that
it was with relief, the scant meal ended, that Johnny shoved back his
chair and arose. He debated for a moment between bed and the front

door, and finally went out the latter. He did not go far. He sat down on the stoop, his knees drawn up and his narrow shoulders drooping forward, his elbows on his knees and the palms of his hand supporting his chin.

As he sat there, he did no thinking. He was just resting. So far as his mind was concerned, it was asleep. His brothers and sisters came out, and with other children played noisily about him. An electric globe on the corner lighted their frolics. He was peevish and irritable, that they knew; but the spirit of adventure lured them into teasing him. They joined hands before him, and, keeping time with their bodies, chanted in his face weird and uncomplimentary doggerel. At first he snarled curses at them—curses he had learned from the lips of various foremen. Finding this futile, and remembering his dignity, he relapsed into dogged silence.

His brother Will, next to him in age, having just passed his tenth birthday, was the ringleader. Johnny did not possess particularly kindly feelings toward him. His life had early been imbittered by continual giving over and giving way to Will. He had a definite feeling that Will was greatly in his debt and was ungrateful about it. In his own playtime, far back in the dim past, he had been robbed of a large part of that playtime by being compelled to take care of Will. Will was a baby then, and then, as now, their mother had spent her days in the mills. To Johnny had fallen the part of little father and little mother as well.

Will seemed to show the benefit of the giving over and the giving way. He was well-built, fairly rugged, as tall as his elder brother and even heavier. It was as though the lifeblood of the one had been diverted into the other's veins. And in spirits it was the same. Johnny was jaded, worn out, without resilience, while his younger brother seemed bursting and spilling over with exuberance.

The mocking chant rose louder and louder. Will leaned closer as he danced, thrusting out his tongue. Johnny's left arm shot out and caught the other around the neck. At the same time he rapped his bony fist to the other's nose. It was a pathetically bony fist, but that it was sharp to hurt was evidenced by the squeal of pain it produced. The other children were uttering frightened cries, while Johnny's sister, Jenny, had dashed into the house.

He thrust Will from him, kicked him savagely on the shins, then reached for him and slammed him face downward in the dirt. Nor did he release him till the face had been rubbed into the dirt several times. Then the mother arrived, an anæmic whirlwind of solicitude and maternal wrath.

"Why can't he leave me alone?" was Johnny's reply to her upbraiding. "Can't he see I'm tired?"

"I'm as big as you," Will raged in her arms, his face a mess of tears, dirt, and blood. "I'm as big as you now, an' I'm goin' to git bigger. Then I'll lick you—see if I don't."

"You ought to be to work, seein' how big you are," Johnny snarled. "That's what's the matter with you. You ought to be to work. An' it's up to your ma to put you to work."

"But he's too young," she protested. "He's only a little boy."

"I was younger'n him when I started to work."

Johnny's mouth was open, further to express the sense of unfairness that he felt, but the mouth closed with a snap. He turned gloomily on his heel and stalked into the house and to bed. The door of his room was open to let in warmth from the kitchen. As he undressed in the semi-darkness he could hear his mother talking with a neighbor woman who had dropped in. His mother was crying, and her speech was punctuated with spiritless sniffles.

"I can't make out what's gittin' into Johnny," he could hear her say. "He didn't used to be this way. He was a patient little angel."

"An' he is a good boy," she hastened to defend. "He's worked faithful, an' he did go to work too young. But it wasn't my fault. I do the best I can, I'm sure."

Prolonged sniffling from the kitchen, and Johnny murmured to himself as his eyelids closed down, "You betcher life I've worked faithful."

The next morning he was torn bodily by his mother from the grip of sleep. Then came the meagre breakfast, the tramp through the dark, and the pale glimpse of day across the housetops as he turned his back on it and went in through the factory gate. It was another day, of all the days, and all the days were alike.

And yet there had been variety in his life—at the times he changed from one job to another, or was taken sick. When he was six, he was little mother and father to Will and the other children still younger. At seven he went into the mills—winding bobbins. When he was eight, he got work in another mill. His new job was marvellously easy. All he had to do was to sit down with a little stick in his hand and guide a stream of cloth that flowed past him. This stream of cloth came out of the maw of a machine, passed over a hot roller, and went on its way elsewhere. But he sat always in the one place, beyond the reach of daylight, a gas-jet flaring over him, himself part of the mechanism.

He was very happy at that job, in spite of the moist heat, for he was still young and in possession of dreams and illusions. And wonderful dreams he dreamed as he watched the steaming cloth streaming endlessly by. But there was no exercise about the work, no call upon his mind, and he dreamed less and less, while his mind grew torpid and drowsy. Nevertheless, he earned two dollars a week, and two dollars represented the difference between acute starvation and chronic underfeeding.

But when he was nine, he lost his job. Measles was the cause of it. After he recovered, he got work in a glass factory. The pay was better, and the work demanded skill. It was piece-work, and the more skillful he was, the bigger wages he earned. Here was incentive. And under this incentive he developed into a remarkable worker.

It was simple work, the tying of glass stoppers into small bottles. At his waist he carried a bundle of twine. He held the bottles between his knees so that he might work with both hands. Thus, in a sitting position and bending over his own knees, his narrow shoulders grew humped and his chest was contracted for ten hours each day. This was not good for the lungs, but he tied three hundred dozen bottles a day.

The superintendent was very proud of him, and brought visitors to look at him. In ten hours three hundred dozen bottles passed through his hands. This meant that he had attained machine-like perfection. All waste movements were eliminated. Every motion of his thin arms, every movement of a muscle in the thin fingers, was swift and accurate. He worked at high tension, and the result was that he grew nervous. At night his muscles twitched in his sleep, and in the daytime he could not relax and rest. He remained keyed up and his muscles continued to twitch. Also he grew sallow and his lint-cough grew worse. Then pneumonia laid hold of the feeble lungs within the contracted chest, and he lost his job in the glassworks.

Now he had returned to the jute mills where he had first begun with winding bobbins. But promotion was waiting for him. He was a good worker. He would next go on the starcher, and later he would go into the loom room. There was nothing after that except increased efficiency.

The machinery ran faster than when he had first gone to work, and his mind ran slower. He no longer dreamed at all, though his earlier

years had been full of dreaming. Once he had been in love. It was
when he first began guiding the cloth over the hot roller, and it was
with the daughter of the superintendent. She was much older than he,
a young woman, and he had seen her at a distance only a paltry half-
dozen times. But that made no difference. On the surface of the cloth
stream that poured past him, he pictured radiant futures wherein he
performed prodigies of toil, invented miraculous machines, won to
the mastership of the mills, and in the end took her in his arms and
kissed her soberly on the brow.

But that was all in the long ago, before he had grown too old and
tired to love. Also, she had married and gone away, and his mind had
gone to sleep. Yet it had been a wonderful experience, and he used
often to look back upon it as other men and women look back upon
the time they believed in fairies. He had never believed in fairies nor
Santa Claus; but he had believed implicitly in the smiling future his
imagination had wrought into the steaming cloth stream.

He had become a man very early in life. At seven, when he drew
his first wages, began his adolescence. A certain feeling of independence crept up in him, and the relationship between him and his
mother changed. Somehow, as an earner and breadwinner, doing his
own work in the world, he was more like an equal with her. Manhood,
full-blown manhood, had come when he was eleven, at which time
he had gone to work on the night shift for six months. No child works
on the night shift and remains a child.

There had been several great events in his life. One of these had
been when his mother bought some California prunes. Two others
had been the two times when she cooked custard. Those had been
events. He remembered them kindly. And at that time his mother had
told him of a blissful dish she would sometime make—"floating island," she had called it, "better than custard." For years he had looked
forward to the day when he would sit down to the table with floating
island before him, until at last he had relegated the idea of it to the
limbo of unattainable ideals.

Once he found a silver quarter lying on the sidewalk. That, also,
was a great event in his life, withal a tragic one. He knew his duty on
the instant the silver flashed on his eyes, before even he had picked
it up. At home, as usual, there was not enough to eat, and home he
should have taken it as he did his wages every Saturday night. Right
conduct in this case was obvious; but he never had any spending of
his money, and he was suffering from candy hunger. He was ravenous

for the sweets that only on red-letter days he had ever tasted in his life.

He did not attempt to deceive himself. He knew it was sin, and deliberately he sinned when he went on a fifteen-cent candy debauch. Ten cents he saved for a future orgy; but not being accustomed to the carrying of money, he lost the ten cents. This occurred at the time when he was suffering all the torments of conscience, and it was to him an act of divine retribution. He had a frightened sense of the closeness of an awful and wrathful God. God had seen, and God had been swift to punish, denying him even the full wages of sin.

In memory he always looked back upon that event as the one great criminal deed of his life, and at the recollection his conscience always awoke and gave him another twinge. It was the one skeleton in his closet. Also, being so made and circumstanced, he looked back upon the deed with regret. He was dissatisfied with the manner in which he had spent the quarter. He could have invested it better, and, out of his later knowledge of the quickness of God, he would have beaten God out by spending the whole quarter at one fell swoop. In retrospect he spent the quarter a thousand times, and each time to better advantage.

There was one other memory of the past, dim and faded, but stamped into his soul everlastingly by the savage feet of his father. It was more like a nightmare than a remembered vision of a concrete thing—more like the race-memory of man that makes him fall in his sleep and that goes back to his arboreal ancestry.

This particular memory never came to Johnny in broad daylight when he was wide awake. It came at night, in bed, at the moment that his consciousness was sinking down and losing itself in sleep. It always aroused him to frightened wakefulness, and for the moment, in the first sickening start, it seemed to him that he lay crosswise on the foot of the bed. In the bed were the vague forms of his father and mother. He never saw what his father looked like. He had but one impression of his father, and that was that he had savage and pitiless feet.

His earlier memories lingered with him, but he had no late memories. All days were alike. Yesterday or last year were the same as a thousand years—or a minute. Nothing ever happened. There were no events to mark the march of time. Time did not march. It stood always still. It was only the whirling machines that moved, and they moved nowhere—in spite of the fact that they moved faster.

When he was fourteen, he went to work on the starcher. It was a colossal event. Something had at last happened that could be remembered beyond a night's sleep or a week's pay-day. It marked an era. It was a machine Olympiad, a thing to date from. "When I went to work on the starcher," or, "after," or "before I went to work on the starcher," were sentences often on his lips.

He celebrated his sixteenth birthday by going into the loom room and taking a loom. Here was an incentive again, for it was piece-work. And he excelled, because the clay of him had been moulded by the mills into the perfect machine. At the end of three months he was running two looms, and, later, three and four.

At the end of his second year at the looms he was turning out more yards than any other weaver, and more than twice as much as some of the less skillful ones. And at home things began to prosper as he approached the full stature of his earning power. Not, however, that his increased earnings were in excess of need. The children were growing up. They ate more. And they were going to school, and schoolbooks cost money. And somehow, the faster he worked, the faster climbed the prices of things. Even the rent went up, though the house had fallen from bad to worse disrepair.

He had grown taller; but with his increased height he seemed leaner than ever. Also, he was more nervous. With the nervousness increased peevishness and irritability. The children had learned by many bitter lessons to fight shy of him. His mother respected him for his earning power, but somehow her respect was tinctured with fear.

There was no joyousness in life for him. The procession of the days he never saw. The nights he slept away in twitching unconsciousness. The rest of the time he worked, and his consciousness was machine consciousness. Outside this his mind was a blank. He had no ideals, and but one illusion; namely, that he drank excellent coffee. He was a work-beast. He had no mental life whatever; yet deep down in the crypts of his mind, unknown to him, were being weighed and sifted every hour in his toil, every movement of his hands, every twitch of his muscles, and preparations were making for a future course of action that would amaze him and all his little world.

It was in the late spring that he came home from work one night aware of unusual tiredness. There was a keen expectancy in the air as he sat down to the table, but he did not notice. He went through the meal in moody silence, mechanically eating what was before him. The children um'd and ah'd and made smacking noises with their mouths. But he was deaf to them.

"D'ye know what you're eatin'?" his mother demanded at last, desperately.

He looked vacantly at the dish before him, and vacantly at her.

"Floatin' island," she announced triumphantly.

"Oh," he said.

"Floating island!" the children chorused loudly.

"Oh," he said. And after two or three mouthfuls, he added, "I guess I ain't hungry to-night."

He dropped the spoon, shoved back his chair, and arose wearily from the table.

"An' I guess I'll go to bed."

His feet dragged more heavily than usual as he crossed the kitchen floor. Undressing was a Titan's task, a monstrous futility, and he wept weakly as he crawled into bed, one shoe still on. He was aware of a rising, swelling something inside his head that made his brain thick and fuzzy. His lean fingers felt as big as his wrist, while in the ends of them was a remoteness of sensation vague and fuzzy like his brain. The small of his back ached intolerably. All his bones ached. He ached everywhere. And in his head began the shrieking, pounding, crashing, roaring of a million looms. All space was filled with flying shuttles. They darted in and out, intricately, amongst the stars. He worked a thousand looms himself, and ever they speeded up, faster and faster, and his brain unwound, faster and faster, and became the thread that fed the thousand flying shuttles.

He did not go to work next morning. He was too busy weaving colossally on the thousand looms that ran inside his head. His mother went to work, but first she sent for the doctor. It was a severe attack of la grippe, he said. Jennie served as nurse and carried out his instructions.

It was a very severe attack, and it was a week before Johnny dressed and tottered feebly across the floor. Another week, the doctor said, and he would be fit to return to work. The foreman of the loom room visited him on Sunday afternoon, the first day of his convalescence. The best weaver in the room, the foreman told his mother. His job would be held for him. He could come back to work a week from Monday.

"Why don't you thank 'im, Johnny?" his mother asked anxiously.

"He's ben that sick he ain't himself yet," she explained apologetically to the visitor.

Johnny sat hunched up and gazing steadfastly at the floor. He sat in the same position long after the foreman had gone. It was warm outdoors, and he sat on the stoop in the afternoon. Sometimes his lips moved. He seemed lost in endless calculations.

Next morning, after the day grew warm, he took his seat on the stoop. He had pencil and paper this time with which to continue his calculations, and he calculated painfully and amazingly.

"What comes after millions?" he asked at noon, when Will came home from school. "An' how d'ye work 'em?"

That afternoon finished his task. Each day, but without paper and pencil, he returned to the stoop. He was greatly absorbed in the one tree that grew across the street. He studied it for hours at a time, and was unusually interested when the wind swayed its branches and fluttered its leaves. Throughout the week he seemed lost in a great communion with himself. On Sunday, sitting on the stoop, he laughed aloud, several times, to the perturbation of his mother, who had not heard him laugh in years.

Next morning, in the early darkness, she came to his bed to rouse him. He had had his fill of sleep all week, and awoke easily. He made no struggle, nor did he attempt to hold on to the bedding when she stripped it from him. He lay quietly, and spoke quietly.

"It ain't no use, ma."

"You'll be late," she said, under the impression that he was still stupid with sleep.

"I'm awake, ma, an' I tell you it ain't no use. You might as well lemme alone. I ain't goin' to git up."

"But you'll lose your job!" she cried.

"I ain't goin' to git up," he repeated in a strange, passionless voice.

She did not go to work herself that morning. This was sickness beyond any sickness she had ever known. Fever and delirium she could understand; but this was insanity. She pulled the bedding up over him and sent Jennie for the doctor.

When that person arrived Johnny was sleeping gently, and gently he awoke and allowed his pulse to be taken.

"Nothing the matter with him," the doctor reported. "Badly debilitated, that's all. Not much meat on his bones."

"He's always been that way," his mother volunteered.

"Now go 'way, ma, an' let me finish my snooze."

Johnny spoke sweetly and placidly, and sweetly and placidly he rolled over on his side and went to sleep.

At ten o'clock he awoke and dressed himself. He walked out into the kitchen, where he found his mother with a frightened expression on her face.

"I'm goin' away, ma," he announced, "an' I jes' want to say good-by."

She threw her apron over her head and sat down suddenly and wept. He waited patiently.

"I might a-known it," she was sobbing.

"Where?" she finally asked, removing the apron from her head and gazing up at him with a stricken face in which there was little curiosity.

"I don't know—anywhere."

As he spoke, the tree across the street appeared with dazzling brightness on his inner vision. It seemed to lurk just under his eyelids, and he could see it whenever he wished.

"An' your job?" she quavered.

"I ain't never goin' to work again."

"My God, Johnny!" she wailed, "don't say that!"

What he had said was blasphemy to her. As a mother who hears her child deny God, was Johnny's mother shocked by his words.

"What's got into you, anyway?" she demanded, with a lame attempt at imperativeness.

"Figures," he answered. "Jes' figures. I've ben doin' a lot of figurin' this week, an' it's most surprisin'."

"I don't see what that's got to do with it," she sniffled.

Johnny smiled patiently, and his mother was aware of a distinct shock at the persistent absence of his peevishness and irritability.

"I'll show you," he said. "I'm plum' tired out. What makes me tired? Moves. I've ben moving' ever since I was born. I'm tired of movin', an' I ain't goin' to move any more. Remember when I worked in the glass-house? I used to do three hundred dozen a day. Now I reckon I made about ten different moves to each bottle. That's thirty-six thousan' moves a day. Ten days, three hundred an' sixty thousan' moves a day. One month, one million an' eighty thousan' moves. Chuck out the eighty thousan'—" he spoke with the complacent beneficence of a philanthropist—"chuck out the eighty thousan', that leaves a million moves a month—twelve million moves a year.

"At the looms I'm movin' twic'st as much. That makes twenty-five million moves a year, an' it seems to me I've ben a-movin' that way 'most a million years.

"Now this week I ain't moved at all. I ain't made one move in hours an' hours. I tell you it was swell, jes' settin' there, hours an' hours, an' doin' nothin'. I ain't never ben happy before. I never had any time. I've ben movin' all the time. That ain't no way to be happy. An' I ain't goin' to do it any more. I'm jes' goin' to set, an' set, an' rest, an' rest, and then rest some more."

"But what's goin' to come of Will an' the children?" she asked despairingly.

"That's it, 'Will an' the children,' " he repeated.

But there was no bitterness in his voice. He had long known his mother's ambition for the younger boy, but the thought of it no longer rankled. Nothing mattered any more. Not even that.

"I know, ma, what you've ben plannin' for Will—keepin' him in school to make a bookkeeper out of him. But it ain't no use, I've quit. He's got to go to work."

"An' after I have brung you up the way I have," she wept, starting to cover her head with the apron and changing her mind.

"You never brung me up," he answered with sad kindliness. "I brung myself up, ma, an' I brung up Will. He's bigger'n me, an' heavier an' taller. When I was a kid, I reckon I didn't git enough to eat. When he come along an' was a kid, I was workin' an' earnin' grub for him too. But that's done with. Will can go to work, same as me, or he can go to hell, I don't care which. I'm tired. I'm goin' now. Ain't you goin' to say good-by?"

She made no reply. The apron had gone over her head again, and she was crying. He paused a moment in the doorway.

"I'm sure I done the best I knew how," she was sobbing.

He passed out of the house and down the street. A wan delight came into his face at the sight of the lone tree. "Jes' ain't goin' to do nothin'," he said to himself, half aloud, in a crooning tone. He glanced wistfully up at the sky, but the bright sun dazzled and blinded him.

It was a long walk he took, and he did not walk fast. It took him past the jute-mill. The muffled roar of the looms came to his ears, and he smiled. It was a gentle, placid smile. He hated no one, not even the pounding, shrieking machines. There was no bitterness in him, nothing but an inordinate hunger for rest.

The houses and factories thinned out and the open spaces increased as he approached the country. At last the city was behind him, and he was walking down a leafy lane beside the railroad track. He did not walk like a man. He did not look like a man. He was a travesty of the human. It was a twisted and stunted and nameless piece of life that shambled like a sickly ape, arms loose-hanging, stoop-shouldered, narrow-chested, grotesque and terrible.

He passed by a small railroad station and lay down in the grass under a tree. All afternoon he lay there. Sometimes he dozed, with muscles that twitched in his sleep. When awake, he lay without movement, watching the birds or looking up at the sky through the branches of the tree above him. Once or twice he laughed aloud, but without relevance to anything he had seen or felt.

After twilight had gone, in the first darkness of the night, a freight train rumbled into the station. When the engine was switching cars on to the sidetrack, Johnny crept along the side of the train. He pulled open the side-door of an empty box-car and awkwardly and laboriously climbed in. He closed the door. The engine whistled. Johnny was lying down, and in the darkness he smiled.

The Dream of Debs

I awoke fully an hour before my customary time. This in itself was remarkable, and I lay very wide awake, pondering over it. Something was the matter, something was wrong—I knew not what. I was oppressed by a premonition of something terrible that had happened or was about to happen. But what was it? I strove to orientate myself. I remembered that at the time of the Great Earthquake of 1906 many claimed they awakened some moments before the first shock and that during those moments they experienced strange feelings of dread. Was San Francisco again to be visited by earthquake?

I lay for a full minute, numbly expectant, but there occurred no reeling of walls nor shock and grind of falling masonry. All was quiet. That was it! The silence! No wonder I had been perturbed. The hum of the great live city was strangely silent. The surface cars passed along my street at that time of day, on an average of one every three minutes; but in the ten succeeding minutes not a car passed. Perhaps it was a street railway strike, was my thought; or perhaps there had been an accident and the power was shut off. But no, the silence was too profound. I heard no jar and rattle of wagon-wheels, nor stamp of iron-shod hoofs straining up the steep cobble-stones.

Pressing the push-button beside my bed, I strove to hear the sound of the bell, though I knew it was impossible for the sound to rise three stories to me even if the bell did ring. It rang all right, for a few minutes later Brown entered with the tray and morning paper. Though his features were impassive as ever, I noted a startled, apprehensive light in his eyes. I noted, also, that there was no cream on the tray.

"The creamery did not deliver this morning," he explained; "nor did the bakery."

I glanced again at the tray. There were no fresh French rolls—only slices of stale graham bread from yesterday, the most detestable of bread so far as I was concerned.

"Nothing was delivered this morning, sir." Brown started to explain apologetically; but I interrupted him.

"The paper?"

"Yes, sir, it was delivered, but it was the only thing, and it is the last time, too. There won't be any paper tomorrow. The paper says so. Can I send out and get you some condensed milk?"

I shook my head, accepted the coffee black, and spread open the paper. The headlines explained everything—explained too much, in fact, for the lengths of pessimism to which the journal went, were ridiculous. A general strike, it said, had been called all over the United States; and most foreboding anxieties were expressed concerning the provisioning of the great cities.

I read on hastily, skimming much and remembering much of the labor troubles in the past. For a generation the general strike had been the dream of organized labor, which dream had arisen originally in the mind of Debs, one of the great leaders of thirty years before. I recollected that in my young college-settlement days I had even written an article on the subject for one of the magazines and that I had entitled it, "The Dream of Debs." And I must confess that I had treated the idea very carefully and academically as a dream and nothing more. Time and the world had rolled on, Gompers was gone, the American Federation of Labor was gone, and gone was Debs with all his wild revolutionary ideas; but the dream had persisted, and here it was at last realized in fact. But I laughed, as I read, at the journal's gloomy outlook. I knew better. I had seen organized labor worsted in too many conflicts. It would be a matter only of days when the thing would be settled. This was a national strike, and it wouldn't take the government long to break it.

I threw the paper down and proceeded to dress. It would certainly be interesting to be out in the streets of San Francisco when not a wheel was turning and the whole city was taking an enforced vacation.

"I beg your pardon, sir," Brown said, as he handed me my cigar case, "but Mr. Harmmed has asked to see you before you go out."

"Send him in right away," I answered.

Harmmed was the butler. When he entered I could see he was laboring under controlled excitement. He came at once to the point.

"What shall I do, sir? There will be needed provisions, and the delivery drivers are on strike. And the electricity is shut off—I guess they're on strike, too."

"Are the shops open?" I asked.

"Only the small ones, sir. The retail clerks are out and the big ones can't open; but the owners and their families are running the little ones themselves."

"Then take the machine," I said, "and go the rounds and make your purchases. Buy plenty of everything you need or may need. Get a box of candles—no, get half a dozen boxes. And when you're done, tell Harrison to bring the machine around to the club for me—not later than eleven."

Harmmed shook his head gravely. "Mr. Harrison has struck along with the Chauffeurs' Union, and I don't know how to run the machine myself."

"Oh, ho, he has, has he?" I said. "Well, when next Mister Harrison happens around you tell him that he can look elsewhere for a position."

"Yes, sir."

"You don't happen to belong to a Butlers' Union, do you Harmmed?"

"No, sir," was the answer. "And even if I did I'd not desert my employer in a crisis like this. No, sir, I would—"

"All right, thank you," I said. "Now you get ready to accompany me. I'll run the machine myself, and we'll lay in a stock of provisions to stand a siege."

It was a beautiful first of May, even as May days go. The sky was cloudless, there was no wind, and the air was warm—almost balmy. Many autos were out, but the owners were driving them themselves. The streets were crowded but quiet. The working class, dressed in its Sunday best, was out taking the air and observing the effects of the strike. It was all so unusual, and withal so peaceful, that I found myself enjoying it. My nerves were tinkling with mild excitement. It was a sort of placid adventure. I passed Miss Chickering. She was at the helm of her little runabout. She swung around and came after me, catching me at the corner.

"Oh, Mr. Cerf!" she hailed. "Do you know where I can buy candles?

I've been to a dozen shops, and they're all sold out. It's dreadfully awful, isn't it?"

But her sparkling eyes gave the lie to her words. Like the rest of us, she was enjoying it hugely. Quite an adventure it was, getting those candles. It was not until we went across the city and down into the working class quarter south of Market street that we found small corner groceries that had not yet sold out. Miss Chickering thought one box was sufficient, but I persuaded her into taking four. My car was large, and I laid in a dozen boxes. There was no telling what delays might arise in the settlement of the strike. Also I filled the car with sacks of flour, baking powder, tinned goods, and all the ordinary necessities of life suggested by Harmmed, who fussed around and clucked over the purchases like an anxious old hen.

The remarkable thing, that first day of the strike, was that no one really apprehended anything serious. The announcement of organized labor in the morning papers that it was prepared to stay out a month or three months was laughed at. And yet that very first day we might have guessed as much from the fact that the working class took practically no part in the great rush to buy provisions. Of course not. For weeks and months, craftily and secretly, the whole working class had been laying in private stocks of provisions. That was why we were permitted to go down and buy out the little groceries in the working class neighborhood.

It was not until I arrived at the Club that afternoon that I began to feel the first alarm. Everything was in confusion. There were no olives for the cocktails, and the service was by hitches and jerks. Most of the men were angry, and all were worried. A babel of voices greeted me as I entered. General Folsom, nursing his capacious paunch in a window-seat in the smoking-room, was defending himself against half a dozen excited gentlemen who were demanding that he do something.

"What can I do more than I have done?" he was saying. "There are no orders from Washington. If you gentlemen will get a wire through I'll do anything I am commanded to do. But I don't see what can be done. The first thing I did this morning, as soon as I learned of the strike, was to order in the troops from the Presidio—three thousand of them. They're guarding the banks, the mint, the post office, and all the public buildings. There is no disorder whatever. The strikers are keeping the peace perfectly. You can't expect me to shoot them down as they walk along the streets with wives and children all in their best bib and tucker."

"I'd like to know what's happening on Wall street," I heard Jimmy Wombold say as I passed along. I could imagine his anxiety, for I knew that he was deep in the big Consolidated-Western deal.

"Say, Cerf," Atkinson bustled up to me. "Is your machine running?"

"Yes," I answered, "but what's the matter with your own?"

"Broken down, and the garages are all closed. And my wife's somewhere around Truckee, I think, stalled on the Overland. Can't get a wire to her for love or money. She should have arrived this evening. She may be starving. Lend me your machine."

"Can't get it across the bay," Halsted spoke up. "The ferries aren't running. But I tell you what you can do. There's Rollinson—oh, Rollinson, come here a moment. Atkinson wants to get a machine across the bay. His wife is stuck on the Overland at Truckee. Can't you bring the 'Lurlette' across from Tiburon and carry the machine over for him?"

The "Lurlette" was a two-hundred-ton ocean-going schooner-yacht.

Rollinson shook his head. "You couldn't get a longshoreman to load the machine on board, even if I could get the 'Lurlette' over, which I can't for the crew are members of the Coast Seamen's Union, and they're on strike along with the rest."

"But my wife may be starving." I could hear Atkinson wailing as I moved on.

At the other end of the smoking-room I ran into a group of men bunched excitedly and angrily around Bertie Messener. And Bertie was stirring them up and prodding them in his cool, cynical way. Bertie didn't care about the strike. He didn't care much about anything. He was blasé—at least in all the clean things of life; the nasty things had no attraction for him. He was worthy twenty millions, all of it in safe investments, and he had never done a tap of productive work in his life—inherited it all from his father and two uncles. He had been everywhere, seen everything, and done everything but get married, and this last in the face of the grim and determined attack of a few hundred ambitious mammas. For years he had been the greatest catch, and as yet he had avoided being caught. He was disgracefully eligible. On top of his wealth, he was young and handsome, and, as I said before, clean. He was a great athlete, a young blond god that did everything perfectly and admirably with the solitary exception of matrimony. And he didn't care about anything, had no

ambitions, no passions, no desire to do the very things he did so much
better than other men.

"This is sedition!" one man in the group was crying. Another
called it revolt and revolution, and another called it anarchy.

"I can't see it," Bertie said. "I have been out in the streets all morning. Perfect order reigns. I never saw a more law-abiding populace.
There's no use calling it names. It's not any of these things. It's just
what it claims to be, a general strike, and it's your turn to play,
gentlemen."

"And we'll play alright!" cried Garfield, one of the traction millionaires. "We'll show this dirt where its place is—the beasts! Wait
till the government takes a hand."

"But where is the government?" Bertie interposed. "It might as
well be at the bottom of the sea so far as you're concerned. You
don't know what's happening at Washington. You don't know whether
you've got a government or not."

"Don't you worry about that!" Garfield blurted out.

"I assure you I'm not worrying," Bertie smiled languidly. "But it
seems to me it's what you fellows are doing. Look in the glass, Garfield."

Garfield did not look, for had he looked, he would have seen a very
excited gentleman with rumpled, iron-gray hair, a flushed face, mouth
sullen and vindictive, and eyes wildly gleaming.

"It's not right, I tell you," little Hanover said; and from his tone
I was sure that he had already said it a number of times.

"Now, that's going too far, Hanover," Bertie replied. "You fellows
make me tired. You're all open-shop men. You've eroded my eardrums
with your endless gabble for the open-shop and the right of a man to
work. You've harangued along those lines for years. Labor is doing
nothing wrong in going out on this general strike. It is violating no
law of God nor man. Don't you talk, Hanover. You've been ringing
the changes too long on the God-given right to work . . . . or not to
work; you can't escape the corollary. It's a dirty little sordid scrap,
that's all the whole thing is. You've got labor down and gouged it,
and now labor's got you down and is gouging you, that's all, and
you're squealing."

Every man in the group broke out in indignant denials that labor
had ever been gouged.

"No, sir!" Garfield was shouting, "we've done the best for labor.

Instead of gouging it, we've given it a chance to live. We've made work for it. Where would labor be if it hadn't been for us?"

"A whole lot better off," Bertie sneered. "You've got labor down and gouged it every time you got a chance, and you went out of your way tô make chances."

"No! No!" were the cries.

"There was the teamster's strike right here in San Francisco," Bertie went on imperturbably. "The Employers' Association precipitated that strike. You know that. And you know I know it, too, for I've sat in these very rooms and heard the inside talk and news of the fight. First you precipitated the strike, then you bought the Mayor and the Chief of Police and broke the strike. A pretty spectacle, you philanthropists getting the teamsters down and gouging them.

"Hold on, I'm not through with you. It's only last year that the labor ticket of Colorado elected a Governor. He was never seated. You know why. You know how your brother philanthropists and capitalists of Colorado worked it. It was a case of getting labor down and gouging it. You kept the President of the Southwestern Amalgamated Association of Miners in jail for three years on trumped up murder charges, and with him out of the way you broke up the Association. That was gouging labor; you'll admit. The third time the graduated income tax was declared unconstitutional was a gouge. So was the Eight-hour Bill you killed in the last Congress.

"And of all the unmitigated immoral gouges, your destruction of the closed-shop principle was the limit. You know how it was done. You bought out Farburg, the last president of the old American Federation of Labor. He was your creature—or the creature of all the trusts and employers' associations, which is the same thing. You precipitated the big Closed Shop Strike. Farburg betrayed that strike. You won, and the old American Federation of Labor crumbled to pieces. You fellows destroyed it, and by so doing undid yourselves; for right on top of it began the organization of the I.L.W.—the biggest and solidest organization of labor the United States has even seen, and you are responsible for its existence and for the present general strike. You smashed all the old federations and drove labor into the I.L.W., and the I.L.W. called the general strike—still fighting for the closed shop. And then you have the effrontery to stand here face to face and tell me that you never got labor down and gouged it. Bah!!"

This time there was no denials. Garfield broke out in self-defense:

"We've done nothing we were not compelled to do, if we were to win."

"I'm not saying anything about that," Bertie answered. "What I am complaining about is your squealing now that you're getting a taste of your own medicine. How many strikes have you won by starving labor into submission? Well, labor's worked out a scheme whereby to starve you into submission. It wants the closed shop, and if it can get it by starving you, starve you shall."

"I notice that you have profited in the past by those very labor-gouges you mentioned," insinuated Brentwood, one of the wiliest and most astute of our corporation lawyers. "The receiver is as bad as the thief," he sneered. "You had no hand in the gouging, but you took your whack out of the gouge."

"That is quite beside the question, Brentwood," Bertie drawled. "You're as bad as Hanover, intruding the moral element. I haven't said that anything is right or wrong. It's all a rotten game, I know; and my sole kick is that you fellows are squealing now that you're down and labor's taking a gouge out of you. Of course I've taken the profits from the gouging, and, thanks to you, gentlemen, without having personally to do the dirty work. You did that for me—oh, believe me, not because I am more virtuous than you, but because my good father and his various brothers left me a lot of money with which to pay for the dirty work."

"If you mean to insinuate—" Brentwood began hotly.

"Hold on, don't get all ruffled up," Bertie interposed insolently. "There's no use in playing hypocrites in this thieves' den. The high and lofty is all right for the newspapers, boys' clubs and Sunday schools—that's part of the game; but for heaven's sake, don't let's play it on one another. You know, and you know I know, just what jobbery was done in the building trades' strike last fall, who put up the money, who did the work, and who profited by it." (Brentwood flushed darkly.) "But we are all tarred with the same brush, and the best thing for us to do is to leave the morality out of it. Again I repeat, play the game, play it to the last finish, but for goodness sake, don't squeal when you get hurt."

When I left the group Bertie was off on a new tack, tormenting them with the more serious aspects of the situation, pointing out the shortage of supplies that was already making itself felt, and asking them what they were going to do about it. A little later I met him in the cloak room, leaving, and gave him a lift home in my machine.

"It's a great stroke, this general strike," he said, as we bowled along through the crowded but orderly streets. "It's a smashing body-blow. Labor caught us napping and struck at our weakest place, the stomach. I'm going to get out of San Francisco, Cerf. Take my advice and get out, too. Head for the country, anywhere. You'll have more chance. Buy up a stock of supplies and get into a tent or cabin somewhere. Soon there'll be nothing but starvation in this city for such as we."

How correct Bertie Messener was, I never dreamed. I decided mentally that he was an alarmist. As for myself I was content to remain and watch the fun. After I dropped him, instead of going directly home, I went on in a hunt for more food. To my surprise, I learned that the small groceries where I had bought in the morning were sold out. I extended my search to the Potrero, and by good luck managed to pick up another box of candles, two sacks of wheat flour, ten pounds of graham flour (which would do for the servants), a case of tinned corn, and two cases of tinned tomatoes. It did look as though there was going to be at least a temporary food shortage, and I hugged myself over the goodly stock of provisions I had laid in.

The next morning I had my coffee in bed as usual, and, more than the cream, I missed the daily paper. It was this absence of knowledge of what was going on in the world that I found the chiefest hardship. Down at the club there was little news. Rider had crossed from Oakland in his launch, and Halstead had been down to San José and back in his machine. They reported the same condition in those places as in San Francisco. Everything was tied up by the strike. All grocery stocks had been bought out by the upper classes. And perfect order reigned. But what was happening over the rest of the country—in Chicago? New York? Washington? Most probably the same things that were happening with us, we concluded; but the fact that we did not know with absolute surety was irritating.

General Folsom had a bit of news. An attempt had been made to place army telegraphers in the telegraph offices, but the wires had been cut in every direction. This was, so far, the one unlawful act committed by labor, and that it was a concerted act he was fully convinced. He had communicated by wireless with the army post at Benicia, the telegraph lines were even then being patrolled by soldiers all the way to Sacramento. Once, for one short instant, they had got the Sacramento call, then the wires, somewhere, were cut again. General Folsom reasoned that similar attempts to open communication were

being made by the authorities all the way across the continent, but he
was non-committal as to whether or not he thought the attempt would
succeed. What worried him was the wire-cutting, he could not but
believe that it was an important part of the deep-laid labor conspiracy.
Also, he regretted that the government had not long since established
its projected chain of wireless stations.

The days came and went, and for a time it was a humdrum time.
Nothing happened. The edge of excitement had become blunted. The
streets were not so crowded. The working class did not come up town
any more to see how we were taking the strike. And there were not
so many automobiles running around. The repair shops and garages
were closed, and whenever a machine broke down it went out of commission. The clutch on mine broke and love nor money could not get
it repaired. Like the rest, I now was walking. San Francisco lay dead,
and we did not know what was happening over the rest of the country.
But from the very fact that we did not know we could conclude only
that the rest of the country lay as dead as San Francisco. From time to
time the city was placarded with the proclamations of organized
labor—these had been printed months before and evidenced how
thoroughly the I.L.W. had prepared for the strike. Every detail had
been worked out long in advance. No violence had occurred as yet,
with the exception of the shooting of a few wire-cutters by the soldiers,
but the people of the slums were starving and growing ominously
restless.

The business men, the millionaires, and the professional class held
meetings and passed proclamations, but there was no way of making
the proclamations public. They could not even get them printed. One
result of these meetings, however, was that General Folsom was
persuaded into taking military possession of the wholesale houses and
of all the flour, grain and food warehouses. It was high time, for suffering was becoming acute in the homes of the rich, and breadlines
were necessary. I know that my servants were beginning to draw long
faces, and it was amazing—the hole they made in my stock of provisions. In fact, as I afterward surmised, each servant was stealing
from me and secreting a private stock of provisions for himself.

But with the formation of the breadlines came new troubles. There
was only so much of a food reserve in San Francisco, and at the best
it could not last long. Organized labor, we knew, had its private supplies; nevertheless, the whole working class joined the bread lines.
As a result, the provisions General Folsom had taken possession of

diminished with perilous rapidity. How were the soldiers going to distinguish between a shabby middle-class man, a member of the I.L.W., or a slum-dweller? The first and the last had to be fed, but the soldiers did not know all the I.L.W. men in the city, much less the wives and sons and daughters of the I.L.W. men. The employers help-ing, a few of the known union men were flung out of the breadlines; but that amounted to nothing. To make matters worse, the govern-ment tugs that had been hauling food from the army depots on Mare Island to Angel Island found no more food to haul. The soldiers now received their rations from the confiscated provisions, and they re-ceived them first.

The beginning of the end was in sight. Violence was beginning to show its awful face. Law and order were passing away, and passing away, I must confess, among the slum people and the upper classes. Organized labor still maintained perfect order. It could well afford to—it had plenty to eat. I remember the afternoon at the Club when I caught Halsted and Brentwood whispering in a corner. They took me in on the venture. Brentwood's machine was still in running order, and they were going out cow-stealing. Halsted had a long butcher-knife and a cleaver. We went out to the outskirts of the city. Here and there were cows grazing, but always guarded by their owners. We pursued our quest, following along the fringe of the city to the east, and on the hills near Hunter's Point we came upon a cow guarded by a little girl. There was also a young calf with the cow. We wasted no time on preliminaries. The little girl ran away screaming, while we slaughtered the cow. I omit the details, for they are not nice—we were unaccustomed to such work, and we bungled it.

But in the midst of it, working with the haste of fear, we heard cries, and we saw a number of men running toward us. We abandoned the spoils and took to our heels. To our surprise we were not pursued. Looking back, we saw the men hurriedly cutting up the cow. They had been on the same lay as ourselves. We argued that there was plenty for all, and ran back. The scene that followed beggars descrip-tion. We fought and squabbled over the division like savages. Brent-wood, I remember, was a perfect brute, snarling and snapping and threatening that murder would be done if we did not get our proper share.

And we were getting our share when there occurred a new irruption on the scene. This time it was the dreaded peace officers of the I.L.W. The little girl had brought them. They were armed with whips and clubs, and there were a score of them. The little girl danced up and down in anger, the tears streaming down her cheeks, crying, "Give it to 'em! Give it to 'em! That guy with the specs—he did it! Mash his face for him! Mash his face!" That guy with the specs was I and I got my face mashed, too, though I had the presence of my mind to take off my glasses at the first. My! but we did receive a trouncing as we scattered in all directions. Brentwood, Halsted and I flew away for the machine. Brentwood's nose was bleeding, while Halstead's cheek was cut across with the scarlet slash of a blacksnake whip.

And lo, when the pursuit ceased and we had gained the machine, there, hiding behind it, was the frightened calf. Brentwood warned us to be cautious and crept upon it like a wolf or tiger. Knife and cleaver had been left behind, but Brentwood still had his hands, and over and over on the ground he rolled with the poor little calf as he throttled it. We threw the carcass into the machine, covered it over with a robe, and started home. But our misfortunes had only begun. We blew out a tire. There was no way of fixing it, and twilight was coming on. We abandoned the machine, Brentwood puffing and staggering along in advance, the calf, covered by the robe, slung across his shoulders. We took turn about carrying that calf, and it nearly killed us. Also we lost our way. And then, after hours of wandering and toil, we encountered a gang of hoodlums. They were not I.L.W. men and I guess they were as hungry as we. At any rate, they got the calf and we got the thrashing. Brentwood raged like a madman the rest of the way home, and he looked like one, what of his torn clothes, swollen nose, and blackened eyes.

There wasn't any more cow-stealing after that. General Folsom sent his troopers out and confiscated all the cows, and his troopers, aided by the militia, ate most of the meat. General Folsom was not to be blamed; it was his duty to maintain law and order, and he maintained it by means of the soldiers, wherefore he was compelled to feed them first of all.

It was about this time that the great panic occurred. The wealthy classes precipitated the flight, and then the slum people caught the contagion and stampeded wildly out of the city. General Folsom was pleased. It was estimated that at least 200,000 had deserted San Francisco, and by that much was his food problem solved. Well do I remember that day. In the morning I had eaten a crust of bread. Half of the afternoon I had stood in the bread line; and after dark I returned home, tired and miserable, carrying a quart of rice and a slice of bacon. Brown met me at the door. His face was worn and terrified. All the servants had fled, he informed me. He alone remained. I was touched by his faithfulness, and when I learned that he had eaten nothing all day, I divided my food with him. We cooked half the rice and half the bacon, sharing it equally and reserving the other half for morning. I went to bed with my hunger, and tossed restlessly all night. In the morning I found Brown had deserted me, and, greater misfortune still, he had stolen what remained of the rice and bacon.

It was a gloomy handful of men that came together at the Club that morning. There was no service at all. The last servant was gone. I noticed, too, that the silver was gone, and I learned where it had gone. The servants had not taken it, for the reason, I presume, that the club members got to it first. Their method of disposing of it was simple. Down south of Market street, in the dwellings of the I.L.W., the housewives had given square meals in exchange for it. I went back to my house. Yes, my silver was gone all but a massive pitcher. This I wrapped up and carried down south of Market.

I felt better after the meal, and returned to the Club to learn if there was anything new in the situation. Hanover, Collins and Dakon were just leaving. There was no one inside, they told me, and they invited me to come along with them. They were leaving the city, they said, on Dakon's horses, and there was a spare one for me. Dakon had four magnificent carriage horses that he wanted to save, and General Folsom had given him the tip that next morning all the horses that remained in the city were to be confiscated for food. There were not many horses left, for tens of thousands of them had been turned loose into the country when the hay and grain gave out during the first days. Birdall, I remember, who had great draying interests had turned loose 300 dray horses. At an average value of five hundred dollars this had amounted to $150,000. He had hoped, at first, to recover most of the horses after the strike was over, but in the end he never recovered one of them. They were all eaten by the people that fled from San Francisco. For that matter the killing of the army mules and horses for food had already begun.

Fortunately for Dakon, he had had a plentiful supply of hay and grain stored in his stable. We managed to raise four saddles, and we found the animals in good condition and spirited, withal unused to being ridden. I remembered the San Francisco of the Great Earthquake as we rode through the streets, but this San Francisco was vastly more pitiable. No cataclysm of nature had caused this, but

rather the tyranny of the labor unions. We rode down past Union
Square and through the theatre, hotel and shopping districts. The
streets were deserted. Here and there stood automobiles, abandoned
where they had broken down or when the gasoline had given out.
There was no sign of life, save for the occasional policeman and the
soldiers, guarding the banks and public buildings. Once we came
upon an I.L.W. man pasting up the latest proclamation. We stopped
to read. "We have maintained an orderly strike," it ran ; "and we shall
maintain order to the end. The end will come when our demands are
satisfied, and our demands will be satisfied when we have starved our
employers into submission, as we ourselves in the past have often been
starved into submission."

"Messener's very words," Collins said. "And I, for one, am ready
to submit, only they won't give me a chance to submit. I haven't had a
full meal in an age. I wonder what horse-meat tastes like."

We stopped to read another proclamation : "When we think our
employers are ready to submit, we shall open up the telegraphs and
place the employers' associations of the United States in communication. But only messages relating to peace terms shall be permitted over
the wires."

We rode on, crossed Market street, and a little later were passing
through the working class districts. Here the streets were not deserted.
Leaning over gates or standing in groups, were the I.L.W. men. Happy,
well-fed children were playing games, and stout housewives sat on the
front steps gossiping. One and all cast amused glances at us. Little
children ran after us crying : "Hey, mister, ain't you hungry ?" And
one woman, a nursing child at her breast, called at Dakon, "Say, Fatty,
I will give you a square meal for your skate—ham and potatoes, cur-
rant jelly, white bread, canned butter, and two cups of coffee."

"Have you noticed, the last few days," Hanover remarked to me,
"that there's not been a stray dog in the streets ?"

I had noticed, but I had not thought about it before. It was high
time to leave the unfortunate city. We at last managed to connect with
the San Bruno Road, along which we headed south. I had a country
place near Menlo, and it was our objective. But soon we began to
discover that the country was worse off and far more dangerous than
the city. There, the soldiers and the I.L.W. kept order ; but the
country had been turned over to anarchy. Two hundred thousand
people had fled south from San Francisco, and we had countless evi-
dences that their flight had been like that of an army of locusts. They

had swept everything clean. There had been robbery and fighting. Here and there we passed bodies by the roadside and saw the blackened ruins of farmhouses. The fences were down, and the crops had been trampled by the feet of a multitude. All the vegetable patches had been rooted up by the famished hordes. All the chickens and farm animals had been slaughtered. This was true of all the main roads that led out of San Francisco. Here and there, away from the roads, farmers had held their own with shotguns and revolvers, and were still holding their own. They warned us away and refused to parley with us. And all the destruction and violence had been done by the slum-dwellers and the upper classes. The I.L.W. men, with plentiful food supplies, remained quietly in their homes in the cities.

Early in the day we received concrete proof of how desperate was the situation. To the right of us we heard cries and rifle shots. Bullets whistled dangerously near. There was a crashing in the underbrush; then a magnificent black truck-horse broke across the road in front of us and was gone. We had barely time to notice that he was bleeding and lame. He was followed by three soldiers. The chase went on amongst the trees on the left. We could hear the soldiers calling to one another. A fourth soldier limped out upon the road from the right, sat down on a boulder, and mopped the sweat from his face.

The man grinned up at us and asked for a match. In reply to Dakon's "What's the word?" he informed us that the militiamen were deserting. "No grub," he explained. "They're feedin' it all to the regulars." We also learned from him that the military prisoners had been released from Alcatraz Island because they could no longer be fed.

I shall never forget the next sight we encountered. We came upon it abruptly, around a turn of the road. Overhead arched the trees. The sunshine was filtering down through the branches. Butterflies were fluttering by, and from the fields came the song of larks. And there stood a powerful touring car. About it and in it lay a number of corpses. It told its own tale. Its occupants, fleeing from the city, had been attacked and dragged down by a gang of slum-dwellers—hoodlums. The thing had occurred within twenty-four hours. Freshly opened meat and fruit tins explained the reason for the attacks. Dakon examined the bodies.

"I thought so," he reported. "I've ridden in that car. It was Periton—the whole family. We've got to watch out for ourselves from now on."

"But we have no food with which to invite attack," I objected.

Dakon pointed to the horse I rode, and I understood.

Early in the day Dakon's horse had cast a shoe. The delicate hoof had split, and by noon the animal was limping. Dakon refused to ride it further, and refused to desert it. So, on his solicitation, we went on. He would lead the horse and join us at my place. That was the last we saw of him; nor did we ever learn his end.

By one o'clock we arrived at the town of Menlo, or rather at the site of Menlo, for it was in ruins. Corpses lay everywhere. The business part of the town, as well as part of the residences, had been gutted by fire. Here and there a residence still held out; but there was no getting near them. When we approached too closely we were fired upon. We met a woman who was poking about in the smoking ruins of her cottage. The first attack, she told us, had been on the stores, and as she talked we could picture that raging, roaring, hungry mob flinging itself upon the handful of townspeople. Millionaires and paupers had fought side by side for the food, and then fought with one another after they got it. The town of Palo Alto and Stanford University had been sacked in similar fashion, we learned. Ahead of us lay a desolate wasted land; and we thought we were wise in turning off to my place. It lay three miles to the west, snuggling among the first rolling swells of the foothills.

But as we rode along we saw that the devastation was not confined to the main roads. The van of the flight had kept to the roads, sacking the small towns as it went; while those that followed had scattered out and swept the whole countryside, like a great broom. My place was built of concrete, masonry, and tiles, and so had escaped being burned, but it was gutted clean. We found the gardener's body in the windmill, littered around with empty shotgun shells. He had put up a good fight. But no trace could be found of the two Italian laborers, nor of the housekeeper and her husband. Not a living thing remained. The calves, the colts, all the fancy poultry and thoroughbred stock, everything was gone. The kitchen and the fireplace where the mob had cooked, were a mess, while many campfires outside bore witness to the large number that had fed and spent the night. What they had not eaten they had carried away. There was not a bite for us.

We spent the rest of the night vainly waiting for Dakon, and in the morning, with our revolvers, fought off half a dozen marauders. Then we killed one of Dakon's horses, hiding for the future what meat we did not immediately eat. In the afternoon Collins went out for a walk,

but failed to return. This was the last straw to Hanover. He was for
flight there and then, and I had great difficulty in persuading him to
wait for daylight. As for myself, I was convinced that the end of the
general strike was near, and I was resolved to return to San Francisco.
So, in the morning we parted company, Hanover heading south, fifty
pounds of horse-meat strapped to his saddle, while I, similarly loaded,
headed north. Little Hanover pulled through all right, and to the
end of his life he will persist, I know, in boring everybody with the
narrative of his subsequent adventures.

I got as far as Belmont, on the main road back, when I was robbed
of my horse-meat by three militiamen. There was no change in the
situation, they said, except that it was going from bad to worse. The
I.L.W. had plenty of provisions hidden away and could last out for
months. I managed to get as far as Baden, when my horse was taken
away from me by a dozen men. Two of them were San Francisco
policemen, and the remainder were regular soldiers. This was ominous. The situation was certainly extreme when the regulars were
beginning to desert. When I continued my way on foot, they already
had the fire started, and the last of Dakon's horses lay slaughtered
on the ground.

As luck would have it, I sprained my ankle, and succeeded in getting
no further than South San Francisco. I lay there that night in an out-
house, shivering with the cold and at the same time burning with
fever. Two days I lay there, too sick to move, and on the third, reeling
and giddy, supporting myself on an extemporized crutch I tottered
on toward San Francisco. I was weak as well, for it was the third day
since food had passed my lips. It was a day of nightmare and torment. As in a dream I passed hundreds of regular soldiers drifting
along in the opposite direction, and many policemen, with their families, organized in large groups for mutual protection.

As I entered the city I remembered the workman's house at which
I had traded the silver pitcher, and in that direction my hunger drove
me. Twilight was falling when I came to the place. I passed around
by the alleyway and crawled up the back steps, on which I collapsed.
I managed to reach out with the crutch and knocked at the door.
Then I must have fainted, for I came to in the kitchen, my face wet
with water and whisky being poured down my throat. I choked and
spluttered and tried to talk; I began by saying something about not
having any more silver pitchers, but that I would make it up to them

afterward if they would only give me something to eat. But the house-wife interrupted me.

"Why, you poor man!" she said. "Haven't you heard? The strike was called off this afternoon. Of course we'll give you something to eat."

She hustled around, opening a tin of breakfast bacon and preparing to fry it.

"Let me have some now, please," I begged; and I ate the raw bacon on a slice of bread, while her husband explained that the demands of the I.L.W. had been granted. The wires had been opened up in the early afternoon, and everywhere the Employers' Association had given in. There hadn't been any employers left in San Francisco, but General Folsom had spoken for them. The trains and steamers would start running in the morning, and so would everything else just as soon as system could be established.

And that was the end of the general strike. I never want to see an-other one. It was worse than a war. A general strike is a cruel and im-moral thing, and the brain of man should be capable of running industry in a more rational way. Harrison is still my chauffeur. It was part of the conditions of the I.L.W. that all of its members should be reinstated in their old positions. Brown never came back, but the rest of the servants are with me. I hadn't the heart to discharge them—poor creatures, they were pretty hard pressed when they deserted with the food and silver. And now I can't discharge them. They have all been unionized by the I.L.W. The tyranny of organized labor is getting beyond human endurance. Something must be done.

South of the Slot

Old San Francisco, which is the San Francisco of only the other day, the day before the Earthquake, was divided midway by the Slot. The Slot was an iron crack that ran along the center of Market Street, and from the Slot arose the burr of the ceaseless, endless cable that was hitched at will to the cars it dragged up and down. In truth, there were two Slots, but, in the quick grammar of the West, time was saved by calling them, and much more that they stood for, The Slot. North of the Slot were the theaters, hotels and shopping district, the banks and the staid, respectable business houses. South of the Slot were the factories, slums, laundries, machine-shops, boiler-works and the abodes of the working class.

The Slot was the metaphor that expressed the class cleavage of Society, and no man crossed this metaphor, back and forth, more successfully than Freddie Drummond. He made a practice of living in both worlds and in both worlds he lived signally well. Freddie Drummond was a professor in the Sociology Department of the University of California, and it was as a professor of sociology that he first crossed over the Slot, lived for six months in the great labor ghetto and wrote The Unskilled Laborer—a book that was hailed everywhere as an able contribution to the Literature of Progress and as a splendid reply to the Literature of Discontent. Politically and economically, it was nothing if not orthodox. Presidents of great railway systems bought whole editions of it to give to their employees. A manufacturers' association alone distributed fifty thousand copies of it. In its preachment of thrift and content it ran Mrs. Wiggs of the Cabbage Patch a close second.

At first, Freddie Drummond found it monstrously difficult to get along among the working people. He was not used to their ways, and they certainly were not used to his. They were suspicious. He had no antecedents. He could talk of no previous jobs. His hands were soft. His extraordinary politeness was ominous. His first idea of the rôle he would play was that of a free and independent American who chose to work with his hands and no explanations given. But it wouldn't do, as he quickly discovered. At the beginning they accepted him, very provisionally, as a freak. A little later, as he began to know his way about better, he insensibly drifted into the only rôle that he could play with some degree of plausibility—namely, that of a man who had seen better days, very much better days, but who was down in his luck, though, to be sure, only temporarily.

He learned many things and generalized much and often erroneously, all of which can be found in the pages of The Unskilled Laborer. He saved himself, however, after the sane and conservative manner of his kind, by labeling his generalizations as "tentative." One of his first experiences was in the great Wilmax Cannery, where he was put on piecework making small packing-cases. A box-factory supplied the parts, and all Freddie Drummond had to do was to fit the parts into a form and drive in the wire nails with a light hammer.

It was not skilled labor, but it was piecework. The ordinary laborers in the cannery got a dollar and a half a day. Freddie Drummond found the other men on the same job with him jogging along and earning a dollar and seventy-five cents a day. By the third day he was able to earn the same. But he was ambitious. He did not care to jog along, and, being unusually able and fit, on the fourth day earned two dollars. The next day, having keyed himself up to an exhausting high tension, he earned two dollars and a half. His fellow-workers favored him with scowls and black looks and made remarks, slangily witty and which he did not understand, about sucking up to the boss, and pace-making, and holding her down when the rains set in. He was astonished at their malingering on piecework, generalized about the laziness of the unskilled laborer, and proceeded next day to hammer out three dollars' worth of boxes.

And that night, coming out of the cannery, he was interviewed by his fellow-workmen, who were very angry and incoherently slangy. He failed to comprehend the motive behind their action. The action itself was strenuous. When he refused to ease down his pace and bleated about freedom of contract, independent Americanism and the dignity of toil they proceeded to spoil his pace-making ability. It was a fierce battle, for Drummond was a large man and an athlete; but the crowd finally jumped on his ribs, walked on his face and stamped on his fingers, so that it was only after lying in bed for a week that he was able to get up and look for another job. All of this is duly narrated in that first book of his, in the chapter entitled The Tyranny of Labor.

A little later, in another department of the Wilmax Cannery, lumping as a fruit-distributor among the women, he essayed to carry two boxes of fruit at a time and was promptly reproached by the other fruit-lumpers. It was palpable malingering; but he was there, he decided, not to change conditions, but to observe. So he lumped one box thereafter, and so well did he study the art of shirking that he wrote a special chapter on it, with the last several paragraphs devoted to tentative generalizations.

In those six months he worked at many jobs and developed into a very good imitation of a genuine worker. He was a natural linguist and he kept notebooks, making a scientific study of the workers' slang or argot until he could talk quite intelligibly. This language also enabled him more intimately to follow their mental processes and thereby to gather much data for a projected chapter in some future book which he planned to entitle Synthesis of Working-Class Psychology.

Before he arose to the surface from that first plunge into the underworld, he discovered that he was a good actor and demonstrated the plasticity of his nature. He was himself astonished at his own fluidity. Once having mastered the language and conquered numerous fastidious qualms he found that he could flow into any nook of working-class life and fit it so snugly as to feel comfortably at home. As he said in the preface to his second book, The Toiler, he endeavored really to know the working people; and the only possible way to achieve this was to work beside them, eat their food, sleep in their beds, be amused with their amusements, think their thoughts and feel their feelings.

He was not a deep thinker. He had no faith in new theories. All his norms and criteria were conventional. His Thesis on the French Revolution was noteworthy in college annals, not merely for its painstaking and voluminous accuracy, but for the fact that it was the dryest, deadest, most formal and most orthodox screed ever written on the subject. He was a very reserved man, and his natural inhibition was large in quantity and steel-like in quality. He had but few friends.

He was too undemonstrative, too frigid. He had no vices, nor had any one ever discovered any temptations. Tobacco he detested, beer he abhorred, and he was never known to drink anything stronger than an occasional light wine at dinner.

When a freshman he had been baptized Ice-Box by his warmer-blooded fellows. As a member of the Faculty he was known as Cold-Storage. He had but one grief, and that was Freddie. He had earned it when he played fullback on the Varsity eleven, and his formal soul had never succeeded in living it down. Freddie he would ever be, except officially, and through nightmare vistas he looked into a future when his world would speak of him as Old Freddie.

For he was very young to be a doctor of sociology—only twenty-seven, and he looked younger. In appearance and atmosphere he was a strapping big college man, smooth-faced and easy-mannered, clean and simple and wholesome, with a known record of being a splendid athlete and an implied vast possession of cold culture of the inhibited sort. He never talked shop out of class and committee-rooms, except later when his books showered him with distasteful public notice and he yielded to the extent of reading occasional papers before certain literary and economic societies.

He did everything right—too right; and in dress and comportment was inevitably correct. Not that he was a dandy. Far from it. He was a college man, in dress and carriage as like as a pea to the type that of late years is being so generously turned out of our institutions of higher learning. His handshake was satisfyingly strong and stiff. His blue eyes were coldly blue and convincingly sincere. His voice, firm and masculine, clean and crisp of enunciation, was pleasant to the ear. The one drawback to Freddie Drummond was his inhibition. He never unbent. In his football days the higher the tension of the game the cooler he grew. He was noted as a boxer, but he was regarded as an automaton, with the inhuman action of a machine judging distance and timing blows, guarding, blocking and stalling. He was rarely punished himself, while he rarely punished an opponent. He was too clever and too controlled to permit himself to put a pound more weight into a punch than he intended. With him it was a matter of exercise. It kept him fit.

As time went by Freddie Drummond found himself more frequently crossing the Slot and losing himself in South of Market. His summer and winter holidays were spent there, and, whether it was a week or a week-end, he found the time spent there to be valuable and enjoyable. And there was so much material to be gathered. His third book, Mass and Master, became a textbook in the American universities, and almost before he knew it he was at work on a fourth one, The Fallacy of the Inefficient.

Somewhere in his make-up there was a strange twist or quirk. Perhaps it was a recoil from his environment and training, or from the tempered seed of his ancestors, who had been bookmen generation preceding generation; but, at any rate, he found enjoyment in being down in the working-class world. In his own world he was Cold-Storage, but down below he was Big Bill Totts, who could drink and smoke and slang and fight and be an all-around favorite. Everybody liked Bill, and more than one working-girl made love to him. At first he had been merely a good actor, but as time went on simulation became second nature. He no longer played a part, and he loved sausages —sausages and bacon, than which, in his own proper sphere, there was nothing more loathsome in the way of food.

From doing the thing for the need's sake he came to doing the thing for the thing's sake. He found himself regretting it as the time drew near for him to go back to his lecture-room and his inhibition. And he often found himself waiting with anticipation for the dreary time to pass when he could cross the Slot and cut loose and play the devil. He was not wicked, but as Big Bill Totts he did a myriad things that Freddie Drummond would never have been permitted to do. Moreover, Freddie Drummond never would have wanted to do them. That was the strangest part of his discovery. Freddie Drummond and Bill Totts were two totally different creatures. The desires and tastes and impulses of each ran counter to the other's. Bill Totts could shirk at a job with a clear conscience, while Freddie Drummond condemned shirking as vicious, criminal and un-American, and devoted whole chapters to condemnation of the vice. Freddie Drummond did not care for dancing, but Bill Totts never missed the nights at the various dancing clubs, such as The Magnolia, The Western Star, and The Élite; while he won a massive silver cup standing thirty inches high for being the best-sustained character at the butchers' and meat-workers' annual grand masked ball. And Bill Totts liked the girls, and the girls liked him, while Freddie Drummond enjoyed playing the ascetic in this particular, was open in his opposition to equal suffrage and cynically bitter in his secret condemnation of co-education.

Freddie Drummond changed his manners with his dress and without effort. When he entered the obscure little room used for his transformation scenes he carried himself just a bit too stiffly. He was too erect, his shoulders were an inch too far back, while his face was grave, almost harsh, and practically expressionless. But when he emerged in Bill Totts' clothes he was another creature. Bill Totts did not slouch, but somehow his whole form limbered up and became graceful. The very sound of the voice was changed and the laugh was loud and hearty, while loose speech and an occasional oath were as a matter of course on his lips. Also Bill Totts was a trifle inclined to late hours, and at times, in saloons, to be good-naturedly bellicose with other workmen. Then, too, at Sunday picnics or when coming home from the show either arm betrayed a practiced familiarity in stealing around girls' waists, while he displayed a wit keen and delightful in the flirtatious badinage that was expected of a good fellow in his class.

So thoroughly was Bill Totts himself, so thoroughly a workman, a genuine denizen of South of the Slot, that he was as class-conscious as the average of his kind, and his hatred for a scab even exceeded that of the average loyal union man. During the water-front strike Freddie Drummond was somehow able to stand apart from the unique combination, and, coldly critical, watch Bill Totts hilariously slug scab longshoremen. For Bill Totts was a dues-paying member of the Longshoremen's Union and had a right to be indignant with the usurpers of his job. Big Bill Totts was so very big and so very able that it was Big Bill to the front when trouble was brewing. From acting outraged feelings Freddie Drummond, in the rôle of his other self, came to experience genuine outrage, and it was only when he returned to the classic atmosphere of the university that he was able, sanely and conservatively, to generalize upon his underworld experiences and put them down on paper as a trained sociologist should. That Bill Totts lacked the perspective to raise him above class-consciousness Freddie Drummond clearly saw. But Bill Totts could not see it. When he saw a scab taking his job away he saw red at the same time and little else did he see. It was Freddie Drummond, irreproachably clothed and comported, seated at his study desk or facing his class in Sociology 17, who saw Bill Totts and all around Bill Totts, and all around the whole scab and union-labor problem and its relation to the economic welfare of the United States in the struggle for the world-market. Bill Totts really wasn't able to see beyond the next meal and the prize-fight the following night at the Gayety Athletic Club.

It was while gathering material for Women and Work that Freddie

received his first warning of the danger he was in. He was too successful at living in both worlds. This strange dualism he had developed was, after all, very unstable, and as he sat in his study and medi-
tated he saw that it could not endure. It was really a transition stage;
and if he persisted he saw that he would inevitably have to drop one
world or the other. He could not continue in both. And as he looked
at the row of volumes that graced the upper shelf of his revolving
bookcase, his volumes, beginning with his Thesis and ending with
Women and Work, he decided that that was the world he would hold
on to and stick by. Bill Totts had served his purpose, but he had become a too-dangerous accomplice. Bill Totts would have to cease.

Freddie Drummond's fright was due to Mary Condon, president
of the International Glove-Workers' Union No. 974. He had seen her
first from the spectators' gallery at the annual convention of the
Northwest Federation of Labor, and he had seen her through Bill
Totts' eyes, and that individual had been most favorably impressed
by her. She was not Freddie Drummond's sort at all. What if she were
a royal-bodied woman, graceful and sinewy as a panther, with amazing black eyes that could fill with fire or laughter-love, as the mood
might dictate? He detested woman with a too-exuberant vitality and
a lack of—well, of inhibition. Freddie Drummond accepted the doctrine of evolution because it was quite universally accepted by college
men, and he flatly believed that man had climbed up the ladder of
life out of the weltering muck and mess of lower and monstrous organic things. But he was a trifle ashamed of their genealogy. Wherefore, probably, he practiced his iron inhibition and preached it to
others, and preferred women of his own type who could shake free of
this bestial and regrettable ancestral line and by discipline and control emphasize the wideness of the gulf that separated them from
what their dim forebears had been.

Bill Totts had none of these considerations. He had liked Mary
Condon from the moment his eyes first rested on her in the convention
hall, and he had made it a point, then and there, to find out who she
was. The next time he met her, and quite by accident, was when he
was driving an express wagon for Pat Morrissey. It was in a lodging-
house in Mission Street, where he had been called to take a trunk into
storage. The landlady's daughter had called him and led him to the
little bedroom, the occupant of which, a glove-maker, had just been
removed to a hospital. But Bill did not know this. He stooped, up-
ended the trunk, which was a large one, got it on his shoulder and

struggled to his feet with his back toward the open door. At that moment he heard a woman's voice.

"Belong to the union?" was the question asked.

"Aw, what's it to you?" he retorted. "Run along now, an' git outa my way. I wanta turn 'round."

The next he knew, big as he was, he was whirled half around and sent reeling backward, the trunk overbalancing him, till he fetched up with a crash against the wall. He started to swear, but at the same instant found himself looking into Mary Condon's flashing, angry eyes.

"Of course I b'long to the union," he said. "I was only kiddin' you."

"Where's your card?" she demanded in businesslike tones.

"In my pocket. But I can't git it out now. This trunk's too damn heavy. Come on down to the wagon an' I'll show it to you."

"Put that trunk down," was the command.

"What for? I got a card, I'm tellin' you."

"Put it down, that's all. No scab's going to handle that trunk. You ought to be ashamed of yourself, you big coward, scabbing on honest men. Why don't you join the union and be a man?"

Mary Condon's color had left her face and it was apparent that she was in a white rage.

"To think of a big man like you turning traitor to his class. I suppose you're aching to join the militia for a chance to shoot down union drivers the next strike. You may belong to the militia already, for that matter. You're the sort—"

"Hold on now; that's too much!" Bill dropped the trunk to the floor with a bang, straightened up and thrust his hand into his inside coat pocket. "I told you I was only kiddin'. There, look at that."

It was a union card properly enough.

"All right, take it along," Mary Condon said. "And the next time don't kid."

Her face relaxed as she noticed the ease with which he got the big trunk to his shoulder and her eyes glowed as they glanced over the graceful massiveness of the man. But Bill did not see that. He was too busy with the trunk.

The next time he saw Mary Condon was during the laundry strike. The laundry workers, but recently organized, were green at the business, and had petitioned Mary Condon to engineer the strike. Freddie Drummond had had an inkling of what was coming and had sent Bill Totts to join the union and investigate. Bill's job was in the wash-

room, and the men had been called out first that morning in order to
stiffen the courage of the girls; and Bill chanced to be near the door
to the mangle-room when Mary Condon started to enter. The superintendent, who was both large and stout, barred her way. He wasn't
going to have his girls called out and he'd teach her a lesson to mind
her own business. And as Mary tried to squeeze past him he thrust
her back with a fat hand on her shoulder. She glanced around and saw
Bill.

"Here you, Mr. Totts," she called. "Lend a hand. I want to get in."

Bill experienced a startle of warm surprise. She had remembered
his name from his union card. The next moment the superintendent
had been plucked from the doorway, raving about rights under the
law, and the girls were deserting their machines. During the rest of
that short and successful strike, Bill constituted himself Mary Condon's henchman and messenger, and when it was over returned to the
university to be Freddie Drummond and to wonder what Bill Totts
could see in such a woman.

Freddie Drummond was entirely safe, but Bill had fallen in love.
There was no getting away from the fact of it, and it was this fact
that had given Freddie Drummond his warning. Well, he had done
his work and his adventures could cease. There was no need for him
to cross the Slot again. All but the last three chapters of his latest,
Labor Tactics and Strategy, was finished, and he had sufficient material on hand adequately to supply those chapters.

Another conclusion he arrived at was that, in order to sheet-anchor
himself as Freddie Drummond, closer ties and relations in his own
social nook were necessary. It was time that he was married, anyway,
and he was fully aware that if Freddie Drummond didn't get married Bill Totts assuredly would, and the complications were too awful
to contemplate. And so enters Catherine Van Vorst. She was a college
woman herself, and her father, the one wealthy member of the
Faculty, was the head of the philosophy department. It would be a
wise marriage from every standpoint, Freddie Drummond concluded
when the engagement was entered into and announced. In appearance, cold and reserved, aristocratic and wholesomely conservative,
Catherine Van Vorst, though warm in her way, possessed an inhibition equal to Drummond's.

All seemed well with him, but Freddie Drummond could not quite
shake off the call of the underworld, the lure of the free and open, of
the unhampered, irresponsible life South of the Slot. As the time of

his marriage approached he felt that he had indeed sowed wild oats, and he felt, moreover, what a good thing it would be if he could have but one wild fling more, play the good fellow and the wastrel one last time ere he settled down to gray lecture-rooms and sober matrimony. And, further to tempt him, the very last chapter of Labor Tactics and Strategy remained unwritten for lack of a trifle more of essential data which he had neglected to gather.

So, Freddie Drummond went down for the last time as Bill Totts, got his data, and, unfortunately, encountered Mary Condon. Once more installed in his study it was not a pleasant thing to look back upon. It made his warning doubly imperative. Bill Totts had behaved abominably. Not only had he met Mary Condon at the Central Labor Council, but he had stopped in at a creamery with her, on the way home, and treated her to oysters. And before they parted at her door his arms had been about her and he had kissed her on the lips and kissed her repeatedly. And her last words in his ear, words uttered softly with a catchy sob in the throat that was nothing more nor less than a love-cry, were, "Bill—dear, dear Bill."

Freddie Drummond shuddered at the recollection. He saw the pit yawning for him. He was not by nature a polygamist, and he was appalled at the possibilities of the situation. It would have to be put an end to, and it would end in one only of two ways: either he must become wholly Bill Totts and be married to Mary Condon, or he must remain wholly Freddie Drummond and be married to Catherine Van Vorst. Otherwise, his conduct would be horrible and beneath contempt.

In the several months that followed, San Francisco was torn with labor strife. The unions and the employers' associations had locked horns with a determination that looked as if they intended to settle the matter one way or the other for all time. But Freddie Drummond corrected proofs, lectured classes and did not budge. He devoted himself to Catherine Van Vorst and day by day found more to respect and admire in her—nay, even to love in her. The street-car strike tempted him, but not so severely as he would have expected; and the great meat strike came on and left him cold. The ghost of Bill Totts had been successfully laid, and Freddie Drummond with rejuvenescent zeal tackled a brochure, long planned, on the topic of Diminishing Returns.

The wedding was two weeks off when, on one afternoon, in San Francisco, Catherine Van Vorst picked him up and whisked him away to see a Boys' Club recently instituted by the settlement workers with whom she was interested. They were in her brother's machine, but they were alone except for the chauffeur. At the junction with Kearny Street, Market and Geary Streets intersect like the sides of a sharp-angled letter V. They, in the auto, were coming down Market with the intention of negotiating the sharp apex and going up Geary. But they did not know what was coming down Geary, timed by Fate to meet them at the apex. While aware from the papers that the meat strike was on and that it was an exceedingly bitter one, all thought of it at that moment was farthest from Freddie Drummond's mind. Was he not seated beside Catherine? And besides, he was carefully expounding to her his views on settlement work—views that Bill Totts' adventures had played a part in formulating.

Coming down Geary Street were six meat wagons. Beside each scab driver sat a policeman. Front and rear, and along each side of this procession, marched a protecting escort of one hundred police. Behind the police rear-guard, at a respectful distance, was an orderly but vociferous mob several blocks in length, that congested the street from sidewalk to sidewalk. The Beef Trust was making an effort to supply the hotels and, incidentally, to begin the breaking of the strike. The St. Francis had already been supplied at a cost of many broken windows and broken heads, and the expedition was marching to the relief of the Palace Hotel.

All unwitting, Drummond sat beside Catherine talking settlement work as the auto, honking methodically and dodging traffic, swung in a wide curve to get around the apex. A big coal wagon, loaded with lump coal and drawn by four huge horses, just debouching from Kearny Street as though to turn down Market, blocked their way. The driver of the wagon seemed undecided, and the chauffeur, running slow but disregarding some shouted warning from the policemen, swerved the auto to the left, violating the traffic rules in order to pass in front of the wagon.

At that moment Freddie Drummond discontinued his conversation. Nor did he resume it again, for the situation was developing with the rapidity of a transformation scene. He heard the roar of the mob at the rear and caught a glimpse of the helmeted police and the lurching meat wagons. At the same moment, laying on his whip and standing up to his task, the coal-driver rushed horses and wagon squarely in front of the advancing procession, pulled the horses up sharply and put on the brake. Then he made his lines fast to the brake-handle and sat down with the air of one who had stopped to stay. The auto had been brought to a stop, too, by his big, panting leaders.

Before the chauffeur could back clear, an old Irishman, driving a rickety express wagon and lashing his one horse to a gallop, had locked wheels with the auto. Drummond recognized both horse and wagon, for he had driven them often himself. The Irishman was Pat Morrissey. On the other side a brewery wagon was locking with the coal wagon, and an east-bound Kearny Street car, wildly clanging its gong, the motorman shouting defiance at the crossing policemen, was dashing forward to complete the blockade. And wagon after wagon was locking and blocking and adding to the confusion. The meat wagons halted. The police were trapped. The roar at the rear increased as the mob came on to the attack, while the vanguard of the police charged the obstructing wagons.

"We're in for it," Drummond remarked coolly to Catherine.

"Yes," she nodded with equal coolness. "What savages they are!"

His admiration for her doubled on itself. She was indeed his sort. He would have been satisfied with her even if she had screamed and clung to him, but this—this was magnificent. She sat in that storm-center as calmly as if it had been no more than a block of carriages at the opera.

The police were struggling to clear a passage. The driver of the coal wagon, a big man in shirt sleeves, lighted a pipe and sat smoking. He glanced down complacently at a captain of police who was raving and cursing at him, and his only acknowledgment was a shrug of the shoulders. From the rear arose the rat-tat-tat of clubs on heads and a pandemonium of cursing, yelling and shouting. A violent accession of noise proclaimed that the mob had broken through and was dragging a scab from a wagon. The police captain was reënforced from his vanguard and the mob at the rear was repelled. Meanwhile, window after window in the high office-building on the right had been opened and the class-conscious clerks were raining a shower of office furniture down on the heads of police and scabs. Waste-baskets, ink-bottles, paper-weights, typewriters—anything and everything that came to hand was filling the air.

A policeman, under orders from his captain, clambered to the lofty seat of the coal wagon to arrest the driver. And the driver, rising leisurely and peacefully to meet him, suddenly crumpled him in his arms and threw him down on top of the captain. The driver was a young giant, and when he climbed on top his load and poised a lump

of coal in both hands a policeman, who was just scaling the wagon
from the side, let go and dropped back to earth. The captain ordered
half a dozen of his men to take the wagon. The teamster, scrambling
over the load from side to side, beat them down with huge lumps of
coal.

The crowd on the sidewalks and the teamsters on the locked wagons
roared encouragement and their own delight. The motorman, smashing helmets with his controller-bar, was beaten into insensibility and
dragged from his platform. The captain of police, beside himself at
the repulse of his men, led the next assault on the coal wagon. A score
of police were swarming up the tall-sided fortress. But the teamster
multiplied himself. At times there were six or eight policemen rolling
on the pavement and under the wagon. Engaged in repulsing an attack on the rear end of his fortress the teamster turned about to see
the captain just in the act of stepping on to the seat from the front
end. He was still in the air and in most unstable equilibrium when
the teamster hurled a thirty-pound lump of coal. It caught the captain
fairly on the chest and he went over backward, striking on a wheeler's
back, tumbling to the ground and jamming against the rear wheel
of the auto.

Catherine thought he was dead, but he picked himself up and
charged back. She reached out her gloved hand and patted the flank
of the snorting, quivering horse. But Drummond did not notice the
action. He had eyes for nothing save the battle of the coal wagon,
while somewhere in his complicated psychology one Bill Totts was
heaving and straining in an effort to come to life. Drummond believed
in law and order and the maintenance of the established; but this
riotous savage within him would have none of it. Then, if ever, did
Freddie Drummond call upon his iron inhibition to save him. But it
is written that the house divided against itself must fall. And Freddie
Drummond found that he had divided all the will and force of him
with Bill Totts, and between them the entity that constituted the
pair of them was being wrenched in twain.

Freddie Drummond sat in the auto quite composed, alongside Catherine Van Vorst; but looking out of Freddie Drummond's eyes was
Bill Totts, and somewhere behind those eyes, battling for the control
of their mutual body, was Freddie Drummond, the sane and conservative sociologist, and Bill Totts, the class-conscious and bellicose
union working-man. It was Bill Totts looking out of those eyes who
saw the inevitable end of the battle on the coal wagon. He saw a

policeman gain the top of the load, a second and a third. They lurched clumsily on the loose footing, but their long riot-clubs were out and swinging. One blow caught the teamster on the head. A second he dodged, receiving it on the shoulder. For him the game was plainly up. He dashed in suddenly, clutched two policemen in his arms, and hurled himself a prisoner to the pavement.

Catherine Van Vorst was sick and faint at sight of the blood and brutal fighting. But her qualms were vanquished by the sensational and most unexpected happening that followed. The man beside her emitted an unearthly yell and rose to his feet. She saw him spring over the front seat, leap to the broad rump of the wheeler and from there gain the wagon. His onslaught was like a whirlwind. Before the bewildered officer on top the load could guess the errand of this conventionally-clad but excited-seeming gentleman he was the recipient of a punch that arched him back through the air to the pavement. A kick in the face led an ascending policeman to follow his example. A rush of three more gained the top and locked with Bill Totts in a gigantic clinch, during which his scalp was opened up by a club, and coat, vest and half his starched shirt were torn from him. But the three policemen were flung wide and far, and Bill Totts, raining down lumps of coal, held the fort.

The captain led gallantly to the attack, but was bowled over by a chunk of coal that burst on his head in black baptism. The need of the police was to break the blockade in front before the mob could break in at the rear, and Bill Totts' need was to hold the wagon till the mob did break through. So the battle of the coal went on.

The crowd had recognized its champion. Big Bill, as usual, had come to the front, and Catherine Van Vorst was bewildered by the cries of "Bill! Oh, you Bill!" that arose on every hand. Pat Morrissey, on his wagon-seat, was jumping and screaming in an ecstasy: "Eat 'em, Bill! Eat 'em! Eat 'em alive!" From the sidewalk she heard a woman's voice cry out, "Look out, Bill—front end!" Bill took the warning, and with well-directed coal cleaned the front end of the wagon of assailants. Catherine Van Vorst turned her head and saw on the curb of the sidewalk a woman with vivid coloring and flashing black eyes who was staring with all her soul at the man who had been Freddie Drummond a few minutes before.

The windows of the office-building became vociferous with applause. The mob had broken through on one side the line of wagons and was advancing, each segregated policeman the center of a fighting group. The scabs were torn from their seats, the traces of the horses cut and the frightened animals put in flight. Many policemen crawled under the coal wagon for safety, while the loose horses, with here and there a policeman on their backs or struggling at their heads to hold them, surged across the sidewalk opposite the jam and broke into Market Street.

Catherine Van Vorst heard the woman's voice calling in warning. She was back on the curb again and crying out:

"Beat it, Bill! Now's your time! Beat it!"

The police for the moment had been swept away. Bill Totts leaped to the pavement and made his way to the woman on the sidewalk. Catherine Van Vorst saw her throw her arms around him and kiss him on the lips; and Catherine Van Vorst watched him curiously as he went on down the sidewalk, one arm around the woman, both talking and laughing, and he with a volubility and abandon she could never have dreamed possible.

The police were back again and clearing the jam while waiting for reënforcements and new drivers and horses. The mob had done its work and was scattering, and Catherine Van Vorst, still watching, could see the man she had known as Freddie Drummond. He towered a head above the crowd. His arm was still about the woman. And she in the motor car, watching, saw the pair cross Market Street, cross the Slot and disappear down Third Street into the labor ghetto.

In the years that followed no more lectures were given in the University of California by one Freddie Drummond and no more books on economics and the labor question appeared over the name of Frederick A. Drummond. On the other hand, there arose a new labor leader, William Totts by name. He it was who married Mary Condon, president of the International Glove-Workers' Union No. 974, and he it was who called the notorious cooks' and waiters' strike, which, before its successful termination, brought out with it scores of other unions, among which, of the more remotely allied, were the chicken-pickers and the undertakers.

The Strength of the Strong

Parables don't lie, but liars will parable.
—LIP-KING

Old Long-Beard paused in his narrative, licked his greasy fingers and wiped them on his naked sides where his one piece of ragged bear-skin failed to cover him. Crouched around him, on their hams, were three young men, his grandsons, Deer-Runner, Yellow-Head and Afraid-of-the-Dark. In appearance they were much the same. Skins of wild animals partially covered them. They were lean and meager of build, narrow-hipped and crooked-legged, and at the same time deep-chested with heavy arms and enormous hands. There was much hair on their chests and shoulders, and on the outsides of their arms and legs. Their heads were matted with uncut hair, long locks of which often strayed before their eyes, beady and black and glittering like the eyes of birds. They were narrow between the eyes and broad between the cheeks, while their lower jaws were projecting and massive.

It was a night of clear starlight, and below them, stretching away remotely, lay range on range of forest-covered hills. In the distance the heavens were red from the glow of a volcano. At their backs yawned the black mouth of a cave, out of which, from time to time, blew draughty gusts of wind. Immediately in front of them blazed a fire. At one side, partly devoured, lay the carcass of a bear, with about it, at a respectable distance, several large dogs, shaggy and wolflike. Beside each man lay his bow and arrows and a huge club. In the cave-mouth a number of rude spears leaned against the rock.

"So that was how we moved from the cave to the tree," old Long-Beard spoke up.

They laughed boisterously, like big children, at recollection of a previous story his words called up. Long-Beard laughed, too, the five-inch bodkin of bone thrust midway through the cartilage of his nose leaping and dancing and adding to his ferocious appearance. He did not exactly say the words recorded, but he made animal-like sounds with his mouth that meant the same thing.

"And that is the first I remember of the Sea Valley," Long-Beard went on. "We were a very foolish crowd. We did not know the secret of strength. For behold, each family lived by itself and took care of itself. There were thirty families, but we got no strength from one another. We were in fear of each other all the time. No one ever paid visits. In the top of our tree we built a grass house, and on the platform outside was a pile of rocks which were for the heads of any that might chance to try to visit us. Also, we had our spears and arrows. We never walked under the trees of the other families, either. My brother did, once, under old Boo-oogh's tree, and he got his head broken and that was the end of him.

"Old Boo-oogh was very strong. It was said he could pull a grown man's head right off. I never heard of him doing it, because no man would give him a chance. Father wouldn't. One day when father was down on the beach, Boo-oogh took after mother. She couldn't run fast, for the day before she had got her leg clawed by a bear when she was up on the mountain gathering berries. So Boo-oogh caught her and carried her up into his tree. Father never got her back. He was afraid. Old Boo-oogh made faces at him.

"But father did not mind. Strong-Arm was another strong man. He was one of the best fishermen. But one day, climbing after sea-gull eggs, he had a fall from the cliff. He was never strong after that. He coughed a great deal, and his shoulders drew near to each other. So father took Strong-Arm's wife. When he came around and coughed under our tree, father laughed at him and threw rocks at him. It was our way in those days. We did not know how to add strength together and become strong."

"Would a brother take a brother's wife?" Deer-Runner demanded.

"Yes, if he had gone to live in another tree by himself."

"But we do not do such things now," Afraid-of-the-Dark objected.

"It is because I have taught your fathers better." Long-Beard thrust his hairy paw into the bear meat and drew out a handful of

suet, which he sucked with a meditative air. Again he wiped his hands
on his naked sides and went on. "What I am telling you happened in
the long ago, before we knew any better."

"You must have been fools not to know better," was Deer-Runner's
comment, Yellow-Head grunting approval.

"So we were, but we became bigger fools, as you shall see. Still, we
did learn better, and this was the way of it. We Fish-Eaters had not
learned to add our strength until our strength was the strength of all
of us. But the Meat-Eaters, who lived across the divide in the Big
Valley, stood together, hunted together, fished together, and fought
together. One day they came into our valley. Each family of us got
into its own cave and tree. There were only ten Meat-Eaters, but
they fought together, and we fought each family by itself."

Long-Beard counted long and perplexedly on his fingers.

"There were sixty men of us," was what he managed to say with
fingers and lips combined. "And we were very strong, only we did not
know it. So we watched the ten men attack Boo-oogh's tree. He made
a good fight, but he had no chance. We looked on. When some of the
Meat-Eaters tried to climb the tree, Boo-oogh had to show himself
in order to drop stones on their heads, whereupon the other Meat-
Eaters, who were waiting for that very thing, shot him full of arrows.
And that was the end of Boo-oogh.

"Next, the Meat-Eaters got One-Eye and his family in his cave.
They built a fire in the mouth and smoked him out, like we smoked
out the bear there to-day. Then they went after Six-Fingers, up his
tree, and while they were killing him and his grown son, the rest of us
ran away. They caught some of our women, and killed two old men
who could not run fast and several children. The women they carried
away with them to the Big Valley.

"After that the rest of us crept back, and somehow, perhaps because we were in fear and felt the need for one another, we talked the
thing over. It was our first council—our first real council. And in that
council we formed our first tribe. For we had learned the lesson. Of
the ten Meat-Eaters, each man had had the strength of ten, for the
ten had fought as one man. They had added their strength together.
But of the thirty families and the sixty men of us, we had had the
strength of but one man, for each had fought alone.

"It was a great talk we had, and it was hard talk, for we did not
have the words then as now with which to talk. The Bug made some
of the words long afterwards, and so did others of us make words from

time to time. But in the end we agreed to add our strength together and to be as one man when the Meat-Eaters came over the divide to steal our women. And that was the tribe.

"We set two men on the divide, one for the day and one for the night, to watch if the Meat-Eaters came. These were the eyes of the tribe. Then, also, day and night, there were to be ten men awake with their clubs and spears and arrows in their hands, ready to fight. Before, when a man went after fish or clams or gull eggs, he carried his weapons with him and half the time he was getting food and half the time watching for fear some other man would get him. Now that was all changed. The men went out without their weapons and spent all their time getting food. Likewise, when the women went into the mountains after roots and berries, five of the ten men went with them to guard them, while all the time, day and night, the eyes of the tribe watched from the top of the divide.

"But troubles came. As usual, it was about the women. Men without wives wanted other men's wives, and there was much fighting between men, and now and again one got his head smashed or a spear through his body. While one of the watchers was on the top of the divide another man stole his wife, and he came down to fight. Then the other watcher was in fear that some one would take his wife, and he came down likewise. Also, there was trouble among the ten men who carried always their weapons, and they fought five against five, till some ran away down the coast and the others ran after them.

"So it was that the tribe was left without eyes or guards. We had not the strength of sixty. We had no strength at all. So we held a council and made our first laws. I was but a cub at the time, but I remember. We said that in order to be strong we must not fight one another, and we made a law that when a man killed another, him would the tribe kill. We made another law that whoso stole another man's wife, him would the tribe kill. We said that whatever man had too great strength, and by that strength hurt his brothers in the tribe, him would we kill that his strength might hurt no more. For if we let his strength hurt, the brothers would become afraid and the tribe would fall apart, and we would be as weak as when the Meat-Eaters first came upon us and killed Boo-oogh.

"Knuckle-Bone was a strong man, a very strong man, and he knew not law. He knew only his own strength, and in the fullness thereof he went forth and took the wife of Three-Clams. Three-Clams tried to fight, but Knuckle-Bone clubbed out his brains. Yet had Knuckle-

Bone forgotten that all the men of us had added our strength to keep the law among us, and him we killed, at the foot of his tree, and hung his body on a branch as a warning that the law was stronger than any man. For we were the law, all of us, and no man was greater than the law.

"Then there were other troubles, for know, O Deer-Runner and Yellow-Head and Afraid-of-the-Dark, that it is not easy to make a tribe. There were many things, little things, that it was a great trouble to call all the men together to have a council about. We were having councils morning, noon and night, and in the middle of the night. We could find little time to go out and get food, what of the councils, for there was always some little thing to be settled, such as naming two new watchers to take the place of the old ones on the hill, or naming how much food should fall to the share of the men who kept their weapons always in their hands and got no food for themselves.

"We stood in need of a chief man to do these things, who would be the voice of the council and who would account to the council for the things he did. So we named Fith-Fith the chief man. He was a strong man, too, and very cunning, and when he was angry he made noises just like that, *fith-fith*, like a wildcat.

"The ten men who guarded the tribe were set to work making a wall of stones across the narrow part of the valley. The women and large children helped, as did other men, until the wall was strong. After that, all the families came down out of their caves and trees and built grass houses behind the shelter of the wall. These houses were large and much better than the caves and trees, and everybody had a better time of it because the men had added their strength together and become a tribe. Because of the wall and the guards and the watchers, there was more time to hunt and fish and pick roots and berries; there was more food, and better food, and no one went hungry. And Three-Legs, so named because his legs had been smashed when a boy and he walked with a stick, Three-Legs got the seed of the wild corn and planted it in the ground in the valley near his house. Also, he tried planting fat roots and other things he found in the mountain valleys.

"Because of the safety in the Sea Valley, which was because of the wall and the watchers and the guards, and because there was food in plenty for all without having to fight for it, many families came in from the coast valleys on both sides and from the high back mountains where they had lived more like wild animals than men. And it

was not long before the Sea Valley filled up, and in it were countless
families. But before this happened the land, which had been free to all
and belonged to all, was divided up. Three-Legs began it when he
planted corn. But most of us did not care about the land. We thought
the marking of the boundaries with fences of stone was a foolishness.
We had plenty to eat, and what more did we want? I remember that
my father and I built stone fences for Three-Legs and were given
corn in return.

"So only a few got all the land, and Three-Legs got most of it.
Also, others that had taken land gave it to the few that held on, being
paid in return with corn and fat roots and bearskins and fishes which
the farmers got from the fishermen in exchange for corn. And the first
thing we knew, all the land was gone.

"It was about this time that Fith-Fith died, and Dog-Tooth, his
son, was made chief. He demanded to be made chief anyway, because
his father had been chief before him. Also, he looked upon himself
as a greater chief than his father. He was a good chief at first, and
worked hard, so that the council had less and less to do. Then arose a
new voice in the Sea Valley. It was Twisted-Lip. We had never
thought much of him, until he began to talk with the spirits of the
dead. Later we called him Big-Fat, because he ate overmuch and did
no work and grew round and large. One day Big-Fat told us that the
secrets of the dead were his, and that he was the voice of God. He
became great friends with Dog-Tooth, who commanded that we build
Big-Fat a grass house. And Big-Fat put taboos all around this house
and kept God inside.

"More and more Dog-Tooth became greater than the council, and
when the council grumbled and said it would name a new chief, Big-
Fat spoke with the voice of God and said no. Also, Three-Legs and
the others who held the land stood behind Dog-Tooth. Moreover, the
strongest man in the council was Sea-Lion, and him the landowners
gave land to secretly, along with many bearskins and baskets of corn.
So Sea-Lion said that Big-Fat's voice was truly the voice of God and
must be obeyed. And soon afterwards Sea-Lion was named the voice of
Dog-Tooth and did most of his talking for him.

"Then there was Little-Belly, a little man, so thin in the middle
that he looked as if he never had had enough to eat. Inside the mouth
of the river, after the sand-bar had combed the strength of the
breakers, he built a big fish trap. No man had ever seen or dreamed
of a fish trap before. He worked weeks on it, with his son and his wife,

while the rest of us laughed at their labors. But when it was done, the first day he caught more fish in it than could the whole tribe in a week, whereat there was great rejoicing. There was only one other place in the river for a fish trap; but when my father and I and a dozen other men started to make a very large trap, the guards came from the big grass house we had built for Dog-Tooth. And the guards poked us with their spears and told us begone, because Little-Belly was going to build a trap there himself on the word of Sea-Lion, who was the voice of Dog-Tooth.

"There was much grumbling, and my father called a council. But when he rose to speak, him the Sea-Lion thrust through the throat with a spear, and he died. And Dog-Tooth and Little-Belly and Three-Legs and all that held land said it was good. And Big-Fat said it was the will of God. And after that all men were afraid to stand up in the council, and there was no more council.

"Another man, Pig-Jaw, began to keep goats. He had heard about it among the Meat-Eaters, and it was not long before he had many flocks. Other men, who had no land and no fish traps and who else would have gone hungry were glad to work for Pig-Jaw, caring for his goats, guarding them from wild dogs and tigers and driving them to the feeding pastures in the mountains. In return Pig-Jaw gave them goat meat to eat, and goatskins to wear, and sometimes they traded the goat meat for fish and corn and fat roots.

"It was this time that money came to be. Sea-Lion was the man who first thought of it, and he talked it over with Dog-Tooth and Big-Fat. You see, these three were the ones that got a share of everything in the Sea Valley. One basket out of every three of corn was theirs, one fish out of every three, one goat out of every three. In return, they fed the guards and the watchers, and kept the rest for themselves. Sometimes, when a big haul of fish was made, they did not know what to do with all their share. So Sea-Lion set the women to making money out of shell—little round pieces, with a hole in each one, and all made smooth and fine. These were strung on strings, and the strings were called money.

"Each string was of the value of thirty fish, or forty fish, but the women who made a string a day were given two fish each. The fish came out of the shares of Dog-Tooth, Big-Fat and Sea-Lion, which they three did not eat. So all the money belonged to them. Then they told Three-Legs and the other landowners that they would take their share of corn and roots in money, Little-Belly that they would take their share of fish in money, and Pig-Jaw that they would take their share of goat and cheese in money. Thus, a man who had nothing worked for one who had and was paid in money. With this money he bought corn and fish and meat and cheese. And Three-Legs and all owners of things paid Dog-Tooth and Sea-Lion and Big-Fat their share in money. And they paid the guards and watchers in money, and the guards and watchers bought their food with the money. And because money was cheap, Dog-Tooth made many more men into guards. And because money was cheap to make, a number of men began to make money out of shells themselves. But the guards stuck spears in them and shot them full of arrows, because they were trying to break up the tribe. It was bad to break up the tribe, for then the Meat-Eaters would come over the divide and kill them all.

"Big-Fat was the voice of God, but he took Broken-Rib and made him into a priest, so that he became the voice of Big-Fat and did most of his talking for him. And both had other men to be servants to them. So also did Little-Belly and Three-Legs and Pig-Jaw have other men to lie in the sun about their grass houses and carry messages for them and give commands. And more and more were men taken away from work, so that those that were left worked harder than ever before. It seemed that men desired to do no work and strove to seek out other ways whereby men should work for them. Crooked-Eyes found such a way. He made the first firebrew out of corn. And thereafter he worked no more, for he talked secretly with Dog-Tooth and Big-Fat and the other masters, and it was agreed that he should be the only one to make firebrew. But Crooked-Eyes did no work himself. Men made the brew for him, and he paid them in money. Then he sold the firebrew for money, and all men bought. And many strings of money did he give Dog-Tooth and Sea-Lion and all of them.

"Big-Fat and Broken-Rib stood by Dog-Tooth when he took his second wife, and his third wife. They said Dog-Tooth was different from other men and second only to God that Big-Fat kept in his taboo house, and Dog-Tooth said so, too, and wanted to know who were they to grumble about how many wives he took. Dog-Tooth had a big canoe made, and many more men he took from work, who did nothing and lay in the sun save only when Dog-Tooth went in the canoe when they paddled for him. And he made Tiger-Face head man over all the guards, so that Tiger-Face became his right arm, and when he did not like a man Tiger-Face killed that man for him. And Tiger-Face, also, made another man to be his right arm, and to give commands and to kill for him.

"But this was the strange thing: as the days went by, we who were left worked harder and harder and yet did we get less and less to eat."

"But what of the goats and the corn and the fat roots and the fish trap?" spoke up Afraid-of-the-Dark. "What of all this? Was there not more food to be gained by a man's work?"

"It is so," Long-Beard agreed. "Three men on the fish trap got more fish than the whole tribe before there was a fish trap. But have I not said we were fools? The more food we were able to get, the less food did we have to eat."

"But was it not plain that the many men who did not work ate it all up?" Yellow-Head demanded.

Long-Beard nodded his head sadly. "Dog-Tooth's dogs were stuffed with meat, and the men who lay in the sun and did no work were rolling in fat, and at the same time there were little children crying themselves to sleep with hunger biting them with every wail."

Deer-Runner was spurred by the recital of famine to tear out a chunk of bear meat and broil it on a stick over the coals. This he devoured with smacking lips while Long-Beard went on.

"When we grumbled, Big-Fat arose and with the voice of God said that God had chosen the wise men to own the land and the goats and the fish trap and the firebrew and that without these wise men we would all be animals as in the days when we lived in trees.

"And there arose one who became a singer of songs for the king. Him they called the Bug, because he was small and ungainly of face and limb and excelled not in work or deed. He loved the fattest marrowbones, the choicest fish, the milk warm from the goats, the first corn that was ripe, and the snug place by the fire. And thus, becoming singer of songs to the king, he found a way to do nothing and be fat. And when the people grumbled more and more, and some threw stones at the king's big grass house, the Bug sang a song of how good it was to be a Fish-Eater. In his song he told that the Fish-Eaters were the chosen of God and the finest men God had made. He sang of the Meat-Eaters as pigs and crows, and sang how fine and good it was for the Fish-Eaters to fight and die doing God's work, which was the killing of Meat-Eaters. The words of his song were like fire in us, and we clamored to be led against the Meat-Eaters. And we forgot that we were hungry and why we had grumbled, and were glad to be led by Tiger-Face over the divide where we killed many Meat-Eaters and were content.

"But things were no better in the Sea Valley. The only way to get food was to work for Three-Legs or Little-Belly or Pig-Jaw; for there was no land that a man might plant with corn for himself. And often there were more men than Three-Legs and the others had work for. So these men went hungry, and so did their wives and children and their old mothers. Tiger-Face said they could become guards if they wanted to, and many of them did; and thereafter they did no work except to poke spears in the men who did work and who grumbled at feeding so many idlers.

"And when we grumbled, ever the Bug sang new songs. He said that Three-Legs and Pig-Jaw and the rest were strong men, and that that was why they had so much. He said that we should be glad to have strong men with us, else would we perish of our own worthlessness and the Meat-Eaters. Therefore we should be glad to let such strong men have all they could lay hands on. And Big-Fat and Pig-Jaw and Tiger-Face and all the rest said it was true.

" 'All right,' said Long-Fang, 'then will I, too, be a strong man.' And he got himself corn and began to make firebrew and sell it for strings of money. And when Crooked-Eyes complained, Long-Fang said that he was himself a strong man, and that if Crooked-Eyes made any more noise he would dash his brains out for him. Whereat Crooked-Eyes was afraid and went and talked with Three-Legs and Pig-Jaw. And all three went and talked to Dog-Tooth. And Dog-Tooth spoke to Sea-Lion, and Sea-Lion sent a runner with a message to Tiger-Face. And Tiger-Face sent his guards, who burned Long-Fang's house along with the firebrew he had made. Also, they killed him and all his family. And Big-Fat said it was good, and the Bug sang another song about how good it was to observe the law, and what a fine land the Sea Valley was, and how every man who loved the Sea Valley should go forth and kill the bad Meat-Eaters. And again his song was as fire to us, and we forgot to grumble.

"It was very strange. When Little-Belly caught too many fish, so that it took a great many to sell for a little money, he threw many of the fish back into the sea so that more money would be paid for what was left. And Three-Legs often let many large fields lie idle so as to get more money for his corn. And the women, making so much money out of shell that much money was needed to buy with, Dog-Tooth stopped the making of money. And the women had no work, so they took the places of the men. I worked on the fish trap, getting a string of money every five days. But my sister now did my work, getting a string of money for every ten days. The women worked cheaper, and there was less food, and Tiger-Face said for us to become guards. Only I could not become a guard, because I was lame of one leg and Tiger-Face would not have me. And there were many like me. We were broken men and only fit to beg for work or to take care of the babies while the women worked."

Yellow-Head, too, was made hungry by the recital, and broiled a piece of bear meat on the coals.

"But why didn't you rise up, all of you, and kill Three-Legs and Pig-Jaw and Big-Fat and the rest, and get enough to eat?" Afraid-of-the-Dark demanded.

"Because we could not understand," Long-Beard answered. "There was too much to think about, and also there were the guards sticking spears into us, and Big-Fat talking about God, and the Bug singing new songs. And when any man did think right, and said so, Tiger-Face and the guards got him and he was tied out to the rocks at low tide so that the rising waters drowned him.

"It was a strange thing—the money. It was like the Bug's songs. It seemed all right, but it wasn't, and we were slow to understand. Dog-Tooth began to gather the money in. He put it in a big pile, in a grass house, with guards to watch it day and night. And the more money he piled in the house, the dearer money became, so that a man worked a longer time for a string of money than before. Then, too, there was always talk of war with the Meat-Eaters, and Dog-Tooth and Tiger-Face filled many houses with corn and dried fish and smoked goat meat and cheese. And with the food piled there in mountains, the people had not enough to eat. But what did it matter? Whenever the people grumbled too loudly, the Bug sang a new song, and Big-Fat said it was God's word that we should kill Meat-Eaters, and Tiger-Face led us over the divide to kill and be killed. I was not good enough to be a guard and lie fat in the sun, but when we made war Tiger-Face was glad to take me along. And when we had eaten all the food stored in the houses we stopped fighting and went back to work to pile up more food."

"Then were you all crazy," commented Deer-Runner.

"Then were we indeed all crazy," Long-Beard agreed. "It was strange, all of it. There was Split-Nose. He said everything was wrong. He said it was true that we grew strong by adding our strength together. And he said that when we first formed the tribe it was right that the men whose strength hurt the tribe should be shorn of their strength—men who bashed their brothers' heads and stole their brothers' wives. And now, he said, the tribe was not getting stronger but was getting weaker, because there were men with another kind of strength that were hurting the tribe—men who had the strength of the land, like Three-Legs; who had the strength of the fish trap, like Little-Belly; who had the strength of all the goat meat, like Pig-Jaw. The thing to do, Split-Nose said, was to shear these men of their evil strength; to make them go to work, all of them, and to let no man eat who did not work.

"And the Bug sang another song about men like Split-Nose, who wanted to go back and live in trees.

"Yet Split-Nose said no; that he did not want to go back but ahead; that they grew strong only as they added their strength together; and that if the Fish-Eaters would add their strength to the Meat-Eaters, there would be no more fighting and no more watchers and no more guards, and that with all men working there would be so much food that each man would have to work not more than two hours a day.

"Then the Bug sang again, and he sang that Split-Nose was lazy, and he sang also the 'Song of the Bees.' It was a strange song, and those who listened were made mad as from the drinking of strong firebrew. The song was of a swarm of bees, and of a robber wasp who had come in to live with the bees, and who was stealing all their honey. The wasp was lazy and told them there was no need to work; also, he told them to make friends with the bears who were not honey stealers but only very good friends. And the Bug sang in crooked words, so that those who listened knew that the swarm was the Sea Valley tribe, that the bears were the Meat-Eaters, and that the lazy wasp was Split-Nose. And when the Bug sang that the bees listened to the wasp till the swarm was near to perishing, the people growled and snarled; and when the Bug sang that at last the good bees arose and stung the wasp to death, the people picked up stones from the ground and stoned Split-Nose to death till there was naught to be seen of him but the heap of stones they had flung on top of him. And there were many poor people who worked long and hard and had not enough to eat that helped throw the stones on Split-Nose.

"And after the death of Split-Nose there was but one other man that dared rise up and speak his mind, and that man was Hair-Face. 'Where is the strength of the strong?' he asked. 'We are the strong, all of us, and we are stronger than Dog-Tooth and Tiger-Face and Three-Legs and Pig-Jaw and all the rest who do nothing and eat much and weaken us by the hurt of their strength, which is bad strength. Men who are slaves are not strong. If the man who first found the virtue and use of fire had used his strength, we would have been his slaves, as we are the slaves to-day of Little-Belly who found the virtue and use of the fish trap, and of the men who found the virtue and use of the land and the goats and the firebrew. Before, we lived in trees, my brothers, and no man was safe. But we fight no more with one another. We have added our strength together. Then let us fight no more with the Meat-Eaters. Let us add our strength and their strength together. Then will we be indeed strong. And then we will go out together, the Fish-Eaters and the Meat-Eaters, and we will kill the tigers and the lions and the wolves and the wild dogs, and we will pasture our goats on all the hillsides and plant our corn and fat roots in all the high mountain valleys.

" 'In that day we will be so strong that all the wild animals will flee before us and perish. And nothing will withstand us, for the strength of each man will be the strength of all men in the world.'

"So said Hair-Face, and they killed him, because they said he was a wild man and wanted to go back and live in a tree. It was very strange. Whenever a man arose and wanted to go forward all those that stood still said he went backward and should be killed. And the poor people helped stone him, and were fools. We were all fools, except those who were fat and did no work. The fools were called wise, and the wise were stoned. Men who worked did not get enough to eat, and the men who did not work ate too much.

"And the tribe went on losing strength. The children were weak and sickly. And because we ate not enough, strange sicknesses came among us and we died like flies. And then the Meat-Eaters came upon us. We had followed Tiger-Face too often over the divide and killed them. And now they came to repay in blood. We were too weak and sick to man the big wall. And they killed us, all of us, except some of the women which they took away with them. The Bug and I escaped, and I hid in the wildest places, and became a hunter of meat and went hungry no more. I stole a wife from among the Meat-Eaters, and went to live in the caves of the high mountains where they could not find me. And we had three sons, and each son stole a wife from the Meat-Eaters. And the rest you know, for are you not the sons of my sons?"

"But the Bug?" queried Deer-Runner. "What became of him?"

"He went to live with the Meat-Eaters and to be a singer of songs to the king. He is an old man now, but he sings the same old songs; and when a man rises up to go forward he sings that that man is walking backward to live in a tree."

Long-Beard dipped into the bear carcass and sucked with tooth-less gums at a fist of suet.

"Someday," he said, wiping his hands on his sides, "all the fools will be dead, and then all live men will go forward. The secret of the strength of the strong will be theirs, and they will add their strength together, so that of all the men in the world not one will fight with another. There will be no guards nor watchers on the walls. And all the hunting animals will be killed, and, as Hair-Face said, all the hillsides will be pastured with goats, and all the high mountain val-leys will be planted with corn and fat roots. And all men will be brothers, and no man will lie idle in the sun and be fed by his fellows. And all that will come to pass in the time when the fools are dead, and when there will be no more singers to stand still and sing the 'Song of the Bees.' Bees are not men."

In the Laundry

A SELECTION FROM Martin Eden

EDITOR'S NOTE: *On the verge of starvation and unable to pay his bills, Martin Eden is forced to interrupt his work on his manuscripts and to seek a job. The only work he can find is in a laundry. Having himself worked in the laundry of the Belmont Academy, London knew how to invest the laundry scene in his great autobiographical novel with authenticity. This section is not only among the finest parts of* Martin Eden, *but has few equals in realistic fiction.*

For a fuller discussion of Martin Eden, *see pages 100–106.*

The alarm-clock went off, jerking Martin out of sleep with a suddenness that would have given headache to one with less splendid constitution. Though he slept soundly, he awoke instantly, like a cat, and he awoke eagerly, glad that the five hours of unconsciousness were gone. He hated the oblivion of sleep. There was too much to do, too much of life to live. He grudged every moment of life sleep robbed him of, and before the clock had ceased its clattering he was head and ears in the wash-basin and thrilling to the cold bite of the water.

But he did not follow his regular programme. There was no unfinished story waiting his hand, no new story demanding articulation. He had studied late, and it was nearly time for breakfast. He tried to read a chapter in Fiske, but his brain was restless and he closed the book. To-day witnessed the beginning of the new battle, wherein for some time there would no writing. He was aware of a sadness akin to that with which one leaves home and family. He looked at the manuscripts in the corner. That was it. He was going away from them, his pitiful, dishonored children that were welcome nowhere. He went over and began to rummage among them, reading snatches here and there, his favorite portions. "The Pot" he honored with reading aloud, as he did "Adventure." "Joy," his latest-born, completed the day before and tossed into the corner for lack of stamps, won his keenest approbation.

"I can't understand," he murmured. "Or maybe it's the editors who can't understand. There's nothing wrong with that. They publish worse every month. Everything they publish is worse—nearly everything, anyway."

After breakfast he put the typewriter in its case and carried it down into Oakland.

"I owe a month on it," he told the clerk in the store. "But you tell the manager I'm going to work and that I'll be in in a month or so and straighten up."

He crossed on the ferry to San Francisco and made his way to an employment office. "Any kind of work, no trade," he told the agent; and was interrupted by a newcomer, dressed rather foppishly, as some workingmen dress who have instincts for finer things. The agent shook his head despondently.

"Nothin' doin', eh?" said the other. "Well, I got to get somebody to-day."

He turned and stared at Martin, and Martin, staring back, noted the puffed and discolored face, handsome and weak, and knew that he had been making a night of it.

"Lookin' for a job?" the other queried. "What can you do?"

"Hard labor, sailorizing, run a typewriter, no shorthand, can sit on a horse, willing to do anything and tackle anything," was the answer.

The other nodded.

"Sounds good to me. My name's Dawson, Joe Dawson, an' I'm tryin' to scare up a laundryman."

"Too much for me." Martin caught an amusing glimpse of himself ironing fluffy white things that women wear. But he had taken a liking to the other, and he added: "I might do the plain washing. I learned that much at sea."

Joe Dawson thought visibly for a moment.

"Look here, let's get together an' frame it up. Willin' to listen?"

Martin nodded.

"This is a small laundry, up country, belongs to Shelly Hot Springs,—hotel, you know. Two men do the work, boss and assistant.

I'm the boss. You don't work for me, but you work under me. Think
you'd be willin' to learn?"

Martin paused to think. The prospect was alluring. A few months
of it, and he would have time to himself for study. He could work
hard and study hard.

"Good grub an' a room to yourself," Joe said.

That settled it. A room to himself where he could burn the midnight oil unmolested.

"But work like hell," the other added.

Martin caressed his swelling shoulder-muscles significantly. "That
came from hard work."

"Then let's get to it." Joe held his hand to his head for a moment.
"Gee, but it's a stem-winder. Can hardly see. I went down the line
last night—everything—everything. Here's the frame-up. The wages
for two is a hundred and board. I've been drawin' down sixty, the
second man forty. But he knew the biz. You're green. If I break you
in, I'll be doing plenty of your work at first. Suppose you begin at
thirty, an' work up to the forty. I'll play fair. Just as soon as you can
do your share you get the forty."

"I'll go you," Martin announced, stretching out his hand, which
the other shook. "Any advance?—for railroad ticket and extras?"

"I blew it in," was Joe's sad answer, with another reach at his
aching head. "All I got is a return ticket."

"And I'm broke—when I pay my board."

"Jump it," Joe advised.

"Can't. Owe it to my sister."

Joe whistled a long, perplexed whistle, and racked his brains to little
purpose.

"I've got the price of the drinks," he said desperately. "Come on,
an' mebbe we'll cook up something."

Martin declined.

"Water-wagon?"

This time Martin nodded, and Joe lamented, "Wish I was."

"But I somehow just can't," he said in extenuation. "After I've
ben workin' like hell all week I just got to booze up. If I didn't, I'd
cut my throat or burn up the premises. But I'm glad you're on the
wagon. Stay with it."

Martin knew of the enormous gulf between him and this man—the
gulf the books had made; but he found no difficulty in crossing back
over the gulf. He had lived all his life in the working-class world,

and the *camaraderie* of labor was second nature with him. He solved
the difficulty of transportation that was too much for the other's
aching head. He would send his trunk up to Shelly Hot Springs on
Joe's ticket. As for himself, there was his wheel. It was seventy miles,
and he could ride it on Sunday and be ready for work Monday morning. In the meantime he would go home and pack up. There was no one
to say good-by to. Ruth and her whole family were spending the long
summer in the Sierras, at Lake Tahoe.

He arrived at Shelly Hot Springs, tired and dusty, on Sunday night.
Joe greeted him exuberantly. With a wet towel bound about his aching brow, he had been at work all day.

"Part of last week's washin' mounted up, me bein' away to get you,"
he explained. "Your box arrived all right. It's in your room. But it's
a hell of a thing to call a trunk. An' what's in it? Gold bricks?"

Joe sat on the bed while Martin unpacked. The box was a packing-
case for breakfast food, and Mr. Higginbotham had charged him half
a dollar for it. Two rope handles, nailed on by Martin, had technically
transformed it into a trunk eligible for the baggage-car. Joe watched,
with bulging eyes, a few shirts and several changes of underclothes
come out of the box, followed by books, and more books.

"Books clean to the bottom?" he asked.

Martin nodded, and went on arranging the books on a kitchen table
which served in the room in place of a washstand.

"Gee!" Joe exploded, then waited in silence for the deduction to
arise in his brain. At last it came.

"Say, you don't care for the girls—much?" he queried.

"No," was the answer. "I used to chase a lot before I tackled the
books. But since then there's no time."

"And there won't be any time here. All you can do is work an'
sleep."

Martin thought of his five hours' sleep a night, and smiled. The
room was situated over the laundry and was in the same building with
the engine that pumped water, made electricity, and ran the laundry
machinery. The engineer, who occupied the adjoining room, dropped
in to meet the new hand and helped Martin rig up an electric bulb, on
an extension wire, so that it travelled along a stretched cord from
over the table to the bed.

The next morning, at quarter-past six, Martin was routed out for
a quarter-to-seven breakfast. There happened to be a bath-tub for the

servants in the laundry building, and he electrified Joe by taking a
cold bath.

"Gee, but you're a hummer!" Joe announced, as they sat down to
breakfast in a corner of the hotel kitchen.

With them were the engineer, the gardener, and the assistant gardener, and two or three men from the stable. They ate hurriedly and
gloomily, with but little conversation, and as Martin ate and listened
he realized how far he had travelled from their status. Their small
mental caliber was depressing to him, and he was anxious to get away
from them. So he bolted his breakfast, a sickly, sloppy affair, as
rapidly as they, and heaved a sigh of relief when he passed out through
the kitchen door.

It was a perfectly appointed, small steam laundry, wherein the
most modern machinery did everything that was possible for machinery to do. Martin, after a few instructions, sorted the great heaps
of soiled clothes, while Joe started the masher and made up fresh
supplies of soft-soap, compounded of biting chemicals that compelled
him to swathe his mouth and nostrils and eyes in bathtowels till he
resembled a mummy. Finished the sorting, Martin lent a hand in
wringing the clothes. This was done by dumping them into a spinning
receptacle that went at a rate of a few thousand revolutions a minute,
tearing the water from the clothes by centrifugal force. Then Martin
began to alternate between the dryer and the wringer, between times
"shaking out" socks and stockings. By the afternoon, one feeding and
one stacking up, they were runnings socks and stockings through the
mangle while the irons were heating. Then it was hot irons and underclothes until six o'clock, at which time Joe shook his head dubi-
ously.

"Way behind," he said. "Got to work after supper."

And after supper they worked until ten o'clock, under the blazing
electric lights, until the last piece of underclothing was ironed and
folded away in the distributing room. It was a hot California night,
and though the windows were thrown wide, the room, with its red-
hot ironing-stove, was a furnace. Martin and Joe, down to undershirts,
bare armed, sweated and panted for air.

"Like trimming cargo in the tropics," Martin said, when they went
upstairs.

"You'll do," Joe answered. "You take hold like a good fellow. If
you keep up the pace, you'll be on thirty dollars only one month. The

second month you'll be gettin' your forty. But don't tell me you never ironed before. I know better."

"Never ironed a rag in my life, honestly, until to-day," Martin protested.

He was surprised at his weariness when he got into his room, forgetful of the fact that he had been on his feet and working without let up for fourteen hours. He set the alarm at six, and measured back five hours to one o'clock. He could read until then. Slipping off his shoes, to ease his swollen feet, he sat down at the table with his books. He opened Fiske, where he had left off two days before, and began to read. But he found trouble with the first paragraph and began to read it through a second time. Then he awoke, in pain from his stiffened muscles and chilled by the mountain wind that had begun to blow in through the window. He looked at the clock. It marked two. He had been asleep four hours. He pulled off his clothes and crawled into bed, where he was asleep the moment after his head touched the pillow.

Tuesday was a day of similar unremitting toil. The speed with which Joe worked won Martin's admiration. Joe was a dozen of demons for work. He was keyed up to concert pitch, and there was never a moment in the long day when he was not fighting for moments. He concentrated himself upon his work and upon how to save time, pointing out to Martin where he did in five motions what could be done in three, or in three motions what could be done in two. "Elimination of waste motion," Martin phrased it as he watched and patterned after. He was a good workman himself, quick and deft, and it had always been a point of pride with him that no man should do any of his work for him or outwork him. As a result, he concentrated with a similar singleness of purpose, greedily snapping up the hints and suggestions thrown out by his working mate. He "rubbed out" collars and cuffs, rubbing the starch out from between the double thicknesses of linen so that there would be no blisters when it came to the ironing, and doing it at a pace that elicited Joe's praise.

There was never an interval when something was not at hand to be done. Joe waited for nothing, waited on nothing, and went on the jump from task to task. They starched two hundred white shirts, with a single gathering movement seizing a shirt so that the wristbands, neckband, yoke, and bosom protruded beyond the circling right hand. At the same moment the left hand held up the body of the shirt so that it would not enter the starch, and at the same moment the right hand dipped into the starch—starch so hot that, in order to wring it out, their hands had to be thrust, and thrust continually, into a bucket of cold water. And that night they worked till half-past ten, dipping "fancy starch"—all the frilled and airy, delicate wear of ladies.

"Me for the tropics and no clothes," Martin laughed.

"And me out of a job," Joe answered seriously. "I don't know nothin' but laundrying."

"And you know it well."

"I ought to. Began in the Contra Costa in Oakland when I was eleven, shakin' out for the mangle. That was eighteen years ago, an' I've never done a tap of anything else. But this job is the fiercest I ever had. Ought to be one more man on it at least. We work to-morrow night. Always run the mangle Wednesday nights—collars an' cuffs."

Martin set his alarm, drew up to the table, and opened Fiske. He did not finish the first paragraph. The lines blurred and ran together and his head nodded. He walked up and down, batting his head savagely with his fists, but he could not conquer the numbness of sleep. He propped the book before him, and propped his eyelids with his fingers, and fell asleep with his eyes wide open. Then he surrendered, and, scarcely conscious of what he did, got off his clothes and into bed. He slept seven hours of heavy, animal-like sleep, and awoke by the alarm, feeling that he had not had enough.

"Doin' much readin'?" Joe asked.

Martin shook his head.

"Never mind. We got to run the mangle to-night, but Thursday we'll knock off at six. That'll give you a chance."

Martin washed woollens that day, by hand, in a large barrel, with strong soft-soap, by means of a hub from a wagon wheel, mounted on a plunger-pole that was attached to a spring-pole overhead.

"My invention," Joe said proudly. "Beats a washboard an' your knuckles, and, besides, it saves at least fifteen minutes in the week, an' fifteen minutes ain't to be sneezed at in this shebang."

Running the collars and cuffs through the mangle was also Joe's idea. That night, while they toiled on under the electric lights, he explained it.

"Something no laundry ever does, except this one. An' I got to do it if I'm goin' to get done Saturday afternoon at three o'clock. But I know how, an' that's the difference. Got to have right heat, right pres-

sure, and run 'em through three times. Look at that!" He held a cuff
aloft. "Couldn't do it better by hand or on a tiler."

Thursday, Joe was in a rage. A bundle of extra "fancy starch" had
come in.

"I'm goin' to quit," he announced. "I won't stand for it. I'm goin'
to quit it cold. What's the good of me workin' like a slave all week,
a-savin' minutes, an' them a-comin' an' ringing' in fancy-starch extras
on me? This is a free country, an' I'm goin' to tell that fat Dutchman
what I think of him. An' I won't tell 'im in French. Plain United States
is good enough for me. Him a-ringin' in fancy starch extras!

"We got to work to-night," he said the next moment, reversing his
judgment and surrendering to fate.

And Martin did no reading that night. He had seen no daily paper
all week, and, strangely to him, felt no desire to see one. He was not
interested in the news. He was too tired and jaded to be interested in
anything, though he planned to leave Saturday afternoon, if they
finished at three, and ride on his wheel to Oakland. It was seventy
miles, and the same distance back on Sunday afternoon would leave
him anything but rested for the second week's work. It would have
been easier to go on the train, but the round trip was two dollars and
a half, and he was intent on saving money.

Martin learned to do many things. In the course of the first week, in
one afternoon, he and Joe accounted for the two hundred white shirts.
Joe ran the tiler, a machine wherein a hot iron was hooked on a steel
string which furnished the pressure. By this means he ironed the
yoke, wristbands, and neckband, setting the latter at right angles to
the shirt, and put the glossy finish on the bosom. As fast as he finished
them, he flung the shirts on a rack between him and Martin, who
caught them up and "backed" them. This task consisted of ironing
all the unstarched portions of the shirts.

It was exhausting work, carried on, hour after hour, at top speed.
Out on the broad verandas of the hotel, men and women, in cool
white, sipped iced drinks and kept their circulation down. But in the
laundry the air was sizzling. The huge stove roared red hot and white
hot, while the irons, moving over the damp cloth, sent up clouds
of steam. The heat of these irons was different from that used by
housewives. An iron that stood the ordinary test of a wet finger was too
cold for Joe and Martin, and such test was useless. They went wholly
by holding the irons close to their cheeks, gauging the heat by some

secret mental process that Martin admired but could not understand. When the fresh irons proved too hot, they hooked them on iron rods and dipped them into cold water. This again required a precise and subtle judgment. A fraction of a second too long in the water and the fine and silken edge of the proper heat was lost, and Martin found time to marvel at the accuracy he developed—an automatic accuracy, founded upon criteria that were machine-like and unerring.

But there was little time in which to marvel. All Martin's consciousness was concentrated in the work. Ceaselessly active, head and hand, an intelligent machine, all that constituted him a man was devoted to furnishing that intelligence. There was no room in his brain for the universe and its mighty problems. All the broad and spacious corridors of his mind were closed and hermetically sealed. The echoing chamber of his soul was a narrow room, a conning tower, whence were directed his arm and shoulder muscles, his ten nimble fingers, and the swift-moving iron along its steaming path in broad, sweeping strokes, just so many strokes and no more, just so far with each stroke and not a fraction of an inch farther, rushing along interminable sleeves, sides, backs, and tails, and tossing the finished shirts, without rumpling, upon the receiving frame. And even as his hurrying soul tossed, it was reaching for another shirt. This went on, hour after hour, while outside all the world swooned under the overhead California sun. But there was no swooning in that superheated room. The cool guests on the verandas needed clean linen.

The sweat poured from Martin. He drank enormous quantities of water, but so great was the heat of the day and of his exertions, that the water sluiced through the interstices of his flesh and out at all his pores. Always, at sea, except at rare intervals, the work he performed had given him ample opportunity to commune with himself. The master of the ship had been lord of Martin's time; but here the manager of the hotel was lord of Martin's thoughts as well. He had no thoughts save for the nerve-racking, body-destroying toil. Outside of that it was impossible to think. He did not know that he loved Ruth. She did not even exist, for his driven soul had no time to remember her. It was only when he crawled to bed at night, or to breakfast in the morning, that she asserted herself to him in fleeting memories.

"This is hell, ain't it?" Joe remarked once.

Martin nodded, but felt a rasp of irritation. The statement had been obvious and unnecessary. They did not talk while they worked. Conversation threw them out of their stride, as it did this time, compelling Martin to miss a stroke of his iron and to make two extra motions before he caught his stride again.

On Friday morning the washer ran. Twice a week they had to put through hotel linen,—the sheets, pillow-slips, spreads, table-cloths, and napkins. This finished, they buckled down to "fancy starch." It was slow work, fastidious and delicate, and Martin did not learn it so readily. Besides, he could not take chances. Mistakes were disastrous.

"See that," Joe said, holding up a filmy corset-cover that he could have crumpled from view in one hand. "Scorch that an' it's twenty dollars out of your wages."

So Martin did not scorch that, and eased down on his muscular tension, though nervous tension rose higher than ever, and he listened sympathetically to the other's blasphemies as he toiled and suffered over the beautiful things that women wear when they do not have to do their own laundering. "Fancy starch" was Martin's nightmare, and it was Joe's, too. It was "fancy starch" that robbed them of their hard-won minutes. They toiled at it all day. At seven in the evening they broke off to run the hotel linen through the mangle. At ten o'clock, while the hotel guests slept, the two laundrymen sweated on at "fancy starch" till midnight, till one, till two. At half-past two they knocked off.

Saturday morning it was "fancy starch," and odds and ends, and at three in the afternoon the week's work was done.

"You ain't a-goin' to ride them seventy miles into Oakland on top of this?" Joe demanded, as they sat on the stairs and took a triumphant smoke.

"Got to," was the answer.

"What are you goin' for?—a girl?"

"No; to save two and a half on the railroad ticket. I want to renew some books at the library."

"Why don't you send 'em down an' up by express? That'll cost only a quarter each way."

Martin considered it.

"An' take a rest to-morrow," the other urged. "You need it. I know I do. I'm plumb tuckered out."

He looked it. Indomitable, never resting, fighting for seconds and minutes all week, circumventing delays and crushing down obstacles, a fount of resistless energy, a high-driven human motor, a demon for work, now that he had accomplished the week's task he was in a state of collapse. He was worn and haggard, and his handsome face drooped in lean exhaustion. He puffed his cigarette spiritlessly, and his voice was peculiarly dead and monotonous. All the snap and fire had gone out of him. His triumph seemed a sorry one.

"An' next week we got to do it all over again," he said sadly. "An' what's the good of it all, hey? Sometimes I wish I was a hobo. They don't work, an' they get their livin'. Gee! I wish I had a glass of beer; but I can't get up the gumption to go down to the village an' get it. You'll stay over, an' send your books down by express, or else you're a damn fool."

"But what can I do here all day Sunday?" Martin asked.

"Rest. You don't know how tired you are. Why, I'm that tired Sunday I can't even read the papers. I was sick once—typhoid. In the hospital two months an' a half. Didn't do a tap of work all that time. It was beautiful.

"It was beautiful," he repeated dreamily, a minute later.

Martin took a bath, after which he found that the head laundry-man had disappeared. Most likely he had gone for the glass of beer, Martin decided, but the half-mile walk down to the village to find out seemed a long journey to him. He lay on his bed with his shoes off, trying to make up his mind. He did not reach out for a book. He was too tired to feel sleepy, and he lay, scarcely thinking, in a semi-stupor of weariness, until it was time for supper. Joe did not appear for that function, and when Martin heard the gardener remark that most likely he was ripping the slats off the bar, Martin understood. He went to bed immediately afterward, and in the morning decided that he was greatly rested. Joe being still absent, Martin procured a Sunday paper and lay down in a shady nook under the trees. The morning passed, he knew not how. He did not sleep, nobody disturbed him, and he did not finish the paper. He came back to it in the afternoon, after dinner, and fell asleep over it.

So passed Sunday, and Monday morning he was hard at work, sorting clothes, while Joe, a towel bound tightly around his head, with groans and blasphemies, was running the washer and mixing soft-soap.

"I simply can't help it," he explained. "I got to drink when Saturday night comes around."

Another week passed, a great battle that continued under the electric lights each night and that culminated on Saturday afternoon

at three o'clock, when Joe tasted his moment of wilted triumph and
then drifted down to the village to forget. Martin's Sunday was the
same as before. He slept in the shade of the trees, toiled aimlessly
through the newspaper, and spent long hours lying on his back, doing
nothing, thinking nothing. He was too dazed to think, though he
was aware that he did not like himself. He was self-propelled, as
though he had undergone some degradation or was intrinsically foul.
All that was god-like in him was blotted out. The spur of ambition
was blunted; he had no vitality with which to feel the prod of it. He
was dead. His soul seemed dead. He was a beast, a work-beast. He
saw no beauty in the sunshine sifting down through the green leaves,
nor did the azure vault of the sky whisper as of old and hint of cosmic
vastness and secrets trembling to disclosure. Life was intolerably
dull and stupid, and its taste was bad in his mouth. A black screen
was drawn across his mirror of inner vision, and fancy lay in a darkened sick-room where entered no ray of light. He envied Joe, down in
the village, rampant, tearing the slats off the bar, his brain gnawing
with maggots, exulting in maudlin ways over maudlin things, fan-
tastically and gloriously drunk and forgetful of Monday morning and
the week of deadening toil to come.

A third week went by, and Martin loathed himself, and loathed
life. He was oppressed by a sense of failure. There was reason for the
editors refusing his stuff. He could see that clearly now, and laugh at
himself and the dreams he had dreamed. Ruth returned his "Sea
Lyrics" by mail. He read her letter apathetically. She did her best to
say how much she liked them and that they were beautiful. But she
could not lie, and she could not disguise the truth from herself. She
knew they were failures, and he read her disapproval in every per-
functory and unenthusiastic line of her letter. And she was right. He
was firmly convinced of it as he read the poems over. Beauty and
wonder had departed from him, and as he read the poems he caught
himself puzzling as to what he had had in mind when he wrote them.
His audacities of phrase struck him as grotesque, his felicities of expression were monstrosities, and everything was absurd, unreal, and
impossible. He would have burned the "Sea Lyrics" on the spot, had
his will been strong enough to set them aflame. There was the engine-
room, but the exertion of carrying them to the furnace was not worth
while. All his exertion was used in washing other persons' clothes. He
did not have any left for private affairs.

He resolved that when Sunday came he would pull himself together and answer Ruth's letter. But Saturday afternoon, after work was finished and he had taken a bath, the desire to forget overpowered him. "I guess I'll go down and see how Joe's getting on," was the way he put it to himself; and in the same moment he knew that he lied. But he did not have the energy to consider the lie. If he had had the energy, he would have refused to consider the lie, because he wanted to forget. He started for the village slowly and casually, increasing his pace in spite of himself as he neared the saloon.

"I thought you was on the water-wagon," was Joe's greeting.

Martin did not deign to offer excuses, but called for whiskey, filling his own glass brimming before he passed the bottle.

"Don't take all night about it," he said roughly.

The other was dawdling with the bottle, and Martin refused to wait for him, tossing the glass off in a gulp and refilling it.

"Now, I can wait for you," he said grimly; "but hurry up."

Joe hurried, and they drank together.

"The work did it, eh?" Joe queried.

Martin refused to discuss the matter.

"It's fair hell, I know," the other went on, "but I kind of hate to see you come off the wagon, Mart. Well, here's how!"

Martin drank on silently, biting out his orders and invitations and awing the barkeeper, an effeminate country youngster with watery blue eyes and hair parted in the middle.

"It's something scandalous the way they work us poor devils," Joe was remarking. "If I didn't bowl up, I'd break loose an' burn down the shebang. My bowlin' up is all that saves me, I can tell you that."

But Martin made no answer. A few more drinks, and in his brain he felt the maggots of intoxication beginning to crawl. Ah, it was living, the first breath of life he had breathed in three weeks. His dreams came back to him. Fancy came out of the darkened room and lured him on, a thing of flaming brightness. His mirror of vision was silver-clear, a flashing, dazzling palimpsest of imagery. Wonder and beauty walked with him, hand in hand, and all power was his. He tried to tell it to Joe, but Joe had visions of his own, infallible schemes whereby he would escape the slavery of laundry-work and become himself the owner of a great steam laundry.

"I tell yeh, Mart, they won't be no kids workin' in my laundry— not on yer life. An' they won't be no workin' a livin' soul after six P.M. You hear me talk! They'll be machinery enough an' hands enough to do it all in decent workin' hours, an' Mart, s'help me, I'll make yeh superintendent of the shebang—the whole of it, all of it. Now here's the scheme. I get on the water-wagon an' save my money for two years—save an' then—"

But Martin turned away, leaving him to tell it to the barkeeper, until that worthy was called away to furnish drinks to two farmers who, coming in, accepted Martin's invitation. Martin dispensed royal largess, inviting everybody up, farm-hands, a stableman, and the gardener's assistant from the hotel, the barkeeper, and the furtive hobo who slid in like a shadow and like a shadow hovered at the end of the bar.

Monday morning, Joe groaned over the first truck load of clothes to the washer.

"I say," he began.

"Don't talk to me," Martin snarled.

"I'm sorry, Joe," he said at noon, when they knocked off for dinner.

Tears came into the other's eyes.

"That's all right, old man," he said. "We're in hell, an' we can't help ourselves. An', you know, I kind of like you a whole lot. That's what made it hurt. I cottoned to you from the first."

Martin shook his hand.

"Let's quit," Joe suggested. "Let's chuck it, an' go hoboin'. I ain't never tried it, but it must be dead easy. An' nothin' to do. Just think of it, nothin' to do. I was sick once, typhoid, in the hospital, an' it was beautiful. I wish I'd get sick again."

The week dragged on. The hotel was full, and extra "fancy starch" poured in upon them. They performed prodigies of valor. They fought late each night under the electric lights, bolted their meals, and even got in a half hour's work before breakfast. Martin no longer took his cold baths. Every moment was drive, drive, drive, and Joe was the masterful shepherd of moments, herding them carefully, never losing one, counting them over like a miser, counting gold, working on in a frenzy, toil-mad, a feverish machine, aided ably by that other machine that thought of itself as once having been one Martin Eden, a man.

But it was only at rare moments that Martin was able to think. The house of thought was closed, its windows boarded up, and he was its shadowy caretaker. He was a shadow. Joe was right. They were both shadows, and this was the unending limbo of toil. Or was it a dream? Sometimes, in the steaming, sizzling heat, as he swung the heavy irons back and forth over the white garments, it came to him that it was a dream. In a short while, or maybe after a thousand years or so, he would awake, in his little room with the ink-stained table, and take up his writing where he had left off the day before. Or maybe that was a dream, too, and the awakening would be the changing of the watches, when he would drop down out of his bunk in the lurching forecastle and go up on deck, under the tropic stars, and take the wheel and feel the cool tradewind blowing through his flesh.

Came Saturday and its hollow victory at three o'clock.

"Guess I'll go down an' get a glass of beer," Joe said, in the queer, monotonous tones that marked his week-end collapse.

Martin seemed suddenly to wake up. He opened the kit bag and oiled his wheel, putting graphite on the chain and adjusting the bearings. Joe was halfway down to the saloon when Martin passed by, bending low over the handle-bars, his legs driving the ninety-six gear with rhythmic strength, his face set for seventy miles of road and grade and dust. He slept in Oakland that night, and on Sunday covered the seventy miles back. And on Monday morning, weary, he began the new week's work, but he had kept sober.

A fifth week passed, and a sixth, during which he lived and toiled as a machine, with just a spark of something more in him, just a glimmering bit of soul, that compelled him, at each week-end, to scorch off the hundred and forty miles. But this was not rest. It was super-machine-like, and it helped to crush out the glimmering bit of soul that was all that was left him from former life. At the end of the seventh week, without intending it, too weak to resist, he drifted down to the village with Joe and drowned life and found life until Monday morning.

Again, at the week-ends, he ground out the one hundred forty miles, obliterating the numbness of too great exertion by the numbness of still greater exertion. At the end of three months he went down a third time to the village with Joe. He forgot, and lived again, and, living, he saw, in clear illumination, the beast he was making of himself—not by the drink, but by the work. The drink was an effect, not a cause. It followed inevitably upon the work, as the night follows upon the day. Not by becoming a toil-beast could he win to the heights, was the message the whiskey whispered to him, and he nodded approbation. The whiskey was wise. It told secrets on itself.

He called for paper and pencil, and for drinks all around, and while they drank his very good health, he clung to the bar and scribbled.

"A telegram, Joe," he said. "Read it."

Joe read it with a drunken, quizzical leer. But what he read seemed to sober him. He looked at the other reproachfully, tears oozing into his eyes and down his cheeks.

"You ain't goin' back on me, Mart?" he queried hopelessly.

Martin nodded, and called one of the loungers to him to take the message to the telegraph office.

"Hold on," Joe muttered thickly. "Lemme think."

He held on to the bar, his legs wobbling under him, Martin's arm around him and supporting him, while he thought.

"Make that two laundrymen," he said abruptly. "Here, lemme fix it."

"What are you quitting for?" Martin demanded.

"Same reason as you."

"But I'm going to sea. You can't do that."

"Nope," was the answer, "but I can hobo all right, all right."

Martin looked at him searchingly for a moment, then cried:—

"By God, I think you're right! Better a hobo than a beast of toil. Why, man, you'll live. And that's more than you ever did before."

"I was in hospital once," Joe corrected. "It was beautiful. Typhoid—did I tell you?"

While Martin changed the telegram to "two laundrymen," Joe went on:—

"I never wanted to drink when I was in hospital. Funny, ain't it? But when I've ben workin' like a slave all week, I just got to bowl up. Ever noticed that cooks drink like hell?—an' bakers, too? It's the work. They've sure got to. Here, lemme pay half of that telegram."

"I'll shake you for it," Martin offered.

"Come on, everybody drink," Joe called, as they rattled the dice and rolled them out on the damp bar.

Monday morning Joe was wild with anticipation. He did not mind his aching head, nor did he take interest in his work. Whole herds of moments stole away and were lost while their careless shepherd gazed out of the window at the sunshine and the trees.

"Just look at it!" he cried. "An' it's all mine! It's free. I can lie down under them trees an' sleep for a thousan' years if I want to. Aw, come on, Mart, let's chuck it. What's the good of waitin' another moment. That's the land of nothin' to do out there, an' I got a ticket for it—an' it ain't no return ticket, b'gosh!"

A few minutes later, filling the truck with soiled clothes for the washer, Joe spied the hotel manager's shirt. He knew its mark, and with a sudden glorious consciousness of freedom he threw it on the floor and stamped on it.

"I wish you was in it, you pig-headed Dutchman!" he shouted. "In it, an' right there where I've got you! Take that! an' that! an' that! damn you! Hold me back, somebody! Hold me back!"

Martin laughed and held him to his work. On Tuesday night the new laundrymen arrived, and the rest of the week was spent breaking them into the routine. Joe sat around and explained his system, but he did no more work.

"Not a tap," he announced. "Not a tap. They can fire me if they want to, but if they do, I'll quit. No more work in mine, thank you kindly. Me for the freight cars an' the shade under the trees. Go to it, you slaves! That's right. Slave and sweat! Slave and sweat! An' when you're dead, you'll rot the same as me, an' what's it matter how you live?—eh? Tell me that—what's it matter in the long run?"

On Saturday they drew their pay and came to the parting of the ways.

"They ain't no use in me askin' you to change your mind an' hit the road with me?" Joe asked hopelessly.

Martin shook his head. He was standing by his wheel, ready to start. They shook hands, and Joe held on to his for a moment, as he said:—

"I'm going to see you again, Mart, before you an' me die. That's straight dope. I feel it in my bones. Good-by, Mart, an' be good. I like you like hell, you know."

He stood, a forlorn figure, in the middle of the road, watching until Martin turned a bend and was gone from sight.

"He's a good Indian, that boy," he muttered. "A good Indian."

Then he plodded down the road himself, to the water tank, where half a dozen empties lay on a side-track waiting for the up freight.

Autobiographical Writings

In the Powerhouse

A SELECTION FROM John Barleycorn

EDITOR'S NOTE: *The chief emphasis in* John Barleycorn, *published in August, 1913, is on the role which drink played in the life of Jack London, his introduction to it and the reasons for his succumbing to its lure. The following selection, however, tells of his experiences in the power plant of the Oakland Street Railway. The description of the back-breaking toil is filled with a grim humor, but no one will miss the burning anger against merciless exploitation.*

The jute mills failed in their agreement to increase my pay to a dollar and a quarter a day; and I, a freeborn American boy, whose direct ancestors had fought in all the wars, from the old pre-Revolutionary Indian wars down, exercised my right of free contract by quitting the job.

I was still resolved to settle down, and I looked about me. One thing was clear: unskilled labor did not pay. I must learn a trade, and I decided on electricity. The need for electricians was constantly growing. But how to become an electrician? I had not the money to go to a technical school or a university; besides, I did not think much of schools. I was a practical man in a practical world. Also I still believed in the old myths that were the heritage of the American boy when I was a boy.

A canal boy could become a president. Any boy who took employment with any firm could, by thrift, energy and sobriety, learn the business and rise from position to position until he was taken in as a junior partner. After that the senior partnership was only a matter of time. Very often—so ran the myth—the boy, by reason of his steadiness and application, married his employer's daughter. By this time I had been encouraged to such faith in myself in the matter of girls that I was quite certain I could marry my employer's daughter. There was not a doubt of it. All the little boys in the myths did it as soon as they were old enough.

So I bade farewell forever to the adventure path and went out to the power plant of one of our Oakland street railroads. I saw the superintendent himself—in a private office so fine it almost stunned me. But I talked straight up. I told him I wanted to become a practical electrician; that I was unafraid of work; that I was used to hard work; and that all he had to do was look at me to see I was fit and strong. I told him I wanted to begin right at the bottom and work up; that I wanted to devote my life to this one occupation and this one employment.

The superintendent beamed as he listened. He told me that I was the right stuff for success, and that he believed in encouraging American youth who wanted to rise. Why, employers were always on the lookout for young fellows like me. And, alas! they found them all too rarely. My ambition was fine and worthy, and he would see to it that I got my chance. And as I listened with swelling heart I wondered if it was his daughter I was to marry.

"Before you can go out on the road and learn the more complicated and higher details of the profession," he said, "you will, of course, have to work in the carhouse with the men who install and repair the motors." By this time I was sure that it was his daughter, and I was wondering how much stock he might own in the company. "But," he said, "as you yourself so plainly see, you could not expect to begin as a helper to the carhouse electricians. That will come when you have worked up to it. You will really begin at the bottom. In the carhouse your first employment will be sweeping up, washing the windows, keeping things clean. And, after you have shown yourself satisfactory at that, then you may become a helper to the electricians."

I did not see how sweeping and scrubbing a building was any preparation for the trade of electrician; but I did know that in the books all the boys started with the most menial tasks and by making good ultimately won to the ownership of the whole concern.

"When shall I come to work?" I asked, eager to launch on this dazzling career.

"As you and I have already agreed, you must begin at the bottom," said the superintendent. "Not immediately can you in any capacity enter the carhouse. Before that you must pass through the engine room as an oiler."

My heart went down slightly for the moment as I saw the road lengthen between his daughter and myself; then it rose again. I should be a better electrician with knowledge of steam engines. As an oiler in the great engine room I was confident that few things concerning steam would escape me. Heavens! My career shone more dazzling than ever.

"When shall I come to work?" I asked gratefully.

"You should not expect to enter immediately into the engine room," said the superintendent. "There must be preparation for that—and through the fireroom of course. Come—you see the matter clearly, I know. And you will see that even the mere handling of coal is a scientific matter and not to be sneezed at. Do you know that we weigh every pound of coal we burn? Thus we learn the value of the coal we buy; we know to the last penny the cost of every item of production; and we learn which firemen are the most wasteful, and which firemen, out of stupidity or carelessness, get the least out of the coal they fire." The superintendent beamed again. "You see how very important the little matter of coal is; and by as much as you learn of this little matter you will become that much better workman—more valuable to us; more valuable to yourself. Now are you prepared to begin?"

"Any time," I said valiantly. "The sooner the better."

"Very well," he answered. "You will come tomorrow morning at seven o'clock."

I was taken out and shown my duties. Also I was told the terms of my employment—a ten-hour day every day in the month, including Sundays and holidays, with one day off each month and a salary of thirty dollars a month. It was not exciting. Years before, at the cannery, I had earned a dollar a day for a ten-hour day. I consoled myself with the thought that the reason my earning capacity had not increased with my years and strength was because I had remained an unskilled laborer. But it was different now. I was beginning to work for skill, for a trade, for a career and a fortune—and the superintendent's daughter.

And I was beginning in the right way—right at the beginning. That was the thing. I was passing coal to the firemen, who shoveled it into the furnaces, where its energy was transformed into steam, which in the engine room was transformed into the electricity with which the electricians worked. This passing coal was surely the very beginning—unless the superintendent should take it into his head to send me to work in the mines from which the coal came in order to get a completer understanding of the genesis of electricity for street railroads.

Work! I, who had worked with men, found that I did not know the first thing about real work. A ten-hour day! I had to pass coal for the day and the night shifts; and, despite working through the noon hour, I never finished my task before eight at night. I was working a twelve or thirteen hour day, and I was not being paid overtime as in the cannery.

I might as well give the secret away right here. I was doing the work of two men. Before me, one mature, able-bodied laborer had done the day shift and another equally mature able-bodied laborer had done the night shift. They had received forty dollars a month each. The superintendent, bent on an economical administration, had persuaded me to do the work of both men for thirty dollars a month. I thought he was making an electrician of me. In truth and fact he was saving fifty dollars a month in operating expenses for the company.

However, I did not know I was displacing two men. Nobody told me. On the contrary the superintendent warned everybody not to tell me. How valiantly I went at it that first day! I worked at top speed, filling the iron wheelbarrow with coal, running it on the scales and weighing the load, then trundling it into the fireroom and dumping it on the plates before the fires.

Work! I did more than the two men I had displaced. They had merely wheeled in the coal and dumped it on the plates. But though I did this for the day coal, the night coal I had to pile against the wall of the fireroom. Now the fireroom was small. It had been planned for a night coalpasser. So I had to pile the night coal higher and higher, buttressing up the heap with stout plates. Toward the top of the heap I had to handle the coal a second time, tossing it up with a shovel.

I dripped with sweat, but I never ceased from my stride, though I could feel exhaustion coming on. By ten o'clock in the morning so much of my body's energy had I consumed I felt hungry and snatched a thick double slice of bread and butter from my dinner pail. This I devoured standing, grimed with coal dust, my knees trembling under me. By eleven o'clock, in this fashion, I had consumed my whole lunch. But what of it? I realized that it would enable me to continue working through the noon hour, and I worked all the afternoon. Darkness came on and I worked under the electric lights. The day fireman went off and the night fireman came on. I plugged away.

At half past eight, famished, tottering, I washed up, changed my clothes and dragged my weary body to the car. It was three miles to where I lived, and I had received a pass, with the stipulation that I could sit down so long as there were no paying passengers in need of a seat. As I sank into a corner outside seat I prayed that no passenger might require my seat. But the car filled up, and halfway in a woman came on board and there was no seat for her. I started to get up, and to my astonishment I found that I could not. With the chill wind blowing on me my spent body had stiffened into the seat. It took me the rest of the run in to unkink my complaining joints and muscles and get into a standing position on the lower step. And when the car stopped at my corner I nearly fell to the ground when I stepped off.

I hobbled two blocks to the house and limped into the kitchen. While my mother started to cook I plunged into bread and butter; but before my appetite was appeased or the steak fried I was sound asleep. In vain my mother strove to shake me awake enough to eat the meat. Failing in this, with the assistance of my father she managed to get me to my room, where I collapsed dead asleep on the bed. They undressed me and covered me up. In the morning came the agony of being awakened. I was terribly sore and, worst of all, my wrists were swelling. But I made up for my lost supper by eating an enormous breakfast, and when I hobbled to catch my car I carried a lunch twice as big as the one the day before.

Work! Let any youth just turned eighteen try to outshovel two man-grown coal-shovelers! Work! Long before midday I had eaten the last scrap of my huge lunch. But I was resolved to show them what a husky young fellow determined to rise could do. The worst of it was that my wrists were swelling and going back on me. There are few who do not know the pain of walking on a sprained ankle. Then imagine the pain of shoveling coal with two sprained wrists!

Work! More than once I sank down on the coal where no one could see me and cried with rage, mortification, exhaustion and despair. That second day was my hardest; and all that enabled me to survive it and get in the last of the night coal at the end of thirteen hours was the day fireman who bound both my wrists with broad leather straps. So tightly were they buckled that they were like slightly flexible plaster-casts. They took the stresses and pressures which thitherto had been borne by my wrists; and they were so tight that there was no room for the inflammation to rise in the sprains.

In this fashion I continued to learn to be an electrician. Night after night I limped home, fell asleep before I could eat my supper, and was undressed and helped into bed. Morning after morning, always with huger lunches in my dinner pail, I limped out of the house on my way to work.

I no longer read my library books. I made no dates with the girls. I was a proper workbeast. I worked and ate and slept, while my mind slept all the time. The whole thing was a nightmare. I worked every day, including Sunday; and I looked far ahead to my one day off at the end of the month, resolved to lie abed all that day and just sleep and rest up.

The strangest part of this experience was that I never took a drink or thought of taking a drink. Yet I knew that men under hard pressure almost invariably drank. I had seen them do it and in the past had often done it myself. But so sheerly non-alcoholic was I that it never entered my mind that a drink might be good for me. I instance this to show how entirely lacking from my make-up was any predisposition toward alcohol. And the point of this instance is that later on, after more years had passed, contact with John Barleycorn at last did induce in me the alcoholic desire.

I had often noticed the day fireman staring at me in a curious way. At last one day he spoke. He began by swearing me to secrecy. He had been warned by the superintendent not to tell me and in telling me he was risking his job. He told me of the day coalpasser and the night coalpasser, and of the wages they had received. I was doing for thirty dollars a month what they had received eighty dollars for doing. He would have told me sooner, the fireman said, had he not been so certain that I would break down under the work and quit. As it was I was killing myself, and all to no good purpose. I was merely cheapening the price of labor, he argued, and keeping two men out of a job.

Being an American boy—and a proud American boy—I did not immediately quit. This was foolish of me, I know; but I resolved to continue the work long enough to prove to the superintendent that I could do it without breaking down. Then I would quit and he would realize what a fine young fellow he had lost. All of which I faithfully and foolishly did. I worked on until the time came when I got in the last of the night coal by six o'clock. Then I quit the job of learning electricity by doing more than two men's work for a boy's wages, went home, and proceeded to sleep the clock round.

Fortunately I had not stayed by the job long enough to injure myself—though I was compelled to wear straps on my wrists for a year afterward; but the effect of this work orgy in which I had indulged was to sicken me with work. I just would not work. The thought of work was repulsive. I did not care if I never settled down. Learning a trade could go hang. It was a whole lot better to roister and frolic over the world in the way I had previously done. So I headed out on the adventure path again, starting to tramp East by beating my way on the railroads.

Tramp Days

SELECTIONS FROM My Life in the Underworld

EDITOR'S NOTE: *The series of articles which recounted Jack London's experiences as a hobo were first published in the summer and fall of 1907 in the* Cosmopolitan Magazine. *Today, forty years later, they still retain the remarkable qualities which caused the* Los Angeles Times *to describe them as a "veritable novel of adventure . . . as thrilling and breath-bating as a fragment from Dumas." And as the editor of* Cosmopolitan *pointed out: "They reveal Jack London's initiation into the real mysteries and tragedies of existence. In these youthful experiences was developed that remarkable sympathy for those who are brought into strenuous contact with the harsher problems of life, which has made him one of the most popular and sincere fiction writers of the day."*

A REMINISCENCE AND A CONFESSION

There is a woman in the state of Nevada to whom I once lied continuously, consistently, and shamelessly, for the matter of a couple of hours. I don't want to apologize to her. Far be it from me. But I do want to explain. Unfortunately, I do not know her name, much less her present address. If her eyes should chance upon these lines, I hope she will write to me.

It was in Reno, Nevada, in the summer of 1892. Also, it was fair-time, and the town was filled with petty crooks and tin-horns, to say nothing of a vast horde of hungry hoboes. It was the hungry hoboes that made the town a "hungry" town. They "battered" the back doors of the homes of the citizens until the back doors became unresponsive.

A hard town for "scoffings," was what the hoboes called it at that time. I know that I missed many a meal, in spite of the fact that I could "throw my feet" with the next one when it came to "slamming a gate" for a "poke-out" or a "set-down," or hitting for a "light piece" on the street. Why, I was so hard put in that town, one day, that I gave the porter the slip and invaded the private car of some itinerant millionaire. The train started as I made the platform, and I headed for the aforesaid millionaire with the porter one jump behind and reaching for me. It was a dead heat, for I reached the millionaire at the same instant that the porter reached me. I had no time for formalities. "Gimme a quarter to eat on," I blurted out. And as I live, that millionaire dipped into his pocket and gave me—just precisely a quarter. It is my conviction that he was so flabbergasted that he obeyed automatically, and it has been a matter of keen regret ever since, on my part, that I didn't ask him for a dollar. I know that I'd have got it. I swung off the platform of that private car with the porter maneuvering to kick me in the face. He missed me. But I got the quarter! I got it!

But to return to the woman to whom I so shamelessly lied. It was in the evening of my last day in Reno. I had been out to the racetrack watching the ponies run, and had missed my dinner (*i. e.*, the mid-day meal). I was hungry, and, furthermore, a committee of public safety had just been organized to rid the town of just such hungry mortals as I. Already a lot of my brother hoboes had been gathered in by John Law, and I could hear the sunny valleys of California calling to me over the cold crests of the Sierras. Two acts remained for me to perform before I shook the dust of Reno from my feet. One was to catch the blind baggage on the westbound overland that night. The other was first to get something to eat. Even youth will hesitate at an all-night ride, on an empty stomach, outside a train that is tearing the atmosphere through the snowsheds, tunnels, and eternal snows of heaven-aspiring mountains.

But that something to eat was a hard proposition. I was "turned down" at a dozen houses. Sometimes I received insulting remarks and was informed of the barred domicile that would be mine if I had my just deserts. The worst of it was that such assertions were only too true. That was why I was pulling west that night.

At other houses the doors were slammed in my face, cutting short

my politely and humbly couched request for something to eat. At one
house they did not open the door. I stood on the porch and knocked,
and they looked out at me through the window. They even held one
sturdy little boy aloft so that he could see over the shoulders of his
elders the tramp who wasn't going to get anything to eat at their
house.

It began to look as if I should be compelled to go to the very poor
for my food. The very poor constitute the last sure recourse of the
hungry tramp. The very poor can always be depended upon. They
never turn away the hungry. Time and again, all over the United
States, have I been refused food at the big house on the hill; and always have I received food from the little shack down by the creek or
marsh, with its broken windows stuffed with rags and its tired-faced
mother broken with labor. Oh! you charity-mongers, go to the poor
and learn, for the poor alone are the charitable. They neither give
nor withhold from their excess. They have no excess. They give, and
they withhold never, from what they need for themselves, and very
often from what they cruelly need for themselves. A bone to the dog
is not charity. Charity is the bone shared with the dog when you are
just as hungry as the dog.

There was one house in particular where I was turned down that
evening. The porch windows opened on the dining-room, and through
them I saw a man eating pie—a big meat pie. I stood in the open door,
and while he talked with me he went on eating. He was prosperous,
and out of his prosperity had been bred resentment against his less
fortunate brothers. He cut short my request for something to eat,
snapping out,

"I don't believe you want to work."

Now this was irrelevant. I hadn't said anything about work. The
topic of conversation I had introduced was "food." In fact, I didn't
want to work. I wanted to take the westbound overland that night.

"You wouldn't work if you had a chance," he bullied.

I glanced at his meek-faced wife, and knew that but for the presence of this Cerberus I'd have a whack at that meat pie myself. But
Cerberus sopped himself in the pie, and I saw that I must placate him
if I were to get a share of it. So I sighed to myself and accepted his
work morality.

"Of course I want work," I bluffed.

"Don't believe it," he snorted.

"Try me," I answered, warming to the bluff.

"All right," he said. "Come to the corner of blank and blank streets" —I have forgotten the address—"to-morrow morning—you know where that burned building is—and I'll put you to work tossing bricks."

"All right, sir, I'll be there."

He grunted and went on eating. I waited. After a couple of minutes he looked up with an I-thought-you-were-gone expression on his face, and demanded,

"Well?"

"I—I am waiting for something to eat," I said gently.

"I knew you wouldn't work!" he roared.

He was right, of course; but his conclusion must have been reached by mind-reading, for his logic wouldn't bear it out. But the beggar at the door must be humble, so I accepted his logic as I had accepted his morality.

"You see, I am now hungry," I said, still gently. "To-morrow morning I shall be hungrier. Think how hungry I shall be when I have tossed bricks all day without anything to eat. Now, if you will give me something to eat, I'll be in great shape for those bricks."

He gravely considered my plea, at the same time going on eating, while his wife nearly trembled into propitiatory speech, but refrained.

"I'll tell you what I'll do," he said, between mouthfuls. "You come to work to-morrow, and in the middle of the day I'll advance you enough for your dinner. That will show whether you are in earnest or not."

"In the meantime—" I began; but he interrupted.

"If I gave you something to eat now, I'd never see you again. Oh, I know your kind. Look at me. I owe no man. I have never descended so low as to ask anyone for food. I have always earned my food. The trouble with you is that you are idle and dissolute. I can see it in your face. I have worked and been honest. I have made myself what I am. And you can do the same, if you work and are honest."

"Like you?" I queried.

Alas! no ray of humor had ever penetrated the somber, work-sodden soul of that man. "Yes, like me," he answered.

"All of us?" I queried.

"Yes, all of you," he answered.

"But if we all became like you," I said, "allow me to point out that there'd be nobody to toss bricks for you."

I swear there was a flicker of a smile in his wife's eye. As for him, he was aghast.

"I'll not waste words on you," he roared. "Get out of here, you ungrateful whelp!"

I scraped my feet to advertise my intention of going, and queried, "And I don't get anything to eat?"

He arose suddenly to his feet. He was a large man. I was a stranger in a strange land, and John Law was looking for me. I went away hurriedly. "But why ungrateful?" I asked myself as I slammed his gate. "What in the dickens did he give me to be ungrateful about?" I looked back. He had returned to his pie.

By this time I had lost heart. I passed many houses by without venturing up to them. After walking half a dozen blocks I shook off my despondency and gathered my "nerve." This begging for food was all a game, and if I didn't like the cards I could always call for a new deal. I made up my mind to tackle the next house. I approached it in the deepening twilight, going around to the kitchen-door.

I knocked softly, and when I saw the kind face of the middle-aged woman who answered, as by inspiration came to me the "story" I was to tell. For know that upon his ability to tell a good story depends the success of the beggar. First of all, and on the instant, the beggar must "size up" his victim. After that he must tell a story that will appeal to the peculiar personality and temperament of that particular victim. And right here arises the great difficulty: in the instant that he is sizing up the victim he must begin his story. Not a minute is allowed for preparation. As in a lightning flash he must divine the nature of the victim and conceive a tale that will hit home. The successful hobo must be an artist. He must create spontaneously and instantaneously —and not upon a theme selected from the plenitude of his own imagination, but upon the theme he reads in the face of the person who opens the door, be it man, woman, or child, sweet or crabbed, generous or miserly, good-natured or cantankerous, Jew or Gentile, black or white, race-prejudiced or brotherly, provincial or universal, or whatever else it may be. I have often thought that to this training of my tramp days is due much of my success as a story-writer. In order to get the food whereby I lived, I was compelled to tell tales that rang true. At the back door, out of inexorable necessity, is developed the convincingness and sincerity laid down by all authorities on the art of the short story. Also, I quite believe it was my tramp apprentice-

ship that made a realist out of me. Realism constitutes the only goods
one can exchange at the kitchen-door for grub.

After all, art is only consummate artfulness, and artfulness saves
many a "story." I remember lying in a police station at Winnipeg,
Manitoba. I was bound west over the Canadian Pacific. Of course
the police wanted my story, and I gave it to them—on the spur of the
moment. They were landlubbers, in the heart of the continent, and
what better story for them than a sea-story? They could never trip
me up on that. And so I told a tearful tale of my life on the hell-ship
Glenmore. (I had once seen the *Glenmore* lying at anchor in San
Francisco Bay.) I was an English apprentice, I said. And they said
that I didn't talk like an English boy. It was up to me to create on
the instant. I had been born and reared in the United States. On the
death of my parents, I had been sent to England to my grandparents.
It was they who had apprenticed me on the *Glenmore*. I hope the captain of the *Glenmore* will forgive me, for I gave him a character that
night in the Winnipeg police station. Such cruelty! Such brutality!
Such diabolical ingenuity of torture! It explained why I had deserted
the *Glenmore* at Montreal.

But why was I in the middle of Canada going west, when my grandparents lived in England? Promptly I created a married sister who
lived in California. She would take care of me. I developed at length
her loving nature. But they were not done with me, those hard-
hearted policemen. I had joined the *Glenmore* in England; in the
two years that had elapsed before my desertion at Montreal, what
had the *Glenmore* done and where had she been? And thereat I took
those landlubbers around the world with me. Buffeted by pounding
seas and stung with flying spray, they fought a typhoon with me off
the coast of Japan. They loaded and unloaded cargo with me in all
the ports of the Seven Seas. I took them to India and Rangoon and
China, had them hammer ice with me around the Horn, and at last
come to moorings at Montreal.

And then they said to wait a moment, and one policeman went forth
into the night while I warmed myself at the stove, all the while racking my brains for the trap they were going to spring on me.

I groaned to myself when I saw him come in the door at the heels
of the policeman. No gypsy prank had thrust those tiny hoops of
gold through the ears; no prairie winds had beaten that skin into
wrinkled leather; nor had snow-drift and mountain-slope put in his

walk that reminiscent roll. And in those eyes, when they looked at me, I saw the unmistakable sun-wash of the sea. Here was a theme, alas! with half a dozen policemen to watch me read, and I had never sailed the China seas, nor been around the Horn, nor seen India and Rangoon.

I was desperate. Disaster stalked before me incarnate in the form of that gold-ear-ringed, weather-beaten son of the sea. Who was he? What was he? I must solve him ere he solved me. If he questioned me first, before I knew how much he knew, I was lost.

But did I betray my desperate plight to those lynx-eyed guardians of the public welfare of Winnipeg? Not I. I met that aged sailorman glad-eyed and beaming, with all the simulated relief at deliverance that a drowning man would display on finding a life-preserver in his last despairing clutch. Here was a man who understood and who would verify my true story to the faces of those sleuth-hounds. I seized upon him. I volleyed at him questions about himself. Before my judges, I would prove the character of my savior before he saved me.

He was a kindly sailorman—an "easy mark." The policemen grew impatient while I questioned him. At last one of them told me to shut up. I shut up, but while I remained shut up I was busy creating, busy sketching the scenario of the next act. I had learned enough to go on with. He was a Frenchman. He had sailed always on French merchant vessels, with the one exception of a voyage on a "lime-juicer." And last of all—blessed fact!—he had not been on the sea for twenty years.

The policemen urged him to examine me.

"You called in at Rangoon?" he queried.

I nodded. "We put our third mate ashore there. Fever."

If he had asked me what kind of fever, I should have answered, "Enteric," though for the life of me I didn't know what enteric was. But his next question was,

"And how is Rangoon?"

"All right. It rained a whole lot when we were there."

"Did you get shore-leave?"

"Sure," I answered.

"Do you remember the temple?"

"Which temple?" I parried.

"The big one, at the top of the stairway."

If I remembered that temple, I knew I'd have to describe it. I shook my head.

"You can see it from all over the harbor," he informed me. "You don't need shore-leave to see that temple."

I never loathed a temple so in my life. But I fixed that particular temple at Rangoon. "You can't see it from the harbor," I contradicted, "you can't see it from the town, you can't see it from the top of the stairway, because"—I paused for the effect—"because there isn't any temple there."

"But I saw it with my own eyes!" he cried.

"That was in—?" I queried.

"Seventy-one."

"It was destroyed in the great earthquake of 1887," I explained. "It was very old."

There was a pause. He was busy reconstructing in his old eyes his youthful vision of that fair temple by the sea.

"The stairway is still there," I aided him. "You can see it from all over the harbor. And you remember that little island on the right-hand side coming into the harbor?" I guess there must have been one there (I was prepared to shift it over to the left-hand side), for he nodded. "Gone," I said. "Seven fathoms of water there now."

I had gained a moment for breath. While he pondered on time's changes, I prepared the finishing touches of my story.

"You remember the custom house at Bombay?" He remembered it.

"Burned to the ground," I announced.

"Do you remember Jim Wan?" he came back at me.

"Dead," I said, but who the devil Jim Wan was I hadn't the slightest idea. I was on thin ice again. "Do you remember Billy Harper, at Shanghai?" I queried.

That aged sailorman worked hard to recollect, but the Billy Harper of my imagination was beyond his faded memory.

"Of course you remember Billy Harper," I insisted. "Everybody knows him. He's been there forty years. Well, he's still there, that's all."

And then the miracle happened. The sailorman remembered Billy Harper. Perhaps there was a Billy Harper, and perhaps he had been in Shanghai for forty years and was still there; but it was news to me.

For fully half an hour longer the sailorman and I talked on in similar fashion. In the end he told the policeman that I was what I represented myself to be, and after a night's lodging and a breakfast I was released to wander on westward to my married sister in San Francisco.

But to return to the woman in Reno who opened her door to me in the deepening twilight. At the first glimpse of her kindly face I took my cue. I became a sweet, innocent, unfortunate lad. I couldn't speak. I opened my mouth and closed it again. Never in my life before had I asked anyone for food. My embarrassment was painful, extreme. I was ashamed. I, who looked upon begging as a delightful whimsicality, thumbed myself over into a true son of Mrs. Grundy, burdened with all her bourgeois morality. Only the harsh pangs of the belly-need could compel me to do so degraded and ignoble a thing as beg for food. And into my face I strove to throw all the wan wistfulness of famished and ingenuous youth unused to mendicancy.

"You are hungry, my poor boy," she said. I had made her speak first.

I nodded my head and gulped. "It is the first time I have ever—asked," I faltered.

"Come right in." The door swung open. "We have already finished eating, but the fire is burning, and I can get something up for you." She looked at me closely when she got me into the light. "I wish my boy were as healthy and strong as you," she said. "But he is not strong. He sometimes falls down. He fell down just this afternoon and hurt himself badly, the poor dear."

She mothered him with her voice, with an ineffable tenderness in it that I yearned to appropriate. I glanced at him. He sat across the table, slender and pale, his head swathed in bandages. He did not move, but his eyes, bright in the lamplight, were fixed upon me in a wondering stare.

"Just like my poor father," I said. "He had the falling sickness. Some kind of vertigo. It puzzled the doctors."

"He is dead?" she queried gently, setting before me half a dozen soft-boiled eggs.

"Dead," I gulped. "Two weeks ago. I was with him when it happened. We were crossing the street together. He fell right down. He was never conscious again. They carried him into a drug store. He died there."

And thereat I developed the pitiful tale of my father—how, after my mother's death, he and I had gone to San Francisco from the ranch; how his pension (he was an old soldier), and the little other money he had, was not enough; and how he had tried book-canvassing. Also, I narrated my own woes during the few days after his death that I had spent alone and forlorn on the streets of San Francisco. While that good woman warmed up biscuits, fried bacon, and cooked more eggs, and while I kept pace with her in taking care of all that she placed before me, I enlarged the picture of that poor orphan boy and filled in the details. I became that poor boy. I believed in him as I believed in the beautiful eggs I was devouring. I could have wept for myself. I know the tears did get into my voice at times.

It was very effective. In fact, with every touch I added to the picture that kind soul gave me something else. She made up a lunch for me to carry away. She put in many boiled eggs, pepper and salt, and other things, and a big apple. She provided me with three pairs of thick red woolen socks. She gave me clean handkerchiefs and other things which I have since forgotten. And all the time she cooked more and more, and I ate more and more. I gorged like a savage; but then it was a far cry across the Sierras on a blind baggage, and I knew not when nor where I should find my next meal. And all the while, like a death's-head at the feast, silent and motionless, her own unfortunate boy sat and stared at me across the table. I suppose I represented to him mystery and romance and adventure—all that was denied the feeble flicker of life that was in him. And yet I could not forbear, once or twice, from wondering if he saw through me down to the bottom of my mendacious heart.

"But where are you going?" she asked.

"Salt Lake City," said I. "I have a sister there, a married sister. Her husband is a plumber, a contracting plumber."

Now, I knew that contracting plumbers were usually credited with making lots of money. But I had spoken. It was up to me to qualify.

"They would have sent me the money for my fare if I had asked for it," I explained, "but they have had sickness and business troubles. His partner cheated him. And so I wouldn't write for the money. I knew I could make my way there somehow. I let them think I had enough to get me to Salt Lake City. She is lovely, and so kind. She was always kind to me. I guess I'll go into the shop and learn the trade. She has two daughters. They are younger than I. One is only a baby."

Of all my married sisters that I have distributed among the cities of the United States, that Salt Lake sister is my favorite. She is quite real, too. When I tell about her I can see her and her two little girls and her plumber husband. She is a large, motherly woman, just verging on beneficent stoutness—the kind, you know, that always cooks nice things and that never gets angry. She is a brunette. Her husband is a quiet, easy-going fellow. Sometimes I almost know him quite well. And who knows but some day I may meet him?

On the other hand, I have a feeling of certitude within me that I shall never meet in the flesh my many parents and grandparents—you see, I invariably killed them off. Heart disease was my favorite way of getting rid of my mother, though on occasions I did away with her by means of consumption, pneumonia, and typhoid fever.

I hope that woman in Reno will read these lines and forgive me my gracelessness and unveracity. I do not apologize, for I am unashamed. It was youth, delight in life, zest for experience, that brought me to her door. It did me good. It taught me the intrinsic kindliness of human nature. I hope it did her good. Anyway, she may get a good laugh out of it, now that she learns the real inwardness of the situation.

To her my story was "true." She believed in me and all my family, and she was filled with solicitude for the dangerous journey I must make ere I won to Salt Lake City. This solicitude nearly brought me to grief. Just as I was leaving, my arms full of lunch and my pockets bulging with fat woolen socks, she bethought herself of a nephew, or uncle, or relative of some sort, who was in the railway mail service, and who, moreover, would come through that night on the very train on which I was going to steal my ride. The very thing! She would take me down to the station, tell him my story, and get him to hide me in the mail-car. Thus, without danger or hardship, I would be carried straight through to Ogden. Salt Lake City was only a few miles farther on. My heart sank. She grew excited as she developed the plan, and with my heart sinking I had to feign unbounded gladness and enthusiasm at this solution of my difficulties.

Solution! Why, I was bound west that night, and here I was being trapped into going east. It *was* a trap, and I hadn't the heart to tell her that it was all a miserable lie. And while I made believe that I was delighted, I was busy racking my brains for some way to escape. But there was no way. She would see me into the mail-car—she said so herself—and then that mail-clerk relative of hers would carry me to Ogden. And then I would have to beat my way back all over those hundreds of miles of desert.

But luck was with me that night. Just about the time she was get-

ting ready to put on her bonnet and accompany me, she discovered
that she had made a mistake. Her mail-clerk relative was not scheduled to come through that night. His run had been changed; he would
not come through until two nights afterward. I was saved, for of
course my boundless youth would never permit me to wait those two
days. I optimistically assured her that I'd get to Salt Lake City
quicker if I started immediately, and I departed with her blessings
and best wishes ringing in my ears.

But those woolen socks were great. I know. I wore a pair of them
that night on the blind baggage of the overland, and that overland
went west.

"HOLDING HER DOWN"

Barring accidents, a good hobo, with youth and agility, can hold a
train down despite all the efforts of the train-crew to "ditch" him—
given, of course, night-time as an essential condition. When such a
hobo, under such conditions, makes up his mind that he is going to
hold her down, either he does hold her down or chance trips him up.
There is no legitimate way, short of murder, whereby the train-crew
can ditch him. That train-crews have not stopped short of murder
is a current belief in the tramp world. Not having had that particular experience in my tramp days, I cannot vouch for it personally.

But this I have heard of the bad roads. When a tramp has "gone
underneath," on the rods, and the train is in motion, there is apparently no way of dislodging him until the train stops. The tramp,
snugly ensconced inside the truck, with the four wheels and all the
framework around him, has the "cinch" on the crew—or so he thinks,
until some day he rides the rods on a bad road. A "bad" road is usually
one on which a short time previously one or several trainmen have
been killed by tramps. Heaven pity the tramp who is caught "underneath" on such a road—for caught he is, though the train be going
sixty miles an hour.

The "shack" (brakeman) takes a steel coupling-pin and a length
of bell-cord to the platform in front of the truck in which the tramp is
riding. He fastens the coupling-pin to the bell-cord, drops it down
between the platforms, and pays out the cord. The coupling-pin
strikes the ties between the rails, rebounds against the bottom of the
car, and again strikes the ties. The shack plays it back and forth, now
to one side, now to the other, lets it out a bit and hauls it in a bit,

giving his weapon opportunity for every variety of impact and re-bound. Every blow of that flying coupling-pin is freighted with death, and at sixty miles an hour it beats a veritable tattoo of death. The next day the remains of that tramp are gathered up along the right of way, and a line in the local paper mentions the unknown man, un-doubtedly a tramp, assumably drunk, who had probably fallen asleep on the track.

As a characteristic illustration of how a capable hobo can hold her down, I am minded to give the following experience:

I was in Ottawa, bound west over the Canadian Pacific. Three thousand miles of that road stretched before me, it was the fall of the year, and I had to cross Manitoba and the Rocky Mountains. I could expect "crimpy" weather, and every moment of delay increased the frigid hardships of the journey. Furthermore, I was disgusted. The distance between Montreal and Ottawa is one hundred and twenty miles. I ought to know, for I had just come over it, and it had taken me six days. By mistake I had missed the main line and come over a small "jerk" with only two locals a day on it. And during those six days I had lived on dry crusts, and not enough of them, begged from the French peasants.

Furthermore, my disgust had been heightened by the one day I had spent in Ottawa trying to get an outfit of clothing for my long jour-ney. Let me put it on record right here that Ottawa, with one excep-tion, is the hardest town in the United States and Canada to beg clothes in; the one exception is Washington, D.C. The latter fair city is the limit. I spent two weeks there trying to beg a pair of shoes, and then had to go to Jersey City before I got them.

But to return to Ottawa. At eight sharp in the morning I started out after clothes. I worked energetically all day. I swear I walked forty miles. I interviewed the housewives of a thousand homes. I did not even knock off work for dinner. And at six in the afternoon, after ten hours of unremitting and depressing toil, I was still shy one shirt, while the pair of trousers I had managed to acquire was tight and was showing all the signs of an early disintegration.

At six I quit work and headed for the railroad-yards, expecting to pick up something to eat on the way. But my hard luck was still with me. I was refused food at house after house. Then I got a "hand-out." My spirits soared, for it was the largest hand-out I had ever seen in a long and varied experience. It was a parcel wrapped in newspapers and as big as a mature suit-case. I hurried to a vacant lot and opened it. First I saw cake, then more cake, all kinds and makes of cake, and then some. It was all cake. No bread and butter with thick firm slices of meat between—nothing but cake; and of all things I abhorred cake most! In another age and clime they sat down by the waters of Babylon and wept. And in a vacant lot in Canada's proud capital, I, too, sat down and wept—over a mountain of cake. As one looks upon the face of his dead son, so looked I upon that multitudinous pastry. I suppose I was an ungrateful tramp, for I refused to partake of the bounteousness of the house that had had a party the night before. Evidently the guests hadn't liked cake, either.

That cake marked the crisis in my fortunes. Than it nothing could be worse; therefore things must begin to mend. And they did. At the very next house I was given a "set-down." Now a "set-down" is the height of bliss. One is taken inside, very often is given a chance to wash, and is then "set down" at a table. Tramps love to throw their legs under a table. The house was large and comfortable, in the midst of spacious grounds and fine trees, and sat well back from the street. They had just finished eating, and I was taken right into the dining-room—in itself a most unusual happening, for the tramp who is lucky enough to win a set-down usually receives it in the kitchen. A grizzle-haired and gracious Englishman, his matronly wife, and a beautiful young Frenchwoman talked with me while I ate.

I wonder if that beautiful young Frenchwoman would remember, at this late day, the laugh I gave her when I uttered the barbaric phrase, "two bits." You see, I was trying delicately to hit them for a "light-piece." That was how the sum of money came to be mentioned. "What?" she said. "Two bits," said I. Her mouth was twitching as she again said, "What?" "Two bits," said I. Whereat she burst into laughter. "Won't you repeat it?" she said when she had regained control of herself. "Two bits," said I. And once more she rippled into uncontrollable silvery laughter. "I beg your pardon," said she; "but what—what was it you said?" "Two bits," said I. "Is there anything wrong about it?" "Not that I know of," she gurgled between gasps; "but what does it mean?" I explained; but I do not remember now whether or not I got that two bits out of her; but I have often wondered as to which of us was the provincial.

When I arrived at the station I found, much to my disgust, a bunch of at least twenty tramps that were waiting to ride out the blind baggages of the overland. Now, two or three tramps on the blind baggage are all right. They are inconspicuous. But a score! That meant trouble. No train-crew would ever let all of us ride.

I may as well explain here what a "blind baggage" is. Some mail-cars are built without doors in the ends; hence such a car is "blind." The mail-cars that possess end doors have those doors always locked. Suppose, after the train has started, that a tramp gets onto the platform of one of these blind cars. There is no door, or the door is locked. No conductor or brakeman can get to him to collect fare or throw him off. It is clear that the tramp is safe until the next time the train stops. Then he must get off, run ahead in the darkness, and when the train pulls by jump onto the blind again. But there are ways and ways, as you shall see.

When the train pulled out, those twenty tramps swarmed upon the three blinds. Some climbed on before the train had run a car's length. They were awkward dubs, and I saw their speedy finish. Of course the train-crew was "on," and at the first stop the trouble began. I jumped off and ran forward along the track. I noticed that I was accompanied by a number of the tramps. They evidently knew their business. When one is beating an overland, he must always keep well ahead of the train at the stops. I ran ahead, and as I ran, one by one those that accompanied me dropped out. This dropping out was the measure of their skill and nerve in boarding a train.

For this is the way it works. When the train starts, the shack rides out the blind. There is no way for him to get back into the train proper except by jumping off the blind and catching a platform where the car-ends are not "blind." When the train is going as fast as the shack cares to risk, he jumps off the blind, lets several cars go by and gets onto the train. So it is up to the tramp to run so far ahead that before the blind is opposite him the shack will have already vacated it.

I dropped the last tramp about fifty feet, and waited. The train started. I saw the lantern of the shacks on the first blind; he was riding her out. And I saw the dubs stand forlornly by the track as the blind went by. They made no attempt to get on. They were beaten by their own inefficiency at the very start. After them, in the line-up, came the tramps that knew a little something about the game. They let the first blind, occupied by the shack, go by, and jumped on the second and third blinds. Of course the shack jumped off the first and onto the second as it went by, and scrambled around there, throwing off the men who had boarded it. But the point is that I was so far ahead that when the first blind came opposite me, the shack had already left it and was tangled up with the tramps on the second blind. A half-dozen of the more skillful tramps, who had run far enough ahead, made for the first blind, too.

At the next stop, as we ran forward along the track, I counted but fifteen of us. Five had been ditched. The weeding-out process had begun nobly, and it continued station by station. Now we were fourteen, now twelve, now eleven, now nine, now eight. It reminded me of the ten little niggers of the nursery rhyme. I was resolved that I should be the last little nigger of all. And why not? Was I not blessed with strength, agility, and youth? (I was eighteen, and in perfect condition.) And didn't I have my "nerve" with me? And furthermore, was I not a tramp royal? Were not these other tramps mere dubs and "gay-cats" and amateurs alongside of me? If I weren't the last little nigger, I might as well quit the game and get a job on an alfalfa-farm somewhere.

By the time our number had been reduced to four the whole train-crew had become interested. From then on it was a contest of skill and wits, with the odds in favor of the crew. One by one the three other survivors turned up missing, until I alone remained. My, but I was proud of myself! No Crœsus was ever prouder of his first million. I was holding her down in spite of two brakemen, a conductor, a fireman, and an engineer.

And here are a few samples of the way I held her down. Out ahead, in the darkness—so far ahead that the shack riding out the blind must perforce get off before it reaches me—I get on. Very well; I am good for another station. When that station is reached, I again dart ahead to repeat the maneuver. The train pulls out. I watch her coming. There is no light of a lantern on the blind. Has the crew abandoned the fight? I do not know. One never knows, and one must be prepared every moment for anything. As the first blind comes opposite me, and I run to leap aboard, I strain my eyes to see if the shack is on the platform. For all I know he may be there, with his lantern doused, and even as I spring upon the steps that lantern may smash down upon my head. I ought to know. I have been hit by lanterns two or three times.

But no, the first blind is empty. The train is gathering speed. I am safe for another station. But am I? I feel the train slacken speed. On the instant I am alert. A maneuver is being executed against me, and I do not know what it is. I try to watch on both sides at once, not forgetting to keep track of the tender in front of me. From any one, or all, of these three directions, I may be assailed.

Ah! there it comes. The shack has ridden out the engine. My first warning is when his feet strike the steps of the right-hand side of the blind. Like a flash I am off the blind to the left and running ahead past the engine. I lose myself in the darkness. The situation is where it has been ever since the train left Ottawa. I am ahead, and the train must come past me if it is to proceed on its journey. I have as good a chance as ever for boarding her.

I watch carefully. I see a lantern come forward to the engine and I do not see it go back. It must therefore be still on the engine, and it is a fair assumption that attached to the handle of that lantern is a shack. That shack is lazy, or he would have put out his lantern instead of trying to shield it as he came forward. The train pulls out. The first blind is empty, and I gain it. As before, the train slackens, the shack from the engine boards the blind from one side, and I go off the other side and run forward.

As I wait in the darkness I am conscious of a big thrill of pride. The overland has stopped twice for me—for me, a poor hobo on the bum. I alone have twice stopped the overland with its many passengers and coaches, its government mail, and its two thousand steam horses straining at the engine. And I weigh only one hundred and sixty pounds, and I haven't a five-cent piece in my pocket!

Again I see the lantern come forward to the engine. But this time it comes conspicuously—a bit too conspicuously to suit me, and I wonder what is up. At any rate, I have something more to be afraid of than the shack on the engine. The train pulls by. Just in time, before I make my spring, I see the dark form of a shack, without a lantern, on the first blind. I let it go by, and prepare to board the second blind. But the shack on the first blind has jumped off and is at my heels. Also, I have a fleeting glimpse of the lantern of the shack who rode out the engine. He has jumped off, and now both shacks are on the ground on the same side with me. The next moment the second blind comes by and I am aboard it. But I do not linger. I have figured out my countermove. As I dash across the platform, I hear the impact of the shack's feet against the steps as he boards. I jump off the other side and run forward with the train. My plan is to run forward and get on the first blind. It is nip and tuck, for the train is gathering speed. Also, the shack is behind me and running after me. I guess I am the better sprinter, for I make the first blind. I stand on the steps and watch my pursuer. He is only about ten feet back and running hard; but now the train has approximated his own speed, and, relative to me, he is standing still. I encourage him, hold out my hand to him; but he explodes in a mighty oath, gives up, and makes the train several cars back.

The train is speeding along, and I am still chuckling to myself, when, without warning, a spray of water strikes me. The fireman is playing the hose on me from the engine. I step forward from the car-platform to the rear of the tender, where I am sheltered under the overhang. The water flies harmlessly over my head. My fingers itch to climb up on the tender and lam that fireman with a chunk of coal; but I know if I do that I'll be massacred by him and the engineer, and I refrain.

At the next stop I am off and ahead in the darkness. This time, when the train pulls out, both shacks are on the first blind. I divine their game. They have blocked the repetition of my previous play. I cannot again take the second blind, cross over, and run forward to the first. As soon as the first blind passes and I do not get on, they swing off, one on each side of the train. I board the second blind, and as I do so I know that a moment later, simultaneously, those two shacks will arrive on both sides of me. It is like a trap. Both ways are blocked. Yet there is another way out, and that way is up.

So I do not wait for my pursuers to arrive. I climb upon the upright ironwork of the platform and stand upon the wheel of the hand-brake. This has taken up the moment of grace, and I hear the shacks strike the steps on either side. I don't stop to look. I raise my arms overhead until my hands rest upon the downcurving ends of the roofs of the two cars. One hand, of course, is on the curved roof of one car, the other hand on the curved roof of the other car. By this time both shacks are coming up the steps. I know it, though I am too busy to see them. All this is happening in the space only of several seconds. I make a spring with my legs, and "muscle" myself up with my arms. As I draw up my legs, both shacks reach for me and clutch empty air. I know this, for I look down and see them. Also, I hear them swear.

I am now in a precarious position, riding the ends of the down-curving roofs of two cars at the same time. With a quick, tense movement I transfer both legs to the curve of one roof and both hands to the curve of the other roof. Then, gripping the edge of that curving roof, I climb over the curve to the level roof above, where I sit down to catch my breath, holding on the while to a ventilator that projects above the surface. I am on top of the train—on the "decks," as the tramps call it, and this process I have described is by them called "decking her." And let me say right here that only a young and vigorous tramp is able to "deck" a passenger-train, and also, that the young and vigorous tramp must have his nerve with him as well.

The train goes on gathering speed, and I know I am safe until the next stop—but only until the next stop. If I remain on the roof after the train stops, I know those shacks will fusillade me with rocks. A healthy shack can "dew-drop" a pretty heavy chunk of stone on top of a car—say anywhere from five to twenty pounds. On the other hand, the chances are large that at the next stop the shacks will be waiting for me to descend at the place I climbed up. It is up to me to climb down at some other platform.

Registering a fervent hope that there are no tunnels in the next half-mile, I rise to my feet and walk down the train half a dozen cars. And let me say that one must leave timidity behind him on such a pasear. The roofs of passenger-coaches are not made for midnight promenades. And if anyone thinks they are, let me advise him to try it. Just let him walk along the roof of a jolting, lurching car, with nothing to hold on to but the black and empty air, and when he comes to the downcurving end of the roof, all wet and slippery with dew, let him accelerate his speed so as to step across to the next roof, downcurving and wet and slippery. Believe me, he will learn whether his heart is weak or his head is giddy.

As the train slows down for a stop, half a dozen platforms from where I decked her I come down. No one is on the platform. When the train comes to a standstill, I slip off to the ground. Ahead, and between me and the engine, are two moving lanterns. The shacks are looking for me on the roofs of the cars. I note that the car beside which I am standing is a "four-wheeler"—by which is meant that it has only four wheels to each truck. (When you go underneath on the rods, be sure to avoid the "six-wheelers"; they lead to disaster.) I duck under the train and make for the rods, and I can tell you I am mighty glad that the train is standing still. It is the first time I have ever gone underneath on the Canadian Pacific, and the internal arrangements are new to me. I try to crawl over the top of the truck, between the truck and the bottom of the car, but the space is not large enough for me to squeeze through. This is new to me. Down in the United States I am accustomed to going underneath on rapidly moving trains, seizing a gunnel and swinging my feet under to the brake-beam and from there crawling over the top of the truck and down inside the truck to a seat on the cross-rod.

Feeling with my hands in the darkness, I learn that there is room between the brake-beam and the ground. It is a tight squeeze. I have to lie flat and worm my way through. Once inside the truck, I take my seat on the rod and wonder what the shacks are wondering has become of me. The train gets under way again. They have given me up at last.

But have they? At the very next stop I see a lantern thrust under the next truck to mine at the other end of the car. They are searching the rods for me. I must make my get-away pretty lively. I crawl on my stomach under the brake-beam. They see me and run for me, but I crawl on hands and knees across the rail on the opposite side and gain my feet. Then away I go for the head of the train. I run past the engine and hide in the sheltering darkness. It is the same old situation. I am ahead of the train, and the train must go past me.

The train pulls out. There is a lantern on the first blind. I lie low, and see the peering shack go by. But there is also a lantern on the second blind. That shack spots me and calls to the shack who has gone past on the first blind. Both jump off. Never mind, I'll take the third blind and deck her. But heavens! there is a lantern on the third blind, too. It is the conductor. I let it go by. At any rate I have now the full train-crew in front of me. I turn and run back toward the rear of the train. I look over my shoulder. All three lanterns are on the ground and wobbling along in pursuit. I sprint. Half the train has gone by, and it is going quite fast, when I spring aboard. I know that the two shacks and the conductor will arrive like ravening wolves in about two seconds. I spring upon the wheel of the hand-brake, get my hands on the curved ends of the roofs, and muscle myself up to the decks; while my disappointed pursuers, clustering on the platform beneath like dogs that have treed a cat, howl curses up at me and say uncivil things about my ancestors.

But what does that matter? It is five to one, including the engineer and fireman, and the majesty of the law and the might of a great corporation are behind them, and I am beating them out. I am too far down the train, and I run ahead over the roofs of the coaches until I am over the fifth or sixth platform from the engine. I peer down cautiously. A shack is on that platform. That he has caught sight of me I know from the way he makes a swift sneak inside the car; and I know, also, that he is waiting inside the door, ready to pounce out on

me when I climb down. But I make believe that I don't know, and I
remain there to encourage him in his error. I do not see him, yet I
know that he opens the door once and peeps up to assure himself
that I am still there.

The train slows down for a station. I dangle my legs down in a tentative way. The train stops. My legs are still dangling. I hear the door
unlatch softly. He is all ready for me. Suddenly I spring up and run
forward over the roof. This is right over his head where he lurks inside the door. The train is standing still, the night is quiet, and I take
care to make plenty of noise on the metal roof with my feet. I don't
know, but my assumption is that he is now running forward to catch
me as I descend at the next platform. But I don't descend there.
Halfway along the roof of the coach, I turn, retrace my way softly and
quickly to the platform both the shack and I have just abandoned.
The coast is clear. I descend to the ground on the off-side of the train
and hide in the darkness. Not a soul has seen me.

I go over to the fence, at the edge of the right of way, and watch.
Aha! What's that? I see a lantern on top of the train, moving along
from front to rear. They think I haven't come down, and they are
searching the roofs for me. And better than that, on the ground on
the sides of the train, moving abreast with the lantern on top, are two
other lanterns. It is a rabbit drive, and I am the rabbit. When the
shack on top flushes me, the one on the side will nab me. I roll a cigarette and watch the procession go by. Once past me, I am safe to
proceed to the front of the train. She pulls out, and I make the front
blind without opposition. But before she is fully under way, and just
as I am lighting my cigarette, I am aware that the fireman has
climbed over the coal to the back of the tender and is looking down
at me. I am filled with apprehension. From his position he can mash
me to a jelly with lumps of coal. Instead of which, he addresses me,
and I note with relief the admiration in his voice.

"You son of a gun," is what he says.

It is a high compliment, and I thrill as a schoolboy thrills on receiving a reward of merit. "Say," I call up to him; "don't you play the
hose on me any more."

"All right," he answers, and goes back to his work.

I have made friends with the engine, but the shacks are still looking
for me. At the next stop, the shacks ride out all three blinds, and, as
before, I let them go by and deck in the middle of the train. The crew
is on its mettle by now, and the train stops. The shacks are going to

ditch me or know the reason why. Three times the mighty overland stops for me at that station, and each time I elude the shacks and make the decks. But it is hopeless, for they have finally come to an understanding of the situation. I have taught them that they cannot guard the train from me. They must do something else.

And they do it. When the train stops the last time, they take after me hot-footed. Ah! now I see their game. They are trying to run me down. At first they herd me back toward the rear of the train. I know my peril. Once to the rear of the train, it will pull out with me left behind. I double, and twist, and turn, dodge through my angry pursuers, and gain the front of the train.

One shack still hangs on after me. All right, I'll give him the run of his life, for my wind is good. I run straight ahead along the track. It doesn't matter; if he chases me ten miles, he'll nevertheless have to catch the train, and I can board her at any speed that he can.

So I run on, keeping just comfortably ahead of him and straining my eyes in the gloom for cattle-guards and switches that may bring me to grief. Alas! I strain my eyes too far ahead, and trip over something just under my feet, I know not what, some little thing, and go down to earth in a long, stumbling fall. The next moment I am on my feet, but the shack has me by the collar. I do not struggle. I am busy with breathing deeply and with sizing him up. He is narrow-shouldered, and I have at least thirty pounds the better of him in weight. Besides, he is just as tired as I am, and if he tries to slug me I'll teach him a few things.

But he doesn't try to slug me, and that problem is settled. Instead, he starts to lead me back toward the train, and another possible problem arises. I see the lanterns of the conductor and the other shack. We are approaching them. Not for nothing have I made the acquaintance of the New York police. Not for nothing, in box-cars, by water-tanks, and in prison cells, have I listened to bloody tales of manhandling. What if these three men are about to manhandle me? Heaven knows I have given them provocation enough. I think quickly. We are drawing nearer and nearer to the other two trainmen. I line up the stomach and the jaw of my captor, and plan the right and left I'll give him at the first sign of trouble.

Pshaw! I know another trick I'd like to work on him, and I almost regret that I did not do it at the moment I was captured. I could make him sick, what of his clutch on my collar. His fingers, tight-gripping, are buried inside my collar. My coat is tightly buttoned. Did you ever see a tourniquet? Well, this is one. All I have to do is to duck my head under his arm and begin to twist. I must twist rapidly—very rapidly. I know how to do it, twisting in a violent, jerky way, ducking my head under his arm with each revolution. Before he knows it, those detaining fingers of his will be detained. He will be unable to withdraw them. It is a powerful leverage. Twenty seconds after I have started revolving, the blood will be bursting out of his finger-ends, the delicate tendons will be rupturing, and all the muscles and nerves will be mashing and crushing together in a shrieking mass. Try it some time when somebody has you by the collar. But be quick—quick as lightning. Also, be sure to hug yourself while you are revolving—hug your face with your left arm and your abdomen with your right. You see, the other fellow might try to stop you with a punch from his free arm. It would be a good idea, too, to revolve away from that free arm rather than toward it. A punch going is never so bad as a punch coming.

That shack will never know how near he was to being made very, very sick. All that saves him is that it is not in their plan to man-handle me. When we draw near enough, he calls out that he has me, and they signal the train to come on. The engine passes us, and the three blinds. After that, the conductor and the other shack swing aboard. But still my captor holds on to me. I see the plan. He is going to hold me until the train goes by. Then he will hop on, and I shall be left behind—ditched.

But the train has pulled out fast, the engineer trying to make up for lost time. Also, it is a long train. It is going very lively, and I know the shack is measuring its speed with apprehension.

"Think you can make it?" I query innocently.

He releases my collar, makes a quick run, and swings aboard. A number of coaches are yet to pass by. He knows it, and remains on the steps, his head poked out and watching me. In that moment my next move comes to me. I'll take the last platform. I know she's going fast and faster, and I'll only get a roll in the dirt if I fail, and the optimism of youth is mine. I do not give myself away. I stand with a dejected droop of shoulder, advertising that I have abandoned hope. But at the same time I am feeling with my feet the good gravel. It is perfect footing. Also, I am watching the poked-out head of the shack. I see it withdrawn. He is confident that the train is going too fast for me ever to make it.

And the train *is* going fast—faster than any train I have ever tackled. As the last coach comes by, I sprint in the same direction with it. It is a swift, short sprint. I cannot hope to equal the speed of the train, but I can reduce the difference of our speeds to the minimum, and hence reduce the shock of impact, when I leap on board. In the fleeting instant of darkness I do not see the iron hand-rail of the last platform; nor is there time for me to locate it. I reach for where I think it ought to be, and at the same instant my feet leave the ground. It is all in the toss. The next moment I may be rolling in the gravel with broken ribs, or arms, or head. But my fingers grip the handhold, there is a jerk on my arms that slightly pivots my body, and my feet land on the steps with sharp violence.

I sit down, feeling very proud of myself. In all my hoboing it is the best bit of train-jumping I have done. I know that late at night one is always good for several stations on the last platform, but I do not care to trust myself at the rear of the train. At the first stop I run forward on the off-side of the train, pass the Pullmans, and duck under and take a rod under a day-coach. At the next stop I run forward again and take another rod. I am now comparatively safe. The shacks think I am ditched. But the long day and the strenuous night are beginning to tell on me. Also, it is not so windy nor cold underneath, and I begin to doze. This will never do. Sleep on the rods spells death, so I crawl out at a station and go forward to the second blind. Here I can lie down and sleep; and here I do sleep—how long I do not know, for I am awakened by a lantern thrust into my face. The two shacks are staring at me. I scramble up on the defensive, wondering as to which one is going to make the first "pass" at me. But slugging is far from their minds.

"I thought you was ditched," says the shack who had held me by the collar.

"If you hadn't let go of me when you did, you'd have been ditched along with me," I answer.

"How's that?" he asks.

"I'd have gone into a clinch with you, that's all," is my reply.

They hold a consultation, and their verdict is summed up in:

"Well, I guess you can ride, Bo. There's no use trying to keep you off." And they go away and leave me in peace to the end of their division.

I have given the foregoing as a sample of what "holding her down," means. Of course I have selected a fortunate night out of my experiences, and said nothing of the nights—and many of them—when I was tripped up by accident and ditched.

In conclusion, I want to tell of what happened when I reached the end of the division. On single-track, transcontinental lines, the freight-trains wait at the divisions and follow out after the passenger-trains. When the division was reached, I left my train and looked for the freight that would pull out behind it. I found the freight, made up and waiting on a side-track. I climbed into a box-car half full of coal, and lay down. In no time I was asleep.

I was awakened by the sliding open of the door. Day was just dawning, cold and gray, and the freight had not yet started. A "con" (conductor) was poking his head inside the door.

"Get out of that, you blankety-blank-blank!" he roared at me.

I got, and outside I watched him go down the line inspecting every car in the train. When he got out of sight I thought to myself that he would never think I'd have the nerve to climb back into the very car out of which he had fired me. So back I climbed and lay down again.

Now that con's mental processes must have been paralleling mine, for he reasoned that it was the very thing I would do. For back he came and fired me out.

Now, surely, I reasoned, he will never dream that I'd do it a third time. Back I went, into the very same car. But I decided to make sure. Only one side door could be opened; the other side door was nailed up. Beginning at the top of the coal, I dug a hole alongside that door and lay down in it. I heard the other door open. The con climbed up and looked in over the top of the coal. He couldn't see me. He called to me to get out. I tried to fool him by remaining quiet. But when he began tossing chunks of coal into the hole on top of me, I gave up and for the third time was fired out. Also, he informed me in warm terms of what would happen to me if he caught me in there again.

I changed my tactics. When a man is paralleling your mental processes, ditch him. Abruptly break off your line of reasoning, and go off on a new line. This I did. I hid between some cars on an adjacent side-track, and watched. Sure enough, that con came back again to the car. He opened the door, he climbed up, he called, he threw coal into the hole I had made. He even crawled over the coal and looked into the hole. That satisfied him. Five minutes later the freight was pulling out, and he was not in sight. I ran alongside the car, pulled the door open, and climbed in. He never looked for me again, and I rode that coal-car precisely one thousand and twenty-two miles, sleeping most of the time and getting out at divisions (where the freights always stop for an hour or so) to beg my food. And at the end of the thousand and twenty-two miles I lost that car through a happy incident. I got a set-down, and the tramp doesn't live who won't miss a train for a set-down any time.

"PINCHED"

I rode into Niagara Falls in a "side-door Pullman," or, in common parlance, a box-car. A flat car, by the way, is known among the fraternity as a "gondola," with the second syllable emphasized and pronounced long. But to return. I arrived in the afternoon and headed straight from the freight-train to the falls. Once my eyes were filled with that wonderful vision of downrushing water, I was lost. I could not tear myself away long enough to "batter" the "privates" (domiciles) for my supper. Even a set-down could not have lured me away. Night came on, a beautiful night of moonlight, and I lingered by the falls until after eleven. Then it was up to me to hunt for a place to "kip."

"Kip," "doss," "flop," "pound your ear," all mean the same thing, namely, to sleep. Somehow I had a "hunch" that Niagara Falls was a "bad" town for hoboes, and I headed out into the country. I climbed a fence and "flopped" in a field. John Law would never find me there, I flattered myself. I lay on my back in the grass and slept like a babe. It was so balmy warm that I woke up not once all night. But with the first gray daylight my eyes opened, and I remembered the wonderful falls. I climbed the fence and started down the road to have another look at them. It was early—not more than five o'clock—and not until eight o'clock could I begin to batter for my breakfast. I could spend at least three hours by the river. Alas! I was fated never to see the river nor the falls again.

The town was asleep when I entered it. As I came along the quiet street, I saw three men coming toward me along the sidewalk. They were walking abreast. Hoboes, I decided, who, like myself, had got up early. In this surmise I was not quite correct. I was only sixty-six and two-thirds per cent correct. The men on each side were hoboes all right, but the man in the middle wasn't. I directed my steps to the

edge of the sidewalk in order to let the trio go by. But it didn't go by.
At some word from the man in the center, all three halted, and he of
the center addressed me.

I piped the lay on the instant. He was a "fly-cop," and the two
hoboes were his prisoners. John Law was up and out after the early
worm. I was a worm. Had I been richer by the experiences that were
to befall me in the next several months, I should have turned and run
like the very devil. He might have shot at me, but he'd have had to
hit me to get me. He'd never have run after me, for two hoboes in the
hand are worth more than one on the getaway. But like a dummy I
stood still when he halted me. Our conversation was brief.

"What hotel are you stopping at?" he queried.

He had me. I wasn't stopping at any hotel, and, since I did not
know the name of a hotel in the place, I could not claim residence in
any of them. Also, I was up too early in the morning. Everything was
against me.

"I just arrived," I said.

"Well, you turn around and walk in front of me, and not too far in
front. There's somebody wants to see you."

I was "pinched." I knew who wanted to see me. With that "fly-
cop" and the two hoboes at my heels, and under the direction of the
former, I led the way to the city jail. There we were searched and our
names registered. I have forgotten now under which name I was
registered. I gave the name of Jack Drake, but when they searched
me they found letters addressed to Jack London. This caused trouble
and required explanation, all of which has passed from my mind, and
to this day I do not know whether I was pinched as Jack Drake or
Jack London. But one or the other, it should be there to-day in the
prison register of Niagara Falls. Reference can bring it to light. The
time was somewhere in the latter part of June, 1894. It was only a
few days after my arrest that the great railroad strike began.

From the office we were led to the "Hobo" and locked in. The
"Hobo" is that part of a prison where the minor offenders are confined together in a large iron cage. Since hoboes constitute the principal division of the minor offenders, the aforesaid iron cage is called
the "Hobo." Here we met several hoboes who had been pinched
already that morning, and every little while the door was unlocked
and two or three more were thrust in with us. At last, when we totaled
sixteen, we were led upstairs into the court-room. And I shall faithfully describe what took place in that court-room, for know that my

patriotic American citizenship there received a shock from which it has never fully recovered.

In the court-room were the sixteen prisoners, the judge, and two bailiffs. The judge seemed to act as his own clerk. There were no witnesses. There were no citizens of Niagara Falls present to look on and see how justice was administered in their community. The judge glanced at the list of cases before him and called out a name. A hobo stood up. The judge glanced at a bailiff. "Vagrancy, your honor," said the bailiff. "Thirty days," said his honor. The hobo sat down, and the judge was calling another name and another hobo was rising to his feet.

The trial of that hobo had taken just about fifteen seconds. The trial of the next hobo came off with equal celerity. The bailiff said, "Vagrancy, your honor," and his honor said, "Thirty days." Thus it went like clockwork, fifteen seconds to a hobo—and thirty days.

They are poor dumb cattle, I thought to myself. But wait till my turn comes; I'll give his honor a "spiel." Part way along in the performance his honor, moved by some whim, gave one of us an opportunity to speak. As chance would have it, this man was not a genuine hobo. He bore none of the earmarks of the professional "stiff." Had he approached the rest of us, while waiting at a water-tank for a freight, we should have unhesitatingly classified him as a gay-cat. "Gay-cat" is the synonym for tenderfoot in Hoboland. This gay-cat was well along in years—somewhere around forty-five, I should judge. His shoulders were humped a trifle, and his face was seamed and weather-beaten.

For many years, according to his story, he had driven team for some firm in (if I remember rightly) Lockport, New York. The firm had ceased to prosper, and finally, in the hard times of 1893, had gone out of business. He had been kept on to the last, though toward the last his work had been very irregular. He went on and explained at length his difficulties in getting work (when so many were out of work) during the succeeding months. In the end, deciding that he would find better opportunities for work on the lakes, he had started for Buffalo. Of course he was "broke," and there he was. That was all.

"Thirty days," said his honor, and called another hobo's name.

Said hobo got up. "Vagrancy, your honor," said the bailiff, and his honor said, "Thirty days."

And so it went, fifteen seconds and thirty days to each hobo. The machine of justice was grinding smoothly. Most likely, considering how early it was in the morning, his honor had not yet had his breakfast and was in a hurry.

But my American blood was up. Behind me were the many generations of my American ancestry. One of the kinds of liberty of those ancestors of mine had fought and died for was the right of trial by jury. This was my heritage, stained sacred by their blood, and it devolved upon me to stand up for it. All right, I threatened myself ; just wait till he gets to me.

He got to me. My name, whatever it was, was called, and I stood up. The bailiff said, "Vagrancy, your honor," and I began to talk. But the judge began talking at the same time, and he said, "Thirty days." I started to protest, but at that moment his honor was calling the name of the next hobo on the list. His honor paused long enough to say to me, "Shut up!" The bailiff forced me to sit down. And the next moment that next hobo had received thirty days, and the succeeding hobo was just in process of getting his.

When we had all been disposed of, thirty days to each stiff, his honor, just as he was about to dismiss us, suddenly turned to the teamster from Lockport, the one man he had allowed to talk.

"Why did you quit your job?" his honor asked.

Now the teamster had already explained how his job had quit him, and the question took him aback. "Your honor," he began confusedly, "isn't that a funny question to ask?"

"Thirty days more for quitting your job," said his honor, and the court was closed. That was the outcome. The teamster got sixty days altogether, while the rest of us got thirty days.

We were taken down below, locked up, and given breakfast. It was a pretty good breakfast, as prison breakfasts go, and it was the best I was to get for a month to come.

As for me, I was dazed. Here was I, under sentence, after a farce of a trial wherein I was denied not only my right of trial by jury, but my right to plead guilty or not guilty. Another thing my fathers had fought for flashed through my brain—habeas corpus. I'd show them. But when I asked for a lawyer, I was laughed at. Habeas corpus was all right, but of what good was it to me when I could communicate with no one outside the jail? But I'd show them. They couldn't keep me in jail forever. Just wait till I got out, that was all. I'd make them sit up. I knew something about the law and my own rights, and I'd expose their maladministration of justice. Visions of damage suits and sensational newspaper head-lines were dancing before my eyes, when the jailers came in and began hustling us out into the main office.

A policeman snapped a handcuff on my right wrist. (Aha! thought I, a new indignity. Just wait till I get out.) On the left wrist of a Negro he snapped the other handcuff of that pair. He was a very tall Negro, well past six feet—so tall was he that when we stood side by side his hand lifted mine up a trifle in the manacles. Also, he was the happiest and the raggedest Negro I have ever seen.

We were all handcuffed similarly, in pairs. This accomplished, a bright, nickel-steel chain was brought forth, run down through the links of all the handcuffs, and locked at front and rear of the double line. We were now a chain-gang. The command to march was given, and out we went upon the street, guarded by two officers. The tall Negro and I had the place of honor. We led the procession.

After the tomb-like gloom of the jail, the outside sunshine was dazzling. I had never known it to be so sweet as now when, a prisoner with clanking chains, I knew that I was soon to see the last of it for thirty days. Down through the streets of Niagara Falls we marched to the railroad station, stared at by curious passers-by and, especially, by a group of tourists on the veranda of a hotel that we marched past.

There was plenty of slack in the chain, and with much rattling and clanking we sat down, two and two, in the seats of the smoking-car. Afire with indignation as I was at the outrage that had been perpetrated on me and my forefathers, I was nevertheless too prosaically practical to lose my head over it. This was all new to me. Thirty days of mystery were before me, and I looked about me to find somebody who knew the ropes. For I had already learned that I was not bound for a petty jail with a hundred or so prisoners in it, but for a full-grown penitentiary with a couple of thousand prisoners in it doing anywhere from ten days to ten years.

In the seat behind me, attached to the chain by his wrist, was a squat, heavily built, powerfully muscled man. He was somewhere between thirty-five and forty years of age. I sized him up. In the corners of his eyes I saw humor and laughter and kindliness. As for the rest of him, he was a brute beast, wholly unmoral, and with all the passion and turgid violence of the brute beast. What saved him, what made him possible for me, were those corners of his eyes—the humor and laughter and kindliness of the beast when unaroused.

He was my "meat." I cottoned to him. While my cuff-mate, the tall Negro, mourned with chucklings and laughter over some laundry he was sure to lose through his arrest, and while the train rolled on

toward Buffalo, I talked with the man in the seat behind me. He had
an empty pipe. I filled it for him with my precious cigarette tobacco
—enough in a single filling to make a dozen cigarettes. Nay, the more
we talked the surer I was that he was my meat, and I divided all my
tobacco with him.

Now it happens that I am a fluid sort of organism, with sufficient
kinship with life to fit myself in 'most anywhere. I laid myself out to
fit in with that man, though little did I dream to what extraordinary
good purpose I was succeeding. He had never been in the particular
penitentiary to which we were going, but he had done "one," "two,"
and "five spots" in various other penitentiaries (a "spot" is a year),
and he was filled with wisdom. We became pretty chummy, and my
heart bounded when he cautioned me to follow his lead. He called
me "Jack," and I called him "Jack."

The train stopped at a station about five miles from Buffalo, and
we, the chain-gang, got off. I do not remember the name of the station,
but I am confident that it is someone of the following: Rocklyn,
Rockwood, Black Rock, Rockcastle, or Newcastle. But whatever the
name of the place, we were walked a short distance and then put on a
street-car. It was an old-fashioned car, with a seat, running the full
length, on each side. All the passengers who sat on one side were asked
to move over to the other side, and we, with a great clanking of chain,
took their places. We sat facing them, I remember, and I remember,
too, the awed expression on the faces of the women, who took us, un-
doubtedly, for convicted murderers and bank-robbers. I tried to look
my fiercest, but that cuff-mate of mine, the too happy Negro, insisted
on rolling his eyes, laughing and reiterating, "Oh, Lawdy! Lawdy!"

We left the car, walked some more, and were led into the office
of the Erie County penitentiary. Here we were to register, and on that
register one or the other of my names will be found. Also, we were informed that we must leave in the office all our valuables, money, tobacco, matches, pocket-knives, and so forth.

My new pal shook his head at me.

"If you do not leave your things here, they will be confiscated inside," warned the official.

Still my pal shook his head. He was busy with his hands, hiding his
movements behind the other fellows. (Our handcuffs had been removed.) I watched him and followed suit, wrapping up in a bundle in
my handkerchief all the things I wanted to take in. These bundles the
two of us thrust into our shirts. I noticed that our fellow-prisoners,

with the exception of one or two who had watches, did not turn over their belongings to the man in the office. They were determined to smuggle them in somehow, trusting to luck; but they were not so wise as my pal, for they did not wrap their things in bundles.

Our erstwhile guardians gathered up the handcuffs and chain and departed for Niagara Falls, while we, under new guardians, were led away into the prison. While we were in the office our number had been added to by other squads of newly arrived prisoners, so that we were now a procession forty or fifty strong.

Know, ye unimprisoned, that traffic is as restricted inside a large prison as commerce was in the Middle Ages. Once inside a penitentiary, one cannot move about at will. Every few steps are encountered great steel doors or gates which are always kept locked. We were bound for the barber-shop, but we encountered delays in the unlocking of doors for us. We were thus delayed in the first hall we entered. A "hall" is not a corridor. Imagine an oblong structure, built of bricks and rising six stories high, each story a row of cells, say fifty cells in a row—in short, imagine an oblong of colossal honey-comb. Place this on the ground and enclose it in a building with a roof overhead and walls all around. Such an oblong and encompassing building constitute a "hall" in the Erie County penitentiary. Also, to complete the picture, see a narrow gallery, with steel railing, running the full length of each tier of cells, and at the ends of the oblong see all these galleries, from both sides, connected by a fire-escape system of narrow steel stairways.

We were halted in the first hall, waiting for some guard to unlock a door. Here and there, moving about, were convicts, with close-cropped heads and shaven faces, and garbed in prison stripes. One such convict I noticed above us on the gallery of the third tier of cells. He was standing on the gallery and leaning forward, his arms resting on the railing, apparently oblivious of our presence. He seemed staring into vacancy. My pal made a slight hissing noise. The convict glanced down. Motioned signals passed between them. Then through the air soared the handkerchief bundle of my pal. The convict caught it, and like a flash it was out of sight in his shirt, and he was staring into vacancy. My pal had told me to follow his lead. I watched my chance when the guard's back was turned, and my bundle followed the other one into the shirt of the convict.

A minute later the door was unlocked, and we filed into the barber-shop. Here were more men in convict stripes. They were prison barbers. Also, there were bath-tubs, hot water, soap, and scrubbing-brushes. We were ordered to strip and bathe, each man to scrub his neighbor's back—a needless precaution, this compulsory bath, for the prison swarmed with vermin. After the bath, we were each given a canvas clothes-bag.

"Put all your clothes in the bags," said the guard. "It's no good trying to smuggle anything in. You've got to line up naked for inspection. Men for thirty days or less keep their shoes and suspenders. Men for more than thirty days keep nothing."

This announcement was received with consternation. How could naked men smuggle anything past an inspection? Only my pal and I were safe. But it was right here that the convict barbers got in their work. They passed among the poor newcomers, kindly volunteering to take charge of their precious little belongings, and promising to return them later in the day. Those barbers were philanthropists—to hear them talk. As in the case of Fra Lippo Lippi, there was prompt disemburdening. Matches, tobacco, rice-paper, pipes, knives, money, everything, flowed into the capacious shirts of the barbers. They fairly bulged with the spoil, and the guards made believe not to see. To cut the story short, nothing was ever returned. The barbers never had any intention of returning what they had taken. They considered it legitimately theirs. It was the barber-shop graft. There were many grafts in that prison, as I was to learn, and I, too, was destined to become a grafter—thanks to my new pal.

There were several chairs, and the barbers worked rapidly. The quickest shaves and hair-cuts I have ever seen were given in that shop. The men lathered themselves, and the barbers shaved them at the rate of a man a minute. A hair-cut took a trifle longer. In three minutes the down of eighteen was scraped from my face and my head was as smooth as a billiard-ball just sprouting a crop of bristles. Beards, mustaches, like our clothes and everything, came off. Take my word for it, we were a villainous-looking gang when they got through with us. I had not realized before how really altogether bad we were.

Then came the line-up, forty or fifty of us, naked as Kipling's heroes who stormed Lungtungpen. To search us was easy. There were only our shoes and ourselves. Two or three rash spirits, who had doubted the barbers, had the goods found on them—which goods, namely, tobacco, pipes, matches, and small change, were quickly confiscated. This over, our new clothes were brought to us—stout prison shirts, and coats and trousers conspicuously striped. I had always lin-

gered under the impression that the convict stripes were put on a
man only after he had been convicted of a felony. I lingered no
longer, but put on the insignia of shame and got my first taste of
marching the lock-step.

In single file, close together, each man's hands on the shoulders of
the man in front, we marched on into another large hall. Here we were
ranged up against the wall in a long line and ordered to strip our left
arms. A youth, a medical student who was getting in his practice on
cattle such as we, came down the line. He vaccinated just about four
times as rapidly as the barbers shaved. With a final caution to avoid
rubbing our arms against anything, we were led away to our cells.

In my cell was another man who was to be my cell-mate. He was a
young, manly fellow, not talkative, but very capable, indeed as splendid a fellow as one could meet with in a day's ride, and this in spite of
the fact that he had just recently finished a two-year term in some
Ohio penitentiary.

Hardly had we been in our cell half an hour when a convict saun-
tered down the gallery and looked in. It was my pal. He had the freedom of the hall, he explained. He was to be unlocked at six in the
morning and not locked up again till nine at night. He was in with
the "push" in that hall, and had been promptly appointed a trusty of
the kind technically known as "hall-man." The man who had appointed him was also a prisoner and a trusty, and was known as "first
hall-man." There were thirteen hall-men in that hall. Ten of them had
charge each of a gallery of cells, and over them were the first, second,
and third hall-men.

We newcomers were to stay in our cells for the rest of the day, my
pal informed me, so that the vaccine would have a chance to take.
The next morning we would be put to hard labor in the prison-yard.

"But I'll get you out of the work as soon as I can," he promised.
"I'll get one of the hall-men fired and have you put in his place."

He put his hand into his shirt, drew out the handkerchief containing my precious belongings, passed it in to me through the bars, and
went on down the gallery.

I opened the bundle. Everything was there. Not even a match was
missing. I shared the makings of a cigarette with my cell-mate. When
I started to strike a match for a light, he stopped me. A flimsy, dirty
comforter lay in each of our bunks for bedding. He tore off a narrow
strip of the thin cloth and rolled it tightly and telescopically into a
long and slender cylinder. This he lighted with a precious match. The

cylinder of tight-rolled cotton cloth did not flame. On the end a coal
of fire slowly smoldered. It would last for hours, and my cell-mate
called it a "punk." When it burned short, all that was necessary was to
make a new punk, put the end of it against the old, blow on them, and
so transfer the glowing coal. Why, we could have given Prometheus
pointers on the conserving of fire.

At twelve o'clock dinner was served. At the bottom of our cage-
door was a small opening like the entrance of a runway in a chicken-
yard. Through this were thrust two hunks of dry bread and two pan-
nikins of "soup." A portion of soup consisted of about a quart of hot
water with a lonely drop of grease floating on its surface. Also, there
was some salt in that water.

We drank the soup, but we did not eat the bread. Not that we were
not hungry, and not that the bread was uneatable. It was fairly good
bread. But we had reasons. My cell-mate had discovered that our cell
was alive with bedbugs. In all the cracks and interstices between the
bricks where the mortar had fallen out great colonies flourished. The
natives even ventured out in the broad daylight and swarmed over
the walls and ceilings by hundreds. My cell-mate was wise in the ways
of the beasts. Like Childe Roland, dauntless the slug-horn to his lips
he bore. Never was there such a battle. It lasted for hours. It was a
shambles. And when the last survivors fled to their brick-and-mortar
fastnesses, our work was only half done. We chewed mouthfuls of
our bread until it was reduced to the consistency of putty, and when
a fleeing belligerent escaped into a crevice between the bricks, we
promptly walled him in with a daub of the chewed bread. We toiled
on until the light grew dim and until every hole, nook, and cranny
was closed. I shudder to think of the tragedies of starvation and
cannibalism that must have ensued behind those bread-plastered
ramparts.

We threw ourselves on our bunks, tired out and hungry, to wait
for supper. It was a good day's work well done. In the weeks to come
we at least should not suffer from the hosts of vermin. We had fore-
gone our dinner, saved our hides at the expense of our stomachs; but
we were content. Alas for the futility of human effort! Scarcely was
our long task completed when a guard unlocked our door. A redistri-
bution of prisoners was being made, and we were taken to another
cell and locked in two galleries higher up.

Early next morning our cells were unlocked, and down in the hall
the several hundred prisoners of us formed the lock-step and marched

out into the prison-yard to go to work. The Erie Canal runs right by the back yard of the Erie County penitentiary. Our task was to unload canal-boats, carrying huge stay-bolts on our shoulders, like railroad ties, into the prison. As I worked I sized up the situation and studied the chances for a get-away. There wasn't the ghost of a show. Along the tops of the walls marched guards armed with repeating rifles, and I was told, furthermore, that there were machine-guns in the sentry-towers.

I did not worry. Thirty days were not so long. I'd stay those thirty days, and add to the store of material I intended to use, when I got out, against the harpies of justice. I'd show what an American boy could do when his rights and privileges had been trampled on the way mine had. I had been denied my right of trial by jury. I had been denied my right to plead guilty or not guilty; I had been denied a trial even (for I couldn't consider that what I had received at Niagara Falls was a trial); I had not been allowed to communicate with a lawyer or anyone, and hence had been denied my right of suing for a writ of habeas corpus; my face had been shaved, my hair cropped close, convict stripes had been put upon my body; I was forced to toil hard on a diet of bread and water and to march the shameful lock-step with armed guards over me—and all for what? What had I done? What crime had I committed against the good citizens of Niagara Falls that all this vengeance should be wreaked upon me? I had not even violated their "sleeping-out" ordinance. I had slept in the country, outside their jurisdiction, that night. I had not even begged for a meal, or battered for a "light-piece" on their streets. All that I had done was to walk along their sidewalk and gaze at their picayune waterfall. And what crime was there in that? Technically I was guilty of no misdemeanor. All right, I'd show them when I got out.

The next day I talked with a guard. I wanted to send for a lawyer. The guard laughed at me. So did the other guards. I really was *incommunicado* so far as the outside world was concerned. I tried to write a letter out, but I learned that all letters were read and censored or confiscated by the prison authorities, and that "short-timers" were not allowed to write letters, anyway. A little later I tried smuggling letters out by men who were released, but I learned that they were searched and the letters found and destroyed. Never mind. It all helped to make it a blacker case when I did get out.

But as the prison days went by (which I shall describe in the next chapter), I "learned a few." I heard tales of the police, and police courts, and lawyers, that were unbelievable and monstrous. Men, prisoners, told me of personal experiences with the police of great cities that were awful. And more awful were the hearsay tales they told me concerning men who had died at the hands of the police and who therefore could not testify for themselves. Years afterward, in the report of the Lexow Committee, I was to read tales true and more awful than those told to me. But in the meantime, during the first days of my imprisonment, I scoffed at what I heard.

As the days went by, however, I began to be convinced. I saw with my own eyes, there in that prison, things unbelievable and monstrous. And the more convinced I became, the profounder grew the respect in me for the sleuth-hounds of the law and for the whole institution of criminal justice. My indignation ebbed away, and into my being rushed the tides of fear. I saw at last, clear-eyed, what I was up against. I grew meek and lowly. Each day I resolved more emphatically to make no rumpus when I got out. All I asked, when I got out, was a chance to fade away from the landscape. And that was just what I did do when I was released. I kept my tongue between my teeth, walked softly, and sneaked for Pennsylvania, a wiser and a humbler man.

THE "PEN"

For two days I toiled in the prison-yard. It was heavy work, and, in spite of the fact that I malingered at every opportunity, I was played out. This was because of the food. No man could work hard on such food. Bread and water, that was all that was given us. Once a week we were supposed to get meat; but this meat did not always go around, and since all nutriment had first been boiled out of it in the making of soup, it didn't matter much whether one got a taste of it once a week or not.

Furthermore, there was one vital defect in the bread-and-water diet. While we got plenty of water, we did not get enough of the bread. A ration of bread was about the size of one's two fists, and three rations a day were given to each prisoner. There was one good thing, I must say, about the water: it was hot. In the morning it was called "coffee," at noon it was dignified as "soup," and at night it masqueraded as "tea." But it was the same old water all the time. The prisoners called it "water bewitched." In the morning it was black water, the color being due to boiling it with burnt bread-crusts. At

noon it was served minus the color, with salt and a drop of grease
added. At night it was served with purplish-auburn hue that defied all
speculation; it was darn poor tea, but it was dandy hot water.

We were a hungry lot in the Erie County pen. Only the long-timers
knew what it was to have enough to eat. The reason for this was that
they would have died after a time on the fare we short-timers received. I know that the long-timers got more substantial grub, because there was a whole row of them on the ground floor in our hall,
and when I was a trusty I used to steal from their grub while serving
them. Man cannot live on bread alone and not enough of it.

My pal delivered the goods. After two days of work in the yard
I was taken out of my cell and made a trusty, a hall-man. At morning
and night we served the bread to the prisoners in their cells; but at
twelve o'clock a different method was used. The convicts marched in
from work in a long line. As they entered the door of our hall, they
broke the lock-step and took their hands down from the shoulders of
their line-mates. Just inside the door were piled trays of bread, and
here also stood the first hall-man and two ordinary hall-men. I was
one of the two. Our task was to hold the trays of bread as the line of
convicts filed past. As soon as the tray, say that I was holding, was
emptied, the other hall-man took my place with a full tray; and when
his was emptied, I took his place with a full tray. Thus the line
tramped steadily by, each man reaching with his right hand and taking one ration of bread from the extended tray.

The task of the first hall-man was different. He used a club. He
stood beside the tray and watched. The hungry wretches could never
get over the delusion that some time they could manage to get two
rations of bread out of the tray. But in my experience that time never
came. The club of the first hall-man had a way of flashing out, quick
as the stroke of a tiger's paw, to the hand that dared ambitiously.
The first hall-man was a good judge of distance, and he had smashed
so many hands with that club that he had become infallible. He never
missed, and he usually punished the offending convict by taking his
one ration away from him and sending him to his cell to make his
meal on hot water.

And at times, while all these men lay hungry in their cells, I have
seen a hundred or so extra rations of bread hidden away in the cells
of the hall-men. It would seem absurd, our retaining this bread. But it
was one of our grafts. We were economic masters inside our hall, turning the trick in ways quite similar to the economic masters of civiliza-

tion. We controlled the food supply of the population, and, just like our brother bandits outside, we made the people pay for it. We peddled the bread. Once a week the men who worked in the yard received a five-cent plug of chewing-tobacco. This chewing-tobacco was the coin of the realm. Two or three rations of bread for a plug was the way we exchanged, and they traded, not because they loved tobacco less, but because they loved bread more. Oh, I know it was like taking candy from a baby, but what would you? We had to live. And certainly there should be some reward for initiative and enterprise. Besides, we but patterned ourselves after our betters outside the walls, who, on a larger scale and under the respectable disguise of speculators, promoters, and captains of industry, did precisely what we were doing. What awful things would have happened to those poor wretches if it hadn't been for us, I can't imagine. Heaven knows we put bread into circulation in the Erie County pen. Aye, and we encouraged frugality and thrift—in the poor devils who forewent their tobacco. And then there was our example. In the breast of every convict there we implanted the ambition to become even as we and run a graft. Saviors of society—I guess yes!

Here was a hungry man without any tobacco. Maybe he was a profligate and had used it all up on himself. Very good; he had a pair of suspenders. I exchanged half a dozen rations of bread for them, or a dozen rations if the suspenders were very good. Now I never wore suspenders, but that didn't matter. Around the corner lodged a long-timer, doing ten years for manslaughter. He wore suspenders, and he wanted a pair. I could trade them to him for some of his meat. Meat was what I wanted. Or perhaps he had a tattered, paper-covered novel. That was a treasure-trove. I could read it and then trade it off to the bakers for cake, or to the cooks for meat and vegetables, or to the firemen for decent coffee, or to some one or other for the newspaper that occasionally filtered in, heaven alone knows how. The cooks, bakers, and firemen were prisoners like myself, and they lodged in our hall in the first row of cells over us.

In short, a full-grown system of barter obtained in the Erie County pen. There was even money in circulation. This money was sometimes smuggled in by the short-timers, more frequently it came from the barber-shop graft where the newcomers were mulcted, but most of all flowed from the cells of the long-timers, though how they got it I don't know.

What of his preeminent position, the first hall-man was reputed to be quite wealthy. In addition to his miscellaneous grafts, he grafted on us. We farmed the general wretchedness, and the first hall-man was farmer-general over all of us. We held our particular grafts by his permission, and we had to pay for that permission. As I say, he was reputed to be wealthy; but we never saw his money, and he lived in a cell all to himself in solitary grandeur. But that money was made in the pen I had direct evidence, for I was cell-mate quite a time with the third hall-man. He had over sixteen dollars. He used to count his money every night after nine o'clock when we were locked in. Also, he used to tell me each night what he would do to me if I gave him away to the other hall-men. You see, he was afraid of being robbed, and danger threatened him from three different directions. First, there were the guards. A couple of them might jump upon him, give him a good beating for alleged insubordination, and throw him into the "solitaire" (the dungeon); and in the mix-up that sixteen dollars of his would take wings. Then again, the first hall-man could have taken it all away from him by threatening to dismiss him and fire him back to hard labor in the prison-yard. And yet again, there were the ten of us who were ordinary hall-men. If we got an inkling of his wealth there was a large likelihood, some quiet day, of the whole bunch of us getting him into a corner and dragging him down. Oh, we were wolves, believe me—just like some of the fellows who do business in Wall Street.

He had good reason to be afraid of us, and so had I to be afraid of him. He was a huge, illiterate brute, an ex-Chesapeake Bay oyster-pirate, an "ex-con" who had done five years in Sing Sing, and a general all-around stupidly carnivorous beast. Oh, no, I never gave him away to the other hall-men. This is the first time I have mentioned his sixteen dollars. But I grafted on him just the same. He was in love with a woman prisoner who was confined in the "female department." He could neither read nor write, and I used to read her letters to him and write his replies. And I made him pay for it, too. But they were good letters. I laid myself out on them, put in my best licks, and, furthermore, I won her for him; though I shrewdly guess that she was in love, not with him, but with the humble scribe. I repeat, those letters were great.

Another one of our grafts was "passing the punk." We were the celestial messengers, the fire-bringers, in that iron world of bolt and bar. When the men came in from work at night and were locked in their cells, they wanted to smoke. Then it was that we restored the divine spark, running the galleries, from cell to cell, with our smoldering punks. Those who were wise, or with whom we did business, had their punks all ready to light. Not everyone got divine sparks, however. The guy who refused to dig up went sparkless and smokeless to bed. But what did we care? We had the immortal cinch on him, and if he got fresh two or three of us would pitch on him and give him "what-for." You see, this was the working theory of the hall-men. There were thirteen of us. We had something like half a thousand prisoners in our hall. We were supposed to do the work, and to keep order. The latter was the function of the guards, which they turned over to us. It was up to us to keep order; if we didn't we'd be fired back to hard labor, most probably with a taste of the dungeon thrown in. But so long as we maintained order, that long could we work our own particular grafts.

Bear with me a moment and look at the problem. Here were thirteen beasts of us over half a thousand other beasts. It was a living hell, that prison, and it was up to us thirteen there to rule. It was impossible, considering the nature of the beasts, for us to rule by kindness. We ruled by fear. Of course, behind us, backing us up, were the guards. In extremities we called upon them for help; but it would bother them if we called upon them too often, in which event we could depend upon it that they would get more efficient trusties to take our places. But we did not call upon them often, except in a quiet sort of way, when we wanted a cell unlocked in order to get at a refractory prisoner inside. In such cases all the guard did was to unlock the door and walk away so as not to be a witness of what happened when half a dozen hall-men went inside and did a bit of manhandling.

As regards the details of that manhandling, I shall say nothing. And after all, manhandling was merely one of the very minor unprintable horrors of the Erie County pen. I say "unprintable"; and in justice I must also say unthinkable. They were unthinkable to me until I saw them, and I was no spring chicken in the ways of the world and the awful abysses of human degradation. It would take a deep plummet to reach bottom in the Erie County pen of that day, and I do but skim lightly the surface of things as I there saw them.

At times, say in the morning when prisoners came down to wash, the thirteen of us would be practically alone in the midst of them, and every last one of them had it in for us. Thirteen against five hundred, and we ruled by fear. We could not permit the slightest infraction of the rules, the slightest insolence. If we did we were lost. Our rule was to hit a man as soon as he opened his mouth—hit him hard, hit him with anything. A broom-handle, end on, in the face had a very sobering effect. But that was not all. Such a man must be made an example of; so the next rule was to wade right in and follow him up. Of course one was sure that every hall-man in sight would come on the run to join in the chastisement; this also was a rule. Whenever any hall-man was in trouble with a prisoner, the duty of any other hall-man who happened to be around was to lend a fist. Never mind the merits of the case—wade in and hit, and hit with anything; in short, lay the man out.

I remember a handsome young mulatto of about twenty who got the insane idea into his head that he should stand up for his rights. And he did have the right of it, too; but that didn't help him any. He lived on the topmost gallery. Eight hall-men took the conceit out of him in just about a minute and a half; for that was the length of time required to travel along his gallery to the end and down five flights of steel stairs. He traveled the whole distance on every portion of his anatomy except his feet, and the eight hall-men were not idle. The mulatto struck the pavement where I was standing watching it all. He regained his feet and stood upright for a moment. In that moment he threw his arms wide apart and emitted an awful scream of terror and pain and heart-break. At the same instant, as in a transformation scene, the shreds of his stout prison clothes fell from him, leaving him wholly naked and streaming blood from every portion of the surface of his body. Then he collapsed in a heap, unconscious. He had learned his lesson, and every convict within those walls who heard him scream had learned a lesson. So had I learned mine. It is not a nice thing to see a man's heart broken in a minute and a half.

The following will illustrate how we drummed up business in the graft of passing the punk. A row of newcomers is installed in your hall. You pass along before the bars with your punk. "Hey, Bo, give us a light," some one calls to you. Now this is an advertisement that that particular man has tobacco on him. You pass in the punk and go your way. A little later you come back and lean up casually against the bars. "Say, Bo, can you let us have a little tobacco?" is what you say. If he is not wise to the game the chances are that he solemnly avers that he hasn't any more tobacco. All very well. You condole with him and go your way. But you know that his punk will last him only the rest of that day. Next day you come by, and he says again, "Hey, Bo, give us a light." And you say, "You haven't any tobacco and you don't need a light." And you don't give him any, either. Half an hour after, or an hour, or two or three hours, you will be passing by, and the man will call out to you in mild tones, "Come here, Bo." And you come. You thrust your hand between the bars and have it filled with precious tobacco. Then you give him a light.

Sometimes, however, a newcomer arrives upon whom no grafts are to be worked. The mysterious word is passed along that he is to be treated decently. Where this word originates I could never learn. The one thing patent is that the man has a "pull." It may be with one of the superior hall-men; it may be with one of the guards in some other part of the prison; it may be that good treatment has been purchased from grafters higher up; but be it as it may, we know that it is up to us to treat him decently if we want to avoid trouble.

We hall-men were middlemen and common carriers. We arranged trades between convicts confined in different parts of the prison, and we put through the exchange. Also, we took our commissions coming and going. Sometimes the objects traded had to go through the hands of half a dozen middlemen, each of whom took his whack, or, in some way or another, was paid for his services.

Sometimes one was in debt for services, and sometimes one had others in his debt. Thus I entered the prison in debt to the convict who smuggled in my things for me. A week or so afterward one of the firemen passed a letter into my hand. It had been given to him by a barber. The barber had received it from the convict who had smuggled in my things. Because of my debt to him I was to carry the letter on. But he had not written the letter. The original sender was a long-timer in his hall. The letter was for a woman prisoner in the female department. But whether it was intended for her, or whether she, in turn, was one of the chain of go-betweens, I did not know. All that I knew was her description, and that it was up to me to get the letter into her hands.

Two days passed, during which time I kept the letter in my possession; then the opportunity came. The women did the mending of all the clothes worn by the convicts. A number of our hall-men had to go to the female department to bring back huge bundles of clothes. I fixed it with the first hall-man that I was to go along. Door after door was unlocked for us as we threaded our way across the prison to the women's quarters. We entered a large room where the women sat working at their mending. My eyes were "peeled" for the woman who had been described to me. I located her and worked near to her.

Two eagle-eyed matrons were on watch. I held the letter in my palm,
and looked my intention at the woman. She knew I had something for
her : she must have been expecting it, and had set herself to divining,
at the moment we entered, which of us was the messenger. But one of
the matrons stood within two feet of her. Already the hall-men were
picking up the bundles they were to carry away. The moment was
passing. I delayed with my bundle, making believe that it was not tied
securely. Would that matron ever look away? Or was I to fail? Just
then another woman cut up playfully with one of the hall-men—
stuck out her foot and tripped him, or pinched him, or did something
or other. The matron looked that way and reprimanded the woman
sharply. I do not know whether or not this was all planned to distract
the matron's attention, but I did know that it was my opportunity.
The woman's hand dropped from her lap down by her side. I stooped
to pick up my bundle. From my stooping position I slipped the letter
into her hand, and received another in exchange. The next moment
the bundle was on my shoulder, the matron's gaze had returned to me
because I was the last hall-man, and I was hastening to catch up with
my companions.

The letter I had received from the woman I turned over to the fireman, and thence it passed through the hands of the barber, of the
convict who had smuggled in my things, and on to the long-timer at
the other end.

Often we conveyed letters, the chain of communication of which
was so complex that we knew neither sender nor sendee. We were but
links in the chain. Somewhere, somehow, a convict would thrust a
letter into my hand with the instruction to pass it on to the next link.
All such acts were favors to be reciprocated later on, when I should be
acting directly with a principal in transmitting letters, and from whom
I should be receiving my pay. The whole prison was covered by a
network of lines of communication. And we who were in control of
the system of communication naturally exacted heavy tolls from our
customers. It was service for profit with a vengeance, though we were
at times not above giving service for love.

And all the time I was in the pen I was making myself solid with
my pal. He had done much for me, and in return he expected me to
do as much for him. When we got out we were to travel together and,
it goes with the saying, "pull off jobs" together. For my pal was a
criminal—oh, not a constellation of the first water, merely a petty
criminal who would steal and rob, commit burglary, and, if cornered,

not stop at murder. Many a quiet hour we sat and talked together. He had two or three jobs in view for the immediate future, in which my work was cut out for me, and of which I joined in planning the details. I had been with and seen much of criminals, and my pal never dreamed that I was only fooling him, giving him a string thirty days long. He thought I was the real goods, liked me because I was not stupid, and liked me a bit, too, I think, for myself. Of course I had not the slightest intention of joining him in a life of sordid, petty crime; but I'd have been an idiot to throw away all the good things his friendship made possible. When one is on the hot lava of hell he cannot pick and choose his path, and so it was with me in the Erie County pen. I had to stay in with the "push" or do hard labor on bread and water; and to stay in with the push I had to make good with my pal.

Life was not monotonous in the pen. Every day something was happening, men were having fits, going crazy, fighting, or the hall-men were getting drunk. "Rover Jack," one of the ordinary hall-men, was our star "oryide." He was a true "profesh," a "blowed-in-the-glass" stiff, and as such received all kinds of latitude from the hall-men in authority. "Pittsburg Joe," who was second hall-man, used to join "Rover Jack" in his sprees, and it was a saying of the pair that the Erie County pen was the only place where a man could get "slopped" and not be arrested. I never knew, but I was told that bromide of potassium, gained in devious ways from the dispensary, was the dope they used. But I do know, whatever their dope was, that they got good and drunk on occasion.

Our hall was filled with the ruck and the filth, the scum and the dregs, of society—hereditary inefficients, degenerates, wrecks, lunatics, addled intelligences, epileptics, monsters, weaklings, in short, a very nightmare of humanity. Hence fits flourished with us. These fits seemed contagious. When one man began throwing a fit, others followed his lead. I have seen seven men down with fits at the same time, making the air hideous with their cries, while as many more lunatics would be raging and gibbering. Nothing was ever done for the men with fits except to throw water on them. It was useless to send for the medical student or the doctor. They were not to be bothered with such trivial and frequent occurrences.

There was a young Dutch boy, about eighteen years of age, who had fits most frequently of all. He usually threw one every day. It was for that reason that we kept him on the ground floor farther down

in the row of cells in which we lodged. After he had had a few fits
in the prison-yard, the guards refused to be bothered with him any
more, and so he remained locked up in his cell all day with a cockney
cell-mate to keep him company. Not that the cockney was of any use;
whenever the Dutch boy had a fit, the cockney became paralyzed with
terror.

The Dutch boy could not speak a word of English. He was a
farmer's boy, serving ninety days as punishment for having got into
a scrap with some one. He prefaced his fits with howling. He howled
like a wolf. Also, he took his fits standing up, which was very incon-
venient for him, for they always culminated in a headlong pitch to
the floor. Whenever I heard the long wolf-howl rising, I used to grab
a broom and run to his cell. The trusties were not allowed keys to the
cells, so I could not get in to him. He would stand up in the middle
of his narrow cell, shivering convulsively, his eyes rolled backward
till only the whites were visible, and howling like a lost soul. Try as
I would, I could never get the cockney to lend a hand. While he stood
and howled, the cockney crouched and trembled in the upper bunk,
his terror-stricken eyes fixed on that awful figure, with eyes rolled
back, that howled and howled. It was hard on him, too, the poor devil
of a cockney. His own reason was not any too firmly seated, and the
wonder is that he did not go mad.

All that I could do was my best with the broom. I would thrust it
through the bars, train it on Dutchy's chest, and wait. As the crisis approached he would begin swaying back and forth. I would follow this
swaying with the broom, for there was no telling when he would take
that dreadful forward pitch. But when he did I was there with the
broom, catching him and easing him down. Contrive as I would, he
never came down quite gently, and his face was usually bruised by the
stone floor. Once down and writhing in convulsions, I'd throw a
bucket of water over him. I don't know whether cold water was the
right thing or not, but it was the custom in the Erie County pen. Nothing more than that was ever done for him. He would lie there, wet, for
an hour or so, and then crawl into his bunk. I knew better than to run
to a guard for assistance. What was a man with a fit, anyway?

In the adjoining cell lived a strange character, a man who was doing
sixty days for eating out of Barnum's swill-barrel, or at least that was
the way he put it. He was a badly addled creature, but, at first, very
mild and gentle. The facts of his case were as he had stated them. He
had strayed out to the circus grounds and, being hungry, had made

his way to the barrel that contained the refuse from the table of the circus people. "And it *was* good bread," he often assured me; "and the meat was out of sight." A policeman had seen him and arrested him, and there he was.

Once I passed his cell with a piece of stiff thin wire in my hand. He asked me for it so earnestly that I passed it through the bars to him. Promptly, and with no tool but his fingers, he broke it into short lengths and twisted them into half a dozen very creditable safety-pins. He sharpened the points on the stone floor. Thereafter I did quite a trade in safety-pins. I furnished the raw materials and peddled the finished product, and he did the work. As wages, I paid him extra rations of bread and once in a while a chunk of meat or a piece of soup-bone with some marrow inside.

But his imprisonment told on him, and he grew more violent day by day. The hall-men took delight in teasing him. They filled his weak brain with stories of a great fortune that had been left him. It was in order to rob him of it that he had been arrested and sent to jail. Of course, as he himself knew, there was no law against eating out of a barrel. Therefore he was wrongly imprisoned. It was a plot to deprive him of his fortune.

The first I knew of it, I heard the hall-men laughing about the "string" they had given him. Next he held a serious conference with me, in which he told me of his millions and the plot to deprive him of them, and in which he appointed me his detective. I did my best to let him down gently, speaking vaguely of a mistake, and that it was another man with a similar name who was the rightful heir. I left him quite cooled down; but I couldn't keep the hall-men away from him, and they continued to string him worse than ever. In the end, after a most violent scene, he threw me down, revoked my private-detective-ship, and went on strike. My trade in safety-pins ceased. He refused to make any more safety-pins, and he peppered me with raw material through the bars of his cell when I passed by.

I could never make it up with him. The other hall-men told him that I was a detective in the employ of the conspirators, and in the meantime they drove him mad with their stringing. His fictitious wrongs preyed upon his mind, and at last he became a dangerous and homicidal lunatic. The guards refused to listen to his tale of stolen millions, and he accused them of being in the plot. One day he threw a pannikin of hot tea over one of them, and then his case was investigated. The warden talked with him a few minutes through the bars of his cell. Then he was taken away for examination before the doctors. He never came back, and I often wonder if he is dead, or if he still gibbers about his millions in some asylum for the insane.

At last came the day of days, my release. It was the day of release for the third hall-man as well, and the short-time girl I had won for him was waiting for him outside the wall. They went away together, blissfully happy. My pal and I went out together, and together we walked down into Buffalo. Were we not to be together always? We begged together on the "main drag" that day for pennies, and what we received was spent for "shupers" of beer—I don't know how they are spelled, but they are pronounced the way I have spelled them, and they cost three cents. I was watching my chance all the time for a get-away. From some bo on the drag I managed to learn what time a certain freight pulled out. I calculated my time accordingly.When the moment came, my pal and I were in a saloon. Two foaming shupers were before us. I'd have liked to say good-by. He had been good to me. But I did not dare. I went out through the rear of the saloon and jumped the fence. It was a swift sneak, and a few minutes later I was on board a freight and headed south on the Western New York and Pennsylvania Railroad.

How I Became a Socialist

It is quite fair to say that I became a Socialist in a fashion somewhat similar to the way in which the Teutonic pagans became Christians —it was hammered into me. Not only was I not looking for Socialism at the time of my conversion, but I was fighting it. I was very young and callow, did not know much of anything, and though I had never even heard of a school called "Individualism," I sang the pæan of the strong with all my heart.

This was because I was strong myself. By strong I mean that I had good health and hard muscles, both of which possessions are easily accounted for. I had lived my childhood on California ranches, my boyhood hustling newspapers on the streets of a healthy Western city, and my youth on the ozone-laden waters of San Francisco Bay and the Pacific Ocean. I loved life in the open, and I toiled in the open, at the hardest kinds of work. Learning no trade, but drifting along from job to job, I looked on the world and called it good, every bit of it. Let me repeat, this optimism was because I was healthy and strong, bothered with neither aches nor weaknesses, never turned down by the boss because I did not look fit, able always to get a job at shovelling coal, sailorizing, or manual labor of some sort.

And because of all this, exulting in my young life, able to hold my own at work or fight, I was a rampant individualist. It was very natural. I was a winner. Wherefore I called the game, as I saw it played, or thought I saw it played, a very proper game for MEN. To be a MAN was to write man in large capitals on my heart. To adventure like a man, and fight like a man, and do a man's work (even for a boy's pay)—these were things that reached right in and gripped hold of me as no other thing could. And I looked ahead into long vistas of a hazy and interminable future, into which, playing what I conceived to be MAN'S game, I should continue to travel with unfailing health, without accidents, and with muscles ever vigorous. As I say, this future was interminable. I could see myself only raging through life without end like one of Nietzsche's *blond beasts,* lustfully roving and conquering by sheer superiority and strength.

As for the unfortunates, the sick, and ailing, and old, and maimed, I must confess I hardly thought of them at all, save that I vaguely felt that they, barring accidents, could be as good as I if they wanted to real hard, and could work just as well. Accidents? Well, they represented FATE, also spelled out in capitals, and there was no getting around FATE. Napoleon had had an accident at Waterloo, but that did not dampen my desire to be another and later Napoleon. Further, the optimism bred of a stomach which could digest scrap iron and a body which flourished on hardships did not permit me to consider accidents as even remotely related to my glorious personality.

I hope I have made it clear that I was proud to be one of Nature's strong-armed noblemen. The dignity of labor was to me the most impressive thing in the world. Without having read Carlyle, or Kipling, I formulated a gospel of work which put theirs in the shade. Work was everything. It was sanctification and salvation. The pride I took in a hard day's work well done would be inconceivable to you. It is almost inconceivable to me as I look back upon it. I was as faithful a wage slave as ever capitalist exploited. To shirk or malinger on the man who paid me my wages was a sin, first, against myself, and second, against him. I considered it a crime second only to treason and just about as bad.

In short, my joyous individualism was dominated by the orthodox bourgeois ethics. I read the bourgeois papers, listened to the bourgeois preachers, and shouted at the sonorous platitudes of the bourgeois politicians. And I doubt not, if other events had not changed my career, that I should have evolved into a professional strike-breaker, (one of President Eliot's American heroes), and had my head and my earning power irrevocably smashed by a club in the hands of some militant trades-unionist.

Just about this time, returning from a seven months' voyage before the mast, and just turned eighteen, I took it into my head to go tramping. On rods and blind baggages I fought my way from the open West, where men bucked big and the job hunted the man, to the congested labor centres of the East, where men were small potatoes and hunted the job for all they were worth. And on this new *blond-beast* adventure I found myself looking upon life from a new and totally different angle. I had dropped down from the proletariat into what sociologists love to call the "submerged tenth," and I was startled to discover the way in which that submerged tenth was recruited.

I found there all sorts of men, many of whom had once been as good as myself and just as *blond-beastly;* sailor-men, soldier-men, labor-men, all wrenched and distorted and twisted out of shape by toil and hardship and accident, and cast adrift by their masters like so many old horses. I battered on the drag and slammed back gates with them, or shivered with them in box cars and city parks, listening the while to life-histories which began under auspices as fair as mine, with digestions and bodies equal to and better than mine, and which ended there before my eyes in the shambles at the bottom of the Social Pit.

And as I listened my brain began to work. The woman of the streets and the man of the gutter drew very close to me. I saw the picture of the Social Pit as vividly as though it were a concrete thing, and at the bottom of the Pit I saw them, myself above them, not far, and hanging on to the slippery wall by main strength and sweat. And I confess a terror seized me. What when my strength failed? when I should be unable to work shoulder to shoulder with the strong men who were as yet babes unborn? And there and then I swore a great oath. It ran something like this: *All my days I have worked hard with my body, and according to the number of days I have worked, by just that much am I nearer the bottom of the Pit. I shall climb out of the Pit, but not by the muscles of my body shall I climb out. I shall do no more hard work, and may God strike me dead if I do another day's hard work with my body more than I absolutely have to do.* And I have been busy ever since running away from hard work.

Incidentally, while tramping some ten thousand miles through the United States and Canada, I strayed into Niagara Falls, was nabbed by a fee-hunting constable, denied the right to plead guilty or not guilty, sentenced out of hand to thirty days' imprisonment for having no fixed abode and no visible means of support, handcuffed and chained to a bunch of men similarly circumstanced, carted down country to Buffalo, registered at the Erie County Penitentiary, had my head clipped and my budding mustache shaved, was dressed in convict stripes, compulsorily vaccinated by a medical student who practised on such as we, made to march the lock-step, and put to work under the eyes of guards armed with Winchester rifles—all for adventuring in *blond-beastly* fashion. Concerning further details deponent sayeth not, though he may hint that some of his plethoric national patriotism simmered down and leaked out of the bottom of his soul somewhere—at least, since that experience he finds that he cares more for men and women and little children than for imaginary geographical lines.

To return to my conversion. I think it is apparent that my rampant individualism was pretty effectively hammered out of me, and something else as effectively hammered in. But, just as I had been an individualist without knowing it, I was now a Socialist without knowing it, withal, an unscientific one. I had been reborn, but not renamed, and I was running around to find out what manner of thing I was. I ran back to California and opened the books. I do not remember which ones I opened first. It is an unimportant detail anyway. I was already It, whatever It was, and by aid of the books I discovered that It was a Socialist. Since that day I have opened many books, but no economic argument, no lucid demonstration of the logic and inevitableness of Socialism affects me as profoundly and convincingly as I was affected on the day when I first saw the walls of the Social Pit rise around me and felt myself slipping down, down, into the shambles at the bottom.

In the London Slums

SELECTIONS FROM The People of the Abyss

PREFACE

The experiences related in this volume fell to me in the summer of 1902. I went down into the under-world of London with an attitude of mind which I may best liken to that of the explorer. I was open to be convinced by the evidence of my eyes, rather than by the teachings of those who had not seen, or by the words of those who had seen and gone before. Further, I took with me certain simple criteria with which to measure the life of the under-world. That which made for more life, for physical and spiritual health, was good; that which made for less life, which hurt, and dwarfed, and distorted life, was bad.

It will be readily apparent to the reader that I saw much that was bad. Yet it must not be forgotten that the time of which I write was considered "good times" in England. The starvation and lack of shelter I encountered constituted a chronic condition of misery which is never wiped out, even in the periods of greatest prosperity.

Following the summer in question came a hard winter. To such an extent did the suffering and positive starvation increase that society was unable to cope with it. Great numbers of the unemployed formed into processions, as many as a dozen at a time, and daily marched through the streets of London crying for bread. Mr. Justin McCarthy, writing in the month of January, 1903, to the New York *Independent,* briefly epitomizes the situation as follows:—

> *The workhouses have no space left in which to pack the starving crowds who are craving every day and night at their doors for food and shelter. All the charitable institutions have*

exhausted their means in trying to raise supplies of food for famishing residents of the garrets and cellars of London lanes and alleys. The quarters of the Salvation Army in various parts of London are nightly besieged by hosts of the unemployed and the hungry for whom neither shelter nor the means of sustenance can be provided.

It has been urged that the criticism I have passed on things as they are in England is too pessimistic. I must say, in extenuation, that of optimists I am the most optimistic. But I measure manhood less by political aggregations than by individuals. Society grows, while political machines rack to pieces and become "scrap." For the English, so far as manhood and womanhood and health and happiness go, I see a broad and smiling future. But for a great deal of the political machinery, which at present mismanages for them, I see nothing else than the scrap heap.

THE DESCENT

"But you can't do it, you know," friends said, to whom I applied for assistance in the matter of sinking myself down into the East End of London. "You had better see the police for a guide," they added, on second thought, painfully endeavoring to adjust themselves to the psychological processes of a madman who had come to them with better credentials than brains.

"But I don't want to see the police," I protested. "What I wish to do, is to go down into the East End and see things for myself. I wish to know how those people are living there, and why they are living there, and what they are living for. In short, I am going to live there myself."

"You don't want to live down there!" everybody said, with disapprobation writ large upon their faces. "Why, it is said there are places where a man's life isn't worth tu'pence."

"The very places I wish to see," I broke in.

"But you can't, you know," was the unfailing rejoinder.

"Which is not what I came to see you about," I answered brusquely, somewhat nettled by their incomprehension. "I am a stranger here, and I want you to tell me what you know of the East End, in order that I may have something to start on."

"But we know nothing of the East End. It is over there, somewhere." And they waved their hands vaguely in the direction where the sun on rare occasions may be seen to rise.

"Then I shall go to Cook's," I announced.

"Oh, yes," they said, with relief. "Cook's will be sure to know."

But O Cook, O Thomas Cook & Son, pathfinders and trail-clearers, living sign-posts to all the world and bestowers of first aid to bewildered travellers—unhesitatingly and instantly, with ease and celerity, could you send me to Darkest Africa or Innermost Thibet, but to the East End of London, barely a stone's throw distant from Ludgate Circus, you know not the way!

"You can't do it, you know," said the human emporium of routes and fares at Cook's Cheapside branch. "It is so—ahem—so unusual."

"Consult the police," he concluded authoritatively, when I persisted. "We are not accustomed to taking travellers to the East End; we receive no call to take them there, and we know nothing whatsoever about the place at all."

"Never mind that," I interposed, to save myself from being swept out of the office by his flood of negations. "Here's something you can do for me. I wish you to understand in advance what I intend doing, so that in case of trouble you may be able to identify me."

"Ah, I see; should you be murdered, we would be in position to identify the corpse."

He said it so cheerfully and cold-bloodedly that on the instant I saw my stark and mutilated cadaver stretched upon a slab where cool waters trickle ceaselessly, and him I saw bending over and sadly and patiently identifying it as the body of the insane American who would see the East End.

"No, no," I answered; "merely to identify me in case I get into a scrape with the 'bobbies.'" This last I said with a thrill; truly, I was gripping hold of the vernacular.

"That," he said, "is a matter for the consideration of the Chief Office.

"It is so unprecedented, you know," he added apologetically.

The man at the Chief Office hemmed and hawed. "We make it a rule," he explained, "to give no information concerning our clients."

"But in this case," I urged, "it is the client who requests you to give the information concerning himself."

Again he hemmed and hawed.

"Of course," I hastily anticipated, "I know it is unprecedented, but—"

"As I was about to remark," he went on steadily, "it is unprecedented, and I don't think we can do anything for you."

However, I departed with the address of a detective who lived in the East End, and took my way to the American consul-general. And here, at last, I found a man with whom I could 'do business.' There was no hemming and hawing, no lifted brows, open incredulity, or blank amazement. In one minute I explained myself and my project, which he accepted as a matter of course. In the second minute he asked my age, height, and weight, and looked me over. And in the third minute, as we shook hands at parting, he said: "All right, Jack. I'll remember you and keep track."

I breathed a sigh of relief. Having built my ships behind me, I was now free to plunge into that human wilderness of which nobody seemed to know anything. But at once I encountered a new difficulty in the shape of my cabby, a gray-whiskered and eminently decorous personage, who had imperturbably driven me for several hours about the 'City.'

"Drive me down to the East End," I ordered, taking my seat.

"Where, sir?" he demanded with frank surprise.

"To the East End, anywhere. Go on."

The hansom pursued an aimless way for several minutes, then came to a puzzled stop. The aperture above my head was uncovered, and the cabman peered down perplexedly at me.

"I say," he said, "wot plyce yer wanter go?"

"East End," I repeated. "Nowhere in particular. Just drive me around, anywhere."

"But wot's the haddress, sir?"

"See here!" I thundered. "Drive me down to the East End, and at once!"

It was evident that he did not understand, but he withdrew his head and grumblingly started his horse.

Nowhere in the streets of London may one escape the sight of abject poverty, while five minutes' walk from almost any point will bring one to a slum; but the region my hansom was now penetrating was one of unending slum. The streets were filled with a new and different race of people, short of stature, and of wretched or beer-sodden appearance. We rolled along through miles of bricks and squalor, and from each cross street and alley flashed long vistas of bricks and misery. Here and there lurched a drunken man or woman, and the air was obscene with sounds of jangling and squabbling. At

a market, tottery old men and women were searching in the garbage
thrown in the mud for rotten potatoes, beans, and vegetables, while
little children clustered like flies around a festering mass of fruit,
thrusting their arms to the shoulders into the liquid corruption, and
drawing forth morsels, but partially decayed, which they devoured
on the spot.

Not a hansom did I meet with in all my drive, while mine was like
an apparition from another and better world, the way the children
ran after it and alongside. And as far as I could see were the solid
walls of brick, the slimy pavements, and the screaming streets; and
for the first time in my life the fear of the crowd smote me. It was
like the fear of the sea; and the miserable multitudes, street upon
street, seemed so many waves of a vast and malodorous sea, lapping
about me and threatening to well up and over me.

"Stepney, sir; Stepney Station," the cabby called down.

I looked about. It was really a railroad station, and he had driven
desperately to it as the one familiar spot he had ever heard of in all
that wilderness.

"Well?" I said.

He spluttered unintelligibly, shook his head, and looked very miserable. "I'm a strynger 'ere," he managed to articulate. "An' if yer
don't want Stepney Station, I'm blessed if I know wotcher do want."

"I'll tell you what I want," I said. "You drive along and keep your
eye out for a shop where old clothes are sold. Now, when you see
such a shop, drive right on till you turn the corner, then stop and let
me out."

I could see that he was growing dubious of his fare, but not long
afterward he pulled up to the curb and informed me that an old
clothes shop was to be found a bit of the way back.

"Won'tcher py me?" he pleaded. "There's seven an' six owin' me."

"Yes," I laughed, "and it would be the last I'd see of you."

"Lord lumme, but it'll be the last I see of you if yer don't py me,"
he retorted.

But a crowd of ragged onlookers had already gathered around the
cab, and I laughed again and walked back to the old clothes shop.

Here the chief difficulty was in making the shop-man understand
that I really and truly wanted old clothes. But after fruitless attempts
to press upon me new and impossible coats and trousers, he began to
bring to light heaps of old ones, looking mysterious the while and
hinting darkly. This he did with the palpable intention of letting me

know that he had 'piped my lay,' in order to bulldose me, through
fear of exposure, into paying heavily for my purchases. A man in
trouble, or a high-class criminal from across the water, was what he
took my measure for—in either case, a person anxious to avoid the
police.

But I disputed with him over the outrageous difference between
prices and values, till I quite disabused him of the notion, and he settled down to drive a hard bargain with a hard customer. In the end I
selected a pair of stout though well-worn trousers, a frayed jacket
with one remaining button, a pair of brogans which had plainly seen
service where coal was shovelled, a thin leather belt, and a very dirty
cloth cap. My underclothing and socks, however, were new and warm,
but of the sort that any American waif, down in his luck, could acquire in the ordinary course of events.

"I must sy yer a sharp 'un," he said, with counterfeit admiration,
as I handed over the ten shillings finally agreed upon for the outfit.
"Blimey, if you ain't ben up an' down Petticut Lane afore now. Yer
trouseys is wuth five bob to hany man, an' a docker 'ud give two an'
six for the shoes, to sy nothin' of the coat an' cap an' new stoker's
singlet an' hother things."

"How much will you give me for them?" I demanded suddenly. "I
paid you ten bob for the lot, and I'll sell them back to you, right now,
for eight. Come, it's a go!"

But he grinned and shook his head, and though I had made a good
bargain, I was unpleasantly aware that he had made a better one.

I found the cabby and a policeman with their heads together, but
the latter, after looking me over sharply and particularly scrutiniz-
ing the bundle under my arm, turned away and left the cabby to wax
mutinous by himself. And not a step would he budge till I paid him
the seven shillings and sixpence owing him. Whereupon he was willing
to drive me to the ends of the earth, apologizing profusely for his
insistence, and explaining that one ran across queer customers in
London Town.

But he drove me only to Highbury Vale, in North London, where
my luggage was waiting for me. Here, next day, I took off my shoes
(not without regret for their lightness and comfort), and my soft,
gray travelling suit, and, in fact, all my clothing; and proceeded to
array myself in the clothes of the other and unimaginable men, who
must have been indeed unfortunate to have had to part with such
rags for the pitiable sums obtainable from a dealer.

Inside my stoker's singlet, in the armpit, I sewed a gold sovereign
(an emergency sum certainly of modest proportions) ; and inside my
stoker's singlet I put myself. And then I sat down and moralized upon
the fair years and fat, which had made my skin soft and brought the
nerves close to the surface; for the singlet was rough and raspy as a
hair shirt, and I am confident that the most rigorous of ascetics suffer
no more than did I in the ensuing twenty-four hours.

The remainder of my costume was fairly easy to put on, though the
brogans, or brogues, were quite a problem. As stiff and hard as if
made of wood, it was only after a prolonged pounding of the uppers
with my fists that I was able to get my feet into them at all. Then,
with a few shillings, a knife, a handkerchief, and some brown papers
and flake tobacco stowed away in my pockets, I thumped down the
stairs and said good-by to my foreboding friends. As I passed out the
door, the 'help,' a comely, middle-aged woman, could not conquer a
grin that twisted her lips and separated them till the throat, out of
involuntary sympathy, made the uncouth animal noises we are wont
to designate as 'laughter.'

No sooner was I out on the streets than I was impressed by the difference in status effected by my clothes. All servility vanished from
the demeanor of the common people with whom I came in contact.
Presto! in the twinkling of an eye, so to say, I had become one of
them. My frayed and out-at-elbows jacket was the badge and advertisement of my class, which was their class. It made me of like kind,
and in place of the fawning and too-respectful attention I had hitherto received, I now shared with them a comradeship. The man in
corduroy and dirty neckerchief no longer addressed me as 'sir' or
'governor.' It was 'mate,' now—and a fine and hearty word, with a
tingle to it, and a warmth and gladness, which the other term does
not possess. Governor! It smacks of mastery, and power, and high
authority—the tribute of the man who is under to the man on top,
delivered in the hope that he will let up a bit and ease his weight.
Which is another way of saying that it is an appeal for alms.

This brings me to a delight I experienced in my rags and tatters
which is denied the average American abroad. The European traveller
from the States, who is not a Croesus, speedily finds himself reduced
to a chronic state of self-conscious sordidness by the hordes of cring-
ing robbers who clutter his steps from dawn till dark, and deplete his
pocketbook in a way that puts compound interest to the blush.

In my rags and tatters I escaped the pestilence of tipping, and encountered men on a basis of equality, Nay, before the day was out I turned the tables, and said, most gratefully, "Thank you, sir," to a gentleman whose horse I held, and who dropped a penny into my eager palm.

Other changes I discovered were wrought in my condition by my new garb. In crossing crowded thoroughfares I found I had to be, if anything, more lively in avoiding vehicles, and it was strikingly impressed upon me that my life had cheapened in direct ratio with my clothes. When before, I inquired the way of a policeman, I was usually asked, "Bus or 'ansom, sir?" But now the query became, "Walk or ride?" Also, at the railway stations it was the rule to be asked, "First or second, sir?" Now I was asked nothing, a third-class ticket being shoved out to me as a matter of course.

But there was compensation for it all. For the first time I met the English lower classes face to face, and knew them for what they were. When loungers and workmen, on street corners and in public houses, talked with me, they talked as one man to another, and they talked as natural men should talk, without the least idea of getting anything out of me for what they talked, or the way they talked.

And when at last I made into the East End, I was gratified to find that the fear of the crowd no longer haunted me. I had become a part of it. The vast and malodorous sea had welled up and over me, or I had slipped gently into it, and there was nothing fearsome about it— with the one exception of the stoker's singlet.

THOSE ON THE EDGE

My first impression of East London was naturally a general one. Later the details began to appear, and here and there in the chaos of misery I found little spots where a fair measure of happiness reigned, —sometimes whole rows of houses in little out-of-the-way streets, where artisans dwell and where a rude sort of family life obtains. In the evenings the men can be seen at the doors, pipes in their mouths and children on their knees, wives gossiping, and laughter and fun going on. The content of these people is manifestly great, for, relative to the wretchedness that encompasses them, they are well off.

But at the best, it is a dull, animal happiness, the content of the full belly. The dominant note of their lives is materialistic. They are stupid and heavy, without imagination. The Abyss seems to exude a stupefying atmosphere of torpor, which wraps about them and

deadens them. Religion passes them by. The Unseen holds for them
neither terror nor delight. They are unaware of the Unseen; and the
full belly and the evening pipe, with their regular 'arf an' arf,' is all
they demand, or dream of demanding, from existence.

This would not be so bad if it were all; but it is not all. The satisfied torpor in which they are sunk is the deadly inertia that pre-
cedes dissolution. There is no progress, and with them not to progress
is to fall back and into the Abyss. In their own lives they may only
start to fall, leaving the fall to be completed by their children and
their children's children. Man always gets less than he demands from
life; and so little do they demand, that the less than little they get
cannot save them.

At the best, city life is an unnatural life for the human; but the
city life of London is so utterly unnatural that the average workman
or workwoman cannot stand it. Mind and body are sapped by the undermining influences ceaselessly at work. Moral and physical stamina
are broken, and the good workman, fresh from the soil, becomes in
the first city generation a poor workman; and by the second city
generation, devoid of push and go and initiative, and actually unable
physically to perform the labor his father did, he is well on the way
to the shambles at the bottom of the Abyss.

If nothing else, the air he breathes, and from which he never escapes, is sufficient to weaken him mentally and physically, so that he
becomes unable to compete with the fresh virile life from the country
hastening on to London Town to destroy and be destroyed.

Leaving out the disease germs that fill the air of the East End, consider but the one item of smoke. Sir William Thistleton-Dyer, curator
of Kew Gardens, has been studying smoke deposits on vegetation, and
according to his calculations, no less than six tons of solid matter,
consisting of soot and tarry hydrocarbons, are deposited every week
on every quarter of a square mile in and about London. This is
equivalent to twenty-four tons per week to the square mile, or 1248
tons per year to the square mile. From the cornice below the dome of
St. Paul's Cathedral was recently taken a solid deposit of crystallized
sulphate of lime. This deposit had been formed by the action of the
sulphuric acid in the atmosphere upon the carbonate of lime in the
stone. And this sulphuric acid in the atmosphere is constantly being
breathed by the London workmen through all the days and nights of
their lives.

It is incontrovertible that the children grow up into rotten adults, without virility or stamina, a weak-kneed, narrow-chested, listless breed, that crumples up and goes down in the brute struggle for life with the invading hordes from the country. The railway men, carriers, omnibus drivers, corn and timber porters, and all those who require physical stamina, are largely drawn from the country; while in the Metropolitan Police there are, roughly, 12,000 country-born as against 3000 London-born.

So one is forced to conclude that the Abyss is literally a huge man-killing machine, and when I pass along the little out-of-the-way streets with the full-bellied artisans at the doors, I am aware of a greater sorrow for them than for the 450,000 lost and hopeless wretches dying at the bottom of the pit. They, at least, are dying, that is the point; while these have yet to go through the slow and preliminary pangs extending through two and even three generations.

And yet the quality of the life is good. All human potentialities are in it. Given proper conditions, it could live through the centuries, and great men, heroes and masters, spring from it and make the world better by having lived.

I talked with a woman who was representative of that type which has been jerked out of its little out-of-the-way streets and has started on the fatal fall to the bottom. Her husband was a fitter and a member of the Engineers' Union. That he was a poor engineer was evidenced by his inability to get regular employment. He did not have the energy and enterprise necessary to obtain or hold a steady position.

The pair had two daughters, and the four of them lived in a couple of holes, called 'rooms' by courtesy, for which they paid seven shillings per week. They possessed no stove, managing their cooking on a single gas-ring in the fireplace. Not being persons of property, they were unable to obtain an unlimited supply of gas; but a clever machine had been installed for their benefit. By dropping a penny in the slot, the gas was forthcoming, and when a penny's worth had forthcome the supply was automatically shut off. "A penny gawn in no time," she explained, "an' the cookin' not arf done!"

Incipient starvation had been their portion for years. Month in and month out, they had arisen from the table able and willing to eat more. And when once on the downward slope, chronic innutrition is an important factor in sapping vitality and hastening the descent.

Yet this woman was a hard worker. From 4:30 in the morning till the last light at night, she said, she had toiled at making cloth dress-skirts, lined up and with two flounces, for seven shillings a dozen. Cloth dress-skirts, mark you, lined up and with two flounces, for seven shillings a dozen! This is equal to $1.75 per dozen, or 14¾ cents per skirt.

The husband, in order to obtain employment, had to belong to the union, which collected one shilling and sixpence from him each week. Also, when strikes were afoot and he chanced to be working, he had at times been compelled to pay as high as seventeen shillings into the union's coffers for the relief fund.

One daughter, the elder, had worked as green hand for a dress-maker; for one shilling and sixpence per week—37½ cents per week, or a fraction over 5 cents per day. However, when the slack season came she was discharged, though she had been taken on at such low pay with the understanding that she was to learn the trade and work up. After that she had been employed in a bicycle store for three years, for which she received five shillings per week, walking two miles to her work, and two back, and being fined for tardiness.

As far as the man and woman were concerned, the game was played. They had lost handhold and foothold, and were falling into the pit. But what of the daughters? Living like swine, enfeebled by chronic innutrition, being sapped mentally, morally, and physically, what chance have they to crawl up and out of the Abyss into which they were born falling? . . .

THE CARTER AND THE CARPENTER

The Carter, with his clean-cut face, chin beard, and shaved upper lip, I should have taken in the United States for anything from a master workman to a well-to-do farmer. The Carpenter—well, I should have taken him for a carpenter. He looked it, lean and wiry, with shrewd, observant eyes, and hands that had grown twisted to the handles of tools through forty-seven years' work at the trade. The chief difficulty with these men was that they were old, and that their children, in-stead of growing up to take care of them, had died. Their years had told on them, and they had been forced out of the whirl of industry by the younger and stronger competitors who had taken their places.

These two men, turned away from the casual ward of the White-chapel Workhouse, were bound with me for Poplar Workhouse. Not much of a show, they thought, but to chance it was all that remained to us. It was Poplar, or the streets and night. Both men were anxious

for a bed, for they were "about gone," as they phrased it. The Carter,
fifty-eight years of age, had spent the last three nights without shelter
or sleep, while the Carpenter, sixty-five years of age, had been out
five nights.

But, O dear, soft people, full of meat and blood, with white beds
and airy rooms waiting for you each night, how can I make you know
what it is to suffer as you would suffer if you spent a weary night on
London's streets? Believe me, you would think a thousand centuries
had come and gone before the east paled into dawn; you would shiver
till you were ready to cry aloud with the pain of each aching muscle;
and you would marvel that you could endure so much and live. Should
you rest upon a bench, and your tired eyes close, depend upon it the
policeman would rouse you and gruffly order you to "move on." You
may rest upon the bench, and benches are few and far between; but if
rest means sleep, on you must go, dragging your tired body through
the endless streets. Should you, in desperate slyness, seek some forlorn alley or dark passageway and lie down, the omnipresent policeman will rout you out just the same. It is his business to rout you out.
It is a law of the powers that be that you shall be routed out.

But when the dawn came, the nightmare over, you would hie you
home to refresh yourself, and until you died you would tell the story
of your adventure to groups of admiring friends. It would grow into a
mighty story. Your little eight-hour night would become an Odyssey
and you a Homer.

Not so with these homeless ones who walked to Poplar Workhouse
with me. And there are thirty-five thousand of them, men and women,
in London Town this night. Please don't remember it as you go to
bed; if you are as soft as you ought to be you may not rest so well as
usual. But for old men of sixty, seventy, and eighty, ill-fed, with
neither meat nor blood, to greet the dawn unrefreshed, and to stagger
through the day in mad search for crusts, with relentless night rushing down upon them again, and to do this five nights and days—O
dear, soft people, full of meat and blood, how can you ever understand?

I walked up Mile End Road between the Carter and the Carpenter.
Mile End Road is a wide thoroughfare, cutting the heart of East
London, and there were tens of thousands of people abroad on it. I
tell you this so that you may fully appreciate what I shall describe
in the next paragraph. As I say, we walked along, and when they grew
bitter and cursed the land, I cursed with them, cursed as an Ameri-

can waif would curse, stranded in a strange and terrible land. And, as I tried to lead them to believe, and succeeded in making them believe, they took me for a "seafaring man," who had spent his money in riotous living, lost his clothes (no unusual occurrence with seafaring men ashore), and was temporarily broke while looking for a ship. This accounted for my ignorance of English ways in general and casual wards in particular, and my curiosity concerning the same.

The Carter was hard put to keep the pace at which we walked (he told me that he had eaten nothing that day), but the Carpenter, lean and hungry, his gray and ragged overcoat flapping mournfully in the breeze, swung on in a long and tireless stride which reminded me strongly of the plains coyote. Both kept their eyes upon the pavement as they walked and talked, and every now and then one or the other would stoop and pick something up, never missing the stride the while. I thought it was cigar and cigarette stumps they were collecting, and for some time took no notice. Then I did notice.

From the slimy, spittle-drenched side-walk, they were picking up bits of orange peel, apple skin, and grape stems, and they were eating them. The pits of green gage plums they cracked between their teeth for the kernels inside. They picked up stray crumbs of bread the size of peas, apple cores so black and dirty one would not take them to be apple cores, and these things these two men took into their mouths, and chewed them, and swallowed them; and this, between six and seven o'clock in the evening of August 20, year of our Lord 1902, in the heart of the greatest, wealthiest, and most powerful empire the world has ever seen.

These two men talked. They were not fools. They were merely old. And, quite naturally, a-reek with pavement offal, they talked of bloody revolution. They talked as anarchists, fanatics, and madmen would talk. And who shall blame them? In spite of my three good meals that day, and the snug bed I could occupy if I wished, and my social philosophy, and my evolutionary belief in the slow development and metamorphosis of things—in spite of all this, I say, I felt impelled to talk rot with them or hold my tongue. Poor fools! Not of their sort are revolutions bred. And when they are dead and dust, which will be shortly, other fools will talk bloody revolution as they gather offal from the spittle-drenched side-walk along Mile End Road to Poplar Workhouse.

Being a foreigner, and a young man, the Carter and the Carpenter explained things to me and advised me. Their advice, by the way, was brief and to the point; it was to get out of the country. "As fast as God'll let me," I assured them; "I'll hit only the high places, till you won't be able to see my trail for smoke." They felt the force of my figures rather than understood them, and they nodded their heads approvingly.

"Actually make a man a criminal against 'is will," said the Carpenter. " 'Ere I am, old, younger men takin' my place, my clothes gettin' shabbier an' shabbier, an' makin' it 'arder every day to get a job. I go to the casual ward for a bed. Must be there by two or three in the afternoon or I won't get in. You saw what happened today. What chance does that give me to look for work? S'pose I do get into the casual ward? Keep me in all day tomorrow, let me out mornin' o' next day. What then? The law sez I can't get in another casual ward that night less'n ten miles distant. Have to hurry an' walk to be there in time that day. What chance does that give me to look for a job? S'pose I don't walk. S'pose I look for a job? In no time there's night come, an' no bed. No sleep all night, nothin' to eat, what shape am I in in the mornin' to look for work? Got to make up my sleep in the park somehow" (the vision of Christ's Church, Spitalfield, was strong on me) "an' get something to eat. An' there I am! Old, down, 'an no chance to get up."

"Used to be a toll-gate 'ere," said the Carter, "Many's the time I've paid my toll 'ere in my cartin' days."

"I've 'ad three 'a'penny rolls in two days," the Carpenter announced, after a long pause in the conversation.

"Two of them I ate yesterday, an' the third to-day," he concluded, after another long pause.

"I ain't 'ad anything today," said the Carter. "An' I'm fagged out. My legs is hurtin' me somethin' fearful."

"The roll you get in the 'spike' is that 'ard you can't eat it nicely with less than a pint of water," said the Carpenter, for my benefit. And, on asking him what the "spike" was, he answered, "The casual ward. It's a cant word, you know."

But what surprised me was that he should have the word "cant" in his vocabulary that I found was no mean one before we parted.

I asked him what I may expect in the way of treatment, if we succeeded in getting into the Poplar Workhouse, and between them I was supplied with much information. Having taken a cold bath on entering, I would be given for supper six ounces of bread and "three parts of skilly." "Three parts" means three-quarters of a pint, and "skilly" is a fluid concoction of three quarts of oatmeal stirred into three buckets and a half of hot water.

"Milk and sugar, I suppose, and a silver spoon?" I queried.

"No fear. Salt's what you'll get, an' I've seen some places where you'd not get any spoon. 'Old 'er up an' let 'er run down, that's 'ow they do it."

"You do get good skilly at 'Ackney," said the Carter.

"Oh, wonderful skilly, that," praised the Carpenter, and each looked eloquently at the other.

"Flour an' water at St. George's in the East," said the Carter.

The Carpenter nodded. He had tried them all.

"Then what?" I demanded.

And I was informed that I was sent directly to bed. "Call you at half after five in the mornin', an' you get up an' take a 'sluice'—if there's any soap. Then breakfast, same as supper, three parts o' skilly an' a six-ounce loaf."

" 'Tisn't always six ounces," corrected the Carter.

" 'Tisn't, no; an' often that sour you can 'ardly eat it. When first I started I couldn't eat the skilly nor the bread, but now I can eat my own an' another man's portion."

"I could eat three other men's portions," said the Carter. "I 'aven't 'ad a bit this blessed day."

"Then what?"

"Then you've got to do your task, pick four pounds of oakum, or clean an' scrub, or break ten to eleven hundredweight o' stones. I don't 'ave to break stones; I'm past sixty, you see. They'll make you do it, though. You're young an' strong."

"What I don't like," grumbled the Carter, "is to be locked up in a cell to pick oakum. It's too much like prison."

"But suppose after you've had your night's sleep, you refuse to pick oakum, or break stones, or do any work at all?" I asked.

"No fear you'll refuse the second time; they'll run you in," answered the Carpenter. "Wouldn't advise you to try it on, my lad."

"Then comes dinner," he went on. "Eight ounces of bread, one and a 'arf ounces of cheese, an' cold water. Then you finish your task and 'ave supper, same as before, three parts o' skilly an' six ounces of bread. Then to bed, six o'clock, an' next mornin' you're turned loose, provided you've finished your task."

We had long since left Mile End Road, and after traversing a gloomy maze of narrow, winding streets, we came to Poplar Workhouse. On a low stone wall we spread our handkerchiefs, and each in his handkerchief put all his worldly possessions with the exception of the "bit o' baccy" down his sock. And then, as the last light was fading from the drab-colored sky, the wind blowing cheerless and cold, we stood, with our pitiful little bundles in our hands, a forlorn group at the workhouse door.

Three working girls came along, and one looked pityingly at me; as she passed I followed her with my eyes, and she still looked pityingly back at me. The old men she did not notice, Dear Christ, she pitied me, young and vigorous and strong, but she had no pity for the two old men who stood by my side! She was a young woman, and I was a young man, and what vague sex promptings impelled her to pity me put her sentiment on the lowest plane. Pity for old men is an altruistic feeling, and besides, the workhouse door is the accustomed place for old men. So she showed no pity for them, only for me, who deserved it least or not at all. Not in honor do gray hairs go down to the grave in London Town.

On one side the door was a bell handle, on the other side a press button.

"Ring the bell," said the Carter to me.

And just as I ordinarily would at anybody's door, I pulled out the handle and rang a peal.

"Oh! Oh!" they cried in one terrified voice. "Not so 'ard!"

I let go, and they looked reproachfully at me, as though I had imperilled their chance for a bed and three parts of skilly. Nobody came. Luckily, it was the wrong bell, and I felt better.

"Press the button," I said to the Carpenter.

"No, no, wait a bit," the Carter hurriedly interposed.

From all of which I drew the conclusion that a poorhouse porter, who commonly draws a yearly salary of from thirty to forty dollars, is a very finicky and important personage, and cannot be treated too fastidiously by—paupers.

So we waited, ten times a decent interval, when the Carter stealthily advanced a timid forefinger to the button, and gave it the faintest possible push. I have looked at waiting men where life and death was in the issue; but anxious suspense showed less plainly on their faces than it showed on the faces of these two men as they waited for the coming of the porter.

He came. He barely looked at us. "Full up," he said, and shut the door.

"Another night of it," groaned the Carpenter. In the dim light the Carter looked wan and gray.

Indiscriminate charity is vicious, say the professional philanthropists. Well, I resolved to be vicious.

"Come on; get your knife out and come here," I said to the Carter, drawing him into a dark alley.

He glared at me in a frightened manner, and tried to draw back. Possibly he took me for a latter-day Jack-the-Ripper, with a penchant for elderly male paupers. Or he may have thought I was inveigling him into the commission of some desperate crime. Anyway, he was frightened.

It will be remembered, at the outset, that I sewed a pound inside my stoker's singlet under the arm-pit. This was my emergency fund, and I was now called upon to use it for the first time.

Not until I had gone through the acts of a contortionist, and shown the round coin sewed in, did I succeed in getting the Carter's help. Even then his hand was trembling so that I was afraid he would cut me instead of the stitches, and I was forced to take the knife away and do it myself. Out rolled the gold piece, a fortune in their hungry eyes; and away we stampeded for the nearest coffee-house.

Of course, I had to explain to them that I was merely an investigator, a social student, seeking to find out how the other half lived. And at once they shut up like clams. I was not of their kind; my speech had changed, the tones of my voice were different, in short, I was a superior, and they were superbly class conscious.

"What will you have?" I asked, as the waiter came for the order.

"Two slices an' a cup of tea," m ekly said the Carter.

"Two slices an' a cup of tea," meekly said the Carpenter.

Stop a moment, and consider the situation. Here were two men, invited by me into the coffee-house. They had seen my gold piece, and they could understand that I was no pauper. One had eaten a ha'penny roll that day, the other had eaten nothing. And they called for "two slices an' a cup of tea!" Each man had given a tu'penny order. "Two slices," by the way, means two slices of bread and butter.

This was the same degraded humility that had characterized their attitude toward the poorhouse porter. But I wouldn't have it. Step by step I increased their orders—eggs, rashers of bacon, more eggs, more bacon, more tea, more slices, and so forth—they denying wistfully all the while that they cared for anything more, and devouring it ravenously as fast as it arrived.

"First cup o' tea I've 'ad in a fortnight," said the Carter.

"Wonderful tea, that," said the Carpenter.

They each drank two pints of it, and I assure you that it was slops. It resembled tea less than lager beer resembles champagne. Nay, it was "water-bewitched," and did not resemble tea at all.

It was curious, after the first shock, to notice the effect the food had on them. At first they were melancholy, and talked of the divers times they had contemplated suicide. The Carter, not a week before, had stood on the bridge and looked at the water, and pondered the question. Water, the Carpenter insisted with heat, was a bad route. He, for one, he knew, would struggle. A bullet was " 'andier," but how under the sun was he to get hold of a revolver? That was the rub.

They grew more cheerful as the hot "tea" soaked in, and talked more about themselves. The Carter had buried his wife and children, with the exception of one son, who grew to manhood and helped him in his little business. Then the thing happened. The son, a man of thirty-one, died of the smallpox. No sooner was this over than the father came down with fever and went to the hospital for three months. Then he was done for. He came out weak, debilitated, no strong young son to stand by him, his little business gone glimmering, and not a farthing. The thing had happened, and the game was up. No chance for an old man to start again. Friends all poor and unable to help. He had tried for work when they were putting up stands for the first Coronation parade. "An' I got fair sick of the answer: 'No! no! no!' It rang in my ears at night when I tried to sleep, always the same, 'No! no! no!'" Only the past week he had answered an advertisement in Hackney, and on giving his age was told, "Oh, too old, too old by far."

The Carpenter had been born in the army, where his father had served twenty-two years. Likewise, his two brothers had gone into the army; one, troop sergeant-major of the Seventh Hussars, dying in India after the Mutiny; the other, after nine years under Roberts in the East, had been lost in Egypt. The Carpenter had not gone into the army, so here he was, still on the planet.

"But 'ere, give me your 'and," he said, ripping open his ragged shirt. "I'm fit for the anatomist, that's all. I'm wastin' away, sir, actually wastin' away for want of food. Feel my ribs an' you'll see."

I put my hand under his shirt and felt. The skin was stretched like parchment over the bones, and the sensation produced was for all the world like running one's hand over a washboard.

"Seven years o' bliss I 'ad," he said. "A good missus and three bonnie lassies. But they all died. Scarlet fever took the girls inside a fortnight."

"After this, sir," said the Carter, indicating the spread, and desiring to turn the conversation into more cheerful channels; "after this, I wouldn't be able to eat a workhouse breakfast in the morning."

"Nor I," agreed the Carpenter, and they fell to discussing stomach delights and the fine dishes their respective wives had cooked in the old days.

"I've gone three days and never broke my fast," said the Carter.

"And I, five," his companion added, turning gloomy with the memory of it. "Five days once, with nothing on my stomach but a bit of orange peel, an' outraged nature wouldn't stand it, sir, an' I near died. Sometimes, walkin' the streets at night, I've been that desperate I've made up my mind to win the horse or lose the saddle. You know what I mean sir—to commit some big robbery. But when mornin' come, there was I, too weak from 'unger 'an cold to 'arm a mouse."

As their poor vitals warmed to the food, they began to expand and wax boastful, and to talk politics. I can only say that they talked politics as well as the average middle-class man, and a great deal better than some of the middle-class men I have heard. What surprised me was the hold they had on the world, its geography and peoples, and on recent and contemporaneous history. As I say, they were not fools, these two men. They were merely old, and their children had undutifully failed to grow up and give them a place by the fire.

One last incident, as I bade them good-by on the corner, happy with a couple of shillings in their pockets and the certain prospect of a bed for the night. Lighting a cigarette, I was about to throw away the burning match when the Carter reached for it. I proffered him the box, but he said, "Never mind, won't waste it, sir." And while he lighted the cigarette I had given him, the Carpenter hurried with the filling of his pipe in order to have a go at the same match.

"It's wrong to waste," said he.

"Yes," I said, but I was thinking of the washboard ribs over which I had run my hand.

CARRYING THE BANNER

"To carry the banner" means to walk the streets all night; and I, with the figurative emblem hoisted, went out to see what I could see. Men and women walk the streets at night all over this great city, but I selected the West End, making Leicester Square my base, and scouting about from the Thames Embankment to Hyde Park.

The rain was falling heavily when the theatres let out, and the brilliant throng which poured from the places of amusement was hard put to find cabs. The streets were so many wild rivers of cabs, most of which were engaged, however; and here I saw the desperate attempts of ragged men and boys to get a shelter from the night by procuring cabs for the cabless ladies and gentlemen. I use the word "desperate" advisedly; for these wretched homeless ones were gambling a soaking against a bed; and most of them, I took notice, got the soaking and missed the bed. Now, to go through a stormy night with wet clothes, and, in addition, to be ill nourished and not to have tasted meat for a week or a month, is about as severe a hardship as a man can undergo. Well-fed and well-clad, I have travelled all day with the spirit thermometer down to seventy-four degrees below zero; and though I suffered, it was a mere nothing compared with carrying the banner for a night, ill-fed, ill-clad, and soaking wet.

The streets grew very quiet and lonely after the theatre crowd had gone home. Only were to be seen the ubiquitous policemen, flashing their dark lanterns into doorways and alleys, and men and women and boys taking shelter in the lee of buildings from the wind and rain. Piccadilly, however, was not quite so deserted. Its pavements were brightened by well dressed women without escort, and there was more life and action there than elsewhere, due to the process of finding escort. But by three o'clock the last of them had vanished, and it was then indeed lonely.

At half-past one the steady downpour ceased, and only showers fell thereafter. The homeless folk came away from the protection of the buildings, and slouched up and down and everywhere, in order to rush up the circulation and keep warm.

One old woman, between fifty and sixty, a sheer wreck, I had noticed earlier in the night, standing on Piccadilly, not far from Leicester Square. She seemed to have neither the sense nor the strength to get out of the rain or keep walking, but stood stupidly, whenever she got the chance, meditating on past days, I imagine, when life was young and blood was warm. But she did not get the chance often. She was moved on by every policeman, and it required an average of six moves to send her doddering off one man's beat and on to another's. By three o'clock she had progressed as far as

St. James Street, and as the clocks were striking four I saw her sleeping soundly against the iron railings of Green Park. A brisk shower was falling at the time, and she must have been drenched to the skin.

Now, said I, at one o'clock, to myself, consider that you are a poor young man, penniless, in London Town, and that tomorrow you must look for work. It is necessary, therefore, that you get some sleep in order that you may have strength to look for work and to do work in case you find it.

So I sat down on the stone steps of a building. Five minutes later a policeman was looking at me. My eyes were wide open, so he only grunted and passed on. Ten minutes later my head was on my knees, I was dozing, and the same policeman was saying gruffly, "Ere, you, get outa that!"

I got. And, like the old woman, I continued to get; for every time I dozed a policeman was there to rout me along again. Not long after, when I had given this up, I was walking with a young Londoner (who had been out to the colonies and wished he were out to them again) when I noticed an open passage leading under a building and disappearing in darkness. A low iron gate barred the entrance.

"Come on," I said. "Let's climb over and get a good sleep."

"Wot?" he answered, recoiling from me. "An' get run in fer three months! Blimey if I do!"

Later on, I was passing Hyde Park with a young boy of fourteen or fifteen, a most wretched-looking youth, gaunt, and hollow-eyed and sick.

"Let's go over the fence," I proposed, "and crawl into the shrubbery for a sleep. The bobbies couldn't find us there."

"No fear," he answered. "There's the park guardians, and they'd run you in for six months."

Times have changed, alas! When I was a youngster I used to read of homeless boys sleeping in doorways. Already the thing has become a tradition. As a stock situation it will doubtlessly linger in literature for a century to come, but as a cold fact it has ceased to be. Here are the doorways, and here are the boys, but happy conjunctions are no longer effected. The doorways remain empty, and the boys keep awake and carry the banner.

"I was down under the arches," grumbled another young fellow. By "arches" he meant the shore arches where begin the bridges that span the Thames. "I was down under the arches, w'en it was ryning its 'ardest, an' a bobby comes in an' chyses me out. But I come back, an' 'e come too. ' 'Ere,' sez 'e, 'wot you doin' ere?' An' out I goes, but I sez, 'Think I want to pinch the bleeding bridge?' "

Among those who carry the banner, Green Park has the reputation of opening its gates earlier than the other parks, and at quarter-past four in the morning, I, and many more, entered Green Park. It was raining again, but they were worn out with the night's walking, and they were down on the benches and asleep at once. Many of the men stretched out full length on the dripping wet grass, and, with the rain falling steadily upon them, were sleeping the sleep of exhaustion.

And now I wish to criticise the powers that be. They *are* the powers, therefore they may decree whatever they please; so I make bold only to criticise the ridiculousness of their decrees. All night long they make the homeless ones walk up and down. They drive them out of doors and passages, and lock them out of the parks. The evident intention of all this is to deprive them of sleep. Well and good, the powers have the power to deprive them of sleep, or of anything else for that matter; but why under the sun do they open the gates of the parks at five o'clock in the morning and let the homeless ones go inside and sleep? If it is their intention to deprive them of sleep, why do they let them sleep after five in the morning? And if it is not their intention to deprive them of sleep, why don't they let them sleep earlier in the night?

In this connection, I will say that I came by Green Park that same day, at one in the afternoon, and that I counted scores of the ragged wretches asleep in the grass. It was Sunday afternoon, the sun was fitfully appearing, and the well-dressed West Enders, with their wives and progeny, were out by thousands, taking the air. It was not a pleasant sight for them, those horrible, unkempt, sleeping vagabonds; while the vagabonds themselves, I know, would rather have done their sleeping the night before.

And so, dear soft people, should you ever visit London Town, and see these men asleep on the benches and in the grass, please do not think they are lazy creatures, preferring sleep to work. Know that the powers that be have kept them walking all the night long, and that in the day they have nowhere else to sleep.

THE MANAGEMENT

In this final chapter it were well to look at the Social Abyss in its widest aspect, and to put certain questions to Civilization, by the answers to which Civilization must stand or fall. For instance, has Civilization bettered the lot of man? "Man" I use in its democratic sense, meaning the average man. So the question reshapes itself: *Has Civilization bettered the lot of the average man?*

Let us see. In Alaska, along the banks of the Yukon River, near its mouth, live the Innuit folk. They are a very primitive people, manifesting but mere glimmering adumbrations of that tremendous artifice, Civilization. Their capital amounts possibly to $10 per head. They hunt and fish for their food with bone-headed spears and arrows. They never suffer from lack of shelter. Their clothes, largely made from the skins of animals, are warm. They always have fuel for their fires, likewise timber for their houses, which they build partly underground, and in which they lie snugly during the periods of intense cold. In the summer they live in tents, open to every breeze and cool. They are healthy and strong and happy. Their one problem is food. They have their times of plenty and times of famine. In good times they feast; in bad times they die of starvation. But starvation, as a chronic condition, present with a large number of them all the time, is a thing unknown. Further they have no debts.

In the United Kingdom, on the rim of the Western Ocean, live the English folk. They are a consummately civilized people. Their capital amounts to at least $1500 per head. They gain their food, not by hunting and fishing, but by toil at colossal artifices. For the most part they suffer from lack of shelter. The greater number of them are vilely housed, do not have enough fuel to keep them warm, and are insufficiently clothed. A constant number never have any house at all, and sleep shelterless under the stars. Many are to be found, winter and summer, shivering on the streets in their rags. They have good times and bad. In good times most of them manage to get enough to eat, in bad times they die of starvation. They are dying now, they were dying yesterday and last year, they will die tomorrow and next year, of starvation; for they unlike the Innuit, suffer from a chronic condition of starvation. There are 40,000,000 of the English folk, and 939 out of every 1000 of them die in poverty, while a constant army of 8,000,000 struggle on the ragged edge of starvation. Further, each babe that is born, is born in debt to the sum of $110. This is because of an artifice called the National Debt.

In a fair comparison of the average Innuit and the average Englishman, it will be seen that life is less rigorous for the Innuit; that while the Innuit suffers only during bad times from starvation, the Englishman suffers during good times as well; that no Innuit lacks fuel, clothing or housing, while the Englishman is in perpetual lack of these three essentials. In this connection it is well to instance the judgment of a man such as Huxley. From the knowledge gained as a medical officer in the East End of London, and as a scientist pursuing investigations among the most elemental savages, he concludes, "Were the alternative presented to me I would deliberately prefer the life of a savage to that of those people of Christian London."

The creature comforts man enjoys are the products of man's labor. Since Civilization has failed to give the average Englishman food and shelter equal to that enjoyed by the Innuit, the question arises: *Has Civilization increased the producing power of the average man?* If it has not increased man's producing power, then Civilization cannot stand.

But it will be instantly admitted, Civilization *has* increased man's producing power. Five men can produce bread for a thousand. One man can produce cotton cloth for 250 people, woolens for 300, and boots and shoes for 1000. Yet it has been shown throughout the pages of this book that English folk by the millions do not receive enough food, clothes and boots. Then arises the third and inexorable question: *If Civilization has increased the producing power of the average man, why has it not bettered the lot of the average man?*

There can be one answer only—MISMANAGEMENT. Civilization has made possible all manner of creature comforts and heart's delights. In these the average Englishman does not participate. If he shall be forever unable to participate, then Civilization falls. There is no reason for the continued existence of an artifice so avowed a failure. But it is impossible that men should have reared this tremendous artifice in vain. It stuns the intellect. To acknowledge so crushing a defeat is to give the death-blow to striving and progress.

One other alternative, and one other only, presents itself. *Civilization must be compelled to better the lot of the average man.* This accepted, it becomes at once a question of business management. Things profitable must be continued; things unprofitable must be eliminated. Either the Empire is a profit to England or it is a loss. If it is a loss, it must be done away with. If it is a profit, it must be managed so that the average man comes in for a share of the profit.

If the struggle for commercial supremacy is profitable, continue it. If it is not, if it hurts the worker and makes his lot worse than the lot of a savage, then fling foreign markets and industrial empire overboard. For it is a patent fact that if 40,000,000 people, aided by Civilization, possess a greater individual producing power than the Innuit, then those 40,000,000 people should enjoy more creature comforts and heart's delights than the Innuits enjoy.

If the 400,000 English gentlemen, "of no occupation," according to their own statement of the census of 1881, are unprofitable, do away with them. Set them to work ploughing game preserves and planting potatoes. If they are profitable, continue them by all means, but let it be seen to that the average Englishman shares somewhat in the profits they produce by working at no occupation.

In short, society must be reorganized, and a capable management put at the head. That the present management is incapable, there can be no discussion. It has drained the United Kingdom of its life-blood. It has enfeebled the stay-at-home folk till they are unable longer to struggle in the van of the competing nations. It has built up a West End and an East End as large as the Kingdom is large, in which one end is riotous and rotten, the other end sickly and underfed.

A vast empire is foundering on the hands of this incapable management. And by empire is meant the political machinery which holds together the English-speaking people of the world outside of the United States. Nor is this charged in a pessimistic spirit. Blood empire is greater than political empire, and the English of the New World and the Antipodes are strong and vigorous as ever. But the political empire under which they are nominally assembled is perishing. The political machine known as the British Empire is running down. In the hands of its management it is losing momentum every day.

It is inevitable that this management, which has grossly and criminally mismanaged, shall be swept away. Not only has it been wasteful and inefficient, but it has misappropriated the funds. Every worn-out, pasty-faced pauper, every blind man, every prison babe, every man, woman and child whose belly is gnawing with hunger pangs, is hungry because the funds have been misappropriated by the management.

Nor can one member of the managing class plead not guilty before the judgment bar of Man. "The living in their houses, and in the graves the dead," are challenged by every babe that dies of innutrition, by every girl that flees the sweater's den to the nightly promenade of Piccadilly, by every worked-out toiler that plunges into the canal. The food this managing class eats, the wine it drinks, the show it makes, and the fine clothes it wears, are challenged by eight million mouths which have never had enough to fill them, and by twice eight million bodies which have never been sufficiently clothed and housed.

There can be no mistake. Civilization has increased man's producing power an hundred fold, and through mismanagement the men of Civilization live worse than the beasts, and have less to eat and wear and protect them from the elements than the savage Innuit in a frigid climate who lives today as he lived in the stone age ten thousand years ago.

What Life Means to Me

I was born in the working-class. Early I discovered enthusiasm, ambition, and ideals; and to satisfy these became the problem of my child-life. My environment was crude and rough and raw. I had no outlook, but an uplook rather. My place in society was at the bottom. Here life offered nothing but sordidness and wretchedness, both of the flesh and the spirit; for here flesh and spirit were alike starved and tormented.

Above me towered the colossal edifice of society, and to my mind the only way out was up. Into this edifice I early resolved to climb. Up above, men wore black clothes and boiled shirts, and women dressed in beautiful gowns. Also, there were good things to eat, and there was plenty to eat. This much for the flesh. Then there were the things of the spirit. Up above me, I knew, were unselfishnesses of the spirit, clean and noble thinking, keen intellectual living. I knew all this because I read "Seaside Library" novels, in which, with the exception of the villains and adventuresses, all men and women thought beautiful thoughts, spoke a beautiful tongue, and performed glorious deeds. In short, as I accepted the rising of the sun, I accepted that up above me was all that was fine and noble and gracious, all that gave decency and dignity to life, all that made life worth living and that remunerated one for his travail and misery.

But it is not particularly easy for one to climb up out of the working-class—especially if he is handicapped by the possession of ideals and illusions. I lived on a ranch in California, and I was hard put to find the ladder whereby to climb. I early inquired the rate of interest on invested money, and worried my child's brain into an understanding of the virtues and excellencies of that remarkable invention of man, compound interest. Further, I ascertained the current rates of wages for workers of all ages, and the cost of living. From all this data I concluded that if I began immediately and worked and saved until I was fifty years of age, I could then stop working and enter into participation in a fair portion of the delights and goodnesses that would then be open to me higher up in society. Of course, I resolutely determined not to marry, while I quite forgot to consider at all that great rock of disaster in the working-class world— sickness.

But the life that was in me demanded more than a meagre existence of scraping and scrimping. Also, at ten years of age, I became a newsboy on the streets of a city, and found myself with a changed uplook. All about me were still the same sordidness and wretchedness, and up above me was still the same paradise waiting to be gained; but the ladder whereby to climb was a different one. It was now the ladder of business. Why save my earnings and invest in government bonds, when, by buying two newspapers for five cents, with a turn of the wrist I could sell them for ten cents and double my capital? The business ladder was the ladder for me, and I had a vision of myself becoming a baldheaded and successful merchant prince.

Alas for visions! When I was sixteen I had already earned the title of "prince." But this title was given me by a gang of cut-throats and thieves, by whom I was called "The Prince of the Oyster Pirates." And at that time I had climbed the first rung of the business ladder. I was a capitalist. I owned a boat and a complete oyster-pirating outfit. I had begun to exploit my fellow-creatures. I had a crew of one man. As captain and owner I took two-thirds of the spoils, and gave the crew one-third, though the crew worked just as hard as I did and risked just as much his life and liberty.

This one rung was the height I climbed up the business ladder. One night I went on a raid amongst the Chinese fishermen. Ropes and nets were worth dollars and cents. It was robbery, I grant, but it was precisely the spirit of capitalism. The capitalist takes away the possessions of his fellow-creatures by means of a rebate, or of a betrayal of trust, or by the purchase of senators and supreme-court judges. I was merely crude. That was the only difference. I used a gun.

But my crew that night was one of those inefficients against whom the capitalist is wont to fulminate, because, forsooth, such inefficients increase expenses and reduce dividends. My crew did both. What of his carelessness he set fire to the big mainsail and totally destroyed it. There weren't any dividends that night, and the Chinese fishermen were richer by the nets and ropes we did not get. I was bankrupt, unable just then to pay sixty-five dollars for a new mainsail. I left my boat at anchor and went off on a bay-pirate boat on a raid up the Sacramento River. While away on this trip, another gang of bay pirates raided my boat. They stole everything, even the anchors; and later on, when I recovered the drifting hulk, I sold it for twenty dollars. I had slipped back the one rung I had climbed, and never again did I attempt the business ladder.

From then on I was mercilessly exploited by other capitalists. I had the muscle, and they made money out of it while I made but a very indifferent living out of it. I was a sailor before the mast, a longshoreman, a roustabout; I worked in canneries, and factories, and laundries; I mowed lawns, and cleaned carpets, and washed windows. And I never got the full product of my toil. I looked at the daughter of the cannery owner, in her carriage, and knew that it was my muscle, in part, that helped drag along that carriage on its rubber tires. I looked at the son of the factory owner, going to college, and knew that it was my muscle that helped, in part, to pay for the wine and good fellowship he enjoyed.

But I did not resent this. It was all in the game. They were the strong. Very well, I was strong. I would carve my way to a place amongst them and make money out of the muscles of other men. I was not afraid of work. I loved hard work. I would pitch in and work harder than ever and eventually become a pillar of society.

And just then, as luck would have it, I found an employer that was of the same mind. I was willing to work, and he was more than willing that I should work. I thought I was learning a trade. In reality, I had displaced two men. I thought he was making an electrician out of me; as a matter of fact, he was making fifty dollars per month out of me. The two men I had displaced had received forty dollars each per month; I was doing the work of both for thirty dollars per month.

This employer worked me nearly to death. A man may love oysters, but too many oysters will disincline him toward that particular diet. And so with me. Too much work sickened me. I did not wish ever to see work again. I fled from work. I became a tramp, begging my way from door to door, wandering over the United States and sweating bloody sweats in slums and prisons.

I had been born in the working-class, and I was now, at the age of eighteen, beneath the point at which I had started. I was down in the cellar of society, down in the subterranean depths of misery about which it is neither nice nor proper to speak. I was in the pit, the abyss, the human cesspool, the shambles and charnel-house of our civilization. This is the part of the edifice of society that society chooses to ignore. Lack of space compels me here to ignore it, and I shall say only that the things I there saw gave me a terrible scare.

I was scared into thinking. I saw the naked simplicities of the complicated civilization in which I lived. Life was a matter of food and shelter. In order to get food and shelter men sold things. The merchant sold shoes, the politician sold his manhood, and the representative of the people, with exceptions, of course, sold his trust; while nearly all sold their honor. Women, too, whether on the street or in the holy bond of wedlock, were prone to sell their flesh. All things were commodities, all people bought and sold. The one commodity that labor had to sell was muscle. The honor of labor had no price in the market-place. Labor had muscle, and muscle alone, to sell.

But there was a difference, a vital difference. Shoes and trust and honor had a way of renewing themselves. They were imperishable stocks. Muscle, on the other hand, did not renew. As the shoe merchant sold shoes, he continued to replenish his stock. But there was no way of replenishing the laborer's stock of muscle. The more he sold of his muscle, the less of it remained to him. It was his one commodity, and each day his stock of it diminished. In the end, if he did not die before, he sold out and put up his shutters. He was a muscle bankrupt, and nothing remained to him but to go down into the cellar of society and perish miserably.

I learned, further, that brain was likewise a commodity. It, too, was different from muscle. A brain seller was only at his prime when he was fifty or sixty years old, and his wares were fetching higher prices than ever. But a laborer was worked out or broken down at forty-five or fifty. I had been in the cellar of society, and I did not like the place as a habitation. The pipes and drains were unsanitary, and the air was bad to breathe. If I could not live on the parlor floor of society, I could, at any rate, have a try at the attic. It was true, the diet there was slim, but the air at least was pure. So I resolved to sell no more muscle, and to become a vender of brains.

Then began a frantic pursuit of knowledge. I returned to California and opened the books. While thus equipping myself to become a brain merchant, it was inevitable that I should delve into sociology. There

I found, in a certain class of books, scientifically formulated, the simple sociological concepts I had already worked out for myself. Other and greater minds, before I was born, had worked out all that I had thought and a vast deal more. I discovered that I was a socialist.

The socialists were revolutionists, inasmuch as they struggled to overthrow the society of the present, and out of the material to build the society of the future. I, too, was a socialist and a revolutionist. I joined the groups of working-class and intellectual revolutionists, and for the first time came into intellectual living. Here I found keen-flashing intellects and brilliant wits; for here I met strong and alert-brained, withal horny-handed, members of the working-class; unfrocked preachers too wide in their Christianity for any congregation of Mammon-worshippers; professors broken on the wheel of university subservience to the ruling class and flung out because they were quick with knowledge which they strove to apply to the affairs of mankind.

Here I found, also, warm faith in the human, glowing idealism, sweetnesses of unselfishness, renunciation, and martyrdom—all the splendid, stinging things of the spirit. Here life was clean, noble, and alive. Here life rehabilitated itself, became wonderful and glorious; and I was glad to be alive. I was in touch with great souls who exalted flesh and spirit over dollars and cents, and to whom the thin wail of the starved slum child meant more than all the pomp and circumstance of commercial expansion and world empire. All about me were nobleness of purpose and heroism of effort, and my days and nights were sunshine and starshine, all fire and dew, with before my eyes, ever burning and blazing, the Holy Grail, Christ's own Grail, the warm human, long-suffering and maltreated, but to be rescued and saved at the last.

And I, poor foolish I, deemed all this to be a mere foretaste of the delights of living I should find higher above me in society. I had lost many illusions since the day I read "Seaside Library" novels on the California ranch. I was destined to lose many of the illusions I still retained.

As a brain merchant I was a success. Society opened its portals to me. I entered right in on the parlor floor, and my disillusionment proceeded rapidly. I sat down to dinner with the masters of society, and with the wives and daughters of the masters of society. The women were gowned beautifully, I admit; but to my naïve surprise I discovered that they were of the same clay as all the rest of the women I had known down below in the cellar. "The colonel's lady and Judy O'Grady were sisters under their skins"—and gowns.

It was not this, however, so much as their materialism, that shocked me. It is true, these beautifully gowned, beautiful women prattled sweet little ideals and dear little moralities; but in spite of their prattle the dominant key of the life they lived was materialistic. And they were so sentimentally selfish! They assisted in all kinds of sweet little charities, and informed one of the fact, while all the time the food they ate and the beautiful clothes they wore were bought out of dividends stained with the blood of child labor, and sweated labor, and of prostitution itself. When I mentioned such facts, expecting in my innocence that these sisters of Judy O'Grady would at once strip off their blood-dyed silks and jewels, they became excited and angry, and read me preachments about the lack of thrift, the drink, and the innate depravity that caused all the misery in society's cellar. When I mentioned that I couldn't quite see that it was the lack of thrift, the intemperance, and the depravity of a half-starved child of six that made it work twelve hours every night in a Southern cotton mill, these sisters of Judy O'Grady attacked my private life and called me an "agitator"—as though that, forsooth, settled the argument.

Nor did I fare better with the masters themselves. I had expected to find men who were clean, noble, and alive, whose ideals were clean, noble, and alive. I went about amongst the men who sat in the high places—the preachers, the politicians, the business men, the professors, and the editors. I ate meat with them, drank wine with them, automobiled with them, and studied them. It is true, I found many that were clean and noble; but with rare exceptions, they were not *alive*. I do verily believe I could count the exceptions on the fingers of my two hands. Where they were not alive with rottenness, quick with unclean life, they were merely the unburied dead—clean and noble, like well-preserved mummies, but not alive. In this connection I may especially mention the professors I met, the men who live up to that decadent university ideal, "the passionless pursuit of passionless intelligence."

I met men who invoked the name of the Prince of Peace in their diatribes against war, and who put rifles in the hands of Pinkertons with which to shoot down strikers in their own factories. I met men incoherent with indignation at the brutality of prize-fighting, and who, at the same time, were parties to the adulteration of food that killed each year more babies than even red-handed Herod had killed.

I talked in hotels and clubs and homes and Pullmans and steamer-chairs with captains of industry, and marvelled at how little travelled they were in the realm of intellect. On the other hand, I discovered that their intellect, in the business sense, was abnormally developed. Also, I discovered that their morality, where business was concerned, was nil.

This delicate, aristocratic-featured gentleman, was a dummy director and a tool of corporations that secretly robbed widows and orphans. This gentleman, who collected fine editions and was an especial patron of literature, paid blackmail to a heavy-jowled, black-browed boss of a municipal machine. This editor, who published patent medicine advertisements and did not dare print the truth in his paper about said patent medicines for fear of losing the advertising, called me a scoundrelly demagogue because I told him that his political economy was antiquated and that his biology was contemporaneous with Pliny.

This senator was the tool and the slave, the little puppet of a gross, uneducated machine boss; so was this governor and this supreme court judge; and all three rode on railroad passes. This man, talking soberly and earnestly about the beauties of idealism and the goodness of God, had just betrayed his comrades in a business deal. This man, a pillar of the church and heavy contributor to foreign missions, worked his shop girls ten hours a day on a starvation wage and thereby directly encouraged prostitution. This man, who endowed chairs in universities, perjured himself in courts of law over a matter of dollars and cents. And this railroad magnate broke his word as a gentleman and a Christian when he granted a secret rebate to one of two captains of industry locked together in a struggle to the death.

It was the same everywhere, crime and betrayal, betrayal and crime—men who were alive, but who were neither clean nor noble, men who were clean and noble but who were not alive. Then there was a great, hopeless mass, neither noble nor alive, but merely clean. It did not sin positively nor deliberately; but it did sin passively and ignorantly by acquiescing in the current immorality and profiting by it. Had it been noble and alive it would not have been ignorant, and it would have refused to share in the profits of betrayal and crime.

I discovered that I did not like to live on the parlor floor of society. Intellectually I was bored. Morally and spiritually I was sickened. I remembered my intellectuals and idealists, my unfrocked preachers, broken professors, and clean-minded, class-conscious workingmen. I remembered my days and nights of sunshine and starshine, where life was all a wild sweet wonder, a spiritual paradise of unselfish adventure and ethical romance. And I saw before me, ever blazing and burning, the Holy Grail.

So I went back to the working-class, in which I had been born and where I belonged. I care no longer to climb. The imposing edifice of society above my head holds no delights for me. It is the foundation of the edifice that interests me. There I am content to labor, crowbar in hand, shoulder to shoulder with intellectuals, idealists, and class-conscious workingmen, getting a solid pry now and again and setting the whole edifice rocking. Some day, when we get a few more hands and crowbars to work, we'll topple it over, along with all its rotten life and unburied dead, its monstrous selfishness and sodden materialism. Then we'll cleanse the cellar and build a new habitation for mankind, in which there will be no parlor floor, in which all the rooms will be bright and airy, and where the air that is breathed will be clean, noble, and alive.

Such is my outlook. I look forward to a time when man shall progress upon something worthier and higher than his stomach, when there will be a finer incentive to impel men to action than the incentive of to-day, which is the incentive of the stomach. I retain my belief in the nobility and excellence of the human. I believe that spiritual sweetness and unselfishness will conquer the gross gluttony of to-day. And last of all, my faith is in the working-class. As some Frenchman has said, "The stairway of time is ever echoing with the wooden shoe going up, the polished boot descending."

Newspaper Articles

Explanation of the Great Socialist Vote of 1904

The only people surprised by the heavy Socialist vote throughout the United States are the Democrats and Republicans.[1] The Socialists knew it all the time. Their campaign is twelve months long and they have a campaign every year, wherefore it was to be expected that they should know what was coming.

However, during the last several weeks of the campaign, the professional politicians began to awaken to something, they knew not what, that was in the air. In a remarkably quiet campaign, when their own rallies and mass meetings were unremarkable for size and enthusiasm, they were astonished at the sight of Debs and Hanford and the rest of the Socialist orators speaking continually to crowded houses.

Nay, the professional, old-party politicians were puzzled. Never in their experience had they witnessed mass meetings with a charge for admission, and it was beyond their imagination to conceive of such mass meetings being jammed to the doors, with overflow meetings taking place in the street and in nearby halls. Yet this was precisely what they witnessed in every large city of the United States when the Socialist candidates passed through.

Mark Hanna was, possibly, the only old party politician who saw clearly the Socialist trend. "The next great issue this country will have to meet will be Socialism," he said not long before he died.

It was his last political prophecy.

Ever since the 1900 campaign the National Committee of the Republican party, through its paid agents, has been gathering informa-

[1] For a discussion of the election see pages 59–61.—EDITOR.

tion concerning the strength of the Socialist movement in the United States. At the end of this careful canvass the Republican National Committee conceded 600,000 votes to Debs for the election just past. Full returns will show that the estimate was rather a conservative one.

A table of the Socialist vote in the United States, since the first Socialist ballots were cast, should be of interest.

1888	2,068	1897	55,550
1892	21,512	1898	82,204
1894	30,120	1900	98,424
1895	34,869	1902	225,903
1896	36,275		

The most notable thing in connection with the above table is the steady growth of the Socialist vote. Socialism has not arisen in a day, and by the same token it will not subside in a day. Whether it will ever subside is a question.

It has fastened upon every civilized country in the world, and in no country has it subsided. Not only that, but in every country it is stronger to-day than ever before, is constantly adding to its strength and constantly gaining a footing in new countries.

The thunder of the guns of the Spanish-American War had not yet died away when the Socialist group were forming in Cuba. No sooner had Japan joined the ranks of the manufacturing nations and begun to build machines and factories, than she found the Socialist organizers in her midst, bombarding the workingmen with pamphlets and speeches. And to-day the Socialists of Japan send greeting to the Socialists of Russia of which the following is an excerpt:

"Dear comrades, your government and ours have recently plunged into war to carry out their imperialistic tendencies, but for us Socialists there are no boundaries, race, country or nationality. We are comrades, brothers and sisters, and have no reason to fight. Your enemies are not the Japanese people, but our militarism and so-called patriotism."

There has been nothing mushroom-like in the growth of Socialism in the United States. It has been slow, and steady, and sure. "Once a Socialist always a Socialist," is the saying; and in truth, backsliding is a rare occurrence. Populism sprang up in a day and died down in a day. It was a mushroom growth. Its roots were not sunk into permanence. It was superficial, a surface issue which attracted a few million people who had been hurt by social wrong but who did not know what it was. They thought it was the gold standard, and they flocked to populism. But there was nothing fundamental to populism, in the very nature of things it could not last, and it perished as it had spawned, in unseemly haste.

But there is something fundamental to Socialism. It is nothing at all, if it is not in its very essence fundamental. It is a revolutionary movement that aims to pull down society to its foundation, and upon a new foundation to build a new society where shall reign order, equity and justice. "The capitalist must go!" is the battle-cry. "The brother-hood of man has waited long enough!"

In the history of man, Socialism is the first movement of men to involve the whole globe. None has been so widespreading, so far-reaching. It is international and world-wide. Compared with it, the supremacy of any ancient people was quite local; likewise the waves of Arabian fanaticism and the medieval crusades to the holy sepulchre. The Socialist movement is limited only by the limits of the planet.

Its banner is blood red (symbolizing the blood of man), and it preaches the passionate gospel of the brotherhood of man. It is an ethi-cal movement as well as an economic and political movement and, one may say, a religious movement as well. It is the politics and the gospel of the common man in his struggle against the uncommon man who has expressed his uncommonness by gathering to himself the wealth of the world.

Behind the Socialist movement in the United States is a most im-posing philosophic and scientific literature. It owns illustrated maga-zines and reviews high in quality, dignity and restraint; it possesses hundreds of weekly papers which circulate throughout the land, single papers which have subscribers by the hundreds of thousands, and it literally swamps the working classes in a vast sea of tracts and pam-phlets.

No political party in the United States, no church organization nor mission effort has as indefatigable workers as has the Socialist party. They multiply themselves, know of no effort or sacrifice too great to make for the cause, and "cause" with them is spelled out in capitals.

Let these men tell what they are doing, what is their aim; and the Debs vote will take on greater significance. They are preaching an uncompromising and deadly class struggle. In fact, they are organized upon the basis of a class struggle. The history of society, they say, is a history of class struggles. Patrician struggled with plebeian in early Rome, the nobles and the kings with merchant class at the close of the middle ages, and to-day the struggle is on between the triumphant merchant class and the rising working class.

That the working class shall conquer (mark the note of fatalism) is as certain as the rising of the sun. Just as the merchant class of the eighteenth century wanted democracy applied to politics, so the working class of the twentieth century wants democracy applied to industry, and to this end they organize the working classes into a political party that is a party of revolt.

This working-class, socialist revolt is a revolt against the capitalist class. The Socialist party aims to capture the political machinery of society. With the political machinery in its hands, which will also give it the control of the police, the army, the navy and the courts, its plan is to confiscate, with or without remuneration, all the possessions of the capitalist class which are used in the production and distribution of the necessaries and luxuries of life.

By this it means to apply the law of eminent domain to the land and to extend the law of eminent domain till it embraces the mines, the factories, the railroads and the ocean carriers. In short, the Socialist party intends to destroy present day society, which, it contends, is run in the interest of the merchant or capitalist class, and from the materials to construct a new society which will be run in the interest of the working class. And in that day, say the Socialists, all men will be workers, and there will be but one class, the working class.

This, in short, is the aim of the Socialist party of the United States and of the world. The vote cast for Debs day before yesterday was the tally of the American citizens who have raised the red banner of revolt. It is a working-class revolt against the economic masters of the United States.

How will the masters quell the revolt? That remains to be seen, but the masters must take one thing into consideration—there was never the like of this revolt in the world before. It is without precedent. It is a democratic revolt and must be fought out with ballots.

It is not a strife of lockout and blacklist, strike and boycott, employers' associations and labor unions, strike-breakers and broken heads, armed Pinkertons and injunctions, policemen's clubs and machine guns. It is a peaceable and orderly revolt at the ballot box, under democratic conditions, where the majority rules.

My masters, you are in the minority. How will you manage to keep the majority of the votes?

What will you, my masters; what will you?

Something Rotten in Idaho

THE TALE OF THE CONSPIRACY AGAINST MOYER, PETTIBONE AND HAYWOOD

Up in the State of Idaho, at the present moment, are three men lying in jail.[1] Their names are Moyer, Haywood and Pettibone. They are charged with the murder of Governor Steunenberg. Incidentally they are charged with thirty, sixty or seventy other atrocious murders. Not alone are they labor leaders and murderers, but they are anarchists. They are guilty, and they should be swiftly and immediately executed. It is to be regretted that no severer and more painful punishment than hanging awaits them. At any rate there is consolation in the knowledge that these men will surely be hanged.

The foregoing epitomises the information and beliefs possessed by the average farmer, lawyer, professor, clergyman and businessman in the United States. His belief is based upon the information he has gained by reading the newspapers. Did he possess different information, he might possibly believe differently. It is the purpose of this article to try to furnish information such as is not furnished by 99% of the newspapers of the United States.

In the first place, Moyer, Haywood and Pettibone were not even in the State of Idaho at the time the crime with which they are charged was committed. In the second place, they are at present in jail in the State of Idaho because of the perpetration of lawless acts by officers of the law, from the chief of the state executives down to the petty deputy chiefs—and this in collusion with mine owners' associations and railroad companies.

Here is conspiracy self-confessed and openly flaunted. And it is con-

[1] For a discussion of the Moyer-Haywood-Pettibone case see pages 85–86.— EDITOR

spiracy and violation of law on the part of the very men who claim that they are trying to bring punishment for conspiracy and violation of law. This is inconsistency, to say the least. It may be added that it is criminal inconsistency. Two wrongs have never been known to make a right. Yet the mine owners begin their alleged crusade for the right by committing wrong.

This is a bad beginning, and it warrants investigation and analysis of the acts, motives and characters of the mine owners; and incidentally an examination of the evidence they claim to have against Moyer, Haywood and Pettibone.

The evidence against these labor leaders is contained in the confession of one Harry Orchard. It looks bad, in the face of it, when a man confesses that at the instigation of another, and for money received from that other, he had committed murder. This is what Harry Orchard confesses.

But this is not the first time that these same labor leaders have been charged with murder; and this is not the first confession implicating them. Colorado is a fertile soil for confessions. Moyer, in particular, has been in jail many times charged with other murders. At least five men have solemnly sworn that at his instigation they have committed murder. Now it is a matter of history that when the tool confesses, the principal swings.

Moyer gives the lie to history. In spite of the many confessions he has never been convicted. This would make it look bad for the confessions. Not only does it make the confession look rotten, but the confessions, in turn, cast a doubt on the sweetness and purity of the present confession of Harry Orchard. In a region noted for the rottenness of its confession-fruit, it would be indeed remarkable to find this latest sample clean and wholesome.

When a man comes into court to give testimony, it is well to know what his character is, what his previous acts are, and whether or not self-interest enters into the case. Comes the mine owners' association of Colorado and Idaho to testify against Moyer, Haywood and Pettibone. Well, then, what sort of men are the mine owners? What have they done in the past?

That the mine owners have violated the laws countless times, there is no discussion. That they have robbed thousands of voters of their suffrage is common knowledge. That they have legalized lawlessness is history. But these things have only a general bearing on the matter at issue.

In particular, during and since the labor war that began in Colorado in 1903, the mine owners have charged the members of the Western Federation of Miners with all manner of crimes. There have been many trials, and in every trial the verdict has been acquittal. The testimony in these trials has been given by hired Pinkertons and spies. Yet the Pinkertons and spies, masters in the art of gathering evidence, have always failed to convict in the courts. This looks bad for the sort of evidence that grows in the fertile Colorado soil.

But it is worse than that. While the Pinkertons and spies have proved poor evidence-farmers, they have demonstrated they are good criminals. Many of them have been convicted by the courts and sent to jail for the commission of crimes ranging from theft to manslaughter.

Are the mine owners law abiding citizens? Do they believe in law? Do they uphold the law? "To hell with the Constitution" was their clearly enunciated statement in Colorado in 1903. Their military agent, General Sherman Bell said: "To hell with habeas corpus! We will give them post-mortems instead!" Governor Gooding, the present governor of Idaho, has recently said: "To hell with the people."

Now it is but natural to question the good citizenship of an organization of men that continuously and consistently consigns to hell the process of habeas corpus, the people and the Constitution. In Chicago a few years ago some men were hanged for uttering incendiary language not half so violent as this. But they were workingmen. The mine owners of Colorado and Idaho are the chief executives, or capitalists. They will not be hanged. On the contrary, they have their full liberty, such liberty they are exercising in an effort to hang some other men whom they do not like.

Why do some mine owners dislike Moyer, Haywood and Pettibone? Because these men stand between the mine owners and a pot of money. These men are leaders of organized labor. They plan and direct the efforts of the workingmen to get better wages and shorter hours. The operation of their mines will be more expensive. The higher the running expenses, the smaller the profits. If the mine owners could disrupt the Western Federation of Miners, they would increase the hours of labor, lower wages, and thereby gain millions of dollars. This is the pot of money.

It is a fairly respectable pot of money. Judas betrayed Christ to crucifixion for thirty pieces of silver. Human nature has not changed since that day, and it is conceivable that Moyer, Haywood and Pettibone may be hanged for the sake of a few millions of dollars. Not that the mine owners have anything personally against Moyer, Haywood and Pettibone, (Judas had nothing against Christ), but because the mine owners want the pot of money. Judas wanted the thirty pieces of silver.

That the foregoing is not merely surprising, it would be well to state that the mine owners have frequently and outspokenly announced that it is their intention to exterminate the Western Federation of Miners. Here is the motive clearly shown and expressed. It merits consideration on the part of every thoughtful and patriotic citizen.

In brief, the situation at present in Idaho is as follows: following a long struggle between capital and labor, the capitalist organization has jailed the leaders of the labor organization. The capitalist organization is trying to hang the labor leaders. It has tried to do this before, but its evidence and its "confessions" were always too rotten and corrupt. Its hired spies and Pinkertons have themselves been sent to prison for the commission of all manner of crimes, while they have never succeeded in sending one labor leader to prison.

The capitalist organization has been incendiary in speech, and by unlawful acts has lived up to its speech. It will profit by exterminating the labor organization. The capitalist organization has a bad character. It has never hesitated at anything to attain its ends. By sentiment and act it has behaved unlawfully, as have its agents whom it hired. The situation in Idaho? There can be but one conclusion—THERE IS SOMETHING ROTTEN IN IDAHO!

Strike Methods:
American and Australian

Australia is so different from other civilized countries that a new-comer is hard put to orientate himself.[1] Disregarding her various other unique characteristics, the man just landed on her shores is puzzled by Australia's economic and political situation. It is not until one comprehends that capitalism has not been permitted an unhindered development that he can understand, say, the conditions that obtain at present at Broken Hill.

When I read in the daily press of the pickets granting safe-conduct to persons entering or leaving the Proprietary mine, and venturing, on occasion, to hoot and jeer, I am amazed. In the United States, according to the law as interpreted at present, the union picket is a negligible quantity. He has no reason for existence. If he dared to assume the function of granting a safe-conduct to a man entering or leaving a private property, he would be assaulted by the police, both foot and horse, be charged by soldiers, and be swept out of existence by the fire of magazine rifles and machine guns. Nay, in the United States, a picket may not even venture to address a blackleg in terms of most conciliatory speech. Moral suasion of that order is considered an incendiary attack upon the constitution of the land and the liberty of the people, and any picket rash enough to say "Good morning" to a blackleg is hustled off immediately to gaol. And he is lucky, too, if the treasury of his union is not mulcted by due process of law of heavy civil damages.

Frankly and flatly, our police, private detectives, Pinkertons, and

[1] For a discussion of London's visit to Australia see page 99.—EDITOR.

professional gun-fighters, our constables, sheriffs, and United States marshals, our militia, regular army, and even our courts, fight the battles for capital against labor. Australia is so retarded in her development, or so advanced, if you please, that in industrial conflicts the function of civil and military authorities is the preservation of order merely. As a result industrial conflicts are carried on far more peacefully, and with much less disorder and violence than with us.

For with us a strike is practically civil war—a revolt against all the powers of government. Deny a union picket the right to attempt to exercise moral suasion on a blackleg, and he will the more readily hit the blackleg with a brick. Violence begets violence. Suppression causes explosion. Force is met with force, and when capital bombards labor with rifle-bullets, court injunctions, and suits for damages, Labor fights back with every weapon it can lay hands on. Primitive savagery takes the place of civilisation, and the officials of the morgues and the emergency hospitals work overtime.

Australia is fortunate. The uniqueness of her development—which I, for one, am too new a stranger to attempt to formulate—makes possible a more peaceable and orderly solution of her industrial difficulties. On the other hand, while Australia is so different in many phases, there are certain underlying principles that are universal, and that are as true of Australia as of all other countries in the world. The law of gravitation still obtains in the Antipodes; two plus two is neither more nor less than four, and the three angles of a triangle are equal to two right-angles. Human psychology is very much the same all over the earth's surface, and it is precisely the same where certain phases of the conduct of strikes are concerned. The average strike, in order to succeed, must have public opinion in favor of the strikers. This is true in Europe, in England, in America, and in Australia. Another general principle, equally true, is that the favor of public opinion is always lost when the strikers proceed to the destruction of property. Out of this has arisen the policy of Labor leaders to avoid the destruction of property.

So I make bold to assert that in the matter of blowing up watermains and wrecking railroad tracks at Broken Hill, the men who are conducting the strike have had no part. Tom Mann, for instance, is too wise a veteran in Labor struggles to enter upon such a suicidal course. And I make bold further to assert that the capitalists of Australia were no more elated by the petty destructions of property that have taken place than was Tom Mann grieved by them. Every such petty destruction constitutes a point in favor of the owners and against the strikers. If time ever clears such matters up, it is safe to surmise that the guilt will attach itself to isolated individuals of the larrikin order.

Were the scene in America, where we are more advanced in industrial warfare, the odds would favor that it was the captalists themselves who were responsible for the destruction of property. It is a way we have in the United States. I would not venture to charge the owners of Broken Hill with having a hand in the property destruction. It is true that such destruction is of signal benefit to the owners, insofar as it affects public opinion. But, on the other hand, I am a stranger in Australia, and I do not know how wise the employers are. Besides, I think they are such tyros in industrial warfare that they have not yet risen to the effrontery of destroying their own property in order to break a strike.

In America the capitalists destroy their own property as a matter of course. Mr. Carroll D. Wright, United States Commissioner of Labor, in his report to the Government upon the great railroad strike, announced that the railroads themselves had been responsible for burning many freight cars. It is such a simple device. And so handy. It always turns public opinion against the strikers, and enables the authorities to call out the troops. In the labor troubles in the mining regions of the west, the owners blew up their mines, and, on one occasion, blew up a railroad station, killing a score or more of scab miners. This latter was not intended, of course. The explosion was intended to occur before the scabs arrived on the scene. But, as some poet has said, it is an awkward thing to play with gunpowder.

Another trick of the capitalists in the United States is to get the strike leaders in gaol. This is equivalent to removing the general from the battlefield in the midst of the battle. In the A.R.U. strike, Eugene Debs was thus hustled away and put into gaol for six months for contempt of court. It was like removing Wellington from Waterloo in the middle of the day. Naturally, the A.R.U. strike was broken.

In 1894, under stress of hard times many thousands of the unemployed banded into "armies," and marched to Washington to demand work from the Government. The leader was one Coxey. It was a grave situation. But the authorities solved it. The day the great demonstration took place in front of the Capitol at Washington the police shoved Coxey on to the grass and then arrested him for trespass. I see that Tom Mann has been arrested for trespass at Broken

Hill. This leads one to the tentative generalisation that Australia is retarded in her development, rather than advanced, for our authorities in the United States worked that same trick fifteen years ago.

Why do we have strikes, anyway? The average man accepts them as uncomfortable but natural phenomena which must be put up with, but seems to be without any clear understanding of the underlying reason for the existence of strikes.

In order to get a glimpse of this reason, analyze any particular industrial process. Consider that here is a shoe factory. Raw leather, say, to the value of £100, goes into the factory and comes out as finished shoes, say, to the value of £200. What has happened? In some way a value of £100 has been added. How was it added? Capital and labor combined to add it. Capital furnished the factory, the machines, the raw leather, and the running expenses. Labor furnished the labor. Thus, this £100 of added value is the joint product of capital and labor.

Now comes the question of the division of the joint product. Capital takes its share in profits. Labor takes its share in wages. And it is right here, over this division of the joint product, that all the trouble arises. The laborers are men, the capitalists are men, and one of the fundamental traits of human nature is selfishness. In the division of the joint product, capital wants all its can get, and labor wants all it can get. Capital and labor therefore proceed to squabble over the division. When the squabbling becomes intense, there is a strike. Labor calls all the gods to witness that if it doesn't get more of the joint product it will be blowed if it makes any more joint product. And capital says the same thing. And there you are, two kiddies quarreling over the same piece of bread and butter.

And remember this: whatever is true of this particular industrial process is true of every other industrial process. Capital and labor, combining to produce joint products, quarrel over the division of the joint products. Many will ask the question: Will industrial peace ever come? And the only answer is that it will never come so long as the present system of industrial production obtains. Human nature will not change. Capital will continue to want all it can get, and labor will continue to want all it can get. And on both sides they will fight to get it. No, the lion and lamb will never lie down together in vegetarian pastures.

"Then must we forever endure the irrational anarchy of strikes and lockouts?" some one asks. Not so, is the answer. There are two ways by which industrial peace may be achieved. Either capital will own labor absolutely, and there will be no more strikes, or labor will own capital absolutely, and there will be no more strikes. Personally, I think labor will come to own capital. Every capitalist might die to-night, but the capital would remain. Labor could blow the whistle and go to work to-morrow morning as it did this morning. But if all labor died to-night it would take its labor-power with it. There would be no whistle blown to-morrow morning, for, alas! there would be no labor getting up steam in the boiler.

Furthermore, it is illogical to think of capital absolutely owning labor. It would mean chattel slavery, a trend backward to primeval night out of which civilisation has emerged. And civilisation has marked the rise of the common man, of labor, if you please. It would seem, from reading the past, that the future belongs to labor. And in the day that industrial democracy is added to political democracy, all will be laborers. There will be far vaster capital in existence, but there will be no capitalists. In other words, the system of production for profit will have been replaced by the system of production for service.

Essays

What Communities Lose
by the Competitive System

Man's primacy in the animal kingdom was made possible, first, by his
manifestation of the gregarious instinct; and second, by his becoming
conscious of this instinct and the power within it which worked for
his own good and permitted him to endure. Natural selection, un-
deviating, pitiless, careless of the individual, destroyed or allowed to
perpetuate, as the case might be, such breeds as were unfittest or fittest
to survive. In this sternest of struggles man developed the greatest
variability, the highest capacity for adaptation; thus he became the
favored child of the keenest competition ever waged on the planet.
Drawing his strength and knowledge from the dugs of competition,
he early learned the great lesson: that he stood alone, unaided, in a
mighty battle wherein all the natural forces and the myriad forms of
organic life seethed in one vast, precarious turmoil. From this he
early drew the corollary, that his strength lay in numbers, in unity
of interests, in solidarity of effort—in short, in combination against
the hostile elements of his environment. His history substantiates it.
From the family to the tribe, to the federation of tribes, to the nation,
to the (to-day) growing consciousness of the interdependence of nations, he has obeyed it; by his successes, his mistakes and his failures,
he has proved it. There is much to condemn, much which might have
been better, but in the very nature of things, not one jot or tittle could
have been otherwise than it has. And to-day, while he may felicitate
himself on his past, none the less vigilant must be his scrutiny of the
future. He cannot stop. He must go on.

But of the various forms of combination or coöperation which have
marked the progress of man, none has been perfect; yet have they

possessed, in a gradually ascending scale, less and less of imperfection. Every working political and social organism has maintained, during the period of its usefulness and in accordance with time and place, an equilibrium between the claims of the individual and the claims of society. When the balance was destroyed, either by too harsh an assertion of the right of the single life or the right of the type, the social organism has passed away, and another, adjusted to the changed conditions, replaced it. While the individual has made apparent sacrifices in the maintenance of this equilibrium, and likewise society, the result has been identity of interest, and good, both for the single life and the type. And in pursuance of this principle of the coöperation of man against the hostile elements of his environment, social compacts or laws have been formulated and observed. By the surrender of certain rights, the friction between the units of the social organism has been reduced, so that the organism might continue to operate. The future and inevitable rise of the type and the social organism, must necessitate a still further reduction in the friction of its units. Internal competition must be minimized, or turned into channels other than those along which it works to-day. This brings us to a discussion of the present: What the community loses by the competitive system.

All things being equal, ten thousand acres of arable land, under one executive, worked en bloc, say for the purpose of growing wheat, utilizing the most improved methods of plowing, sowing and harvesting, will produce greater returns at less expense than can an equal number of acres, divided into one hundred plots, and worked individually by one hundred men. If the community, believing this friction of its units to be logical, farms in the latter manner, it must suffer a distinct pecuniary loss. And the effects of this loss—call it lack of gain if you will—though apparently borne by the agrarian population, are equally felt by the urban population. Of the many items which at once suggest themselves, consider the simple one of fences. For the division of land in the state of Indiana alone, their cost is computed at two hundred million dollars, and if placed in single file at the equator, they would encircle the globe fourteen times. Under a scientific system of agriculture they could be almost wholly dispensed with. As it is, they represent just so much waste of energy, just so much real loss of wealth. And these losses, of which the preceding is but one of a host, may be attributed to a certain asserted right of the individual to private ownership in land.

To this division of land among individuals, whether in the country, in the city or in franchises, may be traced numerous other losses and grotesque features of the community. Lack of combination in the country causes expensive crops; in the city, expensive public utilities and service, and frightful architectural monstrosities. If a street railway corporation can issue an annual dividend of ten per cent to its shareholders, the community, through lack of the coöperation necessary to run that railway for itself, has lost the ten per cent, which otherwise it might have enjoyed in bettering its transit service, by the building of recreative parks, by the founding of libraries, or by increasing the efficiency of its schools. With regard to architecture, the presence of coöperation among individuals is most notable where it occurs, most notorious where it is absent. Some few of the public buildings, and many tasteful portions of the select resident districts, are examples of the one; sky-scrapers and rattle-trap tenements, of the other. A pumpkin between two planks, unable to obtain a proper rotundity, will lengthen out. Want of combination among adjacent property-owners, and the sky-scraper arises. A pumpkin is denied volition; man is not. The pumpkin cannot help itself; man may remove the planks. There is a certain identity in the raison d'être of the pumpkin and the sky-scraper. Man may remedy either, for to him is given the power of reacting against his environment.

If one were to hire two men to do his gardening when there was no more work than could reasonably be done by one, how quickly his neighbor would decry his extravagance! Yet in the course of the day, with the greatest equanimity, that same neighbor will fare forth and pay his quota for a score of services each performed by two or more men where only one is required. But he is dense to this loss to the community, which he, as a member, must pay. On his street from two to a dozen milkmen deliver their wares, likewise as many butchers, bakers and grocers; yet one policeman patrols and one postman serves the whole district. Downtown are a dozen groceries, each paying rent, maintaining fixtures and staffs of employees, and doing business within half as many blocks. One big store could operate the distributing function performed by these dozen small ones, and operate it more efficiently and at far less cost and labor. The success of the great department stores is a striking proof of this. The department store, in wiping out competition, gets greater returns out of less effort. And having destroyed competition, there is no longer any reason that it should exist, save as the common property of the community to be

operated for the community's common good. It cannot be denied that
the community would gain by so operating it, and not only in this but
in all similar enterprises.

Take, for instance, because of this prerogative of friction the units
of society maintain as their right, another series of burdens borne by
the community. To make it concrete, let the drummer class serve as an
illustration. Certainly fifty thousand is a conservative estimate for the
drummers or traveling men of the United States. And it is very conservative to place their hotel bills, traveling expenses, commissions
and salaries at five dollars a day per man. Since the producer must
sell his wares at a profit or else go out of business, the consumer must
pay the actual cost of the article—whether it be the legitimate cost or
not—plus the per cent increment necessary for the continued existence of the producer's capital. Therefore the community, being the
consumer, must support these fifty thousand five-dollar-a-day drummers; this, aggregated, forms a daily loss to the community of a
quarter of a million, or an annual loss of upward of a hundred millions
of dollars. Nor, from the economic view, is this the sum total of the
community's loss. These drummers are not legitimate creators of
wealth. The cost they add to the articles they sell is an unnecessary
one. The function they carry on in society is absolutely useless. Their
labor is illegitimately expended. Not only have they done nothing,
but they have been paid as though they had done something. Assuming eight hours to be the normal working day, they have, in the
course of the year, taking Sundays and holidays into consideration,
thrown away one hundred and twenty millions of working hours. The
community has paid for this and lost it. It possesses nothing to show
for their labor, save a heavy item in its expense account. But what a
gain there would have been had they devoted their time to the planting of potatoes or the building of public highways! And it must be
borne in mind that this is but one of a long series of similar burdens
which may be assembled under the head of "commercial waste." Consider the one item of advertisement. To make the advertisements
which litter the streets, desecrate the air, pollute the country, and
invade the sanctity of the family circle, a host of people are employed,
such as draftsmen, paper-makers, printers, bill-posters, painters, carpenters, gilders, mechanics, et cetera. Soap and patent-medicine firms
have been known to expend as high as half a million dollars a year
for their advertising. All this appalling commercial waste is drained
from the community. Commercial waste exists in many forms, one

of which is the articles made to sell, not use, such as adulterated foods and shoddy goods; or, to travesty Matthew Arnold, razors which do not shave, clothing which does not wear, watches which will not run.

Let one other example of the loss of effort suffice: that of competing corporations. Again to be concrete, let the example be a public municipal utility. A water company has the necessary water supply, the necessary facilities for distributing it, and the necessary capital with which to operate the plant. It happens to be a monopoly, and the community clamors for competition. A group of predatory capitalists invades the established company's territory, tears up the streets, parallels the other company's mains, and digs, tunnels and dams in the hills to get the necessary commodity. In view of the fact that the other company is fully capacitated to supply the community, this is just so much waste of effort; and equally so, some one must pay for it. Who? Let us see. A rate war ensues. Water becomes a drug on the market. Both companies are operating at ruinous losses, which must ultimately destroy them. There are three ways by which the struggle may be concluded. First, the company with the smallest capital may go under. In this case the capitalists have lost the money invested, the community the labor. But this rarely happens. Second, the wealthier company may buy out the poorer one. In this case it has been forced to double its invested capital. Since it is now become a monopoly, and since capital requires a certain definite rate of interest, the community's water bills must rise to satisfy it. Third, both companies being of equal strength, and a Kilkenny-cat conclusion being impossible, they combine, with doubled capital which demands a double return. In one of these three ways the competition of corporations must inevitably result; nor can the community escape the consequent loss, save by the coöperative operation of all such industries.

Because of the individual performance of many tasks which may be done collectively, effort entails a corresponding costliness. Since much that might have been included under this head has been previously discussed, such labors as may be purely individual shall be here handled. In the field of household economics there are numerous losses of this nature. Of these, choose one. Contemplate that humble but essentially necessary item, the family wash. In a hundred houses, on washing-day, are one hundred toiling housewives, one hundred homes for the time being thrown out of joint, one hundred fires, one hundred tubs being filled and emptied, and so forth and so on—

soap, powder, bluing, fuel and fixtures, all bought at expensive retail prices. Two men, in a well-appointed small steam-laundry, could do their washing for them, year in and year out, at a tithe the expense and toil. Disregarding the saving gained by the wholesale purchase of supplies, by system, and by division of labor, these two men, by machinery alone, increase their power tenfold. By means of a proper domestic coöperation, if not municipal, each of these housewives would save a sum of money which would go far in purchasing little luxuries and recreations.

Again, consider the example of the poorer families of a large town, who buy their food and other necessaries from at least one hundred shops of one sort and another. Here, the costliness of effort for which they pay is not theirs but that of the people they deal with. Instead of one large distributing depot, these one hundred petty merchants each order and handle separate parcels of goods, write separate letters and checks, and keep separate books, all of which is practically unnecessary. Somebody pays for all this, for the useless letters, checks, parcels, clerks, bookkeepers and porters, and assuredly it is not the shopkeeper. And aside from all this, suppose each shop clears for its owner ten dollars a week—a very modest sum—or five hundred dollars a year. For the one hundred shops this would equal fifty thousand dollars. And this the poorer members of the community must pay.

The people have come partially to recognize this, however. To-day no man dreams of keeping his own fire-fighting or street-lighting apparatus, of maintaining his own policeman, keeping his street in repair, or seeing to the proper disposition of his sewage. Somewhere in the past his ancestors did all this for themselves, or else it was not done at all; that is to say, there was greater friction or less coöperation among the units of society then than now.

At one time our forefathers, ignorant of hygiene, sanitation and quarantine, were powerless before the plagues which swept across the earth; yet we, their enlightened descendants, find ourselves impotent in the face of the great social cataclysms known as trade and commercial crises. The crises are peculiarly a modern product—made possible by the specialization of industry and the immense strides which have been taken in the invention of labor-saving machinery, but due, and directly so, to the antagonism of the units which compose society. A competent coöperative management could so operate all the implements and institutions of the present industrial civilization, that there need never be a fear of a trade or commercial crisis. Boards or departments, scientifically conducted, could ascertain, first, the consuming power of the community ; second, its producing power ; and then, by an orderly arrangement, adjust these two, one to the other. These boards or departments would have to study all the causes which go to make the community's producing power inconstant— such as failure of crops, drouths, et cetera—and so to direct the energy of the community that equilibrium between its production and consumption might still be maintained. And to do this is certainly within the realm of man's achievement.

But instead of this logical arrangement of industry, the community to-day possesses the chaotic system of competitive production. It is a war of producers, also of distributors. Success depends on individual knowledge of just how much and at what cost all others are producing, and of just how much and at what prices they are selling. All the factors which decide the fluctuations of the world's markets or the purchasing power of its peoples, must be taken into account. A war-cloud in the Balkans, a failure of crops in the Argentine, the thoughtless word of a kaiser, or a strike of organized labor, and success or failure depends on how closely the results of this event have been foreseen. And even then, because of a thousand and one fortuitous happenings, chance plays an important part. Even the footing of the wisest and the surest is precarious. Risk is the secret of gain. Lessen the risk, the gain is lessened; abolish it, and there can be no gain. Individual strives against individual, producing for himself, buying for himself, selling for himself, and keeping his transactions secret. Everybody is in the dark. Each is planning, guessing, chancing ; and because of this, the competitive system of industry, as a whole, may be justly characterized as planless. The effort lost is tremendous, the waste prodigal. A favorable season arrives. Increased orders accelerate production. Times are prosperous. All industries are stimulated. Little heed is taken of the overstocking of the markets, till at last they are flooded with commodities. This is the danger-point. The collapse of a land-boom in Oregon, the failure of a building association in Austria—anything may start the chain of destruction. Speculations begin to burst, credits to be called in, there is a rush to realize on commodities produced, prices fall, wages come down, factories close up, and consumption is correspondingly reduced. The interdependence of all forms of industry asserts itself. One branch of trade stops, and those branches dependent upon it, or allied with it, cannot

continue. This spreads. Depression grows, failures increase, industry
is paralyzed. The crisis has come! And then may be observed the
paradoxical spectacle of glutted warehouses and starving multitudes.
Then comes the slow and painful recovery of years, then an accelera-
tion of planless production, and then another crisis. This is friction,
the inevitable correlative of a disorderly system of production and
distribution. And the losses incurred by such friction are incalculable.

The forces of evolution, effecting their ends under various guises,
are, after all, one and the same in principle. They are conscious of
neither good nor evil, and work blindly. In any given environment
they decide which are to survive and which to perish. But the environment they do not question; it is no concern of theirs, for they work
only with the material that is. Nor are they to be bribed or deceived.
If it be a good environment, they will see to it that the good endure
and the race be lifted; if an evil environment, they will select the evil
for survival, and degeneration or race deterioration will follow.

In the world primeval, man was almost utterly the creature of his
natural environment. Possessing locomotion, he could change the
conditions which surrounded him only by removing himself to some
other portion of the earth's surface. But man so developed that the
time came when he could change his natural environment, not by
removing but by reacting upon it. If there were ferocious animals, he
destroyed them; pestilential marshes, he drained them. He cleared
the ground that he might till it, made roads, built bridges—in short,
conquered his natural environment. Thus it was that the road-maker
and bridge-builder survived, and those who would make neither
roads nor bridges were stamped out.

But to-day, in all but the most primitive communities, man has
conquered his natural environment and become the creature of an
artificial environment which he himself has created. Natural selection
has seemingly been suspended; in reality, it has taken on new forms.
Among these may be noted military and commercial selection. In-
tertribal warfare, in which farming and fighting are carried on alike
by all male members of the community, does not give rise to military
selection. This arises only when tribes have united to form the state,
and division of labor decides it to be more practicable that part of the
community farm all the time, and part of the community fight all the
time. Thus is created the standing army and the regular soldier. The
stronger, the braver, the more indomitable, are selected to go to the
wars, and to die early, without offspring. The weaker are sent to the

plow and permitted to perpetuate their kind. As Doctor Jordan has remarked, the best are sent forth, the second-best remain. But it does not stop at this. The best of the second-best are next sent, and the third-best is left. The French peasant of to-day demonstrates what manner of man is left to the soil after one hundred years or so of military selection. Where are the soldiers of Greece, Sparta and Rome? They lie on countless fields of battle, and with them their descendants which were not. The degenerate peoples of those countries are the descendants of those who remained to the soil—"of those who were left," as Doctor Jordan aptly puts it.

To-day, however, more especially among ourselves, military selection has waned, but commercial selection has waxed. Those members of the social organism who are successful in the warfare of the units, are the ones selected to survive. Regardless of the real welfare of the race, those individuals who better adapt themselves to the actual environment are permitted to exist and perpetuate themselves. Under the industrial system as at present conducted, in all branches the demand for units is less than is the supply. This renders the unit helpless. Trade is unsentimental, unscrupulous. The man who succeeds in acquiring wealth, is assured of his own survival and that of his progeny. Much selfishness and little altruism must be his, and the heritage he passes down; otherwise he will not acquire his wealth, nor his descendants retain theirs, and both he and they will be relegated to the middle class. Here the keenest and usually the more conscienceless trader survives. If he be unwise or lenient in his dealings, he will fail and descend to the working class. Conditions here change. The individual who can work most, on least, and bow his head best to the captains of industry, survives. If he cannot do these things well, his place is taken by those who can, and he falls into the slum class. Again conditions change. In the slums, the person who brings with him or is born there with normal morals, et cetera, must either yield or be exterminated; for the criminal, the beggar and the thief are best fitted to survive in such an environment and to propagate their kind.

Briefly outlined, this is commercial selection. The individual asserts its claims, to the detriment and injury of the type. It is well known that the intensity of the struggle has increased many fold in the last five decades, and it is self-evident that its intensity must still further and frightfully increase in the next five decades, unless the present system of production and distribution undergoes a modification for the better. Retaining it in its entirety, there are two salutary but at the same time absurd ways of ameliorating things: either kill off half the units, or destroy all machinery. But this is as temporary as it is unwise. Only a little while and commercial selection would again prevail. Besides, man must go forward; he can neither stop nor turn back. Commercial selection means race prostitution, and if continued, race deterioration. Internal competition must be minimized and industry yield more and more to the coöperative principle. For the good of the present and the future generations, certain rights of the individual must be curtailed or surrendered. Yet this is nothing new to the individual; his whole past is a history of such surrenders.

The old indictment that competitive capital is soulless, still holds. Altruism and industrial competition are mutually destructive. They cannot exist together. The struggling capitalist who may entertain philanthropic notions concerning the conduct of his business, is illogical, and false to his position and himself, and if he persist he will surely fail. Competitive industry is not concerned with right or wrong; its sole and perpetual query is, How may I undersell my competitors? And one answer only is vouchsafed: By producing more cheaply. The capitalist who wishes to keep his head above the tide must scale his labor and raw material as relentlessly as do his business rivals, or even a little more so. There are two ways of scaling raw material: by reducing quality and adulterating, or by forcing the producer to sell more cheaply. But the producer cannot scale nature; there is nothing left for him to do but scale his labor. Altruism is incompatible with business success. This being so, foul air, vile water, poor and adulterated foods, unhealthy factory work, crowding, disease, and all that drags down the physical, mental and moral tone of the community, are consistent and essential adjuncts of the competitive system.

As being the more striking, the only form of art here considered will be that which appears to the mind through the eye; but what is said will apply, subject to various modifications, to all other forms of the esthetic. Art is at present enjoyed by a greatly favored but very small portion of the community—the rich and those that are permitted to mingle with them. The poor, lacking not only in time and means but in the training so essential to a just comprehension of the beautiful, and having offered to them only the inferior grades, and because of all this, reacting upon an already harsh environment, live unlovely lives and die without having feasted their souls on the real treasures of life.

And even to the rich and those that cling about their skirts, only fleeting visions may be had of art. Their homes and galleries may be all the soul desires; but the instant they venture on the streets of the city, they have left the realm of beauty for an unsightly dominion, where the utilitarian makes the world hideous and survives, and the idealist is banished or exterminated.

Art, to be truly effective, should be part and parcel of life, and pervade it in all its interstices. It should be work-a-day as well as idle-day. Full justice should be accorded the artist of the period; to do this the whole community should enjoy, appreciate and understand the work of one who has toiled at creating the beautiful. Nor can this be done till the belly-need is made a subsidiary accompaniment of life, instead of being, as it now is to so many, the sole and all-important aim.

Present-day art may be characterized as a few scattered oases amid a desert of industrial ugliness. Not even among the rich can all refresh themselves at the founts. The nineteenth-century business man has no time for such. He is the slave of his desk, the genie of the dollar.

The artist exerts himself for a very small audience indeed. The general public never attains a standard of comprehension; it cannot measure his work. It looks upon his wares in the light of curiosities, baubles, luxuries, blind to the fact that they are objects which should conduce to the highest pleasure. And herein great injury is done the artist, and heavy limitations are laid upon him. But so long as "society flourishes by the antagonism of its units," art, in its full, broad scope, will have neither place nor significance; the artist will not receive justice for his travail, nor the people compensation for their labor in the common drudgery of life.

Variety is the essence of progress; its manifestation is the manifestation of individuality. Man advanced to his dominant position among the vertebrate because his "apelike and probably arboreal ancestors" possessed variety to an unusual degree. And in turn, the races of man possessing the greatest variability advanced to the center of the world-stage, while those possessing the least retreated to the background or to oblivion.

There should be no one type of man. A community in which all men are run in the same mold is virtually bankrupt, though its strong-boxes be overflowing with the treasures of the world. Such a community can endure only through a process of vegetation; it must remain silent or suffer ignominy. An instance of this is afforded by Spain and her Invincible Armada. The Spaniards were great fighting-men; so were the

English. But the English could also build ships and sail them, cast cannon and shoot them. In short, the English possessed and utilized variety. Spain, through a vicious social selection, had lost the greater part of the variety which was hers in former times. Nor was this loss due to an innate degeneracy of her people, but to her social, political and religious structures.

A people must have some standard by which to measure itself and its individuals; then it must shape its institutions in such manner as will permit its attaining this standard. If the measure of individual worth be, *How much have I made?* the present competitive system is the best medium by which to gain that end; but under all its guises it will form a certain type—from the factory hand to the millionaire there will be the one stamp of material acquisitiveness. But if the measure be, *What have I made of myself?* it cannot be attained by the present system. The demand of the belly-need is too strong; the friction too great: individuality is repressed, forced to manifest itself in acquisitiveness and selfishness. And after all, the greatness of a community lies not in the strength of its strong-boxes, nor in the extravagant follies of a few of its members, but in its wisdom, its power for good, and its possibility of realizing in itself the highest and the best. It were well to stand, as Doctor Jordan has said, "for civic ideals, and the greatest of these, that government should make men by giving them freedom to make themselves."

Wanted: A New Law
of Development

Evolution is no longer a mere tentative hypothesis. One by one, step by step, each division and subdivision of science has contributed its evidence, until now the case is complete and the verdict rendered. While there is still discussion as to the method of evolution, none the less, as a process sufficient to explain all biological phenomena, all differentiations of life into widely diverse species, families, and even kingdoms, evolution is flatly accepted. Likewise has been accepted its law of development: That, in the struggle for existence, the strong and fit and the progeny of the strong and fit have a better opportunity for survival than the weak and less fit and the progeny of the weak and less fit.[1]

It is in the struggle of the species with other species and against all other hostile forces in the environment, that this law operates; also in the struggle between the individuals of the same species. In this struggle, which is for food and shelter, the weak individuals must obviously win less food and shelter than the strong. Because of this, their hold on life relaxes and they are eliminated forthwith. And for the same reason that they may not win for themselves adequate food and shelter, the weak cannot give to their progeny the chance for survival that the strong do. And thus, since the weak are prone to beget weakness, the species is constantly purged of its inefficient members.

Because of this a premium is placed upon strength, and so long as the struggle for food and shelter obtains, just so long will the average strength of each generation rise. On the other hand, should conditions

[1] Benjamin Kidd has well worded this biological law.

so change that all, and the progeny of all, the weak as well as the
strong, have an equal chance for survival, then, at once, the average
strength of each generation will begin to fall. Never yet, however, in
animal life, has there been such a state of affairs. Natural selection
has always obtained. The strong and their progeny, at the expense of
the weak, have always survived. This law of development has operated
down all the past upon all life; it so operates to-day, and it is not rash
to say that it will continue to operate in the future—at least upon all
life existing in a state of nature.

Man, pre-eminent though he is in the animal kingdom and capable
of reacting upon and making suitable an unsuitable environment,
nevertheless remains the creature of this same law of development.
The social selection he is subject to is merely another form of natural
selection. True, within certain narrow limits he modifies the struggle
for existence and renders less precarious the tenure of life for the weak.
The extremely weak, diseased, and inefficient, are housed in hospitals
and asylums. The strength of the viciously strong, when inimical to
society, is tempered by penal institutions and by the gallows. The
shortsighted are provided with spectacles, and the sickly (when they
can pay for it) with sanitariums. Pestilential marshes are drained,
plagues are checked, and disasters averted. Yet, for all that, the strong
and the progeny of the strong survive, and the weak are crushed out.
The men, strong of brain, are masters as of yore. They dominate society and gather to themselves the wealth of society. With this wealth
they maintain themselves and equip their progeny for the struggle.
They build their homes in healthy places, purchase the best fruits,
meats, and vegetables the market affords, and buy themselves the
ministrations of the most brilliant and learned of the professional
classes. The weak man, as of yore, is the servant, the doer of things at
the master's beck and call. The weaker and less efficient he is, the
poorer is his reward. The weakest work for a living wage (when they
can get work), live in unsanitary slums, on vile and insufficient food,
at the lowest depths of human degradation. Their grasp on life is indeed precarious, their mortality excessive, their infant death rate appalling.

That some should be born to preferment and others to ignominy
in order that the race may progress, is cruel and sad; but none the less
they are so born. The weeding out of human souls, some for fatness
and smiles, some for leanness and tears, is surely a heartless selective
process—as heartless as it is natural. And the human family, for all its

wonderful record of adventure and achievement, has not yet succeeded in abolishing this process. That it is incapable of doing this is not to be hazarded. Not only is it capable, but the whole trend of society is in that direction. All the social forces are driving man on to a time when the old selective law will be annulled. There is no escaping it, save by the intervention of catastrophes and cataclysms utterly unthinkable. It is inexorable. It is inexorable because the common man demands it. The twentieth century, the common man says, is his day; the common man's day, or, rather, the dawning of the common man's day.

Nor can it be denied. The evidence is with him. The previous centuries, and more notably the nineteenth, have marked the rise of the common man. From chattel slavery to serfdom, and from serfdom to what he bitterly terms "wage slavery," he has upreared. Never was he so strong as he is to-day, and never so menacing. He does the work of the world, and he is beginning to know it. The world cannot get along without him, and this also he is beginning to know. All the human knowledge of the past, all the scientific discovery, governmental experiment, and invention of machinery, have tended to his advancement. His standard of living is higher. His common school education would shame princes ten centuries past. His civil and religious liberty make him a free man, and his ballot the peer of his betters. And all this has tended to make him conscious, conscious of himself, conscious of his class. He looks about him and questions that ancient law of development. It is cruel and wrong, he is beginning to declare. It is an anachronism. Let it be abolished. Why should there be one empty belly in all the world, when the work of ten men can feed a hundred? What if my brother be not so strong as I? He has not sinned. Wherefore should he hunger? he and his sinless little ones? Down with the old law. There is food and shelter for all, therefore let all receive food and shelter.

As fast as labor has become conscious, it has organized. The ambition of these class-conscious men is that the movement shall become general, that all labor shall become conscious of itself and its class interests. And the day that witnesses the solidarity of labor, they triumphantly affirm, will be a day when labor dominates the world. This growing consciousness has led to the organization of two movements, both separate and distinct, but both converging toward a common goal —one, the labor movement, known as Trade Unionism; the other, the political movement, known as Socialism. Both are grim and silent forces, unheralded, and virtually unknown by the general public save in moments of stress. The sleeping labor giant receives no notice from the capitalistic press, and when he stirs uneasily, a column of surprise, indignation, and horror suffices.

It is only now and then, after long periods of silence, that the labor movement puts in its claim for notice. All is quiet. The kind old world spins on, and the bourgeois masters clip their coupons in smug complacency. But the grim and silent forces are at work. Suddenly, like a clap of thunder from a clear sky, comes a disruption of industry. From ocean to ocean the wheels of a great chain of railroads cease to run. A quarter of a million miners throw down pick and shovel and outrage the sun with their pale, bleached faces. The street railways of a swarming metropolis stand idle, or the rumble of machinery in vast manufactories dies away to shocking silence. There is alarm and panic. Arson and homicide stalk forth. There is a cry in the night, and quick anger and sudden death. Peaceful cities are affrighted by the crack of rifles and the snarl of machine guns, and the hearts of the shuddering are shaken by the roar of dynamite. There is hurrying and skurrying. The wires are kept hot between the center of government and the seat of trouble. The chiefs of state ponder gravely and advise, and governors of States implore. There is assembling of militia and massing of troops, and the streets resound to the tramp of armed men. There are separate and joint conferences between the captains of industry and the captains of labor. And then, finally, all is quiet again, and the memory of it is like the memory of a bad dream.

But these strikes become hegiras, olympiads, things to date from; and common on the lips of men become such phrases as "The Great Dock Strike," "The Great Coal Strike," "The Great Railroad Strike." Never before did labor do these things. After the Great Plague in England labor, finding itself in demand, and innocently obeying the economic law, asked higher wages. But the masters set a maximum wage, restrained workingmen from moving about from place to place, refused to tolerate idlers, and by most barbarous legal methods punished those who disobeyed. But labor is accorded greater respect today. Such a policy, put into effect in this the first decade of the twentieth century, would sweep the masters from their seats in one mighty crash. And the masters know it and are respectful.

A fair instance of the growing solidarity of labor is afforded by an unimportant strike in San Francisco. The restaurant cooks and waiters were completely unorganized, working at any and all hours for whatever wages they could get. A representative of the American Federation of Labor went among them and organized them. Within a few weeks nearly two thousand men were enrolled, and they had five thousand dollars on deposit. Then they put in their demand for increased wages and shorter hours. Forthwith their employers organized. The demand was denied, and the Cooks' and Waiters' Union walked out.

All organized employers stood back of the restaurant owners, in sympathy with them and willing to aid them if they dared. And at the back of the Cooks' and Waiters' Union stood the organized labor of the city, 40,000 strong. If a business man were caught patronizing an "unfair" restaurant, he was boycotted; if a union man were caught, he was fined heavily by his union. The oyster companies and the slaughter houses made an attempt to refuse to sell oysters and meat to union restaurants. The Butchers and Meat Cutters, and the Teamsters, in retaliation, refused to work for or to deliver to non-union restaurants. Upon this the oyster companies and slaughter houses backed down and peace reigned. But the Restaurant Bakers in non-union places were ordered out, and the Bakery Wagon Drivers declined to deliver to unfair houses.

Every American Federation of Labor union in the city is prepared to strike, and waits only the word. And behind all, a handful of men, known as the Labor Council, direct the fight. One by one, blow upon blow, they are able to call out the unions—the Laundry Workers, who do the washing; the Hackmen, who haul men to and from restaurants; the Butchers, Meat Cutters, and Teamsters; and the Milkers, Milk Drivers, and Chicken Pickers; and after that, in pure sympathy, the Retail Clerks, the Horse Shoers, the Gas and Electrical Fixture Hangers, the Metal Roofers, the Blacksmiths, the Blacksmiths' Helpers, the Stablemen, the Machinists, the Brewers, the Coast Seamen, the Varnishers and Polishers, the Confectioners, the Upholsterers, the Paper Hangers and Fresco Painters, the Drug Clerks, the Fitters and Helpers, the Metal Workers, the Boiler Makers and Iron Ship Builders, the Assistant Undertakers, the Carriage and Wagon Workers, and so on down the lengthy list of organizations. And over all these trades, over all these thousands of men, is the Labor Council. When it speaks its voice is heard, and when it orders it is obeyed. But it, in turn, is dominated by the National Labor Council, with which it is constantly in touch.

In this wholly unimportant little local strike it is of interest to note the stands taken by the different sides. The legal representative and official mouthpiece of the Employers' Association says: "This organization is formed for defensive purposes, and it may be driven to take offensive steps, and if so, will be strong enough to follow them up. Labor cannot be allowed to dictate to capital and say how business shall be conducted. There is no objection to the formation of unions and trades councils, but membership must not be compulsory. It is repugnant to the American idea of liberty and cannot be tolerated."

On the other hand, the president of the Team Drivers' Union says: "The employers of labor in this city are generally against the trade union movement, and there seems to be a concerted effort on their part to check the progress of organized labor. Such action as has been taken by them in sympathy with the present labor troubles may, if continued, lead to a serious conflict, the outcome of which might be most calamitous for the business and industrial interests of San Francisco."

And the secretary of the United Brewery Workmen: "I regard a sympathetic strike as the last weapon which organized labor should use in its defense. When, however, associations of employers band together to defeat organized labor, or one of its branches, then we should not and will not hesitate ourselves to employ the same instrument in retaliation."

Thus, in a little corner of the world, is exemplified the growing solidarity of labor. The organization of labor has not only kept pace with the organization of industry, but it has gained upon it. In one winter, in the anthracite coal region, $160,000,000 in mines and $600,-000,000 in transportation and distribution consolidated its ownership and control. And at once, arrayed as solidly on the other side, where the 150,000 anthracite miners. The bituminous mines, however, were not consolidated; yet the 250,000 men employed therein were already combined. And not only that, but they were also combined with the anthracite miners, these 400,000 men being under the control and direction of one supreme labor council. And in this and the other great councils are to be found captains of labor of splendid abilities, who, in understanding of economic and industrial conditions, are undeniably equal to the best of their opponents, the captains of industry.

Just the other day the United States Steel Corporation was organized with total securities issued of $1,404,000,000. The workers in many of the lesser corporations absorbed, such as the American Tin Plate Company and the Steel Hoop Company, were organized under the Amalgamated Iron, Steel and Tin Workers' Association. But the workers in a number of the corporations absorbed, were not, but proceeded at once to organize. Seven men were discharged for taking part in the forming of an Amalgamated union in one of the mills of the American Sheet Steel Company. Their four hundred fellow workmen immediately walked out, and the great United States Steel Corporation found itself face to face with its bristling 200,000 employees. President Schwab, who receives a salary of a million a year for his wisdom, wisely ordered the seven discharged men back, and an armed truce for a few weeks was established.

The United States is honeycombed with labor organizations. And the big federations which these go to compose aggregate millions of members, and in their various branches handle millions of dollars yearly. And not only this; for the international brotherhoods and unions are forming, and moneys for the aid of strikers pass back and forth across the seas. The Machinists, in their demand for a nine-hour day, affect 500,000 men in the United States, Mexico, and Canada. In England the membership of working class organizations is approximated by Keir Hardie at 2,500,000, with reserve funds of $18,000,000. There the co-operative movement has a membership of 1,500,000, and every year turns over in distribution more than $100,000,000. In France, one-eighth of the whole working class is unionized. In Belgium the unions are very rich and powerful, and so able to defy the masters that many of the smaller manufacturers, unable to resist, "are removing their works to other countries where the workmen's organizations are not so potential." And in all other countries, according to the stage of their economic and political development, like figures obtain. And Europe, to-day, confesses that her greatest social problem is the labor problem, and that it is the one most closely engrossing the attention of her statesmen.

The organization of labor is one of the chief acknowledged factors in the retrogression of British trade. The workers have become class conscious as workers have never before. The wrong of one is the wrong of all. They have come to realize, in a short-sighted way, that their master's interests are not their interests. The harder they work, they believe, the more wealth they create for their masters. Further, the more work they do in one day, the fewer men will be needed to do the work. So the unions place a day's stint upon their members, beyond which they are not permitted to go. In "A Study of Trade Unionism," by Benjamin Taylor, in the *Nineteenth Century* of April, 1898, are furnished some interesting corroborations. The facts here set forth were collected by the Executive Board of the Employers' Federation, the documentary proofs of which are in the hands of the secretaries. In a certain firm the union workmen made eight ammunition boxes a day. Nor could they be persuaded into making more. A young Swiss, who could not speak English, was set to work, and in the first day he made fifty boxes. In the same firm the skilled union hands filed up the outside handles of one machine gun a day. That was their stint. No one was known to ever do more. A non-union filer came into the shop and did twelve a day. A Manchester firm found that to plane a large bedcasting took union workmen 190 hours, and non-union workmen 135 hours. In another instance a man, resigning from his union, day by day did double the amount of work he had done formerly. And to cap it all, an English gentleman, going out to look at a wall being put up for him by union bricklayers, found one of their number with his right arm strapped to his body, doing all the work with his left arm—forsooth, because he was such an energetic fellow that otherwise he would involuntarily lay more bricks than his union permitted.

All England resounds to the cry: "Wake up, England!" But the sulky giant is not stirred. "Let England's trade go to pot," he says, "what have I to lose?" And England is powerless. The capacity of her workmen is represented by 1, in comparison with the $2\frac{1}{4}$ capacity of the American workman. And because of the solidarity of labor and the destructiveness of strikes, British capitalists dare not even strive to emulate the enterprise of American capitalists. So England watches trade slipping through her fingers and wails unavailingly. As a correspondent writes: "The enormous power of the trade unions hangs, a sullen cloud, over the whole industrial world here, affecting men and masters alike."

The political movement known as Socialism is, perhaps, even less realized by the general public. The great strides it has taken and the portentous front it to-day exhibits are undreamed of; and, fastened though it is to every land, it is given little space by the capitalistic press. For all its plea and passion and warmth, it wells upward like a great cold tidal wave, irresistible, inexorable, ingulfing present-day society level by level. By its own preachment it is inexorable. Just as sure as societies have sprung into existence, fulfilled their function, and passed away, just so sure is present society hastening on to its dissolution. This is a transition period—and destined to be a very short one. Barely a century old, capitalism is ripening so rapidly that it can never live to see a second birthday. There is no hope for it, the Socialists say. It is doomed, doomed, doomed.

The cardinal tenet of Socialism is that forbidding doctrine, the materialistic conception of history. Men are not the masters of their souls. They are the puppets of great, blind forces. The lives they live and the deaths they die are compulsory. All social codes are but the reflexes of existing economic conditions, plus certain survivals of past economic conditions. The institutions men build they are compelled to build. Economic laws determine at any given time what these institutions shall be, how long they shall operate, and by what they shall be replaced. And so, through the economic process, the Socialist preaches the ripening of the capitalistic society and the coming of the new co-operative society.

The second great tenet of Socialism, itself a phase of the materialistic conception of history, is the class struggle. In the social struggle for existence, men are forced into classes. "The history of all society thus far is the history of class strife." In existing society the capitalist class exploits the working class, the proletariat. The interests of the exploiter are not the interests of the exploited. "Profits are legitimate," says the one. "Profits are unpaid wages," replied the other, when he has become conscious of his class, "therefore, profits are robbery." The capitalist enforces his profits because he is the legal owner of all the means of production. He is the legal owner, because he controls the political machinery of society. The Socialist sets himself to work to capture the political machinery, so that he may make illegal the capitalist's ownership of the means of production, and make legal his own ownership of the means of production. And it is this struggle, between these two classes, upon which the world has at last entered.

Scientific Socialism is very young. Only yesterday it was in swaddling clothes. But to-day it is a vigorous young giant, well-braced to battle for what it wants, and knowing precisely what it wants. It holds its international conventions, where world-policies are formulated by the representatives of millions of Socialists. In little Belgium there are three-quarters of a million of men who work for the cause; in Germany, 2,500,000; Austria, between 1895 and 1897, raised her Socialist vote from 90,000 to 750,000. France in 1871 had a whole generation of Socialists wiped out, yet in 1885 there were 30,000, and in 1898, 1,000,000. And so in various countries.

Ere the last Spaniard had evacuated Cuba, Socialist groups were forming. And from far Japan, in these first days of the twentieth century, writes one, Tomoyoshi Murai: "The interest of our people on Socialism has been greatly awakened these days, especially among our laboring people on one hand and young students' circle on the other, as much as we can draw an earnest and enthusiastic audience and fill our hall, which holds two thousand. . . . It is gratifying to say that we have a number of fine and well-trained public orators among our leaders of Socialism in Japan. The first speaker to-night is Mr. Kiyoshi Kawakami, editor of one of our city (Tokyo) dailies, a strong, independent, and decidedly socialistic paper, circulated far and wide. Mr. Kawakami is a scholar as well as a popular writer. He is going to speak to-night on the subject, 'The Essence of Socialism—the Fundamental Principles.' The next speaker is Professor Iso Abe, president of our association, whose subject of address is, 'Socialism and the Existing Social System.' The third speaker is Mr. Naoe Kinosita, the editor of another strong journal of the city. He speaks on the subject, 'How to Realize the Socialist Ideals and Plans.' Next is Mr. Shigeyoshi Sugiyama, a graduate of Hartford Theological Seminary and an advocate of Social Christianity, who is to speak on 'Socialism and Municipal Problems.' And the last speaker is the editor of the 'Labor World,' the foremost leader of the labor union movement in our country, Mr. Sen Katayama, who speaks on the subject, 'The Outlook of Socialism in Europe and America.' These addresses are going to be published in book form and to be distributed among our people to enlighten their minds on the subject."

And in the struggle for the political machinery of society, Socialism is no longer confined to mere propaganda. Italy, Austria, Belgium, England, have Socialist members in their national bodies. Out of the one hundred and thirty-two members of the London County Council, ninety-one are denounced by the conservative element as Socialists. The Emperor of Germany grows anxious and angry at the increasing number which are returned to the Reichstag. In France, many of the large cities, such as Marseilles, are in the hands of the Socialists. A large body of them are in the Chamber of Deputies, and Millerand, Socialist, sits in the cabinet. Of him M. Leroy-Beaulieu says with horror: "M. Millerand is the open enemy of private property, private capital, the resolute advocate of the socialization of production. . . . a constant incitement to violence. . . . a collectivist, avowed and militant, taking part in the government, dominating the departments of commerce and industry, preparing all the laws and presiding at the passage of all measures which should be submitted to merchants and tradesmen."

In the United States there are already Socialist mayors of towns and members of State legislatures, a vast literature, and single Socialist papers with subscription lists running up into the hundreds of thousands. In 1896, 36,000 votes were cast for the Socialist candidate for president; in 1900, nearly 200,000. And the United States, young as it is, is ripening rapidly, and the Socialists claim, according to the materialistic conception of history, that the United States will be the first country in the world wherein the toilers will capture the political machinery and expropriate the bourgeoisie.

But the Socialist and labor movements have recently entered upon a new phase. There has been a remarkable change in attitude on both sides. For a long time the labor unions refrained from going in for political action. On the other hand, the Socialists claimed that without political action labor was utterly powerless. And because of this there was much ill feeling between them, even open hostilities, and no concerted action. But now the Socialists grant that the labor movement has held up wages and decreased the hours of labor, and the labor unions find that political action is absolutely necessary. To-day both parties have drawn closely together in the common fight. In the United States this friendly feeling grows. The Socialist papers espouse the cause of labor, and the unions have opened their ears once more to the wiles of the Socialists. They are all leavened with Socialist workmen, "boring from within," and many of their leaders have already succumbed to the inevitable. In England, where class consciousness is more developed, the name "Unionism" has been replaced by "The New Unionism," the main object of which is "to capture existing social structures in the interests of the wage earners." There the Socialist, trade union, and other working class organizations are beginning to co-operate in securing the return of representatives to the House of Commons. And in France, where the city councils and mayors of Marseilles and Monteau-les-Mines are Socialistic, thousands of francs were voted for the aid of the unions in the recent great strikes.

For centuries the world has been preparing for the coming of the common man. And the period of preparation virtually past, labor, conscious of itself and its desires, has begun a definite movement toward solidarity. It believes the time is not far distant when the historian will speak not only of the dark ages of feudalism, but also of the dark ages of capitalism. And labor sincerely believes itself justified in this by the terrible indictment it brings against capitalistic society. In the face of its enormous wealth, capitalistic society forfeits its right to existence when it permits wide-spread, bestial poverty. The philosophy of the survival of the fittest does not soothe the class-conscious worker when he learns through his class literature that among the Italian pants-finishers of Chicago [2] the average weekly wage is $1.31, and the average number of weeks employed in the year is 27.85. Likewise when he reads: [3] "Every room in these reeking tenements houses a family or two. In one room a missionary found a man ill with smallpox, his wife just recovering from her confinement, and the children running about half naked and covered with dirt. Here are seven people living in one under-ground kitchen, and a little dead child lying in the same room. Here live a widow and her six children, two of whom are ill with scarlet fever. In another, nine brothers and sisters from twenty-nine years of age downward, live, eat, and sleep together." And likewise, when he reads: [4] "When one man fifty years old, who has worked all his life, is compelled to beg a little money to bury his dead baby, and another man fifty years old can give ten million dollars to enable his daughter to live in luxury and bolster up a decaying foreign aristocracy, do you see nothing amiss?"

And on the other hand, the class-conscious worker reads the statistics of the wealthy classes, knows what their incomes are, and just how they get them. True, down all the past he has known his own material misery and the material comfort of the dominant classes, and often has this knowledge led him to intemperate acts and unwise rebellion. But to-day, and for the first time, because both society and he have evolved, he is beginning to see a possible way out. His ears are opening to the vast propaganda of Socialism, the passionate gospel of the dispossessed. But it does not inculcate a turning back. The way through is the way out, he understands, and with this in mind he draws up the program.

It is quite simple, this program. Instead of struggling against forces, the plan is to work with forces. Everything is moving in his direction,

---

[2] From figures presented by Miss Nellie Mason Auten in the *American Journal of Sociology,* and copied extensively by the trade union and socialist press.

[3] *The Bitter Cry of Outcast London.*

[4] An item from the *Social Democratic Herald.* Hundreds of these items, culled from current happenings, are published weekly in the papers of the workers.

toward the day when he will take charge. The trust? Ah, no. Unlike the trembling middle-class man and the small capitalist, he sees nothing to be affrighted at. He likes the trust. He exults in the trust, for it is largely doing the task for him. It socializes production; this done, there remains nothing for him to do but socialize distribution, and all is accomplished. The trust? "It organizes industry on an enormous, labor-saving scale, and abolishes childish, wasteful competition." It is a gigantic object lesson, and it preaches his political economy far more potently than he ever possibly could. He points to it, laughing scornfully in the face of the orthodox economists. "You told me this thing could not be," [5] he thunders. "Behold! the thing is!"

He sees competition in the realm of production passing away. When the captains of industry have thoroughly organized production, and got everything running smoothly, it will be very easy for him to eliminate the profits by stepping in and having the thing run for himself. And the captain of industry, if he be good, may be given the privilege of continuing the management on a fair salary. The sixty millions of dividends which the Standard Oil Company annually declares will be distributed among the workers. The same with the great United States Steel Corporation. Schwab is a pretty good man. He knows his business. Very good. Let him become Secretary of the Department of Iron and Steel Industry of the United States. But, since the chief executive of a nation of seventy-odd millions works for fifty thousand a year, Secretary Schwab must expect to have his salary cut accordingly. And not only will the workers take to themselves the profits of national and municipal monopolies, but also the hundreds and billions of revenue which the dominant classes to-day draw from rents, and mines, and factories, and all manner of enterprises.

All this would seem very like a dream, even to the workers, if it were not for the fact that like things have been done before. He points triumphantly to the aristocrat of the eighteenth century, who fought, legislated, governed, and dominated society; but who was shorn of power and displaced by the rising bourgeoisie. Ay, the thing was done, he holds. And it shall be done again, but this time it is the proletariat who does the shearing. Sociology has taught him that m-i-g-h-t spells "right." Every society has been ruled by classes, and the classes have ruled by sheer strength, and have been overthrown by sheer strength.

[5] Karl Marx, the great Socialist, worked out the trust development **forty years ago**, for which he was laughed at by the orthodox economists.

The bourgeoisie, because they were the stronger, dragged down the nobility of the sword; and the proletariat, because it is the strongest of all, can and will drag down the bourgeoisie.

And in that day, for better or worse, the common man becomes the master—for better, he believes. It is his intention to make the sum of human happiness far greater. No man shall work for a bare living wage, which is degradation. Every man will have work to do, and will be paid exceeding well for doing it. There shall be no slum classes, no beggars. Nor shall there be hundreds of thousands of men and women condemned, for economic reasons, to lives of celibacy or sexual infertility. Every man shall be able to marry, to live in healthy, comfortable quarters, and to have all he wants to eat as many times a day as he wishes. There shall no longer be a life and death struggle for food and shelter. The old heartless law of development shall be annulled.

All of which is very good and very fine. And when these things have come to pass, as they inevitably will, what then? Of old, by virtue of their weakness and inefficiency in the struggle for food and shelter, the race was purged of its weak and inefficient members. But this will no longer obtain. Under the new order the weak and the progeny of the weak will have a chance for survival equal to that of the strong and the progeny of the strong. This being so, the premium upon strength will have been withdrawn, and on the face of it the average strength of each generation, instead of continuing to rise, will begin to decline. And if the strength of the race thus begins to decline, is it not plausible that the race will be displaced by other races yet rising in strength under the old law of development?

This, in turn, is nothing new. Time and again, in the struggles of the classes in past societies, it has been exemplified, and it is so exemplified to-day. For the old law, when working for development, after insuring a better chance for survival to the strong, only insured a better chance to the progeny of the strong during that period which lies between conception and full maturity. After maturity, the progeny of the strong had also to enter the struggle and succeed in order to perpetuate the strength. In the genesis of the old French nobility, for instance, the strongest became the founders of the dominant class. This class gradually built up an institution in society, which, especially in its latter days, permitted the weak to survive and to propagate weakness. Consequently, this class grew weaker and weaker. In England, on the contrary, the institution of aristocracy was so different that the younger sons were forced to shift for themselves, "To win to hearth and saddle of their own." Also, there was much intermarriage with the classes lower in the social scale, and with those classes nearer the soil. And in these classes the struggle for food and shelter was keen, and it is patent that it was the strong ones among them who were chosen for translation into the nobility for breeding purposes. Constantly revivified, the English nobility was thus naturally more virile than the French. And in society to-day the progeny of the captains of industry tends to grow weaker and weaker, and are largely preserved by the social institutions which prevent them from being forced into the struggle for food and shelter.

And likewise, when the common man's day will have arrived, the new social institutions of that day will prevent the weeding out of weakness and inefficiency. All, the weak and the strong, will have an equal chance for procreation. And the progeny of all, of the weak as well as the strong, will have an equal chance for survival. This being so, and if no new effective law of development be put into operation, then progress must cease. And not only progress, for there is high probability that deterioration would set in. It is a pregnant problem. What will be the nature of this new and most necessary law of development? Can the common man pause long enough from his undermining labors to answer? Since he is bent upon dragging down the bourgeoisie and reconstructing society, can he so reconstruct that a premium, in some unguessed way or other, will still be laid upon the strong and efficient so that the human type will continue to develop? Can the common man, or the uncommon men who are allied with him, devise such a law? Or have they already devised one? And if so, what is it? The answer rests with the common man. Dare he answer?

The Class Struggle

Unfortunately or otherwise, people are prone to believe in the reality of the things they think ought to be so. This comes of the cheery optimism which is innate with life itself; and, while it may sometimes be deplored, it must never be censured, for, as a rule, it is productive of more good than harm, and of about all the achievement there is in the world. There are cases where this optimism has been disastrous, as with the people who lived in Pompeii during its last quivering days; or with the aristocrats of the time of Louis XVI, who confidently expected the Deluge to overwhelm their children, or their children's children, but never themselves. But there is small likelihood that the case of perverse optimism here to be considered will end in such disaster, while there is every reason to believe that the great change now manifesting itself in society will be as peaceful and orderly in its culmination as it is in its present development.

Out of their constitutional optimism, and because a class struggle is an abhorred and dangerous thing, the great American people are unanimous in asserting that there is no class struggle. And by "American people" is meant the recognized and authoritative mouthpieces of the American people, which are the press, the pulpit, and the university. The journalists, the preachers, and the professors are practically of one voice in declaring that there is no such thing as a class struggle now going on, much less that a class struggle will ever go on, in the United States. And this declaration they continually make in the face of a multitude of facts which impeach, not so much their sincerity, as affirm, rather, their optimism.

There are two ways of approaching the subject of the class struggle.

The existence of this struggle can be shown theoretically, and it can be shown actually. For a class struggle to exist in society there must be, first, a class inequality, a superior class and an inferior class (as measured by power) ; and, second, the outlets must be closed whereby the strength and ferment of the inferior class have been permitted to escape.

That there are even classes in the United States is vigorously denied by many; but it is incontrovertible, when a group of individuals is formed, wherein the members are bound together by common interests which are peculiarly their interests and not the interests of individuals outside the group, that such a group is a class. The owners of capital, with their dependents, form a class of this nature in the United States; the working people form a similar class. The interest of the capitalist class, say, in the matter of income tax, is quite contrary to the interest of the laboring class; and, *vice versa,* in the matter of poll-tax.

If between these two classes there be a clear and vital conflict of interest, all the factors are present which make a class struggle; but this struggle will lie dormant if the strong and capable members of the inferior class be permitted to leave that class and join the ranks of the superior class. The capitalist class and the working class have existed side by side and for a long time in the United States; but hitherto all the strong, energetic members of the working class have been able to rise out of their class and become owners of capital. They were enabled to do this because an undeveloped country with an expanding frontier gave equality of opportunity to all. In the almost lottery-like scramble for the ownership of vast unowned natural resources, and in the exploitation of which there was little or no competition of capital, (the capital itself rising out of the exploitation), the capable, intelligent member of the working class found a field in which to use his brains to his own advancement. Instead of being discontented in direct ratio with his intelligence and ambitions, and of radiating amongst his fellows a spirit of revolt as capable as he was capable, he left them to their fate and carved his own way to a place in the superior class.

But the day of expanding frontier, of a lottery-like scramble for the ownership of natural resources, and of the upbuilding of new industries, is past. Farthest West has been reached, and an immense volume of surplus capital roams for investment and nips in the bud the patient efforts of the embryo capitalist to rise through slow increment from small beginnings. The gateway of opportunity after opportunity has been closed, and closed for all time. Rockefeller has shut the door on oil, the American Tobacco Company on tobacco, and Carnegie on steel. After Carnegie came Morgan, who triple-locked the door. These doors will not open again, and before them pause thousands of ambitious young men to read the placard: No THOROUGHFARE.

And day by day more doors are shut, while the ambitious young men continue to be born. It is they, denied the opportunity to rise from the working class, who preach revolt to the working class. Had he been born fifty years later, Andrew Carnegie, the poor Scotch boy, might have risen to be president of his union, or of a federation of unions; but that he would never have become the builder of Homestead and the founder of multitudinous libraries, is as certain as it is certain that some other man would have developed the steel industry had Andrew Carnegie never been born.

Theoretically, then, there exist in the United States all the factors which go to make a class struggle. There are the capitalists and working classes, the interests of which conflict, while the working class is no longer being emasculated to the extent it was in the past by having drawn off from it its best blood and brains. Its more capable members are no longer able to rise out of it and leave the great mass leaderless and helpless. They remain to be its leaders.

But the optimistic mouthpieces of the great American people, who are themselves deft theoreticians, are not to be convinced by mere theoretics. So it remains to demonstrate the existence of the class struggle by a marshalling of the facts.

When nearly two millions of men, finding themselves knit together by certain interests peculiarly their own, band together in a strong organization for the aggressive pursuit of those interests, it is evident that society has within it a hostile and warring class. But when the interests which this class aggressively pursues conflict sharply and vitally with the interests of another class, class antagonism arises and a class struggle is the inevitable result. One great organization of labor alone has a membership of 1,700,000 in the United States. This is the American Federation of Labor, and outside of it are many other large organizations. All these men are banded together for the frank purpose of bettering their condition, regardless of the harm worked thereby upon all other classes. They are in open antagonism with the capitalist class, while the manifestos of their leaders state that the struggle is one which can never end until the capitalist class is exterminated.

Their leaders will largely deny this last statement, but an examination of their utterances, their actions, and the situation will forestall such denial. In the first place, the conflict between labor and capital is over the division of the joint product. Capital and labor apply themselves to raw material and make it into a finished product. The difference between the value of the raw material and the value of the finished product is the value they have added to it by their joint effort. This added value is, therefore, their joint product, and it is over the division of this joint product that the struggle between labor and capital takes place. Labor takes its share in wages; capital takes its share in profits. It is patent, if capital took in profits the whole joint product, that labor would perish. And it is equally patent, if labor took in wages the whole joint product, that capital would perish. Yet this last is the very thing labor aspires to do, and that it will never be content with anything less than the whole joint product is evidenced by the words of its leaders.

Mr. Samuel Gompers, president of the American Federation of Labor, has said: "The workers want more wages; more of the comforts of life; more leisure; more chance for self-improvement as men, as trade-unionists, as citizens. *These were the wants of yesterday; they are the wants of to-day; they will be the wants of to-morrow, and of to-morrow's morrow.* The struggle may assume new forms, but the issue is the immemorial one,—an effort of the producers to obtain an increasing measure of the wealth that flows from their production."

Mr. Henry White, secretary of the United Garment Workers of America and a member of the Industrial Committee of the National Civic Federation, speaking of the National Civic Federation soon after its inception, said: "To fall into one another's arms, to avow friendship, to express regret at the injury which has been done, would not alter the facts of the situation. Workingmen will continue to demand more pay, and the employer will naturally oppose them. The readiness and ability of the workmen to fight will, as usual, largely determine the amount of their wages or their share in the product. . . . But when it comes to dividing the proceeds, there is the rub. We can also agree that the larger the product through the employment of labor-saving methods the better, as there will be more to be divided, but again the question of the division. . . . A Concilia-

tion Committee, having the confidence of the community, and composed of men possessing practical knowledge of industrial affairs, can
therefore aid in mitigating this antagonism, in preventing avoidable
conflicts, in bringing about a *truce;* I use the word 'truce' because
understandings can only be temporary."

Here is a man who might have owned cattle on a thousand hills,
been a lumber baron or a railroad king, had he been born a few years
sooner. As it is, he remains in his class, is secretary of the United
Garment Workers of America, and is so thoroughly saturated with the
class struggle that he speaks of the dispute between capital and labor
in terms of war,—workmen *fight* with employers; it is possible to
avoid some *conflicts;* in certain cases *truces* may be, for the time being, effected.

Man being man and a great deal short of the angels, the quarrel
over the division of the joint product is irreconcilable. For the last
twenty years in the United States, there has been an average of over
a thousand strikes per year; and year by year these strikes increase
in magnitude, and the front of the labor army grows more imposing.
And it is a class struggle, pure and simple. Labor as a class is fighting
with capital as a class.

Workingmen will continue to demand more pay, and employers
will continue to oppose them. This is the key-note to *laissez faire,*—
everybody for himself and devil take the hindmost. It is upon this
that the rampant individualist bases his individualism. It is the let-
alone policy, the struggle for existence, which strengthens the strong,
destroys the weak, and makes a finer and more capable breed of men.
But the individual has passed away and the group has come, for better or worse, and the struggle has become, not a struggle between individuals, but a struggle between groups. So the query rises: Has the
individualist never speculated upon the labor group becoming strong
enough to destroy the capitalist group, and take to itself and run for
itself the machinery of industry? And, further, has the individualist
never speculated upon this being still a triumphant expression of individualism,—of group individualism,—if the confusion of terms
may be permitted?

But the facts of the class struggle are deeper and more significant
than have so far been presented. A million or so of workmen may
organize for the pursuit of interests which engender class antagonism
and strife, and at the same time be unconscious of what is engendered.
But when a million or so of workmen show unmistakable signs of being

conscious of their class,—of being, in short, class conscious,—then the situation grows serious. The uncompromising and terrible hatred of the trade-unionist for a scab is the hatred of a class for a traitor to that class,—while the hatred of a trade-unionist for the militia is the hatred of a class for a weapon wielded by the class with which it is fighting. No workman can be true to his class and at the same time be a member of the militia: this is the dictum of the labor leaders.

In the town of the writer, the good citizens, when they get up a Fourth of July parade and invite the labor unions to participate, are informed by the unions that they will not march in the parade if the militia marches. Article 8 of the constitution of the Painters' and Decorators' Union of Schenectady provides that a member must not be a "militiaman, special police officer, or deputy marshal in the employ of corporations or individuals during strikes, lockouts, or other labor difficulties, and any member occupying any of the above positions will be debarred from membership." Mr. William Potter was a member of this union and a member of the National Guard. As a result, because he obeyed the order of the Governor when his company was ordered out to suppress rioting, he was expelled from his union. Also his union demanded his employers, Shafer & Barry, to discharge him from their service. This they complied with, rather than face the threatened strike.

Mr. Robert L. Walker, first lieutenant of the Light Guards, a New Haven militia company, recently resigned. His reason was, that he was a member of the Car Builders' Union, and that the two organizations were antagonistic to each other. During a New Orleans street-car strike not long ago, a whole company of militia, called out to protect non-union men, resigned in a body. Mr. John Mulholland, president of the International Association of Allied Metal Mechanics, has stated that he does not want the members to join the militia. The Local Trades' Assembly of Syracuse, New York, has passed a resolution, by unanimous vote, requiring union men who are members of the National Guard to resign, under pain of expulsion, from the unions. The Amalgamated Sheet Metal Workers' Association has incorporated in its constitution an amendment excluding from membership in its organization "any person a member of the regular army, or of the State militia or naval reserve." The Illinois State Federation of Labor at a recent convention, passed without a dissenting vote a resolution declaring that membership in military organizations is a violation of labor union obligations, and requesting all union men to withdraw from the militia. The president of the Federation, Mr. Albert Young, declared that the militia was a menace not only to unions, but to all workers throughout the country.

These instances may be multiplied a thousand fold. The union workmen are becoming conscious of their class, and of the struggle their class is waging with the capitalist class. To be a member of the militia is to be a traitor to the union, for the militia is a weapon wielded by the employers to crush the workers in the struggle between the warring groups.

Another interesting, and even more pregnant, phase of the class struggle is the political aspect of it as displayed by the socialists. Five men, standing together, may perform prodigies; 500 men, marching as marched the historic Five Hundred of Marseilles, may sack a palace and destroy a king; while 500,000 men, passionately preaching the propaganda of a class struggle, waging a class struggle along political lines, and backed by the moral and intellectual support of 10,000,000 more men of like convictions throughout the world, may come pretty close to realizing a class struggle in these United States of ours.

In 1900 these men cast 150,000 votes; two years later, in 1902, they cast 300,000 votes; and in 1904 they cast 450,000. They have behind them a most imposing philosophic and scientific literature; they own illustrated magazines and reviews, high in quality, dignity, and restraint; they possess countless daily and weekly papers which circulate throughout the land, and single papers which have subscribers by the hundreds of thousands; and they literally swamp the working classes in a vast sea of tracts and pamphlets. No political party in the United States, no church organization nor mission effort, has as indefatigable workers as has the socialist party. They multiply themselves, know of no effort nor sacrifice too great to make for the Cause; and "Cause," with them, is spelled out in capitals. They work for it with a religious zeal, and would die for it with a willingness similar to that of the Christian martyrs.

These men are preaching an uncompromising and deadly class struggle. In fact, they are organized upon the basis of a class struggle. "The history of society," they say, "is a history of class struggles. Patrician struggled with plebeian in early Rome; the king and the burghers, with the nobles in the Middle Ages; later on, the king and the nobles with the bourgeoisie; and to-day the struggle is on between the triumphant bourgeoisie and the rising proletariat. By 'proletariat' is meant the class of people without capital which sells its labor for a living.

"That the proletariat shall conquer," (mark the note of fatalism), "is as certain as the rising sun. *Just as the bourgeoisie of the eighteenth century wanted democracy applied to politics, so the proletariat of the twentieth century wants democracy applied to industry.* As the bourgeoisie complained against the government being run by and for the nobles, so the proletariat complains against the government and industry being run by and for the bourgeoisie; and so, following in the footsteps of its predecessor, the proletariat will possess itself of the government, apply democracy to industry, abolish wages, which are merely legalized robbery, and run the business of the country in its own interest.

"Their aim," they say, "is to organize the working class, and those in sympathy with it, into a political party, with the object of conquering the powers of government and using them for the purpose of transforming the present system of private ownership of the means of production and distribution into collective ownership by the entire people."

Briefly stated, this is the battle plan of these 450,000 men who call themselves "socialists." And, in the face of the existence of such an aggressive group of men, a class struggle cannot very well be denied by the optimistic Americans who say: "A class struggle is monstrous. Sir, there is no class struggle." The class struggle is here, and the optimistic American had better gird himself for the fray and put a stop to it, rather than sit idly declaiming that what ought not to be is not, and never will be.

But the socialists, fanatics and dreamers though they may well be, betray a foresight and insight, and a genius for organization, which put to shame the class with which they are openly at war. Failing of rapid success in waging a sheer political propaganda, and finding that they were alienating the most intelligent and most easily organized portion of the voters, the socialists lessoned from the experience and turned their energies upon the trade-union movement. To win the trade unions was well-nigh to win the war, and recent events show that they have done far more winning in this direction than have the capitalists.

Instead of antagonizing the unions, which had been their previous policy, the socialists proceeded to conciliate the unions. "Let every good socialist join the union of his trade," the edict went forth.

"Bore from within and capture the trade-union movement." And this policy, only several years old, has reaped fruits far beyond their fondest expectations. To-day the great labor unions are honeycombed with socialists, "boring from within," as they picturesquely term their undermining labor. At work and at play, at business meeting and council, their insidious propaganda goes on. At the shoulder of the trade-unionist is the socialist, sympathizing with him, aiding him with head and hand, suggesting—perpetually suggesting—the necessity for political action. As the *Journal*, of Lansing, Michigan, a republican paper, has remarked: "The socialists in the labor unions are tireless workers. They are sincere, energetic, and self-sacrificing. . . . They stick to the union and work all the while, thus making a showing which, reckoned by ordinary standards, is out of all proportion to their numbers. . . . Their cause is growing among union laborers, and their long fight, intended to turn the Federation into a political organization, is likely to win."

They miss no opportunity of driving home the necessity for political action, the necessity for capturing the political machinery of society whereby they may master society. As an instance of this is the avidity with which the American socialists seized upon the famous Taft-Vale Decision in England, which was to the effect that an unincorporated union could be sued and its treasury rifled by process of law. Throughout the United States, the socialists pointed the moral in similar fashion to the way it was pointed by the *Social-Democratic Herald*, which advised the trade-unionists, in view of the decision, to stop trying to fight capital with money, which they lacked, and to begin fighting with the ballot, which was their strongest weapon.

Night and day, tireless and unrelenting, they labor at their self-imposed task of undermining society. Mr. M. G. Cunniff, who lately made an intimate study of trade-unionism, says: "All through the unions socialism filters. Almost every other man is a socialist, preaching that unionism is but a makeshift." "Malthus be damned," they told him, "for the good time was coming when every man should be able to rear his family in comfort." In one union, with two thousand members, Mr. Cunniff found every man a socialist, and from his experiences Mr. Cunniff was forced to confess, "I lived in a world that showed our industrial life a-tremble from beneath with a never-ceasing ferment."

The socialists have already captured the Western Federation of Miners, the Western Hotel and Restaurant Employees' Union, and the Patternmakers' National Association. The Western Federation of Miners, at a recent convention, declared: "The strike has failed to secure to the working classes their liberty; we therefore call upon the workers to strike as one man for their liberties at the ballot box. . . . We put ourselves on record as committed to the programme of independent political action. . . . We indorse the platform of the socialist party, and accept it as the declaration of principles of our organization. We call upon our members as individuals to commence immediately the organization of the socialist movement in their respective towns and states, and to coöperate in every way for the furtherance of the principles of socialism and of the socialist party. In states where the socialist party has not perfected its organization, we advise that every assistance be given by our members to that end. . . . We therefore call for organizers, capable and well-versed in the whole programme of the labor movement, to be sent into each state to preach the necessity of organization on the political as well as on the economic field."

The capitalist class has a glimmering consciousness of the class struggle which is shaping itself in the midst of society; but the capitalists, as a class, seem to lack the ability for organizing, for coming together, such as is possessed by the working class. No American capitalist ever aids an English capitalist in the common fight, while workmen have formed international unions, the socialists a worldwide international organization, and on all sides space and race are bridged in the effort to achieve solidarity. Resolutions of sympathy, and, fully as important, donations of money, pass back and forth across the sea to wherever labor is fighting its pitched battles.

For divers reasons the capitalist class lacks this cohesion or solidarity, chief among which is the optimism bred of past success. And, again, the capitalist class is divided; it has within itself a class struggle of no mean proportions, which tends to irritate and harass it and to confuse the situation. The small capitalist and the large capitalist are grappled with each other, struggling over what Achille Loria calls the "bi-partition of the revenues." Such a struggle, though not precisely analogous, was waged between the landlords and manufacturers of England when the one brought about the passage of the Factory Acts and the other the abolition of the Corn Laws.

Here and there, however, certain members of the capitalist class see clearly the cleavage in society along which the struggle is beginning to show itself, while the press and magazines are beginning to raise

an occasional and troubled voice. Two leagues of class-conscious capitalists have been formed for the purpose of carrying on their side
of the struggle. Like the socialists, they do not mince matters, but
state boldly and plainly that they are fighting to subjugate the opposing class. It is the barons against the commons. One of these
leagues, the National Association of Manufacturers, is stopping short
of nothing in what it conceives to be a life-and-death struggle. Mr. D.
M. Parry, who is the president of the league, as well as president of
the National Metal Trades' Association, is leaving no stone unturned
in what he feels to be a desperate effort to organize his class. He has
issued the call to arms in terms everything but ambiguous: *"There is
still time in the United States to head off the socialistic programme,
which, unrestrained, is sure to wreck our country."*

As he says, the work is for "federating employers in order that we
may meet with a united front all issues that affect us. We must come
to this sooner or later. . . . The work immediately before the National Association of Manufacturers is, first, *keep the vicious Eight-
hour Bill off the books;* second, to *destroy the Anti-injunction Bill,*
which wrests your business from you and places it in the hands of
your employees; third, to secure the *passage of the Department of
Commerce and Industry Bill;* the latter would go through with a rush
were it not for the hectoring opposition of Organized Labor." By this
department, he further says, "business interests would have direct
and sympathetic representation at Washington."

In a later letter, issued broadcast to the capitalists outside the
League, President Parry points out the success which is already beginning to attend the efforts of the League at Washington. "We have
contributed more than any other influence to the quick passage of the
new Department of Commerce Bill. It is said that the activities of this
office are numerous and satisfactory; but of that I must not say too
much—or anything. . . . At Washington the Association is not represented too much, either directly or indirectly. Sometimes it is known
in a most powerful way that it is represented vigorously and unitedly.
Sometimes it is not known that it is represented at all."

The second class-conscious capitalist organization is called the
National Economic League. It likewise manifests the frankness of
men who do not dilly-dally with terms, but who say what they mean,
and who mean to settle down to a long, hard fight. Their letter of
invitation to prospective members opens boldly. "We beg to inform
you that the National Economic League will render its services in an

impartial educational movement *to oppose socialism and class hatred."* Among its class-conscious members, men who recognize that the opening guns of the class struggle have been fired, may be instanced the following names: Hon. Lyman J. Gage, Ex-Secretary U.S. Treasury; Hon. Thomas Jefferson Coolidge, Ex-Minister to France; Rev. Henry C. Potter, Bishop New York Diocese; Hon. John D. Long, Ex-Secretary U.S. Navy; Hon. Levi P. Morton, Ex-Vice President United States; Henry Clews; John F. Dryden, President Prudential Life Insurance Co.; John A. McCall, President New York Life Insurance Co.; J. L. Greatsinger, President Brooklyn Rapid Transit Co.; the shipbuilding firm of William Cramp & Sons, the Southern Railway system, and the Atchison, Topeka, & Santa Fé Railway Company.

Instances of the troubled editorial voice have not been rare during the last several years. There were many cries from the press during the last days of the anthracite coal strike that the mine owners, by their stubbornness, were sowing the regrettable seeds of socialism. The *World's Work* for December, 1902, said: "The next significant fact is the recommendation by the Illinois State Federation of Labor that all members of labor unions who are also members of the state militia shall resign from the militia. This proposition has been favorably regarded by some other labor organizations. It has done more than any other single recent declaration or action to cause a public distrust of such unions as favor it. *It hints of a class separation that in turn hints of anarchy."*

The *Outlook,* February 14, 1903, in reference to the rioting at Waterbury, remarks, "That all this disorder should have occurred in a city of the character and intelligence of Waterbury indicates that the industrial war spirit is by no means confined to the immigrant or ignorant working classes."

That President Roosevelt has smelt the smoke from the firing line of the class struggle is evidenced by his words, "Above all we need to remember that any kind of *class animosity in the political world* is, if possible, even more destructive to national welfare than sectional, race, or religious animosity." The chief thing to be noted here is President Roosevelt's tacit recognition of class animosity in the industrial world, and his fear, which language cannot portray stronger, that this class animosity may spread to the political world. Yet this is the very policy which the socialists have announced in their declaration of war against present-day society—to capture the political machinery of society and by that machinery destroy present-day society.

The New York *Independent* for February 12, 1903, recognized without qualification the class struggle. "It is impossible fairly to pass upon the methods of labor unions, or to devise plans for remedying their abuses, until it is recognized, to begin with, that unions are based upon class antagonism and that their policies are dictated by the necessities of social warfare. A strike is a rebellion against the owners of property. The rights of property are protected by government. And a strike, under certain provocation, may extend as far as did the general strike in Belgium a few years since, when practically the entire wage-earning population stopped work in order to force political concessions from the property-owning classes. This is an extreme case, but it brings out vividly the real nature of labor organization as a species of warfare whose object in the coercion of one class by another class."

It has been shown, theoretically and actually, that there is a class struggle in the United States. The quarrel over the division of the joint product is irreconcilable. The working class is no longer losing its strongest and most capable members. These men, denied room for their ambition in the capitalist ranks, remain to be the leaders of the workers, to spur them to discontent, to make them conscious of their class, to lead them to revolt.

This revolt, appearing spontaneously all over the industrial field in the form of demands for an increased share of the joint product, is being carefully and shrewdly shaped for a political assault upon society. The leaders, with the carelessness of fatalists, do not hesitate for an instant to publish their intentions to the world. They intend to direct the labor revolt to the capture of the political machinery of society. With the political machinery once in their hands, which will also give them the control of the police, the army, the navy, and the courts, they will confiscate with or without remuneration, all the possessions of the capitalist class which are used in the production and distribution of the necessaries and luxuries of life. By this, they mean to apply the law of eminent domain to the land, and to extend the law of eminent domain till it embraces the mines, the factories, the railroads, and the ocean carriers. In short, they intend to destroy present-day society, which they contend is run in the interest of another class, and from the materials to construct a new society, which will be run in their interest.

On the other hand, the capitalist class is beginning to grow conscious of itself and of the struggle which is being waged. It is already forming offensive and defensive leagues, while some of the most prominent figures in the nation are preparing to lead it in the attack upon socialism.

The question to be solved is not one of Malthusianism, "projected efficiency," nor ethics. It is a question of might. Whichever class is to win, will win by virtue of superior strength; for the workers are beginning to say, as they said to Mr. Cunniff, "Malthus be damned." In their own minds they find no sanction for continuing the individual struggle for the survival of the fittest. As Mr. Gompers has said, they want more, and more, and more. The ethical import of Mr. Kidd's plan of the present generation putting up with less in order that race efficiency may be projected into a remote future, has no bearing upon their actions. They refuse to be the "glad perishers" so glowingly described by Nietzsche.

It remains to be seen how promptly the capitalist class will respond to the call to arms. Upon its promptness rests its existence, for if it sits idly by, soothfully proclaiming that what ought not to be cannot be, it will find the roof beams crashing about its head. The capitalist class is in the numerical minority, and bids fair to be outvoted if it does not put a stop to the vast propaganda being waged by its enemy. It is no longer a question of whether or not there is a class struggle. The question now is, what will be the outcome of the class struggle?

The Scab

In a competitive society, where men struggle with one another for food and shelter, what is more natural than that generosity, when it diminishes the food and shelter of men other than he who is generous, should be held an accursed thing? Wise old saws to the contrary, he who takes from a man's purse takes from his existence. To strike at a man's food and shelter is to strike at his life; and in a society organized on a tooth-and-nail basis, such an act, performed though it may be under the guise of generosity, is none the less menacing and terrible.

It is for this reason that a laborer is so fiercely hostile to another laborer who offers to work for less pay or longer hours. To hold his place, (which is to live), he must offset this offer by another equally liberal, which is equivalent to giving away somewhat from the food and shelter he enjoys. To sell his day's work for $2, instead of $2.50, means that he, his wife, and his children will not have so good a roof over their heads, so warm clothes on their backs, so substantial food in their stomachs. Meat will be bought less frequently and it will be tougher and less nutritious, stout new shoes will go less often on the children's feet, and disease and death will be more imminent in a cheaper house and neighborhood.

Thus the generous laborer, giving more of a day's work for less return (measured in terms of food and shelter), threatens the life of his less generous brother laborer, and at the best, if he does not destroy that life, he diminishes it. Whereupon the less generous laborer looks upon him as an enemy, and, as men are inclined to do in a tooth-and-nail society, he tries to kill the man who is trying to kill him.

When a striker kills with a brick the man who has taken his place, he has no sense of wrong-doing. In the deepest holds of his being, though he does not reason the impulse, he has an ethical sanction. He feels dimly that he has justification, just as the home-defending Boer felt, though more sharply, with each bullet he fired at the invading English. Behind every brick thrown by a striker is the selfish will "to live" of himself, and the slightly altruistic will "to live" of his family. The family group came into the world before the State group, and society, being still on the primitive basis of tooth and nail, the will "to live" of the State is not so compelling to the striker as is the will "to live" of his family and himself.

In addition to the use of bricks, clubs, and bullets, the selfish laborer finds it necessary to express his feelings in speech. Just as the peaceful country-dweller calls the sea-rover a "pirate," and the stout burgher calls the man who breaks into his strong-box a "robber," so the selfish laborer applies the opprobrious epithet "scab" to the laborer who takes from him food and shelter by being more generous in the disposal of his labor power. The sentimental connotation of "scab" is as terrific as that of "traitor" or "Judas," and a sentimental definition would be as deep and varied as the human heart. It is far easier to arrive at what may be called a technical definition, worded in commercial terms, as, for instance, that *a scab is one who gives more value for the same price than another.*

The laborer who gives more time or strength or skill for the same wage than another, or equal time or strength or skill for a less wage, is a scab. This generousness on his part is hurtful to his fellow-laborers, for it compels them to an equal generousness which is not to their liking, and which gives them less of food and shelter. But a word may be said for the scab. Just as his act makes his rivals compulsorily generous, so do they, by fortune of birth and training, make compulsory his act of generousness. He does not scab because he wants to scab. No whim of the spirit, no burgeoning of the heart, leads him to give more of his labor power than they for a certain sum.

It is because he cannot get work on the same terms as they that he is a scab. There is less work than there are men to do work. This is patent, else the scab would not loom so large on the labor-market horizon. Because they are stronger than he, or more skilled, or more energetic, it is impossible for him to take their places at the same wage. To take their places he must give more value, must work longer hours or receive a smaller wage. He does so, and he cannot help it, for his will "to live" is driving him on as well as they are being driven on by their will "to live"; and to live he must win food and shelter, which he can do only by receiving permission to work from some man who owns a bit of land or a piece of machinery. And to receive permission from this man, he must make the transaction profitable for him.

Viewed in this light, the scab, who gives more labor power for a certain price than his fellows, is not so generous after all. He is no more generous with his energy than the chattel slave and the convict laborer, who, by the way, are the almost perfect scabs. They give their labor power for about the minimum possible price. But, within limits, they may loaf and malinger, and, as scabs, are exceeded by the machine, which never loafs and malingers and which is the ideally perfect scab.

It is not nice to be a scab. Not only is it not in good social taste and comradeship, but, from the standpoint of food and shelter, it is bad business policy. Nobody desires to scab, to give most for least. The ambition of every individual is quite the opposite, to give least for most; and, as a result, living in a tooth-and-nail society, battle royal is waged by the ambitious individuals. But in its most salient aspect, that of the struggle over the division of the joint product, it is no longer a battle between individuals, but between groups of individuals. Capital and labor apply themselves to raw material, make something useful out of it, add to its value, and then proceed to quarrel over the division of the added value. Neither cares to give most for least. Each is intent on giving less than the other and on receiving more.

Labor combines into its unions, capital into partnerships, associations, corporations, and trusts. A group-struggle is the result, in which the individuals, as individuals, play no part. The Brotherhood of Carpenters and Joiners, for instance, serves notice on the Master Builders' Association that it demands an increase of the wage of its members from $3.50 a day to $4, and a Saturday half-holiday without pay. This means that the carpenters are trying to give less for more. Where they received $21 for six full days, they are endeavoring to get $22 for five days and a half,—that is, they will work half a day less each week and receive a dollar more.

Also, they expect the Saturday half-holiday to give work to one additional man for each eleven previously employed. This last affords a splendid example of the development of the group idea. In this par-

ticular struggle the individual has no chance at all for life. The individual carpenter would be crushed like a mote by the Master Builders' Association, and like a mote the individual master builder would
be crushed by the Brotherhood of Carpenters and Joiners.

In the group-struggle over the division of the joint product, labor
utilizes the union with its two great weapons, the strike and the boycott; while capital utilizes the trust and the association, the weapons
of which are the black-list, the lockout, and the scab. The scab is by
far the most formidable weapon of the three. He is the man who breaks
strikes and causes all the trouble. Without him there would be no
trouble, for the strikers are willing to remain out peacefully and in-
definitely so long as other men are not in their places, and so long as
the particular aggregation of capital with which they are fighting is
eating its head off in enforced idleness.

But both warring groups have reserve weapons. Were it not for the
scab, these weapons would not be brought into play. But the scab
takes the place of the striker, who begins at once to wield a most
powerful weapon, terrorism. The will "to live" of the scab recoils
from the menace of broken bones and violent death. With all due
respect to the labor leaders, who are not to be blamed for volubly
asseverating otherwise, terrorism is a well-defined and eminently successful policy of the labor unions. It has probably won them more
strikes than all the rest of the weapons in their arsenal. This terrorism, however, must be clearly understood. It is directed solely
against the scab, placing him in such fear for life and limb as to drive
him out of the contest. But when terrorism gets out of hand and in-
offensive non-combatants are injured, law and order threatened, and
property destroyed, it becomes an edged tool that cuts both ways.
This sort of terrorism is sincerely deplored by the labor leaders, for
it has probably lost them as many strikes as have been lost by any
other single cause.

The scab is powerless under terrorism. As a rule, he is not so good
nor gritty a man as the men he is displacing, and he lacks their fighting organization. He stands in dire need of stiffening and backing.
His employers, the capitalists, draw their two remaining weapons, the
ownership of which is debatable, but which they for the time being
happen to control. These two weapons may be called the political
and judicial machinery of society. When the scab crumples up and
is ready to go down before the fists, bricks, and bullets of the labor
group, the capitalist group puts the police and soldiers into the field,

and begins a general bombardment of injunctions. Victory usually follows, for the labor group cannot withstand the combined assault of gatling guns and injunctions.

But it has been noted that the ownership of the political and judicial machinery of society is debatable. In the Titanic struggle over the division of the joint product, each group reaches out for every available weapon. Nor are they blinded by the smoke of conflict. They fight their battles as coolly and collectedly as ever battles were fought on paper. The capitalist group has long since realized the immense importance of controlling the political and judicial machinery of society. Taught by gatlings and injunctions, which have smashed many an otherwise successful strike, the labor group is beginning to realize that it all depends upon who is behind and who is before the gatlings and the injunctions. And he who knows the labor movement knows that there is slowly growing up and being formulated a clear and definite policy for the capture of the political and judicial machinery.

This is the terrible spectre which Mr. John Graham Brooks sees looming portentously over the twentieth century world. No man may boast a more intimate knowledge of the labor movement than he; and he reiterates again and again the dangerous likelihood of the whole labor group capturing the political machinery of society. As he says in his recent book:[1] "It is not probable that employers can destroy unionism in the United States. Adroit and desperate attempts will, however, be made, if we mean by unionism the undisciplined and aggressive fact of vigorous and determined organizations. If capital should prove too strong in this struggle, the result is easy to predict. The employers have only to convince organized labor that it cannot hold its own against the capitalist manager, and the whole energy that now goes to the union will turn to an aggressive political socialism. It will not be the harmless sympathy with increased city and state functions which trade unions already feel; it will become a turbulent political force bent upon using every weapon of taxation against the rich."

This struggle not to be a scab, to avoid giving more for less and to succeed in giving less for more, is more vital than it would appear on the surface. The capitalist and labor groups are locked together in desperate battle, and neither side is swayed by moral considera-

---

[1] *The Social Unrest.* Macmillan Company.

tions more than skin-deep. The labor group hires business agents, lawyers, and organizers, and is beginning to intimidate legislators by the strength of its solid vote; and more directly, in the near future, it will attempt to control legislation by capturing it bodily through the ballot-box. On the other hand, the capitalist group, numerically weaker, hires newspapers, universities, and legislatures, and strives to bend to its need all the forces which go to mould public opinion.

The only honest morality displayed by either side is white-hot indignation at the iniquities of the other side. The striking teamster complacently takes a scab driver into an alley, and with an iron bar breaks his arms, so that he can drive no more, but cries out to high Heaven for justice when the capitalist breaks his skull by means of a club in the hands of a policeman. Nay, the members of a union will declaim in impassioned rhetoric for the God-given right of an eight-hour day, and at the time be working their own business agent seventeen hours out of the twenty-four.

A capitalist such as Collis P. Huntington, and his name is Legion, after a long life spent in buying the aid of countless legislatures, will wax virtuously wrathful, and condemn in unmeasured terms "the dangerous tendency of crying out to the Government for aid" in the way of labor legislation. Without a quiver, a member of the capitalist group will run tens of thousands of pitiful child-laborers through his life-destroying cotton factories, and weep maudlin and constitutional tears over one scab hit in the back with a brick. He will drive a "compulsory" free contract with an unorganized laborer on the basis of a starvation wage, saying, "Take it or leave it," knowing that to leave it means to die of hunger, and in the next breath, when the organizer entices that laborer into a union, will storm patriotically about the inalienable right of all men to work. In short, the chief moral concern of either side is with the morals of the other side. They are not in the business for their moral welfare, but to achieve the enviable position of the non-scab who gets more than he gives.

But there is more to the question than has yet been discussed. The labor scab is no more detestable to his brother laborers than is the capitalist scab to his brother capitalists. A capitalist may get most for least in dealing with his laborers, and in so far be a non-scab; but at the same time, in his dealings with his fellow-capitalists, he may give most for least and be the very worst kind of scab. The most heinous crime an employer of labor can commit is to scab on his fellow-employers of labor. Just as the individual laborers have organized into

groups to protect themselves from the peril of the scab laborer, so
have the employers organized into groups to protect themselves from
the peril of the scab employer. The employers' federations, associa-
ations, and trusts are nothing more nor less than unions. They are
organized to destroy scabbing amongst themselves and to encourage
scabbing amongst others. For this reason they pool interests, determine prices, and present an unbroken and aggressive front to the
labor group.

As has been said before, nobody likes to play the compulsorily
generous rôle of scab. It is a bad business proposition on the face of it.
And it is patent that there would be no capitalist scabs if there were
not more capital than there is work for capital to do. When there are
enough factories in existence to supply, with occasional stoppages, a
certain commodity, the building of new factories by a rival concern,
for the production of that commodity, is plain advertisement that that
capital is out of a job. The first act of this new aggregation of capital
will be to cut prices, to give more for less,—in short to scab, to strike
at the very existence of the less generous aggregation of capital the
work of which it is trying to do.

No scab capitalist strives to give more for less for any other reason
than that he hopes, by undercutting a competitor and driving that
competitor out of the market, to get that market and its profits for
himself. His ambition is to achieve the day when he shall stand alone
in the field both as buyer and seller,—when he will be the royal non-
scab, buying most for least, selling least for most, and reducing all
about him, the small buyers and sellers, (the consumers and the laborers), to a general condition of scabdom. This, for example, has been
the history of Mr. Rockefeller and the Standard Oil Company.
Through all the sordid villainies of scabdom he has passed, until to-day
he is a most regal non-scab. However, to continue in this enviable
position, he must be prepared at a moment's notice to go scabbing
again. And he is prepared. Whenever a competitor arises, Mr. Rockefeller changes about from giving least for most and gives most for
least with such a vengeance as to drive the competitor out of existence.

The banded capitalists discriminate against a scab capitalist by refusing him trade advantages, and by combining against him in most
relentless fashion. The banded laborers, discriminating against a
scab laborer in more primitive fashion, with a club, are no more
merciless than the banded capitalists.

Mr. Casson tells of a New York capitalist who withdrew from the Sugar Union several years ago and became a scab. He was worth something like twenty millions of dollars. But the Sugar Union, standing shoulder to shoulder with the Railroad Union and several other unions, beat him to his knees till he cried "Enough." So frightfully did they beat him that he was obliged to turn over to his creditors his home, his chickens, and his gold watch. In point of fact, he was as thoroughly bludgeoned by the Federation of Capitalist Unions as ever scab workman was bludgeoned by a labor union. The intent in either case is the same,—to destroy the scab's producing power. The labor scab with concussion of the brain is put out of business, and so is the capitalist scab who has lost all his dollars down to his chickens and his watch.

But the rôle of scab passes beyond the individual. Just as individuals scab on other individuals, so do groups scab on other groups. And the principle involved is precisely the same as in the case of the simple labor scab. A group, in the nature of its organization, is often compelled to give most for least, and, so doing, to strike at the life of another group. At the present moment all Europe is appalled by that colossal scab, the United States. And Europe is clamorous with agitation for a Federation of National Unions to protect her from the United States. It may be remarked, in passing, that in its prime essentials this agitation in no wise differs from the trade-union agitation among workmen in any industry. The trouble is caused by the scab who is giving most for least. The result of the American scab's nefarious actions will be to strike at the food and shelter of Europe. The way for Europe to protect herself is to quit bickering among her parts and to form a union against the scab. And if the union is formed, armies and navies may be expected to be brought into play in fashion similar to the bricks and clubs in ordinary labor struggles.

In this connection, and as one of many walking delegates for the nations, M. Leroy-Beaulieu, the noted French economist, may well be quoted. In a letter to the Vienna *Tageblatt,* he advocates an economic alliance among the Continental nations for the purpose of barring out American goods, an economic alliance, in his own language, *"which may possibly and desirably develop into a political alliance."*

It will be noted, in the utterances of the Continental walking delegates, that, one and all, they leave England out of the proposed union. And in England herself the feeling is growing that her days are numbered if she cannot unite for offence and defence with the great American scab. As Andrew Carnegie said some time ago, "The only course for Great Britain seems to be reunion with her grandchild or sure decline to a secondary place, and then to comparative insignificance in the future annals of the English-speaking race."

Cecil Rhodes, speaking of what would have obtained but for the pig-headedness of George III, and of what will obtain when England and the United States are united, said, *"No cannon would . . . be fired on either hemisphere but by permission of the English race."* It would seem that England, fronted by the hostile Continental Union and flanked by the great American scab, has nothing left but to join with the scab and play the historic labor rôle of armed Pinkerton. Granting the words of Cecil Rhodes, the United States would be enabled to scab without let or hindrance on Europe, while England, as professional strike-breaker and policeman, destroyed the unions and kept order.

All this may appear fantastic and erroneous, but there is in it a soul of truth vastly more significant than it may seem. Civilization may be expressed to-day in terms of trade-unionism. Individual struggles have largely passed away, but group-struggles increase prodigiously. And the things for which the groups struggle are the same as of old. Shorn of all subtleties and complexities, the chief struggle of men, and of groups of men, is for food and shelter. And, as of old they struggled with tooth and nail, so to-day they struggle with teeth and nails elongated into armies and navies, machines, and economic advantages.

Under the definition that a scab is *one who gives more value for the same price than another,* it would seem that society can be generally divided into the two classes of the scabs and the non-scabs. But on closer investigation, however, it will be seen that the non-scab is a vanishing quantity. In the social jungle, everybody is preying upon everybody else. As in the case of Mr. Rockefeller, he who was a scab yesterday is a non-scab to-day, and to-morrow may be a scab again.

The woman stenographer or bookkeeper who receives forty dollars per month where a man was receiving seventy-five is a scab. So is the woman who does a man's work at a weaving-machine, and the child who goes into the mill or factory. And the father, who is scabbed out of work by the wives and children of other men, sends his own wife and children to scab in order to save himself.

When a publisher offers an author better royalties than other publishers have been paying him, he is scabbing on those other publishers. The reporter on a newspaper, who feels he should be receiving a larger salary for his work, says so, and is shown the door, is replaced by a reporter who is a scab; whereupon, when the belly-need presses, the displaced reporter goes to another paper and scabs himself. The minister who hardens his heart to a call, and waits for a certain congregation to offer him say $500 a year more, often finds himself scabbed upon by another and more impecunious minister; and the next time it is *his* turn to scab while a brother minister is hardening his heart to a call. The scab is everywhere. The professional strike-breakers, who as a class receive large wages, will scab on one another, while scab unions are even formed to prevent scabbing upon scabs.

There are non-scabs, but they are usually born so, and are protected by the whole might of society in the possession of their food and shelter. King Edward is such a type, as are all individuals who receive hereditary food-and-shelter privileges,—such as the present Duke of Bedford, for instance, who yearly receives $75,000 from the good people of London because some former king gave some former ancestor of his the market privileges of Covent Garden. The irresponsible rich are likewise non-scabs,—and by them is meant that coupon-clipping class which hires its managers and brains to invest the money usually left it by its ancestors.

Outside these lucky creatures, all the rest, at one time or another in their lives, are scabs, at one time or another are engaged in giving more for a certain price than any one else. The meek professor in some endowed institution, by his meek suppression of his convictions, is giving more for his salary than gave the other and more outspoken professor whose chair he occupies. And when a political party dangles a full dinner-pail in the eyes of the toiling masses, it is offering more for a vote than the dubious dollar of the opposing party. Even a money-lender is not above taking a slightly lower rate of interest and saying nothing about it.

Such is the tangle of conflicting interests in a tooth-and-nail society that people cannot avoid being scabs, are often made so against their desires, and are often unconsciously made so. When several trades in a certain locality demand and receive an advance in wages, they are unwittingly making scabs of their fellow-laborers in that district who have received no advance in wages. In San Francisco the barbers, laundry-workers, and milk-wagon drivers received such an advance

in wages. Their employers promptly added the amount of this advance
to the selling price of their wares. The price of shaves, of washing,
and of milk went up. This reduced the purchasing power of the unorganized laborers, and, in point of fact, reduced their wages and
made them greater scabs.

Because the British laborer is disinclined to scab,—that is, because he restricts his output in order to give less for the wage he
receives,—it is to a certain extent made possible for the American
capitalist, who receives a less restricted output from his laborers,
to play the scab on the English capitalist. As a result of this, (of course
combined with other causes), the American capitalist and the American laborer are striking at the food and shelter of the English capitalist and laborer.

The English laborer is starving to-day because, among other things,
he is not a scab. He practices the policy of "ca' canny," which may be
defined as "go easy." In order to get most for least, in many trades he
performs but from one-fourth to one-sixth of the labor he is well able
to perform. An instance of this is found in the building of the Westinghouse Electric Works at Manchester. The British limit per man was
400 bricks per day. The Westinghouse Company imported a "driving"
American contractor, aided by half a dozen "driving" American foremen, and the British bricklayer swiftly attained an average of 1800
bricks per day, with a maximum of 2500 bricks for the plainest work.

But the British laborer's policy of "ca' canny," which is the very
honorable one of giving least for most, and which is likewise the
policy of the English capitalist, is nevertheless frowned upon by the
English capitalist, whose business existence is threatened by the
great American scab. From the rise of the factory system, the English
capitalist gladly embraced the opportunity, wherever he found it, of
giving the least for most. He did it all over the world whenever he
enjoyed a market monopoly, and he did it at home with the laborers
employed in his mills, destroying them like flies till prevented, within
limits, by the passage of the Factory Acts. Some of the proudest
fortunes of England to-day may trace their origin to the giving of least
for most to the miserable slaves of the factory towns. But at the present time the English capitalist is outraged because his laborers are
employing against him precisely the same policy he employed against
them, and which he would employ again did the chance present itself.

Yet "ca' canny" is a disastrous thing to the British laborer. It has
driven ship-building from England to Scotland, bottle-making from

Scotland to Belgium, flint-glass-making from England to Germany, and to-day is steadily driving industry after industry to other countries. A correspondent from Northampton wrote not long ago: "Factories are working half and third time. . . . There is no strike, there is no real labor trouble, but the masters and men are alike suffering from sheer lack of employment. Markets which were once theirs are now American." It would seem that the unfortunate British laborer is 'twixt the devil and the deep sea. If he gives most for least, he faces a frightful slavery such as marked the beginning of the factory system. If he gives least for most, he drives industry away to other countries and has no work at all.

But the union laborers of the United States have nothing of which to boast, while, according to their trade-union ethics, they have a great deal of which to be ashamed. They passionately preach short hours and big wages, the shorter the hours and the bigger the wages the better. Their hatred for a scab is as terrible as the hatred of a patriot for a traitor, of a Christian for a Judas. And in the face of all this, they are as colossal scabs as the United States is a colossal scab. For all of their boasted unions and high labor ideals, they are about the most thoroughgoing scabs on the planet.

Receiving $4.50 per day, because of his proficiency and immense working power, the American laborer has been known to scab upon scabs (so called) who took his place and received only $0.90 per day for a longer day. In this particular instance, five Chinese coolies, working longer hours, gave less value for the price received from their employer than did one American laborer.

It is upon his brother laborers overseas that the American laborer most outrageously scabs. As Mr. Casson has shown, an English nail-maker gets $3 per week, while an American nail-maker gets $30. But the English worker turns out 200 pounds of nails per week, while the American turns out 5500 pounds. If he were as "fair" as his English brother, other things being equal, he would be receiving, at the English worker's rate of pay, $82.50. As it is, he is scabbing upon his English brother to the tune of $79.50 per week. Dr. Schultze-Gaevernitz has shown that a German weaver produces 466 yards of cotton a week at a cost of .303 per yard, while an American weaver produces 1200 yards at a cost of .02 per yard.

But, it may be objected, a great part of this is due to the more improved American machinery. Very true, but none the less a great part is still due to the superior energy, skill, and willingness of the Ameri-

can laborer. The English laborer is faithful to the policy of "ca'
canny." He refuses point-blank to get the work out of a machine that
the New World scab gets out of a machine. Mr. Maxim, observing a
wasteful hand-labor process in his English factory, invented a machine
which he proved capable of displacing several men. But workman after
workman was put at the machine, and without exception they turned
out neither more nor less than a workman turned out by hand. They
obeyed the mandate of the union and went easy, while Mr. Maxim
gave up in despair. Nor will the British workman run machines at as
high speed as the American, nor will he run so many. An American
workman will "give equal attention simultaneously to three, four, or
six machines or tools, while the British workman is compelled by his
trade union to limit his attention to one, so that employment may be
given to half a dozen men."

But, for scabbing, no blame attaches itself anywhere. With rare
exceptions, all the people in the world are scabs. The strong, capable
workman gets a job and holds it because of his strength and capacity.
And he holds it because out of his strength and capacity he gives a
better value for his wage than does the weaker and less capable workman. Therefore he is scabbing upon his weaker and less capable
brother workman. He is giving more value for the price paid by the
employer.

The superior workman scabs upon the inferior workman because
he is so constituted and cannot help it. The one, by fortune of birth
and upbringing, is strong and capable; the other, by fortune of birth
and upbringing, is not so strong nor capable. It is for the same reason
that one country scabs upon another. That country which has the
good fortune to possess great natural resources, a finer sun and soil,
unhampering institutions, and a deft and intelligent labor class and
capitalist class is bound to scab upon a country less fortunately situated. It is the good fortune of the United States that is making her the
colossal scab, just as it is the good fortune of one man to be born with
a straight back while his brother is born with a hump.

It is not good to give most for least, not good to be a scab. The
word has gained universal opprobrium. On the other hand, to be a
non-scab, to give least for most, is universally branded as stingy,
selfish, and unchristian-like. So all the world, like the British workman, is 'twixt the devil and the deep sea. It is treason to one's fellows
to scab, it is unchristian-like not to scab.

Since to give least for most, and to give most for least, are universally bad, what remains? Equity remains, which is to give like for like, the same for the same, neither more nor less. But this equity, society, as at present constituted, cannot give. It is not in the nature of present-day society for men to give like for like, the same for the same. And so long as men continue to live in this competitive society, struggling tooth and nail with one another for food and shelter, (which is to struggle tooth and nail with one another for life), that long will the scab continue to exist. His will "to live" will force him to exist. He may be flouted and jeered by his brothers, he may be beaten with bricks and clubs by the men who by superior strength and capacity scab upon him as he scabs upon them by longer hours and smaller wages, but through it all he will persist, giving a bit more of most for least than they are giving.

The Tramp

Mr. Francis O'Neil, General Superintendent of Police, Chicago, speaking of the tramp, says: "Despite the most stringent police regulations, a great city will have a certain number of homeless vagrants to shelter through the winter." "Despite,"—mark the word, a confession of organized helplessness as against unorganized necessity. If police regulations are stringent and yet fail, then that which makes them fail, namely, the tramp, must have still more stringent reasons for succeeding. This being so, it should be of interest to inquire into these reasons, to attempt to discover why the nameless and homeless vagrant sets at naught the right arm of the corporate power of our great cities, why all that is weak and worthless is stronger than all that is strong and of value.

Mr. O'Neil is a man of wide experience on the subject of tramps. He may be called a specialist. As he says of himself: "As an old-time desk sergeant and police captain, I have had almost unlimited opportunity to study and analyze this class of floating population, which seeks the city in winter and scatters abroad through the country in the spring." He then continues: "This experience reiterated the lesson that the vast majority of these wanderers are of the class with whom a life of vagrancy is a chosen means of living without work." Not only is it to be inferred from this that there is a large class in society which lives without work, for Mr. O'Neil's testimony further shows that this class is forced to live without work.

He says: "I have been astonished at the multitude of those who have unfortunately engaged in occupations which practically force them to become loafers for at least a third of the year. And it is from this class that the tramps are largely recruited. I recall a certain winter when it seemed to me that a large portion of the inhabitants of Chicago belonged to this army of unfortunates. I was stationed at a police station not far from where an ice harvest was ready for the cutters. The ice company advertised for helpers, and the very night this call appeared in the newspapers our station was packed with homeless men, who asked shelter in order to be at hand for the morning's work. Every foot of floor space was given over to these lodgers and scores were still unaccommodated."

And again: "And it must be confessed that the man who is willing to do honest labor for food and shelter is a rare specimen in this vast army of shabby and tattered wanderers who seek the warmth of the city with the coming of the first snow." Taking into consideration the crowd of honest laborers that swamped Mr. O'Neil's station-house on the way to the ice-cutting, it is patent, if all tramps were looking for honest labor instead of a small minority, that the honest laborers would have a far harder task finding something honest to do for food and shelter. If the opinion of the honest laborers who swamped Mr. O'Neil's station-house were asked, one could rest confident that each and every man would express a preference for fewer honest laborers on the morrow when he asked the ice foreman for a job.

And, finally, Mr. O'Neil says: "The humane and generous treatment which this city has accorded the great army of homeless unfortunates has made it the victim of wholesale imposition, and this well-intended policy of kindness has resulted in making Chicago the winter Mecca of a vast and undesirable floating population." That is to say, because of her kindness, Chicago had more than her fair share of tramps; because she was humane and generous she suffered wholesale imposition. From this we must conclude that it does not do to be *humane* and *generous* to our fellow-men—when they are tramps. Mr. O'Neil is right, and that this is no sophism it is the intention of this article, among other things, to show.

In a general way we may draw the following inferences from the remarks of Mr. O'Neil: (1) The tramp is stronger than organized society and cannot be put down; (2) The tramp is "shabby," "tattered," "homeless," "unfortunate"; (3) There is a "vast" number of tramps; (4) Very few tramps are willing to do honest work; (5) Those tramps who are willing to do honest work have to hunt very hard to find it; (6) The tramp is undesirable.

To this last let the contention be appended that the tramp is only *personally* undesirable; that he is *negatively* desirable; that the function he performs in society is a negative function; and that he is the by-product of economic necessity.

It is very easy to demonstrate that there are more men than there is work for men to do. For instance, what would happen to-morrow if one hundred thousand tramps should become suddenly inspired with an overmastering desire for work? It is a fair question. "Go to work" is preached to the tramp every day of his life. The judge on the bench, the pedestrian in the street, the housewife at the kitchen door, all unite in advising him to go to work. So what would happen to-morrow if one hundred thousand tramps acted upon this advice and strenuously and indomitably sought work? Why, by the end of the week one hundred thousand workers, their places taken by the tramps, would receive their time and be "hitting the road" for a job.

Ella Wheeler Wilcox unwittingly and uncomfortably demonstrated the disparity between men and work.[1] She made a casual reference, in a newspaper column she conducts, to the difficulty two business men found in obtaining good employees. The first morning mail brought her seventy-five applications for the position, and at the end of two weeks over two hundred people had applied.

Still more strikingly was the same proposition recently demonstrated in San Francisco. A sympathetic strike called out a whole federation of trades' unions. Thousands of men, in many branches of trade, quit work,—draymen, sand teamsters, porters and packers, longshoremen, stevedores, warehousemen, stationary engineers, sailors, marine firemen, stewards, sea-cooks, and so forth,—an interminable list. It was a strike of large proportions. Every Pacific coast shipping city was involved, and the entire coasting service, from San Diego to Puget Sound, was virtually tied up. The time was considered auspicious. The Philippines and Alaska had drained the Pacific coast of surplus labor. It was summer-time, when the agricultural demand for laborers was at its height, and when the cities were bare of their floating populations. And yet there remained a body of surplus labor sufficient to take the places of the strikers. No matter what occupation, sea-cook or stationary engineer, sand teamster or warehouseman, in every case there was an idle worker ready to do the work. And not only ready but anxious. They fought for a chance to work. Men were killed, hundreds of heads were broken, the hospitals were filled with injured

---

[1] "From 43 to 52 per cent of all applicants need work rather than relief."— *Report of the Charity Organization Society of New York City.*

men, and thousands of assaults were committed. And still surplus laborers, "scabs," came forward to replace the strikers.

The question arises: *Whence came this second army of workers to replace the first army?* One thing is certain: the trades' unions did not scab on one another. Another thing is certain: no industry on the Pacific slope was crippled in the slightest degree by its workers being drawn away to fill the places of the strikers. A third thing is certain: the agricultural workers did not flock to the cities to replace the strikers. In this last instance it is worth while to note that the agricultural laborers wailed to High Heaven when a few of the strikers went into the country to compete with them in unskilled employments. So there is no accounting for this second army of workers. It simply was. It was there all this time, a surplus labor army in the year of our Lord 1901, a year adjudged most prosperous in the annals of the United States.[2]

The existence of the surplus labor army being established, there remains to be established the economic necessity for the surplus labor army. The simplest and most obvious need is that brought about by the fluctuation of production. If, when production is at low ebb, all men are at work, it necessarily follows that when production increases there will be no men to do the increased work. This may seem almost childish, and, if not childish, at least easily remedied. At low ebb let the men work shorter time; at high flood let them work overtime. The main objection to this is, that it is not done, and that we are considering what is, not what might be or should be.

Then there are great irregular and periodical demands for labor which must be met. Under the first head come all the big building and engineering enterprises. When a canal is to be dug or a railroad put through, requiring thousands of laborers, it would be hurtful to withdraw these laborers from the constant industries. And whether it is a canal to be dug or a cellar, whether five thousand men are required or five, it is well, in society as at present organized, that they be taken from the surplus labor army. The surplus labor army is the reserve fund of social energy, and this is one of the reasons for its existence.

Under the second head, periodical demands, come the harvests. Throughout the year, huge labor tides sweep back and forth across the

---

[2] Mr. Leiter, who owns a coal mine at the town of Zeigler, Illinois, in an interview printed in the *Chicago Record-Herald* of December 6, 1904, said: "When I go into the market to purchase labor, I propose to retain just as much freedom as does a purchaser in any other kind of a market. . . . There is no difficulty whatever in obtaining labor, *for the country is full of unemployed men.*"

United States. That which is sown and tended by few men, comes to sudden ripeness and must be gathered by many men; and it is inevitable that these many men form floating populations. In the late spring the berries must be picked, in the summer the grain garnered, in the fall the hops gathered, in the winter the ice harvested. In California a man may pick berries in Siskiyou, peaches in Santa Clara, grapes in the San Joaquin, and oranges in Los Angeles, going from job to job as the season advances, and traveling a thousand miles ere the season is done. But the great demand for agricultural labor is in the summer. In the winter, work is slack, and these floating populations eddy into the cities to eke out a precarious existence and harrow the souls of the police officers until the return of warm weather and work. If there were constant work at good wages for every man, who would harvest the crops?

But the last and most significant need for the surplus labor army remains to be stated. This surplus labor acts as a check upon all employed labor. It is the lash by which the masters hold the workers to their tasks, or drive them back to their tasks when they have revolted. It is the goad which forces the workers into the compulsory "free contracts" against which they now and again rebel. There is only one reason under the sun that strikes fail, and that is because there are always plenty of men to take the strikers' places.

The strength of the union to-day, other things remaining equal, is proportionate to the skill of the trade, or, in other words, proportionate to the pressure the surplus labor army can put upon it. If a thousand ditch-diggers strike, if is easy to replace them, wherefore the ditch-diggers have little or no organized strength. But a thousand highly skilled machinists are somewhat harder to replace, and in consequence the machinist unions are strong. The ditch-diggers are wholly at the mercy of the surplus labor army, the machinists only partly. To be invincible, a union must be a monopoly. It must control every man in its particular trade, and regulate apprentices so that the supply of skilled workmen may remain constant; this is the dream of the "Labor Trust" on the part of the captains of labor.

Once, in England, after the Great Plague, labor awoke to find there was more work for men than there were men to work. Instead of workers competing for favors from employers, employers were competing for favors from the workers. Wages went up and up, and continued to go up, until the workers demanded the full product of their toil. Now it is clear that, when labor receives its full product, capital must perish. And so the pygmy capitalists of that post-Plague day found their existence threatened by this untoward condition of affairs To save themselves, they set a maximum wage, restrained the workers from moving about from place to place, smashed incipient organization, refused to tolerate idlers, and by most barbarous legal penalties punished those who disobeyed. After that, things went on as before.

The point of this, of course, is to demonstrate the need of the surplus labor army. Without such an army, our present capitalist society would be powerless. Labor would organize as it never organized before, and the last least worker would be gathered into the unions. The full product of toil would be demanded, and capitalist society would crumble away. Nor could capitalist society save itself as did the post-Plague capitalist society. The time is past when a handful of masters, by imprisonment and barbarous punishment, can drive the legions of the workers to their tasks. Without a surplus labor army, the courts, police, and military are impotent. In such matters the function of the courts, police, and military is to preserve order, and to fill the places of strikers with surplus labor. If there be no surplus labor to instate, there is no function to perform; for disorder arises only during the process of instatement, when the striking labor army and the surplus labor army clash together. That is to say, that which maintains the integrity of the present industrial society more potently than the courts, police, and military is the surplus labor army.

It has been shown that there are more men than there is work for men, and that the surplus labor army is an economic necessity. To show how the tramp is a by-product of this economic necessity, it is necessary to inquire into the composition of the surplus labor army. What men form it? Why are they there? What do they do?

In the first place, since the workers must compete for employment, it inevitably follows that it is the fit and efficient who find employment. The skilled worker holds his place by virtue of his skill and efficiency. Were he less skilled, or were he unreliable or erratic, he would be swiftly replaced by a stronger competitor. The skilled and steady employments are not cumbered with clowns and idiots. A man finds his place according to his ability and the needs of the system, and those without ability, or incapable of satisfying the needs of the system, have no place. Thus, the poor telegrapher may develop into an excellent wood-chopper. But if the poor telegrapher cherishes the delusion that he is a good telegrapher, and at the same time disdains all other employments, he will have no employment at all, or he will be so poor at all other employments that he will work only now and again in lieu of better men. He will be among the first let off when times are dull, and among the last taken on when times are good. Or, to the point, he will be a member of the surplus labor army.

So the conclusion is reached that the less fit and less efficient, or the unfit and inefficient, compose the surplus labor army. Here are to be found the men who have tried and failed, the men who cannot hold jobs,—the plumber apprentice who could not become a journeyman, and the plumber journeyman too clumsy and dull to retain employment; switchmen who wreck trains; clerks who cannot balance books; blacksmiths who lame horses; lawyers who cannot plead; in short, the failures of every trade and profession, and failures, many of them, in divers trades and professions. Failure is writ large, and in their wretchedness they bear the stamp of social disapprobation. Common work, any kind of work, wherever or however they can obtain it, is their portion.

But these hereditary inefficients do not alone compose the surplus labor army. There are the skilled but unsteady and unreliable men; and the old men, once skilled, but, with dwindling powers, no longer skilled.[3] And there are good men, too, splendidly skilled and efficient, but thrust out of the employment of dying or disaster-smitten indus-

[3] "Despondent and weary with vain attempts to struggle against an unsympathetic world, two old men were brought before Police Judge McHugh this afternoon to see whether some means could not be provided for their support, at least until springtime.

"George Westlake was the first one to receive the consideration of the court. Westlake is seventy-two years old. A charge of habitual drunkenness was placed against him, and he was sentenced to a term in the county jail, though it is more than probable that he was never under the influence of intoxicating liquor in his life. The act on the part of the authorities was one of kindness for him, as in the county jail he will be provided with a good place to sleep and plenty to eat.

"Joe Coat, aged sixty-nine years, will serve ninety days in the county jail for much the same reason as Westlake. He states that, if given a chance to do so, he will go out to a wood-camp and cut timber during the winter, but the police authorities realize that he could not long survive such a task."—*From the Butte (Montana) Miner, December 7th, 1904.*

" 'I end my life because I have reached the age limit, and there is no place for me in this world. Please notify my wife, No. 222 West 129th Street, New York.' Having summed up the cause of his despondency in this final message, James Hollander, fifty-six years old, shot himself through the left temple, in his room at the Stafford Hotel, to-day."—*New York Herald.*

tries. In this connection it is not out of place to note the misfortune of the workers in the British iron trades, who are suffering because of American inroads. And, last of all, are the unskilled laborers, the hewers of wood and drawers of water, the ditch-diggers, the men of pick and shovel, the helpers, lumpers, roustabouts. If trade is slack on a seacoast of two thousand miles, or the harvests are light in a great interior valley, myriads of these laborers lie idle, or make life miserable for their fellows in kindred unskilled employments.

A constant filtration goes on in the working world, and good material is continually drawn from the surplus labor army. Strikes and industrial dislocations shake up the workers, bring good men to the surface and sink men as good or not so good. The hope of the skilled striker is in that the scabs are less skilled, or less capable of becoming skilled; yet each striker attests to the efficiency that lurks beneath. After the Pullman strike, a few thousand railroad men were chagrined to find the work they had flung down taken up by men as good as themselves.

But one thing must be considered here. Under the present system, if the weakest and least fit were as strong and fit as the best, and the best were correspondingly stronger and fitter, the same condition would obtain. There would be the same army of employed labor, the same army of surplus labor. The whole thing is relative. There is no absolute standard of efficiency.

Comes now the tramp. And all conclusions may be anticipated by saying at once that he is a tramp because some one has to be a tramp. If he left the "road" and became a *very* efficient common laborer, some *ordinarily* efficient common laborer would have to take to the "road." The nooks and crannies are crowded by the surplus laborers; and when the first snow flies, and the tramps are driven into the cities, things become overcrowded and stringent police regulations are necessary.

The tramp is one of two kinds of men: he is either a discouraged worker or a discouraged criminal. Now a discouraged criminal, on investigation, proves to be a discouraged worker, or the descendant of discouraged workers; so that, in the last analysis, the tramp is a discouraged worker. Since there is not work for all, discouragement for some is unavoidable. How, then, does this process of discouragement operate?

The lower the employment in the industrial scale, the harder the conditions. The finer, the more delicate, the more skilled the trade, the higher is it lifted above the struggle. There is less pressure, less sordidness, less savagery. There are fewer glass-blowers proportionate to the needs of the glass-blowing industry than there are ditch-diggers proportionate to the needs of the ditch-digging industry. And not only this, for it requires a glass-blower to take the place of a striking glass-blower, while any kind of a striker or out-of-work can take the place of a ditch-digger. So the skilled trades are more independent, have more individuality and latitude. They may confer with their masters, make demands, assert themselves. The unskilled laborers, on the other hand, have no voice in their affairs. The settlement of terms is none of their business. "Free contract" is all that remains to them. They may take what is offered, or leave it. There are plenty more of their kind. They do not count. They are members of the surplus labor army, and must be content with a hand-to-mouth existence.

The reward is likewise proportioned. The strong, fit worker in a skilled trade, where there is little labor pressure, is well compensated. He is a king compared with his less fortunate brothers in the unskilled occupations where the labor pressure is great. The mediocre worker not only is forced to be idle a large portion of the time, but when employed is forced to accept a pittance. A dollar a day on some days and nothing on other days will hardly support a man and wife and send children to school. And not only do the masters bear heavily upon him, and his own kind struggle for the morsel at his mouth, but all skilled and organized labor adds to his woe. Union men do not scab on one another, but in strikes, or when work is slack, it is considered "fair" for them to descend and take away the work of the common laborers. And take it away they do; for, as a matter of fact, a well-fed, ambitious machinist or a coremaker will transiently shovel coal better than an ill-fed, spiritless laborer.

Thus there is no encouragement for the unfit, inefficient, and mediocre. Their very inefficiency and mediocrity make them helpless as cattle and add to their misery. And the whole tendency for such is downward, until, at the bottom of the social pit, they are wretched, inarticulate beasts, living like beasts, breeding like beasts, dying like beasts. And how do they fare, these creatures born mediocre, whose heritage is neither brains nor brawn nor endurance? They are sweated in the slums in an atmosphere of discouragement and despair. There is no strength in weakness, no encouragement in foul air, vile food, and dank dens. They are there because they are so made that they are not fit to be higher up; but filth and obscenity do not strengthen the neck, nor does chronic emptiness of belly stiffen the back.

For the mediocre there is no hope. Mediocrity is a sin. Poverty is the penalty of failure,—poverty, from whose loins spring the criminal and the tramp, both failures, both discouraged workers. Poverty is the inferno where ignorance festers and vice corrodes, and where the physical, mental, and moral parts of nature are aborted and denied.

That the charge of rashness in splashing the picture be not incurred, let the following authoritative evidence be considered: first, the work and wages of mediocrity and inefficiency, and, second, the habitat:

The *New York Sun* of February 28, 1901, describes the opening of a factory in New York City by the American Tobacco Company. Cheroots were to be made in this factory in competition with other factories which refused to be absorbed by the trust. The trust advertised for girls. The crowd of men and boys who wanted work was so great in front of the building that the police were forced with their clubs to clear them away. The wage paid the girls was $2.50 per week, sixty cents of which went for car fare.[4]

Miss Nellie Mason Auten, a graduate student of the department of sociology at the University of Chicago, recently made a thorough investigation of the garment trades of Chicago. Her figures were published in the *American Journal of Sociology,* and commented upon by the *Literary Digest.* She found women working ten hours a day, six days a week, for forty cents per week (a rate of two-thirds of a cent an hour). Many women earned less than a dollar a week, and none of them worked every week. The following table will best summarize Miss Auten's investigations among a portion of the garment-workers:

INDUSTRY	AVERAGE INDIVIDUAL WEEKLY WAGES	AVERAGE NUMBER OF WEEKS EMPLOYED	AVERAGE YEARLY EARNINGS
Dressmakers	$ .90	42.	$37.00
Pants-finishers	1.31	27.58	42.41
Housewives and pants-finishers	1.58	30.21	47.49
Seamstresses	2.03	32.78	64.10
Pants-makers	2.13	30.77	75.61
Miscellaneous	2.77	29.	81.80
Tailors	6.22	31.96	211.92
General averages	$2.48	31.18	$76.74

[4] In the *San Francisco Examiner* of November 16, 1904, there is an account

Walter A. Wyckoff, who is as great an authority upon the worker as Josiah Flynt is on the tramp, furnishes the following Chicago experience:

"Many of the men were so weakened by the want and hardship of the winter that they were no longer in condition for effective labor. Some of the bosses who were in need of added hands were obliged to turn men away because of physical incapacity. One instance of this I shall not soon forget. It was when I overheard, early one morning at a factory gate, an interview between a would-be laborer and the boss. I knew the applicant for a Russian Jew, who had at home an old mother and a wife and two young children to support. He had had intermittent employment throughout the winter in a sweater's den,[5] barely enough to keep them all alive, and, after the hardships of the cold season, he was again in desperate straits for work.

"The boss had all but agreed to take him on for some sort of unskilled labor, when, struck by the cadaverous look of the man, he told him to bare his arm. Up went the sleeve of his coat and his ragged flannel shirt, exposing a naked arm with the muscles nearly gone, and the blue-white transparent skin stretched over sinews and the outline of the bones. Pitiful beyond words was his effort to give a semblance of strength to the biceps which rose faintly to the upward movement of the forearm. But the boss sent him off with an oath and a contemptuous laugh; and I watched the fellow as he turned down the street, facing the fact of his starving family with a despair at his heart which only mortal man can feel and no mortal tongue can speak."

Concerning habitat, Mr. Jacob Riis has stated that in New York City, in the block bounded by Stanton, Houston, Attorney, and Ridge streets, the size of which is 200 by 300, there is a warren of 2244 human beings.

In the block bounded by Sixty-first and Sixty-second streets, and

---

of the use of fire-hose to drive away three hundred men who wanted work at unloading a vessel in the harbor. So anxious were the men to get the two or three hours' job that they made a veritable mob and had to be driven off.

[5] "It was no uncommon thing in these sweatshops for men to sit bent over a sewing-machine continuously from eieven to fifteen hours a day in July weather, operating a sewing-machine by foot-power, and often so driven that they could not stop for lunch. The seasonal character of the work meant demoralizing toil for a few months in the year, and a not less demoralizing idleness for the remainder of the time. Consumption, the plague of the tenements and the especial plague of the garment industry, carried off many of these workers; poor nutrition and exhaustion, many more."—*From McClure's Magazine.*

Amsterdam and West End avenues, are over four thousand human creatures,—quite a comfortable New England village to crowd into one city block.

The Rev. Dr. Behrends, speaking of the block bounded by Canal, Hester, Eldridge, and Forsyth streets, says: "In a room 12 by 8 and 5½ feet high, it was found that nine persons slept and prepared their food. . . . In another room, located in a dark cellar, without screens or partitions, were together two men with their wives and a girl of fourteen, two single men and a boy of seventeen, two women and four boys,—nine, ten, eleven, and fifteen years old,—fourteen persons in all."

Here humanity rots. Its victims, with grim humor, call it "tenant-house rot." Or, as a legislative report puts it: "Here infantile life unfolds its bud, but perishes before its first anniversary. Here youth is ugly with loathsome disease, and the deformities which follow physical degeneration."

These are the men and women who are what they are because they were not better born, or because they happened to be unluckily born in time and space. Gauged by the needs of the system, they are weak and worthless. The hospital and the pauper's grave await them, and they offer no encouragement to the mediocre worker who has failed higher up in the industrial structure. Such a worker, conscious that he has failed, conscious from the hard fact that he cannot obtain work in the higher employments, finds several courses open to him. He may come down and be a beast in the social pit, for instance; but if he be of a certain caliber, the effect of the social pit will be to discourage him from work. In his blood a rebellion will quicken, and he will elect to become either a felon or a tramp.

If he has fought the hard fight, he is not unacquainted with the lure of the "road." When out of work and still undiscouraged, he has been forced to "hit the road" between large cities in his quest for a job. He has loafed, seen the country and green things, laughed in joy, lain on his back and listened to the birds singing overhead, unannoyed by factory whistles and bosses' harsh commands; and, most significant of all, *he has lived.* That is the point! He has not starved to death. Not only has he been care-free and happy, but he has lived! And from the knowledge that he has idled and is still alive, he achieves a new outlook on life; and the more he experiences the unenviable lot of the poor worker, the more the blandishments of the "road" take hold of him. And finally he flings his challenge in the face of society, imposes

a valorous boycott on all work, and joins the far-wanderers of Hoboland, the gypsy folk of this latter day.

But the tramp does not usually come from the slums. His place of
birth is ordinarily a bit above, and sometimes a very great bit above.
A confessed failure, he yet refuses to accept the punishment, and
swerves aside from the slum to vagabondage. The average beast in
the social pit is either too much of a beast, or too much of a slave to
the bourgeois ethics and ideals of his masters, to manifest this flicker
of rebellion. But the social pit, out of its discouragement and vicious-
ness, breeds criminals, men who prefer being beasts of prey to being
beasts of work. And the mediocre criminal, in turn, the unfit and inefficient criminal, is discouraged by the strong arm of the law and
goes over to trampdom.

These men, the discouraged worker and the discouraged criminal,
voluntarily withdraw themselves from the struggle for work. Industry
does not need them. There are no factories shut down through lack of
labor, no projected railroads unbuilt for want of pick-and-shovel men.
Women are still glad to toil for a dollar a week, and men and boys to
clamor and fight for work at the factory gates. No one misses these
discouraged men, and in going away they have made it somewhat
easier for those that remain.

So the case stands thus: There being more men than there is work
for men to do, a surplus labor army inevitably results. The surplus
labor army is an economic necessity; without it, present society would
fall to pieces. Into the surplus labor army are herded the mediocre, the
inefficient, the unfit, and those incapable of satisfying the industrial
needs of the system. The struggle for work between the members of
the surplus labor army is sordid and savage, and at the bottom of the
social pit the struggle is vicious and beastly. This struggle tends to discouragement, and the victims of this discouragement are the criminal
and the tramp. The tramp is not an economic necessity such as the
surplus labor army, but he is the by-product of an economic necessity.

The "road" is one of the safety-valves through which the waste of
the social organism is given off. And *being given off* constitutes the
negative function of the tramp. Society, as at present organized, makes
much waste of human life. This waste must be eliminated. Chloroform
or electrocution would be a simple, merciful solution of this problem of
elimination; but the ruling ethics, while permitting the human waste,
will not permit a humane elimination of that waste. This paradox

demonstrates the irreconcilability of theoretical ethics and industrial need.

And so the tramp becomes self-eliminating. And not only self! Since he is manifestly unfit for things as they are, and since kind is prone to beget kind, it is necessary that his kind cease with him, that his progeny shall not be, that he play the eunuch's part in this twentieth century after Christ. And he plays it. He does not breed. Sterility is his portion, as it is the portion of the woman on the street. They might have been mates, but society has decreed otherwise.

And, while it is not nice that these men should die, it is ordained that they must die, and we should not quarrel with them if they cumber our highways and kitchen stoops with their perambulating carcasses. This is a form of elimination we not only countenance but compel. Therefore let us be cheerful and honest about it. Let us be as stringent as we please with our police regulations, but for goodness' sake let us refrain from telling the tramp to go to work. Not only is it unkind, but it is untrue and hypocritical. We know there is no work for him. As the scapegoat to our economic and industrial sinning, or to the plan of things, if you will, we should give him credit. Let us be just. He is so made. Society made him. He did not make himself.

Revolution

"The present is enough for common souls,
Who, never looking forward, are indeed
Mere clay, wherein the footprints of their age
Are petrified forever."

I received a letter the other day. It was from a man in Arizona. It began, "Dear Comrade." It ended, "Yours for the Revolution." I replied to the letter, and my letter began, "Dear Comrade." It ended, "Yours for the Revolution." In the United States there are 400,000 men, of men and women nearly 1,000,000, who begin their letters, "Dear Comrade," and end them, "Yours for the Revolution." In Germany there are 3,000,000 men who begin their letters, "Dear Comrade," and end them, "Yours for the Revolution"; in France, 1,000,000 men; in Austria, 800,000 men; in Belgium, 300,000 men; in Italy, 250,000 men; in England, 100,000 men; in Switzerland, 100,000 men; in Denmark, 55,000 men; in Sweden, 50,000 men; in Holland, 40,000 men; in Spain, 30,000 men—comrades all, and revolutionists.

These are numbers which dwarfed the grand armies of Napoleon and Xerxes. But they are numbers not of conquest and maintenance of the established order, but of conquest and revolution. They compose, when the roll is called, an army of 7,000,000 men, who, in accordance with the conditions of to-day, are fighting with all their might for the conquest of the wealth of the world and for the complete overthrow of existing society.

There has never been anything like this revolution in the history of the world. There is nothing analogous between it and the American

Revolution or the French Revolution. It is unique, colossal. Other revolutions compare with it as asteroids compare with the sun. It is alone of its kind, the first world-revolution in a world whose history is replete with revolutions. And not only this, for it is the first organized movement of men to become a world movement, limited only by the limits of the planet.

This revolution is unlike all other revolutions in many respects. It is not sporadic. It is not a flame of popular discontent, arising in a day and dying down in a day. It is older than the present generation. It has a history and traditions, and a martyr-roll only less extensive possibly than the martyr-roll of Christianity. It has also a literature a myriad times more imposing, scientific, and scholarly than the literature of any previous revolution.

They call themselves "comrades," these men, comrades in the socialist revolution. Nor is the word empty and meaningless, coined of mere lip service. It knits men together as brothers, as men should be knit together who stand shoulder to shoulder under the red banner of revolt. This red banner, by the way, symbolizes the brotherhood of man, and does not symbolize the incendiarism that instantly connects itself with the red banner in the affrighted bourgeois mind. The comradeship of the revolutionists is alive and warm. It passes over geographical lines, transcends race prejudice, and has even proved itself mightier than the Fourth of July, spread-eagle Americanism of our forefathers. The French socialist workingmen and the German socialist workingmen forget Alsace and Lorraine, and, when war threatens, pass resolutions declaring that as workingmen and comrades they have no quarrel with each other. Only the other day, when Japan and Russia sprang at each other's throats, the revolutionists of Japan addressed the following message to the revolutionists of Russia: "Dear Comrades—Your government and ours have recently plunged into war to carry out their imperialistic tendencies, but for us socialists there are no boundaries, race, country, or nationality. We are comrades, brothers and sisters, and have no reason to fight. Your enemies are not the Japanese people, but our militarism and so-called patriotism. Patriotism and militarism are our mutual enemies."

In January, 1905, throughout the United States the socialists held mass-meetings to express their sympathy for their struggling comrades, the revolutionists of Russia, and, more to the point, to furnish the sinews of war by collecting money and cabling it to the Russian leaders.

The fact of this call for money, and the ready response, and the very wording of the call, make a striking and practical demonstration of the international solidarity of this world revolution: "Whatever may be the immediate results of the present revolt in Russia, the socialist propaganda in that country has received from it an impetus unparalleled in the history of modern class wars. The heroic battle for freedom is being fought almost exclusively by the Russian working-class under the intellectual leadership of Russian socialists, thus once more demonstrating the fact that the class-conscious workingmen have become the vanguard of all liberating movements of modern times."

Here are 7,000,000 comrades in an organized, international, world-wide, revolutionary movement. Here is a tremendous human force. It must be reckoned with. Here is power. And here is romance—romance so colossal that it seems to be beyond the ken of ordinary mortals. These revolutionists are swayed by great passion. They have a keen sense of personal right, much of reverence for humanity, but little reverence, if any at all, for the rule of the dead. They refuse to be ruled by the dead. To the bourgeois mind their unbelief in the dominant conventions of the established order is startling. They laugh to scorn the sweet ideals and dear moralities of bourgeois society. They intend to destroy bourgeois society with most of its sweet ideals and dear moralities, and chiefest among these are those that group themselves under such heads as private ownership of capital, survival of the fittest, and patriotism—even patriotism.

Such an army of revolution, 7,000,000 strong, is a thing to make rulers and ruling classes pause and consider. The cry of this army is, "No quarter! We want all that you possess. We will be content with nothing less than all that you possess. We want in our hands the reins of power and the destiny of mankind. Here are our hands. They are strong hands. We are going to take your governments, your palaces, and all your purpled ease away from you, and in that day you shall work for your bread even as the peasant in the field or the starved and runty clerk in your metropolises. Here are our hands. They are strong hands."

Well may rulers and ruling classes pause and consider. This is revolution. And, further, these 7,000,000 men are not an army on paper. Their fighting strength in the field is 7,000,000. To-day they cast 7,000,000 votes in the civilized countries of the world. Yesterday they were not so strong. To-morrow they will be still stronger. And they are fighters. They love peace. They are unafraid of war. They intend nothing less than to destroy existing capitalist society and to take possession of the whole world. If the law of the land permits, they fight for this end peaceably, at the ballot-box. If the law of the land does not permit, and if they have force meted out to them, they resort to force themselves. They meet violence with violence. Their hands are strong and they are unafraid. In Russia, for instance, there is no suffrage. The government executes the revolutionists. The revolutionists kill the officers of the government. The revolutionists meet legal murder with assassination.

Now here arises a particularly significant phase which would be well for the rulers to consider. Let me make it concrete. I am a revolutionist. Yet I am a fairly sane and normal individual. I speak, and I *think,* of these assassins in Russia as "my comrades." So do all the comrades in America, and all the 7,000,000 comrades in the world. Of what worth an organized, international, revolutionary movement if our comrades are not backed up the world over! The worth is shown by the fact that we do back up the assassinations by our comrades in Russia. They are not disciples of Tolstoy, nor are we. We are revolutionists.

Our comrades in Russia have formed what they call "The Fighting Organization." This Fighting Organization accused, tried, found guilty, and condemned to death, one Sipiaguin, Minister of Interior. On April 2 he was shot and killed in the Maryinsky Palace. Two years later the Fighting Organization condemned to death and executed another Minister of Interior, Von Plehve. Having done so, it issued a document, dated July 29, 1904, setting forth the counts of its indictment of Von Plehve and its responsibility for the assassination. Now, and to the point, this document was sent out to the socialists of the world, and by them was published everywhere in the magazines and newspapers. The point is, not that the socialists of the world were unafraid to do it, not that they dared to do it, but that they did it as a matter of routine, giving publication to what may be called an official document of the international revolutionary movement.

These are high lights upon the revolution—granted, but they are also facts. And they are given to the rulers and the ruling classes, not in bravado, not to frighten them, but for them to consider more deeply the spirit and nature of this world revolution. The time has come for the revolution to demand consideration. It has fastened upon every civilized country in the world. As fast as a country becomes

civilized, the revolution fastens upon it. With the introduction of
the machine into Japan, socialism was introduced. Socialism marched
into the Philippines shoulder to shoulder with the American soldiers.
The echoes of the last gun had scarcely died away when socialist
locals were forming in Cuba and Porto Rico. Vastly more significant
is the fact that of all the countries the revolution has fastened upon,
on not one has it relaxed its grip. On the contrary, on every country its
grip closes tighter year by year. As an active movement it began ob-
scurely over a generation ago. In 1867, its voting strength in the
world was 30,000. By 1871, its vote had increased to 100,000. Not till
1884 did it pass the half-million point. By 1889, it had passed the
million point. It had then gained momentum. In 1892 the socialist vote
of the world was 1,798,391; in 1893, 2,585,898; in 1895, 3,033,718;
in 1898, 4,515,591; in 1902, 5,253,054; in 1903, 6,285,374; and in the
year of our Lord 1905 it passed the seven-million mark.

Nor has this flame of revolution left the United States untouched.
In 1888, there were only 2,068 socialist votes. In 1902, there were
127,713 socialist votes. And in 1904, 435,040 socialist votes were cast.
What fanned this flame? Not hard times. The first four years of the
twentieth century were considered prosperous years, yet in that time
more than 300,000 men added themselves to the ranks of the revolutionists, flinging their defiance in the teeth of bourgeois society and
taking their stand under the blood-red banner. In the state of the
writer, California, one man in twelve is an avowed and registered
revolutionist.

One thing must be clearly understood. This is no spontaneous and
vague uprising of a large mass of discontented and miserable people—
a blind and instinctive recoil from hurt. On the contrary, the propaganda is intellectual; the movement is based upon economic necessity
and is in line with social evolution; while the miserable people have
not yet revolted. The revolutionist is no starved and diseased slave in
the shambles at the bottom of the social pit, but is, in the main, a
hearty, well-fed workingman, who sees the shambles waiting for him
and his children and recoils from the descent. The very miserable
people are too helpless to help themselves. But they are being helped,
and the day is not far distant when their numbers will go to swell
the ranks of the revolutionists.

Another thing must be clearly understood. In spite of the fact that
middle-class men and professional men are interested in the movement, it is nevertheless a distinctly working-class revolt. The world

over, it is a working-class revolt. The workers of the world, as a class,
are fighting the capitalists of the world, as a class. The so-called great
middle class is a growing anomaly in the social struggle. It is a perishing class (wily statisticians to the contrary), and its historic mission
of buffer between the capitalist- and working-classes has just about
been fulfilled. Little remains for it but to wail as it passes into oblivion, as it has already begun to wail in accents Populistic and
Jeffersonian-Democratic. The fight is on. The revolution is here now,
and it is the world's workers that are in revolt.

Naturally the question arises: Why is this so? No mere whim of
the spirit can give rise to a world revolution. Whim does not conduce
to unanimity. There must be a deep-seated cause to make 7,000,000
men of the one mind, to make them cast off allegiance to the bourgeois
gods and lose faith in so fine a thing as patriotism. There are many
counts of the indictment which the revolutionists bring against the
capitalist class, but for present use only one need be stated, and it is a
count to which capital has never replied and can never reply.

The capitalist class has managed society, and its management has
failed. And not only has it failed in its management, but it has failed
deplorably, ignobly, horribly. The capitalist class had an opportunity
such as was vouchsafed no previous ruling class in the history of the
world. It broke away from the rule of the old feudal aristocracy and
made modern society. It mastered matter, organized the machinery of
life, and made possible a wonderful era for mankind, wherein no
creature should cry aloud because it had not enough to eat, and
wherein for every child there would be opportunity for education, for
intellectual and spiritual uplift. Matter being mastered, and the
machinery of life organized, all this was possible. Here was the chance,
God-given, and the capitalist class failed. It was blind and greedy.
It prattled sweet ideals and dear moralities, rubbed its eyes not once,
nor ceased one whit in its greediness, and smashed down in a failure as
tremendous only as was the opportunity it had ignored.

But all this is like so much cobwebs to the bourgeois mind. As it
was blind in the past, it is blind now and cannot see nor understand.
Well, then, let the indictment be stated more definitely, in terms sharp
and unmistakable. In the first place, consider the caveman. He was
a very simple creature. His head slanted back like an orang-utan's and
he had but little more intelligence. He lived in a hostile environment,
the prey of all manner of fierce life. He had no inventions nor artifices.
His natural efficiency for food-getting was, say, 1. He did not even

till the soil. With his natural efficiency of 1, he fought off his carnivorous enemies and got himself food and shelter. He must have done all this, else he would not have multiplied and spread over the earth and sent his progeny down, generation by generation, to become even you and me.

The caveman, with his natural efficiency of 1, got enough to eat most of the time, and no caveman went hungry all the time. Also, he lived a healthy, open-air life, loafed and rested himself, and found plenty of time in which to exercise his imagination and invent gods. That is to say, he did not have to work all his waking moments in order to get enough to eat. The child of the caveman (and this is true of the children of all savage peoples) had a childhood, and by that is meant a happy childhood of play and development.

And now, how fares modern man? Consider the United States, the most prosperous and most enlightened country of the world. In the United States there are 10,000,000 people living in poverty. By poverty is meant that condition of life in which, through lack of food and adequate shelter, the mere standard of working efficiency cannot be maintained. In the United States there are 10,000,000 people who have not enough to eat. In the United States, because they have not enough to eat, there are 10,000,000 people who cannot keep the ordinary measure of strength in their bodies. This means that these 10,000,000 people are perishing, are dying, body and soul, slowly, because they have not enough to eat. All over this broad, prosperous, enlightened land, are men, women, and children who are living miserably. In all the great cities, where they are segregated in slum ghettos by hundreds of thousands and by millions, their misery becomes beastliness. No caveman ever starved as chronically as they starve, ever slept as vilely as they sleep, ever festered with rottenness and disease as they fester, nor ever toiled as hard and for as long hours as they toil.

In Chicago there is a woman who toiled sixty hours per week. She was a garment worker. She sewed buttons on clothes. Among the Italian garment workers of Chicago, the average weekly wage of the dressmakers is 90 cents, but they work every week in the year. The average weekly wage of the pants finishers is $1.31, and the average number of weeks employed in the year is 27.85. The average yearly earnings of the dressmakers is $47.00; of the pants finishers, $37.00. Such wages means no childhood for the children, beastliness of living, and starvation for all.

Unlike the caveman, modern man cannot get food and shelter whenever he feels like working for it. Modern man has first to find the work, and in this he is often unsuccessful. Then misery becomes acute. This acute misery is chronicled daily in the newspapers. Let several of the countless instances be cited.

In New York City lived a woman, Mary Mead. She had three children: Mary, one year old; Johanna, two years old; Alice, four years old. Her husband could find no work. They starved. They were evicted from their shelter at 160 Steuben Street. Mary Mead strangled her baby, Mary, one year old; strangled Alice, four years old; failed to strangle Johanna, two years old, and then herself took poison. Said the father to the police: "Constant poverty had driven my wife insane. We lived at No. 160 Steuben Street until a week ago, when we were dispossessed. I could get no work. I could not even make enough to put food into our mouths. The babies grew ill and weak. My wife cried nearly all the time."

> *"So overwhelmed is the Department of Charities with tens of thousands of applications from men out of work that it finds itself unable to cope with the situation."*—New York Commercial, *January 11, 1905.*

In a daily paper, because he cannot get work in order to get something to eat, modern man advertises as follows:—

> *Young man, good education, unable to obtain employment, will sell to physician and bacteriologist for experimental purposes all right and title to his body. Address for price, box 3466, Examiner.*

> *Frank A. Mallin went to the central police station Wednesday night and asked to be locked up on a charge of vagrancy. He said he had been conducting an unsuccessful search for work so long that he was sure he must be a vagrant. In any event, he was so hungry he must be fed. Police Judge Graham sentenced him to ninety days' imprisonment.*—San Francisco Examiner.

In a room at the Soto House, 32 Fourth Street, San Francisco, was found the body of W. G. Robbins. He had turned on the gas. Also was found his diary, from which the following extracts are made:—

March 3.—No chance of getting anything here. What will I do?

March 7.—Cannot find anything yet.

March 8.—Am living on doughnuts at five cents a day.

March 9.—My last quarter gone for room rent.

March 10.—God help me. Have only five cents left. Can get nothing to do. What next? Starvation or—? I have spent my last nickel to-night. What shall I do? Shall it be steal, beg, or die? I have never stolen, begged, or starved in all my fifty years of life, but now I am on the brink—death seems the only refuge.

March 11.—Sick all day—burning fever this afternoon. Had nothing to eat to-day or since yesterday noon. My head, my head. Good-by, all.

How fares the child of modern man in this most prosperous of lands? In the city of New York 50,000 children go hungry to school every morning. From the same city on January 12, a press despatch was sent out over the country of a case reported by Dr. A. E. Daniel, of the New York Infirmary for Women and Children. The case was that of a babe, eighteen months old, who earned by its labor fifty cents per week in a tenement sweat-shop.

In the United States 80,000 children are toiling out their lives in the textile mills alone. In the South they work twelve-hour shifts. They never see the day. Those on the night shift are asleep when the sun pours its life and warmth over the world, while those on the day shift are at the machines before dawn and return to their miserable dens, called "homes," after dark. Many receive no more than ten cents a day. There are babies who work for five and six cents a day. Those who work on the night shift are often kept awake by having cold water dashed in their faces. There are children six years of age who have already to their credit eleven months' work on the night shift. When they become sick, and are unable to rise from their beds to go to work, there are men employed to go on horseback from house to house, and cajole and bully them into arising and going to work. Ten per cent of them contract active consumption. All are puny wrecks, distorted, stunted, mind and body. Elbert Hubbard says of the child-laborers of the Southern cotton-mills:—

I thought to lift one of the little toilers to ascertain his weight. Straightaway through his thirty-five pounds of skin

*and bones there ran a tremor of fear, and he struggled forward
to tie a broken thread. I attracted his attention by a touch, and
offered him a silver dime. He looked at me dumbly from a face
that might have belonged to a man of sixty, so furrowed, tightly
drawn, and full of pain it was. He did not reach for the money
—he did not know what it was. There were dozens of such children in this particular mill. A physician who was with me said
that they would all be dead probably in two years, and their
places filled by others—there were plenty more. Pneumonia
carries off most of them. Their systems are ripe for disease,
and when it comes there is no rebound—no response. Medicine
simply does not act—nature is whipped, beaten, discouraged,
and the child sinks into a stupor and dies.*

So fares modern man and the child of modern man in the United
States, most prosperous and enlightened of all countries on earth. It
must be remembered that the instances given are instances only, but
that they can be multiplied myriads of times. It must also be remembered that what is true of the United States is true of all the
civilized world. Such misery was not true of the caveman. Then what
has happened? Has the hostile environment of the caveman grown
more hostile for his descendants? Has the caveman's natural efficiency
of 1 for food-getting and shelter-getting diminished in modern man
to one-half or one-quarter?

On the contrary, the hostile environment of the caveman has been
destroyed. For modern man it no longer exists. All carnivorous enemies, the daily menace of the younger world, have been killed off.
Many of the species of prey have become extinct. Here and there, in
secluded portions of the world, still linger a few of man's fiercer enemies. But they are far from being a menace to mankind. Modern
man, when he wants recreation and change, goes to the secluded portions of the world for a hunt. Also, in idle moments, he wails regret-
fully at the passing of the "big game," which he knows in the not
distant future will disappear from the earth.

Nor since the day of the caveman has man's efficiency for food-
getting and shelter-getting diminished. It has increased a thousand-
fold. Since the day of the caveman, matter has been mastered. The
secrets of matter have been discovered. Its laws have been formulated. Wonderful artifices have been made, and marvellous inventions,
all tending to increase tremendously man's natural efficiency of 1 in

every food-getting, shelter-getting exertion, in farming, mining, manufacturing, transportation, and communication.

From the caveman to the hand-workers of three generations ago,
the increase in efficiency for food- and shelter-getting has been very
great. But in this day, by machinery, the efficiency of the hand-
worker of three generations ago has in turn been increased many times.
Formerly it required 200 hours of human labor to place 100 tons of
ore on a railroad car. To-day, aided by machinery, but two hours of
human labor is required to do the same task. The United States Bureau of Labor is responsible for the following table, showing the comparatively recent increase in man's food- and shelter-getting efficiency:

	MACHINE HOURS	HAND HOURS
Barley (100 bushels)	9	211
Corn (50 bushels shelled, stalks, husks, and blades cut into fodder)	34	228
Oats (160 bushels)	28	265
Wheat (50 bushels)	7	160
Loading ore (loading 100 tons iron ore on cars)	2	200
Unloading coal (transferring 200 tons from canal-boats to bins 400 feet distant)	20	240
Pitchforks (50 pitchforks, 12-inch tines)	12	200
Plough (one landside plough, oak beams and handles)	3	118

According to the same authority, under the best conditions for organization in farming, labor can produce 20 bushels of wheat for 66
cents, or 1 bushel for 3⅓ cents. This was done on a bonanza farm of
10,000 acres in California, and was the average cost of the whole
product of the farm. Mr. Carroll D. Wright says that to-day 4,500,000
men, aided by machinery, turn out a product that would require the
labor of 40,000,000 men if produced by hand. Professor Herzog, of
Austria, says that 5,000,000 people with the machinery of to-day, employed at socially useful labor, would be able to supply a population
of 20,000,000 people with all the necessaries and small luxuries of life
by working 1½ hours per day.

This being so, matter being mastered, man's efficiency for food- and
shelter-getting being increased a thousand-fold over the efficiency of
the caveman, then why is it that millions of modern men live more

miserably than lived the caveman? This is the question the revolutionist asks, and he asks it of the managing class, the capitalist class. The capitalist class does not answer it. The capitalist class cannot answer it.

If modern man's food- and shelter-getting efficiency is a thousand-fold greater than that of the caveman, why, then, are there 10,000,000 people in the United States to-day who are not properly sheltered and properly fed? If the child of the caveman did not have to work, why, then, to-day, in the United States, are 80,000 children working out their lives in the textile factories alone? If the child of the caveman did not have to work, why, then, to-day, in the United States, are there 1,752,187 child-laborers?

It is a true count in the indictment. The capitalist class has mismanaged, is to-day mismanaging. In New York City 50,000 children go hungry to school, and in New York City there are 1320 millionaires. The point, however, is not that the mass of mankind is miserable because of the wealth the capitalist class has taken to itself. Far from it. The point really is that the mass of mankind is miserable, not for want of the wealth taken by the capitalist class, *but for want of the wealth that was never created.* This wealth was never created because the capitalist class managed too wastefully and irrationally. The capitalist class, blind and greedy, grasping madly, has not only not made the best of its management, but made the worst of it. It is a management prodigiously wasteful. This point cannot be emphasized too strongly.

In face of the facts that modern man lives more wretchedly than the caveman, and that modern man's food- and shelter-getting efficiency is a thousand-fold greater than the cave-man's, no other solution is possible than that the management is prodigiously wasteful.

With the natural resources of the world, the machinery already invented, a rational organization of production and distribution, and an equally rational elimination of waste, the able-bodied workers would not have to labor more than two or three hours per day to feed everybody, clothe everybody, house everybody, educate everybody, and give a fair measure of little luxuries to everybody. There would be no more material want and wretchedness, no more children toiling out their lives, no more men and women and babes living like beasts and dying like beasts. Not only would matter be mastered, but the machine would be mastered. In such a day incentive would be

finer and nobler than the incentive of to-day, which is the incentive
of the stomach. No man, woman, or child would be impelled to action
by an empty stomach. On the contrary, they would be impelled to
action as a child in a spelling match is impelled to action, as boys
and girls at games, as scientists formulating law, as inventors applying law, as artists and sculptors painting canvases and shaping clay,
as poets and statesmen serving humanity by singing and by state-
craft. The spiritual, intellectual, and artistic uplift consequent upon
such a condition of society would be tremendous. All the human world
would surge upward in a mighty wave.

This was the opportunity vouchsafed the capitalist class. Less blind-
ness on its part, less greediness, and a rational management, were all
that was necessary. A wonderful era was possible for the human race.
But the capitalist class failed. It made a shambles of civilization.
Nor can the capitalist class plead not guilty. It knew of the opportunity. Its wise men told it of the opportunity, its scholars and its
scientists told it of the opportunity. All that they said is there to-day
in the books, just so much damning evidence against it. It would not
listen. It was too greedy. It rose up (as it rises up to-day), shamelessly,
in our legislative halls, and declared that profits were impossible without the toil of children and babes. It lulled its conscience to sleep with
prattle of sweet ideals and dear moralities, and allowed the suffering
and misery of mankind to continue and to increase. In short, the
capitalist class failed to take advantage of the opportunity.

But the opportunity is still here. The capitalist class has been tried
and found wanting. Remains the working-class to see what it can do
with the opportunity. "But the working-class is incapable," says the
capitalist class. "What do you know about it?" the working-class
replies. "Because you have failed is no reason that we shall fail.
Furthermore, we are going to have a try at it, anyway. Seven millions
of us say so. And what have you to say to that?"

And what can the capitalist class say? Grant the incapacity of the
working-class. Grant that the indictment and the argument of the
revolutionists are all wrong. The 7,000,000 revolutionists remain.
Their existence is a fact. Their belief in their capacity, and in their
indictment and their argument, is a fact. Their constant growth is a
fact. Their intention to destroy present-day society is a fact, as is also
their intention to take possession of the world with all its wealth and
machinery and governments. Moreover, it is a fact that the working-
class is vastly larger than the capitalist class.

The revolution is a revolution of the working-class. How can the capitalist class, in the minority, stem this tide of revolution? What has it to offer? What does it offer? Employers' associations, injunctions, civil suits for plundering of the treasuries of the labor-unions, clamor and combination for the open shop, bitter and shameless opposition to the eight-hour day, strong efforts to defeat all reform child-labor bills, graft in every municipal council, strong lobbies and bribery in every legislature for the purchase of capitalist legislation, bayonets, machine-guns, policemen's clubs, professional strike-breakers, and armed Pinkertons—these are the things the capitalist class is dumping in front of the tide of revolution, as though, forsooth, to hold it back.

The capitalist class is as blind to-day to the menace of the revolution as it was blind in the past to its own God-given opportunity. It cannot see how precarious is its position, cannot comprehend the power and the portent of the revolution. It goes on its placid way, prattling sweet ideals and dear moralities, and scrambling sordidly for material benefits.

No overthrown ruler or class in the past ever considered the revolution that overthrew it, and so with the capitalist class of to-day. Instead of compromising, instead of lengthening its lease of life by conciliation and by removal of some of the harsher oppressions of the working-class, it antagonizes the working-class, drives the working class into revolution. Every broken strike in recent years, every legally plundered trades-union treasury, every closed shop made into an open shop, has driven the members of the working-class directly hurt over to socialism by hundreds and thousands. Show a working-man that his union fails, and he becomes a revolutionist. Break a strike with an injunction or bankrupt a union with a civil suit, and the workingmen hurt thereby listen to the siren song of the socialist and are lost forever to the *political capitalist* parties.

Antagonism never lulled revolution, and antagonism is about all the capitalist class offers. It is true, it offers some few antiquated notions which were very efficacious in the past, but which are no longer efficacious. Fourth-of-July liberty in terms of the Declaration of Independence and of the French Encyclopedists is scarcely apposite to-day. It does not appeal to the workingman who has had his head broken by a policeman's club, his union treasury bankrupted by a court decision, or his job taken away from him by a labor-saving invention. Nor does the Constitution of the United States appear so glorious and constitutional to the workingman who has experienced a bull pen or been unconstitutionally deported from Colorado. Nor are this particular workingman's hurt feelings soothed by reading in the newspapers that both the bull pen and the deportation were preëminently just, legal, and constitutional. "To hell, then, with the Constitution!" says he, and another revolutionist has been made—by the capitalist class.

In short, so blind is the capitalist class that it does nothing to lengthen its lease of life, while it does everything to shorten it. The capitalist class offers nothing that is clean, noble, and alive. The revolutionists offer everything that is clean, noble, and alive. They offer service, unselfishness, sacrifice, martyrdom—the things that sting awake the imagination of the people, touching their hearts with the fervor that arises out of the impulse toward good and which is essentially religious in its nature.

But the revolutionists blow hot and blow cold. They offer facts and statistics, economic and scientific arguments. If the workingman be merely selfish, the revolutionists show him, mathematically demonstrate to him, that his condition will be bettered by the revolution. If the workingman be the higher type, moved by impulses toward right conduct, if he have soul and spirit, the revolutionists offer him the things of the soul and the spirit, the tremendous things that cannot be measured by dollars and cents, nor be held down by dollars and cents. The revolutionist cries out upon wrong and injustice, and preaches righteousness. And, most potent of all, he sings the eternal song of human freedom—a song of all lands and all tongues and all time.

Few members of the capitalist class see the revolution. Most of them are too ignorant, and many are too afraid to see it. It is the same old story of every perishing ruling class in the world's history. Fat with power and possession, drunken with success, and made soft by surfeit and by cessation of struggle, they are like the drones clustered about the honey vats when the worker-bees spring upon them to end their rotund existence.

President Roosevelt vaguely sees the revolution, is frightened by it, and recoils from seeing it. As he says: "Above all, we need to remember that any kind of class animosity in the political world is, if possible, even more wicked, even more destructive to national welfare, than sectional, race, or religious animosity."

Class animosity in the political world, President Roosevelt maintains, is wicked. But class animosity in the political world is the preachment of the revolutionists. "Let the class war in the industrial world continue," they say, "but extend the class war to the political world." As their leader, Eugene V. Debs, says: "So far as this struggle is concerned, there is no good capitalist and no bad workingman. Every capitalist is your enemy and every workingman is your friend."

Here is class animosity in the political world with a vengeance. And here is revolution. In 1888 there were only 2,000 revolutionists of this type in the United States; in 1900 there were 127,000 revolutionists; in 1904, 435,000 revolutionists. Wickedness of the President Roosevelt definition evidently flourishes and increases in the United States. Quite so, for it is the revolution that flourishes and increases.

Here and there a member of the capitalist class catches a clear glimpse of the revolution, and raises a warning cry. But his class does not heed. President Eliot of Harvard raised such a cry: "I am forced to believe there is a present danger of socialism never before so imminent in America in so dangerous a form, because never before imminent in so well organized a form. The danger lies in the obtaining control of the trades-unions by the socialists." And the capitalist employers, instead of giving heed to the warnings, are perfecting their strike-breaking organization and combining more strongly than ever for a general assault upon that dearest of all things to the trades-unions,—the closed shop. In so far as this assault succeeds, by just that much will the capitalist class shorten its lease of life. It is the old, old story, over again and over again. The drunken drones still cluster greedily about the honey vats.

Possibly one of the most amusing spectacles of to-day is the attitude of the American press toward the revolution. It is also a pathetic spectacle. It compels the onlooker to be aware of a distinct loss of pride in his species. Dogmatic utterance from the mouth of ignorance may make gods laugh, but it should make men weep. And the American editors (in the general instance) are so impressive about it! The old "divide-up," "men-are-*not*-born-free-and-equal" propositions are enunciated gravely and sagely, as things white-hot and new from the forge of human wisdom. Their feeble vaporings show no more than a schoolboy's comprehension of the nature of the revolution. Parasites themselves on the capitalist class, serving the capitalist class by moulding public opinion, they, too, cluster drunkenly about the honey vats.

Of course, this is true only of the large majority of American editors.

To say that it is true of all of them would be to cast too great obloquy
upon the human race. Also, it would be untrue, for here and there an
occasional editor does see clearly—and in his case, ruled by stomach-
incentive, is usually afraid to say what he thinks about it. So far
as the science and the sociology of the revolution are concerned, the
average editor is a generation or so behind the facts. He is intellectually slothful, accepts no facts until they are accepted by the majority, and prides himself upon his conservatism. He is an instinctive
optimist, prone to believe that what ought to be, is. The revolutionist
gave this up long ago, and believes not that what ought to be, is, but
what is, is, and that it may not be what it ought to be at all.

Now and then, rubbing his eyes vigorously, an editor catches a sudden glimpse of the revolution and breaks out in naïve volubility, as,
for instance, the one who wrote the following in the *Chicago Chronicle*:
"American socialists are revolutionists. They know that they are
revolutionists. It is high time that other people should appreciate the
fact." A white-hot, brand-new discovery, and he proceeded to shout
it out from the housetops that we, forsooth, were revolutionists. Why,
it is just what we have been doing all these years—shouting it out
from the housetops that we are revolutionists, and stop us who can.

The time should be past for the mental attitude: "Revolution is
atrocious. Sir, there is no revolution." Likewise should the time be
past for that other familiar attitude: "Socialism is slavery. Sir, it will
never be." It is no longer a question of dialectics, theories, and dreams.
There is no question about it. The revolution is a fact. It is here now.
Seven million revolutionists, organized, working day and night, are
preaching the revolution—that passionate gospel, the Brotherhood of
Man. Not only is it a cold-blooded economic propaganda, but it is in
essence a religious propaganda with a fervor in it of Paul and Christ.
The capitalist class has been indicted. It has failed in its management
and its management is to be taken away from it. Seven million men
of the working-class say that they are going to get the rest of the
working-class to join with them and take the management away. The
revolution is here, now. Stop it who can.

Reviews and Comments

"The Octopus"

There it was, the Wheat, the Wheat! The little seed long planted, germinating in the deep, dark furrows of the soil, straining, swelling, suddenly in one night had burst upward to the light. The wheat had come up. It was before him, around him, everywhere, illimitable, immeasurable. The winter brownness of the ground was overlaid with a little shimmer of green. The promise of the sowing was being fulfilled. The earth, the loyal mother who never failed, who never disappointed, was keeping her faith again.

Very long ago, we of the West heard it rumored that Frank Norris had it in mind to write the *Epic of the Wheat*. Nor can it be denied that many of us doubted—not the ability of Frank Norris merely, but the ability of the human, of all humans. This great, incoherent, amorphous West! Who could grip the spirit and the essence of it, the luster and the wonder, and bind it all, definitely and sanely, within the covers of a printed book? Surely we of the West, who knew our West, may have been pardoned our lack of faith.

And now Frank Norris has done it; has, in a machine age, achieved what has been peculiarly the privilege of the man who lived in an heroic age; in short, has sung the *Epic of the Wheat*. "More power to his elbow," as Charles F. Lummis would say.

On first sight of the Valley of the San Joaquin, one can not help but call it the "new and naked land." There is apparently little to be seen. A few isolated ranches in the midst of the vastness, no timber, a sparse population—that is all. And the men of the ranches, sweating in bitter toil, they must likewise be new and naked. So it would seem; but Norris has given breadth to both, and depth. Not only has

he gone down into the soil, into the womb of the passionate earth,
yearning for motherhood, the sustenance of nations; but he has gone
down into the heart of its people, simple, elemental, prone to the ruder
amenities of existence, growling and snarling with brute anger under
cruel wrong. One needs must feel a sympathy for these men, workers
and fighters, and for all of their weakness, a respect. And, after all, as
Norris has well shown, their weakness is not inherent. It is the weakness of unorganization, the weakness of the force which they represent
and of which they are a part, the agricultural force as opposed to
the capitalistic force, the farmer against the financier, the tiller of
the soil against the captain of industry.

No man, not large of heart, lacking in spontaneous sympathy, incapable of great enthusiasms, could have written *The Octopus*.[1] Presley, the poet, dreamer and singer, is a composite fellow. So far as mere
surface incident goes, he is audaciously Edwin Markham; but down
in the heart of him he is Frank Norris. Presley, groping vaguely in
the silence of the burning night for the sigh of the land; Presley, with
his great Song of the West forever leaping up in his imagination and
forever eluding him; Presley, wrestling passionately for the swing
of his "thundering progression of hexameters"—who is this Presley
but Norris, grappling in keen travail with his problem of *The Octopus*, and doubting often, as we of the West have doubted?

Men obtain knowledge in two ways: by generalizing from experience; by gathering to themselves the generalizations of others.
As regards Frank Norris, one can not avoid pausing for speculation.
It is patent that in this, his last and greatest effort, he has laid down
uncompromisingly the materialistic conception of history, or, more
politely, the economic interpretation of history. Now the question
arises: Did Frank Norris acquire the economic interpretation of history from the printed records of the thoughts of other men, and thus
equipped, approach his problem of *The Octopus*? or, rather, did he
approach it, naive and innocent? and from direct contact with the
great social forces was he not forced to so generalize for himself?
It is a pretty question. Will he some day tell us?

Did Norris undergo the same evolution he has so strongly depicted
in Presley? Presley's ultimate sociological concept came somewhat in
this fashion: Shelgrim, the president and owner of the Pacific and
Southwestern, laid "a thick, powerful forefinger on the table to

[1] *The Octopus*. By Frank Norris. New York, Doubleday, Page & Co., 1901.

emphasize his words. 'Try to believe this—to begin with—that railroads build themselves. Where there is a demand, sooner or later there
will be a supply. Mr. Derrick, does he grow his wheat? The wheat
grows itself. What does he count for? Does he supply the force? What
do I count for? Do I build the railroad? You are dealing with forces,
young man, when you speak of wheat and the railroads, not with men.
There is the wheat, the supply. It must be carried to feed the people.
There is the demand. The wheat is one force, the railroad another,
and there is the law that governs them—supply and demand. Men
have only little to do in the whole business. Complications may arise,
conditions that bear hard on the individual—crush him, maybe—but
the wheat will be carried to feed the people as inevitably as it will
grow.' "

One feels disposed to quarrel with Norris for his inordinate realism.
What does the world care whether Hooven's meat safe be square or
oblong; whether it be lined with wire screen or mosquito netting;
whether it be hung to the branches of the oak tree or to the ridge-
pole of the barn; whether, in fact, Hooven has a meat safe or not?
"Feels disposed" is used advisedly. In truth, we can not quarrel
with him. It is confession and capitulation. The facts are against us.
He *has* produced results, Titanic results. Never mind the realism, the
unimportant detail, minute description, Hooven's meat safe and the
rest. Let it be stated flatly that by no other method could Frank
Norris or anybody else have handled the vast Valley of the San Joaquin and the no less vast-tentacled *Octopus*. Results? It was the only
way to get results, the only way to paint the broad canvas he has
painted, with the sunflare in his brush.

But he gives us something more than realism. Listen to this:

> Once more the pendulum of the seasons swung in its mighty
> arc.

> Then, faint and prolonged, across the levels of the ranch, he
> heard the engine whistling for Bonneville. Again and again, at
> rapid intervals in its flying course, it whistled for road crossings,
> for sharp curves, for trestles; ominous notes, hoarse, bellowing,
> ringing with the accents of menace and defiance; and abruptly
> Presley saw again, in his imagination, the galloping monster,
> the terror of steel and steam, with its single eye, cyclopean, red,
> shooting from horizon to horizon; but saw it now as the symbol
> of a vast power, huge, terrible, flinging the echo of its thunder

*over all the reaches of the valley, leaving blood and destruction
in its path; the leviathan, with tentacles of steel clutching into
the soil, the soulless Force, the iron-hearted Power, the monster, the Colossus, the Octopus.*

*The direct brutality of ten thousand acres of wheat, nothing
but wheat as far as the eye could see, stunned her a little. There
was something vaguely indecent in the sight, this food of the
people, this elemental force, this basic energy, weltering here
under the sun in all the unconscious nakedness of a sprawling,
primordial Titan.*

*Everywhere throughout the great San Joaquin, unseen and
unheard, a thousand ploughs up-stirred the land, tens of thousands of shears clutched deep into the warm, moist soil. It was
the long, stroking caress, vigorous, male, powerful, for which
the Earth seemed panting. The heroic embrace of a multitude
of iron hands, gripping down into the brown, warm flesh of the
land that quivered responsive and passionate under this rude
advance, so robust as to be almost an assault, so violent as to be
veritably brutal. There, under the sun and under the speckless
sheen of the sky, the wooing of the Titan began, the vast primal
passion, the two world-forces, the elemental Male and Female,
locked in a colossal embrace, at grapples in the throes of an infinite desire, at once terrible and divine, knowing no law, un-
tamed, savage, natural, sublime.*

Many men, and women, too, pass through the pages of *The Octopus,*
but one, greatest of all, we can not forbear mentioning in passing—
Annixter. Annixter, rough almost to insolence, direct in speech, intol-
erant in his opinions, relying upon absolutely no one but himself;
crusty of temper, bullying of disposition, a ferocious worker, and as
widely trusted as he was widely hated; obstinate and contrary, cantankerous, and deliciously afraid of "feemale women"—this is Annixter. He is worth knowing. In such cunning fashion has Norris blown
the breath of life into him, that his death comes with a shock which
is seldom produced by deaths in fiction. Osterman, laying his head on
his arms like a tired man going to rest, and Delaney, crawling instinctively out of the blood-welter to die in the growing wheat; but it is
Annixter, instantly killed, falling without movement, for whom we
first weep. A living man there died.

Well, the promise of *Moran* and *McTeague* has been realized. Can we ask more? Yet we have only the first of the trilogy. *The Epic of the Wheat* is no little thing. Content with *The Octopus,* we may look forward to *The Pit* and *The Wolf.* We shall not doubt this time.

"Fomá Gordyéeff"

What, without asking, hither hurried Whence?
And, without asking, Whither hurried hence!
Oh, many a Cup of this forbidden Wine
Must drown the memory of that insolence!

Fomá Gordyéeff [1] is a big book—not only is the breadth of Russia in it, but the expanse of life. Yet, though in each land, in this world of marts and exchanges, this age of trade and traffic, passionate figures rise up and demand of life what its fever is, in *Fomá Gordyéeff* it is a Russian who so arises up and demands. For Gorky, the Bitter One, is essentially a Russian in his grasp on the facts of life and in his treatment. All the Russian self-analysis and insistent introspection are his. And, like all his brother Russians, ardent, passionate protest impregnates his work. There is a purpose to it. He writes because he has something to say which the world should hear. From that clenched fist of his, light and airy romances, pretty and sweet and beguiling, do not flow, but realities—yes, big and brutal and repulsive, but real.

He raises the cry of the miserable and the despised, and in a masterly arraignment of commercialism, protests against social conditions, against the grinding of the faces of the poor and weak, and the self-pollution of the rich and strong, in this mad lust for place and power. It is to be doubted strongly if the average bourgeois, smug and fat and prosperous, can understand this man Fomá Gordyéeff. The rebellion in his blood is something to which their own does not thrill. To them

[1] *Fomá Gordyéeff*. By Maxim Gorky. New York, Charles Scribner's Sons, 1901.

it will be inexplicable that this man, with his health and his millions, could not go on living as his class lived, keeping regular hours at desk and stock exchange, driving close contracts, underbidding his competitors, and exulting in the business disasters of his fellows. It would appear so easy, and, after such a life, well appointed and eminently respectable, he could die. "Ah," Fomá will interrupt rudely,—he is given to rude interruptions,—"if to die and disappear is the end of these money-grubbing years, why money-grub?" And the bourgeois whom he rudely interrupted will not understand. Nor did Mayákin understand as he labored holily with his wayward godson.

"Why do you brag?" Fomá bursts out upon him. "What have you to brag about? Your son—where is he? Your daughter—what is she? Ekh, you manager of life! Come, now you're clever, you know everything—tell me, why do you live! Why do you accumulate money? Aren't you going to die? Well, what then?" And Mayákin finds himself speechless and without answer, but unshaken and unconvinced.

Receiving by heredity the fierce, bull-like nature of his father plus the passive indomitableness and groping spirit of his mother, Fomá, proud and rebellious, is repelled by the selfish, money-seeking environment into which his is born. Ignát, his father, and Mayákin, his godfather, and all the horde of successful merchants singing the pæan of the strong and the praises of merciless, remorseless laissez faire, cannot entice him. Why? he demands. This is a nightmare, this life! It is without significance! What does it all mean? What is there underneath? What is the meaning of that which is underneath?

"You do well to pity people," Ignát tells Fomá, the boy, "only you must use judgment with your pity. First consider the man, find out what he is like, what use can be made of him; and if you see that he is a strong and capable man, help him if you like. But if a man is weak, not inclined to work—spit upon him and go your way. And you must know that when a man complains about everything, and cries out and groans,—he is not worth more than two kopéks, he is not worthy of pity, and will be no use to you if you do help him."

Such the frank and militant commercialism, bellowed out between glasses of strong liquor. Now comes Mayákin, speaking softly and without satire:

"Eh, my boy, what is a beggar? A beggar is a man who is forced, by fate, to remind us of Christ; he is Christ's brother; he is the bell of the Lord, and rings in life for the purpose of awakening our conscience, of stirring up the satiety of man's flesh. He stands under the

window and sings, 'For Christ's sa-ake!' and by that chant he reminds
us of Christ, of His holy command to help our neighbor. But men
have so ordered their lives that it is utterly impossible for them to
act in accordance with Christ's teaching, and Jesus Christ has become
entirely superfluous to us. Not once, but, in all probability, a thousand times, we have given Him over to be crucified, but still we cannot banish Him from our lives so long as His poor brethren sing His
name in the streets and remind us of Him. And so now we have hit
on the idea of shutting up the beggars in such special buildings, so that
they may not roam about the streets and stir up our consciences."

But Fomá will have none of it. He is neither to be enticed or cajoled.
The cry of his nature is for light. He must have light. And in burning
revolt he goes seeking the meaning of life. "His thoughts embraced all
those petty people who toiled at hard labor. It was strange—why did
they live? What satisfaction was it to them to live on the earth? All
they did was to perform their dirty, arduous toil, eat poorly; they were
miserably clad, addicted to drunkenness. One was sixty years old,
but he still toiled side by side with young men. And they all presented
themselves to Fomá's imagination as a huge heap of worms, who were
swarming over the earth merely to eat."

He becomes the living interrogation of life. He cannot begin living
until he knows what living means, and he seeks its meaning vainly.
"Why should I try to live life when I do not know what life is?" he
objects when Mayákin strives with him to return and manage his
business. Why should men fetch and carry for him? be slaves to him
and his money?

"Work is not everything to a man," he says; "it is not true that
justification lies in work. . . . Some people never do any work at all,
all their lives long—yet they live better than the toilers. Why is that?
And what justification have I? And how will all the people who give
their orders justify themselves? What have they lived for? But my
idea is that everybody ought, without fail, to know solidly what he is
living for. Is it possible that a man is born to toil, accumulate money,
build a house, beget children, and—die? No; life means something in
itself. . . . A man has been born, has lived, has died—why? All of
us must consider why we are living, by God, we must! There is no
sense in our life—there is no sense at all. Some are rich—they have
money enough for a thousand men all to themselves—and they live
without occupation; others bow their backs in toil all their life, and
they haven't a penny."

But Fomá can only be destructive. He is not constructive. The dim groping spirit of his mother and the curse of his environment press too heavily upon him, and he is crushed to debauchery and madness. He does not drink because liquor tastes good in his mouth. In the vile companions who purvey to his baser appetites he finds no charm. It is all utterly despicable and sordid, but thither his quest leads him and he follows the quest. He knows that everything is wrong, but he cannot right it, cannot tell why. He can only attack and demolish. "What justification have you all in the sight of God? Why do you live?" he demands of the conclave of merchants, of life's successes. "You have not constructed life—you have made a cesspool! You have disseminated filth and stifling exhalations by your deeds. Have you any conscience? Do you remember God! But you have excelled your conscience!"

Like the cry of Isaiah, "Go to, now, ye rich men, weep and howl for your misfortunes that shall come upon you," is Fomá's: "You bloodsuckers! You live on other people's strength; you work with other people's hands! For all this you shall be made to pay! You shall perish—you shall be called to account for all! For all—to the last little teardrop!"

Stunned by this puddle of life, unable to make sense of it, Fomá questions, and questions vainly, whether of Sófya Medýnsky in her drawing-room of beauty, or in the foulest depths of the first chance courtesan's heart. Linboff, whose books contradict one another, cannot help him; nor can the pilgrims on crowded steamers, nor the verse writers and harlots in dives and boozing-kens. And so, wondering, pondering, perplexed, amazed, whirling through the mad whirlpool of life, dancing the dance of death, groping for the nameless, indefinite something, the magic formula, the essence, the intrinsic fact, the flash of light through the murk and dark,—the rational sanction for existence, in short,—Fomá Gordyéeff goes down to madness and death.

It is not a pretty book, but it is a masterful interrogation of life— not of life universal, but of life particular, the social life of to-day. It is not nice; neither is the social life of to-day nice. One lays the book down sick at heart—sick for life with all its "lyings and its lusts." But it is a healthy book. So fearful is its portrayal of social disease, so ruthless its stripping of the painted charms from vice, that its tendency cannot but be strongly for good. It is a goad, to prick sleeping human consciences awake and drive them into the battle for humanity.

But no story is told, nothing is finished, some one will object.

Surely, when Sásha leaped overboard and swam to Fomá, something happened. It was pregnant with possibilities. Yet it was not finished, was not decisive. She left him to go with the son of a rich vodka-maker. And all that was best in Sófya Medýnsky was quickened when she looked upon Fomá with the look of the Mother-Woman. She might have been a power for good in his life, she might have shed light into it and lifted him up to safety and honor and understanding. Yet she went away next day, and he never saw her again. No story is told, nothing is finished.

Ah, but surely the story of Fomá Gordyéeff is told; his life is finished, as lives are being finished each day around us. Besides, it is the way of life, and the art of Gorky is the art of realism. But it is a less tedious realism than that of Tolstoy or Turgenev. It lives and breathes from page to page with a swing and dash and to that they rarely attain. Their mantle has fallen on his young shoulders, and he promises to wear it royally.

Even so, but so helpless, hopeless, terrible is this life of Fomá Gordyéeff that we would be filled with profound sorrow for Gorky did we not know that he has come up out of the Valley of Shadow. That he hopes, we know, else would he not now be festering in a Russian prison because he is brave enough to live the hope he feels. He knows life, why and how it should be lived. And in conclusion, this one thing is manifest: Fomá Gordyéeff is no mere statement of an intellectual problem. For as he lived and interrogated living, so, in sweat and blood and travail, has Gorky lived.

"The Jungle"

At first, this Earth, a stage so gloomed with woe
You all but sicken at the shifting of the scenes.
And yet be patient. Our Playwright may show
In some fifth Act what this Wild Drama means.

When John Burns, the great English labor leader and present member of the Cabinet, visited Chicago, he was asked by a reporter for his opinion of that city. "Chicago," he answered, "is a pocket edition of hell." Some time later, when Burns was going aboard his steamer to sail to England, he was approached by another reporter, who wanted to know if he had yet changed his opinion of Chicago. "Yes, I have," was the prompt reply. "My present opinion is that hell is a pocket edition of Chicago."

Possibly Upton Sinclair was of the same opinion when he selected Chicago for the scene of his novel of industry, *The Jungle*.[1] At any rate, he selected the greatest industrial city in the country, the one city of the country that is ripest industrially, that is the most perfect specimen of jungle-civilization to be found. One cannot question the wisdom of the author's choice, for Chicago certainly is industrialism incarnate, the storm-center of the conflict between capital and labor, a city of street battles and blood, with a class-conscious capitalist organization and a class-conscious workman organization, where the school teachers are formed into labor unions and are affiliated with the hod carriers and bricklayers of the American Federation of Labor, where the very office clerks rain office furniture out of the windows

[1] *The Jungle*. By Upton Sinclair. New York, 1906, Doubleday & Page.

of the sky-scrapers upon the heads of the police who are trying to deliver scab meat in a beef strike, and where practically as many policemen as strikers are carried away in the ambulances.

This, then, is the scene of Upton Sinclair's novel, Chicago, the industrial jungle of twentieth century civilization. And right here it may be just as well to forestall the legions who will rise up and say that the book is untrue. In the first place, Upton Sinclair himself says: "The book is a true book, true in substance and in detail, an exact and faithful picture of life with which it deals."

Nevertheless, and in spite of the intrinsic evidence of truth, there will be many who will call *The Jungle* a tissue of lies, and first among them may be expected the Chicago newspapers. They are quick to resent the bald truth about their beloved city. Not more than three months ago, a public speaker,[2] in New York City, instancing extreme cases of the smallness of wage in the Chicago sweat shops, spoke of women receiving ninety cents per week. He was promptly called a liar by the Chicago newspapers—all except one paper, that really investigated, and that found not only many who were receiving no more than ninety cents per week, but found some receiving as low as fifty cents per week.

For that matter, when the New York publishers of *The Jungle* first read it, they sent it on to the editor of one of the largest Chicago newspapers, and that gentleman's written opinion was that Upton Sinclair was "the damndest liar in the United States." Then the publishers called Upton Sinclair upon the carpet. He gave his authorities. The publishers were still dubious—no doubt worried by visions of bankrupting libel suits. They wanted to make sure. They sent a lawyer to Chicago to investigate. And after a week or so the lawyer's report came back to the effect that Sinclair had left the worst untold.

Then the book was published, and here it is, a story of human destruction, of poor broken cogs in the remorseless grind of the industrial machine. It is essentially a book of to-day. It is alive and warm. It is brutal with life. It is written of sweat and blood, and groans and tears. It depicts, not what man ought to be, but what man is compelled to be in this, our world, in the twentieth century. It depicts, not what our country ought to be, nor what our country seems to be to those who live in softness and comfort far from the labor-ghetto, but it depicts what our country really is, the home of oppression and in-

[2] The speaker referred to was Jack London himself. See page 78.—EDITOR.

justice, a nightmare of misery, an inferno of suffering, a jungle wherein wild beasts eat and are eaten.

For a hero, Upton Sinclair did not select an American-born man, who, through the mists of Fourth of July oratory and campaign spellbinding, sees clearly in a way the ferocious facts of the American workingman's life. Upton Sinclair made no such mistake. He selected a foreigner, a Lithuanian, fleeing from the oppression and injustice of Europe and dreaming of liberty and freedom and equal rights with all men in the pursuit of happiness.

This Lithuanian was one Jurgis (pronounced Yoorghis), a young giant, broad of back, spilling over with vigor, passionately enamored of work, ambitious, a workingman in a thousand. He was the sort of a man that can set a work-pace that is heart-breaking and soul-killing to the men who work beside him and who must keep his pace despite the fact that they are weaklings compared with him.

In short, Jurgis was "the sort the bosses like to get hold of, the sort they make it a grievance they cannot get hold of." Jurgis was indomitable. This was because of his mighty muscles and superb health. No matter what the latest misfortune that fell upon him, he squared his shoulders and said, "Never mind, I will work harder." That was his clarion cry, his Excelsior! "Never mind, I will work harder!" He had no thought of the time to come when his muscles would not be so mighty, nor his health so superb, and when he would not be able to work harder.

On his second day in Chicago he stood in the crowd at the gates of the packing-houses. "All day long these gates were besieged by starving and penniless men; they came, literally, by the thousands every single morning, fighting with each other for a chance for life. Blizzards and cold made no difference to them, they were always on hand two hours before the sun rose, an hour before the work began. Sometimes their faces froze, sometimes their feet and their hands— but still they came, for they had no other place to go."

But Jurgis stood only half an hour in this crowd. His huge shoulders, his youth and health and unsullied strength marked him out in the crowd like a virgin in the midst of many hags. For he was a labor-virgin, his magnificent body yet unbroken by toil, and he was quickly picked out by a boss and set to work. Jurgis was the one workingman in a thousand. There were men in that crowd who had stood there every day for a month. They were of the nine hundred and ninety-nine.

Jurgis was prosperous. He was getting seventeen and one-half cents per hour, and just then it happened that he worked many hours. The next thing he did needed no urging from President Roosevelt. With the joy of youth in his blood and the cornucopia of prosperity spilling over him, he got married. "It was the supreme hour of ecstasy in the life of one of God's gentlest creatures, the wedding feast and the joy transfiguration of little Ona Lukozaite."

Jurgis worked on the killing floor, wading through the steaming blood that flowed upon the floor, with a street sweeper's broom sweeping the smoking entrails into a trap as fast as they were drawn from the carcasses of the steers. But he did not mind. He was wildly happy. He proceeded to buy a house—on the installment plan.

Why pay rent when one could buy a house for less? That was what the advertisement asked. "And why, indeed?" was what Jurgis asked. There were quite a number in the combined families of Jurgis and Ona, and they studied the house proposition long and carefully, and then paid all their old country savings (three hundred dollars) down, agreeing to pay twelve dollars per month until the balance of twelve hundred was paid. Then the house would be theirs. Until such time, according to the contract that was foisted on them, they would be renters. Failure to pay an installment would lose for them all they had already paid. And in the end they lost the three hundred dollars and the rent and interest they had paid, because the house was built, not as a home, but as a gamble on misfortune, and resold many times to just such simple folk as they.

In the meantime Jurgis worked and learned. He began to see things and to understand. He saw "How there were portions of the work which determined the pace of the rest, and for these they had picked out men whom they paid high wages, and whom they changed frequently. This was called 'speeding up the gang,' and if any man could not keep up with the pace, there were hundreds outside begging to try.

"He saw that the bosses grafted off the men, and they grafted off each other, while the superintendents grafted off the bosses. Here was Durham's, owned by a man who was trying to make as much money of it as he could, and did not care in the least how he did it; and underneath, ranged in ranks and grades like an army, were managers, superintendents and foremen, each man driving the man next below him and trying to squeeze out of him as much work as possible. And all the men of the same rank were pitted against each other; the accounts of each were kept separately, and every man lived in terror of

losing his job if another made a better record than he. There was
no loyalty or decency anywhere about it, there was no place in it
where a man counted for anything against a dollar. The man who
told tales and spied upon his fellow creatures would rise; but the
man who minded his own business and did his work—why, they
would 'speed him up' till they had worn him out, and then they would
throw him into the gutter."

And why should the bosses have any care for the men. There were
always plenty more. "One day Durham advertised in the paper for
two hundred men to cut ice; and all that day the homeless and
starving of the city came trudging through the snow from all of its
two hundred square miles. That night forty score of them crowded
into the station house of the stockyards district—they filled the rooms,
sleeping on each other's laps, toboggan fashion, and they piled on
top of one another in the corridors, till the police shut the doors and
left some to freeze outside. On the morrow, before daybreak, there
were three thousand at Durham's, and the police reserves had to be
sent for to quell the riot. Then Durham's bosses picked out twenty of
the biggest," and set them to work.

And the accident began to loom big to Jurgis. He began to live in
fear of the accident. The thing, terrible as death, that was liable to
happen any time. One of his friends, Mikolas, a beef-boner, had been
laid up at home twice in three years with blood poisoning, once for
three months and once for seven months.

Also, Jurgis saw how the "speeding up" made the accident more
imminent. "In the winter time, on the killing floor, one was apt to be
covered with blood, and it would freeze solid. The men would tie up
their feet in newspapers and old sacks, and these would be soaked in
blood and frozen. All of them that used knives were unable to wear
gloves, and their arms would be white with frost, and their hands
would grow numb, and then of course there would be accidents." Now
and then, when the bosses were not looking, the men, for very relief
from the cold, would plunge their feet and ankles into the steaming
carcasses of the fresh-killed steers.

Another thing that Jurgis saw, and gathered from what was told
him, was the procession of the nationalities. At one time "the workers
had all been Germans. Afterwards, as cheaper labor came, these Germans had moved away. The next had been the Irish. The Bohemians
had come then, and after them the Poles. The people had come in
hordes; and old Durham had squeezed them tighter and tighter,

speeding them up and grinding them to pieces. The Poles had been driven to the wall by the Lithuanians, and now the Lithuanians were giving way to the Slovaks. Who there was poorer and more miserable than the Slovaks, there was no telling; but the packers would find them, never fear. It was easy to bring them, for wages were really much higher, and it was only when it was too late that the poor people found out that everything else was higher, too."

Then there was the lie of society, or the countless lies, for Jurgis to learn. The food was adulterated, the milk for the children was doctored, the very insect-powder for which Jurgis paid twenty-five cents was adulterated and harmless to insects. Under his house was a cesspool containing the sewage of fifteen years. "Jurgis went about with his soul full of suspicion; he understood that he was environed by hostile powers that were trying to get his money. The storekeepers plastered up their windows with all sorts of lies to entice him, the very fences by the wayside, the lampposts and telegraph poles were pasted over with lies. The great corporation that employed him lied to him, and lied to the whole country—from top to bottom it was nothing but one gigantic lie."

Work became slack, and Jurgis worked part time and learned what the munificent pay of seventeen and one-half cents per hour really meant. There were days when he worked no more than two hours, and days when there was no work at all. But he managed to average nearly six hours a day, which meant six dollars per week.

Then came to Jurgis that haunting thing of the labor world, the accident. It was only an injured ankle. He worked on it till he fainted. After that he spent three weeks in bed, went to work on it again too soon, and went back to bed for two months. By that time everybody in the combined families had to get to work. The children sold papers on the streets. Ona sewed hams all day long, and her cousin, Marija, painted cans. And little Stanislovas worked on a marvelous machine that almost did all the work. All Stanislovas had to do was to place an empty lard-can every time the arm of the machine reached out to him.

"And so was decided the place in the universe for little Stanislovas, and his destiny till the end of his days. Hour after hour, day after day, year after year, it was fated that he should stand on a certain square-foot of floor from seven in the morning until noon, and again from half-past twelve to half-past five, making never a motion and thinking never a thought, save for the setting of lard-cans." And for this he received something like three dollars per week, which was his proper share of the total earnings of the million and three-quarters of child laborers in the United States. And his wages a little more than paid the interest on the house.

And Jurgis lay on his back, helpless, starving, in order that the payments and interest on the house should be met. Because of this, when he got on his feet again he was no longer the finest-looking man in the crowd. He was thin and haggard, and he looked miserable. His old job was gone, and he joined the crowd at the gate, morning after morning, striving to keep to the front and to look eager.

"The peculiar bitterness of all this was that Jurgis saw so plainly the meaning of it. In the beginning he had been fresh and strong, and he had gotten a job the first day; but now he was second-hand, a damaged article, so to speak, and they did not want him. They had got the best out of him—they had worn him out, with their speeding up and their carelessness, and now they had thrown him away."

The situation was now desperate. Several of the family lost their jobs, and Jurgis, as a last resort, descended into the inferno of the fertilizer-works and went to work. And then came another accident, of a different sort. Ona, his wife, was vilely treated by her foreman (too vilely treated for narration here), and Jurgis thrashed the foreman and was sent to jail. Both he and Ona lost their jobs.

In the working-class world, disasters do not come singly. The loss of the house followed the loss of the jobs. Because Jurgis had struck a boss he was blacklisted in all the packing-houses and could not even get back his job in the fertilizer-works. The family was broken up, and its members went their various ways to living hell. The lucky ones died, such as Jurgis' father, who died of blood-poisoning, contracted by working in chemicals, and Jurgis' little son, Antanas, who was drowned in the street. (And in this connection I wish to say that this last is a fact. I have personally talked with a man in Chicago, a charity-worker, who buried the child drowned in the streets of Packingtown.)

And Jurgis, under the ban of the blacklist, mused thus: "There was no justice, there was no right, anywhere in it—it was only force, it was tyranny, the will and the power, reckless and unrestrained. They had ground him beneath their heel, they had devoured all his substance, they had murdered his old father, they had broken and wrecked his wife, they had crushed and cowed his whole family. And now they were through with him. They had no further use for him."

"Then men gazed on him with pitying eyes—poor devil, he was blacklisted. He stood as much chance of getting a job in Packingtown as of being chosen Mayor of Chicago. They had his name on a secret list in every office, big and little, in the place. They had his name in St. Louis and New York, in Omaha and Boston, in Kansas City and St. Joseph. He was condemned and sentenced without trial and without appeal; he could never work for the packers again."

Nor does *The Jungle* end here. Jurgis lives to get on the inside of the rottenness and corruption of the industrial and political machinery; and of all that he sees and learns nothing less than the book itself can tell.

It is a book well worth the reading, and it is a book that may well make history, as *Uncle Tom's Cabin* made history. For that matter, there are large chances that it may prove to be the *Uncle Tom's Cabin* of wage slavery. It is dedicated, not to a Huntington nor to a Carnegie, but to the Workingmen of America. It has truth and power, and it has behind it in the United States over four hundred thousand men and women who are striving to give it a wider hearing than any book has been given in fifty years. Not only may it become one of the "great sellers," but it is very likely to become the greatest seller. And yet, such is the strangeness of modern life, *The Jungle* may be read by the hundreds of thousands and by the millions of copies and yet not be listed as a "best seller" in the magazines. The reason for this will be that it will be read by the working-class, as it has already been read by hundreds of thousands of the working class. Dear masters, would it not be wise to read for once the literature that all your working-class is reading?

Introduction to
"The Cry for Justice"

This anthology,[1] I take it, is the first edition, the first gathering to-gether of the body of the literature and art of the humanist thinkers of the world. As well done as it has been done, it will be better done in the future. There will be much adding, there will be a little sub-tracting, in the succeeding editions that are bound to come. The result will be a monument of the ages, and there will be none fairer.

Since reading of the Bible, the Koran, and the Talmud has en-abled countless devout and earnest right-seeking souls to be stirred and uplifted to higher and finer planes of thought and action, then the reading of this humanist Holy Book cannot fail similarly to serve the needs of groping, yearning humans who seek to discern truth and justice amid the dazzle and murk of the thought-chaos of the present-day world.

No person, no matter how soft and secluded his own life has been, can read this Holy Book and not be aware that the world is filled with a vast mass of unfairness, cruelty, and suffering. He will find that it has been observed, during all the ages, by the thinkers, the seers, the poets, and the philosophers.

And such person will learn, possibly, that this fair world so brutally unfair, is not decreed by the will of God nor by any iron law of Nature. He will learn that the world can be fashioned a fair world indeed by the humans who inhabit it, by the very simple, and yet most difficult process of coming to an understanding of the world. Understanding, after all, is merely sympathy in its fine correct sense.

[1] *The Cry for Justice.* An Anthology edited by Upton Sinclair. New York, The John C. Winston Co., 1915.

And such sympathy, in its genuineness, makes toward unselfishness. Unselfishness inevitably connotes service. And service is the solution of the entire vexatious problem of man.

He, who by understanding becomes converted to the gospel of service, will serve truth to confute liars and make them truth-tellers; will serve kindness so that brutality will perish; will serve beauty to the erasement of all that is not beautiful. And he who is strong will serve the weak that they may become strong. He will devote his strength, not to the debasement and defilement of his weaker fellows, but to the making of opportunity for them to make themselves into men rather than into slaves and beasts.

One has but to read the names of the men and women whose words burn in these pages, and to recall that by far more than average intelligence have they won to their place in the world's eye and in the world's brain long after the dust of them has vanished, to realize that due credence must be placed in their report of the world herein recorded. They were not tyrants and wastrels, hypocrites and liars, brewers and gamblers, market-riggers and stock-brokers. They were givers and servers, and seers and humanists. They were unselfish. They conceived of life, not in terms of profit, but of service.

Life tore at them with its heart-break. They could not escape the hurt of it by selfish refuge in the gluttonies of brain and body. They saw, and steeled themselves to see, clear-eyed and unafraid. Nor were they afflicted by some strange myopia. They all saw the same thing. They are all agreed upon what they saw. The totality of their evidence proves this with unswerving consistency. They have brought the report, these commissioners of humanity. It is here in these pages. It is a true report.

But not merely have they reported the human ills. They have proposed the remedy. And their remedy is of no part of all the jangling sects. It has nothing to do with the complicated metaphysical processes by which one may win to other worlds and imagined gains beyond the sky. It is a remedy for this world, since worlds must be taken one at a time. And yet, that not even the jangling sects should receive hurt by the making fairer of this world for this own world's sake, it is well, for all future worlds of them that need future worlds, that their splendor be not tarnished by the vileness and ugliness of this world.

It is so simple a remedy, merely service. Not one ignoble thought or act is demanded of any one of all men and women in the world to make fair the world. The call is for nobility of thinking, nobility of doing. The call is for service, and, such is the wholesomeness of it, he who serves all, best serves himself.

Times change, and men's minds with them. Down the past, civilizations have exposited themselves in terms of power, of world-power or of other-world power. No civilization has yet exposited itself in terms of love-of-man. The humanists have no quarrel with the previous civilizations. They were necessary in the development of man. But their purpose is fulfilled, and they may well pass, leaving man to build the new and higher civilization that will exposit itself in terms of love and service and brotherhood.

To see gathered here together this great body of human beauty and fineness and nobleness is to realize what glorious humans have already existed, do exist, and will continue increasingly to exist until all the world beautiful be made over in their image. We know how gods are made. Comes now the time to make a world.

Sources

Sources

FICTION

The Iron Heel—The Macmillan Company, February, 1908.
"The Apostate"—*Woman's Home Companion*, September, 1906.
"The Dream of Debs"—*International Socialist Review*, January-February, 1909.
"South of the Slot"—*Saturday Evening Post*, May 22, 1909.
"The Strength of the Strong"—*Hampton's Magazine*, March, 1911.
Martin Eden—The Macmillan Company, September, 1909.

AUTOBIOGRAPHICAL WRITINGS

John Barleycorn—The Century Company, August, 1913.
"My Life in the Underworld"
 "A Confession"—*Cosmopolitan*, May, 1907.
 "Holding Her Down"—*Cosmopolitan*, June, 1907.
 "Pinched"—*Cosmopolitan*, July, 1907.
 "The Pen"—*Cosmopolitan*, August, 1907.
"How I Became a Socialist"—*The Comrade*, March, 1903.
The People of the Abyss—The Macmillan Company, November, 1903.
"What Life Means to Me"—*Cosmopolitan*, March, 1906.

NEWSPAPER ARTICLES

"Explanation of the Great Socialist Vote of 1904"—*San Francisco Examiner*, November 10, 1904.

"Something Rotten in Idaho"—*Chicago Daily Socialist*, November
   4, 1906.
"Strike Methods: American and Australian"—*Sydney (Australia)
   Star*, January, 1909.

ESSAYS

"What Communities Lose by the Competitive System"—*Cosmo-
   politan*, November, 1900.
"Wanted: A New Law of Development"—*International Socialist Re-
   view*, August, 1902.
"The Class Struggle"—*The Independent*, November 5, 1903.
"The Scab"—*Atlantic Monthly*, January, 1904.
"The Tramp"—*Wilshire's Magazine*, February, 1904.
"Revolution"—*Contemporary Review*, January, 1908.

REVIEWS AND COMMENT

"The Octopus"—*Impressions*, June, 1901.
"Fomá Gordyéeff"—*Impressions*, November, 1901.
"The Jungle"—*Wilshire's Magazine*, August, 1906.
The Cry for Justice—John C. Winston Co., 1915.

Supplementary Material

Supplementary Material

Page 24, line 4:

Jack London later illustrated how important it was to have English-speaking lecturers in the Socialist movement. "I remember," he told an interviewer in 1912, "that in Oakland, for example, it was a couple of little Russian Jews who first organized our local and started the free speech scrap up in Washington. They got up to their little soap boxes in Spokane and fairly jumped out of their skins trying to get themselves arrested in the cause of free speech. But in a few days they came to us with tears in their eyes, and said that the people were paying no attention to them. The Spokaners had told them to learn to speak English before they undertook to teach them anything. . . ." (*New York Call*, January 28, 1912.) London, however, paid tribute in the same interview to these Jewish Socialists, observing that it "was the same little, narrow-chested foreign Comrades who started the whole shooting match in the way of Socialism in our parts."

Page 27, line 18:

London's debut as a street speaker for the Socialist cause took place on February 12, 1897. He was arrested and jailed, but acquitted with a warning.

Page 48, line 26:

Russell Ames, in his unpublished study of Jack London as a social critic, believes that the Kempton-Wace letters have a greater importance than I have indicated. He points out that "London's in-

sistence that reproduction was woman's peculiar function and
nutrition man's, and his claim that women cannot reason about
love, do not make up a major part of the book." As he sees it, the
important part of the book is the picture London gives "of the pri-
mary creative and revolutionary role in history of the 'doer,' the
scientist and technician, as opposed to the artist subservient to the
demands made by the ruling classes." While I would agree with this
point, I still believe that the Kempton-Wace letters truly reflect
London's backward ideas on women.

Page 52, line 4:
   The flyleaf of a copy of *The People of the Abyss,* in the posses-
sion of Mr. Ray Evans of Toronto, Canada, has the following in-
scription:
   "My Dear Geneva Boggs
   "Walk with me here & find a few more reasons why I am a
Socialist.
                    "Sincerely yours,
                    "Jack London
                    "Glen Ellen, Calif., Oct. 12, 1911."

Page 58, line 4:
   There is increasing doubt among Jack London scholars as to the
authenticity of this piece. During his lifetime, articles were often
attributed to Jack London which he denied writing. The problem
with establishing the authenticity of the description of a scab is that
it appears to have been published after his death and no evidence
thus far has appeared which establishes it as having been published
during his lifetime. Hensley C. Woodbridge of Murray State College
of Murray, Kentucky, who is preparing a bibliography of all of
Jack London's writings, wrote to me on December 21, 1962: "Of
course, at the moment, I am most doubtful as to the authenticity of
the scab piece and will continue to be until I can discover some
printings over his name during his lifetime. . . . In sum, if it were
published during his lifetime and not disowned by him, I would be
glad to call it his; otherwise there is no alternative but to call it
spurious."
   Labor papers have frequently published the scab definition and
attributed it to Jack London, but thus far no labor paper published
during London's lifetime has been found which carried the definition.

There is, however, significant internal evidence that the piece was written by London. He was fond of using Judas Iscariot as a symbol of the traitor. Indeed, the language used in the definition of the scab and that used by London in his definition of "the pot of money" in his article "Something Rotten in Idaho" is almost identical. (*See below*, pp. 134–35.)

Page 59, line 13:

In fairness to London, it must be noted that the "Yellow Peril," as he saw it, was not the usual nonsense about the danger of great waves of people of different color entering our land to sully white "purity." In his essay "The Yellow Peril" (1904), London asks if the Japanese religion may not be as great a religion as Christianity, and he concedes that any great race adventure "must have behind it an ethical impulse, a sincerely conceived righteousness." Then he adds: "But it must be taken into consideration that the above postulate is itself a product of Western race-egotism, urged by our belief in our own righteousness and fostered by a faith in ourselves which may be as erroneous as are most fond race fancies." Only London's questioning of the correctness of "fond race fancies" makes it possible to believe that the same man wrote in "Revolution" (1908):

"The comradeship of the revolutionists is alive and warm. It passes over geographical lines, transcends race prejudice, and has even proved itself mightier than the Fourth of July, spread-eagle Americanism of our forefathers. The French socialist workingmen and the German socialist workingmen forget Alsace and Lorraine, and, when war threatens, pass resolutions declaring that as workingmen and comrades they have no quarrel with each other. Only the other day, when Japan and Russia sprang at each other's throats, the revolutionists of Japan addressed the following message to the revolutionists of Russia: 'Dear Comrades— Your government and ours have recently plunged into war to carry out their imperialistic tendencies, but for us socialists there are no boundaries, race, country, or nationality. . . .'"

Page 70, line 16:

Of the sponsors, only Leonard D. Abbott, Jack London, and Upton Sinclair were members of the Socialist Party at that time.

Page 70, line 36:

Many of the sponsoring organizations billed London as "Daring Traveler," "An Original Klondiker," "Experienced Seaman," and "The American Kipling." Radical groups, however, billed him as "Prominent Socialist" and "Novelist and Socialist Friend of the Underdog."

Page 71, line 33:

London spoke at New York's Grand Central Palace on January 19, 1906. Before he spoke, hawkers sold ten-cent red flags described as "genuine, blood-red, Jack London souvenirs of a great and momentous occasion." The *New York Times* announced the following day: "They All Wear Red to Hear Jack London."

Page 76, line 21:

This had already been made clear during London's Grand Central Palace speech in New York on January 19, which a *New York Times* reporter had covered. During his speech, London had suggested that the workers might be forced to say, "To hell with the Constitution." He was interrupted by an old soldier in the audience who asked if the speaker were quoting someone or expressing an opinion. London answered that he was quoting a soldier who had used the remark in justifying the unconstitutional imprisonment of striking miners in Colorado by the militia. "Mother" Mary Jones, the veteran labor organizer, who had herself been frequently imprisoned during strikes, leaned out from her honored position in one of the boxes to shout, "Yes, and it was a general." All this was reported the next day in the *New York Times,* which also mentioned that as London continued the address, the old soldier stalked from the hall "with his head high."

Actually, it was not Adjutant General Brigadier General Sherman M. Bell, commander of the Colorado Militia, who made the remark, as "Mother" Jones and Upton Sinclair stated, but Judge Advocate Major Thomas McClelland. In her *Autobiography,* published twenty years later, "Mother" Jones corrected the remark about General Bell and charged McClelland with it. (Chicago, 1925, pp. 107–08.)

Page 86, line 24:

London defined "the pot of money" as follows:

"Why do some mine owners dislike Moyer, Haywood and Pettibone? Because these men stand between the mine owners and a pot of money. These men are leaders of organized labor. They plan and direct the efforts of the workingmen to get better wages and shorter hours. The operation of their mills will be more expensive. The higher the running expenses, the smaller the profits. If the mine owners could disrupt the Western Federation of Miners, they would increase the hours of labor, lower wages, and thereby gain millions of dollars. This is the pot of money.

"It is a fairly respectable pot of money. Judas betrayed Christ to crucifixion for thirty pieces of silver. Human nature has not changed since that day, and it is conceivable that Moyer, Haywood and Pettibone may be hanged for the sake of a few millions of dollars. Not that the mine owners have anything personally against Moyer, Haywood and Pettibone (Judas had nothing against Christ), but because the mine owners want the pot of money. Judas wanted the thirty pieces of silver."

Page 87, line 22:

Ghent's book grew out of an article he had written for the *Independent,* "The Next Step: A Benevolent Feudalism." Published on April 6, 1902, it aroused such widespread discussion that Ghent decided to expand it into a book.

Page 87, line 24:

"The future society that Ghent pictured," writes Harold Sherburn Smith, ". . . was not the pleasant land of equality and harmony portrayed in [Edward Bellamy's] *Looking Backward* or in William Dean Howells' *A Traveller from Altruria,* the best known of the recent utopian works. A spirit of sardonic pessimism suffused Ghent's description of a reborn feudalism. He professed to see peace in the society of the future, but it was a regimented peace, the peace of the modern police state, of fascism." ("William James Ghent, Reformer and Historian," unpublished Ph.D. thesis, University of Wisconsin, 1957, pp. 82–83.)

Page 87, line 29:

London's review appeared in the May, 1903, issue of the *International Socialist Review* (vol. IX, pp. 648–52) under the heading "Contradictory Teachers." This was a reference to the two books which were reviewed: Ghent's *Our Benevolent Feudalism* and John

Graham Brooks' *The Social Unrest*. London felt that the "two books
should be read together." Ghent, whom he describes as "sympathetic
to the Socialist movement," followed "with cynic fear every aggressive act of the capitalist class." Brooks, who "yearns for the perpetu-
ation of the capitalist system as long as possible," viewed with
"grave dismay each aggressive act of labor and Socialist organization." The two books thus represented "the two sides which go to
make a struggle so great that even the French Revolution is insignificant beside it; for this latter struggle, for the first time in the
history of struggles, is not confined to any particular portion of the
globe, but involves the whole of it."

London summarizes Ghent's view as follows: "The coming status
which Mr. Ghent depicts, is a class domination by the capitalists.
Labor will take its definite place as a dependent class, living in a
condition of machine servitude fairly analogous to the land servitude
of the middle ages. That is to say, labor will be bound to the machine,
though less harshly, in a fashion somewhat similar to that in which
the earlier serf was bound to the soil." He describes Ghent's arguments "as cunningly contrived and arrayed. They must be read to
be appreciated."

In commenting on Brooks' *The Social Unrest,* London points out
that the author reveals the existence in the United States "of an extreme and tyrannically benevolent feudalism very like to Mr.
Ghent's. . . ." The example he cites in this connection demonstrates
that this "feudalism" was "tyrannical," but the "benevolent" side of
it is difficult to discern. Thus London advises his readers to "witness
the following" from Brooks' work:

"I asked one of the largest employers of labor in the South if he
feared the coming of the trade union. 'No,' he said, 'it is one good
result of race prejudice that the negro will enable us in the long run
to weaken the trade union so that it cannot harm us. We can keep
wages down with the negro, and we can prevent too much organization.'

"It is in this spirit that the lower standards are to be used. If this
purpose should succeed, it has but one issue—the immense strength-
ening of a plutocratic administration at the top, served by an army
of high-salaried helpers, with an elite of skilled and well-paid workmen, but all resting on what would essentially be a serf class of low-
paid labor and this mass kept in order by an increased use of military
force."

In quoting the above from Brooks' *The Social Unrest*, London reveals an understanding that racial prejudice is a device of the employer class to keep the workers under domination. It is unfortunate that this understanding was lacking in so many of his writings.

Page 89, line 8:

Ghent predicted that under the new feudalism the masses, in exchange for liberty, would have security. Here is how Ghent described the approaching utopia:

"Gradually the various processes in the social life merge . . . into a definite and confined stream of tendency. A more perfect, a better coordinated unity develops in the baronial class, and the measure of its control is heightened and extended to a golden mean which insures supremacy with peace. The under-classes settle in their appointed grooves, and the professional intermediaries definitely and openly assume their dual function of advisers to the barons and of interpreters to the people of the baronial will and ways. Laws, customs, and arts, all the institutions and social forces, change with the industrial transformation, and attain a finer harmony with the actual facts of life." (*Our Benevolent Feudalism*, pp. 196–97.)

Ghent also predicted that the masses, "remembering the chaos, the turmoil, the insecurity of the past, will bless its reign" and remain supine under the new feudalism. However, London, in *The Iron Heel*, describes the organization of the movement, based on the discontent of the masses, to overthrow the Oligarchy. Even though the revolt is crushed, it is clear that London believes that the masses will eventually triumph.

Page 90, line 37:

Sam S. Baskett asserts that London derived the sections dealing with the role of the church in American capitalist society from material on this subject appearing in the *Socialist Voice* of Oakland, California. ("A Source of *The Iron Heel*," *American Literature*, May, 1955, pp. 268–70.) Probably this is true, though much the same type of material was appearing in socialist newspapers and magazines all over the country. What is strange is Baskett's conclusion: "This dependence [on the *Socialist Voice*] should serve as further evidence that London was not deeply versed in the works of Karl Marx, that he either preferred or found it necessary to obtain much of his knowledge of socialism indirectly from secondary ma-

terials." (p. 270.) While it is true that London read little of Marx
and Engels besides the *Communist Manifesto,* there would have
been nothing strange, even if he had been steeped in *Das Kapital*
and other works of Marx, in his using contemporary American
socialist sources to describe the role of the clergy in American society.

Page 96, line 36:
   London developed this theme in a number of interviews. On
January 28, 1912, the *New York Call,* a Socialist daily, carried an
interview with Jack London by Joseph Gollomb under the heading:
"London Tells of Social Revolution. Scouts Idea That It Will Be
Realized Without Force." The interview opened:
   "Do you still think," I asked him, "in view of the big strides we
are making, that there is going to be the big flare-up, the huge shindy
that you speak of in your 'Iron Heel'?"
   "I don't see how it can be avoided," he remarked placidly.
   "But suppose we get, as we shall, a sweeping plurality of a thousand to one over the capitalists—"
   "Why, bless it all—(only he did not say 'bless')*—why, bless it
all, you don't suppose the caps are going to hand over peacefully their
nice, fat holdings simply because we shall win on a legal technicality!
(Shade of Marx! a technicality!) You don't for one moment suppose they will lie down simply because we count more noses than
they! Not on your life! Not as long as $5 a day will buy whole
regiments of trained killers like the Pennsylvania State Constabu-
lary!"
   'But there'll be a thousand to every handful of them!"
   "And a lovely chance your untrained, unorganized thousands will
have against a compact little group of these fellows with the lust and
talent for killing in their hearts and the latest thing in machine guns
in their hands!"

   * Gollomb explained that Charmian London had asked him "not to publish
what she called her husband's 'profanity.' " He added: "With deep regret, I
shall not. But I must say with all deep respect for the fine sensibilities of
women in general and Comrade Mrs. London in particular, there are some
beauties to which they are not alive. To call Jack London's swearing 'profanity' is it iself almost profanity. For keep in mind that Comrade London
is a literary artist and that joyous vitality is his dominant note. So that
when he swears it gives fellowship, exuberance, emphasis to what he says,
like the echo of the hunting horn, the clink of glasses to the toast, or the
pistol-crack of a well-snapped whip. 'Profanity,' indeed."

"But do you think there will be enough of these to put up much of an argument?"

"Yes. And don't forget the army of dependents and parasites on the capitalist class who are attached to them and to the present order. Together they make up quite an item and will stick to their masters and fight for them, especially as their masters will make it worth their while to stay by them. Oh, never you fear . . . the Big Scrap is coming!"

"All right," I assented. "When?"

Comrade London laughed a disclaimer.

"I've quit prophesying dates for the social revolution. In high school I laid a lot of bets that it was due in ten years and felt sure of my money. Well I hope none of the fellows come around to collect."

"You don't think, then, that peaceful propaganda of reasoning education and conversion will do the trick?" I asked, to bring him back to his strenuous theme.

"Great Caesar" (or words to that effect). "No! I went through that stage when I believed in my salad days. I said to myself then: 'Now look here. Socialism is as plain as 2 plus 2 equates 4. All I need to do is to show the next fellow that and he'll tell the next fellow and in this way it will become 4 plus 4 equals 8, 8 plus 8 equals 16— and in just no time Socialism will be all over the shop, and come riding in on a flowing decked triumphal car.'

"There I saw the fellow whom I thought I had converted the day before was doing the same blessed thing and thinking the same as before I struck him. Furthermore, I saw while we were carrying on our little propaganda talk the capitalists were not losing time or ground themselves—not by a good deal. Why don't you know the caps are a good deal stronger today than they were ten years ago!

"Oh yes, I've changed my tune since those young days. I used to say of the caps and those who didn't come around to Socialism, 'We'll love them to it.' That's all behind me now. That's the only spirit in which to carry on our propaganda. Don't lose yourselves on a fog of talk, in oceans of hog-wash, softsoap and rose water. Get down to the brass tacks of the struggle. By all means get the ballot. But better still get the spirit. Get the good Western fighting spirit that gets up and shouts and keeps on shouting, 'Fight, damn you, fight!'"

Page 96, line 38:

Later, London added to this concept the idea that the capitalist use of force was teaching the workers to reply in kind, a policy of which he approved. He expressed this most clearly in an interview published in the *San Francisco Bulletin* of December 12, 1913, discussing the Wheatland Hop-Fields Riot, which occurred on August 3, 1913, on the Durst Brothers ranch in Wheatland, California. When the hop pickers, led by the I.W.W., revolted against abominable wages and working conditions, a posse, called in by the Dursts, attempted to disperse the striking hop pickers and arrest their leaders, especially Richard Ford and Herman Suhr. In the riot that followed the sheriff's firing a shot in the air, two county officials and two striking hop pickers were killed. Jack London, who met and interviewed many of the hop pickers after they fled in terror from the scene of the riot to escape arrest, was asked by a reporter for the *Bulletin* to explain the incident. The interview appeared under the heading: "Novelist Explains Hop Riots. Jack London Says Ruling Class Is Responsible for Workers' Use of Force." London explained:

"These men were not organized. There was only one among the 2,300 that held an I.W.W. card.* But they did not need organization. They have seen the cost of living go higher and higher, their purchasing power get less and less; they have all felt within themselves, 'Something has got to be done.'

"They have seen the aristocrats of labor, with their organizations become less oppressed than themselves, having greater purchasing power. They have heard the Socialists talking about the miraculous things to come through voting, but they themselves had no vote.**

"And, above all, they have had force preached to them, pounded into them, from the beginning—by whom? By the employers. By the Government. These things were in their mind when that Sheriff's automobile came rushing into their midst, and set fire to the powder.

"Of course, the employers have always ruled the working class with force. One incident happened that was strangely typical. One of

* Actually, there were about 100 I.W.W. card-carrying workers on the Durst ranch.

** London here was referring to the fact that the hop pickers were migratory workers who did not live in one area long enough to qualify for voting. Moreover, many were foreign-born, Japanese, Hindu, Cubans, Italians, Finns, etc., and were not yet naturalized citizens.

the Durst brothers struck one of the leading workmen over the face.* He said he did it 'facetiously.' Maybe he did; it isn't likely. But facetious or not, that blow symbolized the whole relation between employer and employe. Where they do not actually strike blows it is because the blows will be struck back.

"Now, the Sheriff and the District Attorney came on the scene, not at all in the interests of equity, but in the interests of the employer. They were not there to see fair play; they were there to 'keep order'; that is to say, to quell the hop pickers. The Sheriff expected his shot in the air to cow them."

"Why didn't it cow them?" was asked. "It would have done so a few years ago."

"Simply because they are becoming more and more imbued with the belief that force is the only way. I look back over history and I see that never has the ruling class relinquished a single one of its privileges except it was forced to. I do not understand wherein the ruling class today may have any different psychology from the ruling class at any other time in history."

"But," was asked, "does not your reading of history also teach you that the concessions gained by force have failed to stick?"

"No; I can see that the negro was given suffrage without his fighting for it; the masters got together and handed it down to them, and today he stands by, impassive and indifferent, while they take it away from him again.** It is always the things we fight for, bleed for, suffer for, that we care the most for.

* The man who was struck was Richard "Blackie" Ford. Ford and Suhr were tried for murder of District Attorney Manwell, and although it was conceded that neither had fired the fatal shot, they were found guilty of having incited the firing by their agitation to organize the hop pickers and lead them in the strike, and were sentenced to life imprisonment.

** London here revealed his total ignorance of the history of the Negro people in the United States. Not only did the Negroes fight for suffrage, before the Civil War, during the Civil War, in which over 200,000 served in the Union armed forces, and during the Reconstruction period, but they were anything but "impassive and indifferent" in 1913, when London issued this statement. The National Association for the Advancement of Colored People, organized by W. E. B. Du Bois and other Negro leaders and white sympathizers, was waging an active campaign for restoration of the right of suffrage, guaranteed to the Negro people under the Fifteenth Amendment, as well as for other demands as part of its campaign for full equality.

In this connection, the following comment by London on the Abolitionists is of some interest. It was written on August 4, 1902 while he was en route

"And this is just as true of the employers as it is of the men underneath. They have always preached to the workers in terms of force.
The lesson is soaking into the workers; that is all. That is why we
have hop-field riots, and that is why we are going to have more of
them."

Page 97, line 34:

During his interview with Joseph Gollomb, published in the
New York Call of January 28, 1912, London had been asked: "How
can you bear to leave the interesting times that are coming with the
growth of Socialism in Europe and America, and go for years in the
back yards of civilization in Asia and the South Seas?" London explained:

"Well, I love Socialism. But there is the other passion in me. The
sky, the sea, the hills, wilds—I just love them and I must have them.
So I go where I can get them.

"But don't get the notion that when I cruise around the South Seas
that I am letting up on Socialism. Not a bit. Why, I've made speeches
for Socialism in Honolulu, in Samoa, and in Tahiti. And say," he
smiled in reflection, "in Tahiti our Comrades tried to get for me what
would be the Great Central Palace in this city. But the authorities,
as soon as they learned that I was going to speak on Socialism, shut
the door. So the Comrades got the Folies-Bergères, a sort of gay
resort. Even then, the Chief of Police came around and wanted me
to promise that I'd cut a lot of things out of my speech. I balked at
that. Then they got a couple of fellows who knew English to stand
by and listen, and to let the police know when I had said something
that was against the law. But these fellows couldn't make head or

---

to England, as part of a series of comments on Orlando Smith's book,
Eternalism:

"Then the Abolitionists, who were few in numbers, were irrational and
immoral, but became rational and moral when a great many came to believe
as they believed. Always, you will notice, a few men have believed a thing
first, and then, perhaps, the many. For sometimes a few men have believed
an ascertainable truth and have died without convincing their generation.
And it is even possible, considering how utterly apart is your position and
mine, that the few in every generation may believe an ascertainable truth
which the many in every generation will not believe."

London's letter to Orlando Smith, of which the above is a part, makes fourteen single-spaced typewritten pages. It has never been published. The original
is in the possession of U. Grant Roman of Fort Lauderdale, Florida who has
kindly given me permission to quote from the letter.

tail of what I said, even though they knew English, so everything went off all right.

"In Samoa I talked in a beer garden—they're Germans, you know —the audience drank beer and ate while I talked and they listened. Every now and then they'd send up a glass of beer for me. It was very pleasant. In one place the Comrades, after my talk, organized a local on the spot, and affiliated themselves with the French Socialist party.

"And above all, I write all the time. And no matter what I write, whether it be a novel or romance, I can't help putting Socialism into it. . . ."

Gollomb concluded the interview on the following note: "There was no doubt in my mind as I left him that Socialism is as much a part of Jack London as the breath in his lungs. And I feel sure that as long as he breathes he will go on spreading that good, virile spirit that makes him sign himself invariably, 'Yours for the Revolution, Jack London.'"

Page 104, line 6:

Early in 1909, London had taken issue with Reverend Charles Brown, who, in a sermon on *Martin Eden* on January 16, 1909, at Oakland, had charged that the hero of the novel had failed because, as a Socialist, he had "lacked faith in God," an obvious attack on the author of the novel. London replied the very next day:

"Since hearing the Rev. Charles Brown's sermon last night on *Martin Eden*, I can understand why for two thousand years the Church has been rent with dissension over the interpretation of the Scriptures. Mr. Brown gave last night a splendid sample of the churchman's capacity for misinterpretation.

"Mr. Brown interpreted *Martin Eden* as a man who failed because of lack of faith in God. I wrote *Martin Eden*, not as an autobiography, nor as a parable of what dire end awaits an unbeliever in God, but as an indictment of that pleasant, wild-beast struggle of individualism of which Mr. Brown is not among the least of protagonists.

"Contrary to Mr. Brown's misinterpretation last night, Martin Eden was not a Socialist. Mr. Brown, in order to effect a parallel with my own life, said that Martin Eden was a Socialist. On the contrary, I drew him a temperamental, and later on, an intellectual, individualist. So much so was he an individualist that he characterized Mr. Brown's kind of ethics as a ghetto-ethics and Mr. Brown's kind of

individualism as half-baked Socialism. Martin Eden was a proper
Individualist of the extreme Nietzschean type.

"Now to my parable, which I thought I had expounded lucidly in
the pages of this novel. Being an Individualist, being unaware of the
needs of others, of the whole human collective need, Martin Eden
lived only for himself, fought only for himself, and if you please,
died only for himself. He fought for entrance into the bourgeois
circles where he expected to find refinement, culture, high-living and
high-thinking. He won his way into those circles and was appalled
by the colossal, unlovely mediocrity of the bourgeoisie. He fought for
a woman he loved and had idealized. He found that love had tricked
him and failed him, and that he had loved his idealization more than
the woman herself. These were the things he had found life worth
living in order to fight for. When they failed him, being a consistent
Individualist, being unaware of the collective human need, there
remained nothing for which to live and fight. And so he died.

"All this is so clearly stated in the pages of the book that I am
compelled to quote the following, which occurs when Brissenden
asks Martin to go down with him to the Sunday night meeting of the
Socialists. Brissenden says to Martin:

" 'Outsiders are allowed five-minute speeches. Get up and spout.
Tell them what you think about them and their ghetto-ethics. Slam
Nietzsche into them and get walloped for your pains. Make a scrap
of it. It will do them good. Discussion is what they want, and what
you want, too. You see, I'd like to see you a Socialist before I am
gone. It will give you a sanction for your existence. It is the one thing
that will save you in the time of disappointment that is coming to
you. You have health and much to live for, and you must be handcuffed to life somehow.' "

"I cannot comprehend how, after reading such lines, Mr. Brown
conceives Martin Eden to be a Socialist, nor how Mr. Brown failed
so lamentably in grasping the thesis I have expounded.

"Martin Eden failed and died, in my parable, not because of his
lack of faith in God, but because of his lack of faith in man. Even
Mr. Brown will agree that he cannot get to God except through man.
Martin Eden failed because he did not get even to man. He got only
as far as himself, and the rest of humanity did not count.

"Unfortunately, Mr. Brown's sermon was not on *Martin Eden*, but
on Jack London, and Mr. Brown was woefully unacquainted with
the subject. He said that I was Martin Eden. Let me point out the

vital weakness of his parallel—Martin Eden killed himself. I am still alive.

"Why am I alive? Because of my faith in man, a faith which Martin Eden never achieved, and a faith which Mr. Brown evidently did not know appertained to his subject, namely, Jack London. Yet my faith is most readily accessible to all men; my books are in the Public Library. Mr. Brown should have read up on the subject before he expounded it. Let me here quote some of my faith. I take the following from *What Life Means to Me:*

" 'I look forward to a time when man shall progress upon something worthier and higher than his stomach, when there will be a finer incentive to impel men to action than the incentive of today, which is the incentive of the stomach. I retain my belief in the nobility and excellence of the human, I believe that spiritual sweetness and unselfishness will conquer the gross gluttony of today. And last of all, my faith is in the working class. As some Frenchman has said, 'The stairway of time is ever echoing with the wooden shoe going up, the polished boot descending.' "

"Again I quote my faith, this time from the preface of my *War of the Classes:*

" 'He must learn that Socialism deals with what is, not with what ought to be; and that the material with which it deals, is the clay of the common road, the warm human, fallible and frail, sordid and petty, absurd and contradictory, even grotesque, and yet, withal, shot through with flashes and glimmerings of something finer and Godlike, with here and there sweetnesses of service and unselfishness, desires for goodness, for renunciation and sacrifice, and with conscience stern and awful, at times blazing imperious, demanding the right—the right, nothing more nor less than the right.'

"Jack London"

London's letter to Rev. Brown was published in the Seattle *Socialist* of June 18, 1910. He sent it to the editor with the following explanation: "Dear Comrade: In your issue of May 28, you have an aritcle entitle 'A Little Debate,' in which Comrade Armstrong holds that I am a Socialist, and in which L. Manley insists, from his reading of my book, *Martin Eden,* that I am not. Wherefore, I am impelled to send you the reply I made to Rev. Charles Brown, when he misinterpreted *Martin Eden.* Please return this letter. Yours for the Revolution, Jack London."

Page 111, line 39:

The term "Wobbly" was used, especially after 1913, as denoting a member of the Industrial Workers of the World (I.W.W.). Although Jack London was not a member of the I.W.W., he was on very good terms with the organization. He was listed as a contributing editor by the *Industrial Worker*, official organ of the I.W.W. published in Joliet, Illinois, as early as 1906, although there is no evidence in the files of the paper that he ever contributed an article. London expressed his sympathy with the I.W.W.'s belief in sabotage and syndicalism. "I have believed in them for twenty years," he told an interviewer in 1913. (*New York Call*, June 2, 1913.) Upon his death in 1916, the official I.W.W. journal referred to London as "Our literary comrade." (*Industrial Worker*, May 27, 1916.)

Page 112, line 1:

London had been invited to deliver a speech at a meeting in behalf of the Mexican Liberals and their American friends to be held in the Labor Temple in Los Angeles on February 5, 1911. In lieu of the speech, he sent this letter which first appeared in the February 10, 1911, issue of the *People's Paper*, a Socialist journal published in Los Angeles.

Page 113, line 7:

The Junta was organized by Flores Magón. Magón had been editor of *La Revolución*, the socialist-anarchist organ of the Liberal Party formed in Mexico by Camilio Arriago in 1900. Though firmly and unswervingly committed to anarchist objectives, Flores Magón built a broad radical-liberal following both in Mexico and in the United States. Magón was frequently imprisoned in Mexico and the United States as a "socialist agitator." Exiled from Mexico, Magón and other exiled Liberal Party members operated after 1910 from Los Angeles, where they resumed publication of *La Regeneración* in September.

After the Diaz dictatorship was overthrown, the *Magonistas*, as the followers of Magón were called, sought a more thoroughgoing revolution than that promised under Madero. Although Flores Magón himself did not himself cross into Mexico, under his leadership, Mexicans, I.W.W. members, and assorted soldiers of fortune, seldom reaching three hundred men in all, captured Mexicali, Algodones, Tecate, El Alamo, and Tijuana. Unable to obtain ade-

quate munitions and reinforcements, the revolutionists fell back to
Mexicali and Tijuana, and agents of Madero negotiated surrender of
the Mexicali garrison. Before a similar surrender could be achieved
in Tijuana, Celso Vega, the savage but slow-moving territorial governor of Ensenada, aided by 150 southern California Mexicans, recaptured that border town and drove the remnants of the regiment
back into the United States.

Page 114, line 14:

The story is also, like the earlier Jack London story, "A Piece
of Steak," and the later novelette, *The Abysmal Brute,* a brilliant
exposé of the callousness and commercialism of the prize ring. Danny
Ward's handlers, manager, and even the referee are all involved in
the plot to make him lose. The referee counts fast when he is down,
and breaks his clinches. When he is winning, an attempt is made to
bribe him, and when this fails, they plan to make it look as if he has
fouled his opponent.

London, incidentally drops his racism in this story, and seems even
to go out of his way to state, while describing the fight, that Rivera is
"more delicately coordinated, more finely nerved and strung than any
of them"—the white Americans. The hero of this story is not an
Anglo-Saxon, but a Mexican worker, the son of a revolutionary
working man, who has memories of child labor, starvation, exploitation, lock-out, the shooting down of workers, and the finding of the
corpses of his father and mother in the piles of dead.

Page 116, line 33:

"Whose Business to Live," a story probably written by London
during the time he was doing the series for *Collier's Weekly,* is filled
with the same contempt for the Mexicans who are described as
"greasers," "ungrateful," "cowardly," and "stupid." The plot con-
cerns the escape of several American men and women from maddened
"mobs" of Mexicans who were, to London's annoyance, bitter because American sailors and marines landed at Vera Cruz and took
control of the city. The story was published in his final book of
stories, *Dutch Courage and Other Stories,* which appeared in 1922.

Page 122, line 6:

The Little Lady of the Big House is probably the worst novel
London ever wrote, even worse, especially so far as it reveals his

racism, than *The Mutiny of the Elsinore,* published in 1914. Charmian London called the latter novel "a whacking good sea-story, true,
modern, beneath the romance and action a heartfelt protest against
the decayed condition of the American merchant marine." A truer
interpretation would be to say that "beneath the romance and action"
is London's growing contemptuous loathing for nearly all the "lower
class" characters in his books, his idealization of the blond white
man from the northern countries of Europe who is being crowded
out by the overwhelming weight of the Latin, the Slav, and other
Southern European races who were pouring into America. Only by
stamping out, under an iron heel, the rebellious masses who challenge the reign of the "superior" blond white man could the latter's
hold on leadership in society be preserved, and it is clear that London
is beginning to approve of such a program.

All this is developed to its fullest extent in *The Little Lady of the
Big House.* London here finds "very tenable" the hypothesis that
"the white-skinned, blue-eyed Aryan, born to government and command, ever leaving his primeval, overcast and foggy home, ever
commands and governs the rest of the world and ever perishes because of the two-white light he encounters." When the Mate, Mr.
Pike, "killer and slave-driver, it is true," "sprang first into the teeth
of danger so that his slaves might follow," Pathhurst, the hero of the
novel, felt "pride that my eyes were blue, like his; that my skin was
blond, like his; that my place was aft with him, and with the
Samurai in the high place of government and command. As for the
rest—the weaklings and the rejected, and the dark-pigmented things,
the half-castes, the mongrel-bloods, and the dregs of long-conquered
races—how could they count? My heels were iron as I gazed on them
in their peril and weakness. Lord! Lord! For ten thousand generations and centuries we had stamped upon their faces and enslaved
them to the toil of our will."

The low point in the novel comes when Pathurst comments after
one of the leaders of the mutiny, a New York City gangster curses
him: "As I listened I knew why the English had blown their mutinous Sepoys from the mouths of cannon in India long years ago."

There are, to be sure, a few redeeming features in the novel. Dick
Forrest, who is really Jack London, rebukes one of his intellectual
friends for having a Southern prejudice against Negroes, and admits
curiously enough in such a book, that the "average Hottentot, or
the average Melanesian, is pretty close to being on a par with the

average white man." But he goes on to claim that the whites produce a much heavier percentage of men who are above the average. He asserts further that the Hottentots have produced no great man, the "Hawaiian race" but one, the Negroes in the United States but two—Booker T. Washington and W. E. B. Du Bois.

Jacobs, the supreme representation of the workers, the beasts, is the embodiment of all that is ugly, a complete caricature of the superior workers London had described in his socialist essays. To be sure, London pays his respect to Jacobs by picturing him as fearless, but this is only in passing. Jacobs' philosophy is set forth in the following statement he makes to Pathurst:

"Yes, he was a Red and knew his Kropotkin, but he was no anarchist. On the other hand, political action was a blind alley leading to reformism and quietism. Political socialism had gone to pot, while industrial unionism was the logical culmination of Marxism. He was a direct actionist. The mass strike was the thing. Sabotage, not merely as a withdrawal of efficiency, but as a keen destruction of profits policy, was the weapon."

Probably this revealed London's admiration for the philosophy and tactics of the I.W.W., but the rest of the novel showed that he had little respect at this time for that organization's emphasis upon labor solidarity and bitter opposition to racism in all its forms.

As for the "Little Lady" herself, she reveals her viewpoint when she (Paula) tells Dick Forrest and Evan Graham that she must love them both because: "You are successes. Your muscles are blond-beast muscles, your vital organs are blond-beast organs. And from all this emanates your blond-beast philosophy. That's why you are brass tacks and preach realism, and practice realism, shouldering and shoving and walking over lesser and unluckier creatures who don't dare talk back. . . ."

Graham has lost all his capital in the stock market, and has only "an income of several thousand a year left." "But he doesn't whimper." "He's good stuff, old American stock, a *Yale* man." Dick Forrest owns mines in Mexico and he insists that the Mexicans are too stupid to develop them. He praises Diaz and sneers at the Revolution.

These are the heroine and heroes of London's novel. It almost seems as if London had set out to satirize everything he had written only a few years before.

One who reads *The Little Lady of the Big House* and is tempted to dismiss Jack London as a progressive force in American life and literature would do well to bear in mind the following excellent comment by Russell Ames:

"London was such a mixture of . . . socialist worker and bourgois individualist, so glaringly wrong in theories about so many things, that is easy for us to feel superior to him, rightly, and to think we cannot learn from him, wrongly.

"This is not to say that such terrible weaknesses as London's racism should be tolerated. The point is that his enemies and those who should be his friends should not be allowed to use his weaknesses as clubs against his strong and good qualities. No doubt some critics are anxious to prove that London was a bad, phony, insincere and stupid socialist precisely because he was such a good socialist.

"Though London was clearly more patronizing in his view of the workers as a political force than any socialist intellectual would be today, he was also closer to the workers than most of us are.

"Jack London accepted, off and on, many undemocratic ideas; he tended to overestimate the power of the rich and to underestimate the organized strength of the workers (in his time the socialist and labor groups were especially numerous and divided), but there is no real question as to which side he was on." (Unpublished manuscript on Jack London in possession of the author, Oaxaca, Mexico.)

Page 128, line 7:

One story which London never finished has recently been published, called *The Assassination Bureau, Ltd.* London had written 40,000 words of this novel—based on a story idea bought from Sinclair Lewis—when he died. The final 20,000 words are by Robert L. Fish, who completed the book from London's notes. The novel tells of a society for hired assassinations, headed by Ivan Dragomiloff, composed solely of high-minded operatives who will kill only for the benefit of society. Millionaire Socialist Winter Hall hires the society to assassinate its chief, after proving to Dragomiloff (who is also Sergius Constantine, father of Winter's bride to be) that society will benefit by his own death.

The novel contains flashes of London's indictment of capitalist society. There are jibes at social workers who, by operating day nurseries for the children of women workers, enable the employers "more thoroughly . . . to sweat the mothers." There is a portrait of two labor leaders who are in the pay of the employers and have sold out their members in a number of strikes. There is the professor who joins the Assassination Bureau after he was forced to resign from Burlington University because his "economic teachings offended the founder." There are descriptions of crooked stock manipulations by supposedly respectable capitalists. Essentially, however, *The Assassination Bureau, Ltd.* is a clever and lively suspense novel.

London had already used a somewhat similar theme in two previous pieces. One was "The Minions of Midas" (1901) which is discussed above (pp. 45–46.) In "Goliah" (1910) he described the establishment of Socialism by dictatorship, assassination, and other forms of violence. Here again London showed his lack of understanding of the basic tenets of Socialism, which rejected all terrorist, anarchistic, individualistic policies and worked for the broadest of peaceful mass activity, condoning force only in those situations in which self-defense is necessary and peaceful progress barred.

It is interesting, however, to note that in *The Assassination Bureau, Ltd.*, London makes it quite clear that the whole idea of using assassination to benefit society is fundamentally anti-social. Even in "Goliah," he develops the idea that it is not Goliah, the hero of the story, who, through the use of terror, determines the progress, the forms, the institutions of Socialism, but the whole working people themselves. Thus he wrote: "And the beauty of it is that the people of the United States have achieved all this for themselves. . . . The fear of death made those in the high places get out of the way, that was all, and gave the intelligence of man a chance to realize itself socially."

Bibliography

Bibliography

UNPUBLISHED STUDIES

AMES, RUSSELL. "The Writings of Jack London," unpublished manuscript in possession of author, Oaxaca, Mexico.

BASKETT, SAM S. "Jack London's Fiction: The Social Milieu," unpublished Ph.D. thesis, University of California, 1951.

FRAUENGLASS, ETTIE. "Jack London as a Socialist," unpublished M.A. thesis, New York University, 1939.

HOLLAND, ROBERT BELTON. "Jack London: His Thought and Art in Relation to His Time," unpublished Ph.D. thesis, University of Wisconsin, 1950.

POPE, MARGARET L. "Jack London: A Study in Twentieth Century Values," unpublished Ph.D. thesis, University of Wisconsin, 1935.

ROSE, LISLE ABBOTT. "A Descriptive Catalogue of Economic and Politico-Economic Fiction in the United States, 1902–1909," unpublished Ph.D. thesis, University of Chicago, 1935.

ROTHBERG, ABRAHAM. "The House that Jack Built: A Study of Jack London," unpublished Ph.D. thesis, Columbia University, 1952.

SMITH, HAROLD SHERBURN. "William James Ghent; Reformer and Historian," unpublished Ph.D. thesis, University of Wisconsin, 1957.

YOUNG, THOMAS DANIEL. "Jack London and the Era of Social Protest," unpublished Ph.D. thesis, Vanderbilt University, 1950.

BOOKS

BAMFORD, GEORGIA LORING. *The Mystery of Jack London,* Oakland, Calif., 1913.

BLAISDALE, LOWELL L. *The Desert Revolution: Baja California, 1911,* Madison, Wisconsin, 1962.

CALVERTON, V. F. *The Liberation of American Literature,* New York, 1932.

FREEMAN, JOSEPH. *An American Testament,* New York, 1936.

HAZARD, LUCY LOCKWOOD. *The Frontier in American Literature,* New York, 1927.

HICKS, GRANVILLE. *The Great Tradition,* New York, 1933.

KAZIN, ALFRED. *On Native Grounds,* New York, 1942.

KIPNIS, IRA. *The American Socialist Movement,* 1897–1912, New York, 1952.

LAIDLER, HARRY WELLINGTON. *Twenty Years of Social Pioneering,* New York, 1926.

LEWISOHN, LUDWIG. *Expression in America,* New York and London, 1932.

LONDON, CHARMIAN K. *The Book of Jack London,* 2 vols., New York, 1921.

LONDON, JOAN. *Jack London and His Times,* New York, 1939.

MADISON, CHARLES A. *Critics and Crusaders,* New York, 1947.

McDEVITT, WILLIAM. *Jack London as Poet and as Platform Man,* San Francisco, 1947.

PARRINGTON, VERNON LEWIS. *Main Currents in American Thought,* New York, 1922.

PATTEE, FRED LEWIS. *Side-Lights on American Literature,* New York, 1922.

PAYNE, EDWARD BIRON. *The Soul of Jack London,* London, 1926.

RIDEOUT, WALTER B. *The Radical Novel in the United States,* 1900–1954, Cambridge, Mass., 1956.

SINCLAIR, UPTON. *The Cry for Justice,* Pasadena, Calif., 1925.

SINCLAIR, UPTON. *Mommonart,* Pasadena, Calif., 1925.

SPILLER, ROBERT E. and others. *Literary History of the United States,* 2 vols., New York, 1948.

STONE, IRVING. *Jack London: Sailor on Horseback,* Garden City, New York, 1947.

ARTICLES

AMES, RUSSELL. "Jack London: American Radical," *Our Time,* 7: 254–55, July, 1948.

"Attempt to Place Jack London," *Current Literature,* 42: 513–14, May, 1907.

BAGGS, MAE LUCY. "The Real Jack London in Hawaii," *Overland Monthly*, n.s., 69: 405–10, May, 1917.

BAILEY, MILLARD. "Valley of the Moon Ranch," *Overland Monthly*, n.s., 69: 411–15, May, 1917.

"Barbarian in Jack London, The," *Literary Digest*, 45: 564, October 5, 1912.

BASKETT, SAM S. "A Source of *The Iron Heel*," *American Literature*, 27: 268–70, May, 1955.

BASKETT, SAM S. "Jack London on the Oakland Waterfront," *American Literature*, 27: 363–71, May, 1955.

BLAND, HENRY MEADE. "Jack London, Traveler, Novelist and Social Reformer," *The Craftsman*, 9: 607–19, February, 1906.

COLBRON, GRACE ISABEL. "Jack London, What He Was and What He Accomplished," *Bookman*, 44: 441–51, January, 1917.

DARGAN, E. PRESTON. "Jack London in Chancery," *New Republic*, 10: 7–8, April 21, 1917.

EAMES, NINETTA. "Jack London," *Overland Monthly*, 25: 417–25, May, 1900.

FRIEDLAND, L. S. "Jack London as Titan," *Dial*, 62: 49–51, January 25, 1917.

GLANCY, DONALD R. "Socialist With a Valet: Jack London's 'First, Last and Only' Lecture Tour," *Quarterly Journal of Speech*, 99: 30–39, February, 1963.

GOLLOMB, JOSEPH, "London Tells of Social Revolution," New York *Call*, January 28, 1912.

GRATTAN, C. HARTLEY. "Jack London," *Bookman*, 68: 667–71, February, 1929.

HOUCK, C. B. "Jack London's Philosophy of Life," *Overland Monthly*, n.s., 84: 103–04, April, 1926, 156–57, May, 1926.

HUFFER, O. M. "Jack London: A Personal Sketch," *Living Age*, 292: 124–26, January 13, 1917.

"Jack London," *Literary Digest*, 53: 1537, December 9, 1916.

"Jack London as His Wife Charmain Knew Him," *Current Opinion*, 71: 645–48, November, 1920.

"Jack London, Farmer," *Literary Digest*, 46: 1195, May 24, 1913.

"Jack London—In Memoriam," *International Socialist Review*, 17: 624, April, 1917.

"Jack London's Place in American Literature," *The Nation*, 103: 502, November 30, 1916.

"Jack London's Resignation from the Socialist Party," *Overland Monthly*, n.s., 69: 446, May, 1917.

"Jack London's One Great Contribution to American Literature," *Current Opinion*, 62: 46–47, January, 1917.

JAMES GEORGE WHARTON. "A Study of Jack London in His Prime," *Overland Monthly*, n.s., 69: 361–99, May, 1917.

JULIUS, EMANUEL. "The Pessimism of Jack London," New York *Call*, June 2, 1913.

MILLS, GORDON. "Jack London's Quest for Salvation," *American Quarterly*, 7: 3–15, Spring, 1955.

LANE, ROSE WILDER. "Life and Jack London," *Sunset Magazine*, 39: 34–37, 62, January, 1918, 40: 32–33, 68, February, 1918.

"Our National Honor," New York *Call*, April 16, 1913, 6.

"Placing Jack London's Books Under the Ban," *Arena*, 35: 435, April, 1906.

RUSSAK, MARTIN. "Jack London, America's First Proletarian Writer," *New Masses*, January, 1929, 13.

SILVER, G. V. "Jack London's Women," *Overland Monthly*, n.s., 74: 24–28, July, 1919.

SINCLAIR, UPTON. "About Jack London," *The Masses*, 10: 17–20, November and December, 1917.

SOCIALIST PARTY NATIONAL EXECUTIVE COMMITTEE. "Socialist Party Protests to the President," New York *Call*, April 23, 1914, 1.

STILLMAN, LOUIS J. "Jack London, Super-Boy," *Sunset*, 38: 42, February, 1917.

UNTERMANN, ERNEST. "Jack London, wie ich ihn kannte," *Sozialistich Monatshefte*, Berlin, July, 1929, 602–13.

WALLING, ANNA STRUNSKY. "Memories of Jack London," *The Masses*, 9: 13–17, July, 1917.

WALCUTT, CHARLES CHILD. "Naturalism and the Superman in London's Novels," *Papers of the Michigan Academy of Science, Arts and Letters*, 1948, Part IV, 89–107.

WEINSTEIN, JAMES. "The Socialist Party: Its Roots and Strength, 1912–1919," *Studies on the Left*, 1: 5–27, Winter, 1960.

WOODWARD, ROBERT H. "Jack London's Code of Primitivism," *The Folio*, 18: 39–44, May, 1953.